DISCARD

The Antitheatrical Prejudice

The
Antitheatrical
Prejudice

JONAS BARISH

University
of California
Press
Berkeley
Los Angeles
London

University of California Press
Berkeley and Los Angeles, California

University of California Press, Ltd.
London, England

Copyright © 1981 by
The Regents of
the University of California

Printed in the United States of America
1 2 3 4 5 6 7 8 9

Library of Congress Cataloging in Publication Data

Barish, Jonas A
  The antitheatrical prejudice.

  Includes bibliographical references and index.
  1. Theater—Moral and religious aspects. I. Title.
PN2049.B37   809.2'9353   78–59445
ISBN 0–520–03735–9

For Millie, and for Judith and Rachel

Contents

Acknowledgments

My DEBTS are numerous and heavy, and it is a pleasure to record them here. The subject of the present study has interested a number of my friends and acquaintances over the years, and they have lent aid of varying kinds. For assistance great and small I am indebted to Letizia Ciotti, Christopher Ricks, Marvin and Helga Spevack, R. W. Flint, Stephen J. Greenblatt, Paul and Svetlana Alpers, Jocelyn Harris, Marshall Waingrow, and Alex Zwerdling. To Leo Bersani, Leo Lowenthal, and Stephen Greenblatt I owe a reassuringly encouraging perusal of the manuscript; to Lowry Nelson, Jr., and Stephen Orgel the kind of minute and attentive reading, accompanied by copious annotation, that makes revision a challenge and a delight. My colleagues Thomas Rosenmeyer, Anne Middleton, Paul Alpers, and W. E. Rex read portions of the manuscript at various stages of its existence, and contributed hosts of valuable—or, rather, invaluable—suggestions for its improvement. I hope I have been able to profit from their wise counsel. Throughout I have tried to guide myself by the example of scholarly mastery and intellectual scrupulousness set by my former teacher (and still my teacher in the respects that most matter) Harry Levin, whose seven-league boots I have no doubt most rashly tried to put on in the very attempting of the present enterprise.

I am grateful to the University of California, and especially to my department, for twice allowing me to offer a seminar in the topic of this book, and to the students in both classes who helped me explore antitheatrical literature. I owe thanks to the university also for its patient munificence with research funds, and to the American Council for Learned Societies and the National Endowment for the Humanities for their generous fellowship support. I am further beholden to the editors of *Critical Quarterly*, the *University of Toronto Quarterly*, *New Literary History*, *English Literary History*, and the *Stanford French Review* for permission to reprint, with alterations, material which first appeared in their journals, and to the University of Toronto Press for allowing me to reproduce, again with modifications, the chapter "Jonson and the Loathèd Stage" from *A Celebration of Ben Jonson*, edited by William F. Blisset, which originated as a talk at the Ben Jonson Conference in Toronto in October 1972. Permission to reproduce the illustrations is acknowledged in the legends that accompany the plates. Finally, for help in checking a bewildering array of references I must thank Carol E. Collins, and for piloting an unwieldy manuscript through the shoals of typing I am deeply in the debt of Florence Myer, without whose expert cooperation the vessel would never have reached port. To all these, and to many others whose contribution is less easy to isolate and identify, my profound thanks, along with my assurance that any mistakes that remain despite their best efforts are altogether my own.

This book, finally, completed under difficult circumstances, is dedicated to those who made life a joy for its author while he was writing it.

Jonas Barish
December 1979

Introductory

MOST EPITHETS derived from the arts are laudatory when applied to the other arts, or to life. If one describes a landscape as "poetic," or a man's struggle with adversity as "epic," or a woman's beauty as "lyric," one is using terms of praise. In an old movie comedy, an affected matron expressed her appreciation of dinner by declaring that "the fish was a *poem*"—obviously the most rapturous word of approval she could think of. Similarly, terms like *musical, symphonic, graphic, sculptural* (or *sculpturesque*) are nearly always eulogistic.

But with infrequent exceptions, terms borrowed from the theater— *theatrical, operatic, melodramatic, stagey,* etc.—tend to be hostile or belittling. And so do a wide range of expressions drawn from theatrical activity expressly to convey disapproval: *acting, play acting, playing up to, putting on an act, putting on a performance, making a scene, making a spectacle of oneself, playing to the gallery,* and so forth. Nor are such terms confined to English. The French speak cuttingly of those who *jouent la comédie,* or dismissingly of an action that it was merely *du théâtre.* One does not, in Italian, if one is behaving well, *fare la commedia* or *fare il pulcinella,* nor does one, in German, *sich in Szene setzen* or *sich in den Vordergrund spielen.* The European languages abound in such expressions, most of them pejorative. They embody, in current idioms, the vestiges of a prejudice against the theater that goes back as far in European history as the theater itself can be traced. Thespis, who gave his name to the art of acting, was called a liar by Solon because he was pretending to be someone else,[1] and one would not be overstating the case by very much to say that

1. Plutarch, *Life of Solon,* in *Lives,* trans. Bernadotte Perrin, Loeb Classics, I (London, 1914), 488–489.

I

hostility to impersonation forms one of the cornerstones of Plato's *Republic*.

Nor can it be said that the prejudice in question is confined to the West, especially as it applies to actors. In India, until recent times, actors belonged to the despised castes, and were subject to crippling social disabilities. In Indochina, acting was for centuries classified as a vile profession, while in China, until the Communist Revolution, actresses were regularly recruited from prostitutes, had effectively to continue as prostitutes while acting, and accordingly suffered the reprobation and ostracism inherent in that role.[2] The phenomenon, in short, is worldwide. Even in its European dimension, it is dauntingly vast. Specialized studies might be, and indeed have been, written on many of its individual manifestations—on the attitudes of the church fathers, or on the stage controversy in Tudor and Stuart England, on the Jeremy Collier dispute, or on the polemics in France in the seventeenth and eighteenth centuries. The primary literature of these controversies makes wearisome reading in its grittiness, its repetitiousness and garrulousness. An unmistakably crackpot streak runs through much of it. It is tempting to put the whole phenomenon down to mere narrow-mindedness, and to dismiss it as unworthy of the attention of an adult mind, so many legions of hard-shelled, mole-eyed fanatics seem to have enlisted under its banners. Yet one could say the same thing of certain versions of Christianity itself, or of many another large-scale spiritual movement with a mass following. The fact that the prejudice turns out to be of such nearly universal dimension, that it has infiltrated the spirits not only of insignificant criticasters and village explainers but of giants like Plato, Saint Augustine, Rousseau, and Nietzsche, suggests that it is worth looking at more closely—that it is, indeed, more than a prejudice. If it is an aberration, it is one to which virtually our whole species seems in some measure prone. Looked at more attentively, it comes to appear a kind of ontological malaise, a condition inseparable from our beings, which we can no more discard than we can shed our skins. It would seem to reflect something permanent about the way we think of ourselves and our lives.

The following pages make no pretense at being a systematic history. I adopt a chronological approach because the attitudes with which I

2. See André Villiers, *La prostitution de l'acteur* (Paris, 1946), pp. 55–58.

am concerned evolve with time, but I make no attempt to tell a complete or fully connected story. Every reader will detect lacunae in the tale, as well as space devoted to matters which he may well judge to be dispensable. I can plead only that I followed what seemed to me to be the grain of the subject, and also the directions suggested by my own interests. This has doubtless produced eccentricities of emphasis for which it would be idle to apologize. It must also go without further saying that I do not now and do not expect ever in future to regard myself as knowing enough to write this book, that I have had to omit reference to scores of writers, movements, disciplines, cultures, any one of which might justly have claimed a place, doubtless more validly than some to whom a place was accorded.

These pages, again, propose no polemical thesis. They do not seek to explain the antitheatrical prejudice, but to explore the territory within which it operates, to illuminate the major landmarks, and some obscurer ones, with whatever kind of commentary seems relevant. Sometimes I have temerariously engaged in debate with authors dangerous to disagree with. Elsewhere I have been content to annotate and expound and place in relief, occasionally dwelling on writers of small intellectual consequence in themselves, whose crotchets nevertheless help suggest the range and multifariousness of the negative position. I have sought to avoid, where possible, the dogmatism that the subject has often provoked on both sides, and to develop a series of interlocking propositions that may help to further understanding of what seems increasingly to have become a major theme of our own culture—theatricality. As the ancient distrust of the stage itself seems on the point of dissolving, the fascination with life seen under the aspect of theater seems also to have become a central preoccupation of literature, philosophy, psychology, and sociology, not to mention the stage itself. Perhaps one may say that the lessons about mankind implicit in the theater of the past, and responsible for much of the hatred of it, have at last been absorbed into the consciousness of society at large, but that as the old hatred has ebbed, the ontological queasiness that underlies it has simply found subtler and more sophisticated channels of outlet.

One of the acuter adversaries of the stage in the seventeenth century, the Prince de Conti, commences his treatise by declaring that he does not intend to discuss plays from any lofty metaphysical standpoint. He is willing to believe that, abstractly considered, they have many interesting qualities. They may even be ethically innocuous. He will, however, address himself solely to the specific evils of the theater as he is acquainted with it, the plays actually on view in Paris, and the presumptive effects of those same plays and the presence of those actors.[3] The intent of the present essay is the reverse. I should like to pass lightly over such local considerations, and focus on what has been said against plays in their essence. Plainly enough, the two concerns must sometimes merge. The more analytical foes of the stage often themselves attribute its malign effects to its intrinsic nature—to the fact, for example (the putative fact), that the habit of imitating others must necessarily bring out the worst in the actor himself, or that plays lend themselves too readily to the mockery of those in authority, or that they present images of passion so vivid as to produce a fatal moral impact on their audiences. Such considerations will not be ignored here. But we may set aside quantities of diatribes against the unedifying lives of actresses, or against the unruliness of audiences, or the threat to public order and health posed by crowds assembled in places of amusement—objections which, in the startling degree of fury they are capable of provoking, sometimes almost seem to constitute the central grievance. The fact that the disapproval of the theater is capable of persisting through so many transformations of culture, so many dislocations of time and place, suggests a permanent kernel of distrust waiting to be activated by the more superficial irritants. The durability of the prejudice would seem to reflect a basic attitude toward the lives of men in society that deserves to be disengaged and clarified. It is in the hope of linking it to those wider and deeper attitudes that I have not hesitated to range more widely than the strict limits of the subject might seem to suggest, among books in which theatricality in its larger sense seems to be at issue, whether or not the stage itself is explicitly in question. The ultimate hope is to illuminate if possible the nature of the theatrical, and hence, inevitably, of the human.

3. Armand de Bourbon, Prince de Conti, *Traité de la comédie et des spectacles selon la tradition de l'église tirée des Conciles et des saints pères* (Paris, 1669), pp. 6, 8–9.

·I·

The Platonic Foundation

CONSIDERATION of the antitheatrical prejudice must begin with Plato, who first articulated it, and to whom its later exponents regularly return in support of their proscriptions and prohibitions. Plato provides a philosophical framework for the debate over all art, and most of the key terms for a controversy that raged for two millennia after his death and still smoulders today. In Plato, moreover, we find a characteristic conflict: a haunting acknowledgment of the potency of the theater leading to an all the more stinging repudiation of it. We cannot, and with Plato we need not, differentiate the art of the theater sharply from that of epic poetry, painting, sculpture, or music. All are treated by him as forms of imitation, as are a whole range of steps in the creation and performance and reception of a work of art, from the poet's imagining of the fiction he will create, to the embodiment of that imagining in verbal form, to its execution by actor or recitant, to the retracing and recreating of it in his spirit by the listener or spectator or reader.[1] The drama being the mimetic art par excellence, what is alleged against mimesis in general will apply to the drama with particular force, and Plato keeps it more steadily in view than any of the other manifestations of the artistic impulse, perhaps also because of his own early passionate apprenticeship to it, cured, as we are told in Diogenes Laertius, by the teaching of Socrates.[2] Writing at the end

1. The multiple meanings of mimesis as used in the *Republic* have been skilfully disentangled by Eric A. Havelock, *Preface to Plato* (Cambridge, Mass., 1963), pp. 20–26, and the scholarship on the subject reviewed on pp. 57–60.

2. Diogenes Laertius, *Lives of Eminent Philosophers*, trans. R. D. Hicks, Loeb Classics (Cambridge, Mass., 1938), pp. 280–281 (*Plato*, 5–6).

of the world's first great epoch of drama, Plato acknowledges the power of the dramatists over the minds of his countrymen, and at the same time struggles to combat what he has learned to regard as their baneful influence. Book X of the *Republic* makes best sense as an attack on the stage of the theater-loving Athenians, and we can hardly do better, for a start, than to summarize the main points of the attack and rehearse a few simple objections.

Socrates commences by alleging that unless forearmed with philosophical insight, listeners to poetical imitation are liable to have their understandings ruined by it, for reasons inherent in the nature of imitation itself. Imitation, he explains, is the bringing into being of an inferior world, such as anyone can create by whirling a mirror around and allowing it to reflect the earth, the sea, and the sky. The painter, when he paints a bed, paints such a world, and it is a world of appearances, a debased version of what in nature is already only an appearance, since even the carpenter's solid wooden object is no more than a particular instance of the Idea *bed*, which alone can be said to be real and true. The painter's craft thus reduces itself to an effort of slavish mimicry. And the same holds, says Socrates, for the tragic poet, who, like the painter, is an imitator, and hence "thrice removed from the king and from the truth" (597e).[3] Apart from the strangeness of hearing that a manmade artifact like a bed copies an eternal idea from the kingdom of the forms,[4] it is hard not to feel, even at this preliminary stage of the discussion, that the argument has begun to drift uneasily. A new notion has been introduced, that of human actions, which are what the tragic poets imitate. But it is not clear how particular actions of men can be classed with beds or flutes as imperfect approximations of the forms. An individual man presumably participates in the idea of a man as a flute does in the idea of a flute, but a flute is an inert thing with no will of its own, whereas Platonic man possesses a soul, which itself springs from and is destined to rejoin the realm of the forms. A painter, when he paints a bed, may be said to be copying the form of the bed, for his picture captures something of the static quality of its original. Even in the hands of a virtuoso, the flute, as painted,

3. Citations to the *Republic* will be from B[enjamin] Jowett, trans., *The Dialogues of Plato*, 4th ed. (Oxford, 1953), II, 163–499.

4. See Francis Macdonald Cornford, trans., *The Republic of Plato* (Oxford, 1945), pp. 322–323.

must be arrested, removed (in part) from time, transfixed into something approaching its celestial archetype. But actions have no such fixity. They take place wholly in time; they are time-functional. Even when performed so as to realize such ideas as virtue or courage they can hardly be said to correspond to those ideas in the way that a bed can correspond to the idea of a bed. By their nature they must be radically antithetical to the forms, which are by definition motionless and timeless. How can that which is pure process imitate that which is pure essence? Whatever the poet may be doing, it is hard to see how his activity leads back to the world of the archetypes, which stand in eternal frozen rebuke to his world of perpetual motion.

Even Plato's partisans have often confessed themselves dissatisfied with the excessively spatial character of the logic at this point. Plato's visual fixation seems to trivialize the whole argument. On the analogy with painting, the whole poetic enterprise is seen as something parasitic and derivative, painting itself being implicitly reduced to the kind of naive realism which boasts that it can produce grapes so lifelike birds will peck at them, or draperies that flutter so convincingly the hand reaches out to move them aside.[5] Behind the analogy between poet and painter, indeed, lurks an even more damning analogy between poet and sophist, the latter being belittlingly likened to the painter in the *Sophist* dialogue itself. Together with the painter, "*the poet is a sophist, a maker of counterfeits that look like the truth.*"[6] Like the sophist also, he is a "subjectivist," a "relativist,"[7] with no interest in

5. As John Jones has pointed out, "Plato could quite well have said that the painter imitates the transcendent idea visible to his inward eye, not the table made by the carpenter. This obvious step is taken much later by neo-Platonism, never by Plato himself, and the fact that he does not do so is one ground for suspecting him of stubborn initial prejudice against art" (*On Aristotle and Greek Tragedy* [New York, 1968], pp. 23–24).

6. Gerald F. Else, "The Structure and Date of Book X of Plato's *Republic*," *Abhandlungen der Heidelberger Akademie der Wissenschaften* (Heidelberg, 1972), p. 26. Else advances the startling thesis that the section on poetry in Book X represents Plato's answer to critics of his own earlier attack on mimesis in Book III (see below), the critics in question being his young disciples, notably Aristotle, whose views on tragic poetry, as set forth in the *Poetics*, are expressly coming under fire.

7. Iris Murdoch, *The Fire and the Sun: Why Plato Banished the Artists* (Oxford, 1977), p. 31. See also her recent "Platonic Dialogue," *Art and Eros*, performed at the National Theatre, London, in February 1980.

the true, the good, or the beautiful. The question then arises, if poetry is such an inherently second-rate activity, why should anyone ever wish to practice it? The devastating inference turns out to be: to compensate for his own deficiencies, to bolster his own self-esteem. Unable to perform heroic deeds himself, to lead armies or rule cities, the poet falls back on what he pitifully supposes to be the next best thing: he imitates others doing so. He compensates for his own worthlessness in action by making himself expert at the art of mimicking the actions of others.

Cornford has suggested that the argument here turns on the rejection of a claim, made by the sophists and the recitants of the Homeric poems, that Homer possessed a kind of universal wisdom, that he, and the tragic poets, "were masters of all technical knowledge from wagon-building or chariot-driving to strategy, and also moral and religious guides to the conduct of life," and that as such, the poets were being inflated into rivals of the philosophers as a basis for intellectual training.[8] In the same way, Werner Jaeger alludes to the Greek veneration for poetry, their making of it into an "epitome of all knowledge and culture," so that it served as "the chief vehicle of paideia,"[9] the main transmission belt of the national culture from one generation to the next; and Eric Havelock has seen the rejection of poetry as a major battle in the war against an old-fashioned system of instruction, in which the schoolboy absorbed knowledge from epic poems by hearing them recited and having to memorize them himself with appropriate gesture and expression.[10] Plato, in this view, wishing to refound education on true knowledge rather than mere opinion, on analytical thinking rather than anecdote and incident, on philosophy, in short, rather than on poetry, needs to discredit the claims made for poetry by all the exponents of traditional culture. If so, one consequence may be a certain measure of polemical exaggeration. For Socrates' rejection of the claims of Homer's partisans implicitly transfers the claim to Homer himself. The wish to build wagons, drive chariots, and lead armies is imputed not only to his followers and apologists but to the poet himself, and viewed as the wretched shift

8. Cornford, *The Republic*, p. 322.

9. Werner Jaeger, *Paideia: The Ideals of Greek Culture*, trans. Gilbert Highet (Oxford, 1943), II, 214, 359.

10. *Preface to Plato*, passim.

of one who failed to find a foothold of his own in the world of strenuous action he loved to depict.

As so often in later discussions of this sort, little attention is paid to the range of actions actually imitated by the poet. Socrates assumes that anyone would aspire to command troops, like Agamemnon, win battles, like Achilles, or provide sage counsel, like Odysseus. But does the poet also yearn to murder his own children, like Medea, to entrap and betray his spouse, like Clytemnestra, to die consumed with hopeless passion, like Phaedra? Most of the central actions on which stage tragedy turns are those a man would go to any lengths to avoid—as Oedipus, indeed, goes to extreme and desperate lengths to avoid the fate that seems actively to be driving him to perform actions he holds in the utmost abhorrence.

But now the argument sharply alters direction, handing down a newer and sterner indictment. Up to this point the reality status of poetry has been impugned and the poet's own motives downgraded: he engages in a kind of pointless mimicry in order to fend off, as it were, the sense of his own shortcomings. His efforts, however, we now discover, are far from insignificant or feeble; on the contrary they are explosive and dangerous. For they excite in us the very faculties which stand in most need of restraint, and they paralyze those that most need encouragement. Of the two primary properties of our minds, one, the faculty that processes sensory data, is untrustworthy, easily deceived by appearances, and subject to delusions. It takes light for shade and crooked for straight. The other, the "calculating and rational principle," deals in numbers and exact quantities. It sorts out and corrects the disordered impressions of the senses, certifying to the real truth of things. Artists, says Socrates, owe their allegiance to the inferior principle, which trades in fancies and opinions. They depict men divided within themselves, torn between passion and reason, and as they do so, instead of helping us master our passions they inflame them. They pour fuel on the most combustible part of our nature. For they aim not to discover the truth but only to please, and nothing is easier than to follow the line of least resistance, to imitate the passions, which lend themselves to vivid mimetic enactment, and which seduce by their very variety and variability. Far more difficult to render interestingly or convincingly would be the austerity of a truly temperate soul. Artists invite us to sympathize with men racked by emotions we should be ashamed to yield to in our own lives. By foment-ing our irrational selves, they carry us away from the true, the good, and the beautiful.[11]

If poetry owes its degraded metaphysical status to Plato's preference for abstractions over particulars, it owes its unenviable moral status to his division of the soul into higher and lower faculties. More than a simple hierarchy, this division constitutes a fierce dualism in which emotion wars eternally on reason, where all good lodges. Except for the fiery courage, the *thumos* or "spirit" that enables soldiers to defend the state, Plato hardly allows any positive value to the feelings at all. The one significant exception comes about mainly for reasons of po-litical necessity: the survival of the community depends on it. But the normal behavior of the feelings, both the "desires" and the "passions," is to distort our perception of things, and to weaken our self-command. They play the role of a rebellious army, restlessly biding its time till it can stage a *coup d'état* against its rightful ruler, the reason, which for its part must take strict measures, maintain a large police force and a relentless vigilance, to keep mutinous elements in check.

Mimetic experience can imperil even the hardiest soul. All of us "delight in giving way to sympathy, and are in raptures at the excel-lence of the poet who stirs our feelings most" (605d). But even as he stirs our feelings, the poet is subverting our judgment. If he wrings tears from us with his feigned actions, he is softening us up so that we will more readily weep and lament in our daily lives. If he makes us laugh in public, he is prompting us to give way to unseemly hilarity

11. R. G. Collingwood, "Plato's Philosophy of Art," *Mind* 34 (1925): 154–172, argues that *Republic* X contains not an attack on art but simply a theory of art. Despite much clarifying analysis, this argument at its crucial points seems to superimpose on the material a Neoplatonic interpretation not discoverable in Plato himself. See esp. p. 162, where it is claimed that the imaginative character of art, for Plato, lends it a "glamour" which springs from "phantasms" that "indirectly" symbolize the truth, symbolism itself being, by its nature, "the apprehension of truth veiled or disguised in an imaginative form . . . . heavy with an import which can only convey itself in the shape of a feeling of urgency . . . a feeling that we are in the presence of a mystery revealed and yet not revealed." One searches Book X of the *Republic* in vain for anything that might support these Florentine fantasies. On the matter of Plato's attitude toward "art," see Havelock, *Preface to Plato*, pp. 33–35.

at home. In either case we lose our dignity and our powers of dispassionate thought. The imitative poet, then, upsets the order in our souls and fosters what is evil in us. We must be on our guard, warns Socrates, and forbid him to treat of any subject except those officially approved, and in ways officially approved as well. So, he concludes, in his bantering fashion, though we may greatly admire the poets, even revere their talent, we will, nevertheless, firmly escort them to the city gates and usher them out—unless, of course, they can make some irresistibly charming and persuasive defense of themselves in verse, in which case we will hasten to welcome them back.

This jocular palinode, with its disclaimer of excessive solemnity, revives the strain of playfulness always lurking in Plato, and may seem to warn us against taking his theses too solemnly. The attack on mimesis, we reflect, is after all itself conducted in the mimetic mode. Its cast of characters express themselves with a winning and lifelike vividness. They reminisce, they digress, they tease each other, and in a host of ways interfere with the straightforward march of the argument. The Platonic dialogues, in general, one suspects, would have trouble with the proposed Platonic censor. Moreover, we do not need the testimony of Diogenes Laertius to convince us of Plato's own addiction to poetry: page after page of the dialogues betray a long-standing intimacy that only intense and lively engagement can produce. It is clear enough, again, that the *Republic* contemplates not an actual but an ideal state, which could come into existence only in a radically changed world in which virtually all familiar landmarks had long since been swept away, leaving pastimes like the theater irrelevant in a way we find it almost impossible to imagine. We remember, finally, dialogues other than the *Republic*, which seem to render a more gracious verdict on poetry than this one.

Certainly among the middle dialogues the *Republic* gives greatest scope to Plato's puritanism. At the same time, there are good grounds for regarding it as his *summa*, the one that sets forth his central convictions in most comprehensive and deeply pondered fashion. Despite the whimsy and the irony and the Socratic self-deprecation, a careful reading of the dialogue as a whole tends to confirm the hard interpretation, and to make the frequent local concessions, the dramatic touches, the quasi-comic byplay, largely a matter of leavening, to win a favorable hearing for unpalatable doctrine. It would probably be less of an error to take the antipoetic theses of the *Republic* too literally than to write them off as mere turns of an endless dialectical kaleidoscope. Unless the logic implicit in Plato's whole view of society is to be set aside, we must conclude that the hostility to art is real, and the rejection of the theater an integral part of the utopian vision.

A well-known passage in the *Ion* has sometimes been taken, and in the Renaissance was regularly taken,[12] as his espousal of a very different doctrine. Here, it is said, Plato ascribes poetry to divine inspiration. "For the poet," says Socrates on this occasion, "is a light and winged and holy thing, and there is no invention in him until he has been inspired and is out of his senses, and reason is no longer in him" (534b).[13] Poetry, on this account, is a sacred madness, the product of an ecstatic loss of the self, as in the *Phaedrus*. But even in the *Phaedrus* Socrates denies it the title of "art" (*techne*)—of a discipline that can be formulated, studied, and learned. Only the madman may hope to enter the temple of the Muses (245a).[14] In the *Ion*, an earlier dialogue, the quarrel between poetry and philosophy is energetically pursued. Ion himself, the rhapsode, is portrayed as a foolish posturing fellow, naively vain of his talent and quite insensible of Socrates' irony. He displays the same condition of ignorance as the poets in Book X of the *Republic*, knowing nothing of the various skills of which he sings —nothing of fishing, nothing of cowherding, nothing of weaving of baskets or healing the sick—not even so much as would be known by a slave. He is indeed egregiously ignorant and his boast of being a general, based on his recitations of the deeds of warriors, is so patently absurd that it brings his whole calling into contempt. If anything, he ranks lower in the scale of truth than the painter, sculptor, or poet, for where they are interpreters, he is but "the [interpreter] of interpreters" (535a), and so at an even further remove than they "from the king and from the truth."

Socrates rapidly establishes the proposition that Ion's talent as an interpreter cannot be an art, a definable body of knowledge or an ordered system of skills. For if it were, Ion would be able to judge the

12. See Sir Philip Sidney, *An Apology for Poetry*, ed. Geoffrey Shepherd (Manchester, 1973), p. 129, lines 36–39, and p. 209, n. 38.

13. *Dialogues*, trans. Jowett, I, 108.

14. Ibid., III, 151.

worth and accomplishment of poets other than Homer, whereas in fact when it comes to speaking of Hesiod or Archilochus or any other than Homer, he confesses himself helpless. Good-natured Socrates, with his own weakness for poetry, is eager to propitiate the chagrined rhapsode by finding an innocent justification for his calling, some non-pejorative definition that will leave him with a few shreds of dignity. Predictably, the explanatory myth he comes up with proves only ambiguously favorable, since in attributing poetry to moments of ecstasy, it also denies the poet the use of his reason at these moments; it stresses his kinship with the lunatic. Under Socrates' questioning, Ion admits that he too, the poet's interpreter, is subject to ecstasies. He too is carried away by the furious emotion of his verses as he chants them. And so is his audience. At the climax it quite loses its senses, an effect that for more than one reason the rhapsode wishes to encourage. For the more tears he can wring from his listeners, the more he himself will laugh when the time of payment arrives, whereas if now he makes them laugh, it is he who will weep at the hour of reckoning. His inspiration, then, stems at least in part from mercenary motives. The prospect of a handsome fee helps bring on an access of the divine frenzy.

The final twist, once Ion's fatuous pretence to generalship has been exploded, is Socrates' charge that his friend has been practicing the arts of Proteus in their conversation, "twisting and turning up and down" (541e) and trying at length to sneak off in the disguise of a commander of troops. At length he is allowed to choose whether he prefers to be considered dishonest or inspired. No other options are available, and the one claim he will be emphatically forbidden to make is that his trade has anything to do with art.

It is not hard to see in this amiable ridicule most of the antimimetic theses of the *Republic* pursued in a more lighthearted vein. Here too poetry is viewed as a disordering force, capable of unhinging the balance not only of the poet but of his interpreters, the rhapsodes and their hearers. That Ion's audiences love to submit to his deranging influence illustrates the power of poetry to unseat the one faculty which in a well-governed life should never lose control. The *Ion* does not so much present a different view of poetry from that of the *Republic* as a more tentative and ingratiating version of it, without the element of proscription that we find disquieting in the later dialogue. The divine fury must, after all, mean the tyranny of the irrational. The fact that it can be induced in such an insignificant creature as Ion, and for such trivial, not to say unworthy, reasons, casts grave doubt on its divinity.[15]

But the *Ion*, like the *Phaedrus*, reminds us of Plato's own intense and exceptional aesthetic responsiveness, which struggles with his anti-poetic austerity, and finds its chief outlet in his drive to aestheticize politics. The ideal city may exile the poets, but it does so in order to become all the more a poem itself, a beautiful and harmonious totality, every particle of which contributes to the total order. Since, as the Platonic Socrates tells us, whatever impinges on a man's senses or enters into his daily experience has the power to ennoble or degrade him, every aspect of life acquires importance in the fashioning of the good citizen. The interplay between our minds and our surroundings takes on a capital importance. Hence the crucial roles of music, diet, and expressive architecture, and hence also, the climactic onslaught on mimesis with which the *Republic* nears its end, which amounts to the rejection of the arts of poetry, drama, and theater in favor of the art of the state. In the accurate phrase of one critic, politics for Plato is "an art of composition, like music, painting, or architecture. The Platonic politician composes cities, for beauty's sake."[16] The inevitable consequence is that all the particular arts must become subservient *to* politics. If the stage, or other mimetic arts, do not promote the well-being of the body politic, they must be eliminated, much as an ill-drawn line or an ill-placed patch of color must be erased from the canvas in the interests of the design as a whole—or, to use Plato's own figure in a related context, as the color of the eyes of a statue must be

15. Craig LaDrière, "The Problem of Plato's *Ion*," *Journal of Aesthetics and Art Criticism* 10 (1951): 26–34, argues persuasively that the subject of the *Ion* is neither poetry itself nor the recitation of poetry, but "the *criticism* of poetry as Ion practiced it; and, by implication, such criticism of all similar art" (p. 29, my italics). But the fact that the dialogue addresses itself chiefly to criticism does not prevent it, and indeed cannot prevent it, from concerning itself centrally with poetry itself, its creation, performance, and reception, as the passage about the magnet and the iron rings clearly demonstrates.

16. K[arl] R. Popper, *The Open Society and Its Enemies*, I, *The Spell of Plato*, 2d ed. (London, 1952), p. 165.

chosen not for their independent attractiveness but for the sake of the entire statue (420c–d).

To clarify Platonic antitheatricalism, we need to glance at some earlier portions of the *Republic*. Books I and II, it will be remembered, survey the topic which is to dominate the inquiry, the nature of justice. Socrates disposes easily of the crude claims of the sophist Thrasymachus, who promotes the cynical view that justice consists of the will of the stronger. The two young disciples Glaucon and Adeimantus, however, confront their master with a less contemptible challenge. Justice, they point out, has always been defined as an external thing, a matter of reputation. Gyges, the honest shepherd in the myth, turns into a villain from the instant that he acquires the magic ring which makes him invisible. He seduces the queen, plots with her to kill the king, and seizes the kingdom for himself. Would any man, demands Glaucon, act otherwise? Would anyone resist the temptation to gratify his appetites, irrespective of the harm he might do to others, if he knew that there was no possible way he could be called to account for his actions? Would anyone, conversely, endure a lonely martyrdom for truth, if the very stuff of martyrdom—witnesses and fellow-sufferers—were denied him? Surely, "no man would keep his hands off what was not his own when he could safely take what he liked out of the market, or go into houses and lie with any one at his pleasure, or kill or release from prison whom he would, and in all respects be like a god among men. Then the actions of the just would be as the actions of the unjust; they would both tend to the same goal" (360b–c). To which Adeimantus subjoins that justice has always been recommended to us for the blessings it brings, the honor it earns for us among our fellows. It seems to be no more than a reflex of our need to be loved and respected and to avoid punishment. We care nothing for it as it may be in itself, irrespective of its rewards, and we need care as little about the penalties for injustice, since even if these are real they can always be redeemed by last-minute propitiations and sacrifices, leaving us free to pursue our selfish ways until the very end.

Unlike Thrasymachus, with his boorish sophistries, Glaucon and Adeimantus have posed a genuine challenge, which it will take much of the rest of the dialogue to answer. Socrates from the outset will be seeking to define justice as a kind of primary truth, something with the absolute and sacrosanct character of mathematics, independent of appearances and unaffected by individual caprice. He starts, however, by shifting the angle of vision away from individual men to the state as a whole, so as to be able to view the question "macroscopically." But this shift holds portentous consequences. By taking the state rather than the individual as the standard, Plato subordinates ethics to politics. Not man but the state becomes the measure of all things, and the way is open for a series of inhibiting actions against the individual, who is henceforth to be constrained by the requirements of the polity as a whole.

The inquiry gets under way with a highly conjectural, highly schematic account of the origins of the state, which lays no claim to historical factuality. Society emerges from chaos, suggests Socrates, because men need each other. Unequally fitted to perform the various tasks required to sustain life, they band together and pool their skills. In this first stage, they will engage only in those occupations directly necessary to survival, those concerned with feeding, clothing, and housing themselves, with defending themselves against attack, and acquiring by trade whatever is in short supply at home. This first society will include no purveyors of pleasure—no hunters, painters, musicians, poets, recitants, players, dancers, barbers, dressmakers, swineherds, or soldiers. The practitioners of the arts of adornment and enhancement begin to appear only when the citizens have developed a taste for luxury, and demand specialists who can provide it. Although this second stage represents a long-consolidated advance from which it would be futile to wish to retreat, Plato makes it clear that he regards it as pathological. The healthy condition is the earlier one, in which only basic natural necessities are appeased. Even in this provisional sketch one is struck by the intensity of Plato's nostalgia for a simpler existence, and by the invidiousness of his tone toward the artists, who are lumped together with dressmakers and barbers as a race of drones, supplying trivial amusements which the community would be better off without. In the primitive community, men spend their leisure feasting at home, "drinking of the wine which they have made, wearing garlands on their heads, and hymning the praises of the gods, in happy converse with one another" (372c). Neither poets nor musicians have anything to contribute to this idyll, and they are firmly excluded from it. Even before poetry has come under direct scrutiny, then, it has already been stigmatized as a fever symptom, an adulterating element whose presence helps mark the unwelcome transition from a wholesome, innocent life to a corrupted and enervated one.[17]

Rather abruptly at this point, the conversation takes a new tack. It turns from the innocent community of the past to the ideal state of the future, and specifically to the education of its "guardians," its soldiers and rulers. Disconcertingly, the first topic for discussion concerns the institution of a censorship, to shield the fledgling guardians from malign influences that might injure them as protectors of the state. To put it another way, we start with a species of thought control instituted in the nursery, designed to exclude from the consciousness of the young guardians a wide range of potentially subversive notions. The stories told them are to be carefully expurgated. Brutal tales about the gods, such as the myth of the castration of Uranos by Chronos, or of Chronos devouring his children, are to be forbidden, as are stories of wars, jealousies, revenges, and betrayals among the gods, since "the tales which the young first hear should be models of virtuous thoughts" (378e). Again, the young are not to be allowed to hear that the gods—or God—are authors of evil, but of good only, nor are they to be permitted to suppose, as the myths have it, that he is a magician, "of a nature to appear insidiously now in one shape, and now in another—sometimes really changing and passing into many forms, sometimes deceiving us with the semblance of such transformations." Rather, he must be shown as he truly is, "one and the same immutably fixed in his own proper image" (380d).

17. The *Laws*, too, contain an account of the primitive state, in which men are virtuous because neither rich nor poor. "The community which has neither poverty nor riches will always have the noblest principles; in it there is no insolence or injustice, nor . . . any contentions or envyings." In such a community men are good; men *were* good, "and also because they were what is called simple-minded; and when they were told about good and evil, they in their simplicity believed what they heard to be very truth and practised it. No one had the wit to suspect another of falsehood, as men do now; but what they heard about the Gods and men they believed to be true, and lived accordingly." Moreover, as men were simpler they were "more manly, and also more temperate and altogether more just" (679b–e). Plato's primitivism thus places a premium on naiveté and credulity. These become the handmaidens of virtue, while intelligence, wit, skepticism, and subtlety, which might prompt a man to question what he is told, become its enemies.

For Plato, the force of this precept is overwhelming, since it springs from his profound attachment to what is stable and fixed as against that which flickers or alters, and for what is simple and pure as against that which is compound and corruptible.[18] His theory of personality rests on the premise that each man is endowed by nature with one chief talent which must form the basis for his role in society. Every man in the *Republic* will be assigned one work at which he is to persevere all his life long and at no other. If this is so for men, if their highest virtue is to persist unswervingly in the pursuit of their single natural bent, then the same must apply, a fortiori, to the gods, whose superiority lies precisely in their being, by definition, exempt from change. Since they are already perfect, they must wish to remain so. Change could be only for the worse, and no perfect being would ever willingly degrade himself. Each one of the gods, therefore, "remains absolutely and for ever in his own form" (381c). Poets, consequently, must be forbidden to slander them by telling tales like those of the metamorphoses of Proteus, or of other disguises and deceptions in which the gods trick men into thinking that they can transform themselves.

The whole passage constitutes a remarkable attempt to demythologize religion, to moralize it, to make it transcendental, to banish the animistic pantheon of wood deities, sea nymphs, and mountain gods, and replace it with the heavenly city Plato alone believed in, the kingdom of the forms, simple, abstract, and eternal in its changelessness. The aim of the earthly city, in Plato's mind, should be to conform as closely as possible to its celestial archetype. But the traditional lore

18. On this point see, *inter alia*, Walter Pater, *Plato and Platonism*, 2d ed. (London, 1895), pp. 16 ff.: "To Plato motion becomes the token of unreality in things, of falsity in our thoughts about them. . . . Everywhere he displays himself as an advocate of the immutable" (p. 16); and Popper, p. 37: "In brief Plato teaches *that change is evil, and that rest is divine.*" See also, however, Alban Dewes Winspear, *The Genesis of Plato's Thought*, 2d ed. (New York, 1956), pp. 319–331, for the thesis that Plato modified this view in the later dialogues, largely under the pressure of social and political conditions which led him to a position of activism and reform incompatible with an ideal of total stasis. The problem becomes one not of refusing to recognize change as a reality but of learning how to control it. See also J. B. Skemp, *The Theory of Motion in Plato's Later Dialogues* (Cambridge, 1942).

about the gods has had the opposite effect. It assimilates the ideal realm to the debased human one, making it into a picturesque exaggeration of the changefulness of man and external nature. It attributes every kind of vacillation to supernatural beings whose only claim to reverence is or ought to be their unvarying perfection.

But the account of censorship in the nursery proceeds. If the Olympian gods must not be shown as mutable, neither must the underworld be shown as terrifying, for this would frighten the young guardians, who must be schooled to meet death without fear. The exploits of the heroes will have to be revised, with accounts of the "weepings and wailings of famous men" deleted (387d), since good men ought not to think of death as terrible, either for themselves or others. The same holds for the keening of the gods themselves when they lose their friends and lovers: any serious heed paid to such stories will induce the guardians too to whine and lament on trifling occasions. And on the other hand, since boisterous mirth would likewise be indecent in them, they are not to be told that the gods give way to hilarity, or that they are prone to drunkenness. Gods, sages, and heroes, in short, must never be shown doing anything which the state would not wish its own citizens to do, but rather, the young should be regaled with "instances of endurance of various ills by famous men" (390d), and whatever else may toughen their fibre and instill resolution into them.

We start, then, with a view of art as an adjunct of state policy, an instrument for the shaping of good citizens in accord with approved morality. Anything in the intellectual diet of the guardians that encourages freedom, curiosity, or exploration is to be suppressed. When it comes to stories about ordinary men, as distinct from gods and heroes, Socrates defers answer. He is not yet ready, he says, to speak to this point, since he has not yet proved his central thesis, the paradox that the just are happy and the unjust unhappy, regardless of appearances. But the handwriting is on the wall, and Socrates anticipates the ultimate verdict: poets will be forbidden to show life as it presents itself to their eyes if that view clashes with the one held by the philosophers. Specifically, they will be forbidden to expound the view that the wicked often seem happy and the good miserable, for this would contradict the official position, based on existence as seen from the standpoint of eternity. They will be expected to renounce their own insight and adopt that of the governors.

The principle which thus crystallizes in the course of the *Republic* is spelled out more fully in the *Laws,* and its most repressive consequences drawn without hesitation. Plato's Athenian spokesman tells his hearers that "the true legislator will persuade, and, if he cannot persuade, will compel the poet to express, as he ought, by fair and noble words, in his rhythms, the figures, and in his melodies, the music of temperate and brave and in every way good men" (660a). More specifically, poets will be enjoined to declare that "the good man, if he be temperate and just, is fortunate and happy," whatever the apparent meanness of his worldly circumstances, and that on the other hand, no matter how rich or powerful he may seem to be, "he is wretched and lives in misery" if he is unjust (660e). This prescription, moreover, is to be rigorously enforced. "I would inflict the heaviest penalties on anyone in all the land who should dare to say that there are bad men who lead pleasant lives, or that the profitable and gainful is one thing, and the just another" (662 b–c). The poets, in short, are to say what their rulers order them to say, for their rulers know best.

Freedom, clearly, freedom of the individual, is not an ideal that recommends itself to Plato. It encourages what is emotional and irrational in us. It carries the seeds of diversity and hence of disruption. It leads to waywardness, to multiplicity, to tolerance [*sic!*], carelessness, the cult of pleasure, and other evils, all enumerated in a long sarcastic passage in Book VIII, where democracy is scoffingly likened to "an embroidered robe . . . spangled with every sort of flower" (557c). What makes democracy suspect to Plato is precisely what makes it attractive to us, its variety and freedom, and it is against such freedom, symbolized in the waywardness of the artist, that the Republic is to mobilize its repressive mechanisms. If the state is to achieve the greatness proper to it, it must curb the instinct for self-expression that lodges in us all and tends to thwart the fulfillment of the political ideal. This is not the last occasion we shall have to notice that those who promulgate utopias are often more dangerous enemies of art than simple despots, since they so much more programmatically and ideologically set about to restrict individual expression. It is the deepest urge of art and artists to elude the exactitudes and boundaries which states find it convenient to impose, and which, in their assumption of their own greater dignity and reality, they believe they have the right to impose.

Having disapprovingly surveyed some of the subjects of traditional poetry, Socrates now turns to considerations of style, taking up the question of whether poets are to be allowed to practice the "imitative" as distinct from the "narrative" mode in their poems, and if so, how. Once again the argument proves to hinge on the monolithic theory of personality. Just as human beings are born with a single talent, which it is their mission to cultivate, so they are restricted in their capacity for imitation. "Human nature . . . appears . . . as incapable of imitating many things well, as of performing well the actions of which the imitations are copies" (395b). One may well ask on what grounds, other than those of prejudice and political convenience, Plato makes such claims. Certainly the doctrine of "one man, one talent" makes a useful rule of thumb for bureaucrats. It offers a simple and handy way of dividing men into categories of specialists. Moreover, once implemented, it doubtless tends to become self-perpetuating. A man who cultivates a single talent to the exclusion of all others will no doubt see his other powers atrophy; as he watches his father devotedly refining a single skill throughout a lifetime, he may indeed conclude that he is in the presence of a law of nature, to be obeyed unquestioningly in his own life. But that this process reflects any inherent limitation in our natures, any innate incapacity for excelling at more than one activity, seems utterly unlikely—belied, indeed, by the example of Plato himself and by the actors and poets whom he is at such pains to disparage. It remains, however, a powerful unargued assumption to which the dialogue keeps returning, and which licenses the state to assume a maximum of control over its members, discouraging them from imagining other forms of life for themselves than those they have once chosen or had chosen for them.

Since, in Plato's view, imitation is formative—those who imitate will tend to become what they imitate—it follows that the guardians may be allowed to imitate only characters suitable as models: the courageous, the temperate, the devout. They must be prohibited from miming illiberal or base characters, lest they receive taint from them. They must not imitate women either, or slaves, or villains, or madmen, or "smiths or other artificers, or oarsmen, boatswains, or the like" (396a). They must, in fact, confine themselves to imitations of members of their own sex, their own social level, their own professional class and moral outlook. Whatever takes them into another realm of the mind by distancing them from their "essential" selves, whatever momentarily provides them with an alternate role, a new soul, thereby unfits them for their work in society. Nor may they, needless to add, desert humanity altogether and personate the neighing of horses, the murmur of rivers, or the roll of the oceans. Even when it comes to imitating good men who are their equals, they must take care never to do so when the latter are "overtaken by illness or love or drink; or [when they have] met with any disaster," but only when they are acting "firmly and wisely." Imitation, then, may be used only to reinforce desirable behavior patterns, to confirm the guardians in what (in principle) they already are, and the rule is extended, as we might expect, in the *Laws*, to cover not only the guardians, but all men (656b). Perhaps it would be wrong to deny the name of imitation to this activity— this emulation of one's own "ideal character" in others—but if it is imitation, it is of the narrowest sort, restricted to the tightest range of possible models, excluding the whole realm of unstructured play, of spontaneous self-discovery, of casual and random improvisation.[19] Wherever it might involve imaginative displacement, adoption of unfamiliar psychic hypotheses, experiments with untried states of feeling, wherever it might promise (or threaten) to release the individual from the cage of his ego or his fixed place in the social order, it becomes the first step in a disintegrative process that can only end in anarchy.

For the poet, this means that he must prefer the less perilous narrative style to the mimetic, and when practicing the mimetic must confine himself to setting forth the deeds of the just and the well-tempered (though even this concession seems withdrawn in Book X). Poets desirous of imitating the whole range of human actions must be discouraged, and so must those whose style includes diversity, "for one man plays one part only." But by what authority, we are once more driven to ask, does Plato restrict human nature to "one part only"? Why should a man not attempt many parts? In the ideal state, Socrates triumphantly declares, "we shall find a shoemaker to be a shoemaker and not a pilot also, and a husbandman to be a husbandman and not a dicast also, and a soldier a soldier and not a trader also, and the same throughout" (397e). Socrates' horror of such multiple roles seems

19. See J. Tate, " 'Imitation' in Plato's *Republic*," *Classical Quarterly* 22 (1928): 16–23, pp. 17–18. References such as this will regularly give first the inclusive page numbers of the article or chapter in question, and then the page or pages to which specific citation is made.

both puzzling and irritating. Why should a shoemaker *not* also be a pilot, a husbandman a dicast, and a soldier a trader? May there not be men whose natural versatility enables them to do many things well? May not there also be those who even without special aptitude nevertheless feel themselves more fulfilled by performing a variety of tasks than by adhering inflexibly to a single one? Even from the point of view of social efficiency, might not the alternation between one activity and another relieve the monotony in both, heighten the pleasure, and thereby enhance the very expertness desiderated by the social planner? The most one can say for the Socratic prescription is that it has a certain arithmetical neatness. It sets bounds to the amorphousness of human personality. It reduces each man to a single well-defined entity, firmly linked to his social role. It establishes an unambiguous numerical equivalence between the number of citizens and the approved occupations. It seems to promise a coherent social order, in which each man plies the trade for which nature has intended him, without envious or restless side glances at his neighbor. But from the individual's point of view the principle seems forbiddingly repressive. No one is to be allowed to deviate from his allotted task, to abandon familiar routines or experiment with untried ones. No one is to be allowed to cast off the yoke of his assigned role, however galling he may find it. Frustration, boredom, curiosity, excitement, adventurousness—all such responses are to be invalidated and in effect legislated out of existence.

Built into the foundations of the edifice, then, we find a constraining assumption about the capacities of the individual, and an effort to lock him securely in his place in the social structure, as a piece of movable type is locked into place by the quoins. Plato constructs the entire Republic on the basis of the simplification of the self, and he reinforces it with laws designed to curb any tendency to counteract it, to enlarge, extend, or expand its domain. Ultimately, as we discover, justice itself, the object of the dialectical quest, in its "macrocosmic" aspect proves to be nothing more nor less than the perseverance of each citizen in the role allotted him, and injustice any attempt to cast off that role. That nature has prescribed the course of our lives we learn from the myth of the metals. All men have had infused into their composition at birth an amalgam of gold, silver, and brass, predisposing them to succeed as guardians, soldiers, artisans, or tradesmen. It is the job of the state to reinforce these genetic differences, and to build solid walls between the social classes, since an oracle has predicted that "when a man of brass or iron guards the State, it will be destroyed" (415c). The end result, then, is that,

> when the cobbler or any other man whom nature designed to be a trader . . . attempts to force his way into the class of warriors, or a warrior into that of legislators and guardians, to which he ought not to aspire, and when these exchange their implements and their social position with those above them; or when one man would be trader, legislator, and warrior all in one, then I think you will agree with me in saying that this interchange and this meddling of one with another is the ruin of the State. . . .
> Seeing then . . . that there are three distinct classes, any meddling of one with another, or the change of one into another, is the greatest harm to the State, and may be most justly termed evil-doing? . . . And the greatest degree of evil-doing to one's own city would be termed by you injustice? . . . This then is injustice; and on the other hand when the three main classes, traders, auxiliaries, and guardians, each do their own business, that is justice, and will make the city just. (434b–d)

Justice, in sum, means knowing one's place, acquiescing in one's "natural" limitations, performing one's allotted duties as prescribed by the authorities. Any attempt to cross social barriers, to widen one's horizons, to multiply one's interests, constitutes a dereliction, a breach of justice.

Inevitably, then, one telltale symptom of the downfall of the good state, in its emblematic progress from aristocracy to tyranny, is the crumbling of the fixed callings and a licentious multiplication of roles. In oligarchy, for example, says Socrates, "there is the fault which we blamed long ago: the same persons have too many callings—they are husbandmen, tradesmen, warriors, all in one. Does that look well?" "Very well," we are tempted to reply, but the once irreverent Adeimantus, now totally Socratized, promptly interposes his disapproval: "Anything but well" (552a). In the next stage—democracy—freedom of movement increases. The city is now "full of freedom and frankness," and "the individual is clearly able to order for himself his own life as he pleases," so that "in this kind of State there will be the greatest variety of human natures" (557b–c). The life of the single citizen himself becomes "motley and manifold and an epitome of the lives

of many" (561e). And again we receive the strange sensation of looking down the wrong end of a telescope, where what Plato perceives
as a danger and a decadence we can hardly help seeing—at least in
part—as a liberation and an enrichment.

The Platonic Republic, then, is an inhibitory state, as that of the
Laws is an inquisitorial one. It confines human nature to a single mold,
on doubtful psychological grounds, maintains sharp boundaries between the life styles of its various inhabitants, and penalizes any attempt
to pass freely back and forth among them. Nor are the citizens forbidden to stray from their appointed roles in fact alone, but also in
imagination: it is a crime to invent or "imitate" a situation differing
from the existing one, or tending toward such differences. In music,
only those rhythms and harmonies are to be permitted which foster
resolution and temperance, not those expressive of conviviality or grief,
which might enervate the soul. "Corrupting" harmonies and rhythms
must be purified. Flutes, three-cornered lyres, and complex scales are
to be banned; only the simple lyre and harp are to be allowed for urban
use and the shepherd's pipe for the country, along with the basic scales.[20]
No gourmet diets, either, for as complexity in music engenders license,
so elaborateness in cuisine produces disease. Pleasure itself must be
kept to a minimum, to what will help foster courage in the leaders,
since like pain it is disabling and deranging, robbing a man of the
right use of his faculties. In every conceivable sphere of activity, simplicity is the goal, and complexity the dreaded enemy. Simplicity means
purity, stability, and health. Complexity spells impurity, instability,
distemper.

An especially bizarre kind of simplicity is desiderated for the magistrates. They are to learn about injustice only late in life, "from long
observation of its nature in others . . . knowledge should be [their]
guide, not personal experience" (409b–c). The upright magistrate of

20. Jaeger is reminded, in this connection, of the story that "Spartan officials prohibited the brilliant Timotheus . . . from appearing in Sparta,
because he had abandoned the seven-stringed cithara of Terpander, hallowed by tradition, and played an instrument of more strings and richer
harmonies," thus demonstrating "how the Greeks felt a fundamental alteration in the structure of music to be a political revolution, because it
changed the spirit of education, on which the state depended" (*Paideia*,
II, 226). Perhaps it would be even more to the point to speak of "Plato and
the Spartans" rather than generally "the Greeks."

the Republic, that is, is to remain ignorant of evil, insulated from any consciousness of it in himself, acquainted with it only in an external way by observation of others. He occupies the perilous position of Angelo in *Measure for Measure*, except that Plato, unlike Shakespeare, really believes in the purity of his Angelos, in an invincible ignorance that fits them to become judges of their frailer fellows. Education in the Republic must foster this ignorance, not dispel it. Imitation threatens us because it can acquaint us with evils that have remained chained up in the world of our dreams. It can unshackle the evils, enabling them to claw their way to the surface to break out into savage rebellion against their rightful master, the reason.

Platonic attitudes toward art, then, form a complex of negative injunctions, hinging on the relations between the individual and the state. Art has the disadvantage of springing from the individual and addressing itself, in the last analysis, to the individual. It cares little for the state. From the point of view of the Republic, whatever tends to widen the individual's range tends also to undermine the fixity of his role, and imperils the stability of the social order. If the state is to remain simple and stable, so must each of its members, and for them to do so, imaginative activity must be restricted at every port: the inner lives of the citizens must be as strictly monitored as their outer lives, with every tendency to eccentricity or extravagance sharply curbed. Mimesis, which can place new and unsettling thoughts in the mind, must be treated as a dangerous explosive. Except in rare moments, it works chiefly on the irrational side of us, giving license to our dreams and foul thoughts, to whatever in us is devious, intricate, and disordering. Theater being the quintessentially mimetic art, acting being radically founded in multiplication of roles and transgression of boundaries, all that is urged in suspicion of poetry, music, recitation, and the other arts must apply here with a maximum of force and a minimum of regretful qualification. If any one sphere of activity apart from unabashed crime may be said to embody what Plato fears and distrusts, it is the theater, and his hostility to it, which smolders in the *Republic*, bursts into fiery blaze in the *Laws*, where it is made responsible for the evils and corruptions of the present day. Music, says the Athenian, degenerated because of an "excess of freedom." Once upon a time, poets were restricted to certain prayers and paeans to the gods; other kinds of poetry were forbidden. In those days authority kept a watchful eye

on the public, and wielded a stern hand over it. The "directors of public instruction insisted that the spectators should listen in silence to the
end; and boys and their tutors, and the multitude, in general, were
kept quiet by a hint from a stick." The theater thus resembled a class-
room, with the spectators as schoolchildren. But this wholesome state
of affairs deteriorated when poets, in order to please their listeners,
started to practice "vulgar and lawless innovation," when they began
to experiment with mixtures of genres, new instrumental timbres, and
licentious words, abandoning their adherence to "what is just and lawful." In their license they inspired the crowd in its turn with "lawlessness and boldness," so that whereas formerly an elite of seasoned critics
had served as judges, now "an evil sort of theatrocracy has grown up,"
which not only tyrannizes in the theater but has produced a whole host
of social evils in its wake: "disobedience to rulers," followed by "the
attempt to escape the control of father, mother, elders, and . . . the laws,"
from which has sprung, finally, "the contempt of oaths and pledges,
and no regard at all for the Gods" (700b–701c).

This extraordinary passage, which lays the anarchy of the present
directly at the door of the poets, tracing it to their attempts to please
the public by generic experimentation, and by metrical and harmonic
novelty, not only sets forth Plato's theory of freedom as a curse, but
tries to bolster that theory through a historical analysis. Casting his
mind into the future, then, Plato's Athenian goes on with minute
specificity to formulate the rules for the writing of poems. Poets are
to be forbidden to say anything but what the guardians have declared
to be true, forbidden to show their compositions to anyone before the
guardians have approved them—a species of prior censorship at which
even the framers of the licensing law attacked in Milton's *Areopagitica*
would have quailed. Poets, as in the olden days, are to confine themselves to hymns and panegyrics, but only in honor of the dead, since
it is unsafe—subversive, that is—to praise the living. Poets, moreover,
must be of a certain age; they must be of high moral character; they
must receive their appointments by official decree. Once appointed,
they are in fact to be treated as technicians rather than creators, assigned distinct tasks to be performed under close supervision, required
to compose and emend in accord with the wishes of the judges (802a–c,
829c–e). In the theater itself, the judges will no longer sit as disciples
but as schoolmasters of the people. It will be their mission to oppose

"all pandering to the pleasure of the spectators" (659b). Only, in short, under conditions of authoritarian stringency will Plato allow the theater into his projected state at all, conditions that will nullify it as an artistic event and turn it into an undisguised device of social indoctrination.

The actual theater, the theater as known to Plato and practiced by his contemporaries, can in the last analysis be allowed no virtue. It has corrupted society, and it continues to symbolize the evils which have led to Athens' downfall. And Plato's hostility toward it is destined to become the cornerstone of an antitheatrical edifice that is only now, after two and a half millennia, finally crumbling.

The rehabilitation of mimesis from the low position assigned it by Plato also begins early, with Aristotle. The *Poetics* leaves it at the heart of the educational process, but removes the stigma from it, seeing it not as a menace but a source of value. For Aristotle, mimesis is not the blurred second carbon of a remote ideality, but the filling out of an inherent form which that form requires for its fulfillment. Nor does it mislead men about the nature of reality; instead, it teaches them. It enables them to acquire true knowledge, since in coming to "imitate" particulars, or to witness such imitations, they learn valid general truths about the world.[21] They discover what is real beneath what is immediately apprehended. In its pleasurable aspect, moreover, in its capacity to rouse the emotions, mimesis, far from enfeebling us by putting us at the mercy of our worser instincts, actually fortifies us. By ordering and regulating its materials, tragic mimesis trains our responses, provides a lightning rod for potentially damaging feelings that clamor for expression.[22]

The theory of catharsis has generally been taken—at least since the rediscovery of the *Poetics* in the Renaissance—to entail the notion of a release from repression, and we may think of it as roughly analogous

21. My understanding of *mimesis* as used by Aristotle owes much to Gerald F. Else, *Aristotle's Poetics: The Argument* (1957; rpt. Cambridge, Mass., 1967), pp. 124–132.

22. This traditional view of what Aristotle meant by *catharsis* has come under increasing challenge recently. See Else, *Aristotle's Poetics*, pp. 224–232, 423–450, and H. D. F. Kitto, "Catharsis," in *The Classical Tradition: Literary and Historical Studies in Honor of Harry Caplan*, ed. Luitpold Wallach (Ithaca, N. Y., 1966), pp. 133–147.

to Freud's theory of wit, in which sexual aggression takes the socially acceptable form of a joke. Aristotle and Freud both see the release of irrational impulses as therapeutic, whereas for Plato it means the dangerous raking up of feelings that might better be suppressed. Werner Jaeger has credited Plato with being "the father of psychoanalysis . . . the first to disclose that the horrible Oedipus-complex . . . was part of the unconscious personality,"[23] and it is certainly true that for Plato, as for Freud, our dreams swarm with hostile, predatory fantasies.[24] But Plato deals with this insight in a highly un-Freudian spirit, insisting that the dream state, so highly charged with menace as it is, must not be allowed the encouragement that might enable it to translate itself into waking thought, not to mention waking action. The mimetic copy of a thing, in Plato's view, resembles the dream of a thing in that it is an impure and debased version of it which threatens our wholeness and sanity, and must therefore be subjected to stringent curbs. Paradoxically, Plato makes much of the ontological difference between an actual thing and its mimetic copy (or the dream of it), yet allows little psychological difference. It is nearly as terrible to *imagine* one has married one's mother as it would be to do so in earnest. The first can lead to the second and must be prohibited. The character of the "worst" man may be defined as the "waking reality of what we dreamed" (576b). Aristotle, on the other hand, redeems the ontological validity of the imitation: he refuses to dismiss or demote it as illusory, dreamlike, or secondhand. But since it is after all an imitation and not the thing itself, it must be allowed to involve profound psychological differences for the imitator and those who behold it. An evil imagined in the mind cannot casually be equated with an evil brought about in the visible world.

Twenty-five hundred years have by no means sufficed to settle these disputed claims, or to clarify the problem of how art affects us, especially in an age of mass culture such as our own. At a time when so many forms of art have become so effortlessly, even meaninglessly, absorbed into a homogenizing culture, the question may seem to have

23. *Paideia*, II, 343.
24. Freud in fact regarded himself as greatly indebted to Plato. He thought of his theory of libido as a psychoanalytic version of the Platonic Eros. See the Preface to *Three Essays on Sexuality*, 4th ed., trans. Jas. Strachey et al., VII (London, 1953), 134, and Murdoch, *The Fire and the Sun*, pp. 37–43.

lost some of its urgency. Our own world no longer cares so deeply about art as either Plato or Aristotle, or Freud himself, because we no longer feel its power so keenly. Plato legislated as he did because he recognized that power and was troubled by it. In the words of Edgar Wind, "he rated the strength of man's imagination so high that he thought a man could be transformed by the things he imagined. Hence he found miming a most perilous exercise, and he devised curious laws that would prohibit the miming of extravagant or evil characters."[25] The more seriously, indeed, one credits the power of art to vitalize and transfigure, to heal and sustain, the more seriously one must reckon with its potentiality to debilitate and debase. Certainly it would be reckless to claim that we remain unmoved, or unchanged, by what we see in the theater. If we can be changed, we can presumably be changed for the worse. Perhaps in the case of susceptible people with livelier imaginations, the possibilities for change are greater. Wind notes how guardedly recent psychotherapy deals with such clinical activities as psychodrama. Children and neurotic patients are still occasionally encouraged to act out their fantasies by painting or reenacting traumatic episodes from their past, but for other kinds of patient, notably schizophrenics, such therapy is no longer thought advisable, "because the imaginative activity is likely to reinforce rather than relieve the abnormal condition,"[26] and this same concern would seem to underlie the psychoanalytic distrust of "acting out," in the analytic situation, for patients in whom the acting out is already a symptom of disturbance. In such cases mimesis tends to confirm the imitator in his identification with what he imitates rather than to detach him from it. It functions as self-reinforcing rather than as liberating. Such findings would echo Plato's misgivings. Obviously, no simple answer exists to the question of what happens when the mind retraces its own or another's fantasies. Only an extremely fine-grained phenomenology, of a sort so far never attempted, could begin to provide a satisfactory answer. Meanwhile, the effect of the theater, as of painting or poetry, must be allowed to be at least potentially malign. But that can hardly mean that it *must* be malign, or that its possibilities for good can be strengthened only by authoritarian curbs. The life of reason dreamed of by Plato, the way of geometry, the tortuous ascent to truth along

25. *Art and Anarchy* (London, 1963), p. 3.
26. Ibid., p. 107, n. 5.

the difficult path of dialectic, can hardly become a reality for more than a chosen few. The rest require, one would think, not the sting of the ferule, but emotional sustenance, such as no geometry can be expected to supply. Those who can join Socrates in the quest of the absolute can doubtless dispense with the theater. The rest of us cannot. So long as the malign possibilities remain live ones, however, unverified but also unfalsified, one can hardly dismiss Plato's warnings as mere obscurantist bigotry. Thinking of our own children glued to the television screen, with its saturation advertising and its endless violence and vulgarity, together with the evidence (however fragmentary) of the kind of *anomie* it can induce among children and adults alike,[27] thinking of the well-known phenomenon of "imitative" crime—crimes committed in the wake of those reported in the press or on television— one might be tempted to wonder whether "art," in its currently most demotic form, does not present an even greater danger to us today than it seemed to Plato to present to ancient Athens.

With the exception of the *Poetics*, in which Plato is implicitly being challenged, subsequent writers make little effort to confront or engage Plato's position. The usual response, on the part of adherents and opponents alike, is simply to adopt its dogmas in order to bolster existing prejudice. Such would seem to be the case with Plutarch's fragmentary tract, "Were the Athenians More Famous in War or in Wisdom?", which reads rather like a twisted, gutted version of certain Platonic theses. For it resumes—how seriously it is difficult to tell—a number of Plato's antitheatrical motifs. Probably it constitutes an instance of the "exercise oration," in which the writer, wielding his rhetorical skill, expounds a position not necessarily his own, perhaps even opposite to his own.

There is certainly reason to suspect that Plutarch did not always harbor views of such dismissive harshness as appear in the essay in question. Elsewhere he is capable of entering into debate on related issues in more positive terms. Aristotle, for example, had called attention to a paradox which also created a puzzle, the fact that we enjoy imitations of things that would horrify us in reality, and had suggested that it was the educative element of the imitation that explained our

27. For a recent report, see H. J. Eysenck and D. K. B. Nias, *Sex, Violence and the Media* (London, 1978), passim, and bibliography, pp. 276–292.

otherwise perverse and inexplicable enjoyment. Plutarch probes the question further in one of his *Questiones convivales*, "Why we take pleasure in hearing actors represent anger and pain but not in seeing people actually experience those emotions."[28] His conclusion is that since we are "naturally endowed with reason and love of art, we have an affinity for any performance that exhibits reason or artistry." Children will prefer a piece of bread in the form of a cow or dog to a simple loaf, or a little silver animal to a shapeless lump of the same metal, or a story that includes riddles or a game that involves complications to one that does not. Whatever bears the stamp of human ingenuity pleases us, and the pleasure we take is therefore "not in our sight or our hearing but in our minds." Parmeno's pig, when its squeal was thought to be a product of clever mimicry, produced great amusement, but when it was discovered to be merely natural—the real squeal of a real pig—occasioned only indifference and annoyance.

This would seem to be an instance of Plutarch's addressing himself, with apparently serious intent, to an aesthetic issue raised by Plato, the problem of the differing impact on us of the real and the imaginary. Such passages, scattered about in his loose and baggy collected works, lend some likelihood to the supposition that he is treating the question concerning the Athenians in a wilfully schoolboyish spirit, as a topic for rhetorical highjinks. If so, however, unlike most specimens of its kind, unlike, for example, the dialogues of Lucian, which run to extravagances of ingenuity, exploiting the paradoxes discoverable in bizarre and patently ridiculous propositions, the present essay contains nothing self-evidently sophistical, but seems rather to be straightforwardly marshalling the arguments for a defensible point of view. That point of view, however clumsily and incoherently set forth, seems to lead us back to the attack on mimesis in the *Republic*. It suggests the kind of coarsening to which the Platonic argument was subject, and the kind of philistine prejudice that could unsubtly travesty Plato's own carefully spun texture of argument. By way of coda, then, to our discussion of Plato, we may glance at Plutarch's tract, suspecting that if we cannot confidently attribute its sentiments to Plutarch himself, it at least represents what he imagined might be said in defense of the view advanced. But even on these narrower grounds it falls grievously

28. Plutarch, *Table-Talk*, I–VI, trans. Paul A. Clement and Herbert B. Hoffleit, *Moralia*, VIII, Loeb Classics (London, 1969), 376–383.

short. The question at issue proves to be more far-reaching than the title might imply. For the issue is not simply a matter of fact—*were* the Athenians more renowned for their feats of war or their intellectual efforts—but a matter of evaluation: Which of the two modes of action *deserved* their allegiance, and which should properly command ours? The essay purports to make a contribution to a debate between the active and the contemplative life, but the debate proves to be a one-sided one in which the speaker covertly assumes that whichever of the two in fact brought more "glory" to Athens should be taken as the standard for all states. Like the *Republic*, Plutarch's treatise rests its case on the well-being of society as a whole, but unlike the *Republic*, it takes no account whatever of the individual, either as the basic unit or as the ultimate purpose of the community. Even the common good is considered in purely external terms, as a matter of reputation, while the question of whether reputation is always rightfully earned is never raised.

The inquiry proceeds by way of a series of comments on "wise" callings—historiography, painting, poetry, and oratory—and on the "warlike" callings, statecraft and generalship. From the outset one is struck by the assumption, doubtless derived from Plato, that all artistic activity is mimetic, and mimetic in the crudest sense, a kind of representational plagiarism, and so discreditable. Men of letters, in Plutarch's view, or in that of his imaginary spokesman, depend for their raw material on the exploits of men of action—"if you take away the men of action, you will have no men of letters"[29]—and they are moved to take up the pen largely in order to bask in the reflected glory of their illustrious subjects. Similarly, painters like Euphranor, who painted the cavalry battle against Epaminondas, strive to render historical events as vividly as possible, "but I do not think you would award judgement to the painter in comparison with the general, nor would you bear with those who prefer the picture to the trophy of victory, or the imitation to the actuality" (p. 501). In the case of the historian, however expertly he may recreate past events we read him because of the events themselves, "for the words do not create the deeds, but because of the deeds they are also deemed worthy of being read" (p. 505). In

29. Plutarch, *Moralia*, IV, trans. Frank Cole Babbitt, Loeb Classics (London, 1936), 493–527, p. 493. Parenthetical page references in the discussion that follows will be to this edition.

the case of the poet, he has either won favor for celebrating noble deeds, in which case he is parasitic on them like historians and painters, or else he has dealt with myths, which are merely false tales made to sound true. In the latter event he is even further removed from actuality, since those who describe imaginary exploits "lag as far behind historians as persons who tell of deeds come short of those that do them" (p. 509). The mythic poet, then, instead of being credited with originality, and relieved of the onus of being a copier, is dismissed as a fabricator of falsehoods and reduced to a still lower rank in the mimetic hierarchy.

The whole conception seems to represent a debased version of Plato's views on mimesis, including an unexamined preference for "deeds" over "words." Plutarch has nothing to say about any ulterior realm of reality to which the mimesis may refer, or about its moral or psychological effects, or about its place in human affairs. He, or his spokesman, simply makes the brute assumption that since "deeds" precede in time the "words" about them, they therefore enjoy some mystical superiority. Behind this assumption seems to lie another, doubtless also beholden to Plato, that celebrating the deeds of war betrays a pathetic attempt to compensate for the inability to perform such deeds. The possibility that poems, paintings, and histories might possess their own reality, might require assessment on some basis other than that of a servile aping of "deeds," never comes into question. Instead, all products of the mind are assumed to depend on feats of prowess, to be unoriginal, and therefore in their own right worthless.

One mark of the crassness of the argument is another assumption, also made throughout, that what the Athenians thought about the matter can be treated as definitive wisdom. Received opinion carries the stamp of truth here, as of course it does not in Plato, who labels it *as* opinion and distinguishes it firmly from knowledge. Plutarch confers an authority on the Athenians' prejudices that no impartial inquirer would countenance for a moment, and which he himself is prepared to overthrow when those prejudices fail to confirm his own chosen position. The prejudices in question tend to be grossly materialistic. Poets are measured by the concrete benefits they have brought the city; these are compared unfavorably to the benefits conferred by political and military heroes. Pericles adorned the Acropolis; Themistocles built the city walls; Cleon made the city supreme over its rivals;

but what have the poets, with all their eloquence, accomplished? What advantage has the town reaped from the expense of masks and altars, stage machines, and commemorative tripods purchased for the festivals? The money would have been better spent on fleets and armies. But there is no attempt made to argue this point. It is simply asserted, with complacent brutality, that fleets and armies are "better" than dramatic festivals, that to adorn the Acropolis or to build walls is "better" than to compose tragedies. No argument is offered to defend this preference, except the allegation of cost and waste—but since war is more costly and wasteful by far than dramatic festivals, it is clear that Plutarch's "reasons" presuppose the answer he is ostensibly seeking. On the other hand, an opposite piece of evidence is inserted to prove the same point: the fact that the victorious sponsors receive nothing for their huge expense but a tripod, "an empty memorial of their vanished estates" (p. 515). Here it is baldly assumed that since custom has decreed only a meager reward for the poet's assistant, the poet's art must be inferior to the soldier's deeds; financial recompense is allowed to stand without challenge as a proper standard of evaluation. But on the other hand, the fact that the Athenians lavished great sums on the tragic festivals is taken as a sign of their wastefulness. In short, when it suits his argument the pleader makes custom the arbiter, but throws it aside when it does not. We conclude, then, that what underlies the conclusion is not reasoned argument but a powerful prejudice against the products of the mind.

The poets having supposedly pleaded their cause, the generals are now summoned to plead theirs. At this point the argument becomes more than ever mired in opinion, and more than ever fixated on superficialities. The generals, it is proudly claimed, bring no paltry goat or bull for a prize (as the poets do), but whole cities, islands, and continents, "temples costing a thousand talents," ships, captive soldiers, stores of gold coin and other treasure, while their emblems are buildings "one hundred feet in length," dockyards, long walls, and other architectural solidities. "These are the things," declares the speaker fervently, "which the city celebrates in her festivals, for these she sacrifices to the gods, not for the dramatic victories of Aeschylus and Sophocles" (pp. 517–519). The speaker thus ascribes a purely quantitative standard of success to the citizens, a fondness for palpable plunder and a scorn for the treasures of the spirit; then he endorses that preference without further ado. The citizens' view of the matter is thereby first misrepresented, then assumed to be valid; if *they* rated soldiership above poetry, so should we all. Interestingly, the attack on the theater here takes a turn that will be rare in succeeding centuries. Under Christianity the theater will often be taxed for its excessive materialism and physicality, its too great commitment to the visible and audible and palpable. Plutarch, adopting a materialistic standard at the start, finds the theater too *im*material, too exclusively mental, to compete with such concretely productive activities as politics and soldiering.

A similar unexamined materialism governs the discussion of orators and rhetoricians. Once again, the greater value of military victory over forensic accomplishment is assumed to require no arguing, and the deriding of the wordmongers becomes a form of heckling. Isocrates is ridiculed for having grown old not sharpening his sword or whetting his spear-point but glueing together antitheses, balanced clauses, and inflexional elements: "How could this person do other than fear the clash of arms and the impact of phalanxes, he who feared to let vowel collide with vowel, or to utter a phrase whose balance was upset by the lack of a single syllable?" (pp. 523–525). Earlier, the belittling of the historians might have given rise to a suspicion that Plutarch was indulging in a covert form of self-mockery. Here the rhetorician's ingenuity used to deride rhetorical ingenuity heightens the suspicion. But if the passage is not meant as self-mockery, or as Lucianic satire, then it can only be written off as a species of childish pseudo-thinking, in which all pretense of rational argument has been abandoned. The same holds a moment later for the jeering at Isocrates, who, we are informed, spent years laboring over a single speech, made out of "mere words" (p. 525), while others were leading armies into battle or constructing great buildings. The scornful reference to "mere words" gives the whole discussion away for the know-nothing operation it is. We are urged to admire the accomplishments of Demosthenes the general, but to disdain the eloquence of Demosthenes the orator, to compare half a dozen instances of eloquent speech with as many comparable deeds of arms, in order to see how feeble and inadequate words are by comparison.

Throughout the essay, then, runs a persistent bias in favor of physical prowess and the arts of war as against mental skill and the arts of the study, in favor of tangible as against intangible rewards, nor is there even a perfunctory gesture in the direction of the familiar proposition that deeds *require* words in order to be remembered, that without historians, poets, and painters, the gests of the heroes, going unrecorded, would pass into oblivion. Whether the speaker is Plutarch himself or an imaginary disputant, whether in jest or in earnest, he notably fails to muster or respond to any counterarguments that might help create the illusion, at least, of responsible argument on his own part. The piece is of interest primarily as a curiosity, and because it exposes so baldly some of the prejudice always operating against "wisdom": the distrust of what takes time and skill and patience yet can never be reduced to weights and measures, the suspicion of whatever lacks instant, evident, practical utility, and so looks unreal and unsatisfying to the mind whose only reality is the world of physical things. That this brash materialism could owe its origin to Plato is only one of a number of paradoxes and contradictions in which the antitheatrical prejudice comes to entangle itself as the centuries wear on. The secret bond between Plato and the Plutarch of "Were the Athenians More Famous in War or in Wisdom?" lies not in their view of matter, soul, or society, but in their shared suspicion of the autonomy of art, which persists in eluding exact measurements and exact controls, which cannot bend to the dictates of soldiers, judges, guardians, or lawmakers without, ultimately, ceasing to be itself, and which, when allowed to be itself, almost invariably tends to cast suspicion on the measurements of the soldiers and the judges.

· II ·

Roman Ruins

To TURN FROM Greece to Rome is to turn from a culture in which the theater played an honored role in the state religion, and its practitioners enjoyed special rewards and dignities, to one where despite a nominal connection with religion it did not itself form part of the cult, and where its professors found themselves, as the centuries passed, increasingly stigmatized and ostracized. In Greece the antitheatrical philosopher bases his disapproval on certain metaphysical and moral principles. Plato criticizes not so much the Athenian theater of his day as the Idea of a Theater, and the dominance of tragic poetry (mainly Homer) in the educational system. His attack, moreover, forms part of a comprehensive critique of all mimetic art. The epic poets as well as the stage tragedians, the playwrights as well as the actors, are found guilty of slandering the gods and fomenting the base instincts of spectators and listeners. But Plato is not campaigning against the dramatic festivals. He does not warn his disciples to cease attending them, or imply that there would be merit in crusading against them and stamping them out. He does, in the *Laws*, point to the Athenian stage of his own day as a debased version of what must once, in the time of innocence, have been acceptably edifying, but essentially it is the kind itself that offends, when viewed from the vantage point of the visionary utopia.

In Rome, by puzzling contrast, the theater appears to have aroused antipathy even in its early days, and to have become thoroughly disreputable by the time of the Empire. The evidence for the period of the Republic being equivocal, and fragmentary, the extent of the antipathy during the earliest centuries is not entirely clear. Charles Garton has assembled information about the busy lives of some of the early actor-playwrights which suggests a lively and picturesque art, much appreciated by the public.[1] Classical dramatic forms continued to flourish throughout most of the Republic, the link with religion remaining close enough for the Senate to insist that they be performed regularly in the festival seasons. The link looks tenuous, however, compared to its Greek counterpart. Theatrical events, though technically ceremonial occasions, actually belonged in the hands not of priests or religious groups but of professional theatrical managers, often actors themselves. Much of the personnel consisted of foreigners and freedmen, to whom were later added slaves. The censors, moreover, "repeatedly refused to permit permanent theaters to be built,"[2] as though to advertise how low a priority the theater held in the official scheme of things, whatever its formal ties with religion. By the time the Atellan farces had evolved into a distinct genre in the second century B.C., at least one class of actors, those of the *ars ludicra*—a kind of vaudeville with dancing— were in settled disrepute, subject to crippling disabilities from which the Atellan players could exempt themselves only by carefully preserving their amateur status, wearing masks, and avoiding all contact with the professionals.[3] The professionals of the *ars ludicra* found themselves disenfranchised, forbidden to serve in the army, and subject to maltreatment by the police and the magistrates, who could whip them without any right of appeal or delay. Ultimately their infamy must have extended to nearly all actors, since even Cicero, writing in the time of the tragedian Roscius, his personal friend, could report that his fellow citizens "considered the dramatic art and the theatre in general disgraceful," so that "they desired that all persons connected with such things should not only be deprived of the privileges of other cit-

1. Charles Garton, *Personal Aspects of the Roman Theatre* (Toronto, 1972), chs. 2, 5 (pp. 41–139), and passim.

2. Tenney Frank, "The Status of Actors at Rome," *Classical Philology* 26 (1931): 14. On the history and conditions of the theater in Rome see also James Turney Allen, *Stage Antiquities of the Greeks and Romans and Their Influence* (London, 1927), and Margarete Bieber, *The History of the Greek and Roman Theater* (Princeton, 1939); also Samuel Dill, *Roman Society in the Last Century of the Western Empire*, 2d ed. (London, 1910).

3. Livy, *Ab urbe condita*, VII.ii.12, trans. B. O. Foster, Loeb Classics, III (London, 1924), 362–363.

izens, but should even be removed from their tribes by sentence of the censors"[4]—which is as much as to say, not only denied their civil rights but denied their very identities as members of society, virtually stricken, so far as the law was concerned, from the book of life. Cornelius Nepos tells us in the *Lives of the Commanders* that "Almost everywhere in Greece it was deemed a high honour to be proclaimed victor at Olympia; even to appear on the stage and exhibit oneself to the people was never regarded as shameful by those nations. With us, however, all those acts are classed either as disgraceful, or as low and unworthy of respectable conduct."[5] Nepos does not intend to be invidious, yet it is hard to imagine any fifth-century B.C. Greek using such a phrase as "to appear on the stage and exhibit oneself to the people," the very wording of which, with its suggestion of narcissism, implies a history of cultural disapproval.

Considering their high estate in Athens, the actors' degraded status in Rome is puzzling. One key event in the evolution of the Roman theater was the introduction into it in 240 B.C. of plays adapted and translated from the Greek by a Greek-born actor, Livius Andronicus, after which the theater of Rome bore the stamp of its Greek ancestry for generations. Why should a profession that enjoyed the utmost respect and homage in Greece come to be despised by a culture that to such a significant degree based itself upon Greece? Even allowing for Roman ambivalence toward things Hellenic, why should *this* institution have been singled out so ferociously for reprobation? We are reminded occasionally, as in Ulpian's *Digest*, that the Romans scorned anyone engaged in public service for money,[6] but why should it have been so much more unacceptable for actors to receive pay than for

4. *De re publica*, IV.x, in *De re publica* and *De legibus*, trans. Clinton Walker Keyes, Loeb Classics (London, 1966), pp. 238–239: "Cum artem ludicram scaenamque totam in probro ducerent, genus id hominum non modo honore civium reliquorum carere, sed etiam tribu moveri notatione censoria voluerunt."

5. Cornelius Nepos, *On the Great Generals of Foreign Nations, Praefatio*: "Magnis in laudibus tota fere fuit Graecia victorem Olympiae citari; in scaenam vero prodire ac populo esse spectaculo nemini in eisdem gentibus fuit turpitudini. Quae omnia apud nos partim infamia, partim humilia atque ab honestate remota ponuntur" (*Cornelius Nepos*, trans. John C. Rolfe, Loeb Classics [London, 1929], pp. 370–371).

6. Frank, "Status of Actors," p. 18.

members of other callings? Why should the celebrated Roscius have felt it necessary to decline all reward for his performances? Would he have done so if society had not made it seem ignoble for actors to be remunerated for their work? We learn, too, that the *histriones* came mainly from the ranks of foreigners, most of them freedmen, and were later on recruited from slaves as well, so that the measures against them represented a social judgment: the players were "rated on a level with thieves, panderers, cut-throats and gladiators"[7] as a consequence of their humble status. It is easy to believe that the harsh conditions of their existence could set up a kind of vicious circle, in which it was mainly the more ruffianly stratum of the populace that took to the trade of entertainer, and was then dealt with in so far as it was ruffianly and degraded. But why should the theater have fallen so swiftly into the hands of foreigners and outcasts in the first place? And why should the laws have so rapidly made it impossible for respectable citizens to have anything to do with it? Mommsen puts it down to the dour and blinkered temperament of the Romans themselves, who lacked the sense of freedom or the joy in life that are central to the theater. "The gaping and staring idleness of the theater," he suggests, "was utterly offensive to the sober earnestness and the spirit of activity which animated the Romans of the olden type."[8] But it was after all the same "olden" Romans who themselves frequented the plays, presumably relenting in their grimness and joylessness when they did so. Clearly, no theory of national character, of innate sternness or inflexible humorlessness, can explain such facts, and we might almost be driven to conclude that we are confronting a visceral prejudice which precedes all reason and defeats all argument, a stubborn passion that can encompass the most grotesque contradictions and resist all logical accounting. But even the irrationalities of prejudice have their meaning. In the present case it is likely that one result of the gradually eroding link between religion and theater was to turn the theater, a source of pleasure, adrift from its moorings in morality, and thereby inspire a guilt such that the Romans, recoiling from their own pleasures, came to persecute the purveyors of them even as their addiction to them intensified.

7. Allen, *Stage Antiquities*, p. 134.
8. Theodor Mommsen, *The History of Rome*, trans. W. P. Dickson (London, 1868), II, 394.

Certainly as the centuries wore on, the theaters became more wildly popular. By the late days of the Empire they had turned into little less than a mob craze, to which over half the days in the calendar year were officially dedicated. The fact that the one great imperial playwright, Seneca, seems to have composed his plays with no thought whatever of the theater suggests how unacceptable the stage had become as a vehicle for serious artistic expression. Meanwhile the actors sank deeper into their infamy. The Empire multiplied the disabilities inflicted on them by the Republic.[9] The actors found themselves forbidden to vote, forbidden to hold public office, forbidden to serve as attorneys, or, if women, to appoint attorneys. Under the later Empire they were banned from the very rows of the theater in which they themselves performed. Moreover the law bound them to their trade like serfs, forbade them to leave it for any other, and required their children to follow it in their turn. As it was illegal for an actor to cross the line into honesty and respectability, so it was unthinkable for any regular citizen to cross the other way—to turn actor—unless he wished to feel the full weight of the actor's *infamia*, or, if a soldier, be put to death for his dishonor. The law thus created and maintained a hereditary disgraced caste, whose members were cruelly persecuted and yet at the same time forbidden to take up any honorable calling. Like prostitution, the stage had come to be thought of as a necessary evil. As it was evil, its practitioners had to be humiliated and punished for their part in it. But as it was necessary, they had also to be prevented from making their escape from it, since its continuance needed to be guaranteed. It is easy enough to understand that a Roman citizen might feel uneasy about frequenting prostitutes, and that his guilt might prompt him to favor harsh measures against the women who pleasured him. It is less obvious that the same syndrome should apply to the theater—that the citizen who patronized the public shows should also conspire to make life unendurable for the players. The link is clearly a sexual one: in the mimes and pantomimes women exhibited their bodies, castrated actors played feminine roles with much lascivious realism, and the dramatic fare ran heavily to bawdry and sexual excitation. Going to

9. On the legal disabilities of the actors, especially during the Empire, see Paul Olagnier, *L'infamie légale du comédien: Rome, l'église* (Paris, 1899), and Gaston Maugras, *Les comédiens hors la loi*, 2d ed. (Paris, 1887), pp. 13 ff.

the shows must have seemed to many Romans like visiting the stews—equally urgent, equally provocative of guilt, and hence equally in need of being scourged by a savage backlash of official disapproval.

Christianity added new prohibitions and fresh disparagements of its own, provoked not only by the licentiousness of the spectacles but by the fact that the players of mime had taken to parodying the sacraments on the stage.[10] It forbade the actors to wear gold or to mimic the habit of nuns, to associate with Christian women or to appear in public attended by slaves. Regional church councils in the fourth and fifth centuries added the penalty of excommunication: no actor might receive the sacraments without first renouncing his profession for life —which the civil authorities would not allow him to do—and steps were taken to guard against temporary conversions animated solely by the wish to escape excommunication.

Unlike the civil authorities, however, the church pursued a consistent policy. Where the government on the one hand fanned the theatrical craze but on the other discriminated venomously against the actors, the Fathers of the church fulminated against the stage and used all their eloquence to bring about its suppression.[11] It is helpful to recall, when confronted with the high-pitched antitheatrical rhetoric of the Fathers, that they felt themselves embattled, entrusted with the salvation of masses of tepid converts who understood their new religion ill and had no thought of sacrificing their accustomed pleasures to it. The spectacles themselves, furthermore, had grown steadily more bloodthirsty and obscene. By the second or third century A.D., audiences no longer cared for comedy or tragedy, which had dwindled to insignificance among the scenic activities, their place taken by mimes, wild beast shows, lubricious pantomimes, chariot races, and gladiatorial fights. Without denying a streak of asceticism and prudery in the Fathers we can still appreciate the valid element in their protest. If they are virulent in their invectives it is partly because the spectacles have become intolerable. The Fathers seek to wean Christians away from what they perceive as an irreligious obsession in order to safeguard the very survival of the faith.

10. W. Beare, *The Roman Stage: A Short History of Latin Drama in the Time of the Republic* (London, 1950), p. 232.

11. Cf. J.-B. Ériau, *Pourquoi les pères de l'Église ont condamné le théâtre de leur temps* (Paris, 1914).

The earliest Christian writing against the stage seems to occur in some fragments of Tatian (c. 160 A.D.). Inveighing against the festivals, Tatian specifically denounced the actor, who "outwardly counterfeits what he is not," and who, in his impersonations, must be reckoned "a solitary accuser of all the gods, an epitome of superstition, a vituperator of heroic deeds, an actor of murders, a chronicler of adultery, a storehouse of madness, a teacher of cynaedi," and "an instigator of capital sentences."[12] It is clear that while Tatian correctly locates the essence of acting in impersonation, he also mistakes, perhaps wilfully, the nature of the impersonation, imputing to the actor a kind of didactic identification with his roles, or at least with his scurrilous roles. When he portrays madness or sodomy, he is giving his audience lessons in how to do it, but "heroic deeds" are being simply "vituperated." Tatian himself, it appears, was an unbalanced spirit, exponent of a heretical asceticism that viewed all sexual activity as impure and the eating of meat as a sin—the first, then, in a long succession of Christian moralists to denounce the theater mainly because, like sexual activity and the eating of meat, it gave pleasure.

Tertullian, half a century later, in *De spectaculis*, launches a more systematic onslaught, "a strong, wild eloquent protest" against the frequenting of the shows by Christians.[13] It is plain, on the evidence of all the Fathers, that Christians were continuing to flock to the arenas regardless of pastoral admonition, in so doing imperiling not only their souls but the future of Christianity, which depended on its votaries giving up their pagan habits. It is Tertullian's plan to place in high relief the fact that the spectacles, in all their forms, remained, as they had always been, versions of pagan ritual, officially dedicated to Jupiter, Neptune, Flora, Bacchus, and others in the heathen pantheon. Their costumes, their decor, the nature of their games, races, combats, and shows all stamped them as idolatrous. Unlike Plato, however, Christian controversialists seek a theological basis for the evil of the theater. Plato ascribes it to human frailty: men love the mimetic arts because

---

12. Tatian, *Address to the Greeks*, xxii, in Tatian and Theophilus, *Writings*, trans. B. Pratten, M. Dods, T. Smith, Ante-Nicene Christian Library, III (Edinburgh, 1867), 28.

13. James Walker, "Tertullian," in William Hanna, ed., *Essays by Ministers of the Free Church of Scotland* (Edinburgh, 1858), p. 91.

they love to abandon their reason and luxuriate in passion. Tertullian, following Tatian,[14] seeks a more conspiratorial explanation. His view of the world requires an Adversary on whom to fix the blame. Accordingly, he uncovers a demonic plot to subvert mankind and destroy the authority of the Most High. The spectacles are pagan in no innocent or accidental sense, but carefully chosen instruments of malign spirits, who take credit for them so as to lure men to the worship of false gods and alienate them from the true one. The names of dead men and of pagan gods may seem harmless, but behind them skulk the devils, utilizing the spectacles for their own sinister ends.

Nevertheless, the conspiracy must work through the defects in human nature itself. All pleasure, suggests Tertullian (perhaps in echo of Plato), is disquieting, even when experienced in moderation and calm, but the theater, with its excitements and its maddened crowds, deliberately aims to provoke frenzy. It is the frenzy itself, in fact, that draws spectators, for how else explain the audience's mindless absorption in the imaginary fortunes of nonexistent characters? Even if the theater specialized in tales of innocence it would be a seduction and a snare. But in fact it is disfigured by obscenities that defile actors and spectators alike. Nor does it extenuate filthy things to say that the actors merely feign them and the spectators merely witness them, for in the world of Tertullian's polemic, the difference between art and life has no status. He will allow no distinction between *homo ludens* and *homo laborans,* no realm of play in which feigning is recognized as the rule of a game. For us, to witness a spectacle is to "receive" it only in the sense of attending to it, being absorbed, engrossed, perhaps delighted, possibly even moved by it. For Tertullian it is to approve it in the most primitive and literal sense: to perceive it as raw fact and to rejoice in it as fact. "The calling to mind of a criminal or a shameful thing," he maintains, "is no better than the thing itself: what in act is rejected, is not in speech to be accepted."[15] Here, with a pair of quibbling antitheses ("in facto," "in dicto"; "reicitur," "recipiendum"),

14. *Writings,* III, 28.

15. "Nullius rei aut atrocis aut vilis commemoratio melior est: quod in facto reicitur, etiam in dicto non est recipiendum" (Tertullian, *Apology, De spectaculis,* etc., trans. T. R. Glover, Loeb Classics [London, 1931], p. 276). I have altered the translation slightly.

Tertullian erases the distinction between committing a misdeed and simply describing it: to make it known in words, to "remember" it, is to endorse it, to express a wish that it come to pass in the actual world. To portray a murder is as wicked as to commit one, even if in the first case the murdered man gets up, walks off, and drinks a pint of ale with his assassin. And as wicked as either the real murderer or his scenical counterfeit is the spuriously innocent spectator, whose soul is delightedly following the motions of the enacted crime.

By what logic, moreover, we may ask, should the crime as so portrayed impinge on us any less obliquely than one reported in a book, such as Scripture? When we (or Tertullian) read that a biblical character—Herod, or David—commits murder, or adultery, we do not therefore fly to the conclusion that the story is designed to spur us to imitation, or that we are being urged to take a favorable view of the crime in question. The fact that we "call to mind" the criminal thing in no way constitutes an "acceptance" of it. The effect would as plausibly be to provoke abhorrence by making the crime more vividly disagreeable, painting it out in its full ugliness. The same would have to be said of paintings, sculptures, or any narrative art that in some fashion "called to mind" a shameful original.

One may observe that as in the case of Tatian, neither Tertullian himself nor his followers will extend the same principle in the reverse direction, to include the portrayal of heroic or saintly deeds. These are never accorded the same degree of reality as their offstage counterparts. If the thing represented be bad, it is truly bad, as bad in all respects as its original, but if good, it is merely a lie, a fraud, a scandalous offense against truth—and this despite the later tradition according to which acting the part of a saint or martyr did, from time to time, produce spectacular conversions to Christianity and create new martyrs, whereas in no tradition do actors turn to brigandage as a result of playing criminals. Tertullian seems to think of acting as involving an escalating sequence of falsehoods. First the actor falsifies his identity, and so commits a deadly sin. If he impersonates someone vicious, he compounds the sin. If he happens to impersonate a noble soul he is aggravating the crime another way, by pretending to be someone so unlike himself. Finally, he must necessarily work out his portrayal with a variety of mimetic details—sighs, groans, and tears—but each of these, far from validating the make-believe character of the whole by lending it inner consistency, simply multiplies its fraudulence and adds to the gravity of the offense.

What strikes one throughout in Tertullian's exposition is the literalness with which he lumps together the world of the spectacles with that of everyday existence. The concept of a domain other than that of the everyday, a fictive domain with its own laws of operation, is ignored, or rejected, in favor of a frozen world in which each thing must remain one thing and that thing alone, forbidden ever to modify itself or change, for any purpose or however fleetingly. "Nowhere and never is that permitted which is not permitted always and everywhere. Here is the perfection of truth . . . in that it never changes its decision, never wavers in its judgement. What is good, really good, cannot be anything but good; nor what is evil anything but evil. In God's truth all things are definite."[16] The principle whereby things have come into existence is thus a principle of inflexibility. What has once been decreed remains eternally binding; laws issuing from a changeless deity operate unalterably through all the vicissitudes and ambiguities of human experience, with no modification allowed for time, place, or manner. Inevitably, then, we may no more behold the spectacles in innocence than we may gaze with amusement on theft, adultery, or murder.

Tertullian's literalness, his apparent inability to distinguish between play and nonplay, recalls the condition of a famous World War I patient, Schneider. Schneider's shell wounds brought about a state of mind such that although perfectly capable of doing anything he was asked to do, he no longer did things unless they *were* asked. He seemed to have ceased being a self-directing, self-monitoring organism. He did not *wish* to do anything, or *intend* to do anything, or *conceive of* himself as doing anything; he could not project himself into the future or into any hypothetical situation in the smallest degree. "There is in his whole conduct something meticulous and serious which derives from the fact that he is incapable of play-acting. To act is to place oneself for a moment in an imaginary situation, to find satisfac-

---

16. ". . . nusquam et numquam excusatur quod deus damnat, nusquam et numquam licet quod semper et ubique non licet. Haec est veritatis integritas . . . non inmutare sententiam nec variare iudicium. Non potest aliud esse, quod vere quidem est bonum seu malum. Omnia autem penes veritatem dei fixa sunt" (*Apology*, etc., pp. 280–281).

47

tion in changing one's 'setting.' The patient, on the other hand, cannot enter into a fictitious situation without converting it into a real one: he cannot tell the difference between a riddle and a problem."[17] Like Schneider, Tertullian seems "incapable of play-acting," or of understanding what play-acting means. What Schneider's pathological behavior makes clear is that the power to play-act, to project oneself into imaginary situations, is precisely one of the distinguishing marks of humanity. Without it, a man turns into a piece of clockwork; he loses the faculty of self-distancing that constitutes part of his humanity. Tertullian's literalness seems to envisage a whole world peopled by Schneiders, a population of robots, for whom each and every aspect of life exists on the same level of blank seriousness as every other.

In the case of cruel and unnatural spectacles like the gladiatorial shows, we may concede the validity of Tertullian's objections, though on grounds somewhat different from his. Caligula burning alive in the stadium an actor said to have spoken slightingly of the state, human victims torn apart by wild beasts, combats to the death between reluctant gladiators—these can hardly be classified as harmless sports or lawful diversions. But from all these, precisely, the element of make-believe is absent. The dismembered captive, the stricken gladiator, the incinerated actor cannot rise up to repeat their performances again on the following day. They are truly dead, from which it follows that their "performance" is no performance at all, in the theatrical sense. The element of feigning, were it to be present on such occasions, far from turning the event into a crime, would on the contrary afford its only justification. Where there is real cruelty, actual torture, and death, we are in some realm other than that of theater. Yet this is precisely the distinction Tertullian refuses to countenance.

Even allowing for the heat of polemic, his is a remarkably rigid cleaving of life into absolute good and absolute evil, with no middle ground, no gradations admitted, and no complications allowed for. "The devil owns everything," we are told, "that is not God's or does not please God."[18] The concept of the human self that emerges is marked by the same literalness. One's identity, for Tertullian, is ab-

17. Maurice Merleau-Ponty, *The Phenomenology of Perception*, trans. Colin Smith (London, 1962), p. 135.

18. "... nihil enim non diaboli est quicquid dei non est vel deo displicet" (*Apology*, etc., pp. 288–289).

48

solutely given, as one's sex is given; any deviation from it constitutes a perversion akin to the attempt to change one's sex. The wearing of feminine clothes by actors playing women thus becomes as sinister as the castration of the pantomimists. It falls, moreover, under the well-known prohibition in Deuteronomy: "The woman shall not wear that which pertaineth unto a man, neither shall a man put on a woman's garment: for all that do so are abomination unto the Lord thy God" (22:5).

As one's identity is absolutely given, so it is given *in detail*. Tertullian condemns the shaving of the beard because, to borrow Gibbon's phrase, it is "a lie against our own faces, and an impious attempt to improve the works of the Creator,"[19] and on similar grounds he attacks the dress of actors: by wearing the cothurnus, they blasphemously seek to add a cubit to their stature, and so try to make a liar out of Christ. Athletes who groom their bodies with exercises are infringing the same edict. As for boxers and gladiators, with their split lips, scarred cheeks, and cauliflower ears, they too are infamously striving to disfigure God's handiwork. In each case men are usurping the functions of their creator, tampering with an identity that has been entrusted to them for safekeeping, but is not theirs to alter.

Analogously, in his tracts on feminine dress and adornment, Tertullian attributes all cosmetics, all use of jewelry, all attempts of women to beautify themselves, to the promptings of the Evil One. Ladies who put cream, rouge, or antimony on their faces "are not satisfied with the creative skill of God; in their own person . . . they censure and criticize the Maker of all things! . . . taking these their additions, of course, from a rival artist. This rival artist is the Devil. For, who else would teach how to change the body but he who by wickedness transformed the spirit of man?"[20] To the Devil also belong such inventions

19. *The Decline and Fall of the Roman Empire*, Modern Library (New York, n.d.), I, 414.

20. *De cultu feminarum* (*The Apparel of Women*), trans. Edwin A. Quain, in *Disciplinary Moral and Ascetical Works*, trans. Arbesmann, Daly, and Edwin A. Quain (New York, 1959), p. 136. See Tertullian, I, in J.-P. Migne, *Patrologia latina* (Paris, 1844), 1321: "Displicet nimirum illis plastica Dei, in ipsis redarguunt, reprehendunt artificem omnium. Reprehendunt enim, cum emendant, cum adjiciunt, utique ab adversario artifice sumentes additamenta ista, id est, diabolo. Nam quis corpus mutare monstraret, nisi qui et hominis spiritum malitia transfiguravit?"

as purple or sky-blue dye for use in women's garments, for if God had wished to produce sheep with fleece of such unnatural colors, he would have done so, "and what God refused to do certainly cannot be lawful for man to make."[21] Setting aside the logical and practical absurdities in this line of reasoning—one wonders how Tertullian felt about the roasting of meat or the baking of bread—one finds in it an early instance of a long-lasting motif: prejudice against the theater coupled with prejudice against women, especially beautiful, ornamental, and seductive women. Fair seemings form no recommendation in these eyes, but an offense. Ugliness becomes something to be positively welcomed, "for, where modesty exists there is no need of beauty."[22] As the theater is suspected of ill designs for its attractiveness, so are women. As the theater debases by its counterfeiting, so do women who affect a beauty not theirs by nature. God hath given them one face, and they make themselves another, just as he has given men one identity and they arrogate to themselves another when they pretend to be what they are not in a play.

One tactical argument of Tertullian's, worth noting because it recurs so often in later controversy, involves the claim that actors deserve to be hated by all right-thinking people because the law already proscribes them. An existing injustice thus becomes its own justification. Whatever is, is right—except that Tertullian would never extend this principle to the official protection allowed the spectacles. Illustrative in another way of the temper of later controversy is the finale of *De spectaculis*, in which the "zealous African," as Gibbon terms him, imagines his enemies—the poets, actors, and charioteers—already in hell, gloating over their prospective torments in "a long variety of affected and unfeeling witticisms."[23] Clearly at such moments a strain of suppressed ferocity becomes visible, a craving to inflict dire punishment. One nineteenth-century commentator sees in Tertullian's later tracts something approaching monomania,[24] while a more recent one

21. *Disciplinary Works*, p. 126; Migne, p. 1312: "Quod Deus noluit, utique non licet fingi."
22. *Disciplinary Works*, p. 133; Migne, p. 1319: "Nam ubi pudicitia, ibi vacua pulchritudo."
23. *Decline and Fall*, I, 407.
24. Walker, "Tertullian," in Hanna, p. 97.

finds that "his rigorism, his intolerance, his disputatious nonconformity, and his violent reaction to opposition approach paranoia."[25] Tertullian, like Tatian, ended his days as a heretic, proclaiming an exaggerated and hysterical hatred of all pleasure. Pleasure, for these writers, has become an enemy in itself, something to be combatted and mortified. In the fifth century, Lactantius expressly denounces the pleasures of the senses, "all of which, since they are vicious and deadly, ought to be overcome and subdued by virtue, or . . . be recalled to their proper office. . . . God gave virtue on this account, that it might subdue and conquer pleasure . . . lest it should soothe and captivate man with enjoyments."[26]

For St. John Chrysostom, not only pleasure as such, but the mere talk of pleasure, the mere thought of pleasure, dissolves and enervates the soul. "He who converses of theatres and actors does not benefit [his soul], but inflames it more, and renders it more careless," whereas "he who converses about hell incurs no dangers, and renders it more sober." Hell, unlike the theater, offers a wholesome theme for meditation and converse. "Let it be continually spoken of, that thou mayest never fall into it. It is not possible that a soul anxious about hell should readily sin." One should not even dwell in imagination on the delights of heaven, for in doing so one reduces one's prospects of experiencing them, since "fear has more power than the promise." The thought of hell is like a bitter medicine, which annoys but also heals and strengthens. "No one of those who have hell before their eyes will fall into hell. No one of those who despise hell will escape hell." To think of hell, furthermore, is to steel oneself against a possible martyrdom, for "if

25. Bernhard Nisters, cited by W. Le Saint, "Tertullian," *The New Catholic Encyclopedia* (1967), XIII, 1019.
26. Lactantius, *Divine Institutes*, VI.xx, in *Works*, trans. William Fletcher, Ante-Nicene Christian Library (Edinburgh, 1871), I, 404–405; *Divinarum institutionum liber septimus*, in Migne, *Patrologia latina*, VI (Paris, 1844), 705–706: "Restat ut contra quinque sensuum voluptates dicam breviter; nam et ipsius libri mensura jam modum flagitat: quae omnes, quoniam vitiosae ac mortiferae sunt, virtute superari atque opprimi debent; vel . . . ad rationem suam revocari. . . . Homini vero solertissimi artificis providentia dedit voluptatem infinitam, et in vitium cadentem; quia proposuit ei virtutem, quae cum voluptate semper, tanquam cum domestico hoste pugnaret."

we be habituated to hear of dreadful things, we shall be habituated also to endure dreadful things."[27] In such a context of self-mortification, in which the very thought of the joys of heaven constitutes a dangerous indulgence, and frightening images of punishment are expressly to be cultivated, the theater can hardly do other than attract execration. And Chrysostom is in fact one of the most remorseless of antitheatrical crusaders, returning to the charge again and again, preferring hell, prisons, and whatever is painful to all that the theater can propose of enjoyment. For all these writers, the Christian life involves a sustained struggle against worldly contentments. The theater, which offers pleasure in such intensity and abundance, which for so many thousands of its addicts is virtually synonymous with pleasure, must incur damnation on that score alone. On the other hand, the fact that their increasingly high-strung asceticism led both Tatian and Tertullian into heresy suggests that even in patristic days a more temperate morality was possible, which did not automatically write off all sensory enjoyment as irretrievably sinful.

When we turn to St. Augustine, two centuries later, we encounter a far more powerful intellect as well as a subtler and more complex sensibility. We find a more philosophical view of a subject that Tertullian tends to view in narrow and moralistic terms. Augustine spends less energy on fulmination and more on analysis. In the *Confessions*, moreover, he strikingly attempts to come to terms with his own youthful passion for the theater. The *Confessions* exhibits a personality in its own way theatrical in the extreme. If Plato's theatricality shows itself in his flair for mimetic dialogue, myth, parable, and protective irony, Augustine's betrays itself in the highly rhetorical cast of the whole work. The *Confessions* consists of impassioned, prayerful utterance addressed to God, and also intermittently to the speaker's own self and soul. The tone is exclamatory and ejaculatory throughout. Although Augustine addresses himself formally to God, his address can obviously have meaning only with respect to human listeners. For a written memoir to God can serve no purpose. God knows the state of the speaker's heart already; he needs no further documentation. On

27. St. John Chrysostom, *Homilies on the Epistles of Saint Paul to the Philippians, Colossians, and Thessalonians*, trans. W. C. Cotton, et al., Parker Society (Oxford, 1843), pp. 476–477.

the other hand, a wholly nonrhetorical, nontheatrical address to him could only take the form of silent prayer, or some such spontaneous utterance as that chanted by Adam and Eve in *Paradise Lost*, welling up from the full heart and in no need of rehearsal or study. To commit the prayer to writing, to polish and perfect and publish it, is to make the genuine audience the human audience. Augustine acknowledges as much at various moments in the book:[28] his purpose is not to tell God what God already knows, but to tell his frailer brethren, to dramatize his own psychic journey in the hope of luring others toward his own present state of achieved felicity.

If Augustine's rhetorical training and instinctive theatricality come out in his highly wrought style, his powers of self-analysis emerge in the account of his youthful addiction to the theater during his days in Carthage. He now reviews this juvenile debauch, as he thinks it, and asks some searching questions. Why is it, he asks, that in the theater a man desires to behold sorrows and tragical happenings which, if he actually experienced them, would make him miserable? It can hardly be a simple wish to show mercy to others, for in these circumstances the only mercy possible is toward "feigned and scenical passions,"[29] where he is not called on to relieve, but only to grieve. Yet the more he grieves, the more he appreciates both play and actors, rather like Ion's listeners, who paid him handsomely if he made them weep, and felt cheated if he did not. Why should this be? asks Augustine. Do men love the griefs of others in order to be able to show mercy to them? If so, it would be more charitable and humane of them to wish the causes of grief removed, so that there was no need for mercy at all. But no theatergoer desires that. On the contrary, the theatergoer wishes the sorrows and sufferings of the characters prolonged, so that he may continue to suffer along with them. "Wretched I, loved at that time to be made sorry, and sought out matter to be sorry at."[30] What seems to emerge from the passage, which might in truth have pursued its theme more fully, is the implication that fictive emotion in the theater provokes something potentially and essentially valuable in us,

28. See esp. X.i–iv and XI.i.

29. *Confessions*, III.ii, trans. William Watts (1631), ed. W. H. D. Rouse, Loeb Classics (London, 1912), p. 101: "Rebus fictis et scenicis" (p. 100).

30. Ibid., pp. 104–105: "Ego tunc miser dolere amabam, et quaerebam, ut esset quod dolerem."

our capacity for fellow feeling, but that the theatrical context falsifies it. Our compassion is enlisted in behalf of unworthy or specious misfortunes, such as the tribulations of wanton lovers, and it applies a covert approval of their actions. It becomes an insidious form of self-indulgence; it relieves us of the need to act, and so feeds our passivity and narcissism. The Lord permits us to sorrow, but he does not permit us to court sorrow for its own sake and wallow in it. Stage plays divert healthy feeling into an unhealthy channel. They invite us to luxuriate in questionable feelings and to flee real ones.

This infinitely more sophisticated discussion of playgoing than any to be found in Tertullian stems partly from Augustine's more analytical turn of mind, but also from a more introspective sensibility; Augustine is determined to grapple with the meaning of his own experience. Tertullian, who as a young man had also lived in lust, with "a passion for immoral plays and bloody spectacles in the arena,"[31] seems merely to have traded one extremism for another, a frenetic licentiousness for an exaggerated asceticism. He is content to blame the ills of the stage on a diabolic conspiracy operating through man's nature. But Augustine wishes to fathom the workings of that nature in himself, to find out what lures men to such dangerous pastimes in defiance of all good sense. He would discover, at very least, the nature of the spell the theater once cast over his own youthful spirit. And even in the reprehending of this benighted activity he can sort out the wheat from the chaff, showing the evil to be the abuse of a potential good.

Certainly he launches no such sharp attack on mimesis as we find in Plato. On the contrary, he examines it with sympathetic attention, trying to discover its precise nature and sort it out from phenomena that seem to resemble it. A passage in the early *Soliloquies* on the "false," the "fallacious," and the "fabulous" distinguishes between "that which either feigns to be what it is not, or tends to exist and does not succeed."[32] Among things which tend to exist but do not succeed would go phenomena like images in a mirror, portraits aiming at exact likeness, the delusions of sleepers or madmen, and optical illusions. These fall short usually because of the imperfections of our senses.

31. *The New Catholic Encyclopedia*, XIII, 1019.

32. *The Soliloquies of Saint Augustine*, II.ix, trans. Thomas F. Gilligan (New York, 1943), pp. 102–105: "Quod aut se fingit esse quod non est, aut omnino esse tendit et non est."

Among things which feign to be what they are not, Augustine includes two types of falsehood, the "fallacious" and the "fabulous," the first being born of the wish to deceive, the second of the wish to tell a story. Deceivers all hope to deceive, but the same cannot be said of those who tell tales, "for farces and comedies and many poems are full of fables whose purpose is to give pleasure rather than to deceive, and almost everyone who tells a joke, tells a fable."[33] Augustine thus removes the onus from fabulation by differentiating the impulse behind it (the desire to please) from that behind falsehood (the desire to deceive) and from the errors caused by a faulty sensory apparatus. Where Plato blurs the distinctions, lumping poetical imitations with malicious lies and sensory distortions, Augustine patiently disentangles and reorders.

He goes further, however. He makes the application not to jokes and fables alone, but to plays, and not to plays alone but to those who act in them, thus carrying the argument to what for Plato is perhaps the crucial and most baneful form of mimesis: mimicry. Poems, jokes, and fables should not be thought of as false at all, argues Augustine's Reason, because they are unable to be true. They neither "choose to be false nor are they false, through their own desire to be so; but they are compelled by a kind of necessity to conform as much as they are able to the artist's will." "By a kind of necessity" might be glossed: by the conventions of art, by rules which differ from those of ordinary truth-telling. When it comes to actors, the situation grows more complicated. In their case the intent to be false is undeniable—and necessary. Roscius, the player, was on stage a false Hecuba, though by nature a true man. He was also, and by choice, in so far as he accomplished his purpose, a true tragedian, and at the same time a false Priam, because he played Priam's part though he himself was not Priam. From which it follows, logically enough, yet at the same time startlingly, that all such phenomena as comedies, tragedies, farces, paintings, and sculptures:

Are in some respect true precisely because they are in other respects false; and to establish their truth, the only thing in their favor is that they are false in some other regard. . . . For how could that man I just mentioned [i.e., Roscius] be a true tragedian if he were unwilling to be a false Hector, a false Andromache, a false Hercules and others

33. Ibid., II.ix, pp. 104–105: "Nam et mini et comoediae et multa poemata mendaciorum plena sunt, delectandi potius quam fallendi voluntate, et omnes fere qui jocantur, mentiuntur."

without number? Or how would it be a true picture, if the horse in it were not false? How could it be the true image of a man in a mirror, if it were not a false man?[34]

Or, to put the matter in terms used recently in another connection by W. H. Auden, "If a man can be called to be an actor, then the only way he can be 'true' to himself is by 'acting,' that is to say, pretending to be what he is not."[35] Here we find the sort of discrimination we might have hoped for from Tertullian, not to speak of Plato, both of whom seem strenuously to look the other way so as to avoid seeing it. Augustine allows the activity in question—acting—its own integrity, its own consistency, and its own mode of reality. He discovers a rationale for it rather than simply invidiously classifying it with lies and delusions. Nor does he berate it because it is founded on a wish to please. He makes us see how Roscius' acting may be said to be "truer" than that of his fellows precisely in the degree in which it is more "false," more faithful to the character being portrayed, which is not Roscius' own.

Ultimately, to be sure, Augustine's analysis produces a conclusion not so different from Plato's as the argument might have led us to expect. When Reason pursues the question of acting by asking why it is that—given the fact that in order to be true it sometimes helps to be false—we should so dread falsehood, Augustine replies that that is because "I find in these examples nothing worthy of imitation. To the end that we may be true to our nature, we should not become false by copying and likening ourselves to the nature of another as do the

34. Ibid., II.x, pp. 106–109: "Neque enim falsa esse volunt, aut ullo appetitu suo falsa sunt; sed quadam necessitate, quantum fingentis arbitrium sequi potuerunt. At vero in scena Roscius voluntate falsa Hecuba erat, natura verus homo; sed illa voluntate etiam verus tragoedus, eo videlicet quo implebat institutum: falsus autem Priamus, eo quod Priamum assimilabat, sed ipse non erat. . . . haec omnia inde esse in quibusdam vera, unde in quibusdam falsa sunt, et ad suum verum hoc solum eis prodesse, quod ad aliud falsa sunt. . . . Quo pacto enim iste quem commemoravi, verus tragoedus esset, si nollet esse falsus Hector, falsa Andromache, falsus Hercules, et alia innumera? aut unde vera pictura esset, si falsus equus non esset? unde in speculo vera hominis imago, si non falsus homo?"

35. Foreword to Henrik Ibsen, *Brand*, trans. Michael Meyer (New York, 1960), p. 30.

actors and the reflections in a mirror. . . . We should, instead, seek that truth which is not self-contradictory and two-faced."[36] In short, ethical assumptions from beyond the immediate argument come in to rescue, for morality and for Christianity, the antitheatrical position away from which the logic of the discussion has for some time been moving. By a somewhat awkward and illogical route we arrive at roughly the same final view as Plato's: a condemnation of both painters and players for seeking a truth which is "self-contradictory and two-faced," rather than one which conforms to the single, indivisible, eternal truth promulgated by God.

Nevertheless, Augustine has done much to clarify the nature of theatrical imitation, and it is only when his Reason has fallen silent, and he himself [i.e., Faith?] takes the floor, that Reason's explanation is hastily shelved and a less rigorous argument from prejudice thrust in to replace it. On more than one occasion, moreover, in his later writings, Augustine expressly invokes the facts of theatrical experience to help explain the nature of the Christian life. A particularly vehement antitheatrical outburst, for example, occurs in a sermon in which he invites his hearers to ponder the difference between their present ceremony and those of the public spectacles. "Contrast," he urges them, "that holy spectacle with the pleasures and delights of the theatre. There your eyes are defiled, here your hearts are cleansed. Here the spectator deserves praise if he but imitate what he sees; there he is bad, and if he imitates what he sees he becomes infamous."[37] Here we have a quasi-Platonic acknowledgment of the educative power of imitation, for good as well as ill. "Hic laudabilis est spector, si fuerit imitator; ibi autem et spectator turpis est, et imitator infamis." Instead of Ter-

36. *Soliloquies*, II.x, pp. 108–109: "Quia in exemplis istis nihil imitatione dignum video. Non enim tanquam histriones, aut de speculis quaeque relucentia, . . . ita etiam nos ut in nostro quodam habitu veri simus, ad alienum habitum adumbrati atque assimilati, et ob hoc falsi esse debemus; sed illud verum quaerere, quod non quasi bifronte ratione sibique adversanti. . . ."

37. Cited in Hugh Pope, *Saint Augustine of Hippo* (London, 1937), pp. 246–247; see Migne, *Patrologia latina*, XLVI (Paris, 1842), 879: "Comparate huic sancto spectaculo voluptates et delicias theatrorum. Ibi oculi inquinantur; hic corda mundantur. Hic laudabilis est spectator, si fuerit imitator; ibi autem et spectator turpis est, et imitator infamis."

tullian's ironclad distinction between truth and feigning, we have a theory that appreciates the mimetic and spectacular elements in Christian worship itself, and allows for differences in value depending on the differing objects of imitation.

More striking still is a passage in the *Christian Doctrine* in which Augustine explains the nature of the Christian congregation by analogy with the spectators at a play.

For in the theatres, dens of iniquity though they be, if a man is fond of a particular actor, and enjoys his art as a great or even as the very greatest good, he is fond of all who join with him in admiration of his favourite, not for their own sakes, but for the sake of him whom they admire in common; and the more fervent he is in his admiration, the more he works in every way he can to secure new admirers for him, and the more anxious he becomes to show him to others; and if he find any one comparatively indifferent, he does all he can to excite his interest by urging his favourite's merits: if, however, he meet with any one who opposes him, he is exceedingly displeased by such a man's contempt of his favourite, and strives in every way he can to remove it. Now, if this be so, what does it become us to do who live in the fellowship of the love of God, the enjoyment of whom is the true happiness of life. . . ?[38]

And Augustine goes on to apply this experience of spectatorship to that of divine worship, which also creates an impassioned community of those who revere the same object. The passage is among other things an acute analysis of crowd psychology. It recognizes the way in which the separateness of the spectators is broken down through their response to the actor, so that they fuse into a single entity. In pointing out that

38. Augustine, *On Christian Doctrine*, trans. J. F. Shaw, I.29, in *Works*, ed. Marcus Dods (Edinburgh, 1871–76), IX, 24–25. See Migne, *Patrologia latina*, XXXIV (Paris, 1841), 30: "Si enim in theatris nequitiae qui aliquem diligit histrionem, et tanquam magno vel etiam summo bono ejus arte perfruitur, omnes diligit qui eum diligunt secum, non propter illos, sed propter eum quem pariter diligunt; et quanto est in ejus amore ferventior, tanto agit quibus potest modis, ut a pluribus diligatur, et tanto pluribus eum cupit ostendere; et quem frigidiorem videt, excitat eum quantum potest laudibus illius; si autem contravenientem invenerit, odit in illo vehementer odium dilecti sui, et quibus modis valet, instat ut auferat: quid nos in societate dilectionis Dei agere convenit, quo perfrui, beate vivere est. . . ."

those who admire a gifted player will also feel a bond with his other admirers, not for the sake of those admirers but for the sake of him whom they admire, Augustine brilliantly elucidates the self-congratulatory euphoria which anyone who has ever been carried away or deeply moved in a crowd situation will recognize at once. To carry this insight a stage further, to see it as a paradigm for the gathering of religious worshippers, is an audacious and insightful step. For the same factor of communal responsiveness that welds us into one body in the theater must also be responsible for forging our communion in church in the presence of God. From this nettle, the theatrical audience, Augustine plucks this flower, the Christian congregation. However the theater itself may offend, it addresses itself to, it utilizes, human impulses that are capable of being turned to sanctified ends.

One other passage in the *Confessions* illustrates Augustine's sophisticated approach to the problem of right and wrong in human affairs. He is lamenting his own early blindness, his ignorance of the ways of heavenly justice. This works, he has come to realize, not independently of particular times and places but very much in concord with them. Those who expect justice to be as unchanging to the outer as it is to the inner eye have no understanding of its nature.

. . . just as if in armour, a man being ignorant what piece were appointed for what part, should clap a greave upon his head, and draw a headpiece upon his leg, and then murmur because they would not fit him: or as if upon some set day when the course of Justice is publicly forbidden in the afternoon, a shopkeeper should stomach at it that he may not have leave to sell his wares, because it was lawful for him to do it in the forenoon: or when in some house he observeth some servant to pass that kind of business through his hands, which the butler is not suffered to meddle withal; or some thing done behind the stable, which is forbidden in the dining-room: or as if he should be angry, that where there is one dwelling-house, and one family, the same equality of distribution is not observed everywhere, and to all alike in it. Of the same humour be those who are fretted to hear something to have been lawful for righteous men in the former age, which is not so for righteous men now-a-days. . . . Is Justice thereupon various or mutable? No; but the times rather, which justice governs, are not like one another; for they are times.[39]

39. *Confessions*, III.vii; I, 123–125, 122–124: ". . . tamquam si quis nescius in armamentis, quid cui membro adcommodatum sit, ocrea velit

Heavenly justice, in short, is always the same in its essence, but it differs in its manifestations. It deals with particular events according to particular circumstances; what suits one situation will not necessarily suit others. He who keeps shop in the morning is not automatically licensed thereby to do so in the afternoon; not all servants may handle the same household articles; and what is allowed out of doors may be forbidden inside. So much, then, for Tertullian's fierce and intractable literalism: "Nowhere and never is that permitted which is not permitted always and everywhere. . . . What is good, really good, cannot be anything but good; nor what is evil anything but evil." Even Tertullian's dictum might have been susceptible of modification or mitigation in practice, but in his hands it is not. Augustine's own residual Manicheism does not go to anything like the same lengths.

Nevertheless, that residual Manicheism is a force to be reckoned with. Though formally disavowed, traces of the spirit of it, the view of evil as "some kind of substance" with "its own foul, and hideous bulk," as a "persecutory force" never created by God at all, cannot be said to be absent from the temper of Augustine's mature thinking, and certainly not from the pages of *The City of God* devoted to the theater. Augustine may well be "the great 'secularizer' of the pagan past," who stripped of their religious aura many areas of life in which the gods seemed still to lurk, reducing them to "purely human dimensions" as "traditional forms laid down by men," but the theater is not one of those areas. With respect to the theater, the Manichean sense of evil as a "persecutory force" seems to prevail. Like Tertullian, Augustine very much "believed in demons: a species of beings, superior to men, living forever . . . endowed with supernatural powers of perception; and, as fallen angels, the sworn enemies of the true

caput contegi et galea calciari, et murmuret, quod non apte conveniat; aut in uno die, indicto a pomeridianis horis iustitio, quisquam stomachetur non sibi concedi quod venale proponere, quia mane concessum est; aut in una domo videat aliquid tractari manibus a quoquam servo, quod facere non sinatur qui pocula ministrat; aut aliquid post praesepia fieri, quod ante mensam prohibeatur; et indignetur, cum sit unum habitaculum et una familia, non ubique atque omnibus idem tribui. sic sunt isti qui indignantur, cum audierint illo saeculo licuisse iustis aliquid, quod isto non licet iustis . . . . numquid iustitia varia est et mutabilis? sed tempora, quibus praesidet, non pariter eunt; tempora enim sunt."

happiness of the human race."[40] His comments on the theater, therefore, take for granted Tertullian's thesis of its diabolic origins. He
offers us no picturesque account of the equipment of the games, the
embellishments of the arena, or the nature of the shows themselves,
to demonstrate anew their identity with pagan worship. All this is
assumed to have been proved. Instead, Augustine's inquiry is historical. He devotes himself to an investigation of the decline and
impending fall of the Roman Empire. Throughout the early books
he proceeds on two fronts simultaneously: refuting the pagan charge
that the collapse of Rome and its sack by Alaric in 406 A.D. could be
laid at the door of the Christians, and at the same time mounting a
countercharge to the effect that in truth the descent of the barbarians
might better be ascribed to the degenerate state of the city, for which
the presence of Christianity actually afforded protection, since so many
pagan Romans who would otherwise have been butchered by the in-
vaders sought sanctuary and found safety in the Christian churches.

Rome's degeneracy shows itself above all, in Augustine's account,
in its increasing abandon to debauchery. Scipio knew what he was
about when in the second century B.C. he argued against destroying
Carthage, for he understood that the threat of Carthage kept Rome on
its mettle. Carthage gone, Rome would rapidly grow complacent and
sink into sloth. It was the same Scipio who, with the same wisdom,
blocked the building of a permanent theater in Rome as a threat to
public morals. He would have pursued his austere program even more
implacably, suggests Augustine, had he known that the gods to whom
the theater was to be dedicated were actually devils in disguise seeking
to corrupt Roman citizens. The devils, masquerading as gods, instituted plays with a plausible pretext, to end the plague that was ravaging
the city in 374 B.C., but they harbored ulterior motives. They were, in
reality, scheming to infect men's minds with a far more pernicious
plague, a moral pestilence, in which they succeeded so well that centuries later, those who took refuge in Carthage following Alaric's sack
of Rome "were daily in the theatres, indulging the craze of partisan
support for favourite actors."[41]

Augustine thus articulates closely what Tertullian had merely in-

40. Peter Brown, *Augustine of Hippo* (London, 1967), pp. 266, 395, 311.
41. *The City of God*, I.xxxii, trans. George E. McCracken, Loeb Clas-

dicated in loose and general terms. Not only are theaters a ruse on the part of malignant spirits to enslave human souls, but it is possible to analyze their strategy historically, to scrutinize its specific tactics, and put one's finger on the times and places of its victories. However, whereas in late Roman belief the demons needed only to appear in human form to start a plague or a riot, for Augustine "the nexus between men and demons was purely psychological. Like was drawn to like. Men got the demons they deserved; the demons, for their part, perpetuated this likeness by suggesting to the masses immoral and anarchic gods as symbols of divine power."[42] Through this psychic transference, they accomplished much. They incited the people to every sort of blasphemous ceremony—to dervishes, magicians, and lascivious pantomimes. Needless to say, they carefully avoided supplying anything in the way of ethical principles. They introduced the festivals in order to distract the public from the precepts of its own philosophers. And they succeeded, for the public ignored the philosophers and took its bearings instead from characters like the young rake in Terence's *Eunuch,* who sees in Jupiter's philanderings a warrant for his own. (Despite this hostile reference to Terence, which recurs in several places, Augustine actually distinguishes with some care between the published plays of the dramatic poets and what goes on in the public arena.[43] The former cannot be charged with the same scurrility, and they can form part of a valid educational program, as indeed they came to do in the Middle Ages. Here again, Augustine is capable of perceiving and stressing distinctions to which Tertullian remains blind.) A further tactic of the devils is to let themselves be charged with crimes they did not commit, "so long as they can enmesh men's minds with such beliefs . . . and drag them along with themselves to a predestined punishment."[44] How or by whom the crimes in question were committed, or if indeed they were committed at all, is of no concern to the malevolent ones, whose only objective is to subvert the goodness of their human victims.

---

sics, I (London, 1957), 132–133: "Inde fugientes Carthaginem pervenire potuerunt, in theatris cotidie certatim pro histrionibus insanirent."

42. Brown, *Augustine,* p. 311.

43. *City of God,* II.viii; I, 168–169.

44. Ibid., II.x; I, 174–175: "Dum tamen humanas mentes his opinionibus velut retibus induant et ad praedestinatum supplicium secum trahant."

Surveying the history of Rome, Augustine comments on the inconsistency we have already noted in the Roman attitude toward the actors. The Greeks venerated their theater and all associated with it, whereas the Romans, while professing to honor it, openly degrade and revile its practitioners. Not surprisingly, Augustine finds in this a sign of the greater moral awareness of the Romans. Their hatred for the actors betrays, he thinks, an uneasiness about the nature of the spectacles, a well-founded suspicion of their wickedness, and so with the measures taken against the players under the Republic, which, in his view, needed only to be completed by equally stringent measures against the poets and a refusal of the state to patronize the stage at all. Would it not, he asks heatedly, have been more fitting to pay divine honors to Plato than to the filthy spirits who inspire the foul goings-on in the arena? Those spirits, after all, pretended to be gods, posed as gods, and yet abandoned their supposed people, leaving them to borrow all of their morality from neighboring nations, with the result that the history of Rome has been disfigured from its origin by terrible crimes —the rape of the Sabines, the rape of Lucretia, the expulsion of Collatinus, the trial of Marcus Camillus, and other brutalities of the early Republic. There is something slightly comic about the indignation with which Augustine attacks the demons for failing to provide sound laws and moral precepts in their pretended role as pagan gods, as though instruction in morality was the least they might have done to make their act convincing. Instead of fostering virtue, however, the "gods" made Rome safe for crime. They helped the bloody Marius win the consulship seven times over, and they enabled the ferocious Sulla to keep his odious tyranny alive while upright public servants like Marcus Regulus suffered the direst humiliations. When, in its final years, the Republic lay rotting in its own corruption, the gods made no move to curb the corruption, but deliberately fomented civil war by inciting the lust for battle in the people's hearts. Part of their campaign to destroy the people's fibre involved the encouragement of theatrical performances, at which the worst possible examples of behavior were held up for emulation. Since its inception, then, the theater has formed a key element in a program of subversion by which evil spirits have sought to induce men to cast aside restraint and abandon themselves to vileness. For Augustine, the theater has played the role of a false temple, or anti-temple, standing in mocking antithesis to the true temple, masquerading indeed *as* the true temple, with its own antipriests and antirituals, inhabited by demons, devoted to the Devil, and dedicated to the overthrow of humanity. A clear unspoken corollary of the investigation into Roman history is the implication that in spite of the arrival of Christianity the Empire may yet be ruined by plays and games as was the Republic.

Augustine thus elaborates into a detailed and intelligible plan the murky conspiracy discovered by Tertullian at the root of all theater. It is worth noticing once more, however, what he omits of Tertullian's complaints, and of Plato's. Although, as we have seen, in the *Soliloquies* classifying acting and other imitative arts as the pursuit of a lesser truth, although in *De musica* viewing imitation along with memory and sense as a faculty we share with the lower animals,[45] and so excluding it from the rank of the disciplines and sciences, he nevertheless does not condemn it or imply that it is dangerous in itself. Nor does he condemn the stage on ontological grounds, as a falling away from being, or protest against impersonation as a form of self-betrayal, or imply that the falsity of the spectacles is a calculated affront to the truth of the creation. His argument, grounded in human history, bases itself on considerations of practical morality. It assails the hysteria for the theater as a sign of moral decay because of the specific indecency of the spectacles and because its more fanatical votaries have turned it into a way of life, neglecting more needful pursuits. Augustine recognizes that human nature is composite to begin with, the self a spectrum of selves. The evil of the theater is not that it substitutes a "false" self for a "true" one, but that it licenses the worser self of both players and spectators, and discourages the better. As a rhetorician who had once subscribed to the Manichean heresy and then undergone the experience of a total conversion, Augustine does not need to abuse the "turning" principle as it manifests itself in the theater, but only the perversities to which that form of turning has shown itself liable.

We may conclude this glance at Augustinian attitudes with two observations: one, that Augustine clearly views the theater as symptomatic of something deeper, of a moral disease of which it is not really the cause but merely an aggravating agent, whereas in Tertullian there seems always to lurk the implication that if the stage could be sup-

45. *On Music*, trans. Robert Catesby Taliaferro, in *Writings*, ed. Ludwig Schopp, et al., II (New York, 1947), 178–179.

pressed, or Christians dissuaded from attending it, public morality would instantly regain its health. Augustine sees the theater as only one element in a larger complex, though an especially visible and telltale element. At the same time, and despite his more flexible and analytic approach, he does at times echo the shrill outrage of his more extreme and fundamentalist brethren. Future polemicists against the theater will tend to rehearse the same arguments in even more strident tones while giving little inkling of Augustine's capacity to appreciate the deep and potentially liberating humanity of the institution he is criticizing.

· III ·

Antitheatrical Lollardy

ONE RECURRENT feature of the history of the theater is the fact that outbursts of antitheatrical sentiment tend to coincide with the flourishing of the theater itself. The stage provokes the most active and sustained hostility when it becomes a vital force in the life of a community. It is then that its own values seem most dangerously to collide with the received values of church and state. The denunciations of the Fathers would seem pointless were it not for the theater mania of the Roman populace. The fulminations of the Puritans in sixteenth-century England, or of the Jansenist clergy or the Spanish episcopacy in the seventeenth century, would make no sense except as a response to the vigorous theatrical institutions of the day.

An obvious exception would be the case of the mediaeval church drama and the street drama that grew out of it. Despite the abundance and energy of mediaeval theatrical culture, no sustained body of antitheatrical writing survives from the Middle Ages.[1] Dramatic forms proliferated freely, in mimetic processions, paternoster plays, liturgical plays, scriptural cycle plays, and morality plays, but left behind no corresponding body of condemnatory theory. The occasional reprimands that turn up in the records seem aimed mainly at specific abuses, at the too enthusiastic involvement of the lower clergy, or at the excesses of

1. On the attitudes of mediaeval writers, lay and clerical, toward the drama, see E. K. Chambers, *The Mediaeval Stage* (Oxford, 1903), I, 38–41, 90–95, and II, 97–103; Karl Young, *The Drama of the Mediaeval Church* (Oxford, 1933), II, 410–421; G. R. Owst, *Literature and Pulpit in Mediaeval England*, 2d ed. (Oxford, 1961), pp. 473–485; and Rosemary Woolf, *The English Mystery Plays* (Berkeley, Ca., 1972), pp. 77–101.

folk customs like the *festus stultorum* which had found their way too boisterously into the church itself.

The key to this forbearance lies of course in the fact that the theater this time had sprung not from an alien, hostile religion but from Christianity. It had originated in the church, and it maintained close links with the church. It took its subject matter from the central truths of religion. It reenacted the mysteries of the faith, it made the very altars its stage, and it involved the massive participation of the clergy. For the most part, in consequence, it seems to have been officially tolerated, if not always formally endorsed. Within the ranks of the clergy only an occasional voice of protest carries us back to the mood of Tertullian or St. John Chrysostom. Gerhoh of Reichersberg, in one chapter of his treatise on the Antichrist, alleges that "those who use a church as a theatre for representing the deeds of Antichrist or the rage of Herod are themselves guilty of the vices of the personages portrayed. . . . they don't, as is their intention, lie in their playing, but exhibit the truth."[2] Here, the curt sentence compresses into itself one of the most persistent of antitheatrical theses: that the players' intent is always to lie, that they succeed in doing so whenever they attempt to depict good deeds or saintly doings, but that when they portray wickedness they fail. In this case they are not lying at all, but "exhibiting the truth," the truth of their own foulness, as unequivocal and criminal as in those who perpetrated the crimes being reenacted. So every petty subdeacon who happens to play Herod in a Christmas trope is guilty of the sins of the Tetrarch himself.

The chief surviving antitheatrical document from the Middle Ages, however, is an anonymous fourteenth-century sermon against miracle plays, generally agreed to be of Lollard inspiration, and headed, in manuscript, *A tretise of miraclis pleyinge.*[3] Despite its repetitiveness and monotony, this sermon provides a valuable glimpse of what one may assume to have been a vigorous minority opinion during the growing

2. Young, *Drama of the Mediaeval Church*, II, 412.
3. Printed in Thomas Wright and James Orchard Halliwell, eds. *Reliquiae Antiquae: Scraps from Ancient Manuscripts* (London, 1843), II, 42–57. Page numbers in parentheses following quotations will be to this volume. On the term *miracle* see George R. Coffman, "The Miracle Play in England—Nomenclature," *PMLA* 31 (1916): 448–465.

years of the Wycliffite movement, and it serves as a kind of prelude also to the massive storm of antitheatrical protest that ended by wrecking the English theater entirely in the seventeenth century. Intellectually, it shows little of the complexity or analytic power of Augustine, but reverts, with some parochial variations of its own, to the fierce fundamentalism of Tertullian. Where Tertullian refused to countenance make-believe in plays, or to accord it a separate status, the preacher admits its centrality, but chooses to interpret it in a peculiarly invidious way as a "flouting" or "scorning" of the reality it depicts. Those who enact the Passion of Christ, according to the preacher, since they are not themselves Christ, or the disciples, or even the tormentors, are "playing" at it in a spirit of blasphemous mockery. The possibility that such a reenactment might reverently celebrate the original event, that it might, in a spirit of devotion, be attempting imaginatively to reenter the world in which the original event took place, is not one that the preacher is capable of entertaining. He is, in fact, mesmerized by the very word *play*, which in his eye affixes a stigma onto the whole operation that nothing can remove, and which makes the representation into a calculated affront to the thing it is attempting to represent.

Some of the moroseness of the more ascetic Fathers, and that of the later reformers, seems to creep into such discussions as that on laughter, which the homilist takes to be an offense against God. Christ, he reminds us, never laughed. Christ shed his blood and his tears and did continual penance, thereby admonishing us that "alle oure doyng heere shulde ben in penaunce, in disciplynyng of oure fleyssh" (p. 43). Anything else that we may do in this world "utterly reverses" Christ's works. A basic objection to plays therefore is that they aim to amuse. Pleasure contradicts our purpose here below, which is to harken to God's word in fear and trembling, in quaking and dread. "Drede smyten to Godward holdith and susteyneth oure bileve to hym" (p. 43), whereas mirth "undisposith a man to paciencie and ablith to glotonye and to othere vicis" (p. 44). Here, we feel, we are listening to a lineal descendant of the Fathers and a true ancestor of the zealots of the Reformation. Here we detect puritanism with a small *p*, the same dogmatic fundamentalism, the same posing of absolute alternatives, the same mapping of the world into God's territory and the Devil's, the same rejection of whatever in life is attractive or inviting. Here too we can hardly escape suspecting also the same slightly unwholesome taste for persecution and martyrdom.

The preacher affects a systematic presentation of his case through a point-by-point refutation of the main defenses urged in behalf of plays by their partisans. One is quickly struck, however, by the circularity of most of the reasoning. To the claim that the purpose of those who act in plays is to worship God—unlike, for example, the Jews, who openly scoffed at Christ—the preacher retorts that this is not so: the purpose is "more to ben seen of the world and to plesyn to the world thanne to be seen of God or to plesyn to hym" (p. 46). Hence plays can never be other than mere "syngnis of love withoute dedis, . . . gynnys of the devvel to cacchen men to byleve of Anti-Christ" (p. 46). But this, plainly, merely substitutes one question-begging assertion for another, and leaves the argument where it was. Again, to the claim that men can be moved to compassion, and from there to devotion, by the sight of Christ's sufferings played, the preacher rejoins that when men weep at plays, it is not for their own sins but for the pathos of the story. Their tears therefore are worthless; even Christ reproved the women who wept for him. Here the preacher implicitly sets aside a substantial tradition according to which religious paintings could soften the heart and so help to arouse devotion. He will admit of no form of mediation between the scriptural episode itself and the believer's spirit—no mediation except, presumably, such sermons as his own and those of his colleagues, which didactically expound the meaning of the episode in question.

To the claim that some men can more readily be converted to God by play than by seriousness, the homilist answers scathingly that those who are not converted by the sacraments will never be converted by plays, since a man who was truly penitent would abhor to behold such vanities. To the suggestion that plays offer innocent recreation he answers that they offer false and worldly recreation, "feigned" recreation; the only true recreation would consist of the doing of deeds of mercy for one's unfortunate neighbors. It is true enough that the *action* of plays is "feigned," and that pious offices, almsdeeds, and the practical duties of devotion might be regarded as having priority for the zealous Christian, but that plays therefore provide merely feigned *recreation* comes as a stunning non sequitur. In each of his rejoinders, the stubborn prior assumption of the thing to be proved vitiates the preacher's logic and muddies the waters of his argument almost to the point of impenetrability.

One of the most grievous counts against plays, for the preacher, is that they are not only wicked, but "mayntenyd and prechid as gode and profitable," so that they become "deadely synne." It is the concerted, organized, professionalized nature of the enterprise that offends so deeply, the fact that it entails planning and teamwork and elaborate preparation, making it different from the kind of sin that is committed inadvertently, or in a fit of ungovernable passion. If it is "mannysche," and hence forgivable, to fall into error in the latter way, it is "develiche," and damnable, to "abyden stylle" in error. Adam and Eve lost Paradise not simply for eating the apple but "more for the excusyng therof" (p. 51). It is the actors' insistence on the harmlessness of their playing, the playgoers' conviction that they are being edified, that stamps theatrical activity as sin of the deepest dye.

A further concern of the homilist is to deny any claim made for plays on the basis of their kinship with the other visual arts. Paintings and sculptured images had long been accepted for their pedagogical value, as "books" for the unlettered and as aids to the untrustworthy memory. The primacy of visual experience, its exceptional "nobility" and effectiveness, were thought to enable it to play a powerful role in the awakening of devotion.[4] On such reasoning, it is clear that plays would have a strong claim, and the defenders of miracle drama would seem to have annexed a set of nearly unanswerable arguments. The Wycliffite preacher proves surprisingly ineffective, even evasive, on this point. At a time when Lollardy was rapidly stiffening its antagonism to images of all kinds,[5] he hedgingly concedes that under proper conditions pictures may not be altogether reprehensible. If they tell the truth, if they steer clear of lies, if they refrain from excessive appeals to the senses, if they avoid idolatry, then they may be considered as a kind of

4. See the illuminating discussion of the whole issue in Woolf, *Mystery Plays*, pp. 86–95.

5. On the controversy over images in the fourteenth century, see W. R. Jones, "Lollards and Images: The Defense of Religious Art in Later Medieval England," *Journal of the History of Ideas* 34 (1973): 27–50, esp. 29–36.

book in which to read the truth. But when it comes to plays on similar subjects, the proposition does not hold, for none of the stipulated conditions is considered to obtain. Whatever may be the case with paintings and sculpture, plays "ben made more to deliten men bodily than to ben bokis to lewid men, and therefore gif thei ben quike bookis, thei ben quike bookis to schrewidenesse more than to godenesse" (p. 50). In short, the virtues grudgingly allowed to "peinture" are not extended to plays. In their case, the possibility of being useful and innocent does not exist, not because of any logical distinction that can be drawn between them and paintings, but because the preacher insists on substituting his own preconceptions about them for the claims of their authors: they are *not* books for the unlearned, *not* unmingled with lies; they *are* designed to please the carnal man, to teach "schrewidenesse" rather than godliness. Traditional religious imagery, though it disturbs the preacher, escapes his censure evidently because it is traditional. But plays enjoy no such immunity. And the greater their impact, the greater their offensiveness. Plainly it is their intense immediacy, everything about them that makes them capable of stirring their audiences, as Gregory of Nyssa was said to have been stirred to tears by a painting of the Sacrifice of Isaac—everything, in short, which enhances their efficacy as aids to devotion—which in the preacher's jaundiced eye turns them into something abominable and sinister.

One striking symptom of the "Lollardy" of the sermon appears in its frequent appeal to Scripture. The attack on the drama as a whole is made to hinge on the Second Commandment, "Thou schalt not take Goddis name in idil," which the miracle plays are said to infringe (p. 50). A negative argument is also drawn from the life of Christ. If Christ had wished us to play miracles, he would have done so himself, and set the example, or at least have instructed us to do so. Since he did not, the playing of them must contradict his word and be forbidden. Here the logic resembles that of those Fathers for whom shaving, cosmetics, purple dyes, and pugilism were sinful because not expressly commanded by God.

The preacher also cites a number of particular biblical texts to support his claim, trying to prove, in effect, that since the Bible always refers disparagingly to players and playing, plays and players are always to be disparaged. For example, if Sara, in the Book of Tobit, illustrates her piety by reminding God that she has never consorted with players ("numquam cum ludentibus miscui me" [3:17]),[6] the preacher concludes that "sythen a yonge womman of the Olde Testament, for kepynge of hir bodily vertue of chastité and for to worthily take the sacrament of matrimonye . . . abstenyde hir fro al maner ydil pleiyng and fro al cumpany of idil pleyeris; mychen more a prist of the Newe Testament . . . awʒte to abstene hym fro al ydil pleiyng bothe of myraclys and ellis" (pp. 47–48). We may observe in passing that throughout his tract the preacher reacts badly to the involvement of the clergy in dramatic events, whether as actors or spectators.

The case of Sara happens to be nearly the sole instance among the scriptural citations made by the preacher that supports his own interpretation. Most depend on a strained and unnatural reading of the text, and in particular on a forced glossing of the word *ludere*. The story of Isaac and Ishmael is strenuously allegorized (following Galatians 4: 21–31) as a figure of the war between the spirit and the flesh, the joining of the Old Testament and the New, in which, since spirit always gets the worst of it in any such encounter, it is necessary to separate them. Ishmael was sent away "to exsaumplen that pley of the fleysh is not covenable ne helpely to the spirit, but to the benymmynge of the spiritus heretage." More specifically, "at the biddyng of God, for Ismael pleyide with hys brother Isaac, both Ismael and his modir were throwen out of the hous of Abraham, of the whiche the cause was for by siche pleyinge Ismael, that was the sone of the servant, myʒte han begilid Isaac of his heretage, that was the sone of the fre wif of Abraham" (p. 52). It is true enough that, in the Vulgate, "Cumque vidisset Sara filium Agar aegyptiae ludentem cum Isaac filio suo, dixit ad Abraham: Eiice ancillam hanc et filium eius, non enim erit heres filius ancillae cum filio meo Isaac" (Genesis 21: 9–10). Sara's maternal jealousy and her fears for the inheritance are certainly brought on by the sight of Isaac playing with Ishmael, but nothing suggests a connection between "playing" and "beguiling," nor does anything in Paul's exposition in Galatians 4 suggest it either. The playing of the boys frightens Sara because it symbolizes an intimacy and a potential equality between the two which might one day imperil Isaac's inheritance. The idea

6. Scriptural citations are to the *Biblia sacra, vulgatae editionis*, ed. monachorum abbatiae pontificiae sancti Hieronymi in urbe ordinis sancti Benedicti, 2d ed. (Turin, 1965).

that she finds something inherently wicked in the playing itself is the importation of the preacher, or of the exegetical tradition on which he may be drawing.[7]

It would almost seem as if he has unconsciously conflated this incident with the later one of Jacob and Esau, which does indeed raise awkward questions about "playing," although here the word *ludere* is not invoked. For Jacob defrauds Esau of his blessing by means of a disguise, by *playing* at being Esau, and is rewarded for this deceit by becoming the patriarch of his race. Here might have been a text to ponder. How can the history of God's elect commence with an act of impersonation, an act of theatrical trickery on the part of its founder?[8] Laban, who later defrauds Jacob of his rightful bride by the substitution of Leah, would seem to be doing no more than giving him a taste of his own medicine. And one might raise the same questions, less sharply perhaps, about some of the trickery and deceit practiced by David while king. But such considerations would have been improper to raise concerning the pillars of the House of God, whereas misbehavior on the part of the outcaste Ishmael could be taken for granted, and the use of *ludere* in connection with his childish games could be assumed to be pejorative.

Elsewhere the references to playing seem even further from the point. In the case of the young men who rose up and "played" before Abner and Joab (2 Samuel, 2:14–16), the playing refers unmistakably to fighting, as the context makes clear. The New English Bible translates "join in single combat." It is true that the disastrous bloodbath seems to have resulted from a mock duel of some sort, which got out of hand and turned into a battle to the death. But the fact that the Hebrew term *saḥaq* includes an element of "playfulness and frolic"

7. There may have been a tradition according to which Ishmael's playing was interpreted as containing some sort of threat. For we find in J. Frain du Tremblay, *Conversations morales sur les jeux et les divertissemens* (Paris, 1685), p. 269, à propos of the same verse in Genesis, that "cette sainte mere [i.e., Sara] craignoit que le fils de la servante n'amollît & ne corrompît le coeur de son fils par ces divertissemens." To which he adds, "Il est vray qu'à cause des sens differens dans lesquels se prend ce mot [i.e., *ludere*], les Interpretes ne l'ont pas tous expliqué de la même maniere."

8. See Daniel Dyke, *The Mystery of Self-Deceiving* (London, 1615), Sig. C6ᵛ, where Jacob is cited as an instance of *simulation* for dressing in Esau's clothes to deceive Isaac.

has caused at least one commentator to doubt whether it can even be the correct reading.[9] In the case of Elisha and the children who mocked him (2 Kings 2:23), *illudebant* has to do with direct jeering and flouting, and not at all with theatrical play. "Men shulden not pleyn the passion of Crist," warns the preacher, "upon peyne myche grettere than was the venjaunce of the childre that scornyden Helisee" (p. 56). But men can "play" the Passion of Christ respectfully and reverentially, whereas the children of Bethel could not, in the nature of the case, have reverently or respectfully "scorned" Elisha. So the supposed analogy, instead of clarifying matters, merely introduces another equivocation on the term *play*, adding one more to the tissue of tautologies of which the argument is largely composed.

At length, however, and quite without warning, the preacher introduces a use of *ludere* that completely undermines his own case. Unexpectedly he admits that there may be, after all, such a thing as godly playing. "if we wilen algate pleyen," he advises us, "pleyne we as Davith pleyide bifore the harrke of God, and as he spac byfor Mychel his wif, dispisying his pleyinge" (p. 57). In the passage in question (2 Samuel 6:20–21), David dances before the Lord to celebrate the bringing of the ark to Jerusalem, clad in nothing but the sleeveless ephod of the Israelite priests. Michal's contemptuous reproof on this occasion, apparently for David's frivolity, his exhibitionism, seems very much in the vein of the Lollard preacher; her attitude toward David's playing duplicates his toward theatrical playing. Why then should the preacher relent in this instance? Presumably because David's playing has been sanctified by a tradition too powerful to challenge. But if this instance of play is warranted—and it comes far closer than any of the other instances to being theatrical play, since it involves music and dancing and a joyful displaying of the self—why should playing as such be forbidden? Interestingly, the preacher overlooks, or ignores, other occasions of David's triumphal playing, such as that in a previous verse of the same chapter: "David autem et omnis Israel ludebant coram Domino in omnibus lignis fabrefactis et citharis et lyris, et tympanis et sisris, et cymbalis" (2 Samuel 6:5). Here not David alone but all of Israel "plays" before the Lord, on instruments made of every kind of wood. Earlier we have heard how the Israelite women greeted David and

9. Hans Wilhelm Hertzberg, *I and II Samuel: A Commentary* (London, 1964), pp. 251–252.

Saul upon their return from battle, singing and dancing, playing and chanting. Much later, when Jeremiah and Zechariah wish to prophesy the joyful outpouring of the renewed Israel, they speak of the rebuilt city playing in its triumph, of the children playing in the streets of the new Jerusalem. When Wisdom, again, in the Proverbs of Solomon, wishes to trace her history, she recalls how she played before the Lord at the creation of the world, and then again on the earth when the earth was finished. "Playing," in short, though it occurs in a few unfavorable contexts, more commonly suggests celebration, thanksgiving, and sacred festivity. Why might not these instances have served as text and precedent for fourteenth-century parishioners, as an account of wholesome play, worthy to be emulated, rather than the obscurer citations the homilist has raked together and tormented to make fit his argument? What answer could the moralist make to an actor of "miraclis" who claimed that his kind of playing derived from David's, and bore no resemblance to that of Ishmael or the children of Bethel? Such a claim was in fact to be made shortly in the treatise *Dives et pauper*, whose author takes the episode of David dancing as "scriptural proof that God wishes mirth and gladness from his creatures," and who uses it to defend not only dancing but also miracle plays, and even to defend the performing of them on Sundays and great feast days, on the ground that God commanded mirth and ease on holidays, as a foretaste of the bliss of heaven.[10] Clearly David's dancing forms a far more telling precedent in favor of play than all the unfavorable instances together tell against it, and the homilist's abrupt eleventh-hour endorsement of it merely underscores the fact that the whole case against *ludere* is a house of cards.

Does the Sermon against Miracle Plays concern the outdoor cycle drama alone? Or does it also address itself to the liturgical drama within the church? V. A. Kolve distinguishes between the church drama proper, which "avoided the Crucifixion and had little connection with game," and the street theater, which was "redefined *as* game and allowed to exploit fully its nonearnest, gratuitous nature" (pp. 18–19). The *Tretise* itself, to be sure, speaks only of the impiety of playing the Passion. It makes no mention of plays on other scriptural themes, so it may be that the preacher is thinking only of street drama. On

10. V. A. Kolve, *The Play Called Corpus Christi* (Stanford, 1966), pp. 131–134. Page references in the discussion that follows will be to this edition.

the other hand, he nowhere distinguishes between the two, and his whole line of argument would in consistency require him *not* to distinguish. For he finds the impiety not in the interpolation of alien matter, not in levity of tone, but in the fact of representing sacred story at all, from which it would seem to follow that *any* attempt to depict scriptural episodes mimetically, whether out of doors and in the vernacular, or inside the church and in Latin, must be blasphemous. If it is unlawful to play the Passion of Christ, it must be equally unlawful to play the Resurrection, as in the Easter trope, and the more so the more the trope admits such uncanonical byplay as the Marys haggling with the spice vendor or the jealousy of the cuckold Joseph. It is hard to imagine the author of the *Tretise* viewing even the austerest liturgical drama with anything but indignation.

In this connection it is pertinent that many of the fiercer foes of the stage were also antiliturgical, showing little interest in sacramentalism. What concerns them are actions, not enactments, even in worship itself—hence no doubt the developing stress on preaching. Those who espouse an ecclesiology of action tend to be deeply suspicious of mimesis. This is true of Gerhoh, and also of Wycliffe. It is logical moreover that those who question the mimetic element even in the liturgy should reject the recreational mimesis of the street drama. Apart from practical considerations, philosophical objections enter in. For when a player has given over his consciousness to some form of identification with a character, or when a spectator, identifying with that character, has done the same, what happens to his own self? Is it suspended somehow for the duration of the performance? And if so, is this not a spiritually dangerous state of affairs? Does it not in fact resemble demonic possession? Would not actor and spectator both be better off during their short time on earth giving food to a real beggar rather than watching plays or performing them? The philosophical objection thus reinforces the moral objection. Play, in this view, is no form of true action, and can have no acceptable moral impact at all, either on the player or on the spectator.[11]

"Though the Wycliffite preacher," says Kolve, "shares with the dra-

11. I owe some of the observations in this paragraph to my colleague Professor Anne Middleton, who is not, however, to be charged with any distortions I may have introduced.

matists an exact sense of the drama as play, he understands differently how this play world relates to the world of actual experience. He is unable to see the dramatic artifact as something analogous, but in a root-sense 'unrelated,' to real life. . . . He believes the drama teaches men that hell is only a *locus* on a pageant stage, and that the wrath of God is merely a dramatic attitude, for it is obvious to any spectator that the damned souls are not really punished in any Judgment Day pageant" (p. 21). But this correct assessment of the preacher's attitudes also reveals the crudity and inadequacy of his categories. For he assumes that if the spectator does not credit the literal truth of what he is beholding, if he understands that he is gazing at a pageant at which no one is actually punished, he will be driven to take the entire experience as a falsehood, and as falsehood also the true events being enacted by the players. The element of pretense in the event will prompt him to cast aside all belief in the reality that lies behind the pretense. And this curious notion, though it no doubt constitutes a peculiar tribute to the drama's power of persuasion, also convicts the spectator of a naiveté such as the smallest and dullest child could scarcely be guilty of. "His final answers are confused," pursues Kolve, "because he thought action that was unreal was therefore untrue, clinging rigidly to two polarities: real and unreal, true and false. Whatever was false he considered to be an abomination to God and a peril to men's souls. In this he may have been right, but his categories are muddled: the world of play (and its mode of meaningfulness) lies outside the antithesis, truth or falsehood" (p. 22). We have already encountered in Tertullian the clinging to two polarities of real and unreal, truth and falsehood. But the fourteenth-century moralist is faced with a less clear-cut situation than Tertullian, in which it may not in fact be quite correct to say that the world of play lies "outside" the antithesis true or false. In one sense it does, in another it plainly does not. For in the case of (let us say) a Roman farce, the actors are engaged in playing a fictitious story, a tale of cuckoldry or mistaken identity, which the playwright has invented, or is presumed to have invented, out of whole cloth. The miracle players, by contrast, are engaged in a more serious effort: to render scenes from sacred history, which constitutes not merely truth but the highest possible truth. The miracle plays cannot therefore escape the antithesis true or false. Even considered as "figurative," they deal with "something real and historical which announces something else that is also real and historical."[12] A spectator may know full well that he is not witnessing the original event—the Crucifixion for instance—but he does believe that that event once happened, and that he is watching a more or less believable reenactment of it. Even if he is illiterate, and must rely on sermons, lections, and the visual imagery of the church for his knowledge, that knowledge provides a standard against which he will measure the dramatic performance. And this must make the performance a very different thing from the adultery farce, or the kind of tale in which knights pursue dragons through enchanted forests and rescue princesses from ogres. The scriptural incident as pageanted must be in some degree answerable to a historical original, as the tale of the knight need not. It must not too radically contradict the impressions printed on the spectator's mind by a lifetime of churchgoing, of listening to sermons, of gazing at painted altars and stained-glass windows and carved capitals. To see Christ crucified on the pageant wagon is to see truth renewed, to be forcibly reminded of it, to have it brought powerfully before the spirit, and so, in a sense, to *believe* it once more.

If we set the *Tretise of miraclis pleyinge* alongside *De spectaculis* or Augustine's antitheatrical pronouncements in *The City of God* we can see how the antitheatrical argument transmutes itself, shifts its garments, to fit the changing times. The Fathers had charged the spectacles with being idolatrous, with furthering the worship of Jupiter, Neptune, Bacchus, and the rest of the scandalous pantheon, as part of a diabolic plot to keep men from the true God. The Lollard preacher, a millennium later, is dealing with a Christian drama, born from the liturgy and inspired by the Bible, heavily didactic, moreover, in its emphasis on Christian virtues like obedience, penitence, and piety. The charge of idol worship can hardly now be germane. Its assailants, we imagine, must find grounds more relative than this. Instead, the preacher surprises us by reviving the old accusation in a new form. He devises a fantastic analogy between the playing of miracles and the worship of the golden calf to show that miracle plays, by encouraging gluttony, lechery, and covetise, constitute a dreadful "maumetrie," of which the gilded calf itself was only a relatively modest and innocent prefiguration. In so arguing, of course, he empties the word *maumetry*

12. Erich Auerbach, "Figura," trans. Ralph Manheim, in *Scenes from the Drama of European Literature* (1944; rpt. New York, 1973), p. 29.

—idolatry—of all precision, converting it into little more than a loose synonym for "immorality." But by preserving the term, he evidently preserves in his own mind all the terrific negative force still contained in the term. As we have seen, for him the pious content of the cyclical plays in no way extenuates, but rather aggravates their wickedness. The very thing about them that reveals their devotional purpose—their focus on the biblical story—is the thing that offends the preacher most bitterly, and one suspects he would have had more patience with flat bawdry than with such efforts to turn religion into a source of "idil" amusement.

We may begin to suspect further, then, that the reasons so freely given tend to be in large part rationalizations, that there exists a deep reservoir of prejudice which can lend itself to circumstances, fastening onto local or accidental features of a given theatrical enterprise as if they were permanent and essential. The true meaning of the prejudice is elusive, but it would seem to have to do with the lifelike immediacy of the theater, which puts it in unwelcome competition with the everyday realm and with the doctrines espoused in schools and churches. Moreover, by the element of freedom implicitly claimed in it, it threatens at any moment to depart from the fabric of received belief, even if in all good faith it intends to abide within it. By the closeness of the imitative process, in which it mimes the actual unfolding of events in time, before the spectators' eyes, it has an unsettling way of being received by its audiences, at least for the moment and with whatever necessary mental reserves, as reality pure and simple. As such, it implicitly constitutes a standing threat to the primacy of the reality propounded from lectern and pulpit.

· IV ·

Puritans and Proteans

WHATEVER THE REASON, it is evident that for most antitheatrical polemicists, playgoing tends to rank abnormally high in the hierarchy of sins. Salvianus, a disciple of St. Augustine, points out that other sins defile only those who perpetrate them, but that the theater defiles those who merely see or hear it. If you witness a shocking act like murder, your mind disapproves, so that you yourself are not morally tainted. "The indecencies of the spectacles," however, "involve actors and audience in substantially the same guilt,"[1] for the audience, by attending and enjoying and applauding, approves, in effect, what it sees, and so shares in the sins it beholds. It is the element of spectator complicity which makes the experience perilous.

So, at the close of the seventeenth century, Bourdaloue, in a sermon on worldly amusements, is concerned to curb two dangerous obsessions in his parishioners: gambling and theatergoing. But whereas his reproof of gambling is only partial and contingent, his condemnation

---

1. Salvian, *On the Government of God*, trans. Eva M. Sanford (New York, 1930), VI.3, p. 163. See J.-P. Migne, *Patrologia latina*, LIII (Paris, 1865), 111: "Solae spectaculorum impuritates sunt quae unum admodum faciunt et agentium et aspicientium crimen." See also the same passage as translated in *A Second and Third Blast of Retrait from Plaies and Theaters*, in *The English Drama and Stage under the Tudor and Stuart Princes 1543–1664*, ed. W. C. Hazlitt ([London], 1869), p. 104: "Al other evils pollute the doers onlie, not the beholders, or the hearers. For a man may heare a blasphemer, and not be partaker of his sacriledge, inasmuch as in minde he dissenteth. And if one come while a roberie is a doing, he is cleere, because he abhors the fact. Onlie the filthines of plaies, and spectacles is such, as maketh both the actors & beholders giltie alike. For while they saie nought, but gladlie looke on, they al by sight and assent be actors."

of the theater is total. Gambling, he explains, is sinful in excess, when it involves ruinously high sums, or becomes frenzied, so that it draws the Christian away from the cares of business or family. But indulged in after all needful affairs have been transacted, it can be encouraged as an innocent pastime, to be enjoyed in tranquillity of mind. The ban against playgoing, by contrast, admits of no exceptions. Acting and playgoing, evil intrinsically, remain evil under all circumstances.[2] Gambling, we infer, belongs among the sins attendant on our fallen nature; it reminds us that we are sons of Adam. Playgoing, on the other hand, smells of brimstone; it betokens a settled hardness of heart, a defiance akin to that which produced the revolt in heaven, and enlists its adherents in the ranks of the damned. The Wycliffite preacher had distinguished between "mannysche" and "develiche" sins, ranking acting and playgoing among the latter. Tyndale, similarly, acknowledging that we are born to sin, nevertheless distinguishes between "God's sinners" and "the devil's sinners." God's sinners "consent not to their sin," and "mourn to have [it] taken away." But the devil's sinners consent to theirs, "and would have the law and hell taken away, and are enemies unto the righteousness of God."[3] For the detractors of the stage, any traffic with the theater, whether as participant or spectator, must enroll a man in the legions of the damned. For in neither case can the activity be extenuated, like a crime of passion, as a sudden yielding to a natural urge. The theater involves training, rehearsal, and planning on the part of its producers. On the part of its audiences it requires a sustained imaginative collusion with the events portrayed by the actors. Not many opponents of the stage would have been impressed by the defense of the Italian actor Cecchini, who early in the seventeenth century pointed out that the theater held men from vicious pastimes. When the theater is filled, he suggested, the gaming houses are empty, and those who live by promoting games of chance live in fear of the players, who lure their customers away.[4] For moralists like

2. Le P. Louis Bourdaloue, "Sermon pour le 3e dimanche après Pâques: Sur les divertissements du monde," in *Sermons pour les dimanches*, II (Lyons, 1724), 75–76.

3. "Obedience of a Christian Man," in *Doctrinal Treatises*, ed. Henry Walker (Cambridge, 1848), p. 311.

4. Piermaria Cecchini, *Discorsi intorno alle comedie, comediante, e spettatori* (Vicenza, 1614), Sig. D2ᵛ.

Bourdaloue, the forsaking of the gambling table for the playhouse could only have been viewed as a desperate leap from the frying pan into the fire, the renouncing of a trivial sin in favor of a deadly one.

English Puritans of the sixteenth century reached equally sweeping conclusions, though only after more than a generation of slowly intensifying pamphlet warfare.[5] Early in the century, when the stage served chiefly as an adjunct to pedagogy, helping teach correct pronunciation and good deportment to schoolboys, or when it served as a toy of the court and the great nobility, it was possible for fierce Protestants like John Bale and John Foxe themselves to write plays and destine them for performance. Even as the antitheatrical movement gathered momentum after midcentury, it tended at first to except the academic stage from its strictures. Northbrooke, an early assailant, expressly defends the use of plays in schools,[6] while the first

5. On the history of Puritan opposition to the stage, see Elbert N. S. Thompson, *The Controversy between the Puritans and the Stage*, Yale Studies in English, 20 (New York, 1903); M. M. Knappen, *Tudor Puritanism* (Chicago, 1939), pp. 439–441; William Ringler, "The First Phase of the Elizabethan Attack on the Stage, 1558–1579," *Huntington Library Quarterly* 5 (1941–42): 391–418; Russell Fraser, *The War against Poetry* (Princeton, 1970). I use the convenient shorthand term "Puritan" despite the fact that not all writers against the stage were Puritans. Gosson, for example, according to his biographer, "was actually a vigorous opponent of Puritanism," and a number of Anglican divines were "just as much disturbed over the evils of playgoing and just as outspoken in their opinions as the most rabid Puritans" (William Ringler, *Stephen Gosson: A Biographical and Critical Study*, Princeton Studies in English, 25 [Princeton, 1942], p. 80). Arthur F. Kinney, *Markets of Bawdrie: The Dramatic Criticism of Stephen Gosson*, Salzburg Studies in English Literature, no. 4 (Salzburg, 1974), pp. 5–28, reviews at length the committed Anglicanism of Gosson's career: his education at the Cathedral School in Canterbury and at Corpus Christi College, Oxford, his probable spying for Walsingham (to whom *Plays Confuted* is dedicated), his rapid rise in the Anglican hierarchy, the resolute orthodoxy of his rectorship of St. Botolph's-without-Bishopsgate during the last twenty-five years of his life, and the express anti-Puritanism of some of his opinions. I am mindful, too, of Christopher Hill's warning that "the word 'Puritan' . . . is an admirable refuge from clarity of thought" (*Society and Puritanism in Pre-Revolutionary England* [New York, 1964], p. 13). Nevertheless, the term has come to stand, with some justice, for a complex of attitudes best represented by those strictly designated as Puritans, and it will be adopted here in that sense.

6. John Northbrooke, *A Treatise wherein Dicing, Dauncing, Vaine Plaies*

edition of Stubbes' vehement *Anatomy of Abuses* (1583) carefully exempts from its lash "some kind of playes, tragedies and enterluds," as being both "of great ancie*n*tie," and also "very honest and very commendable exercyses."[7] Discreetly used, these writers intimate, the stage might serve to educate. It might help form sober citizens and godly parishioners. But with the building of the playhouses toward the end of the century, the creation of a permanent class of professional actors under the aegis of the crown, and the gradual tightening of government control over all theatrical activity—in short, with the theater more visibly legitimized and institutionalized than at any time since Greek days—the attack moves into high gear, beginning to take on the rancorous and envenomed character that increasingly stamps it until it reaches a climax with the dissolution of the stage in 1642. Stubbes removes from the second edition of his *Anatomy* the qualifications laid down in the first, and in the final decade of the century an Oxford don, John Rainolds, is found to be fulminating against all theatrical productions, of whatever origin, under whatever auspices, and against all plays, in whatever languages, of whatever apparent harmlessness of subject matter. The attack culminates in 1633 with Prynne's *Histriomastix*, a gargantuan encyclopedia of antitheatrical lore which scourges every form of theater in the most ferocious terms, in a style of paralyzing repetitiousness from which everything resembling nuance has been rigidly excluded.

Doubtless *Histriomastix* deserves a separate word to itself. The title page alone of this extraordinary performance announces that Prynne is the kind of author who must cram the entire argument of his book into every sentence:

Histrio-Mastix, the Players Scourge, or Actors Tragaedie, Divided into Two Parts, Wherein it is largely evidenced, by divers *Arguments*, by the concurring Authorities and Resolutions of *sundry texts of Scripture*; of the *whole Primitive Church*, both under the *Law and Gospell*;

---

or Enterludes with other idle passtimes . . . are reprooved (London, 1579), Sig. L.

7. *Phillip Stubbes's Anatomy of the Abuses in England in Shakspere's Youth, A.D. 1583*, ed. Frederick J. Furnivall, New Shakspere Society (London, 1877–79), p. x (Sigs. 5ᵛ–6, A Preface to the Reader). In citing old texts, and old-spelling reprints such as this, I have normalized *u*, *v*, *i*, and *j* so as to conform with modern usage.

of 55 *Synodes and Councels*; of 71 *Fathers and Christian Writers*, be-fore the yeare of our Lord 1200; of above 150 *foraigne and domestique Protestant and Popish Authors*, since; of 40 *Heathen Philosophers, Historians, Poets*; of many *Heathen*, many *Christian Nations, Repub-liques, Emperors, Princes, Magistrates*; of sundry *Apostolicall, Canon-icall, Imperiall Constitutions*; and of our owne *English Statutes, Mag-istrates, Universities, Writers, Preachers. / That popular Stage-playes (the very Pompes of the Divell which we renounce in Baptisme*, if we beleeve the Fathers) *are sinfull, heathenish, lewde, ungodly Spectacles, and most pernicious Corruptions; condemned in all ages, as intoler-able Mischiefes to Churches, to Republickes, to the manners, mindes, and soules of men. And that the Profession of Play-poets, of Stage players; together with the penning, acting, and frequenting of Stage-playes, are unlawfull, infamous and misbeseeming Christians.* All pretences to the contrary are here likewise fully answered; and the unlawfulnes of acting, of beholding Academicall Enterludes, briefly discussed; besides sundry other particulars concerning *Dancing, Dic-ing, Health-Drinking.* . . .

We are dealing, unmistakably, with a megalomaniac. Prynne him-self, acknowledging the dropsical bulk of his volume, defends it on the ground that since the number of vicious playbooks keeps increas-ing, he must keep up with them. *"Can then one* Quarto *Tractate against Stage-playes be thought too large,"* he demands, *"when as it must as-sault such ample Play-house* Volumes?" He is to enter into a blud-geoning match. His treatise is to swell to such monstrous and unnat-ural size *"because these Play-bookes are so multiplied"* (Sig.**6^v). He will overwhelm the reader with sheer mass, crush the opposition under the tonnage of his prose. It is hard to imagine that Prynne really be-lieves his own logic at this point, yet equally hard to imagine other-wise: he is not a writer given to playfulness, irony, or self-deprecation. But it is not merely the "tedious prolixitie" of the volume he defends, he also excuses those passages that may seem to be "over-sharpe and virulent," "overmalepart and censorious," or "heterogeneall, and im-pertinent to the intended theame," on the ground that in this respect he is conforming to the usage of the Fathers. The wild diversity of his targets he defends as "materially pertinent" to his cause, since the other objects of his attack are all either adjuncts of plays or else in some way closely allied with them, and equally in need of censure. It is:

Manifest to all mens judgements, that effeminate mixt Dancing, Dicing, Stage-playes, lascivious Pictures, wanton Fashions, Face-painting,
Health-drinking, Long haire, Love-lockes, Periwigs, womens curling,
pouldring and cutting of their haire, Bone-fires, New-yeares-gifts, May-
games, amorous Pastoralls, lascivious effeminate Musicke, excessive
laughter, luxurious disorderly Christmas-keeping, Mummeries, . . .
[are all] wicked, unchristian pastimes. (Sigs. **8ᵛ–***)

In this catalogue of horrors we see one staple technique of the radical
antitheatricalists: the dredging up of a whole shoal of evils, of varying
shapes and sizes, from the social sea, minnows along with whales, and
the confounding of all distinction and discrimination in the excited
vehemence against all. The emphasis falls heavily on two sorts of of-
fenses: on sports and games and festive activities—on anything that
gives pleasure and is patently designed as recreation—and even more
obsessively on sexuality and effeminacy, as though to underscore the
author's fearful aversion to anything—dancing, love-making, hair-
curling, elegant attire—that might suggest active or interested sexuality,
this being equated with femininity, with weakness, with the yielding
to feeling, and consequently with the destruction of all assured props
and boundaries.[8] The effect of the whole passage, as of numerous others
like it, is to raise the spectre of an endless feast of fools, a perpetual
carnival, or parody of the good society, in which hectic merriment will
replace ordered work, a *regnum diaboli* dominated by the anarchy of
the sexual instincts. The engorged obsessiveness with which the series
bursts through its logical framework and rounds back on itself constitutes a kind of frantic miming of the chaos to ensue if the theater
and its attendant evils are not swiftly crushed.

In affecting a theatrical subdivision of his topic into acts and scenes,
with Prologue, Chorus, and Catastrophe, Prynne evidently wishes both
to exploit the possibilities for order inherent in such an arrangement,
and also to perpetrate a running irony, to turn the terminology of
dramatic structure against its usual practitioners and make it serve a
godly rather than a satanic purpose. Not surprisingly, he proves un-

8. David Leverenz, "Why Did Puritans Hate Stage Plays?" (ms. article,
1977): "In *Histrio-mastix* . . . language of female contamination is associated not just with sexuality but with the overthrow of maleness itself"
(cited with permission of the author).

equal to the task of following his own models. The endless vistas that open up, of act upon act—6, 7, 8, 9—each containing up to twenty scenes, each scene swollen with its cargo of invective and top-heavy with its freight of learned citations, quickly turns the whole operation into a logorrhaeic nightmare. Nor does the ostentatiously paraded logic fare any better. Each scene purports to establish by syllogism the proposition that plays are unlawful for Christians. But the syllogisms either start by assuming the thing to be proved, or else are founded on gratuitous premises no sane witness could grant for a moment. "Those Playes," we are told, for example, "which are usually accompaned [*sic*] with amorous Pastoralls, lascivious ribaldrous Songs and Ditties, *must needs be unlawfull, yea abominable unto Christians.* But Stageplayes are usually accompanied with such Pastorals, Songs, and Ditties as these. Therefore they must needs be unlawfull, yea abominable unto Christians" (Sig. 2L3ᵛ). Or again, "That which is alwaies accompanied with effeminate lust-provoking Musicke, is doubtlesse inexpedient and unlawfull unto Christians. But Stage-playes are always accompanied with such Musicke," etc. (Sig. 2Nᵛ). Or, "Those Playes which are usually acted and frequented in over-costly effeminate, strange, meretricious, lust-exciting apparell, are questionlesse unseemely, yea unlawfull unto Christians. But our ordinary Theatricall Enterludes, are for the most part acted and frequented in such apparell," etc. (Sig. 2E4ᵛ). All the force of the argument in these "syllogisms" lies in question-begging terms like "effeminate lust-provoking Musicke" and "over-costly effeminate, strange, meretricious, lust-exciting apparell," thrust into the logical slots as if they were dispassionate, neutral data on which reasonable conclusions might be reared.

By the time we are a fourth of the way through, we have heard most of the arguments many times over, and encountered the same quotations in a dozen different contexts. Subsequent repetitions add little. The syllogisms, the citations, the accusations are simply shuffled and reshuffled like a pack of cards, until Prynne is certain that he has amassed enough sheer bulk to suffocate his opponents. The style is correspondingly overloaded and hyperthyroid. Prynne heaps as many injurious epithets as he can collect onto each of the objects of his execration, without the faintest regard for propriety, aptness, or discrimination. Spectators at the theater, for example, are "*Adulterers, Adulteresses, Whore-masters, Whores, Bawdes, Panders, Ruffians, Roarers, Drunk-*

ards, *Prodigals, Cheaters, idle, infamous, base, prophane, and godlesse persons, who hate all grace, all goodnesse, and make a mocke of piety"* (Sig. V). There is something shameless and compulsive about Prynne's tirades. It is as though he were himself goaded by a devil, driven to blacken the theater with lunatic exaggeration and without allowing it the faintest spark of decency or humanity. A minor but telling effect arises from the very typography. The restless switching back and forth between roman and italic type, the lengthy citations from other writers, in English and other languages, in the text itself and streaming in inky rivers down the margins, the thickly strewn superior numerals used to cue in the marginal citations, the parentheses, the unending unparagraphed continuousness of the page, all conspire to chivvy and harass the reader so that he cannot reach a point of rest, to keep up a perpetual din that blocks him from the sound of his own thoughts. Nor is there any inkling of awareness on Prynne's part that he is often misappropriating his own sources. Aristotle is cited as favoring the banning of plays, and the Christians of Tertullian's day are praised as being more abstemious from the theater than Prynne's contemporaries—because Tertullian exhorted them to abstain! (Sig. T4). By this logic, Prynne's contemporaries would have to be reckoned the most abstemious playgoers in history.

One ends, finally, by asking oneself in bewilderment: Why should anyone ever wish to write such a book? The only possible answer can be to work off a staggering load of resentment and anxiety. The whole operation resembles an exercise in pathology. Yet madness tends to be culturally determined. We run amok in ways approved by our fellow citizens. The lunatic who seizes his shotgun and shoots his neighbor in order to start World War III tells the police that he was only trying to save the country from Bolshevism. Prynne, taking up his blunderbuss and charging after the actors with barrels loaded, merely raises to fever pitch themes already familiar in pulpit and pamphlet for over a generation. He expresses, one might say in most agonized form, the fears of impurity, of contamination, of "mixture," of the blurring of strict boundaries, which haunted thousands in the Renaissance as they had haunted Plato and Tertullian. Prynne is terrified, maddened, by the fear of total breakdown. In the uncontrolled outpouring of his style he conjures up a nightmarish vision of a world itself out of control, a horrendous dystopia ruled by the Prince of Darkness, who has made of the theater his chosen weapon for the overthrow of man and the final establishment of his own empire. Prynne's later career shows the kind of inveterate negativism to which his brand of extremism could lead, the compulsion to search and destroy. Pilloried, fined, and imprisoned following the publication of *Histriomastix*, for an offensive remark against actresses thought to be a slur on the queen, who loved to play in court theatricals, he continued his diatribes from prison, was fined a second time, more heavily, lost what remained of his already cropped ears, and had the letters *SL*—for Seditious Libeller—branded onto his cheeks. Released in 1640 by the Long Parliament, with his sentence nullified, he promptly returned to the attack, first against Laud, then against the Independents, then against the Army, finally against the Cromwell government. The return of the monarchy at last met with his approval. Instead of denouncing it he welcomed it back from exile, and for his loyalty was rewarded with the post of the Keeper of the Tower Records, in which fortress of sanctity he ultimately died.[9]

Histriomastix, in any case, though it is a grotesque, is not a freak. It merely caricatures the tendencies of most antitheatrical polemic from 1575 to the closing of the theaters in 1642. None of the pamphlets that dropped from English presses during these years makes an impressive dialectical contribution. Rarely do they pursue an argument closely; more often they disintegrate into free-associative rambles. They repeat themselves, and each other, without shame or scruple. It is perhaps enough to say of most of them that they rehearse all the objections against the stage first formulated by the Fathers, along with a plentiful sprinkling of picturesque anecdote and invective against the loose manners of the London playhouse. It need not be assumed, however, that when they recite grievances dating back to early Christian times they are merely witlessly parrotting their ancestors. The patristic charge of idolatry was one the Puritans could passionately revive, since it expressed so vividly their own hatred of one of the most retrograde features of traditional religion. The Wycliffite preacher in the fourteenth century may grudgingly have conceded the pedagogical usefulness of church images. His successors will make no such concession. In a day when monasteries had been dispossessed and despoiled throughout England, when statues and stained glass had been smashed with icon-

9. On Prynne's career, see William M. Lamont, *Marginal Prynne 1600–1669* (London, 1963).

oclastic fury, it could only have seemed a logical next step to destroy an even more potent competitor for men's imaginations, the secular stage. If the Anglican Church, in its partly reformed condition, could still be the target of fiery curses for its relics of popery and heathenism, how could the stage, an even more mesmerizing relic of popery and heathenism, hope to escape whipping?

The Puritans, and their associates, share the fundamentalist spirit of the sterner Fathers. Not only do they rehearse, ad nauseam, and with endless wrangling and remonstrating, the supposed scriptural injunction against men in women's dress, with its implicit threat to the proper division between the sexes, they also pursue the ontological attack. In Gosson, plays being "consecrated to idolatrie, they are not of God [;] if they proceede not from God, they are the doctrine and inventions of the devill."[10] The human mind, in this reductive view, "is simple without mixture or composition, therefore those instructions that are given to the minde must bee simple without mingle mangle of fish & flesh, good & bad," since "where both are profred, the hereditarie corruption of our nature taketh the worst and leaveth the best" (p. 162). Not for these writers the existential quest that was to inspire Milton, the purification by temptation and trial. Free choice and self-definition form no part of their scheme. The complexity of plays, far from redeeming them, only incriminates them the more deeply, since human beings are predisposed to choose the bad and reject the good.

10. Stephen Gosson, *Plays Confuted in Five Actions* (1582) in Kinney, *Markets of Bawdrie*, p. 151. Further references to Gosson in the discussion that follows will be to this edition. Ringler, *Stephen Gosson*, pp. 26 ff., gives the reasons for thinking that Gosson, along with Munday, was hired by the London authorities to write against the stage. Kinney, *Markets of Bawdrie*, p. 17, n. 40, reviews Ringler's arguments and convincingly refutes most of them, with one or two exceptions, notably the existence of a seventeenth-century manuscript, whose author, a "careful compiler," specifically mentions Gosson as having been "engaged" to combat abuses, by "the Judges, the Templars, and the Puritans of all professions and conditions" (Ringler, p. 28, n. 13). But even if Gosson was being paid by the magistrates to serve as their spokesman against the stage, we would not need to conclude that he was not, in doing so, voicing his own beliefs, or that, apart from his beliefs, he was saying anything other than what he knew would be welcome doctrine to his readers. The swift reprinting of *The School of Abuse* suggests that its views found wide favor among Gosson's fellow citizens.

"The best play you can picke out, is but a mixture of good and evill, how can it be then the schoolemistres of life?" (p. 161). Parenthetically, we may recall that Sidney adopts a similar argument not against plays but against history, holding it to be too mottled, too riddled with inconsistencies, to serve as a moral teacher, preferring imaginative literature precisely because it can create "perfect patterns" of vice and virtue, of a sort not to be found in daily life. Sidney does not, however, suggest that the reader of history will necessarily lean to evil, merely that he will have to bring his own moral standards to the work, instead of having them shaped for him *by* the work.

Gosson reflects a Tertullianesque absoluteness in his refusal to allow good and bad to be subject to modification or interpretation with changing times.

Though the heathen Philosophers which knew not the trueth . . . held one thing to be sometime good, & sometimes evill: yet will not God be mocked *with* Philosophers dreames. Whatsoever he simply pronounceth, evill, can never be conditionally good and lawfull. . . . and shall God in his tables be tyed to specifications, particularities, and exceptions? no, no, the same God that saith thou shalt not covet thy neighbours wife, saith thou shalt in no place, & at no time covet her; . . . and he that chargeth thee not to put on womens garments, chargeth thee in no place, and never to put the*m* on. (p. 176)

Like other antitheatricalists who found their case on the Deuteronomic prohibition against men in women's garments, Gosson stubbornly overlooks the long tradition according to which a number of female saints, in apostolic days, dressed as men in order to escape their persecutors, entered monasteries, lived lives of exemplary sanctity, in disguise, and met with the heroic martyrdoms they craved[11]—striking enough evidence, if evidence were needed, of the fact that the resort to the text in Deuteronomy is a pretext, an evasion of thinking rather than an engagement with it.

Further evidence on the same point appears in the learned debates between Rainolds and the academic playwright Gager, and between Rainolds and the jurist Alberico Gentili, over the nature of the Deu-

11. See John Anson, "The Female Transvestite in Early Monasticism: the Origin and Development of a Motif," *Viator* 5 (1974): 1–32.

teronomic prohibition. Does the prohibition refer to the moral law, or only to the ceremonial law? If to the moral law, then it must include a ban on any appearance, however superficial, of sexual deviation, to be rigorously observed by all Christians, but if to the ceremonial law, then it concerns itself only with differences between ancient Jewish and heathen worship, and holds no lessons for the daily conduct of a sixteenth-century Englishman. Needless to say, "one can find patristic and theological support for either position." The position adopted must therefore be seen not as the *result* of a given interpretation of the disputed verse, but as the *basis* for it. It is worth noting, as a sign of the heightening antitheatrical fever of the 1590s, that even "defenders" of the drama like Gager and Gentili are defending only the academic stage. For them the public playhouse, in which professional actors play lascivious comedies for money, is quite as abominable as its enemies claim, and as little to be countenanced. Soberly managed, the stage may be allowed a role in the educational process. In the ordered life of society at large it can have no role, not even as a vehicle of licensed recreation. As a sign, further, of the double bind in which the fiercer antitheatricalists sought to entrap their adversaries we may cite Rainolds's response to the suggestion that women be allowed to play themselves on the stage, and thereby circumvent the Deuteronomic ban. If this should happen, he declares, "the disgrace to the feminine sense of shame and modesty would be a remedy almost worse than flouting the verse."[12] The theater, then, is damned if it dresses men as women, and damned if it dresses women as themselves.

For polemicists of this retrograde stripe, the most rigid taboos of the Fathers are revived in full force. Prynne restates the charge that acting is based on hypocrisy. For what, he rhetorically demands, is hypocrisy,

in the proper signification of the word, *but the acting of anothers part or person on the Stage*: or what else is an *hypocrite, in his true etimologie, but a Stage-player, or one who acts anothers part*: as sundry Authors and Gramarians teach us. . . . And hence is it, that not onely divers *moderne English* and Latine Writers, but likewise *sundry Fathers* here quoted in the Margent, *stile Stage-players hypocrites; Hyp-*

12. For the controversy between Rainolds and Gentili, see J. W. Binns, "Women or Transvestites on the Elizabethan Stage?: An Oxford Controversy," *Sixteenth Century Journal* 5, no. 2 (October 1974): 95–120, pp. 101, 112.

ocrites, Stage-players, as being one and the same in substance: . . . .
(Sig. X3ᵛ–X4)

And indeed, the "margent" at this point overflows with an inky gutter of references to Tertullian, Cyprian, Chrysostom, Augustine, and "sundry" other Fathers. Having located hypocrisy at the root of the theater, Prynne goes on to make explicit the concept of an absolute identity that was only implied in Tertullian. God, he declares, has conferred on every creature a being that may neither be denied nor altered.

For God, *who is truth it selfe*, in *whom there is no variablenesse, no shadow of change no feining, no hypocrisie*; as he hath given a uniforme distinct and proper being to every creature, *the bounds of which may not be exceeded*: *so he requires that the actions of every creature should be honest and sincere, devoyde of all hypocrisie*, as all his actions, and their natures are. Hence he enjoy[n]es all men at all times, *to be such in shew, as they are in truth*: *to seeme that outwardly which they are inwardly*; to act themselves, not others . . . . (Sig. X4)

God requires us, that is, to live in strict conformity with the self he has bestowed on us, and that in the most minute particulars. Puritan apologists wax clamorous over the offense to nature involved in incorrect dress and the use of cosmetics. "Our Apparell," says Stubbes, "was given us as a signe distinctive to discern betwixt sex and sex, & therfore one to weare the Apparel of another sex is to participate with the same, and to adulterate the veritie of his own kinde. Wherefore these Women may not improperly be called *Hermaphroditi*, that is, Monsters of bothe kindes, half women, half men."[13] Apart from signifying differences of sex, our dress, says Perkins, "must be answerable to our estate and dignitie, for distinction of order and degree in the societies of men." "Wanton and excessive apparrell" is sinful, because "it maketh a confusion of such degrees and callings as God hath ordained, when as men of inferiour degree and calling, cannot be by their attire discerned from men of higher estate."[14] In short, distinctions of dress, however external and theatrical they may seem to us, for Perkins virtually belong to our essence, and may no more be tampered with than that essence itself. God has provided us with not only

13. *Anatomy*, ed. Furnivall, p. 73 (Sig. F5ᵛ).
14. William Perkins, *The Whole Treatise of the Cases of Conscience*, III.4 (Cambridge, 1608), Sig. 2G2ᵛ.

a soul but a body, and not only a body but the prescribed covering for the body, and not only the covering but the precise degree and kind of adornment allowable for that covering. As Tertullian had denounced shaving, so Prynne inveighs against "the common *accursed hellish art of face-painting*," which "*sophisticates and perverts the workes of God, in putting a false glosse upon his creatures*" (Sigs. X4–X4ᵛ). Or, as Perkins less frenetically phrases it,

. . . every one must be content with their owne naturall favour, and complexion, that God hath given them . . . . For the outward forme and favour that man hath, is the worke of God himselfe. . . . Here comes to be justly reprooved, the straunge practise and behaviour of some in these daies, who beeing not contented with that forme and fashion, which God hath sorted unto them, doe devise artificiall formes and favours, to set upon their bodies and faces, by painting and colouring; thereby making themselves seeme that which indeede they are not.[15]

Players are evil because they try to substitute a self of their own contriving for the one given them by God. Plays are evil for analogous reasons: they attempt to substitute "notorious lying fables," in Prynne's phrase (Sig. X2ᵛ), for things that have truly happened. In this respect they resemble chivalric romances, epic poems, and merry tales, and the attack on them forms part of a wider attack on all fiction, all feigning. Plays, like players, threaten God's primacy by challenging his uniqueness; they attempt to wrest from him his most inimitable attribute, his demiurgy. Puritan respect for history stemmed from a reverence for the world as actually, hence divinely, made. History recorded events that had truly happened, had been set in motion by God and brought by him to edifying conclusions. It charted the temporal dimension of the creation, as a cartographer might chart its spatial dimension. But to invent countries that never existed, to people them with the coinages of one's own brain—"the Arimaspie, . . . the Grips, the Pigmeies, the Cranes"[16]—to set them to enacting fables spun from one's own fancy, was to place oneself in blasphemous rivalry with one's maker. It was to imply that what had never happened at all might be more interesting than what had, that God's own efforts had somehow fallen short.

15. Ibid., Sig. 2G7.
16. Anthony Munday, *A Second and Third Blast of Retrait from Plaies and Theaters*, in *The English Drama and Stage*, ed. Hazlitt, p. 145.

Puritan extremists could hardly have been mollified by Sidney's view that the creative powers of the poet were a sign of his celestial origins, or that by his feigning he delivered a golden world in place of nature's brazen one,[17] for to claim so was to ignore the sinfulness of the human imagination, which needed not to be encouraged but tamed and humbled. Uncontrolled imagination, declares Sibbes, in a passage that reads like a direct rebuttal of Sidney, "is a wild and ranging thing; it wrongs not only the frame of God's work in us, setting the baser part of man above the higher, but it wrongs likewise the work of God in creatures, and everything else, for it shapes things as itself pleaseth." In similar vein, Samuel Willard denounces "romances" because they are "adorned with Fictions, or a representation of things according as we fancy they should be, not regarding what they are indeed."[18] No appeal, indeed, to the likeness of God in man was likely to weigh with those concerned above all to stress the *un*likeness, to exalt God as far and as high as possible by making man as contemptible and wormlike as possible.

One corollary of the concept of an absolute identity was the belief in an absolute sincerity. If it was possible truly to know the "uniform, distinct and proper being" one had received from God, then it was possible either to affirm that being in all one's acts—to be "such in truth" as one was "in show"—or to deny it by disguise or pretense. "Every man," declares Gosson, "must show him selfe outwardly to be such as in deed he is."[19] Ideally, all one's acts would be directly revelatory of one's essence. Nor would this necessarily be a complex or laborious task. Polonius' final injunction to Laertes rests on the complacent assumption that knowledge of "thine own self" presents no special difficulties. Even Montaigne tends to assume that good intentions and persistence will suffice. "A generous minde," he tells us, "ought not to belie his thoughts, but make shew of his inmost parts."[20] With self-knowledge so readily available, perfect sincerity moves within

17. *An Apology for Poetry*, in *Elizabethan Critical Essays*, ed. G. Gregory Smith (Oxford, 1904), I, 156–157.

18. Both are cited in Perry Miller, *The New England Mind: The Seventeenth Century* (New York, 1939), p. 258.

19. *Plays Confuted*, in Kinney, *Markets of Bawdrie*, p. 177.

20. *Essays*, II.xvii, trans. John Florio, Everyman ed. (London, 1910), II, 373.

everyone's grasp. One has only to descend into one's own being, consult one's deepest feelings, and report them honestly to the world. It was left to later moralists, in later centuries, to perceive the inner impediments more vividly, and to explore the ways in which pious attempts at self-discovery might be frustrated or twisted by self-deception and bad faith.

Not only the Puritan attack on the stage, but the Puritan attack on the liturgy, it may be suspected, drew strength from the belief in a total sincerity. Worship, to be genuine, could only be a direct translation of one's inner self. It could only be unique, spontaneous, an unpremeditated outpouring from the grateful soul. To reduce it to set forms, to freeze it in ritual repetitions of word or gesture, to commit it to memory, to make it serve a variety of occasions or a diversity of worshippers, was to make the individual a mimic of sentiments not exactly, or not entirely, his own, to introduce a fatal discrepancy between the established gesture and the nuances of feeling. In *Paradise Lost*, Adam and Eve improvise their prayers afresh each morning.

> Lowly they bow'd adoring, and began
> Thir Orisons, each Morning duly paid
> In various style, for neither various style
> Nor holy rapture wanted they to praise
> Thir Maker, in fit strains pronounc't or sung
> Unmeditated, such prompt eloquence
> Flowd from thir lips, in Prose or numerous Verse,
> More tuneable then needed Lute or Harp
> To add more sweetness, and they thus began.
>
> (V. 144–152)[21]

Our first parents thus command a "various style," which flows unhampered, and requires neither study nor memory. Their eloquence is "prompt"; it does not need the services of a prompter. It is "unmeditated," since to meditate would be to introduce the element of reflection, and hence of self-consciousness, that would corrupt sincerity. Worse, it would introduce the element of rehearsal, the element of acting, and hence of falsehood. To adopt the very words today that one

21. *Paradise Lost*, in *The Student's Milton*, ed. Frank Allen Patterson (New York, 1933).

used yesterday, to imitate even one's own previous prayers, let alone those of others, would be to put on a *performance* of piety, instead of simply being pious. But the situation conceals a paradox. The very thing that for Milton guarantees the validity of the prayer—immunizes it, so to speak, *against* theatricality—is the changefulness which for others embodies the most reprehensible feature *of* theatricality. Spontaneous worship, in the Miltonic Eden, resembles a kind of perpetual motion, an endless sequence of unique happenings, in polar contrast to the ideal of stasis held by most Christian antitheatricalists as a prime article of their creed.

At this point we may refocus the discussion by considering two somewhat differing forms of theatricality, mimicry and ostentation. Mimicry —the power to become, or to pretend to become, what one is not—must be reckoned the more fundamental of the two, and the first thing to say about it is that it arouses, and has always aroused, a nearly universal distrust. Somewhere in a corner of all of us lodges the conviction that (as Iago puts it) "Men should be what they seem,"[22] and this conviction, as its dramatic source might suggest, finds its way not only into polemics against plays but into plays themselves. In late sixteenth-century English drama, the villain par excellence is the Machiavellian, who is conceived as possessing exceptional powers of impersonation, which make him sinister. Machiavelli himself had launched a theatrical conception of human behavior upon the world. The essence of the numerous cautions and counsels urged upon the prince, in Machiavelli's much denounced handbook, was that he could acquire the power he sought, and maintain it once he had acquired it, only by showing himself in a certain light. The prince is advised to cultivate a pattern of appearances which may or may not correspond to the truth about himself, but which serve the tactical ends of rule. The only criterion is effectiveness. Men being credulous, eager to believe what they see, it is necessary to arrest their attention and fasten their respect by such *coups de théâtre* as that performed by Cesare Borgia when he first subdued a captive town through the agency of a cruel deputy, then seized a pretext to execute the deputy, having him "cut in half and placed one morning in the public square at Cesena with a piece of wood and blood-stained knife by his side. The ferocity of this spectacle

22. *Othello*, III.iii.126.

caused the people both satisfaction and amazement."[23] And well it might: with one unlooked-for stroke it freed them from a tyrannical overlord, and gave rise to a quite unfounded belief in the beneficence of their conqueror.

Machiavelli rarely asks whether the prince should practice such and such a vice—stinginess, cruelty, duplicity—or should possess such and such a virtue—liberality, kindness, etc.—but rather whether he should be *thought* to practice it, whether he should acquire a name for it, and also in what manner he ought to practice it if he does so. If, for example, his situation requires him to do injuries, he should do them all at once, "so that being less tasted, they will give less offence," while benefits, by contrast, "should be granted little by little, so that they may be better enjoyed."[24] The criterion, to repeat, is effectiveness. What matters is that the prince be able to manipulate appearances and control responses, insofar as circumstances permit. The image is all, the reality nothing. Chapter 18 of *The Prince* notoriously advises the ruler to combine the strength of the lion with the cunning of the fox; to disguise, moreover, the fox's slyness with the appearance of innocence. It helps to be "a great feigner and dissembler; and men are so simple and so ready to obey present necessities, that one who deceives will always find those who allow themselves to be deceived." The main thing, Machiavelli insists, is not to possess the virtues of mercy, faith, integrity, humanity, and religion, but to seem to possess them. "For men in general judge more by the eyes than by the hands, for every one can see, but very few have to feel. Everybody sees what you appear to be, few feel what you are."[25] Expediency, then, with power as

23. *The Prince*, ch. 7, in *The Prince* and *The Discourses*, ed. Max Lerner, trans. Luigi Ricci and E. R. P. Vincent, Modern Library (New York, 1950), p. 27. See Machiavelli, *Opere*, ed. Ezio Raimondi (Milan, 1967), p. 75: "Lo fece a Cesena, una mattina, mettere in dua pezzi in su la piazza, con uno pezzo di legno e uno coltello sanguinoso a canto. La ferocità del quale spettaculo fece quelli populi in uno tempo rimanere satisfatti e stupidi."

24. *The Prince*, ch. 8, p. 35; *Opere*, p. 80: "Perché le iniurie si debbano fare tutte insieme, acciò che, assaporandosi meno, offendino meno; e benefizii si debbano fare a poco a poco, acciò si assaporino meglio."

25. *The Prince*, ch. 18, pp. 64–66; *Opere*, p. 99: "Ma è necessario . . . essere gran simulatore e dissimulatore: e sono tanto semplici gli uomini, e tanto obediscano alle necessità presenti, che colui che inganna, troverrà

its only object, leads to a radically theatrical form of behavior, in which what seems takes precedence over what is, and in which the prince must make himself expert at shows, spectacles, and surfaces. If he is so skilled, the realities may shift for themselves, for few will perceive them, or even care about them.

This nihilistic advice stems ultimately from a cynical view of humanity: that men are always "wicked" (*tristi*) at bottom, "always taken by appearances and the issue of the event,"[26] fickle, selfish, and stupid, incapable of sustaining their own principles, and easily hoodwinked. From this dark view Machiavelli evolves a morality of illusion for his potentates. The prince is forever play-acting before his subjects. Any man who would succeed in the world, it is implied, must do likewise. Small wonder that the stage Machiavel specializes in theatrics, manipulating others under a cloak of friendship, and small wonder that his ethic of deceit should have fed the existing prejudice against the theater and intensified the long-standing equation between acting and duplicity.

For Exhibit A among stage Machiavels we may turn to Shakespeare's Richard III, and to his soliloquy in *3 Henry VI* in which, while still Duke of Gloucester, he confides his ambition to become king.

> Why, I can smile, and murder whiles I smile,
> And cry "Content!" to that which grieves my heart,
> And wet my cheeks with artificial tears,
> And frame my face to all occasions.
> I'll drown more sailors than the mermaid shall;
> I'll slay more gazers than the basilisk;
> I'll play the orator as well as Nestor,
> Deceive more slily than Ulysses could
> And, like a Sinon, take another Troy.
> I can add colors to the chameleon,

sempre chi si lascerà ingannare"; p. 100: "E li uomini, *in universali*, iudicano più alli occhi che alle mani; perché tocca a vedere a ognuno, a sentire a pochi."

26. *The Prince*, p. 66; *Opere*, p. 100: "Il vulgo ne va sempre preso con quello che pare e con lo evento della cosa." See Stephen J. Greenblatt, *Sir Walter Ralegh: The Renaissance Man and His Roles*, Yale Studies in English, 183 (New Haven, 1973), pp. 38–41, for an admirably illuminating account of the role-playing figure projected by Machiavelli.

Change shapes with Proteus for advantages,
And set the murderous Machiavel to school.
Can I do this, and cannot get a crown?
Tut, were it farther off, I'll pluck it down.

(III.ii.182–195)[27]

Richard's trump card, in his own view, is his flair for dissimulation, a control over his face and voice as total as that of a professional actor, which permits him to feign emotions he does not feel and dissemble the emotions he does feel. He likens himself to an imposing array of virtuosos in deceit—the mermaid, the basilisk, Ulysses, Sinon, the chameleon, Proteus, as well as to his great forefather Machiavelli. Two of these—Proteus and the chameleon—deserve particular notice because of the frequency with which they crop up in Renaissance literature, and also because of the implications of the references to them. Unlike the other deceivers listed by Richard, neither Proteus nor the chameleon is bent on harm. Proteus does not lure sailors to their death, as the mermaid does, nor does the chameleon, like the basilisk, kill with its gaze. Neither is known to have ruined cities, like Sinon, promoted murder as an instrument of policy, like Machiavelli, or specialized in guile, like Ulysses. What entitles these two to their place in this formidable company is simply their metamorphic power, their changeability.

We find, when we look further, that this power is widely associated with deceit, and that the same emblems recur to designate it. Reworking Montemayor's *Diana* into *The Two Gentlemen of Verona*, Shakespeare renames the faithless friend Proteus. In one of his satirical excursions in *Cynthia's Revels*, Jonson's virtuous protagonist Crites dismisses the fawning courtier, who can "change, and varie with all formes he sees," as a "subtle PROTEUS," capable of being "any thing but honest";[28] and Volpone, during his attempted seduction of Celia, vows that to possess her he would have contended "with the blue PROTEUS, or the horned *Floud*."[29] Sir John Wrotham, the shifty hedge-

27. Robert K. Turner, Jr. and George Walton Williams, eds., in *The Complete Pelican Shakespeare*, ed. Alfred Harbage, Penguin Books (Baltimore, 1969).

28. III.iv.42–44; C. H. Herford and Percy and Evelyn Simpson, *Ben Jonson* (Oxford, 1925–52), IV, 90.

29. *Volpone*, III.vii.153; Herford and Simpson, V, 81.

priest of *Sir John Oldcastle,* boasts of having "as many shapes as *Proteus* had,"[30] while Massinger's villainous Flaminius, in *Believe As You List,* nearing the climax of a criminal career, muses on the need to show himself, in the "scaene imposed upon" him, "a Protean actor variinge everie shape / with the occasion,"[31] where the theatrical implications of "Protean" crystallize in the terms *scaene* and *actor.* Sejanus, the villain of the anonymous *Tragedy of Tiberius* of 1607, may perhaps be echoing Shakespeare's Richard in his assessment of his own prowess, but more probably he is simply recombining a series of notations that are felt to go naturally together.

> He that wil clime, and aime at honours white,
> Must be a wheeling turning pollitician:
> A changing Proteus, and a seeming all,
> Yet a discoloured Camelion
> Fram'd of an ayrie composition:
> As fickle and unconstant as the ayre:
>
> . . . .
>
> With wisemen sober, with licencious, light:
> With proud men stately, humble with the meeke:
> With old men thirstie, and with young men vaine:
> With angrie, furious, and with mild men calme:
> Humerous with one, and *Cato* with another:
> Effeminate with some, with other chaste,
> Drink with the Germain, with the Spaniard brave:
> Brag with the French, with the AEgyptian lie,
> Flatter in Creet, and fawne in Graecia.
>
> . . . .
>
> If thou doost meane the Empire to obtaine,
> Sweare, flatter, lye, dissemble, cog, & faine.[32]

This Sejanus is more modest than Richard. He does not claim to surpass his mythic predecessors, but merely to equal them, to be able to

30. *The Life of Sir John Oldcastle,* ed. Percy Simpson, Malone Society Reprints (1600; rpt. London, 1908), line 312.

31. *Believe As You List,* ed. Charles J. Sisson, Malone Society Reprints (Oxford, 1927), lines 1202–05.

32. *The Tragedy of Tiberius,* ed. W. W. Greg, Malone Society Reprints (1607; rpt. Oxford, 1914), lines 667–684.

shift his manner in accordance with national characteristics or standard character types. The identification of Proteus and the chameleon with the ambitious actor-politician remains, however, unvarying.

Allusions to Proteus in sermons, moral tracts, and emblem books tend to be similarly invidious, perhaps partly as a consequence of Boccaccio, who construed the god's changing of shapes as an allegory of the passions.[33] Boccaccio's precedent has been cited to explain the otherwise puzzling character given Proteus by Spenser in Book III of *The Faerie Queene*, but one probably does not need to go farther afield than the nearly automatic equation with changefulness and deceit. For Stubbes, attacking feminine cosmetics, *"Proteus,* that Monster, could never chaunge him self into so many fourmes & shapes as these women doo: belike they have made an obligation with hel, and are at agreement with the devil."[34] Sometimes the moralist will spell out the metamorphoses in closely Boccaccian terms, as Stephen Batman does in *The Golden Booke of the Leaden Goddes,* stripping the gilding from the ancient myths in order to expose the rottenness underneath:

Some thincke that by Proteus the dyuers affections, of manns mynde are signified: for somewhyle wee take pleasure, for the chiefeste felicitie, when in verye deede it is but a hoggish affection: otherwhyle Anger haleth vs, and maketh vs more lyke Tygres, than men: somtimes Pryde assaulteth vs, and maketh vs more hautie then Lyons: somtime swynish affections, and then we beecome more Dronken then Hogs: . . .[35]

Batman, we may notice, interprets Proteus in a manner more appropriate to Circe: the metamorphoses proceed through a sequence of lower animals, with emphasis on members of the pig family. Moreover, where Proteus, in the fable, turns himself into one shape after another, Batman makes the protean individual a passive victim of "affections" that "hale" or "assault" him, making him now one thing and now another. Less picturesquely degraded, but equally helpless, is the figure of man in Sir John Hayward, who, "abandoning the dignity of his

33. *Genealogie deorum gentilium* (Venice, 1473), fols. 112–112ᵛ; *Geneologia de gli dei* (Venice, 1547), Sig. Q6ᵛ.

34. *Anatomy*, ed. Furnivall, p. 73 (Sig. F5ᵛ).

35. (London, 1577), Sig. E2. See also Immanuel Bourne, *The Rainebow, or A Sermon Preached at Paul's Cross* (London, 1619), Sig. D2ᵛ.

proper nature, is changed like Proteus into divers forms."[36] Here the passive construction, "is changed," registers the loss of self-propulsion. The resemblance to Circe recurs in Democritus Junior's panoramic vision of humanity shifting its style to suit its surroundings:

To see a man turn himself into all shapes like a Chameleon, or as Proteus transform himself into all that is monstrous; to act twenty parts & persons at once for his advantage, to temporize & vary like Mercury the Planet, good with good, bad with bad; having a several face, garb, & character, for every one he meets; of all religions, humours, inclinations; to fawn like a spaniel, with lying and feigned obsequiousness, rage like a lion, bark like a cur, fight like a dragon, sting like a serpent, as meek as a lamb, & yet again grin like a tiger, weep like a crocodile, insult over some, & yet others domineer over him, here command, there crouch, tyrannize in one place, be baffled in another, a wise man at home, a fool abroad to make others merry![37]

The assumption governing the sequence is that the transformations will be bad. The key to them, as to those of Richard or Sejanus, is self-interest: men "act twenty parts" (the theatrical metaphor is explicit) "for advantage." The random semblance of honor counts for little better than a diversion. To meet good with good hardly qualifies as virtue if followed immediately by meeting bad with bad; to show meek as a lamb in one instant can scarcely be attributed to innocence if it is followed by grinning like a tiger. The goodness and meekness are as calculated as Sejanus' humility, and as insubstantial. Self-transformation, in all these cases, seems conceived as a negative process, a shifting about from one undesirable state to another, and a refusal to maintain one's proper identity. The original Proteus, as described by Virgil and others, turned himself into various natural phenomena and natural creatures—fire, water, tree, lion, panther. But in Burton's reference he transforms himself instead into "all that is monstrous," just as, in Batman, he is thought of as not directing his own transformations at

36. Quoted in E. M. Tillyard, *The Elizabethan World Picture* (London, 1943), p. 68.
37. *The Anatomy of Melancholy*, ed. Floyd Dell and Paul Jordan-Smith (New York, 1941), p. 53. On Proteus, see also A. Bartlett Giamatti, "Proteus Unbound: Some Versions of the Sea God in the Renaissance," in Peter Demetz, Thomas Greene, and Lowry Nelson, Jr., eds., *The Disciplines of Criticism* (New Haven, 1968), pp. 437–475.

all, but passively submitting to them, allowing himself to be degraded into brutish shapes as at the hands of an enchantress.

As an emblem of the perils of mutability and deceit, Proteus often is coupled with a very different sort of creature, the chameleon. Proverbially, the chameleon was said to be able to change to all colors except white, which was taken to mean that it could be anything but truthful or honest.[38] Stubbes, immediately preceding the passage on the monster Proteus, speaks of women who paint their faces: "As in a *Camelion* are said to be all coulours, save white, so I think in these people are all things els, save Vertue and christian sobrietie." According to Alciati, the flattering chameleon imitates every characteristic of his prince except modest shame and innocence.[39] Generally, in Renaissance iconography the chameleon figures as the *adulatore* or flatterer, and often as the courtier, thought to be especially adept at flattery. Ripa's *Iconologia* describes "Adulatione" as a woman "vestita di cangiante," with chameleons painted on her garment.[40] By extension, since flattery springs from ambition, the chameleon can represent the ambitious man in any sphere. Occasionally, also, the little reptile's capacity to feed on air is linked to its changeability, as in Ripa, who explains that it is a cowardly animal with very little blood in its body, causing it to take fright at every trivial encounter, and to keep frantically shifting its hue to escape detection. Its insubstantiality thus accounts for its transformations; it lacks enough blood to be able to sustain a single shape. In Valeriano's *Ieroglifici*, "all agree that by the chameleon one can figure a sly and crafty man, such as a Ulysses, a Lysander, an Alcibiades."[41] According to the same author, the chameleon's changes are "always vicious," prompted by the wish to deceive, whereas those of another notoriously unstable creature, the polyp, may occasionally result from more estimable motives. Other writers,

38. See "Chameleon," in Morris Palmer Tilley, *A Dictionary of the Proverbs in England in the Sixteenth and Seventeenth Centuries* (Ann Arbor, 1950), pp. 91–92.

39. *Emblematum liber* (n.p., 1531), Sig. E4–E4ᵛ.

40. Cesare Ripa, *Iconologia* (Padua, 1611), Sig. A3.

41. Giovanni Piero Valeriano, *Ieroglifici, overo Commentari delle occulte significationi de gli Egittii* (Venice, 1602), Sig. 2L6ᵛ: "Per consentimento d'ogn'uno può esser significato per il camaleonte qual si voglia astuto, come Ulisse, Lisandro, & Alcibiade." Here, and hereafter, when no translator is specified, the translation is my own.

again, group the polyp with the chameleon as an adulator and a prac-
ticer of guile. Even Valeriano cites sources according to which the
polyp represents the too pliant man, the man of every hour, who changes
color from fear and "natural poltroonery."[42]

The chameleon's powers of mimicry, then, signify its craven, fawning, unscrupulous nature. Its changes, like those of Proteus, tend to
be dictated by ruse. Anthony Munday underlines the identity between
chameleons and actors: "As for those stagers," he asks rhetorically,
"are they not commonlie such kind of men in their conversation, as
they are in profession? Are they not variable in hart, as they are in their
parte?" A marginal note hammers home the analogy: "Plaiers cannot
better be compared than to the Camelion."[43]

If we look, in emblem literature, for symbols of constancy to oppose
to the fickle chameleon and polyp, we find them in the figures of the
steadfast rock and the solid club, or in geometrical forms like the
square, the cube, and the pyramid. So Wither, in *A Collection of Emblems, Ancient and Modern* (1634):

> This Cube, which is an equall sided square,
> Doth very well in Emblem-wise, declare
> The temper of that vertuous minded man,
> Whose resolutions nothing alter can.[44]

All the emblems for permanence and dependability come from an inanimate world of minerals or a world of conceptual abstractions, a
world essentially unfeeling and inhuman, and hence exempt from
change. Our own slang preserves echoes of this situation, with justice as "a square deal," or honesty as "on the level," or (pejoratively)
that which is inflexible, rigid, and sharply bounded by convention, as
"square."

Sixteenth-century English drama regularly recommends constancy as
a virtue—constancy, even as it may be, in ill-doing, just as one finds
changeability, even in virtue, to be a fault. Queen Elizabeth's motto,

42. Ibid., Sig. 2L6: "Natural poltroneria."
43. *A Second and Third Blast of Retrait*, in *The English Drama and
Stage*, ed. Hazlitt, p. 148.
44. George Wither, *A Collection of Emblemes, Ancient and Moderne*
(London, 1634–35), Sig. HH2ᵛ.

Semper eadem, speaks only of the certainty with which she can be counted on to remain herself, not of the nature of that self. Marlowe opposes the resolution of Tamburlaine to the irresoluteness of Mycetes, whom his disgusted followers accuse of having been born under the unstable influence of Cynthia, the moon. The vacillations of Edward II cause more trouble between himself and his peers than his perverse clinging to his minion Gaveston, which they can comprehend, if not respect. Something of the same is true of Shakespeare's Henry VI, who may have served as model for Marlowe's Edward. Despite his saintliness, his waverings earn him the contempt of his own most committed followers. In *Richard III*, by contrast, our reluctant admiration for Richard stems from the fact that although changeable in his manner, he steers a fixed course, controls his changes, orchestrates them to a single purpose, whereas his victims, like the luckless Anne, stir impatience for their inability to persevere in their intentions. "Relenting fool, and shallow, changing woman" (IV.iv.431) may not be a judgment we can endorse at the moment it is uttered, against the widowed Queen Elizabeth, but we certainly do so in the case of Anne, and possibly in the case of the old Duchess of York as well.

As the rock, the cube, the square derive their virtue from their changelessness, they resemble God, in whom, as Prynne tells us, there is "no variableness, no shadow of change." Men come closest to God when they preserve themselves as unchanging as possible, when they yield as little as they can to their natural bent for mutability. For moralists like Prynne, change is suspect on principle. It constitutes a lapse, dictated by weakness. Puritan teachers like Perkins stress the need to persevere in one's calling: "Even as the souldiour in the field, must not change his place, wherein he is placed by the Generall, but must abide by it, to the venturing of his life: so must the Christian continue and abide in his calling, without change or alteration."[45] To change, clearly, is to fall, to reenact the first change whereby Lucifer renounced his bliss and man alienated himself from the Being in whose unchanging image he was created. As a result, the actor, his trade founded on change, becomes a lively image of fallen man, the one who renews the primal degradation every day of his life, and so places himself beyond

45. William Perkins, *A Treatise of the Vocations, or, Callings of Men . . .*, in *Works* (Cambridge, 1603), Sig. 4M5.

the pale. "A common Player," says J. Cocke, is *"a daily Counterfeit ... a Motley ... a shifting companion ... compounded of all Natures, all humours, all professions."*[46]

There was, however, another side to the picture. The polyvalence of Renaissance symbology meant that most emblems could be assigned differing, even contradictory meanings, and to this rule Proteus and the chameleon form no exception. Proteus especially, in the Renaissance as in antiquity, lent himself to abstruse, semi-occult interpretations as well as to plebeian and censorious ones. Giulio Camillo sees in him a symbol of the primal stuff of the universe, "natura ostinata e immutabile,"[47] the original chaos; for Capaccio, he represents the realm of created things in all their multiplicity.[48] For both, he seems to signify the physical basis out of which the world is fashioned. For others, he stands for the achievements of the human mind, the arts and disciplines, such as eloquence, which "mens mindes doth change, Even as it lists, to like of thinges most straunge."[49] In one edition of Alciati, Proteus embodies "antique poesy," which men dream of in their varying fashions,[50] and the myths about him represent an effort on the part of ancient writers to get back to things beyond the memory of man. In the realm of society, Conti sees in Proteus the adroit man of affairs in whom the vicissitudes of state call forth a ready adaptability.[51] This interpretation contrasts suggestively with the Machiavellian Proteus of Richard III, the anonymous Sejanus, or Massinger's Flaminius. In all those cases the histrionic versatility serves purely selfish ends, whereas in Conti it reflects a freedom from dogmatism which permits the ruler to respond flexibly to changing circumstances—now severely, now indulgently, but always with regard to the common good. Even in *homo politicus*, then, the protean faculty need not by any prior necessity be construed as malignant. A recent critic has suggested that

46. E. K. Chambers, *The Elizabethan Stage* (Oxford, 1923), IV, 255–257.

47. *Tutte le opere* (Venice, 1552), Sigs. F7, C11ᵛ–C12, D4–D4ᵛ.

48. Giulio Cesare Capaccio, *Il principe* (Venice, 1620), Sig. BB4.

49. Francis Thynne, *Emblemes and Epigrames* [1600], ed. F. J. Furnivall (London, 1876), pp. 34–35.

50. *Emblemes* (Lyons, 1549), Sig. O8.

51. Natalis Comes, *Mythologiae, sive explicationum fabularum, libri decem* (Frankfurt, 1581), HH3ᵛ–HH4.

even the caddishness of Shakespeare's ungentlemanly Proteus may conceal positive mystical meanings.[52]

Most apt of all in this connection would be the appearance of the god himself in Tasso's *Aminta*, who descends to take charge of his proper domain, the world of flux, and specifically of the world of the theater that symbolizes that domain. Proteus here typifies change as it governs the scenic art, in the machines that produce quick changes of locale, or enable deities to emerge from heaven and demons to erupt from hell. Lucian had long ago likened him to "a deliver [i.e., nimble] and crafty dancer,"[53] whose mutations convey the range of human emotion. Tasso now makes him into the benign presiding genius over the entire realm of theatrical illusion.

The chameleon too could evoke favorable as well as invidious glosses. At least one iconographic handbook views him both as the flattering courtier and as the "true and affectionate lover," accustomed with timely conformity to reflect within himself all the changing feelings of his beloved. Elsewhere, more conventionally, as in Shakespeare, he stands for love itself, with its endless metamorphoses. In these cases, as in Conti's and Thynne's versions, we have the notion of a sympathetic identification rather than that of a heartless and promiscuous mimicry.

This secondary strain of interpretation belongs with a secondary strain in European thought. For Christian tradition contained not one God but two. Alongside the God of self-sufficiency, dwelling in his perfect repose and total immobility, there was the Neoplatonic God of emanation, the streaming source of creative energy who delighted to unfold himself in lower forms of being.[54] And alongside the austerer moralists, who summoned men to imitate the perfection of the divine unity, there were others, like the Florentine Neoplatonists, who responded more to the divine multiplicity, and for whom the figures of Proteus and the chameleon took on a more dynamic significance, expressive of the variousness of human potentiality. For Ficino, in the

52. Richard Cody, *The Landscape of the Mind* (Oxford, 1969), pp. 81–104.

53. Sir Thomas Elyot, *The Book Named the Governor*, ed. S. E. Lehmberg, Everyman ed. (London, 1962), p. 72. Lucian, *Works*, ed. A. M. Harmon, Loeb Classics (London, 1936), V, 230–233 (Sect. 19, *De saltatione*).

54. See Arthur O. Lovejoy, *The Great Chain of Being* (Cambridge, Mass., 1936), pp. 82–84.

Theologica Platonica, the soul of every man partakes of both the upper and the lower worlds; it inhabits every gradation of the cosmos; it ascends and descends; it possesses the powers of all things; it transforms itself into all things. Human arts can produce what nature produces; human creativity rivals nature's in the abundance and variety of its issue. Man is not only the vicar of God in this most momentous of senses, he is a kind of god himself—of the animals, of the elements, and of materials, which he shapes and changes; he transcends heaven itself with his mind. Again, the soul of man is by its nature free, unable to endure slavery. It explores, it extends itself; it seeks all things and tries to become all things. The intellect unites itself to all things by transforming them into itself, the will by transforming itself into the things.[55] It is hard to suggest, by a bald summary, the excitement, the exultation even, with which Ficino, in these pages, contemplates the near-divine near-omnipotence of his own species, which springs directly from its self-extending, self-transforming powers. It is hard also to avoid noticing how un-Platonic, how anti-Platonic, even, is the mood of this fervent Platonist as he addresses himself to this aspect of his theme.

Much the same may be said of the celebrated oration of Pico della Mirandola aptly known as *De dignitate hominis*. Pico, like Ficino, strikes a vigorously affirmative note, a note of high confidence in human destiny, of delight at the felicities promised to man, in strongest contrast to the dour and pinched asceticism that marks so much antitheatrical writing. Pico's attitude, which includes a rapturous view of God, may be termed humanistic in that it takes the good of man rather than the will of God as its point of departure. Pico considers first not what will slake God's thirst for justice—the prime preoccupation of Lutheran and Calvinist Protestantism—but what will best fulfill human needs, defined in human terms. Furthermore, he seeks to encompass alternative systems of truth, to reconcile rather than exclude, and here too his syncretism, which welcomes into its eclectic pantheon classical deities like Bacchus and Apollo as mystic symbols for sacred experience, contrasts sharply with the reductionism of the reformers, for whom the same gods were only filthy relics of a discredited creed, to be vituperated, ostracized, and wiped from the imaginations of men.

55. Josephine L. Burroughs, "Translation of Ficino's *Platonic Theology*," *Journal of the History of Ideas* 5 (1944): 227–239.

Pico carries Ficino's conception of the human role one step further by eliminating even the fixed middle place in the hierarchy of being to which Ficino had assigned humanity. The reason, in fact, why, as Pico puts it, man is the supreme creature on the stage of the world is that he has the power to become all things as a result of his free choice. The other denizens of creation each occupy a distinct post. A sponge cannot choose not to be a sponge, nor can it alter its nature as a sponge. Only man possesses no certain position, no traits or functions pre-assigned him, but is invited to find his own level in the scale of creation. In a celebrated passage Pico rhapsodizes on the unprecedented nature of this blessing:

> O supreme generosity of God the Father, O highest and most marvelous felicity of man! To him it is granted to have whatever he chooses, to be whatever he wills. Beasts as soon as they are born ... bring with them from their mother's womb all they will ever possess. Spiritual beings, either from the beginning or soon thereafter, become what they are to be for ever and ever. On man when he came into life the Father conferred the seeds of all kinds and the germs of every way of life. ... Who would not admire this our chameleon? It is man who Asclepius of Athens, arguing from his mutability of character and from his self-transforming nature, on just grounds says was symbolized by Proteus in the mysteries. Hence those metamorphoses renowned among the Hebrews and the Pythagoreans.[56]

Proteus and the chameleon thus become positive symbols of man's self-transforming power, rather than emblems of cunning or shallow

---

56. Elizabeth Livermore Forbes, trans., in *The Renaissance Philosophy of Man*, ed. Ernst Cassirer, Paul Oskar Kristeller, and John Herman Randall, Jr. (Chicago, 1956), pp. 225–226. See *De hominis dignitate, Heptaplus, De ente et uno*, ed. Eugenio Garin (Florence, 1942), pp. 106, 108:

O summam Dei patris liberalitatem, summam et admirandam hominis felicitatem! cui datum id habere quod optat, id esse quod velit. Bruta simul atque nascuntur id secum afferunt ... e bulga matris quod possessura sunt. Supremi spiritus aut ab initio aut paulo mox id fuerunt, quod sunt futuri in perpetuas aeternitates. Nascenti homini omnifaria semina et omnigenae vitae germina indidit Pater. ... Quis hunc nostrum chamaeleonta non admiretur? ... Quem non immerito Asclepius Atheniensis versipellis huius et se ipsam transformantis naturae argumento per Proteum in mysteriis significari dixit. Hinc illae apud Hebraeos et Pythagoricos metamorphoses celebratae.

inconstancy. Changeability of character itself is exalted as a good: the power to change involves the power to experiment with forms of life, to enhance oneself as well as, no doubt, on occasion to debase oneself.

The same idea is elaborated into a specifically theatrical fable by Pico's Spanish disciple, Juan Luis Vives. In Vives' *Fable of Man*, Jupiter creates the universe, for Juno's amusement, in the shape of a giant theater, stationing the other gods about it as spectators, and peopling the stage with the lower creatures as actors. The last actor to take his place is man, who proves also to be the most expert. As the astonished gods look on, man impersonates first a plant, then each of the savage beasts in turn, then a social being, then a star, and finally a god. "O great Jupiter," exclaims the author, "What a spectacle for them! At first they were astonished that they, too, should be brought to the stage and impersonated by such a convincing mime, whom they said to be that multiform Proteus, the son of the Ocean." But when man appears in his last and greatest role, imitating Jupiter himself, the other gods, thunderstruck at such talent, request Jupiter to invite the wondrous creature to join them in heaven. At this point, then, man, "so diverse, so desultory, so changing like a polypus and a chameleon," becomes himself an immortal.[57]

"So diverse, so desultory [so randomly jumping], so changing like a polypus and a chameleon"—such terms imply a profoundly different attitude toward change, and toward acting, from that of more orthodox moralists. Tertullian had used words like *mutare* and *variare* to indicate what men should *not* do, and Socrates had argued against the inclusion of poetry in the Republic on the ground that it imitated the shifting phenomena of the world rather than the changeless archetypes. For the Puritans, as later for the Jansenists, human change reflected human weakness, and was tantamount to a falling away from

57. Nancy Lenkeith, trans., in *The Renaissance Philosophy of Man*, ed. Cassirer, et al., pp. 389–390. See Joannis Ludovici Vivis Valentini, *Opera omnia*, IV (Valencia, 1783), 5–6:

¡Summe Jupiter, quantum illis spectaculum! primum, stupescere se in scenam etiam introductos, expressosque ab hoc tam Ethico mimo, quem plerique multiformem illum Protheum Oceani filium esse affirmabant . . . .

. . . tam varium, tam desultorium, tam versipellem, polypum, et cameleonta.

God. For Ficino, Pico, and Vives, it might represent a way of drawing closer to God.[58] For their follower Giovanni Battista Gelli, even the witch Circe becomes a dignified exponent of human variousness, not so much inflicting loathsome metamorphoses on her victims as inviting them to assume what shapes they please. In all her enchanted herd, Ulysses can find only one who is willing to forsake his bestial form and resume his humanity; that one, however, needless to say, suffices to validate the blessings of free will and adaptability that Gelli has already extolled in his dedicatory epistle. The epistle contains a telling slip, a confusion of Proteus with Prometheus. Alone among the animals, asserts Gelli, paraphrasing Pico, man was invited to fashion his own destiny, "and almost like a newe Prometheus, to transforme him selfe into what he most willed, takynge lyke a Cameleont the colour of al those thinges unto the whiche with thaffecte he is most nyghe."[59]

58. On Pico, Proteus, mutability, and self-transformation, see Edgar Wind, *Pagan Mysteries in the Renaissance*, 2d ed. (London, 1968), pp. 191–217.

59. John Baptista Gelli, *Circes*, trans. Henry Iden (London, 1577), Sig. A3^v. See Gelli, *Circe* (Florence, 1549), Sig. A2^v: "Il potersi eleggere quel modo nelquale piu gli piace vivere: & quasi come un nuovo Prometeo, trasformarsi in tutto quello che egli vuole: prendendo a guisa di Cameleonte il color di tutte quelle cose, a le quali egli piu si avvicina con l'affetto." *Circe*, trans. Thomas Brown, ed. Robert Adams (Ithaca, 1963), p. 3, corrects *Prometheus* to *Proteus*—wrongly, I believe, since none of the early Italian editions I have been able to consult, nor any of the early translations, reads other than *Prometeo* or *Prometheus*. Late in the sixteenth century, the dedicatory epistle drops out of most reprints of the work, thereafter reappearing only sporadically. When it does, there is confusion over the name. H. Layng's translation (London, 1744 and 1745) silently changes *Prometheus* to *Proteus* (p. xx, p. xxii). Bartolommeo Gamba's edition (Venice, 1825) reads *Prometeo* once again (p. xxvi), without comment; that of Severino Ferrari (Florence, 1897) alters to *Proteo* (p. 4), with a note explaining who Proteo was, but no reference to the textual situation; while that of Giuseppe Guido Ferrero (Florence, 1957) once more corrects to *Proteo*, again without explanation or comment. Editors seem to be in a conspiracy to cover up the fact that Gelli (or the printer) wrote the wrong name in the first place. Brown's translation of 1702, utilized by Adams, does not include the epistle dedicatory at all. Adams evidently derives his text of it from the 1855 Florentine edition of Agenore Gelli, which he used as a control when editing Brown, and which reads *Proteo*, without comment. The most recent edition I have been able to consult, that of Roberto

Here Proteus, with his powers of self-transforming creativity, is implicitly seen as a heroic figure, the challenger of the Olympians and the founder of human civilization.

For a later follower, Sidney, the poet's creative power, instead of constituting an impious defiance, constituted further evidence of heavenly bounty, God being so eager to raise his favorite creature to his own level that he endowed him with seeds of the divine creative potency itself.[60] It is noteworthy that the Renaissance writer who perhaps most exalted and exemplified change—Montaigne—should also be one of the most vigorous advocates of the theater, ready to reprove its detractors and to commend it to princes as a valuable recreation for their subjects.[61]

It might appear on the face of it that the Protestant emphasis on "calling" constituted a similar invitation to men to take control over their destinies. But in fact, though the concept of calling stresses the individual's responsibility, by leaving it to him to fathom God's plans for him, it also leaves the plans themselves unequivocally in the hands of God. The individual's task may be construed as one of self-discovery, but not of self-creation. God has called; man must answer. God has decreed how each soul shall live in the world, and it is for each soul to seek out the decree applicable to it and to labor to fulfill it. William Perkins, for example, explains that:

God hath determined what he will doe with every man, and . . . he hath in his eternall counsell assigned every man his office and condition of life. . . . And by his eternall counsell, he separates every man from the very wombe to one calling or other: and accordingly he cals them in time by giving gifts, and will, to doe that, for which they were appointed.[62]

In contrast to the permissive Jupiter of Vives' fable, who encouraged men to choose their parts and write their own dialogue, Perkins' God

---

Tissoni (Bari, 1967), restores the original reading, *Prometeo* (p. 147), and observes aptly, in a note (p. 407), that the confusion of names forms an incident in cultural history which it is an editor's duty to explain but not to alter.

60. Smith, ed. *Elizabethan Critical Essays*, I, 156–157.
61. Montaigne, *Essays*, I.xxv, trans. John Florio, Everyman ed. (London, 1910), I, 190.
62. *Works* (London, 1613), Sig. P5.

has allocated the roles and written out the script in advance. From birth all men are "separated," marked out for some station to which they are to be confined. Perkins does not rule out the possibility of a change of calling, when circumstances necessitate it, but he thinks of it as an escape hatch, a concession to human frailty. Properly, men should be able to resist their bent for change, and cleave to whatever course they have undertaken. When change becomes necessary, it too must also be authorized by God. Perkins takes pains to refute the "heathenish opinion" according to which men's "particular condition and state" in this life come "by the bare wil and pleasure of man himselfe." One consequence of such pernicious doctrine is that "many perswading themselves of their callings, have for all this no calling at al: As for example, such as live by usurie, by carding, and dicing, by maintaining houses of gaming; by plaies and such like: for God is the author of every lawful calling; but these and all such miserable courses of living, are either against the word of God, or else are not grounded thereupon."[63] The Neoplatonic emphasis on self-creation, then, finds no support in the Protestant theory of calling, which emphasizes the stringency of divine surveillance and the close bounds placed on human initiative.

But Christian teaching contained no necessary reason to condemn change—even such expressly histrionic forms of change as disguise. God indeed might be unchanging, and the devil the master of disguise. But at one critical moment in history, God also disguised himself, and assumed the condition of change. There were *two* archetypal disguises, that of Satan as the serpent and that of God made flesh (occasionally, in German, *Verkleidung*); and the latter, no less than the former, contained a significant element of deception.[64] The second

63. *Works* (1603), Sigs. 4K3–4K3ᵛ. See Winthrop D. Jordan, "Searching for Adulthood in America," in *American Civilization: New Perspectives*, *Daedalus* 105, no. 4 (Fall 1976): 2: "No matter how dynamic in the long run, Puritanism spoke for stasis, for striving to know one's existing condition rather than becoming something one was not. To some extent the conversion experience implied change, but it was a limited one since no matter how diligently the individual nurtured the seed of grace, in the end God did all. It is striking that the prevailing imagery of conversion was not one of maturation (despite the seed) but of rebirth."

64. M. C. Bradbrook, "Shakespeare and the Use of Disguise in Elizabethan Drama," *Essays in Criticism* 2 (1952): 161–162.

disguise, doubtless, was necessitated by the unwelcome success of the first. The incarnation came to reverse or mitigate the ill effects of the serpent. Nevertheless, by turning disguise to holy purposes, it sanctified it; it accorded it the highest possible authorization, and this fact was reflected both in the mediaeval drama, with its representation of scriptural history as a contest of guile between Christ and Satan,[65] and in such Renaissance motifs as the character of Duke Vincentio in *Measure for Measure*, using craft against craft for holy ends. One is driven to conclude that the antitheatrical prejudice has little to do with such "facts" as the pagan origin of the stage, or the invention of disguise by the Enemy, but that at certain moments it seizes upon these as upon pretexts by which it can legitimize and validate itself.

On the other hand, it would be equally wrong to ascribe it solely to the social or economic conditions of a given historical moment. No doubt, as Russell Fraser has vigorously argued, serious economic motives underlay the Puritan hatred for the theater.[66] The theater symbolized, or was taken to symbolize, a whole complex of attitudes anathema to the sober burgesses from whose ranks the London magistrates were elected, and whose views weighed heavily on the pulpits of the town. The theater stood for pleasure, for idleness, for the rejection of hard work and thrift as the roads to salvation. Its siren song held prentices from work and fickle parishioners from the church pew. It created disorders. It bred a class of upstart vagabonds who strutted the town in finery it was illegal for them to wear, and it added one more form of conspicuous consumption to the insolence of an already overprivileged aristocracy. It seemed to embody everything wrong with the social order, and doubtless its suppression seemed to some like the first concrete step that could be taken toward the establishment of the rule of the saints. But ostensible reasons have their reality also, even if the clumsier antitheatrical writers often managed to blur the differences between the Roman spectacles and the fare of Elizabethan playhouses. Illogical and irrelevant as their arguments may often seem to us, they plainly mattered to their professors. One does not devote a decade of one's life to blackening a thousand pages of close print,

65. See Alan H. Nelson, "The Temptation of Christ; or, The Temptation of Satan," in *Mediaeval English Drama: Essays Critical and Contextual,* ed. Alan H. Nelson and Jerome Taylor (Chicago, 1972), pp. 219, 229.

66. *The War Against Poetry* (Princeton, 1970).

endlessly vociferating the same furious charges, if one does not believe what one is saying and think that there are others who will believe it as well. What we need to ask ourselves is not merely why the Puritans rehearse the thrice-told tales derived from antiquity, but why they do so with such obstinate and insane repetitiousness, why they seem so morbidly fixated on them, and why they expect their objurgations to be welcome and persuasive to readers. Clearly, the whole complex of theater, dance, music, gorgeous attire, luxurious diet, cosmetics, feminine seductiveness, feminine sexuality, transvestism, etc., aroused a painful anxiety in the foes of the stage, perhaps not only because it symbolized irrational forces threatening chaos, but because it represented a deeply disturbing temptation, which could only be dealt with by being disowned and converted into a passionate moral outrage. Most of the elements in the complex have appeared already, as we have seen, in Plato and the Fathers. The genuineness of the moral complaint then becomes unmistakable when we find it revived within the very different climate of late seventeenth-century France.

Moreover, the caste attitudes of English Puritans cover a wide spectrum, and lead to no unambiguous conclusions. Puritans as Puritans did not necessarily oppose the monarchy. Prynne himself, far from being an enemy to the crown, clashed with Laud because he thought Laud was degrading the institution of kingship. As for the Jansenists in France, they have no social ambitions to further, no economic axes to grind, no New Jerusalem to promulgate. For them it is the moral issues that count. And, on the other side, if in England the court was ruled by queens who loved dancing and play-acting, it came to be ruled in France, as it had been in Spain, by an anxious piety that showed itself willing to heed the antitheatrical clamors of the devout. One of the most odious attacks on Molière comes in a tract entitled *Le roy glorieux au monde*, in which the young Louis XIV is as nauseatingly fawned on as Molière is viperously traduced for his affronts to respectability.[67] And if, again, in England the high-ranking prelates formed part of a theater-loving coterie, in Italy, France, and Spain they spearheaded a turbulent campaign *against* the theater. Even in England, the indulgence accorded the stage by Anglican bishops was

67. Pierre Roulès, *Le roy glorieux au monde, ou Louis XIV le plus glorieux de tous les rois du monde*, ed. M. P. Lacroix (1664; rpt. Geneva, 1867).

scarcely matched by their Catholic counterparts, whose archpriest, William Harrison, in 1618 forbade the priests under his jurisdiction to attend "plays acted by common players upon common stages," on pain of losing their sacerdotal function, and who seems subsequently to have collaborated on an exhaustive defense of his own edict in response to a challenge from an underling London priest.[68]

Similar reservations would have to apply to Pietro Spinucci's more recent thesis, to the effect that the theater in sixteenth-century England was merely one weapon in a game of power politics, which suited the Puritans so long as they could wield it themselves, but against which they turned savagely when it was wrested from their grip to become part of the thought-control machinery of the Elizabethan state.[69] Again, one would have to turn to France and Italy and Spain, where the deeply entrenched episcopal establishment, which could if it wished have used the theater to further its own projects (and did so to a limited extent in the theater of the Jesuit colleges), often did everything it could to dismantle and destroy it.

From such divergencies, as well as from the persistence of the prejudice through so many upheavals, one must suspect that a lively theatrical culture has always tended to generate hostility on moral grounds —that the spectacle, for example in comedy, of authority mocked, social convention flouted, and love gratified provokes an authoritarian backlash from the morally straitlaced elements in a community. Economic, social, and political objections may well constitute almost as much of a pretext as the idolatry and superstitiousness of the spectacles did for the Fathers against the pantomimes. Quite apart from abuse of time, waste of money, and the heeding of false political doctrine, the reformers genuinely do believe the stage to be a vessel of depravity, haunted in the most literal sense by such devils as the one that cavorted on the platform during a notorious performance of Marlowe's *Doctor Faustus*, making himself indistinguishable from those other actors who were merely pretending to be devils.[70]

The prejudice seems too deep-rooted, too widespread, too resistant

68. I. J. Semper, "The Jacobean Theater through the Eyes of Catholic Clerics," *Shakespeare Quarterly* 3 (1952): 45–51.

69. *Teatro elisabettiano teatro di stato: La polemica dei puritani inglesi contro il teatro nei secc. XVI e XVII* (Florence, 1973).

70. See Chambers, *Elizabethan Stage*, III, 423–424.

to changes of place and time to be ascribed entirely, or even mainly, to social, political, or economic factors. It bestrides too many centuries, it encompasses too many different climes and cultures. It wells up from deep sources; it is "ante-predicative," and seems to precede all attempts to explain or rationalize it. It belongs, however, to a conservative ethical emphasis in which the key terms are those of order, stability, constancy, and integrity, as against a more existentialist emphasis that prizes growth, process, exploration, flexibility, variety and versatility of response. In one case we seem to have an ideal of stasis, in the other an ideal of movement, in one case an ideal of rectitude, in the other an ideal of plenitude.

The defenses of the stage that survive from the sixteenth and seventeenth centuries tend to be feebler than the attacks on it. The defenders usually share the assumptions of their opponents. They concede in advance the Christian-Stoic ideal of constancy, and the illusoriness of earthly experience. They equate changeability with hypocrisy. And they shrink sometimes from the brashness and hubbub of the playhouse, preferring not to risk contamination from that quarter. The only passages in Sidney's *Apology* that concern themselves with live theater tend to be negative—that in which he reproaches stage tragedy for its failure to observe the unities, that in which he censures comedy for its licentiousness, which "naughtie Play-makers and Stage-keepers have justly made odious," or that in which he mocks the absurdities of dramatic romance and ridicules "mungrell Tragy-comedie."[71]

But Sidney pleads eloquently for the thing he cares about, narrative and epic poetry. The only comparable attempt to defend the theater itself, as distinct from dramatic poetry, comes from Thomas Heywood, whose *Apology for Actors* proves disappointingly incoherent and slack, a desultory ramble that repeatedly betrays the cause it is attempting to serve. Heywood divides his demonstration into three books, one on the antiquity of actors, one on their dignity, and a third on their "true"

71. Smith, ed. *Elizabethan Critical Essays*, I, 176, 196–199. We may note further that of all the sixteenth-century Italian commentators on Aristotle, poring over the *Poetics* with a reverence due to holy writ, only Castelvetro seems to have recognized the theater as the natural home and indispensable medium for tragedy. See H. B. Charlton, *Castelvetro's Theory of Poetry* (Manchester, 1913), pp. 72–73, 83–84, et seq.

quality. Book I commences with a series of anecdotes about ancient heroes—Hercules, Theseus, Achilles, Alexander, Julius Caesar—all of them traditionally spurred to great deeds by seeing the feats of their predecessors acted out in dramatic form. But the materials here are so shrouded in legend, and the nature of the dramatic enactment in question so murky, that no serious conclusions could possibly be drawn from them. On the other hand, when he attempts to defend the public stage, Heywood manages to push the argument into absurdity at once, by alleging as his prime instance of the power and glory of the stage the rape of the Sabines, the signal for which was given by Romulus *at the theater*. This extraordinary example in effect not only concedes, but actively espouses, the thesis of the opposition. For the adversaries of the stage never doubted its hold over its audiences; they simply considered that hold a malignant one. Northbrooke had actually cited the incident of the Sabine women as an instance of the iniquity of the theater. The women, "being of curiositie desirous to bee present at open spectacles, were rapted and ravished by the Romaines: whereof followed suche warres, that both nations were almost destroied."[72] Heywood, translating the relevant passage from Ovid's *Ars amatoria*, not only contrives to make it sound more approving of Romulus' tactic than Ovid means it to, he omits the last two lines entirely, in which the neophyte lover is informed that the theaters are even today "fraught with danger to the fair"—precisely what the Puritans were saying about the stage of Heywood's own day.[73] For Heywood to boast, then, in effect, that the theater lends itself to violence, fraud, and rapine, and to bend Ovid to his purpose in order to make the boast more authoritative, is simply to repeat contentedly and complacently what the reformers were already saying in accents of indignation and outrage.

Book II, on the dignity of actors, starts with an account of the origins of tragedy in Bacchic sacrifice, of comedy in street songs, and of public theaters in the cult of Dionysus. Whatever the historical correctness of these derivations may be, they constitute another extraordinarily thoughtless piece of polemic, in that they dwell so artlessly on one of the most persistent charges against the stage, its origin in pagan ritual,

72. Northbrooke, *A Treatise*, Sigs. I^v–I2.

73. Ovid, *The Art of Love, and Other Poems*, trans. J. H. Mozley, Loeb Classics (London, 1947), p. 21; *Ars amatoria*, lines 133–134, ibid., p. 20: "Ex illo sollemnia more theatra / Nunc quoque formosis insidiosa manent."

idolatry, and diabolism, without in any way seeming to recognize that such a derivation might rightly be of concern to a Christian. Even more spectacularly inept is the passage that follows, on Julius Caesar and the Julian emperors. The anecdote about Caesar, far from answering the Puritan charge against acting, actually compounds it. For if Caesar, while playing the role of Hercules, really did become "so extremely carryed away with the violence of his practised fury" as to kill the actor playing Lichas, then he provided a perfect instance of what the reformers had all along been saying—that the theater brought out all that was bestial in its practitioners. If it were really true that the actors lost themselves in their parts so completely as to mistake them for reality, committing in raging earnest the crimes they were supposed merely to be feigning, then it would have been perfectly reasonable to suppress their activities altogether. But the crowning absurdity comes with Heywood's attempt to exalt the dignity of the profession by recalling a precedent set by certain Roman emperors:

It was the manner of their Emperours, in those dayes, in their publicke Tragedies to choose out the fittest amongst such, as for capital offences were condemned to dye, and imploy them in such parts as were to be kil'd in the Tragedy, who of themselves would make suit rather so to dye with resolution, and by the hands of such princely *Actors*, then otherwise to suffer a shamefull & most detestable end. And these were Tragedies naturally performed. And such *Caius Caligula, Claudius Nero, Vitellius, Domitianus, Commodus*, & other Emperours of *Rome*, upon their festivals and holy daies of greatest consecration, used to act.[74]

It would be hard to imagine a more inept "apology." Apart from the grotesque nature of the "executions" in question, practiced by only the *worst* emperors, Heywood seems as determined as the Puritans to befog the distinction between the real and the imaginary. To exalt as an "actor" the prince who wears a real dagger in his costume, and in the height of his passion stabs his victim to death, is to confound utterly the difference between life and art. Where Tertullian and the Puritans tend to convert the fictitious occasion—the play—into a real

74. Thomas Heywood, *An Apology for Actors* (1612), with I. G., *A Refutation of the Apology for Actors* (1615), facs. ed. Richard H. Perkinson (New York, 1941), Heywood, Sig. E3ᵛ.

one, Heywood converts a real occasion—the emperor's genuine act of violence—into a fictitious one. The fact that the emperor is striking mythological poses and reciting tragical verses as he delivers the fatal blow does little more than add a bit of fanciful tinsel to a real event, the killing in cold fact of someone who has been judged criminal and condemned to die, in circumstances totally alien to the play, for reasons totally unconnected with his role in it. At such moments one must reluctantly concur with the sharp language of an anonymous "Refuter" to the effect that "Master Actor's" apology has made him "a bold *Sophister* . . . a too cunning, or false reasoner, to knit preposterous and intertangled syllogismes, obscure Sorites, AEnigmaticall Crocodilites and forke-horned *Dilemma's* to ensnare and obnubilate the truth."[75]

Heywood's bungling is such that he is constantly thrusting weapons into the hands of his adversaries. One of his instances of the beneficent power of the stage concerns a party of marauding Spaniards off the Cornish coast, who were frightened away by sounds of battle coming from the town. The sounds were later discovered to have been emanating from a theatrical performance, and the stage is thereby credited with saving the inhabitants from destruction. But one might as well argue that if the robbers had been deterred by a nest of poisonous snakes, one should therefore embark on a program of snake-farming. There can be only the most accidental connection between the players' trade as players and their impact on the invading Spaniards. Even the Lollard preacher did not make this elementary mistake, but distinguished sharply between such good as might by chance come from a theatrical performance and its necessarily evil nature.

When it comes to the content of plays, Heywood tends to rehearse platitudes about their instructional value, and particularly about their social and political utility, conceived in terms of their support of the ruling powers. History plays, for example, besides informing the ignorant about their own national past, also provide valuable lessons in the need for "obedience to [the] King," "the untimely ends of such as have moved tumults, commotions, and insurrections," and "the flourishing estate of such as live in obedience, exhorting them to allegeance, dehorting them from all trayterous and fellonious strategems" (Sig. F3ᵛ). Tragedy, comedy, and pastoral, analogously, have promoted good life, civility, and virtuous morals. Heywood thus adopts most of the

75. Ibid., *A Refutation of the Apology*, Sig. C2.

biases of his antagonists. He accepts the assumption that plays should be ethically wholesome and respectable enough for the respectable, without asking to what degree these propositions ought to govern our judgment. He says nothing about the favorable presentation of love in comedies—a favorite topic of Puritan reprehension—about the outwitting of crabbed age by youth, the flouting of authority, and the triumphs of rascality. The whole subversive aspect of plays is tacitly denied, except to be denounced: "I speake not in the defence of any lascivious shewes, scurrelous jeasts, or scandalous invectives: If there be any such, I banish them quite from my patronage" (Sig. F4). But the very point of the attack on the theater was that lasciviousness, scurrility, and scandal were inseparable from it, and so a sufficient reason for its extirpation. Moreover, from a strictly tactical point of view, to argue the political conservatism of plays, to applaud them for their role in maintaining the status quo, was not necessarily to endear them to a party now beginning to be persecuted by the ruling powers, and whose members were therefore beginning to dream of supplanting the existing order with a revolutionary new one of their own.

The defense of the theater, then, as distinct from the defense of poesy, gets under way slowly and clumsily. The defenders still share too many of the prejudices of their opponents to conduct an effective rebuttal. They do better when, like Nathan Field, they avoid systematic debate. Field expressly declines to "enter . . . the list of contencion" with the fiery preacher who denounced him and his associates from the pulpit in St. Mary Overies in 1616. He contents himself with pointing out the uncharitableness of the attack, its bitter and rancorous tone. "Christ never sought the strayed sheepe in that manner, he never cursed it with acclamacion [i.e., exclamation] or sent a barking dogg to fetch it home, but gently brought it uppon his owne shoulders." Nevertheless Field makes at least one telling point in argument. In answer to the preacher's assertion that because in Old Testament times there were no players, all players are therefore damned, he demands of him, "Why, Sir, there was a tyme there was noe smith in Israel; are all smithes therefore damned?" And further, if in the time of Christ and the Apostles the player's trade was not expressly commended and justified, the same was true of many another trade: "Neither Christ, nor they [the Apostles] by their letters Pattentes incorporated either the mercer, draper, gouldsmith or a hundred trades and misteries that att this day are lawful."[76] With this concise observation Field succeeds in exposing the prejudicial nature of the preacher's case. The actors have been singled out for censure not because of anything said or not said about them in Scripture, but because the preacher has chosen them for damnation. They are not damned for the cause alleged, but damned for they are players.

As in England, so on the Continent, a zealous faction of churchmen —counter-reformers however rather than reformers—launched an energetic antitheatrical campaign in response to similar conditions, to the organizing of theatrical activity into stable companies whose members could claim a serious artistic purpose, and were not so easily to be lumped together as they once had been with pimps, prostitutes, and pickpockets, as criminal vagrants. It became the aim of moralists like the Milanese Saint Carlo Borromeo to discredit the whole theatrical enterprise by tarring the actors with the old brush of vagabondage, and urging repressive edicts that would outlaw them from respectable society. And it became a predictable consequence of Borromeo's high place and his tireless eloquence in denunciation that he unleashed the pens of dozens of hireling moralizers, who took up the cause of outrage against the iniquities of the players. In Spain, the high prelates waged war on the stage both in polemical pamphlets and in memorials addressed to the sovereign urging the suppression of theaters.[77] As in England, moreover, the most effective moments of rebuttal come less in passages of formal dispute than in stretches of folk wisdom and homespun common sense, as when the actor Beltrame, defending his trade, finds in the fearsome Orc of Venice a figure for the shadowy satanism attributed to plays:

Whoever has not heard the old folk of Venice tell of the strange shapes of the Orc [has heard other fantastic tales of a similar nature.] The Orc is supposed to be a malign spirit, who frightens the common people

76. *The Remonstrance of N.F. . . . addressed to a Preacher in Southwark, who had been arraigning against the Players at the Globe Theatre* (1616), ed. J. O. Halliwell (London, 1865), pp. 8–10, 12.

77. For conditions in Italy, see Nicolò Barbieri, *La supplica: discorso famigliare a quelli che trattano de' comici*, ed. Ferdinando Taviani, Archivio del teatro italiano, no. 3 (Milan, 1971), pp. xvi–lxxxv. For Spain, see Hugo Albert Rennert, *The Spanish Stage in the Time of Lope de Vega* (New York, 1909), pp. 137–145, 206–228, and passim.

and harms the poor fellows who go about their business in the streets by night. . . . Many claim to have seen this demon in the shape of a horse, who ran furiously along the quay, whinnied over the bridges, splashed about in the canals, and then disappeared. Some claim to have seen it in the likeness of a barking dog, others of a little pig, others of a goat, and still others in the form of a giant with a collar, which stretched itself up as high as a bell tower. One fellow has seen it all hairy, lurking in the water, as the devil is sometimes shown; another has seen it filch the oars from the gondolas . . . . And these fantastic apparitions are affirmed to be real not only by silly-headed women but by venerable men, with oaths and evidence of injuries received (I suspect) from fear. Now whether this creature exists in truth, or is an illusion begotten by dread, I for my part don't know . . . but I know very well that this Orc has wandered off in our time, and that men with stout hearts no longer meet it either by day or night. The same thing seems to me to be the case with plays: some say that they are the disease, the plague of all good manners, the carnivorous beast and the sink of all mischiefs; but when one examines them, one can find neither this plague, this beast, nor any of these mischievous actions . . . .[78]

78. Barbieri, *La supplica*, ed. Taviani, pp. 31–32:

Chi non ha udito dalla canuta plebe di Venezia raccontar le strane forme dell'Orco . . . . È riputato esser l'Orco uno spirito maligno che intimorisce il volgo e che danneggia i miseri che per loro affari vanno per le vie la notte. . . . Molti dicono aver veduto questo Demonio in forma di cavallo, che furioso correva per le fondamenta, che nitriva sopra de' ponti, che sguazzava canali, e poi spariva. Chi dice averlo veduto in sembianza di cane che latrava, chi di porcello, chi di capra, e chi l'ha veduto che pareva un gigante, con un collo che si slongava alto come un campanile, chi l'ha veduto come si dipinge il Demonio, chi l'ha veduto tutto peloso a star sott'acqua e robbar i remi alle gondole . . . . E queste fantastiche apparenze non solamente vengono da donnicciuole affermate per vere, ma da uomini vecchi, con giuramenti e testimonianze di offese ricevute (cred'io) dalla paura. Ora, che questo sia in realtà o sia illusione di fantasma nata dal timore, io non lo so, e non voglio prendermela né co i filosofi né col popolo . . . . Ma so bene che quest'Orco a' tempi nostri si è smarrito e che gli uomini coraggiosi non l'incontrano né la notte né il giorno.

Il simile mi par vedere della comedia. Alcuni dicono che questa sia il morbo, la peste de' buoni costumi, la fiera della carne e la sentina di tutte le sceleragini; e quando si essamina la comedia non vi è questa peste, questa fiera, né queste viziose azzioni . . . .

Beltrame—Barbieri—himself, it appears, led a life of outstanding piety, generous in alms, diligent in charitable acts, faithful in church observances, a model Christian in all respects. But his blameless career, whose every scene (said a contemporary) might have served to decorate the image of a saint, could hardly by itself provide an answer to the invectives that streamed from the pulpits. In its very character such a life proclaimed itself exceptional, and was so perceived. Acceptance of the actors would have had to mean acceptance of them not as martyrs or plaster saints but as human beings subject to the failings of their fellows, and, even more importantly, as skilled craftsmen with a proper place in society and a valid contribution to make to it.

For a discursive answer of anything approaching adequacy one must await the Restoration in England, and Sir Richard Baker's tract *Theatrum Redevivum, or the Theatre Vindicated, in Answer to Mr. Pryn's Histrio-mastix: Wherein his groundless Assertions against Stage-Plays are discovered, his miss-taken Allegations of the Fathers manifested, as also what he calls his Reasons, to be nothing but his Passions.*[79] Baker's pamphlet, which seems to have caused little stir, owes some of its force no doubt to the lateness of its arrival on the scene, when passions had cooled, the theaters had reopened, and the dispute over their lawfulness had temporarily been shelved. It also benefits from its sharp focus on Prynne himself. In 141 modest octavo pages Baker manages, with expert marksmanship, to shoot down the more than a thousand thickly packed quarto pages of *Histriomastix*. To the claim, for instance, that plays were an invention of idolatrous heathens, Baker coolly reminds his opponent (still alive and on the scene) that the very letters used to write his book derive from the heathens. Are all books therefore to be banned? To the argument from Deuteronomy against the wearing of women's clothes by men, Baker calls attention to a passage from the same chapter which forbids us to wear garments of mixed weave, such as wool and linen together: "Seeing we *lawfully* now wear *Cloaths* of *Linsey-Woolsey*; why may it not be as *lawfull* for *Men* to put on *Womens* Garments?" (p. 16). The Scripture, similarly, forbids us to eat blood. Can Prynne defend his own eating of blood puddings?

As these instances may suggest, Baker is adroit at exposing the passional nature of the attack, the fact that the theater has been *singled out*

79. (London, 1662). Page references in the discussion that follows will be to this edition.

as an object of odium, and that the supposed scriptural injunctions against it, having been picked with high selectivity from a multitude of other injunctions that are ignored, lack all evidential value. Prynne himself, suggests Baker slyly at one point, is the true breaker of the Deuteronomic code, since he argues in the manner of a fishwife: "At least, if we may call it *Womens conditions*, to do nothing else, but *scould*, and *rail*: for what is all his *Book*, but a bundle of *scoulding Invectives*, and *railing*, instead of *reasoning*?" (p. 17). With similar adroitness Baker exposes Prynne's slovenly and dishonest scholarship. The assertion that no reputable authority has ever allowed an exception to the ban in Deuteronomy is countered with citations from both ends of the ecclesiastical spectrum: from Luther, and from a "learned *Jesuite, Lorinuse*," who expressly approves transvestite dress *"ad representandam Comicè Tragicéve personam"*—for the representing of a personage in comedy or tragedy (p. 19). And Baker cites, for perhaps the first time in the literature of theatrical controversy, the holy women who had traditionally gone in men's apparel.

Replying to the charge of hypocrisy, Baker distinguishes, like Augustine, between differences of intention, citing further counter-examples from the Bible to illustrate the coerciveness of Prynne's evidence: "Was it *Hypocrisie* in the *Three Angels*, that appeared to *Abraham*? yet they appeared other, then they were. . . . Did not the *Angel Raphael*, when he conducted young *Tobias* in his *Journey*, both take upon him the *Name*, and *Person*, and counterfeit the *speech*, and *behaviour* of *Azarias*?" (p. 22). Replying, thus, not to Prynne alone but to Tertullian and to multitudes of antitheatrical writers in between, Baker insists on the analogy between theatrical presentation and other narrative forms. If it is lawful for written narratives, including those in Scripture, to trade in fictions and fables and disguises, it must be lawful for the stage to do likewise. However greatly the vividness of stage action may enhance its impact, it cannot magically convert plus into minus, or good into evil.

Considerations of consistency must apply not only to forms of representation but to those who represent, to the actors. Baker is one of the first—perhaps the very first—to appreciate the full absurdity of charging the player with the crimes of his stage personage. "A Player Acts the part of *Solomon*; but is never the wiser for acting his part: why should he be thought the wickeder for acting the part of *Nero*, or the more blasphemous for acting the part of *Porphyrie?*" (p. 43). The point is driven home with reference to the Bible once more—to such instances of wickedness and blasphemy as the cursing of God by Job, the defiance of Christ by the Jews, and the pagan fatalism of Ecclesiastes, none of which provoke diatribes from Prynne, nor any suggestion that they are meant to corrupt the faithful by teaching false doctrine. To the familiar complaint that plays provide a meeting ground for the sinful, and help further lascivious matches, Baker inquires whether markets, fairs, and churches themselves do not do the like? Does the sin lodge in the place itself, or in the abuse of the place by those who frequent it? As for the well-worn charge that plays teach men to cheat and steal, Baker observes, with much sense, that men may more easily acquire an education of the kind gratis, in the street. "This man, with a little help," he observes in summary, "would bring it about, that the very sin of our first Parent *Eve* was nothing else, but her being a *Player*, where she and the *Serpent* were the *Actours*, and *Adam* the *Spectatour*; and not onely that all *Players* are damned, but that none else are damned but they" (pp. 60–61).

As with the Scriptures, so with the Church Councils, and so with the Fathers, the heathen authors, and the philosophers: all of them fulminated against evils that Prynne overlooks in order to wrench their sayings into a campaign against the theater. The Church Councils forbade houses to be decked with green boughs at Christmas, or New Year's gifts to be exchanged at the same season, or fellow gossips at a christening to marry each other. Tertullian himself condemned not only plays, but also second marriages. If these authorities are to be respected in one instance, why not in all? Their authority, then, as officiously summoned by Prynne, remains utterly without weight or value.

We need not pursue Baker's rebuttal further. His treatise carries a sting because it aimed so accurately at *Histriomastix*, unlike *Histriomastix* itself, which sprays its fire promiscuously over the whole social scene, and because of the incisiveness with which Baker reduces Prynne's argumentative tactics to the lunatic's logic they quickly show themselves to be. But by 1662, when *Theatrum redevivum* was printed, Prynne himself had become an aging minion of the restored monarchy, the theaters had reopened without opposition, and the whole pedantic wrangle must have had the air of a ghostly visitation from a forgotten age. Prynne made no known effort to answer Baker, nor does *Theatrum redevivum* seem to have produced anything further in the way of public debate. For the moment, given the failure of the Puritan cause, and the revived condition of the theater, the case rested.

It is above all in the fictive domain of the drama itself, and notably in Shakespeare, that we find theatricality not only criticized, but explored and championed.[80] Shakespeare, with his astounding comprehensiveness, gives us not only the theatrical or histrionic villain, as in Richard III, but the theatrical hero, and the nontheatrical protagonist as well—plenitude and rectitude both. In the latter category we may reckon figures like Desdemona, Cordelia, and Horatio, who do not change, and in whom change would be a denial of their beings; each exemplifies the total sincerity desiderated by the moralists, the unswerving adherence to a single standard of behavior. Looming above them are figures of another sort—Falstaff, Hamlet, Cleopatra—who are conceived as flickering, as multiple, as forever in change, as endlessly engaged in mimicry and metamorphosis: in them multiplicity seems an enlarging and liberating principle, conferring something like heroic stature. All are marked by striking powers of self-transformation, and by resourcefulness in shaping circumstances to their wishes. All are gifted impresarios, not only improvising theatrical performances, but enlisting others in them. Falstaff playing the roles of king and prince, Hamlet presiding over "The Murder of Gonzago," Cleopatra staging the ceremonial climax of her own death—each gives us an image of histrionic power at the point of incandescence. Each of these, more-

80. The most comprehensive discussion of the theatrical motif in Shakespeare appears in Anne Righter [Barton]'s *Shakespeare and the Idea of the Play* (London, 1962). Ms. Barton follows the play metaphor through Shakespeare's career, from the relatively conventional use of it in the early plays for purposes of dramatic heightening, to its more ominous implications in the middle plays, where acting becomes a sign of falsehood and unreality, to the associations of innocence it regains in the late romances. In the mature histories and tragedies, "the actor is a man who cheapens life by the act of dramatising it; the shadows represented on the stage are either corrupt or totally without value, 'signifying nothing' " (p. 171). The dark comedies, too, associate the player with "hollow pretension, negation and pride" (p. 181). The last plays, finally, "[restore] the dignity of the play metaphor and, at the same time, destroy it" (p. 192), by erasing the distinction between art and life.

over, through his rotation of roles, manages to offer himself as quintessentially human: "Banish plump Jack, and banish all the world," "We are arrant knaves all," "No more but e'en a woman."

Falstaff embodies the vitality of life lived on the level of improvisation. Without a trade, without a family, without plans or projects, without a past or a future, contemptuous of consistency, he lives exclusively in the present by a chameleonlike adjustment to the needs of the moment. Past and future, plans and projects imply a part in a regular pattern, a submission, in some measure, to a restriction of one's identity. Falstaff bows to no rule other than that of his pleasure and appetite. Since he possesses no certain identity, he must create one anew at every moment, largely by wit. It is useless to tax him with a tale of what he did on the day before, since the day before scarcely exists for him. He is what he is here and now, what he makes of himself under the stimulus of persons and events. Taxed with his poltroonery of yesterday, he replies by inventing out of whole cloth—buckram or Kendall green—the hero of today. Hence our odd sensation that his explanations are *irrelevant*. They refer to a past that has no meaning for him, or at least, which he is continually rewriting to make conform to his present needs.

Hamlet has been thrust unwillingly into circumstances that require radical action. In this respect he is like Edgar; both may perhaps be said to be less "naturally" histrionic than the others. Yet they reconquer their lost places in the world by giving their metamorphic instincts full scope, by experimenting with a variety of roles, finding the ones that fit, the ones that work best in the situations they face, and finding deep satisfaction in this exercise of their vitality. Hamlet protests, both to the Danish court and to us, that he cannot "play" or "act." Edgar's lack of guile is pointed out to us by his envious brother. Yet each confrontation with friend or enemy, each needful strategem of evasion or attack, finds them inventing new masks and new gestures. Hamlet's excitement over the players stems partly from an envious kinship. He would like to be able to match them in expressive fullness, to manifest himself to the same uninhibited degree. He feels hemmed in by the pressures of his situation. What he does not acknowledge is that those same pressures are conspiring to make him a virtuoso performer in his own right. He comes to encompass in himself, and act out by himself, so many aspects of personality, some of them apparently so contradictory, that we almost lose our way seeking to grasp a central, stable *gestalt*. What we come to admire is precisely his multiplicity, the kaleidoscopic variety with which he responds to the pressures and presences around him. He is like the chameleon in more ways than being promise-crammed.

In Edgar's case, the chameleonic instinct turns into a redemptive force, enabling him to devise and survive through a series of gruelling masquerades that start by nearly erasing his human identity. As Mad Tom, he can claim kinship with the most benighted pariahs and pitiable outcasts of the kingdom. As the country lout in Act IV, he reaches the level of rustic humanity, a denizen of farms and rural settlements, speaking a regional dialect and wielding a sword in behalf of his helpless father. As the masked champion of the finale, he rises to the feudal level embodied in the institution of chivalry and the code of knightly combat. When, finally, he assumes the crown (in the Folio text), he would seem to have been fitted for it by participation in the life of the kingdom at every level, brought forever out of the reckless innocence that made him an easy prey for his brother's intrigues, and identified with as wide a gamut of human possibilities as the society of his world contains.[81]

With Cleopatra, as with Falstaff, change is the law of her being. The imagery of the play identifies her with the sea, in its fluidity, with the moon, in its vacillations, and with the Nile, in its fecundity. Though wrinkled deep in time, she exists, like Falstaff, in a perpetual present that almost excludes history, and her existence takes shape as an unwearying series of improvisings and self-mutations. It is as pointless to accuse her of a past infidelity as it is to tax Falstaff with a past villainy. Like him, she is infinitely various, and, as Francis the tapster with his parrotlike "Anon, anon, sir" served as foil to Falstaff's polyphonic richness, so the holy, cold, and still conversation of Octavia serves to set off Cleopatra's triumphant mutability. Octavia enshrines the Roman value of rectitude, Cleopatra the self-transforming plenitude of all physical life. In the last scene self-transformation turns into self-transcendence. As she fuses all her roles into one—jealous mistress,

81. On Edgar's theatricality, see William R. Elton, *King Lear and the Gods* (San Marino, Ca., 1966), pp. 87–88.

devoted wife, nursing mother, sensual woman, royal queen, goddess—
she achieves the unity that the Neoplatonists thought would emerge
from the quest of the multiform Proteus.

At least one critic has seen in her superlative showmanship a calculated snub to the enemies of the stage. "To the Romans, and to the
critics who follow them in discounting the seductions of rhetoric and
the delusions of the senses, the shows are false and their sublimity
merely 'theatrical.'" To those, on the other hand, who can leave behind
the repressive rationality and the quantitative preoccupations of Rome,
her final performance may be viewed as a rejection of Roman decorum,
the entering of a "fully theatrical world where she can put on her
royalty with its emblems. In this world, the costume we see, the poetry
we hear, and the act we see performed are sufficient, for they satisfy the
only kind of truth-criteria available within the context of the theater"[82]
—criteria, moreover, by which the creator of the play himself demands
to be judged and by which he rules his own existence.

In these four characters, then, Shakespeare provides a positive version
of the phenomenon of self-change, a glimpse into its transfiguring possibilities. In each case he shows the histrionic faculty as a reflection
of life on its deepest level, as perhaps the richest expression of human
temperament, yet he leaves us, all the same, with a tinge of disquiet
toward them, as he does not toward the simpler untheatrical characters
like Desdemona, who never transgress the strict bounds of received
morality. The metamorphic characters know no boundaries. They give
vent to negative impulses as well as benign ones. From the viewpoint
of the scrupulous moralist, Falstaff may well be a thief, a coward, a
parasite, an exploiter of the weak, a disruptive force living in a moral
limbo. Hamlet may be a rash killer, a calculating killer, a harsh abuser
of innocence, a biting manipulator of words and poses. Cleopatra may
be petulant, jealous, cruel, and deceitful. The metamorphic versatility
of all of them adds a cubit to their stature, enables them to encompass
aspects of life that the rest of us seek to repress. Falstaff presents no
danger to Prince Hal because the prince accepts and welcomes his
essential mercuriality. Cleopatra is fatal to Antony because he cannot
rid himself of the expectation that she will behave reasonably, con-

82. Phyllis Rackin, "Shakespeare's Boy Cleopatra, the Decorum of Nature, and the Golden World of Poetry," *PMLA* 87 (1972): 201–212, pp.
204, 209.

sistently, Romanly, even though he himself, under her spell, has ceased to do so. It is in keeping, then, with the persistence of the antitheatrical prejudice in all of us that we should never quite lose, toward these characters, a certain ambiguity of response, a slight uneasiness in the face of their emancipation from conventional restraints, and, also, that in readers in whom the antitheatrical prejudice is strong, these same characters should tend to provoke hostile responses and invite moralistic interpretations, be regarded as incarnations of one deadly sin or another, and the plays in which they appear as digressions upon this pious text or that.

·V·

Jonson and
the Loathèd Stage

SHAKESPEARE, then, keeps us vividly aware of the equivocal nature of the theatrical. His younger contemporary and psychological antithesis, Ben Jonson, reveals a more unsettling ambivalence. Some years ago, when postromantic prejudice was finally on the wane, and Jonson was first beginning to be studied sympathetically, Una Ellis-Fermor made a suggestive comment in her book on the Jacobean drama. "As an artist and as a man," she wrote, "Ben Jonson was originally non-dramatic; at no time did he dramatize himself and it was only with some difficulty that he dramatized anything else. . . . There is, as it were, a deeply inherent non-dramatic principle in him."[1] As phrased, this observation seems open to question in certain ways. Jonson surely did dramatize things and persons other than himself, with such exceptional energy that it sometimes seems as instinctual as breathing, and it might be argued on a priori grounds that far from never dramatizing himself, he could hardly have done otherwise, that a playwright can only give voice to what is already inside him, however he may ventriloquize it and project it onto other imagined creatures. Still, it is hard not to feel, at times, that Jonson's vocation (unlike Shakespeare's) goes against the grain; it can seem to arouse severe inner resistances. Instead of "a deeply inherent non-dramatic principle," however, one might perhaps better speak of a deeply rooted antitheatricalism. In common with many of us, Jonson's attitude toward the theater was split by contradictions. He belongs, in spirit, among a galaxy of talented playwrights

1. *The Jacobean Drama: An Interpretation*, 2d ed. (London, 1947), pp. 99–100.

who at a given moment in their careers have seen their whole enterprise as hollow, and proceeded to renounce it, or else reform it, in more or less spectacular and theatrical fashion. In this company would go Racine, Calderón, Rousseau, and even Plato (if the tradition is correct according to which he wrote tragedies as a young man), not to mention such insignificant Englishmen as Stephen Gosson and Anthony Munday. Other playwrights seem to maintain an endlessly unstable and conflicted relation with the stage. Eugene O'Neill, for example, registered repeated dismay at what he scathingly called the "show-shop" of the theater, recording his sense of betrayal at what actors, including the most gifted and dedicated actors, made of the characters he had forged in the silence of his imagination. Even, as we have seen, in such a born man of the theater as Shakespeare, and, as we might equally see in Molière, we find elements of deep suspicion toward theatricality as a form of behavior in the world.

Jonson is not, therefore, to be thought of as a fluke, but as one in whom a familiar ambivalence remains unresolved, and in whom it produced certain stresses and prompted certain accommodations. To some extent it helped shape his career; it helps us to account for the character of his successes and the accent of his failures. One finds Jonson at loggerheads with his calling in numerous ways: in his prickly relations with his audiences and his caustic view of the stage practice of his day, in his critical theories about the drama and also his larger ethical and philosophical assumptions. An orderly rehearsal of these matters, attempting to set them in proper relation to one another, may help clarify the antitheatricalism of at least one major practitioner of the dramatist's art.

The first thing that needs to be insisted on is that Jonson, despite a lifetime of writing for the stage, never arrived at a comfortable *modus vivendi* with his audiences. His feelings toward them ranged from gingerly to stormy, and by the time he had been at the job of pleasing them for a few years, he had formed some devastating conclusions. Playgoers, he believed, frequented the theater in order to parade their fine clothes and gape at those of their neighbors—to make spectacles of themselves, in fact, and so compete with the play. Or they came clamoring for more of the same empty, noisy amusements that had always diverted them in the past: plays filled with shrieks and battles, plays with ghosts and devils, emperors and clowns. Whatever strained their attention or swerved from stereotype they would "censure" in boorish ways, turning aside with rude remarks, rising noisily from their places to create a disturbance, or even addressing disruptive remarks to the players. To entertain such audiences was to have to cope with them, to devise stratagems to combat their apathy and circumvent their prejudices. Jonson seems to have thought of the good audience as a kind of jury, assembled to render a verdict on a work of art.[2] He asked of it the impartiality appropriate to a court of law rather than the quick emotionality of fellowsharers in a human experience. Alternatively, he thought of it as a panel of tasters scrupulously assaying the quality of the cuisine.[3] In neither of these capacities did the audiences he knew inspire confidence. In the *Discoveries* the craze for playgoing appears along with other frivolous pursuits as a symbol of childishness and abdication of judgment on the part of grown men:

What a deale of cold busines doth a man mis-spend the better part of life in! in scattering *complements*, tendring *visits*, gathering and venting *newes*, following *Feasts* and *Playes*, making a little winter-love in a darke corner.[4]

Certainly the most avid playgoers among Jonsonian *dramatis personae* rank among the most signal fools: Fabian Fitzdottrel, of *The Devil Is an Ass*, hastening to the Blackfriars in order to strut in his new cloak, or Bartholomew Cokes, of *Bartholomew Fair*, unable to distinguish the reality of dolls, puppets, and gingerbread men from that of live people. Jonson's canon, we note, contains no *As You Like Its* or *What You Wills*, no banquets for which the customers are invited to compose their own menus. The closest thing to that would be *Bartholomew Fair*, with its sardonic indenture between poet and pit, in which each side, as in an adversary proceeding, agrees to waive certain claims in return for certain concessions. Only by dint of wary bargaining do the two parties manage to reach a guarded understanding for the duration of the afternoon.

On behalf of this corrupted audience, but without its consent, Jonson

2. Cf. *The Alchemist*, Prologue, 1–4, and V.v.162–163.
3. Cf. *Epicene*, Prologue, 8–11; *The New Inn*, Prologue, 3–9.
4. *Discoveries*, 56–59. All citations to Jonson are from C. H. Herford and Percy and Evelyn Simpson, eds., *Ben Jonson*, 11 vols. (Oxford, 1925–1952).

repudiated nearly all the popular dramatic genres of the day: romance comedy, revenge tragedy, chronicle history, Marlovian tragedy of ambition. All these, in his view, offended nature because they exaggerated. They traded in monsters and chimeras instead of recognizable human types. They bruised the ear with "furious vociferation," or fatigued the eye with "*scenicall* strutting."[5] Taken literally, Jonson's prescriptions of "truth" and "nature" would have forbidden even the kind of heightening he himself freely practiced, not to speak of the grotesques of *Volpone* or the improbabilities of *Epicene.* When it came to stagecraft, he rejected with equal vehemence all the varieties of theatrical claptrap most cherished by Elizabethan audiences: fireworks, thunder, and ordnance, the raising of ghosts from the cellarage and lowering of gods from the hut. In the course of his feud with Inigo Jones, Jonson also ridiculed such newer and more esoteric wonders as the *machina versatilis*, or turning device, and the *machina ductilis*, or tractable scene, both of them among the admired playthings of the court theater. One common factor in these dislikes, as W. A. Armstrong has pointed out, is that "they were all directed against scenes, lights and machines which *moved* before spectators' eyes" and were hence "most likely to distract attention from the spoken word."[6] More may be at stake here, however, than simple attentiveness. Other playwrights managed to preserve the primacy of the spoken word without sacrificing the pleasures of spectacle. Somewhere in Jonson there lurks a puritanical uneasiness about pleasure itself, and also a distrust of movement, which connects with what we shall presently see to be an ideal of stasis in the moral and ontological realm. But whatever exists in time, and unfolds in time, and utilizes human actors, must also involve motion as one of its mainsprings. To banish motion, to attempt to arrest or disguise it by ruling out the devices of stagecraft that exploit it, is in a sense to deny the intrinsically kinetic nature of the theatrical medium.

Jonson himself would not have countenanced the suggestion that he was attacking the theater in its essence. He would have claimed to be reforming it, scouring off its excrescencies, restoring it to nature and truth after its long bondage to false conventions. Jonson belongs,

5. *Discoveries*, 778–779.
6. "Ben Jonson and Jacobean Stagecraft," in *Jacobean Theatre*, ed. John Russell Brown and Bernard Harris, Stratford-upon-Avon Studies I (London, 1960), p. 51.

that is, among the company of artists determined to rescue their art from excessive artifice. Nevertheless his reform aims precisely to de-theatricalize the theater, to strip it of just those attributes which, in the eyes of most of its devotees, made it theater in the first place—not only its gaudiness and bustle, but also its licentious ways with time and space, and its casual recourse to the astounding and the marvellous. Samuel Beckett has pioneered in an analogous reform in our own day, trying to revive an art that has rotted in its own pomp by stripping away all theatrical tinsel, so as to get back to the bedrock of reality, a pair of ragged characters exchanging enigmatic remarks on a few square feet of board. Beckett outdoes Jonson in one significant respect: he eliminates verbal as well as visual luxuriance, turning his back on the whole tradition of stage declamation while still managing to wring a kind of antiphonal poetry from the fragmentary utterances and expressive silences exchanged by the pair. Jonson stops short of such radical measures. He works to make his dialogue less ornamental, more lifelike, more obedient to the twists and turns of the thinking mind, but at the same time he enlarges its role, making it do duty, it would almost seem, for the element of spectacle he has so strenuously downgraded. Even his own rhetorically trained audiences came to rebel. One of his authentic masterpieces, *Sejanus*, was hissed from the stage for the excesses of its verbiage, yet when Jonson sat down to write a second tragedy for the same troupe a few years later, far from conceding anything to the preferences of his audiences he defiantly administered a double dose of what they had already once spat out, as though to coerce them into swallowing his medicine even if they found it unpalatable, on the presumption that he knew better than they what was good for them.

Theatrical performance remained, throughout his career, a hazard for Jonson, fraught with the perils of rejection and trauma. His ambivalence about it emerges plainly in his attitude toward the printing of his plays. As early as 1600 the title page of *Every Man Out of His Humor* informs us that this is "The Comicall Satyre of EVERY MAN OUT OF HIS HUMOR, as it was first composed by the AUTHOR B. I. *Containing more then hath been publickely spoken or acte[d]*. With the severall Character of every person." Now this unusual legend at the same time announces an innovation and issues a challenge. Standard title page salesmanship during the 1590s had stressed the identity of the play as printed with that of the play as acted. Dramatic texts aimed to capitalize on theatrical successes by offering authentic transcripts of what had been well received by audiences. A play was published "as acted by" or "as played by" such and such a company, or as "sundrie time shewed upon Stages," or even "most stately shewed," or as "privately acted," or as "played before the Queen's most excellent Majesty." The 1594 quarto of *A Knack to Know A Knave* advertises proudly that it is "Newlie set foorth, as it hath sundrie tymes bene played by ED. ALLEN and his Companie. With KEMPS applauded Merrimentes," while the 1597 quarto of *Romeo & Juliet* calls attention to the fact that the play has been "often (with great applause) plaid publiquely, by the right Honourable the L. of Hunsdon his Servants."[7]

Jonson completely overturns this custom. Instead of promising us that the printed version will conform to the acted one, he assures us that it will not. It will be "as it was first composed by the author"— presumably superior to, and in any case different from the acted version, about which he leaves us in the dark, not even mentioning the name of the company. Moreover he casts a lure for the browser by first including and then pointing to "the severall Character of every Person," a series of quasi-Theophrastan sketches which could only interest a reader and could not have found any place in performance. Jonson, clearly, is thinking of the play now as a reading experience rather than a theatrical experience, as a literary entity, with rules of its own that dispense it from such purely theatrical constraints as that on length: the text runs to something like 4,500 lines, substantially longer than the longest version of *Hamlet*. Print, again, offered the chance to expatiate on critical questions, to debate disputed points, affix postscripts, and append emendations. The original ending of *Every Man Out* having offended because it contained an impersonation of the queen, Jonson rewrote it, but in the printed text he preserved the original finale along with the altered one, and supplied a learned apology addressed to the "right-ei'd and solide *Reader*" (III. 602).

Analogous considerations, most likely, govern the two states of the

7. Title page citations are from W. W. Greg, *A Bibliography of the English Printed Drama to the Restoration*, I (London, 1939), 171, 172, 194, 234. No attempt has been made to reproduce the type faces of the original (except for capitals), or to indicate line divisions or other title page peculiarities.

text of *Cynthia's Revels*. The quarto would seem to represent an acting version—certainly it is by far the tighter and more concise of the two —while the folio either reverts to an enormous urtext from which the acting script was carved out, or else represents a gigantic expansion of the acted text for inclusion in the later volume. For the folio version of *Poetaster*, again, Jonson seems to have composed an entire new scene, the most striking feature of which is its total unsuitability for performance. The scene, a close paraphrase of a satire of Horace, does nothing to accommodate itself to the dramatic context. It makes no reference to characters or events of the play, but on the other hand it does mention numerous characters and events alien to the play, be-cause they are mentioned in Horace. Of the two speakers of the scene, one is Horace, but the Horace of history rather than the Horace of the play, with no traces of his dramatic self, and the other is Horace's colorless interlocutor Trebatius, who has otherwise nothing at all to do with *Poetaster*. As a contribution to literature, as an excursus on the theory of satire, as an exercise in translation, the scene possesses distinct interest. But interpolated into the dramatic continuum of *Poetaster* it forms a most ill-fitting and unwelcome intrusion. For both these plays, then, when it came to putting them into definitive form for the volume he designed as a monument, Jonson chose to introduce— or reintroduce—extensive literary embellishments that seriously injure them as stage pieces. Even the revised *Every Man In His Humor*, de-spite its greater richness of texture, strikes one as in some respects a more bookish object than its quarto original. The revisions, most of them additions, tend to encrust and at times to encumber with detail what was previously a sparer, sharper pattern of action.

But the very collecting of his plays into the 1616 folio testifies to Jonson's impatience with the fragility of the stage, and his desire to commit his "works"—significantly so named—to a more lasting me-dium. In this respect he forms a sharp contrast to Marston, who in the foreword to *The Malcontent* apologizes for printing his play at all, on the grounds that it does not truly exist apart from its theatrical em-bodiment. "*Onely one thing afflicts me*," he declares mournfully, "*to thinke that Scaenes invented, meerely to be spoken, should be inforcive-ly published to be read.*"[8] Again in the address prefixed to *The Fawne*

8. *The Malcontent* (London, 1604; facs. ed., The Scolar Press, Menston, Yorkshire, 1970), Sig. A2.

he alleges unwillingness and pleads necessity: *"If any shall wonder why I print a Comedie, whose life rests much in the Actors voice, Let such know, that it cannot avoide publishing: let it therefore stand with good excuse, that I have been my owne setter out."*[9] The burden of proof, in Marston's view, is thus on the playwright who would transfer his comedies, meant for the stage, into print. For Jonson, on the other hand, the actor's voice—not to speak of the public's ear—constituted an unpredictable and untrustworthy element over which he had too little control; print offered an escape into a stabler medium. By lifting the play out of the turbulence of the public arena into the still silence of the page, it enabled it to transcend the imperfections and the vicissitudes of live performance. In preface and dedication and apologetical epistle, moreover, Jonson appeals to readers over the heads of playhouse audiences. The latter cannot truly measure the worth of what is offered them; they are bent on instant gratifications of a kind he has little wish to supply, and are, in the nature of things, prone to be swayed by opinion rather than reason. Readers, simply by virtue of literacy, possess a certain irreducible minimum of knowledge and discipline. In addition, they are removed from the passions of the playhouse. They can ponder, instead of reacting blindly, and so bring cool heads and sound judgments to the act of evaluation. The end result of such considerations is to make the printed script rather than the live performance the final authority; the play moves formally into the domain of literature. Jonson makes this clear in the prefatory remarks to *Sejanus* and *Catiline*, when he defends these plays not against the discontented groundlings at the Globe, not against the charges of tedium, insufficient action, and so forth, that had actually caused them to fail, but against what he fancies *might* be said in their reproof by learned commentators steeped in Aristotle and conversant with the erudite debates on tragedy. *Sejanus* lacks "a proper *Chorus*" and does not adhere to "the strict Lawes of *Time*" ("To the Readers," 7–8); *Catiline*, despite *"all noise of opinion,"* is *"a legitimate Poeme"* (Dedication, 6–7). Jonson is not interested in vindicating his plays as theater, but in validating them as literature, as dramatic poems, from pedantic interpreters on the right. And as he appeals to readers to mend the hasty reactions of spectators, so at times he invokes posterity to correct the errors of his contemporaries, thus aiming at a level of disinterested

9. John Marston, *Plays*, ed. H. Harvey Wood, II (Edinburgh, 1938), 143.

judgment unattainable in his own day even in well-instructed readers.

It is no surprise, then, to discover Jonson more concerned with the fate of his plays in the printing-house than any other dramatic author of the period. For the 1616 folio he exercised an unprecedentedly close surveillance over the whole process, supplying corrected copy, reading proof while the volume was in press, and (for the earlier plays at least) entering scores of minute revisions in order to clarify his intentions or enhance the typographical impact of the presentation.

As with the publishing of the plays, so with that of the masques; the purpose is "to redeeme them as well from Ignorance, as Envie, two common evills" (*Masque of Blackness*, 12–14). Here the discrepancy between print and performance widens, since the very essence of the masque lay in its occasional nature and its absolute reliance on spectacle. Far from attempting to deny it this character, Jonson at first puts his whole weight behind it, justifying the cost and sumptuousness of the form as an expression of kingly magnificence, and going to great lengths to make the printed texts recreate as far as possible the brilliant scenic effects of Inigo Jones. With Jones, also, he worked to devise spectacular effects that would function as vehicles of meaning, and could not be written off as mere decoration. But even as he bent his energies to unifying the form and reconciling its disparate elements, Jonson in the depths of his mind preserved a firm belief in the paramountcy of poetry. Spectacle, however splendid, however central and expressive, could never be more than the "carkasse" of an organism whose "spirit" lay in the verses. These terms, from *The Masque of Blackness* (line 8) recur, slightly varied and with renewed emphasis, in the foreword to *Hymenaei*:

It is a noble and just advantage, that the things subjected to *understanding* have of those which are objected to *sense*, that the one sort are but momentarie, and meerely taking; the other impressing, and lasting: Else the glorie of all these *solemnities* had perish'd like a blaze, and gone out, in the *beholders* eyes. So short-liv'd are the *bodies* of all things, in comparison of their *soules*. And, though *bodies* oft-times have the ill-luck to be sensually preferr'd, they find afterwards, the good fortune (when *soules* live) to be utterly forgotten. (1–10)

As carcass to spirit, so body to soul. In the poetic kernel of the masque lies its abiding essence, in the theatrical vesture only a disposable shell.

The poetry addresses itself to the understanding, that faculty which Jonson consistently exalts over its coarser companion "sense," and to which he appeals as the highest faculty he can hope for in a reader or spectator. Sense, indeed, he informs us elsewhere, we should strive to make our "slave" ("Epode," 17–18). By the time we reach *Pleasure Reconciled to Virtue* Jonson's interest in the spectacular side of the masque has unmistakably waned. The text, instead of dwelling lovingly on the details of costume and décor, actually omits some of the most striking visual effects remarked by other observers: the richly decorated front curtain, the pantomime battle between Hercules and Antaeus, the reappearance of the goddess Virtue. "Far from being"— as it would have been earlier—"the record of a particular production on a particular evening in 1618, the text seems almost to testify to the irrelevance of the spectator's experience."[10] Moreover, when members of the audience criticized the entertainment, as they did, they found fault with it not on visual but on poetic grounds. Jonson had trained them to view such shows through his own eyes, and to apply to them his own severe canons of dramatic relevance.[11]

Despite, then, the innovative energy with which Jonson tackled the aesthetic problems of the masque, despite his efforts to forge apt and expressive devices of stage spectacle, he persisted, in the depths of his mind, in holding the spectacular side of the masque in low esteem. Speaking in the *Discoveries* of the quest for magnificence, he reminds us that "Wee covet superfluous things; when it were more honour for us, if wee could contemne necessary."

Have not I seen the pompe of a whole Kingdome, and what a forraigne King could bring hither also to make himselfe gaz'd, and wonder'd at, laid forth as it were to the shew, and vanish all away in a day? And shall that which could not fill the expectation of few houres, entertaine, and take up our whole lives? when even it appear'd as superfluous to the Possessors, as to me that was a Spectator. The bravery was shewne, it was not posses'd; while it boasted it selfe, it perish'd. (1387–89; 1404–12)

Jonson may or may not here be thinking specifically of a masque, but it is hardly to be doubted that behind the description lie his long years

10. Stephen Orgel, *The Jonsonian Masque* (Cambridge, Mass., 1965), p. 150.
11. Ibid., pp. 149–150.

of apprenticeship to court spectacles, and his settled conviction of their wastefulness. Welcoming a newcomer to the Tribe of Ben, he distinguishes between true friendships and flimsy ones, between "Such as are square, wel-tagde, and permanent," and those "built with Canvasse, paper, and false lights, / As are the Glorious Scenes, at the great sights" (63–66). Here the masque becomes an express symbol for what is fleeting, trumped-up, and inauthentic, the antithesis of everything valuable and lasting.

The content itself of one of his most successful masques reflects the same distrust. In *Mercury Vindicated from the Alchemists at Court*, Vulcan and his followers are arraigned for their presumption in thinking to create life in their laboratories. Boasting that they can not only rival nature but outdo her, they succeed only in bringing forth stunted and deformed creatures. At length the sun, the true source of generation, puts them to rout and resumes his proper role as sole fecundating principle of the world. Jonson's myth thus rejects all rivals to great creating nature, and these would have to include not only the alchemists, with their "terms of art," but the poets, with their claim to bring forth a second nature greater than the first. It is not, surely, coincidence that Jonson revered history as he did, that his own historical tragedies follow their sources with such scholarly meticulousness, or that throughout his career he proclaimed his abhorrence of monsters and his adherence to the natural. He rejected dramatic romance because it was the one theatrical genre that openly flouted fact and welcomed into its fold the fantastic creatures relished by Sidney—the pigmies, grips, and hippogriffs which had no counterparts in the actual world. Munday, speaking for hard-shelled antitheatricalists, had charged that the most notable liar had become the best poet. Sidney, on behalf of the poet, replied that the poet could not be said to lie because he made no claim to affirm.[12] Jonson, more perilously, concedes that bad poets may be liars, but that good poets need not be—that poets can choose to respect the truth. They do so when they cling to the observed, the known, the documented, to what can be certified and verified. And having advanced this claim, midway in his career, Jonson in effect set about to

12. W. C. Hazlitt, ed., *The English Drama and Stage under Tudor and Stuart Princes 1543–1664* (London, 1869), p. 145; G. Gregory Smith, ed., *Elizabethan Critical Essays* (Oxford, 1904), I, 184.

substantiate it in his works, pouring his imaginative energy into forms that could be granted to observe the most rigorous correspondence between nature and the world at large.

From a more familiar point of view, his distrust of both play and masque springs from his uneasiness with the impermanence of both forms. Jonson belongs in a Christian-Platonic-Stoic tradition that finds value embodied in what is immutable and unchanging, and tends to dismiss as unreal whatever is past and passing and to come. What endures, for him, has substance. What changes reveals itself thereby as illusory. His nondramatic poems recur repeatedly to the ideal of the unmoved personality, the soul that can sustain itself in virtue when all is flux around it.[13] Men are praised if they can preserve their singleness of mind amid the distractions of the world, their serenity of spirit amid its turbulence. The Earl of Pembroke, in a Senecan paraphrase, is lauded for his perseverance in goodness, for being one "whose noblêsse keeps one stature still, / And one true posture, though besieg'd with ill" ("To William Earle of Pembroke," 13–14). Similarly with Lady Katherine Aubigny; it is her firmness of temper that makes her exemplary: "*Madame*, be bold to use this truest glasse: / Wherein, your forme, you still the same shall finde; / Because nor it can change, nor such a minde" ("To Katherine Lady Aubigny," 122–124). Here the stasis aspired to by the poet, and achieved in the finality of his poem, mirrors the still perfection of its idealized subject. Earlier in the same poem, as often in Jonsonian verse, the satiric vision momentarily gains the ascendant; we glimpse the social turmoil shunned by the lady, the temptations against which she remains steadfast:

> . . . wisely you decline your life,
> Farre from the maze of custome, error, strife,
> And keepe an even, and unalter'd gaite;
>
> . . . .
>
> Which though the turning world may dis-esteeme,
> Because that studies spectacles, and showes,
> And after varyed, as fresh objects goes,
> Giddie with change, and therefore cannot see

13. Cf. Thomas M. Greene, "Ben Jonson and the Centered Self," *Studies in English Literature, 1500–1900* 10 (1970): 325–348.

Right, the right way: yet must your comfort bee
Your conscience, and not wonder, if none askes
For truthes complexion, where they all weare maskes.

(59–70)

One catches a hint of masque terminology here. The "turning world" recalls the revolving microcosm of *Hymenaei*, only now the whole world—masquers and beholders together—have become a *machina versatilis*. Jonson seems to condemn the taste for novelty and the thirst for change independently, as if they constituted separate but related vices, just as on another occasion he makes it more of a sin when vices "do not tary in a place," but shift about.

In "An Epistle to a Friend, to perswade him to the Warres," Jonson urges the friend to keep himself undefiled by the baseness of his surroundings, and to maintain his calm of spirit: "That whatsoever face thy fate puts on, / Thou shrinke or start not, but be alwayes one" (185–186). Fate, like an actor, resourceful in disguise, alters its visage and tries to ensnare the good man, but the good man himself remains "alwayes one," despite all vicissitudes. Such activity as he does engage in, such energy as he does put forth, is exerted to preserve his immobility. Immobility is to be fought for; change is to be fought against. In the dialogue of the One and the Many in the Jonsonian cosmos, it is the Many that must be put to flight, the One that must finally triumph.

Change betokens not only instability, but, as in the emblems of Proteus, deceit, and deceit expresses itself characteristically through change. In "An Epistle to Master Arthur Squib," we learn that "Deceit is fruitfull. Men have Masques and Nets, / But these with wearing will themselves unfold: / They cannot last. No lie grew ever old" (18–20). Only the truth survives; lies perish, and that which perishes thereby shows that it is compounded of lies. The same message meets us more prosaically in the *Discoveries*, where the terms are such as to suggest an indictment of poetry itself. "Nothing is lasting that is fain'd; it will have another face then it had, ere long: As *Euripides* saith, *no lye ever growes old*" (540–542). Even the invocation of the august name of Euripides cannot obscure the hint that the poet's own most hallowed talent, the one that sets the seal on his special status, his "faining," is being called into question as ethically suspect.

Now the bias against change, the allegiance to silence, stasis, and

immobility carry with them an implied bias against the theater that
occasionally erupts into open antagonism. Jonson's fierce epigram "On
the Townes Honest Man," apparently written against Inigo Jones, portrays the title personage making his way in the world by miming.

> At every meale, where it doth dine, or sup,
>   The cloth's no sooner gone, but it gets up
> And, shifting of it's faces, doth play more
>   Parts, than th'*Italian* could doe, with his dore.
> Acts old *Iniquitie*, and in the fit
>   Of miming, gets th'opinion of a wit.
>
> (23-28)

There is no question here about "it's" talent for its degrading feats—
"it" is a past master of them—nor is any gloss needed to underline
Jonson's contempt for the parasite who pays for his dinner by doing
impersonations. When we turn to the plays we find that in them Jonson
does not shed his antitheatrical bias. Rather, he builds it in; he makes
the plays critiques of the instability they incarnate. The plays show us
change as something to be shunned, by presenting us with foolish characters determined to embrace it. Discontented with themselves, barely
able to credit their own reality, addicted to appearances and externals,
they compensate by trying to impose some mimic version of themselves
on their fellows, and characteristically they resort to theatrical means
to make their way. They fall into two well-recognized groups: the gulls,
who witlessly parrot their social or intellectual superiors, and so disavow whatever is true in themselves in favor of some forged identity,
and the rascals, engaged in various games of pretense, in plays-within-
plays which have as object the gulling of the gulls. Thus with Mosca's
aid Volpone plays sick to dupe his heirs, plays the mountebank to
entice Celia, plays the commendatore to needle his victims once he
has gulled them, and teaches Voltore to enact a scene of demonic possession in the courtroom. Subtle, Face, and Doll play an extensive
repertory of roles to hoodwink their clients: learned doctor, saintly
philosopher, professor of quarrelling, gentleman's servant, laboratory
assistant, suburb captain, lord's sister, Queen of Faery. Less malignly,
Truewit plays the solicitous friend to Morose, orchestrating the confusions of the wedding feast, fashioning the quarrel between the two
foolish knights (before a carefully prepared audience), and finally plan-

ning, rehearsing, and executing the parody of legal procedure that terminates Morose's matrimonial misadventures. The degree to which Truewit may be allowed to stand as the authorial spokesman in the play suggests the degree to which, in this play, theatricality is accepted as a necessary evil, reminding us that through all these plays runs a mimetic hierarchy, as we may term it, that cuts across the moral hierarchy, sometimes even seeming to reverse it. According to the negative criteria of change and motion, the rascals and manipulators should attract more odium than their victims. But they are armed against our disapproval with a formidable weapon: the inventiveness of their talent, the gusto with which they exercise it. They command their own changes; they dictate their own motions; they keep the turning world turning; and even as we recognize the subversive nature of their actions we find ourselves drawn to them in admiring fascination.

In the lower reaches of gulldom a comparable hierarchy prevails. Bobadil wrings a paradoxical respect from us for the bizarre extravagance of his style, the brilliance with which he sets about fabricating an inauthentic self. His imitator, Matthew, without his mentor's flair for improvisation, confines himself to purely apish gestures, vain echoes of random words, while the imitator's imitator, Stephen, desperately bringing up the rear, incompetently parrots both, and fails to arrive at anything resembling a coherent role. Similarly, in *The Alchemist* it is Sir Epicure Mammon, with his grandiose fantasies, his readiness to fall into histrionic postures, who among the gulls most notably disarms our sterner morality. The very outlandishness of his folly lends it a heroic accent.

These countermines of theatricality seem sometimes to threaten to blow all antitheatrical doctrine sky high. But on the official level antitheatrical doctrine holds sway, as the ending of *Volpone* clearly shows. The world is one in which sharpsters try to cozen dullards by means of theatrical humbug, and the dullards are bent on foisting some implausible conception of themselves onto the world. Occasionally, in the early plays, we find an express equation between the ductile self and the absence of moral principle. In the quarto of *Every Man In*, Bobadil is scathingly referred to as "signior *Pithagoras*, he thats al manner of shapes" (III.iv.174-175), by his arch-enemy, a character ultimately named Downright, whose property it is to be as stubbornly himself at all times as it is Bobadil's to lack an authentic self, and whose mission it is to expose Bobadil as a braggart. In *Every Man Out* we meet the rascally pseudo-soldier Cavalier Shift, alias Whiff, alias Apple-John, whose self-proclaimed omnicompetence ends with his being shown up as a swaggerer and a coward. And *Cynthia's Revels* brings us acquainted with Amorphus, "a travailer, one so made out of the mixture and shreds of formes, that himselfe is truly deform'd" (II.iii.85–87). Amorphus, like Bobadil and Shift, is arraigned for the crime of wilful self-betrayal, for piecing together a factitious identity from the scraps of those he has met in his travels.

All these characters, as well as less talented, more monochrome gulls like Stephen or Fungoso or Asotus, in the same three plays, may serve as emblems to one of Jonson's most familiar dicta in the *Discoveries*:

> *I have* considered, our whole life is like a *Play*: wherein every man, forgetfull of himselfe, is in travaile with expression of another. Nay, wee so insist in imitating others, as wee cannot (when it is necessary) returne to our selves: like Children, that imitate the vices of *Stammerers* so long, till at last they become such. . . . (1093–98)

What this statement portends is not only that men too often walk their daily rounds as if they were acting on stages, but that this is a self-negating, self-destructive way to live. By their persistence in mimicry they are stunting their own possibilities for self-realization. The sole character who succeeds in avoiding this fate, in transcending the evils of a taste for mimicry, is Brainworm, whose antics spring purely from play, on the success of which neither his economic security nor his sense of his own reality depends. Brainworm embodies the metamorphic power in almost abstract form, and is probably the only character in Jonson in whom it is entirely harmless.

Two passages in *Cynthia's Revels* embroider lavishly on its inherent evils. The first consists of a satirical diatribe spoken by Crites, the authorial spokesman. In the manner of much verse satire of the period, Crites recounts a vision or dream he has had of the hangers-on who infest the court, and compose "the strangest pageant, fashion'd like a court" (III.iv.4). The striking thing about this pageant is its particolored appearance. It has no distinct shape or hue of its own, but remains "diffus'd . . . painted, pyed, and full of rainbow straines." Its individual members share the same unfixed, variegated character, as we discover in Crites' denunciatory portraits of them: the self-important great man, basking haughtily in his "state," attended by "mimiques, jesters, pandars, parasites"; the "mincing marmoset," all clothes and grimaces and starched formality; the venal taker-in of bribes and refuser of honest suits. As the bribe-taker proceeds along,

> With him there meets some subtle PROTEUS, one
> Can change, and varie with all formes he sees;
> Be any thing but honest; serves the time;
> Hovers betwixt two factions, and explores
> The drifts of both . . . .

(III.iv.42–46)

That the Proteus can be "any thing but honest" is almost a tautology. If he were honest, he would not be a Proteus; the two conditions mutually exclude one another.

Crites goes on to recollect a comic scene played by a group of foolish courtiers, all engaged in perfecting their parts as courtly lovers: the neophyte primping and rehearsing his speech beforehand, "like an unperfect *prologue*, at third musike"; another who "sweares / His *Scene* of courtship over," and strikes poses for his mistress; another who acts in more strenuous mode, overwhelming her with ridiculous gallantries, extravagating in vows and kisses; and one, finally, who "onely comes in for a *mute*: / Divides the *act* with a dumbe shew, and *exit*." When the suitors are done, it is their mistresses' turn. "Then must the ladies laugh, straight comes their *Scene*, / A sixt times worse confusion then the rest" (III.iv.58–74). So, implicitly, in the posturing and attitudinizing and protean shifting of these characters, and explicitly in the theatrical images, we find acting used as a synonym for what is false, affected, and empty. Worth, in the Jonsonian universe, as in that of his Stoic guides, is virtually defined as an inner and hence an invisible quality. Whatever can be too readily theatricalized lacks genuineness and substance. We see this comically spelled out again in the scene in which Amorphus tries to coach his oafish pupil Asotus to approach, address, and pay court to his mistress. The fact that courtliness can be conceived in such mechanical terms, that it can be codified into lessons and practiced like acrobatics, tells us all we need to know of its meaning for the characters in the play.

The follies of change appear strikingly exemplified in a character named Phantaste, one of the frivolous nymphs who have desertlessly wormed their way into the purlieus of the court. Phantaste proposes, as a game, that she and her companions imagine whom they would most like to be turned into, if given the chance. Her companions prove to have rather dry imaginations. All that the old bawd, Moria, can think of to wish for is to be "a wisewoman, and know all the secrets of court, citie, and countrie" (IV.i.140–142). Philautia, or self-love, is too pleased with herself as she already is to be much interested in changing; all she craves is more sovereignty. Most of the scene is given over to the musings of Phantaste, who envisages, as her ideal, an endless cycle of shifting identities.

. . . (mee thinkes) I should wish my selfe all manner of creatures. Now, I would bee an empresse; and by and by a dutchesse; then a great ladie of state; then one of your *miscelany* madams; then a waiting-woman; then your cittizens wife; then a course countrey gentlewoman; then a deyrie maide; then a shepheards lasse; then an empresse againe, or the queene of *fayries*: And thus I would proove the vicissitudes, and whirle of pleasures, about, and againe.

This gives us, in stylized form, the insatiable thirst for pleasure that seems automatically to lead to a life of perpetual change. Phantaste's revery puts into systematic and as it were aesthetic form the compulsive flitting about among identities that already constitutes her existence, and her state of mind. "As I were a shepheardesse," she proceeds,

I would be pip'd and sung too; as a deyrie wench, I would dance at *may*-poles, and make sillabubbes; As a countrey gentlewoman, keep a good house, and come up to terme, to see motions; As a cittizens wife, bee troubled with a jealous husband, and put to my shifts; (others miseries should bee my pleasures) As a waiting-woman, I would taste my ladies delights to her; As a *miscellany* madame invent new tyres, and goe visite courtiers; As a great ladie, lye a bed, and have courtiers visite mee; As a dutchesse, I would keepe my state: and as an empresse, I'ld doe any thing. And, in all these shapes, I would ever bee follow'd with the'affections of all that see mee. (IV.i.171–191)

One noteworthy feature of this daydream is that the individual vignettes in it seem innocent enough. There is nothing corrupt or culpable about a shepherdess wishing to be piped and sung to: nothing could be more decorous, or classical. A milkmaid would not have to be ashamed of dancing at maypoles and making syllabubs, or a country gentlewoman of keeping a good house. It is true that Phantaste leans toward pastime rather than honest labor, but the pastimes themselves are mostly harmless ones. What is not harmless is the total vision, the whirligig of metamorphoses which leave no room for a fixed responsible self.

Metamorphic fantasies, it has often been remarked, play a key role in Volpone's advances to Celia. He plies her not only with palpable jewels and the promise of edible delicacies but with the lure of perpetual variety in love, the prospect of an endless charade in which the two will act characters out of history, out of geography, and out of Ovid's *Metamorphoses*. Similarly, Mosca's self-congratulatory euphoria centers on his own dizzying powers of motion, his lightning-like power to "be here, / And there, and here, and yonder, all at once; / Present to any humour, all occasion; / And change a visor, swifter then a thought!" (III.i.26-29). What Mosca is pluming himself on is his power of self-transformation, outrunning thought in its rapidity; this makes him a kind of quintessential opposite to the steadfast characters in the *Epigrams*, inured against time and change—a satanic opposite, perhaps, yet one with whom at some level Jonson profoundly identifies. Again, in the *Epigrams*, the degenerate sensuality of Sir Voluptuous Beast takes the form of a search for unusual ways to arouse and appease his lust; his wife must learn to fit herself to the "varied shapes" of his appetite. And so also for Sir Epicure Mammon, expecting a renewal of youth from the alchemists' elixir: he promises Doll Common "a perpetuitie / Of life, and lust." Like Celia, Doll will have a "wardrobe, / Richer then *Natures*, still, to change thy selfe, / And vary oftener, for thy pride, then shee: / Or *Art*, her wise, and almost-equall servant" (IV.i.166-169). One target of Jonson's antitheatricalism appears here with particular emphasis: the fixation on clothes as a source of pleasure and a basis of identity. Sir Epicure, preoccupied with his visions of sensual sport, harbors the illusion that a "wardrobe, / Richer then *Natures*" will open the door to endless transformations of the self; he and his partner will moult identities, as it were, and experience well-worn pleasures as if for the first time. The same wish, for transformation through costume, appears expressed ironically by Morose, when he tests Epicene by pretending that he expects her to surpass the other beauties of the court in variety and modishness of dress:

... heare me, faire lady, I doe also love to see her, whom I shall choose for my heicfar, to be the first and principall in all fashions; praecede all the dames at court, by a fortnight; have her counsell of taylors, linneners, lace-women, embroyderers, and sit with 'hem sometimes twise a day, upon *French* intelligences; and then come foorth, varied like Nature, or oftner then she, and better, by the helpe of Art, her aemulous servant. (*Epicene*, II.v.68–75)

Jonson seems often to have felt clothes to be (for too many people) disguises, dress-up costumes designed to accompany studied gestures and mannered speech, part of the construction of artificial personalities. Certainly he saw excessive attachment to them as a mark of triviality, an addiction to the inessential and the transitory, as well as a futile and hence perverse attempt to rival nature. Some of his characters display a nearly morbid obsession with them. Nick Stuffe, the tailor in *The New Inn*, when he makes a gown for a lady, uses it to act out a cherished fantasy: he dresses his wife in the commissioned finery, conveys her, in a coach, to an inn, and there throws her down upon a bed. The fact that she is decked in borrowed plumage excites him; it enables him to see her, momentarily, as the great lady herself sumptuously arrayed for his pleasure. Here, in the character who perceives a change of clothes in someone else as a virtual change of identity, we have the reverse of the character who tries to alter his identity by altering his clothes. Each, in comparable ways, finds reality in externals, and each would prefer to replace essences with accidents. Jonson is far from underestimating the expressive power, even the epistemological validity, of externals, but he believes more profoundly in substances and centralities. Carry the assumptions of Sir Epicure and Nick Stuffe far enough, and they lead to a world of total illusion, in which clothes are the only reality—the world of Swift's digression on clothes in *A Tale of a Tub*, or of *Sartor Resartus*—which is also, needless to add, the world of Proteus, the world of the theater.

Wherever we look, then, within the plays or outside them, in structure or in moralizing comment, we find a distrust of theatricality, particularly as it manifests itself in acting, miming, or changing, and a corresponding bias in favor of the "real"—the undisguised, unacted, and unchanging. This is reinforced by a preference for simplicity as against ornament. One of Jonson's most famous poems begins by eulogizing a country house for its unpretentiousness:

> Thou are not, PENSHURST, built to envious show,
>   Of touch, or marble; nor canst boast a row
> Of polish'd pillars, or a roofe of gold:
>   Thou hast no lantherne, whereof tales are told;
> Or stayre, or courts; but stand'st an ancient pile,
>   And these grudg'd at, art reverenc'd the while.
> Thou joy'st in better markes, of soyle, of ayre,
>   Of wood, of water: therein thou art faire.
>
> ("To Penshurst," 1–8)

Nobility here is conceived as a function of plainness, which expresses the sober virtue of the builder. The prized attributes of the house spring from nature—from the attendant soil, air, wood, and water—rather than from art or artifice. Sir Robert Wroth, in the companion poem, is commended for his indifference to public ceremonials. He cares nothing for sheriffs' dinners or lord mayors' feasts,

> Nor throng'st (when masquing is) to have a sight
>   Of the short braverie of the night;
> To view the jewells, stuffes, the paines, the wit
>   There wasted, some not paid for yet!
>
> ("To Sir Robert Wroth," 9–12)

With this disobliging (if witty) reflection on the ostentatiousness of masques, we return to our earlier discussion. The masque proves vulnerable on two related counts—showiness and ephemerality—and the two imply each other. That which is designed for outward show must needs be ephemeral; that which has no solidity to recommend it must perforce resort to display. The same considerations obtain here as apply to the merry-go-round of fashion imagined by Volpone, Morose, and Sir Epicure for their doxies: to lavish ingenuity and cost on mere outsides is to commit oneself to the objects of sense, and to slight the more genuine "subjects" of understanding. But the theater must always do this, and Jonson, in consequence, deeply distrusts it.

It remains to speculate briefly as to why, despite his persistent and at times vehement antitheatricalism, Jonson was nevertheless able to create so many masterpieces for both the public stage and that of the court. We may recall that the wheel of change conjured up in *Cynthia's Revels* originates in the mind of a character named Phantaste. Phantaste alone of the court nymphs is able to let herself go and dream freely. Jonson the moralist may disapprove her refusal to be "herself," but Jonson the dramatist has endowed her with some of the negative capability of his own tribe, the power to imagine herself into a variety of alien shapes. Alongside the well-articulated antitheatricalism, that is, there lurks a less acknowledged but nonetheless potent theatricalism. The fact that Volpone, Morose, and Sir Epicure all think of the garbing of their paramours as "art" serves to underscore the resemblance between the costumer's trade and the poet's, the craft of the cosmetician and that of the playwright. By placing the sanctified term "art" in the unhallowed mouths of these characters, Jonson acknowledges the bond between himself and them even as he repudiates it. The fact that Sir Epicure plans to dress his wench in a "wardrobe / Richer then *Natures*" may chiefly convey the extravagance of his sensuality, but it may also imply that sensual pleasure itself contains an imaginative component which distinguishes it from brute satisfaction of appetite among the brutes, that art can transfigure even the grossest of human activities. One source of ambiguity in the seduction scene in *Volpone* lies in the tension between our sympathy for Celia and our swift responsiveness to Volpone's allurements. How can the plight of the wooden Celia compete with the furious energy of Volpone's mythmaking imagination? How can our integrity resist his spell-binding showmanship? It takes the whiplash of the ending to sting us back to our better selves, and turn us, shamefaced, against the theatrical jugglery we have been cozened into colluding with.

A number of Jonson's most attractive characters possess exceptionally active imaginations, and the power to alchemize other human beings into their own agents—the power to create theatrical illusion. In *Epicene* the power belongs mainly to Truewit and his sly friend Dauphine. In *Bartholomew Fair* it is shared, as a kind of community magic, by all the Smithfield vendors, with their toy shops and gingerbread stalls, their pig tents and ale tables, their games and puppet shows. From a dram of substance they have learned to extract a magnum of illusion. Into all these characters Jonson infuses a heavy current of his own creative energy, which counteracts to some extent the formal disapproval he may think he wishes us to feel. Viewed solely in terms of declared doctrine, we would expect the virtuoso showmanship of Face and Subtle to incur sharp reproof from their creator. In fact we find ourselves inextricably enmeshed in their schemes, and shamefully exhilarated by their triumphs. When, in *Volpone*, the reproof does come, in obedience to a morality imposed from outside, we feel betrayed. It seems likely, in short, that it is precisely the uneasy synthesis between a formal antitheatricalism, which condemns the arts of show and illusion on the one hand, and a subversive hankering after them on the other, that lends to Jonson's comic masterpieces much of their unique high tension and precarious equilibrium.

· VI ·

Puritanism,
Popery, and Parade

"A PERSON," says Hobbes, "is he, *whose words or actions are considered, either as his own, or as representing the words or actions of another man . . . whether truly or by fiction.* When they are considered as his own, then is he called a *natural person*: and when they are considered as representing the words and actions of another, then is he a *feigned* or *artificial person*."[1]

Hobbes' distinction between the two forms of personation may serve to set forth the common ground, as well as to mark the boundary, between what we have already suggested to be two modes of theatricality: the sustaining of a feigned person—or mimicry—and the emphatic maintaining of one's own person, or self-manifestation. The Oxford Dictionary supplies similar coordinates for the verbs *play* and *act*, which may (in general) mean *either* "to sustain a feigned character, make a pretence, act deceitfully"—i.e., engage in mimicry or hypocrisy—*or*, more neutrally, "to pursue a course of action," "to perform a function" —to go about one's business in a normal manner. A man who has "played his part" has done what was expected of him; he has fulfilled the obligations contracted by performing similar actions in the past.

But most men play their parts somewhat inexpertly; they fail to coincide exactly with their assumed roles. And our language, as we have already seen, contains a variety of expressions of disapproval for those who too grossly misplay themselves. In addition to the terms cited above (p. 1), others like *showing off, grandstanding, playing to the crowd*, point to an insistence on being at the center of attention. The

1. *Leviathan*, ed. Michael Oakeshott (Oxford, 1946), p. 105.

155

same notion appears in other languages: in Italian, for example, *sta sempre sul podio*—he's always on a platform—refers bitingly to the man who cannot do without an audience. *To make a spectacle of oneself* means that one is affording undesirable amusement to others, though not necessarily by design. "Stop it! Don't you realize you're making a spectacle of yourself!" constitutes a command to the offending individual, perhaps a child, to take stock of himself, to see that he is engaged in a performance, and to resume control of it rather than be carried away by it.

In all these cases, legitimate self-manifestation seems to have crossed the border into exhibitionism, or into what, borrowing a term more customary in the seventeenth century than today, we might call "parade" (the Oxford Dictionary defines from Blount's *Glossographia* of 1656: "An appearance or shew, a bravado or vaunting offer"). But the border is a shifting one. It varies with time and place, and has altered strikingly in the West in the last four centuries. Compared with the unrelenting antagonism to mimicry, the distrust of exhibitionism is relatively belated and mild, nor does it play a central role in the attacks on the theater proper, except with reference to the immodesty of women who display themselves in public. The word *theatrical* itself seems not to have acquired its overtones of exhibitionism until recently. The first unmistakably unfavorable sense recorded in the Oxford Dictionary dates only from 1649: "That 'plays a part'; that simulates, or is simulated; artificial, affected, assumed." The more invidious sense, and more important to the present discussion, "extravagantly or irrelevantly histrionic; 'stagy'; showy, spectacular," does not occur until 1709. And one curious feature of its later use is that it becomes a term of reproach not only for those behaving flamboyantly in their daily lives, but for those who cannot repress their exhibitionism even within the walls of the theater, as members of a profession proverbially founded on exhibitionism. Stanislavsky employs the term regularly to refer to bad acting, ham acting, and overacting. For Stanislavsky, *theatrical* (*teatralnyj*) means "conventional" in the bad sense. It means "false," "perfunctory," "dead," and "mechanical," the enemy of everything "live," "true," "genuine," "real," "human," "creative," and "natural." *Theatrical* is the word one uses to describe the actor who is aiming merely to amuse his audience, or who practices his craft only to feed his own narcissism. He flirts with his public, "plays up to" it, instead of working out his character in conjunction with the others on the stage. One goal of Stanislavsky's teaching is to train the actor to confine his attention to his own side of the footlights. In this way he learns to shun "the theatre in the theatre," to curb his own driving exhibitionism.[2]

If Stanislavsky, with his naturalistic leanings, seems a biased witness, the same cannot be said for such a pioneer in the overthrow of stage naturalism as Gordon Craig. Yet for Craig as for Stanislavsky, the "theatrical" is "an absurd monster," the deadly enemy of the "natural," which must be rooted out before the theater can regain its true creative function. He explains its derivation thus: the older generation of actors learned to rely on a set of tricks, instead of a genuine discipline, and it bequeathed its tricks to the novices in the profession, who rapidly mastered them. "The young actor," then, "takes the short cut instinctively to these tricks, and this playing of tricks has been the cause of the invention of a word—'Theatrical.' " Craig, like Stanislavsky, is eager to rid the stage of what he terms "the pretty or swaggering artifice of the 'theatrical,' " and to restore to it "the whole spirit of Nature."[3] The term *theatrical* here seems to apply to certain conventions of acting which have excited applause for so long that they have become empty formulae. They promote "effectiveness"; they enhance "prettiness," spectacle cheaply arrived at, or "swaggering artifice," artifice that struts in pampered self-approval and seeks no correspondence with the realities of the mind or the external world.

Theatrical, for these reformers, has come to refer not to the essence of their art, but to its characteristic vices, to the shifts resorted to by second-rate players to compel attention. It is the word Hamlet might have used to describe the ranting of the village Herods, or the mugging and scene-stealing of the clowns. It is what Kim Stanley has in mind when she recalls Lee Strasberg's warning that showing off was not acting,[4] and what Gielgud means when he says that Komisarevsky

2. *Stanislavsky on the Art of the Stage*, trans. David Magarshack (London, 1950), p. 11. See also Constantin Stanislavski, *An Actor Prepares*, trans. Elizabeth Reynolds Hapgood (London, [1937]), and *Building a Character*, trans. Elizabeth Reynolds Hapgood (London, 1950), passim.

3. *On the Art of the Theatre* (London, 1911), pp. 183, 289, 38, 291n.

4. In Lillian and Helen Ross, *The Player* (New York, 1962), p. 14.

taught him "not to act from outside, seizing on obvious effects and histrionics; to avoid the temptations of showing off."[5] Stanislavsky, master of both Strasberg and Komisarevsky, would cordially have endorsed their distaste for "showing off." By all these practitioners of the theater, exhibitionism is rejected as baneful, and their rejection, as spokesmen for an institution that must depend on the exhibitionist impulse for so much of its vitalizing energy, suggests the deep uneasiness felt toward it by society at large.

If exhibitionism has tended, generally, to provoke less indignation than mimicry, the reason is plain enough: mimicry involves conscious deception, nearly always (so it is thought) for wicked purposes—for why would one *want* to depart from truth and nature except to injure others?—whereas exhibitionism merely carries truth to extremes. Even Hobbes, by the language he uses, favors the "natural" as against the "feigned" or "artificial" person. If nature herself, great goddess, collaborates with us in the formation of our ordinary selves, that ordinary self thereby acquires a sanction beyond ourselves that the feigned self, exclusively of our own manufacture, cannot aspire to. Nevertheless, alongside the perdurable hostility toward mimicry, a product of deceit, feigning, and change, one finds a corresponding suspicion of the whole phenomenal world as deceitful and changing. If as for Plato and the severer Christians, the visible is a mere gross caricature of the invisible, then the terms for rendering it acceptable are that it be admitted only on sufferance, without heightening and without being allowed to become a source of interest or pleasure in its own right. Any strong attachment to it necessarily beclouds one's view of the eternal reality behind it. The fact that Plato himself did not always draw this conclusion, or the Neoplatonists, did not deter more otherworldly theologians from doing so, for whom whatever originated in *this* world proclaimed the preeminence of *its* prince. Tertullian's diatribe against feminine dress turns self-adornment into an ontological crime. Since "Whatever is *born* is the work of God. Whatever . . . is *plastered on*, is the devil's work," any attempt to heighten what nature has given is a perversion. By painting their faces, women are announcing their dissatisfaction with what God has made of them, and seeking to improve His handiwork.[6]

5. *Stage Directions* (London, 1963), p. 3.
6. *Writings*, trans. S. Thelwall, P. Holmes, et al., I (Vol. XI in *The*

Tertullian's followers in later centuries ring numerous enthusiastic changes on this theme. They counter the threat of worldly gorgeousness with an ideal of plainness, in dress, architecture, and personality. Not the least grievous offense of the theater, in the eyes of Renaissance Puritans, was the sumptuousness of the playhouses—the marbled columns, the spangled heavens—and the insolent richness of the actors' costumes, emblems of all the carnality that the preachers were struggling to combat from the pulpit.

Similar objections underlay much of the antagonism to the liturgy. The quarrel between Rome and the reformers, according to Calvin, centered on the issue of the visibility of the church. Did the church need to assume visible form at all, or might it exist solely in the hearts of believers? And when it took visible form, was that to be sought in rituals and ceremonies, or in fervor of preaching and due administration of the sacraments?[7] God, avers Tyndale, "dwelleth not in churches or temples made with hands. . . . The temple wherein God will be worshipped, is the heart of man. For God is a Spirit . . . and will be worshipped in the Spirit and in truth."[8] For Hooper, the true church "is invisible to the eye of man, and is only to God known"; "as God is a spirit, so will he be worshipped and served in spirit and in truth."[9] One conclusion to be drawn was that the drama of salvation needed to be shifted from an outer to an inner and invisible stage, with "shews" and "external signs" of worship like kneeling strictly curbed. Works were inadequate as a vehicle of salvation because they too were merely external and "carnal." Those who allowed them priority showed that they were more impressed by the "outward shining" of deeds than by the truth of the law. The effort to purify church observances, to banish incense and images, cap, tippet, and surplice, was an effort to do away with the visible vestures that had come to replace, rather than merely

Writings of the Fathers, ed. Alexander Roberts and James Donaldson [Edinburgh, 1869]), 321. See Tertullian, I, in J.-P. Migne, *Patrologia latina* (Paris, 1844), 1321: "Quod nascitur, opus Dei est; ergo quod fingitur, diaboli negotium est."

7. *Institutes of the Christian Religion*, trans. Henry Beveridge (Edinburgh, 1863), I, 14–17.

8. William Tyndale and John Frith, *Works*, ed. Thomas Russell (London, 1828–31), I, 141.

9. *Later Writings*, ed. Charles Nevinson, Parker Society (Cambridge, 1852), pp. 41, 56.

signify, invisible realities. Tyndale will allow the principle of symbolism in ceremonies, on the precedent of Christ, as signs and promises of grace, but he waxes sarcastic over what the papists have done with it:

... because Christ had instituted the sacrament of his body and blood, to keep us in remembrance of his body breaking, and blood shedding for our sins, therefore went they [i.e., the priests of Rome] and set up this fashion of the mass, and ordained sacraments in the ornaments thereof to signify and express all the rest of his passion. The amice on the head is the kerchief that Christ was blindfolded with . . . . And the flap thereon is the crown of thorns. And the alb is the white garment that Herod put on him. . . . And the two flaps on the sleeves, and the other two on the alb beneath over against his feet behind and before, are the four nails. And the fanon on his hand, the cord that his hands were bound with; and the stool, the rope wherewith he was bound unto the pillar, when he was scourged; and the corporis-cloth, the sindon wherein he was buried; and the altar is the cross, or haply the grave, and so forth. . . . So that in one thing or other, what in the garments, and what in the gestures all [is] played, in so much that before he will go to mass, he will be sure to sell him, lest Judas's part should be left out.[10]

Tyndale thus sees the elaboration of symbolic items of vesture as the useless multiplication of accessories of costume for a part in a play. "What helpeth it," he vehemently demands elsewhere, "that the priest when he goeth to mass disguiseth himself with a great part of the passion of Christ, and playeth out the rest under silence, with signs and proffers, with nodding, becking and mowing, as it were jackanapes . . . . It bringeth them [i.e., the people] into such superstition, that they think they have done abundantly enough for God . . . if they be present once in a day at such mumming."[11]

"Nearly all heresy," Nigel Dennis has quippingly suggested, "is an effort to disestablish the unity of Church and Stage,"[12] and the point is nowhere truer than with respect to sixteenth-century English Protestantism. From Tyndale onward, through the writings of the anti-vestiarian polemicists, the controverters of the mass, the anti-episcopal

10. *Works*, II, 77–78.
11. *Ibid.*, I, 260.
12. *Two Plays and a Preface* (London, 1958), p. 26.

satirists, the admonishers and apologists and animadverters, expounders of doctrine and compilers of cases of conscience, popish liturgy is scornfully likened to the theater, and much picturesque invective mustered to drive the point home. Tyndale himself never wearies of referring to traditional priestly vestments as "disguises." "Behold the monsters," he cries, "how they are disguised with mitres, crosiers, and hats: with crosses, pillars, and poleaxes; and with three crowns!" The true Christian should look only on the word of God, and therein put his trust, "and not in a visor, in a disguised garment, and a cut shoe."[13] For Thomas Becon, the priests come to the altar like "game-players" coming on stage, in "hickscorner's apparel," in "gay, gaudy, gallant, gorgeous game-player's garments."[14] Becon's whole treatise, indeed, *The Displaying of the Popish Mass*, amounts to a sustained attack on the theatricality of traditional worship. The detailed contrast between the Last Supper and its liturgical reenactment turns on the claim that by introducing ceremonial costume, ritual gesture, and symbolic decor, and by separating the clergy from the laity, the church has perverted a simple communal event into a portentous masquerade, a magic show designed to hoodwink the ignorant. Instead of true ministers, the celebrants have become a troupe of actors, a crew of charlatans spouting gibberish to an illiterate crowd. What offends Becon above all is that the spectacular stage effects have actually crowded out the preaching. Their effect is to turn worship into something awesome, wondrous, and remote from daily life, instead of providing sober instruction in the gospel and useful precepts for leading the Christian life. The communicant should not be watching a conjuror perform tricks; he should be listening to the word of God as expounded by a competent elder.[15]

13. *Works*, I, 279, 138.
14. *The Displaying of the Popish Mass*, in *Prayers and Other Pieces*, ed. John Ayre, Parker Society (Cambridge, 1844), pp. 259–260.
15. On the crucial importance of preaching for the reformers, and the consequently heavier emphasis placed on prayer by those of the ecclesiastical establishment, see Christopher Hill, *Society and Puritanism in Pre-Revolutionary England* (New York, 1964), pp. 32–34, 38–39, 46, 49, 52, 67–68, and passim; also *Puritanism and Revolution* (1958; rpt. London, 1965), pp. 48, 269. According to evolved Puritan doctrine, "preaching was the normal way in which God conveyed his spirit into the hearts of men." Sabbath-breaking was hence regularly classed by them as a major sin, "pre-

The charge echoes and re-echoes in the writings of the reformers. For the conciliatory Bishop Jewel, the "scenic apparatus of divine worship" is a "tawdry" thing, which Christians should be able to do without; the sacraments should cease to be ministered "like a masquery or a stage play."[16] For John Foxe, the decay of the primitive church meant that Christ's true votaries were supplanted by "a new sort of players, to furnish the stage, as school-doctors, canonists, and four orders of friars."[17] Ridley informed his superiors that the prescribed ministering garments were "abhominable and foolishe, & to fonde for a vice in a playe,"[18] and when Hooper, in 1551, to the disgust of the zealous, consented to preach in them, he was said to have come forth "as a new player in a strange apparel . . . cometh forth on the stage."[19] Anthony Gilby's *Dialogue between a Soldier and a Chaplain* demands heatedly whether the papists did not play "all their popish pageauntes" in the "garishe geare" of their idolatry in order to blind credulous parishioners.[20] Playing, indeed, and "masking" become tropes as insistent for the ostentatiousness of the prelates as "disguising." Martin Junior enjoins his putative sire, Martin Marprelate, not to fear "these beasts, . . . these *Mar-Martins*, these stage-players, these prelates."[21] And John Rainolds, inveighing against the stage, finds room for particular censure of "the profane and wicked toyes of *Passion-playes*, . . . procured by *Popish Priests*," who, "as they have transformed the celebrating of the Sacrament of the *Lords supper* into a *Masse-game*, and all other

---

sumably because it interfered with the work of instruction and meditation which should take place on that day" (*Puritanism and Revolution*, p. 269). From this point of view, the fulminations against the stage as a sinful distraction from divine workship make good doctrinal sense.

16. John Jewel, *Zur. Letters*, I, 23, quoted in William Pierce, ed., *The Marprelate Tracts 1588–1589* (London, 1911), p. xxi; *An Apology of the Church of England*, ed. J. E. Booty (Ithaca, 1963), p. 144.

17. *Acts and Monuments*, ed. George Townsend and Josiah Pratt, 3d ed. (London, 1870), I, xxi.

18. Anthony Gilby, *A Pleasant Dialogue Betweene a Souldior of Barwicke and an English Chaplaine* ([London], 1581), Sig. G8ᵛ.

19. Foxe, *Acts and Monuments*, VI, 641, quoted in John H. Primus, *The Vestments Controversy* (Kampen, 1960), p. 64.

20. Sigs. E5–E5ᵛ.

21. Pierce, ed., *Marprelate Tracts*, p. 328.

partes of the *Ecclesiasticall service* into *theatricall sights*; so, in steede of *preaching the word*, they caused it to be played; a thing put in practise by their flowres, the *Jesuits*, among the poore *Indians*."[22]

The Jesuits had, in fact, begun using the theater for purposes of religious instruction. As the chief standard-bearers of the theatricalism of traditional religion, they rapidly became a kind of natural antithesis to the Puritans. In France they evolved the custom of staging plays and allegorical ballets of their own composition, with enough decorative finery to attract the fury of their most puritanical cosectarians, the Jansenists. Great was the satisfaction among fierce Protestants when a theatrical performance under Jesuit auspices in Lyons in 1607 met with disaster from the weather—from the hand of God, as it was claimed.[23] And great was the wrath of the Jansenists, a century and a half later, at the costly theatrical spectacles mounted in Jesuit seminaries, with the fathers themselves as playwrights, choreographers, and directors, their pupils as actors and dancers, and the Christian community as paying customers.[24]

"In steede of *preaching the word*, they caused it to be played." Rainolds echoes a charge that Tyndale had repeatedly made, which Becon had made after him, and which had reverberated among midcentury reformers, that traditional liturgy was designed to mystify rather than elucidate. What was merely seen could never be more than an enigmatic tableau until properly glossed and explicated. Tyndale distinguishes sharply between such ceremonies as are accompanied by the word of God and those carried out in silence (or mumbled in an incomprehensible tongue). "The apostles and ministers of God preach God's word; and God's signs or sacraments signify God's word also. . . . Contrariwise, antichrist's bishops preach not, and their sacraments speak not, but as the disguised bishops mum; so are their superstitious sacraments dumb."[25] Without the all-important adjunct of the word, the administering of the sacrament becomes a scene of theater, in which

---

22. *Th' Overthrow of Stage Playes* ([Middleburg], 1599), Sig. X3.

23. *The Iesuites Comedie: Acted at Lyons in France*, with *Recit touchant la comedie jouee par les jesuites, et leurs disciples* (London, 1607).

24. See Ernest Boysse, *Le théâtre des jésuites* (Paris, 1880), pp. 82–83 and passim.

25. *Works*, I, 307.

a pantomime actor, "disguised"—heavily made up and pretending to be a bishop—plays an elaborate charade, "mumming" it in dumb-show.

Plainly, the hardening Protestant attitude toward the Eucharist it-self sprang from a distrust of visible and sensible things. The idea that so much supernatural potency lay in an inert biscuit, or that anything so palpable and localized in space could wield such enormous leverage in the spiritual world, was one that the reformers could not easily ac-cept. The host was too tangible, too readily turned into a fetish, as in Protestant eyes it had become in the ceremonies of reservation and adoration associated with it. It had been turned into a thing of spec-tacle, to be gazed upon and marvelled at. The visual contemplation of it alone, among mediaeval mystics, had come to be credited as "an efficacious means of union with Christ."[26] Becon heaps ridicule upon the paltriness of the wafer itself and the miraculous effects attributed to it:

A wonderful god it is that ye set forth to the people to be wor-shipped. Not many days past it was corn in the ploughman's barn; afterward the miller ground it to meal; then the baker, mingling a little water with it, made dough of it, and with a pair of hot printing-irons baked it. Now at the last come you, blustering and blowing, and with a few words spoken over it, ye charm the bread on such sort that either it trudgeth straightways away beyond the moon, and a fair young child, above fifteen hundred years old, come in the place of the bread; or else, as the most part of you papists teach, of the little thin cake ye make the very same body of Christ that was born of Mary the virgin . . . . O wonderful creators and makers! O marvellous fathers, which beget a child older than the father! And, after ye have made him, ye tear him on pieces, ye eat him, ye digest him, and send him down by a very homely place. O cruel and unmerciful fathers, so to handle your poor young old child![27]

Unsuspected, doubtless, by the reformers was the fact that from the exhibition of the host had sprung the liturgical drama itself and the craft cycles. But most of the implicit connections between ritual and drama seem contained in Jewel's attack on the popes,

26. See C. W. Dugmore, *The Mass and the English Reformers* (London, 1958), pp. 65–72 and passim.
27. *Prayers*, p. 261.

who, without the word of God, without the authority of the holy fathers, without any example of antiquity, after a new guise, do not only set before the people the sacramental bread to be worshiped as God, but do also carry the same about upon an ambling horse, whithersoever themselves journey . . . and have brought the sacraments of Christ to be used now as a stage play and a solemn sight; to the end that men's eyes should be fed with nothing else but with mad gazings and foolish gauds . . . .[28]

There was unwelcome theatricality also in the mimetic aspect of the sacrament, in the idea that the officiating priest was reenacting the original sacrifice, and in the element of displacement, of vicariousness, in the ceremony. It was not for the priest to *represent* the community, as an actor represents other men on a stage, but simply to instruct it. It was for each individual Christian to make his own sacrifice, to offer himself to God as best he could. The mass, like the theater, made the spectator too passive, and the priest-performer too much of a surrogate. The reformers had denied the intercession of the saints; they now denied the intercession of the priests as well. They tried, therefore, to restore the pure sense of the rite by stripping the host of its magical properties, disallowing the ceremony as a fresh act of propitiation, and stressing its "sacramental" force as a sign and memorial of Christ's promise. The ultimate effect, one may suspect, was to downgrade the idea of incarnation, and to make even the original Incarnation look uncomfortably theatrical. Milton's inability to finish his early poem on the Passion seems symptomatic of a certain malaise on this point in the whole Puritan movement.

However, if the Puritans rejected theaters and theatricalism, they gladly adopted the figure of the theater as a metaphor for the condition of sinful man. When they castigated the world, they saw it as the playhouse of God, wherein the virtuous were made to prosper, and the wicked brought to grief, as in Thomas Beard's recital of condign punishments, *The Theatre of God's Judgments* (1597). Gosson and Prynne, in their attacks on the stage, elaborate on their master Tertullian in the use of theatrical imagery, dividing their subject into "acts" and "scenes." Prynne, as we have seen, provides his work with a "prologue" and "choruses," foretells its "catastrophe," and labels it

28. *Apology of the Church of England*, pp. 35–36.

a "tragical discourse."[29] On the title page he translates *Histriomastix* first as "The Player's Scourge," then more freely as "The Actor's Tragaedie." The intent is to use the terminology of the theater as a weapon against the perpetrators of plays. Players are to be shown that whereas they imagine themselves to be acting comedies of their own devising, they are in fact performing tragedies instead, the tragedies of their own damnation composed by the pen of God. The concept of martyrdom, too, was a theatrical one, and necessitated spectators, or at least, a celestial Spectator. *Scaffold*, in Elizabethan English, meant both the executioner's platform and the playhouse stage. To court martyrdom was to claim a starring part on the stage of history, to become a "visible saint," theatricalizing one's sanctity by revealing it triumphantly before the Supreme Gaze. The stage, then, whatever its defects as a human institution, provided a useful set of correlatives for man's relations with the rest of the cosmos, and even offered some serviceable precedents for godly conduct.

Moreover, Puritan repugnance to the visible and the tangible in matters of faith did not prevent their clinging fiercely to it in matters of dress. Opulent attire they may well have mistrusted, but informative attire, which designated the social position of its wearer, they not only approved but doggedly insisted on. No one complained more bitterly than they of the ineffectuality of the sumptuary laws and the consequent breakdown in recognizable social distinctions. On the one hand they believed, or professed to believe, that a man's clothing provided no information about the state of his soul. Thus Stubbes: "It cannot stand with the rule of god his justice, to accept, or not to accept, any man for his apparell." But the most obvious conclusion to which this axiom might be thought to lead—that apparel is a thing indifferent, which should be left to the discretion of every individual—is elbowed aside in favor of a coercive rule prohibiting men from wearing clothes unsuitable to their rank.

As for the privat subjects, it is not at any hand lawful that they should weare silks, velvets, satens, damasks, gould, silver, and what they list . . . . But now there is such a confuse mingle mangle of apparell . . . and suche preposterous excesse therof, as every one is permitted to flaunt it out in what apparell he lust himselfe, or can get by ani kind

29. *Histriomastix*, Sigs. B, B3^v, G^v, 3K4, 5N2^v, 6L2^v.

of meanes. So that it is verie hard to knowe who is noble, who is worshipfull, who is a gentleman, who is not.[30]

What is good enough for God is apparently by no means good enough for man. Similarly, Henry Crosse will first praise the wise heathen ancients for their scorn of external things, which "shewed theyr love to *Vertue*," then fall a-railing at the insolence of base rustics who ruffle it in fashionable apparel, so that "the servant cannot be knowne from the Maister, the maide from the Mistris, nor scarce any mans estate distinguisht by his apparell; but every slovenly servingman, and greasie scrape-trencher will exceede the boundes of his calling, and creepe into acquaintance with velvet, sattin, and such costly stuffe."[31]

We may wonder why Stubbes and Crosse think it so important to be able to tell who is worshipful and who not, who is a gentleman and who not, who is a botcher and who a courtier. If God is unimpressed by finery, and refuses to judge a man by his clothes, should not men aim at a comparable indifference? Should they not try to imitate Him in this, as well as in His constancy, purity, and truth? In principle, we must believe, the state of the soul mattered more to the reformers than the condition of the wardrobe. In practice they feared the blurring of social distinctions just as they feared the blurring of the distinction between the sexes. Any "exceeding of the bounds" prescribed by custom aroused anxiety. In practice, then, their radical theology went hand in hand with a powerful social conservatism. Not only did they wish boundaries preserved, they wished to see them made manifest, inner meanings plainly inscribed on outer casings, and they reacted with defensive hostility to anything that seemed to undermine the traditional reassurances.

The distrust of outward splendor, among the Puritans, must be set against the frank delight in it that characterizes much of Renaissance culture, and the pervasive pleasure taken in the twin roles of actor and spectator. As Northrop Frye has observed, Renaissance (or "high mimetic") literature is full of "the theme of cynosure or centripetal gaze,

30. *Phillip Stubbes's Anatomy of the Abuses in England in Shakspere's Youth, A.D. 1583*, ed. Frederick J. Furnivall, New Shakspere Society (London, 1877–79), pp. 41, 34 (Sigs. C7^v, C2^v).

31. *Vertues Common-wealth: or, the High-way to Honour* (London, 1603), Sigs. F2^v, L.

which, whether addressed to mistress, friend, or deity, seems to have something about it of the court gazing upon its sovereign, the court-room gazing upon the orator, or the audience gazing upon the actor."[32] In certain courtesy books as well, notably in Castiglione, we find, along with routine recommendations of modesty, a wholehearted endorsement of the principle of display of self. The ideal courtier, as sketched by the little academe at Urbino, has as one prime characteristic an unremitting awareness of being on view. It is proper that he seek occasions to exhibit himself, and that he do so with full consciousness of his audience. He will be at pains to do nothing without "a certaine grace," to serve as "an ornament to frame and accompany all his acts," or as a sauce "without the which all his other properties and good conditions were litle worth."[33] He will in fact cherish the grace of his deeds more than the deeds themselves, and avoid deeds that do not allow of it. He will never, for instance, consent to capture a flock of sheep, not even to win a crucial battle: the exploit is too clownish, it invites ridicule, and contains no possibility of being executed elegantly. On the other hand, when he perceives the chance to act so as to enhance his luster, the courtier will try to arrange for his prince to be present, knowing that without the right observers the deed is only half itself.[34] Renaissance literature is full of the metaphor of the jewel and its foil, the book and its frontispiece, the picture and its frame. Precious stones become more precious when beautifully set, as that which is ill-framed loses much of its worth. The courtier will in good conscience therefore do whatever he can to burnish his own brilliance.

And if he happen moreover to be one to shew feates of Chivalrie in open sights, at tilt, turney, or *Joco di canne,* or in any other exercise of the person, remembring the place where he is, and in presence of whom, hee shall provide before hand to be in his armour no lesse handsom and sightly than sure, and feede the eyes of the lookers on

32. *Anatomy of Criticism* (Princeton, 1957), p. 58.
33. *The Book of the Courtier,* trans. Sir Thomas Hoby (1561), ed. W. H. D. Rouse and Drayton Henderson, Everyman ed. (London, 1928), pp. 33, 43. See Baldesar Castiglione, *Il libro del cortegiano,* ed. Bruno Maier, 2d ed. (Turin, 1964), p. 105: "Una certa grazia . . . un ornamento che componga e compagni tutte le operazioni sue"; p. 121: "Un condimento d'ogni cosa, senza il quale tutte l'altre proprietà e bone condicioni sian di poco valore."
34. *The Courtier,* pp. 95–96.

with all thinges that hee shall thinke may give a good grace, and shall doe his best to get him a horse set out with faire harnesse and sightly trappings, and to have proper devises, apt posies, and wittie inventions that may draw unto him the eyes of the lookers on as the Adamant stone doth yron.

"No lesse handsom and sightly than sure"—no less comely and attractive than skilled at his weapon. In this courtier it is a fault *not* to behave theatrically, not to be mindful of beholders, not to afford the fairest possible spectacle. He must estimate the probable impact of his performance as carefully as a professional actor:

He shall never be among the last that come forth into the listes to shew themselves, considering the people, and especially women take much more heede to the first than to the last: because the eyes and mindes that at the beginning are greedy of that noveltie, note every lite matter, and printe it: afterwarde by continuance they are not onely full, but wearie of it.

After this we are scarcely surprised to hear the speaker openly borrow an analogy from the theater: "Therefore was there a noble Stageplayer in olde time that for this respect would alwaies be the first to come forth to play his part."[35] So the fledgling courtier is advised to take lessons from the veteran trouper in how to secure the attention of his audience.

35. *The Courtier*, p. 96; *Il cortegiano*, pp. 201–202:
E se poi si ritroverà armeggiare nei spettaculi publici, giostrando, torneando, o giocando a canne, o facendo qualsivoglia altro esercizio della persona, ricordandosi il loco ove si trova ed in presenza di cui, procurerà esser nell'arme non meno attillato e leggiadro che sicuro, e pascer gli occhi dei spettatori di tutte le cose che gli parrà che possano aggiungergli grazia; e porrà cura d'aver cavallo con vaghi guarnamenti, abiti ben intesi, motti appropriati, invenzioni ingeniose, che a sé tirino gli occhi de'circonstanti, come calamita il ferro. Non sarà mai degli ultimi che compariscano a mostrarsi, sapendo che i populi, e massimamente le donne, mirano con molto maggior attenzione i primi che gli ultimi, perché gli occhi e gli animi, che nel principio son avidi di quella novità, notano ogni minuta cosa e di quella fanno impressione; poi per la continuazione non solamente si saziano, ma ancora si stancano. Però fu un nobile istrione antico, il qual per questo rispetto sempre voleva nelle fabule esser il primo che a recitare uscisse.

The symposium goes on to warn the courtier further that he must not venture to enter a tournament without proper horse, harness, and trappings. He should participate only when rightly accoutered, when adequately costumed for his part. Otherwise he degrades himself and the occasion. Furthermore, he should avoid improper assemblies, such as rustic festivals, where both "lookers on" and "doers" are "of a base sorte."[36] For for him to lend himself to rude sports would be "carterly."

It is clear that the further the courtier can go in the direction of legitimate self-display, the more fully he realizes himself, the more sharply he differentiates himself from the herd. Self-realization *is* self-differentiation. Nowhere in *The Courtier*, except for a minor caveat against boasting, do we find anything resembling the modern notion that deliberate self-exhibition is unseemly. In its place we find only the recommendation that the courtier seem not to be *laboring* to display himself. Instead of an effect of toil, he must cultivate the "Recklessnesse" (*sprezzatura*) that will add spice to whatever he does, make it appear easy, and imply the power to do much more.[37]

But the same precept shows that the principle of ostentation, or parade, can readily shade off into dissimulation. For the laudable aim of self-display, by which the courtier makes himself "acceptable and loving unto who so beholdeth him,"[38] involves a measure of deception. The courtier must acquire as much grace as possible, yet strive to understate it with an air of negligence. The appearance of spontaneity is itself a contrivance, a product of skill and practice. He must use "a certaine disgracing to cover arte withall," and avoid "too much curiousnesse," but the disgracing, the avoiding, are themselves an art. "That," in fact, "may bee saide to be a verie arte, that appeareth not to be arte."[39] The courtier's whole person forms a studied artifact, one prime aim of which is the dissembling of its own artfulness. We could hardly be farther here from the God-oriented ethic of Protestantism, in which eagerness to please others implies a willingness to offend God,

36. *The Courtier*, pp. 97–98; *Il cortegiano*, p. 203: "Dove i spettatori e i compagni fossero gente ignobile."

37. *The Courtier*, pp. 48–49.

38. *The Courtier*, p. 33; *Il cortegiano*, p. 105: "Che lo faccia al primo aspetto a chiunque lo vede grato ed amabile."

39. *The Courtier*, p. 46; *Il cortegiano*, p. 124: "Si po dir quella esser vera arte che non pare esser arte."

where God, and not other men, constitutes the only valid spectator of our doings.

The tension between an older, inner-directed ethic and the other-directed, audience-conscious standard being invoked at Urbino is not lost on Castiglione, who brings it to a crisis between Lord Gaspar Pallavicino and Lord Frederick Fregoso in Book II. We have been listening to a description of the ideal courtier's accomplishments—his dancing, music, dress, choice of friends, playing of cards and dice, handling of weapons, and the like. Repeatedly we have been told, especially by Lord Frederick, that these all must be cultivated, but that the courtier must know how to ply them adroitly, seeking occasions to show off and yet dissembling the intent to show off, mastering a variety of skills and yet giving an impression of negligence, concealing where he can his ignorance or clumsiness, and in general manipulating his talents so as to elicit golden opinions. The long series of prudential maxims finally provokes an outburst from Lord Gaspar, who stands for old-fashioned honesty. All this, he declares heatedly, is not "an arte, but a very deceite . . . it is not meet for him that will be an honest man to deceive at any time." Lord Frederick replies that what has been recommended should be called an adornment rather than a deceit, yet should be allowed even if a deceit. A fencer uses guile in his swordplay, yet we do not call this a deceit. A goldsmith sets a jewel so as to make it sparkle more brilliantly, yet for this deceit "deserveth he prayse, for with judgement and arte a cunning hand doth many times adde a grace and ornament to Ivorie, or to silver, or to a stone that is faire in sight, setting it in gold."[40] No more should we think blameworthy the "wary dissimulation" practiced by our courtier.

The dialectic of the occasion may not require us to take Lord Frederick's rejoinder as definitive, but the drift of *The Courtier* as a whole tells strongly in its favor. Lord Frederick, moreover, couches his reply in terms that ordinarily contain negative implications—"semblant," "deceit," "dissimulation" (*inganno, dissimulazione*, etc.)—but which here

40. *The Courtier*, p. 132; *Il cortegiano*, pp. 252–253: "Questa a me non par arte, ma vero inganno; né credo che si convenga, a chi vol esser omo da bene, mai lo ingannare. . . . Di quello inganno merita laude, perché col bon giudicio e con l'arte le maestrevoli mani spesso aggiungon grazia ed ornamento allo avorio o vero allo argento, o vero ad una bella pietra circondandola di fin oro."

become eulogistic. The domain of artful deception, of skilful fiction, is endorsed not only in works of craftsmen in metal, but in the creation of the human personality. The self is perceived as a theatrical entity, to be planned, constructed, and exhibited much in the manner of an actor's role. Only, the construct must be plausible. It must be capable of being sustained. It cannot depart so far from its natural basis as to turn its possessor into an out-and-out braggart or self-evident liar.

But the theatrical bias of Castiglione's treatise does not end here. We find startlingly approving references to the Roman spectacles, with no mention of their cruelty or obscenity. We find good-natured mimicry recommended as an amusing private pastime, provided it observes decorum, "without speaking filthie wordes, or doing uncomely deedes, without making faces and antiques";[41] it should be suggestive rather than graphic. The provisos are careful, and limiting, yet when we think of the Platonic horror of idle laughter and "recreational" mimicry, we may be tempted to rub our eyes at the distance Castiglione has travelled, in this handbook of Neoplatonism, from Platonism pure and simple.

More anti-Platonic still, and even more theatrical in its implications, is the debate in Book I over the relative merits of sculpture and painting. The sculptor boasts that his art permits an exact reproduction of nature, since "in a figure of Marble or Mettall . . . the members are all rounde proporcioned and measured as nature her selfe shapeth them." To this the painter retorts that sculptured images lack much that only painting can supply, such as lights and shadows. Moreover painters can make things *look* round. They can use perspective to render distance and proportion. They can "counterfeite naturall colours, flesh, cloth, and all other coloured thinges,"[42] none of which would be remotely within the sculptor's power. The engraver in marble can do nothing to convey the glittering of armor, or the glint of yellow hair, or the effect of a tempest at sea, or the smoke and fire of a burning city. And we realize, as we listen, perhaps with a shock, that what

41. *The Courtier*, p. 142; *Il cortegiano*, p. 267: "Senza dir parole sporche o far atti men che onesti, senza distorgersi il viso o la persona così senza ritegno."

42. *The Courtier*, pp. 79–80; *Il cortegiano*, p. 175: "In una figura di marmo o di bronzo . . . sono le membra tutte tonde, formate e misurate come la natura le fa"; pp. 176–177: "Parvi poi che di poco momento sia la imitazione dei colori naturali in contrafar le carni, i panni e tutte l'altre cose colorate?"

this fervent Neoplatonist is recommending is precisely the power to counterfeit appearances, which Plato himself had denounced as trivial and dangerous, and which the ascetic part of the Christian tradition had fully condemned with him. The Neoplatonic tradition has reached the point where it diametrically opposes Plato on one of Plato's own cardinal principles, the delusory and worthless nature of sensory experience, not to speak of the deranging and disturbing effects of sensory pleasure.

For the courtier, a knowledge of painting, if he can acquire it, trains his eye and sharpens his sensibilities. It enables him to respond more fully to the beauty in nature. Pleasure, in this world, is something to be appreciated and cultivated. Far from forming part of the Evil One's design to separate us from God, it forms part of God's design to lure us to Him, part of a method indeed, as Bembo makes clear in Book IV, by which we can aspire to the mystical union. Book I concludes, aptly, with the appearance of "a very pleasant Musition" named Barletta, who plays on his various instruments and sketches out a few dance steps for the company before they all retire for the night.[43] The dialogue throughout thus itself becomes the occasion for pleasure, a mimetic rendering of social pastimes into which we, as readers, are meant to enter, marked by lifelike digressions and casual interruptions, diversionary jocularities, harmless ribaldries. The position of women, we also note, is strikingly high here. They are prized not merely as accessory but as vital to the life of the group, and indeed as its natural leaders and arbiters. All this forms part of Syndrome A, as we may term it, which values abundance, variety, and eclectic appreciativeness, as against singleness, narrowness, and exclusiveness. In Syndrome B women must be either temptresses, daughters of Eve in the most damning sense, or else the submissive underlings that God has commanded them to be. Puritanism, Ernst Cassirer has said, is "a fighting, a thoroughly quarrelsome and quarrel-seeking religion."[44] Italian Neoplatonism, we might add, is a peace-loving and pleasure-valuing creed. Beginning with Ficino, who elaborates on Plotinus by reclassifying *voluptas* as a "noble passion," it is marked, in Wind's words, by "a

43. *The Courtier*, p. 85; *Il cortegiano*, p. 184: "Barletta, musico piacevolissimo e danzator eccellente."

44. *The Platonic Renaissance in England*, trans. James P. Pettegrove (London, 1953), p. 74.

curiously anti-ascetic strain: for however insistent [Ficino] was in explaining the agreement of his philosophy with the Christian creed, he tried to infuse into Christian morals a kind of neo-pagan joy, for which the *passio amatoria* served as model."[45] As for Pico della Mirandola, not only did he welcome and elaborate on this paganizing strain, he also explicitly, and perhaps heretically, denied both original sin and eternal punishment, the latter partly on the logical ground that a finite offense could not justly be made the basis for an infinite penalty,[46] but also, quite clearly, on temperamental grounds, on an aversion to the whole punitive strain in Augustinian Christianity. A positive belief in the value of pleasure implied a refusal to believe in the value of pain. "The Stoic assumption that pleasure must be deficient in virtue, and virtue deficient in pleasure, never gained much credence among Renaissance Neoplatonists. . . . The more comprehensive the virtues and the pleasures become, the more largely they are bound to overlap; and when a pleasure or a virtue becomes all-embracing . . . then goodness becomes indistinguishable from bliss."[47] When we encounter a title like "Pleasure Reconciled to Virtue" as the name of one of Ben Jonson's masques, therefore, we rightly suspect that we have moved into the domain of Neoplatonism, and when the substance of the masque consists of an elaborate series of allegorical demonstrations of this reconciliation, ending with the crowning reconciliation of a dance, we are sure of it. *The Courtier*, a kind of mimetic and practical pendant to the more formal writings of the Florentine philosophers, forms along with their tracts a perfect antithesis to the tradition deriving from Augustinian Christianity, in its frank appeal to aesthetic considerations, its unashamed delight in the life of civilized society, its appreciation of the value of appearances, and its view of morality itself as based on an actor-spectator relation between men.

English courtesy writers, much less given to aesthetic emphasis than Castiglione, are equally emphatic on the importance of appearances. Sir Thomas Elyot, wishing to instill virtue into his magistrates, re-

45. Edgar Wind, *Pagan Mysteries in the Renaissance*, 2d ed. (London, 1968), p. 69.

46. Cassirer, "Giovanni Pico della Mirandola," in *Renaissance Essays from The Journal of the History of Ideas*, ed. Paul O. Kristeller and Philip P. Wiener (New York, 1968), pp. 43–44.

47. Wind, *Pagan Mysteries*, p. 71.

minds them that "by their pre-eminence they sitte, as it were on a piller on the toppe of a mountaine, where all the people do beholde them, nat only in their open affaires, but also in their secrete passetimes, privie daliaunce, or other improfitable or wanton conditions"[48] —a beautiful image of cynosure: the governors perch at so exposed an altitude that even their most intimate doings, which would remain hidden in other men, are plainly beheld, though Elyot adds a characteristically puritanical touch in his suspicion that the "secrete passetimes" and "privie daliaunce" are likely to be nothing but "improfitable or wanton conditions." His strong ethical emphasis is linked to an equally strong Renaissance conviction that substance must be made manifest. Honor, for example, is "but the estimation of people, which estimacion is nat every where perceyved, but by some exterior signe, and that is either by laudable reporte, or excellencie in vesture, or other thinge semblable."[49] For "other thinge semblable" we might read, e.g., "armorial bearings." The value of heraldry, to Henry Peacham, lies in the fact that it publishes to the world the merit that might otherwise remain unguessed at; it provides "outward ensignes and badges of Vertue" which permit men to distinguish "ancient descended & deserved" gentlemen from intruding upstarts, "shot up with the last nights Mushroome."[50] The nobility is exhorted to remember that it stands in the public gaze, and to behave accordingly. Not only must noblemen perform fair deeds, they must set them fairly forth:

There is no one thing that setteth a fairer stampe upon Nobility then evennesse of Carriage, and care of our Reputation, without which our most gracefull gifts are dead and dull, as the Diamond without his foile: for hereupon as on the frontispice of a magnificent Pallace, are fixed the eyes of all passengers, and hereby the heigth of our Judgements (even our selves) is taken; according to that of the wiseman, *By gate, laughter, and apparell, a man is knowne what he is.*[51]

Even the authority of the illustrious "wiseman" (*Ecclesiasticus*) does not alter the fact that gait, laughter, and apparel are precisely the externals that tell in the theater, that have weighty social implications

48. *The Boke Named The Governour*, ed. Foster Watson, Everyman ed. (London, [1907]), p. 119.
49. Ibid., p. 200.
50. *The Compleat Gentleman*, 2d ed. (London, 1634), Sigs. X6ᵛ–X7.
51. Ibid., Sig. 2F2.

but are morally insignificant. Peacham's aristocrats, like Elyot's, sit in a theater of gazes, in "the eyes of all passengers," which they cannot choose but heed.

Just as, for the Puritans, the religion of the papists always comes down to a version of theater, so, for the writers on courtly manners, the court. Eustache du Refuge announces that "the *Court* is an emminent and conspicuous *Theatre*, exposd to the sight and eyes of the world,"[52] and his fellow composers of manuals of courtesy would agree. For Nicholas Faret, the *honnête homme* who is the subject and object of his treatise must learn how to show himself off to best advantage.

It is not sufficient to have merit, he must know how to expose it to view. Industry helps much to make virtue glorious . . . . I would therefore . . . that whensoever our honest man shall make his first entry into any great mans house, or meet in any assembly, whereas all their countenances shall be unknowne unto him, as well as the humors of the persons which are present, he should cause a good opinion to be conceived of his spirit, before hee doth produce his person.[53]

Like a character in a play, the gentleman must make an effective entrance. This he can do by advance planning, so as to predispose others in his favor. Interestingly, this bit of advice, which probably derives from Castiglione, contradicts many of Faret's other prescriptions. His treatise, addressed to the bourgeois social climber, tends generally to recommend self-effacement rather than self-assertion. Like Grimaldi

52. Eustache du Refuge, *A Treatise of the Court, or Instructions for Courtiers*, trans. John Reynolds (London, 1622), Sig. B2. See [Refuge,] *Traicté de la Court* ([Paris], 1615), Sig. A3: "La Court est un theatre haut eslevé & exposé a la veuë de tout le monde."

53. Nicholas Faret, *The Honest Man: or, The Art to please in Court*, trans. E[dward] G[rimestone] (London, 1632), Sigs. K8ᵛ–K9ᵛ. See Faret, *L'honneste homme, ou l'art de plaire à la court*, ed. M. Magendie (Paris, 1925), p. 59: "Ce n'est pas tout que d'avoir du merite, il le faut sçavoir debiter et le faire valoir. L'industrie ayde beaucoup à faire esclater la vertu. . . . Je voudrois donc . . . que toutes les fois que nostre Honeste-homme fera sa premiere entrée dans quelque grande maison, ou qu'il devra se rencontrer en quelque assemblée, où tous les visages luy seront inconneus, aussi bien que les humeurs des personnes qui s'y treuveront, il y eust fait semer une bonne opinion de son esprit, devant que d'y produire sa personne."

Robio, Faret echoes Castiglione's warning against mingling with those of inferior social rank: the prince's followers should shun contact with men of "vile and abject soul."[54] Faret urges his *honnête homme* to avoid associating with the rabble, or those of low reputation, lest he tarnish his own.[55] Even the pragmatic Della Casa declares that "It is not inoughe for a man, to doe things that be good: but hee must also have a care, hee doe them with a good grace."[56]

Francis Bacon probes the morality of display more keenly than most of the courtesy writers. "He that is only Reall, had need have Exceeding great Parts of Vertue: As the Stone had need to be Rich, that is set without Foile."[57] For those aspiring to military command, "*Vaine-Glory* is an Essentiall Point," and even for scholars, the flight of their renown is bound to be sluggish "without some Feathers of *Ostentation*." Some of the greatest men in history—Socrates, Aristotle, Galen —"were Men full of *Ostentation*."[58] An admixture of vanity works, like varnish on ceilings, both to brighten and to preserve reputation. All this is not so much to discommend virtue as to acknowledge the facts of an imperfect world. Bacon neither rejects display as immoral nor endorses it as a principle; he simply bows to its power in human affairs. God can distinguish true worth with or without a "foil"; God can dispense with the theater; men cannot.

The theatricality approved in *The Courtier* differs in obvious ways from that endorsed in *The Prince*, yet the two share some meaningful resemblances. The display of the self, in Castiglione, can no more do without a tinge of calculation than can the program of the successful ruler. Both are achievements of art which may bear only an oblique relation to the underlying facts of nature. Both involve a deliberate

54. Pelegro de Grimaldi Robio, *Discorsi* (Genoa, 1543), Sig. B6ᵛ: "Huomini di animo vile & abietto."

55. *The Honest Man*, Sigs. M3ᵛ–M4ᵛ.

56. Giovanni della Casa, *Galateo of Manners and Behaviours*, trans. Robert Peterson, ed. J. E. Spingarn (1576; rpt. Boston, 1914), p. 102. See *Il Galateo di Mons. Giovanni della Casa*, ed. Giovanni Tinivella, 3 ed. rev. (Milan, 1949), p. 245: "Non si dee adunque l'uomo contentare di fare le cose buone; ma dee studiare di farle anco leggiadre."

57. "Of Ceremonies and Respects," in *Essays*, ed. Geoffrey Grigson (Oxford, 1937), p. 210.

58. "Of Vaine-Glory," in *Essays*, p. 217.

process of self-cultivation and self-transformation. Perhaps the crucial difference lies in the fact that Machiavelli's ruler is assumed to be interested chiefly in the seizure and maintenance of power, whereas the courtier has a loftier aim, the service of his prince. His role is not self-centered, but dictated by a high-minded and disinterested loyalty. Book IV especially shifts the emphasis from the aesthetic to the ethical. It rejects flattery as a betrayal of a sacred trust. It reaches a point, indeed, where the courtier's role is conceived as so exalted that in order to find adequate models for it one must go back to Plato and Aristotle themselves: "It is plainely to be seene that they practised the deeds of Courtiership, and gave themselves to this end, the one with the great Alexander, the other with the kinges of Sicilia."[59]

If there are Machiavellian implications in Castiglione, then, Castiglione takes pains to subordinate them. They surface uncontrolled however in the writings of his disciples, who rapidly lose both the poised aestheticism of their master and his ethical passion. The disciples are more utilitarian in their bent, more coarse-grained in sensibility. Instead of teaching the neophyte how to fashion himself into a harmonious human being, able to adorn his society and inspire virtue in his prince, they would teach him how to survive in a predatory world. Far from rejecting flattery, they recommend it as a practical necessity. Grimaldi Robio tells the novice that he must behave so that his lord will think him valiant.[60] Naturally, it is better if he be so indeed, but the main thing is that he be thought so. In Philibert de Vienne's *Le philosophe de court* we find a curious instance of a subgenre of anti-courtly satire that seems to have come into existence largely in reaction against *The Courtier* itself, in which the lying, the masking, and dissembling recommended by other writers are presented with hot irony as a baseness no good man would stoop to. In its original version a biting attack on the duplicities of the French court under Catherine de Medici, the *Philosophe* seems to have been misconstrued by its English translator and turned into one more straightforward celebration of

59. *The Courtier*, p. 299; *Il cortegiano*, p. 508: "Si vede chiaramente che fecero l'opere della cortegiania ed attesero a questo fine, l'un con Alessandro Magno, l'altro con i re di Sicilia."

60. *Discorsi*, Sig. B3–B3ᵛ: "Conviene, che voi in guisa vi disportiate, che'l Signor vostro si faccia a credere, che voi siete (come se dice hoggidí) valent'huomo."

courtly wiles, in which the duplicities abhorred by Philibert are recommended without irony.[61]

By the time we reach the seventeenth century, in any case, wiliness has become an indispensable part of the courtier's arsenal of qualities. Faret, in a chapter on "suppleness" and "moderation," makes it clear that his honest man will of course be able to dissemble, and that one mark of the noble soul indeed is its capacity to adapt itself to various forms.[62] Without being expressly named, Proteus here moves into the picture as a model and even an ethical ideal. The noble soul must only take care not to let his face contradict his tongue; he must feign skilfully enough to keep from giving himself away. Similarly, for Eustache du Refuge, the successful courtier must number "civility," "affability," "compliments," and "promptitude to give pleasure" among his assets.[63] These need not of themselves entail deceit, yet it is admitted that their honorable possessor may sometimes be required to copy the vices and debaucheries of his associates as well as their virtues, since at court one must be ready to conform to all dispositions.[64] Lying and flattering, though unforgivable if they lead one to praise wickedness, may nevertheless be excused if they are only meant to give pleasure.[65] Moreover, one must protect oneself. To be unable to conceal one's game is to play into the hands of one's enemies.[66] For the hangers-on of princes, then, guile must become a way of life. Without it one can neither please one's lord nor defend oneself against rivals. Castiglione's quest for beauty in daily life and his impassioned idealism now seem equally remote.

Having justified it in theory, Refuge proceeds to inspect dissimulation more practically, describing the specific forms it takes, the occa-

61. My attention was called to this obscure item and its English translation by Daniel Javitch, "*The Philosopher of the Court*: A French Satire Misunderstood," *Comparative Literature* 23 (1971): 97–124.

62. *L'honneste homme*, p. 69: "De la souplesse et moderation d'esprit"; p. 70: "De la complaisance"; p. 72: "Principal precepte de la complaisance," etc.

63. *Traicté de la court*, Sig. A3ᵛ, et seq.: "Les parties plus necessaires a un homme de Court sont la Civilité, et la Promptitude de faire plaisir."

64. Ibid., Sig. G: "Il est bien vray que quelquefoys l'on est contraint d'imiter les vices & desbauches aussy bien que les vertus de ceux avec lesquelz l'on converse."

65. Ibid., Sigs. H7ᵛ–H8.

66. Ibid., Sig. I.

sions on which it is lawful to resort to it, and how it may be detected in others. Book I of his treatise ends with the melancholy reflection that those who truly wish to lead a blameless life must shun the court entirely, for the court, "a great whore," has too often corrupted the chaste and the upright.[67] Book II, picking up at this point, laments the need to practice the ruses already recommended in Book I, and suggests ways to mitigate them, such as mingling truth with one's flattery, soothing the impulsiveness of wilful princes, etc., while all the while still armoring oneself by disguising one's resentments.

This rather uneasy tacking back and forth between a newer, theatrical morality and an older, essentialist ethic lends a slightly schizoid air to Refuge's treatise. A similar discomfort marks the *Politiche considerationi* of Camillo Baldi (1625), which on the one hand strenuously promotes the arts of dissembling, and on the other strenuously denies that it is doing so. Baldi enumerates three "mantles" in which the shrewd courtier must envelop himself: one of religion, one of virtue, a third of dissimulation.[68] The metaphor of the mantles recalls Machiavelli, since it implies that virtue and religion need be no more—indeed should be no more—than wrappings assumed as disguises for practical ends. A second layer of deceit, or perhaps merely of confusion, comes with the mantle of dissimulation, for this would seem to be the mantle of a mantle, the covering up of what is already covered up. Finally, a third injunction appears to add still another mantle: the disguise itself should be carefully disguised, or it will be detected. What emerges from all of this is not so much an intricate layering of deceptions as a simple, though clumsily managed insistence on deception as the master key to success. Instructions on adulation now follow—where, when, and how to practice it. Without warning, however, the author seems to awaken, as from a trance, to the moral heresies he is uttering, and to recoil from them:

It should not for that come into anyone's mind, that I am praising adulation and dissimulation, which are forms of lying, and lying is

67. Ibid., Sig. K7: "Celuy qui veut mener une vie du tout innocente & esloignée du train ordinaire de vivre des hommes, . . . fera beaucoup mieux de ne se point jetter a la Court, qui est . . . une grande putain laquelle corrompt aucunesfoys les plus entiers & les plus chastes."

68. *Politiche considerationi sopra una lettera d'Anton' Perez* (Milan, 1625), Sigs. D5-E^v.

opposed to the truth which is God himself . . . . But I say merely that unfortunately today these are used, and where they are born, and how, so that whoever wishes to profess true honor, must abstain from them.[69]

But the manual, clearly, is not addressed to those who profess "true honor," nor does it indicate the road to it. A moment later, the spell of pragmatism has fallen again, and we are learning how to avoid the fate of Sejanus, who, by becoming too dependent on Tiberius' favor, had nowhere to turn when that was withdrawn. The solution, it seems, is to possess two faces: one for the prince—the face of a young man, humble, docile, eager to please, but of only modest talent—and one for the people—that of an older man, experienced, authoritative, but weary of public service and longing for retirement.[70] Further chapters expound further unedifying maxims. One expatiates on adulation as the staple food of princes, which must be doled out to them by anyone expecting their favor, but cunningly, not poured out heavily as a food in itself, but sprinkled as a condiment to sweeten and enhance the palatability of other food.[71] But, again, before he concludes his tract, Baldi is issuing disclaimers, assuring his readers that they are mistaken if they think he is presenting adulation and feigning as good things. He wishes to make it clear that he regards them as no less deadly than aconite or vipers.[72]

69. Ibid., Sig. F: "Non perciò dovrà cader nell'animo ad alcuno, ch'io lodi l'adulatione, e la simulatione, che sono sorti di bugie, e la bugia è opposta alla verità, ch'è Dio stesso. . . . Ma dico solo, che pur troppo hoggi s'adopera, e dove nasce, e come, accioche chi vuol fare professione d'huomo da bene, se ne debba astenere."

70. Ibid., Sigs. H2ᵛ–H3: "Deve il favorito haver due faccie; . . . la faccia del giovane ubbidiente, umile, mansueta, saggia, e di mediocre prudenza, deve esser voltata al Rè. . . . L'altra faccia, ch'è d'huomo di molta età, di molta sperienza, ed autorità, fastidito da travagli, desideroso di ritirarsi prestissimo alla quiete . . . sia rivolto verso il Popolo. . . ."

71. Ibid., Sigs. L3 ff.: "Dubitatione XVII. Se l'adulatione sia la propria vivanda del Principe."

72. Ibid., Sig. P3:

Se verrà caso già mai, che alcuno legga questa scrittura, potria forsi credere, così à prima vista, che si lodasse l'adulatione, e le fittioni, come cose buone e pur è notorio, ch'elle sono mere bugie, trovate dalla malitia de gl'huomini, per procacciarsi quindi il proprio comodo, con la vergogna, e ruina altrui; cosa totalmente contra la carità, e la retta ragione. Primieramente adunque sarà parte di quell'huomo da bene, in

Baldi thus appears painfully caught between his belief in an older morality and his hard-earned knowledge of how men in courts actually behave. When we reach Torquato Accetto's little treatise, *Della dissimulatione onesta*, the title itself informs us that we have crossed a watershed. Accetto converts dissimulation from a dyslogistic into a eulogistic term, from one suggesting self-serving prudence to one suggesting Christian piety. It began, he tells us, when Adam clothed his nakedness in leaves, and ever since, it has been indispensable in human affairs. More philosophically, it can be explained by the difference between the divine mind and the created world. The divine mind, being invariable, contains but a single immutable truth. This in the created mind must change, passing from true to false as opinion varies, and altering as objects alter. "Only in the eternal light is the truth always true." Dissimulation then is no more than "a veil composed of fair shadows," from which we do not so much project falsehood as "give some respite to the truth." "As nature has wished that in the order of the universe there be day and night, so it is fitting that in the round of human effort there be shadow and light."[73] Physical beauty, we are assured, is no other than a gracious dissimulation of that which at bottom remains unchangeable. In the realm of daily action, dissimulation means patience above all, the power to master one's passions, to bow uncomplainingly to the will of one's superiors, and to conceal unacceptable truths under veils of decency, as his sons covered the naked Noah when they found him drunk, and so performed a pious filial act.

With this fanciful attempt to rehabilitate a suspect word, and indeed a whole suspect concept, Accetto seems to echo the Neoplatonic view of the relations between the divine unity and the created multiplicity, and to draw similar ethical conclusions. Instead of decreeing, with the Puritans, that the oneness of God must serve as model for human ac-

mano di cui capitaranno questi discorsi, di havere per fermo, e sicuro principio, che la bugia, l'adulatione, e la simulatione sono cose di sua natura cattive, e da fuggirsi, come l'Aconito, il Napello, e le vipere stesse.

73. *Della dissimulatione onesta* (1641), con pref. di Benedetto Croce (Bari, 1928), p. 22: "Sol dunque nell'eterna luce il vero è sempre vero"; p. 26: "Non essendo altro il dissimulare che un velo composto di tenebre oneste . . . da che non si forma il falso, ma si dà qualche riposo al vero"; p. 27: "E come la natura ha voluto che nell'ordine dell'universo sia il giorno e la notte, cosí convien che nel giro dell'opere umane sia la luce e l'ombra."

tivity, Accetto follows Ficino and Pico in concluding that it can be apprehended only through joyful participation in the bounty of the universe—that even in the realm of truth, human existence must admit lights and shades, in the form of disguisings and deceptions. Accetto thus elaborates a morality in which the theatrical is not simply tolerated but actively welcomed as a reflection of the diversity of creation. He does so, it must also be added, at a certain cost, keeping himself on a level of rather colorless abstraction, rarely descending into the particulars of daily life in which the courtly manuals, most of them, are so uncomfortably and even painfully enmeshed.

We may seem to have drifted far from our original mooring in ostentation. But the purpose has been to show how a doctrine of ostentation, like Castiglione's, can verge on and ultimately become a doctrine of dissimulation. Exhibitionism inevitably involves exhibiting oneself in a particular way. The more sharply that way is defined, the more it crystallizes into a distinct code of behavior, the more it tends to become an impersonation, a deception. Castiglione thus turns out to be a benign cousin of Machiavelli.

So much becomes plainer still with the seventeenth-century Spanish Jesuit Baltasar Gracián, in whose manuals of courtly service we encounter a truly radical doctrine of ostentation, and an explicit apology for it. If realities are to be apprehended—so runs the argument—appearances are necessary, for what is not seen is as if it were not known. The Puritans might not have been much disturbed by such a prospect, since what was invisible to man would always be seen by God, but for Gracián man is the measure of things, and God's point of view is left out of account. The external world, far from being a mere distracting decor, comes close to being the only reality. Appearance and reality merge confusingly. In an exemplary fable, the peacock, arraigned for pride by his envious fellow birds, defends himself by pointing to his unquestioned beauty. "Why don't they condemn my Beauty it self, as well as the Appearance of it?" he inquires sharply. "Of what Use would all the Wonders of Nature be, if they were doom'd to an eternal Invisibility?" The fox, called to referee the dispute, pronounces in favor of the peacock. " 'Tis . . . undeniable," he concludes, "that Appearance is absolutely necessary, and gives Things in some Measure a second Existence."[74] His final judgment, instead of forbidding the peacock

74. *The Compleat Gentleman* [*El discreto*], trans. T. Saldkeld (London,

to spread his tail, licenses him to do so, with the proviso that to avoid pride, the peacock be also required, whenever he displays himself, to gaze down at his own proverbially ugly feet.

Ostentation, then, is allowed, even encouraged, if reality vouch for it. Otherwise it becomes vanity. But what is the meaning of the distinction between "appearance" and "reality" in the case of the peacock's beauty, which is itself only an appearance? If the peacock, neglecting the second half of the fox's sentence, were to preen himself but ignore his ugly feet, not all the genuine splendor of his plumage could rescue him from vanity. The point of the fable seems to be to discriminate ostentation, or permissible self-revelation, from forbidden vanity, but the fable itself blurs the distinction, and the two qualities end by seeming equally innocent, or equally reprehensible.

Jean Rousset has shown brilliantly that ostentation, in Gracián, is linked to dissimulation: both stem from calculation.[75] The "oracular" maxims range from those favoring judicious self-assertion to those that recommend dissembling pure and simple. At the former end of the scale we find precepts that might have been quarried from Castiglione: "*To be able to put a value upon what one doeth,*" or "*To doe all things, as in the presence of witnesses,*" or, again, "*To revive one's Reputation from time to time* . . . . as the Sun doth, which so often changes Horizons and Theatres."[76] Occupying a more ambiguous middle ground are such rubrics as "*To doe, and make it appear,*" under which we learn that "Things go not for what they are, but for what they appear to be. To know how to doe, and to know how to shew it, is a double knowledge. What is not seen, is as if it had no being."[77] This is the peacock's

1730), pp. 111, 115. See Baltasar Gracián, *Tratados políticos*, ed. Gabriel Juliá Andreu (Barcelona, 1941), pp. 134, 136–137: "¿Que condenáis en mí la ostentación, y no la hermosura? . . . ¿Qué aprovecha ser una cosa relevante en sí, si no lo parece? . . . la ostentación da el verdadero lucimiento a las heroicas prendas y como un segundo ser a todo."

75. *La littérature de l'âge baroque en France: Circé et le paon* (Paris, 1953), p. 221.

76. *The Courtiers Manual Oracle, or, The Art of Prudence* [*Oráculo manual*] (London, 1685), pp. 141, 269, 79. See *Tratados políticos*, p. 251: "*Saber vender sus cosas*"; p. 303: "*Obrar siempre como a vista*"; p. 225: "*Usar el renovar su lucimiento,*" "Como el sol, variando teatros al lucimiento."

77. *The Oracle*, p. 124; *Tratados*, p. 243: "*Hacer y hacer parecer. Las*

morality, where appearance threatens to obliterate and replace reality. From the intense self-reference of all of these, it is a short step to injunctions that recall Machiavelli rather than Castiglione: *"To shape ones self according to people," "Not to be a Dove in all things," "To cover our selves with the Foxe's skin, when we cannot doe it with the Lyon's."*[78] Gracián's view of life in society is thus radically theatrical. The "hero" or "courtier" or "discreet man" is admonished to master his part, to perfect his "natural" person and be able to adopt a feigned or artificial person as well. Above all, he is to refrain from unguarded frankness or spontaneous effusions of feeling. He should seek "the most plausible" employments, the kind that invite praise, that can be "executed in the view and to the satisfaction of all." If these injunctions recall the theater, Gracián will freely confess as much, and declare it a virtue. Though holding the actor's profession in low esteem—presumably because of the actor's social insignificance—he makes no secret of regarding the actor's talent as essential to the gentleman's success. "A stage player lives rich in applause: but dyes poor in reputation. To be eminent, in a gentleman, is an undertaking that's set upon the theater, and must consequently be attended with a large applause."[79] The actor's disgrace, evidently, stems not from his eagerness for applause, or his willingness to exhibit himself, but from his doing so for pay, as a hireling. Under the proper conditions of leisure and courtly service, ostentation becomes a laudable course, a playing of one's natural person almost as though it were feigned, a perpetual exercise in self-manipulation akin to the actor's presentation of himself on stage.

Within the drama, which often presents mimicry so scathingly, exhibitionism is more mildly and ambiguously dealt with. If it is virtue

---

cosas no pasan por lo que son, sino por lo que parecen. Valer y saberlo mostrar es saber dos veces: lo que no se ve es como si no fuese."

78. *The Oracle*, pp. 57, 224, 198; *Tratados*, p. 277: *"Cuando no puede uno vestirse de piel de león, vístase la de la vulpeja"*; p. 217: *"Saberse atemperar"*; p. 285: *"No ser todo columbino."*

79. *The Heroe, of Lorenzo, or the Way to Eminencie and Perfection* [*El héroe*], trans. Sir John Skeffington (London, 1652), Sigs. D8, D10–D10ᵛ; *Tratados*, p. 42: "Empleo plausible llamo aquel que se ejecuta a vista de todos y a gusto de todos. . . . Rico vive de plauso un histrión, y perece de crédito. Ser, pues, eminente en hidalgo, asunto expuesto al universal teatro; eso es conseguir augusta plausibilidad."

in a man to play the part of himself well, it is heroic for him to cast himself in the hero's role, and succeed in filling it. Not to believe in one's part is fatal. Macbeth's borrowed robes symbolize for him the trappings of an alien part, and his failure to learn to wear them comfortably erodes his sense of self until it nearly destroys his sense of reality entirely. For Tamburlaine, by contrast, the shepherd's weeds he disdains to wear belong to an identity he will no longer acknowledge to be his; the armor and the curtle-axe, "adjuncts more beseeming" him, proclaim the new conception of himself that he then proceeds to validate with deeds. Marlowe turns the stage into a battlefield; Tamburlaine, in turn, makes the battlefield into a stage, with captive kings and rival potentates as audience. Each of his acts manifests him to the utmost and consolidates his newly acquired natural person. For Chapman's Bussy D'Ambois, similarly, casting off his base conditions with his mean garments, the court becomes a theater where he can swagger, fulminate, and seduce. For both these heroes a deathbed audience is essential; it would be unthinkable for either to die alone. Tamburlaine bestriding the map of his conquests and showering empires on his sons; Bussy dying upright on his sword, outdoing all example for a valiant death—both depend entirely for their substance on the presence of spectators who surround and admire. The final histrionic flourish affirms the performer's chosen essence for the last time, and settles his claim to be what he has represented himself.

Marlowe and Chapman, however, seem slightly uneasy with this simple exhibitionism, as though it embodied a defective greatness, too empty of the contemplative element. The heroes themselves, Bussy especially, seem ill at ease with their own parading and strutting, and for later heroes such behavior becomes far more difficult. Edward II discovers that one cannot be a peacock through mere will. The plumage he tries to deck himself with proves to possess only theatrical—i.e. illusory—existence; it manifests his craving to be treated as ruler rather than the substance of rule. Or rather, we discover this, but he does not. His bitter degradation is to die unnoticed, the lesson unlearned, in a foul dungeon remote from light. As for Doctor Faustus, he finds himself committed to a titan's role which increasingly frightens and bewilders him, but which he cannot escape. In his case, the role, once chosen, seems to possess the character instead of the other way around.

In the face of the worst the universe can inflict on him, Faustus still cannot retreat from his role as rebel back into that of law-abiding citizen.

With Chapman, the Stoic hero he tried to portray in his later plays proved more refractory to theatrical treatment than the swaggering Bussy. Stoicism being a doctrine of *in*hibition, the true Stoic resists dramatic embodiment. The more absolute his self-mastery, the less need for him to display himself, the less need for the outer world to be called to confirm his stature. His greatness, as in the case of Bussy's avenger-brother, Clermont, consists of his capacity to do nothing— except when goaded beyond endurance by the other characters. Clermont's career, like Cato's in *Caesar and Pompey*, would seem to lend credence to the charge of foes of the stage that virtuous characters could not be theatrically interesting, and that only vicious and unstable personalities possessed enough glamor to be usable in the theater. Cordelia, it may be, puzzled critics for so long because she represents an attempt to project in the theater an untheatrical, even an antitheatrical personality. It belongs to her nature *not* to manifest itself, and this is the aspect of it that Lear, with his craving for the "outward ensigns" of love, finds baffling and infuriating. What he finds baffling we also, to some degree, find baffling. Cordelia's "nothing," however morally right and necessary, is also, theatrically speaking, thin gruel: few of us are prepared to live so far from the theater.

Shakespeare provides us with a whole gamut of self-exhibiters. Kenneth Burke has conveniently distinguished between degrees of "purity" in "persuasion": "Pure persuasion involves the saying of something, not for an extraverbal advantage to be got by the saying, but because of a satisfaction intrinsic to the saying. It summons because it likes the feel of a summons." From which it follows that "perhaps as near an instance of 'pure persuasion' as one could find is in the actor's relation to his audience."[80] The distinction applies also to those characters who are conceived as actors themselves. Richard II would be a purer actor than Richard III—not necessarily a better one—because the aim of his acting is more nearly exhausted in the acting itself. Like the peacock, he exhibits himself for the sheer pleasure or whim of it, whereas for Richard III, however much he enjoys his roles, they remain instru-

80. *A Rhetoric of Motives* (New York, 1950), pp. 269–270.

mental to his primary aim of securing the crown. (At the same time, once he has acquired the crown, and lost some of the scope for his acting, the "natural" person that emerges proves surprisingly thin and peevish, with little of the triumphant confidence of the virtuoso of the earlier scenes.)

In the case of Richard II we find a tinge of slightly feverish excess. When this king drapes himself in the trappings of his office, chants melodious verses, and basks in the gaze of his court, what he is really signalling to us is a defect of function. His characteristic reaction, in a crisis, is not to do what a king should do but to try to look as a king should look, to strike kingly poses. In Sartrean terms, he tries to substitute appearance for being: he performs "gestures" rather than "acts." But to do this is precisely to behave theatrically, to concern oneself with creating an illusion rather than grappling with substance. Richard cannot cope with substance, and is not interested in doing so.

If Richard II represents the overacting king, another Shakespearean monarch, Henry VI, may be taken as the underacter, the halting amateur who cannot persuade himself of the fitness of his part. Henry's taste for sovereignty is faint; he turns over the royal decision-making with relief to his wife and his peers. He steals away from a crucial battle in order to dream longingly of the role he would *like* to have been able to play, that of a simple shepherd, but unlike Tamburlaine he consents to remain a prisoner of his unwelcome identity. His feeling for visual symbolism is as defective as Tamburlaine's is assured: at a moment when York and Lancaster stand on the verge of open war, he negligently pins a red rose onto his robes, pointedly refusing to believe that anyone could attach any importance to such a gesture. He thus dismisses all significance from his own acts, as though he were a simple shepherd indeed, and not the king of England.

"Baroque" tragic heroes like Corneille's Rodrigue or Dryden's Almanzor perpetuate the lineage of Tamburlaine and Bussy. Their flair for the lordly gesture belongs indispensably to their grandeur. Rodrigue must report his victory over the Moors in a tremendous tirade before the king. For anyone else to chronicle it would be to rob him of his most cherished reward, the triumphal reenactment of his exploit before its "real" audience. Though in fact relatively modest himself, Rodrigue has a father who does not hesitate to boast of his own former prowess, and to cite it as example for the king himself to learn from:

Pour s'instruire d'exemple, en dépit de l'envie,
Il lira seulement l'histoire de ma vie.
    Là, dans un long tissu de belles actions,
Il verra comme il faut dompter les nations,
Attaquer une place, ordonner une armée,
Et sur de grands exploits bâtir sa renommée.[81]

The context leaves little doubt that we are expected to accept this as an expression of justifiable self-esteem. In the case of Almanzor, as in the case of Bussy, a certain apology seems indicated for his refusal to submit to normal rule. His flamboyant style is recognized as appropriate only to a superman:

What in another Vanity would seem,
Appears but noble Confidence in him.
No haughty boasting; but a manly pride:
A Soul too fiery, and too great to guide:
He moves excentrique, like a wandring star;
Whose Motion's just; though 'tis not regular.[82]

Almanzor's exhibitionism marks him off from the rest of his kind, and so forms an inseparable aspect of his greatness. The faint absurdity of the whole portrait, of which Dryden was perfectly aware, the fact that Almanzor's vainglory must so explicitly be argued, points to the decline of ostentation as a natural privilege even of those in high place. The hero who exemplifies it is beginning to be felt as an exotic outsider, a meteor to be marvelled at but not imitated. Dryden's pedantic derivation of his hero's lineage from Achilles and Rinaldo and Artaban[83] throws into high relief the extent to which he is a bookish construct; and the bur-

81. *Théâtre complet*, ed. Pierre Lievre and Roger Caillois (Paris, 1934), I, 765. See Corneille, *Seven Plays*, trans. Samuel Solomon (New York, 1969), p. 32:

To learn from example, despite your strife,
He need but read the story of my life.
There, in a long account of noble actions,
He'll see concisely how to conquer nations,
How to attack, how to deploy a host,
And build his fame on deeds—his people's boast.

82. Dryden, *Dramatic Works*, ed. Montague Summers (London, 1932), III, 78.
83. "Of Heroique Plays, An Essay," *Dramatic Works*, III, 23–24.

lesque of Almanzor's bombast in *The Rehearsal* suggests that the moment is nearing when such strutting as his will be its own best parody.

The eighteenth century sees the completion of the process, the metamorphosis of the hero from tragic rufflers like Almanzor into bumpkins like Joseph Andrews and Tom Jones, whose appeal lies in their unaffected naturalness. Now it is the villains, the grand criminals, the seducers in Richardson and Jane Austen, who swagger as the heroes formerly swaggered. Nor is it accidental that the process is consummated in the more intimate medium of the novel, or that, in *Mansfield Park*, private theatricals are viewed with abhorrence by all the morally aware persons of the story. When we reach this point, we arrive at the suspicion of exhibitionism that continues to haunt us today. We replace Gracián's axiom that "Man is born barbarous. He is ransomed from the condition of Beasts, onely by being cultivated. The more he is cultivated, the more he becomes man,"[84] with Rousseau's conviction and that of his followers that man cultivated is man degenerated.

84. *The Oracle*, p. 84; *Tratados*, p. 227: "Nace bárbaro el hombre; redímese de bestia cultivándose. Hace personas la cultura, y más cuanto mayor."

· VII ·

Variations sérieuses

As IN ANCIENT GREECE, as in Renaissance England, so in seventeenth-century France: the bitterest opposition to the theater develops when the theater itself most plentifully prospers. The bright day of Aristophanes and Sophocles brings forth the anxious Platonic reaction, the generation of Marlowe and Shakespeare calls forth the vituperations of the Puritans, and the triumphant artistry of Racine and Molière brings down the anathemas of the sternest moralists in the French religious community, the Jansenists. Plainly the theater comes to be felt as subversive, and its subversive possibilities felt as a real threat, when it counts for something in the emotional and intellectual life of the community. In each case the alleged grounds of the attack are essentially moral: a philosophical or religious movement of some moral intensity (Platonism, Puritanism, Jansenism, post-tridentine Catholicism) mounts a sustained onslaught against the morally insidious effects of the stage, and energetically recommends its suppression.

Another curious phenomenon also emerges, to which we have alluded earlier: the playwright apostate. Plato, who cast his surviving works in the quasi-mimetic form of dialogue, also, according to tradition, wrote tragedies when young, and burned them under the influence of Socrates. Gosson and Munday, possibly from religious motives, possibly for no better reason than to keep the pot boiling, forsook their trade as dramatists in order to promote the Puritan crusade against the stage. Calderón, in the throes of a religious conversion, forswore play-writing, to be lured back to it only by royal command, and then only to compose *autos sacramentales*—acts of faith, which exalted the established religion—while Racine, who during his years as playwright engaged in acrid debate with spokesmen for Port-Royal, abandoned the stage more definitively still after his own conversion to Jansenism, returning to it only twice with *autos sacramentales* of his own, for performance at the convent school patronized by Mme de Maintenon. Finally, one must mention Jean-Jacques Rousseau, who started his career as a successful man of the theater and ended it as one of the most implacable enemies the theater has ever had.

From all this one might perhaps conclude that the writers in question, having glimpsed at first hand the squalors of the theatrical life, experienced a revulsion from it which they turned into a principled repudiation. Such indeed may have been the case with Byron, who found the commercial stage of his day such a school of dullness and petty politicking that he renounced it with a vow never to have anything further to do with it. For the others, a further inference is possible: that some of the moral passion that fueled the polemics against plays also contributed to plays themselves, that the drama was able to do what it did in these epochs because of the intense level of moral awareness in the community at large, which found its direct and unmediated expression in the tracts of the antitheatricalists, its more complex and discriminating expression in the drama itself. A climate of intense moral energy, that is, may have helped nurture both the successes of the theater and the virulence of the campaigns against it.

In any case, as English antitheatricalism radiated from the Puritan movement, the dynamic center of moral consciousness in England, so that in France streamed outward from the dynamic center of French moralism, the Jansenism of Port-Royal. And just as, in England, to justify their regressive onslaught, the Puritans could point to the statutes which classified masterless actors as rogues and vagabonds, so the Jansenists and their cohorts could allege such even more terrible precedents as the sixteenth-century Ritual of Paris, still in force in the seventeenth century, which lumped actors with usurers, magicians, blasphemers, whoremasters, and women of ill life as public sinners forbidden to receive communion during their lives or Christian burial after their deaths.[1] To the French as to the English critics, the very existence of such sanctions seemed to prove the case against the stage,

1. See, e.g., [Joseph de] Voisin, *La défense du traitté de monseigneur le prince de Conti touchant la comédie, et les spectacles* (Paris, 1671), p. 191. Also Gaston Maugras, *Les comédiens hors la loi*, 2d ed. (Paris, 1887), p. 108.

for why would such harsh measures ever have been promulgated if they had not been deserved?

Puritanism and Jansenism resemble each other in their vehemence, their absolutism, and their hatred of compromise, but what tends to strike one first in their antitheatrical writings are the differences. It is a relief to turn from the heavy-handed Puritan tracts, with their clumsy invective and their lumbering repetitiousness, to the Cartesian lucidity of the French treatises. The debate in France proceeds on an altogether more analytical, more intellectually responsible plane. The antagonists attend more carefully to the business of argument and the rules of logic; they indulge less in digression and anecdote. They are not interested, like the Puritans, in rehearsing the diabolic origins of the theater on every occasion, or in prolixly recounting the thrice-recounted objections of the Fathers to the Roman spectacles, nor do they attempt to smother their luckless adversaries under the *peine forte et dure* of a shapeless mountain of detail, or by a comma-by-comma refutation of every micropoint made against them in debate by opponents as long-winded and ill-organized as themselves. When one French polemicist, the Prince de Conti, does wish to survey the contributions of the Fathers, he does so not with an impenetrable jungle of intersecting citations that defeat all rational order, but through a well-defined sequence of chronologically arranged passages from each of the major patristic commentators.[2]

The French controversialists also focus more sharply on the actual stage of their own day. Where the Puritans tend to repeat with tireless persistence the patristic charge that plays are idolatrous and superstitious, Conti, surveying the dramatic fare of the theaters, absolves them from both charges; for him, what offends is their impurity.[3] On the other hand, the French writers refuse to dwell on such matters as the sordid morality of the playhouses. They decline to squander their polemical thunderbolts on the whores and lackeys and petty criminals

2. Armand de Bourbon, Prince de Conti, *Traité de la comédie et des spectacles, selon la tradition de l'église tirée des Conciles et des saints pères* (Paris, 1669), pp. 61–178. On the history of the antitheatrical movement in France in the seventeenth and eighteenth centuries, see M[oses] Barras, *The Stage Controversy in France from Corneille to Rousseau* (New York, 1933). This contains an extensive, though unclassified, bibliography.

3. *Traité*, p. 66.

who infest the theatrical milieu,[4] or on the disorderly lives of the players themselves. What concerns them is the content of plays, and how this affects actors, spectators, and society at large. So Pierre Nicole, perhaps the century's most eloquent spokesman of antitheatricalism, announces that he will have nothing to say about the dissolute manners of the players. He will concern himself only with what is intrinsically corrupting in their craft.

On this crucial issue, he and his colleagues remain deeply in debt to Plato, whose writings they give evidence of having pondered and absorbed, unlike their English predecessors; central to their assault is the Platonic critique of mimesis. Nicole, disclaiming any interest in the private mores of the actors, moves to the more essential fact that their trade requires them to depict the violent passions—love, hate, anger, vengeance, ambition, and despair—as vividly as they can. And this they can only do, he argues, by stirring up in themselves these same feelings, by imprinting them on their own souls.[5] Thirty years later Bossuet, speaking not for Jansenism but for the ecclesiastical establishment itself, makes the same point with express reference to Plato. "In counterfeiting or in imitating something, one takes on its spirit and nature." If one plays the slave, one becomes slavish; if one plays the vicious man, one absorbs his viciousness, since in order to express the passions outwardly it is necessary first to internalize them.[6] The spectator, adds Bossuet, in continuing Platonic vein, is infected in his turn. He admires most the player who can arouse the same emotions in him. And Bossuet follows the vehemently antitheatrical Chrysostom against Aristotle in his disapproval of the *eutrapelos*, the man who can turn easily in every direction. Whoever is so mobile that he is prepared to assume any shape, and with no other purpose than to make the world

4. A subject on which, had they chosen to pursue it, there was much to be said. See, e.g., Barras, *Stage Controversy*, p. 43.

5. *Traité de la comédie* (1667), ed. Georges Couton (Paris, 1961), pp. 41–42.

6. Jacques Benigne Bossuet, *Maximes et réflexions sur la comédie* (1694), in *L'église et le théâtre*, ed. Ch. Urbain et E. Levesque (Paris, 1930), p. 212: "La raison de ce philosophe [i.e., Plato] était qu'en contrefaisant ou en imitant quelque chose, on en prenait l'esprit et le naturel: on devenait esclave avec un esclave, vicieux avec un homme vicieux; et surtout, en représentant les passions, il fallait former au dedans celles dont on voulait porter au dehors l'expression et le caractère."

laugh, is unworthy to be called a Christian. If, says Bossuet, echoing
Tertullian, we must have spectacles in order to be moved, if we must
see bloodshed and love, where can we find anything more touching and
beautiful than the bloody death of Christ and the martyrs?[7]

In all of this, despite its occasional reflexive echoing of Plato, and its
exaggerations, we find the glimmerings of a serious interest in the psychology of acting. Nothing of the kind is to be found among the Puritans, who proceed mainly on the comfortable premise that actors excel
at playing rascals because they *are* rascals:

. . . as for those stagers themselves, are they not commonlie such kind
of men in their conversation, as they are in profession? Are they not
as variable in hart, as they are in their partes? Are they not as good
practisers of Bawderie, as inactors? . . . doth not their talke on the stage
declare the nature of their disposition? doth not everie one take that
part which is proper to his kind? . . . . Aske them, if in their laieng
out of their partes, they choose not those partes which is most agreeing
to their inclination, and that they can best discharge? And looke what
everie of them doth most delight in, that he can best handle to the
contentment of others.[8]

In this view the players simply typecast themselves. Those who play
ruffians and lechers merely extend their private personalities into their
public roles. We can, if we pore closely enough over the thick-tangled
skein of argument that composes Rainolds' *Overthrow of Stage Playes*,
disengage a few comments worked into it on the "inconvenience and
hurt" incurred by actors, "in whom the earnest care of lively representing the lewde demeanour of bad persons doeth worke a great impression of waxing like unto them." Or, as Rainolds elsewhere puts it,

The care of making a shew to doe such feates [such as, i.e., "the playing
of sundry parts in Comedies . . . as of coosening varlets, base parasites,
and the rest . . . of sundry partes in tragedies, as of ambitious, cruell,
blasphemous, godless caitives," etc.], and to doe them as lively as the
beasts them selves in whom the vices raigne, worketh in the actors a
marvellous impression of being like the persons whose qualities they
expresse and imitate: chiefly when earnest and much meditation of

7. *Maximes et réflexions*, pp. 252–257, 274.
8. *Third Blast of Retrait*, in W. C. Hazlitt, ed., *The English Drama and
Stage under the Tudor and Stuart Princes 1543–1664* (London, 1869), p. 148.

sundry dayes and weekes, by often repetition and representation of the partes, shall as it were engrave the things in their minde with a penne of iron, or with the point of a diamond.[9]

Needless to say, neither Rainolds nor any other antitheatrical author would extend the same inference to those playing heroes or men of honor. No amount of repetition would suffice to implant *good* qualities in the false hearts of actors. Plays being by definition a pack of lies, those performing in them could never be other than hypocrites and liars.

Rainolds' remarks, in any event, buried beneath an avalanche of minutiae, remain scattered suppositions rather than articulated theses. As for the hapless Heywood, defending his tiring-house colleagues with the example of Julius Caesar, so crazed with rage in his role as Hercules that he slew the actor playing Lichas, such extravagantly legendary precedents could neither validate the actor's art nor shed light on the workings of his mind. It was the French writers who began to probe the nature of the actor's psychic life. To what extent, they asked, did a player experience the emotions he portrayed while he was portraying them? Did he really feel them, or did he merely simulate them? The seventeenth-century answer was, he really felt them. Georges de Scudéry applauds the comedians for their power to metamorphose themselves into the people they enact, to undergo the joys and sufferings felt by their dramatic selves.[10] Opponents of the stage, like Nicole, agreeing, found in this very circumstance evidence of the corrupting nature of the actor's craft. His trade required the kindling in him of passions which, once aroused, he was powerless to quell, and which henceforth decisively tinged his offstage personality.[11] The actor lived by stirring up in himself—as of course in others—all the violent desires and immoderate affections that it was Christianity's mission to expel or calm.

One corollary of this view was implicitly to exonerate the actor from the charge of hypocrisy. If he really experienced the emotions of his part, then he could hardly be said to be simply counterfeiting them. The Jansenists and their allies, in consequence, more rigorous than the

9. Rainolds, *Th' Overthrow of Stage Playes* ([Middleburg], 1599), Sig. D2.

10. *L'apologie du theatre* (Paris, 1639), Sigs. L3–L3ᵛ.

11. *Traité*, p. 42.

Puritans in following the logic of their own position, ceased to harp on the traditional equation between the actor and the hypocrite. But to them the actor's sincerity was worse than hypocrisy. It sprang from an unholy pact between his conscious self and his own darkest impulses. It created a debased version of the passional existence, which competed, in the minds of spectators, with the passion of Christ.

The French disputants, again, more adept as dramatic critics than their English counterparts, deal more adroitly with the content of plays. They quietly shelve the fanatic charge that all stage action is maliciously calculated to inspire direct imitation, and content themselves with claiming, more simply and more plausibly, that the inherent flamboyance of the theater makes it provoke emulation whatever the playwright's conscious intent. They speak much also of the ubiquitousness of love in both tragedy and comedy, and of how it corrupts by supplying not merely models, but a method that can be copied and a vocabulary that can be learned.[12] To those who instance eleventh-hour repentances and fifth-act marriages as proof of the edifying nature of comedy, they point out in their turn, with some shrewdness, that a last-minute conversion to virtue on the part of a libertine hero will scarcely outweigh, in the minds of impressionable spectators, the effect of three hours of seductive presentation of vice, and that to crown five acts of amorous intrigue with a perfunctory wedding is simply to set the seal of approval on passion: the spectators will remember the passion, but forget the wedding—or if they do remember it, they will remember it as the reward for concupiscence, which marriage was designed to curb, not indulge. Nor does it serve, after an entire evening of delicious poison, in the form of subversive sentiments dispensed by attractive young lovers, for the poet to offer an antidote in the form of a tiresome old king, played by the worst actor in the company, hauled forth to recite a few moral platitudes.[13]

The impact of this clerical position may be judged from the guarded way in which the most illustrious member of the theatrical profession, Corneille, defends himself against the charge of making love too appealing in his plays. He grants its centrality, but begs to point out that love in misfortune arouses only pity, and is more likely to purge us of

12. Ibid., pp. 50–51.

13. Nicole, *Traité*, pp. 43–44; Conti, *Traité*, pp. 28–29; Bossuet, *Maximes et réflexions*, pp. 183–189.

the passion than to make us crave it. There is no man, he observes
acutely in the preface to *Attila*, who, emerging from a performance of
The Cid, would wish to have killed, like the hero, his sweetheart's
father, in order to earn her hand, nor any daughter who would wish
for her lover to have killed her father, so that she could enjoy the
pleasure of being in love with him while she sought his death. There
follows, however, at this point, a startling concession: "The endear-
ments of satisfied love are of another nature, and that is what obliges
me to avoid them. I hope one day to discuss the matter at greater length,
and to make clear what an error it is to say that one can make all sorts
of people speak on the stage throughout the whole range of their characters."[14] The wording here is deliberately guarded and cryptic, but
two points seem clear. First, Corneille is disclaiming a free hand for
the playwright in the treatment of character, and setting unmistakable,
though unspecified boundaries. Second, he agrees, or pretends to agree,
with his critics, that love in plays must not be shown as inviting. It
must appear as agitated, painful, and distressing, never as fulfilled
and peaceful. Yet in going so far to conciliate the clerical opposition
Corneille would seem to be conceding too much, accepting the downgrading of love into something shameful and dangerous, to be allowed
only when carefully framed by signals of disapproval, like the motto
"Crime does not pay" affixed to gangster movies of the 1930s. All that
would be needed to satisfy the most obdurate of his opponents would
be to extend the ban to include *all* representations of love, as too alluring
even in its turbulent moments.

The stage, unquestionably, specializes in volcanic emotions and desperate situations. Nicole, adapting Plato, observes what W. H. Auden,
citing Kierkegaard, has also more recently reiterated, that Christian
virtues like long-suffering make intractable dramatic material,[15] so that
even playwrights who wish to depict saints must make them strutting
and vainglorious. The vogue for sacred subjects in plays, therefore, far
from converting the theater into a school of virtue, as its partisans

14. *Théâtre complet*, ed. Pierre Lievre and Roger Callois (Paris, 1934),
II, 860: "Les tendresses de l'amour content sont d'une autre nature, et c'est
ce qui m'oblige à les éviter. J'espère un jour traiter cette matière plus au
long, et faire voir quelle erreur c'est de dire qu'on peut faire parler sur le
théâtre toutes sortes de gens, selon toute l'étendue de leurs caractères."
15. *The Dyer's Hand and other Essays* (New York, 1962), pp. 199–202.

claim, simply aggravates the evil. In characters like Polyeucte it is not their saintliness but their thirst for glory that endears them to the public. In characters like Theodora it is not their religious fervor but the language of gallantry in which they express it that makes them acceptable.[16] On the especial unsuitability for the stage of subjects drawn from the Bible, Protestant and Catholic polemicists are in firm agreement. The Protestant André Rivet reminds his readers that the discipline of the reformed church in France forbids the faithful to attend theatrical performances, above all when the Scripture is profaned. Occasionally, at school, for the instruction of youth, it may be permissible to present a story in dramatic form, but the story must not be taken from Scripture, which exists to be preached, not played. The Spanish bishop Mariana is called in as witness to testify that "It is not suitable . . . for the deeds of the saints to be represented by infamous men." The *infamia* imputed to the actors is defended on familiar grounds: because it is there. If players of comedies and tragedies have been held to be infamous, that is sufficient argument that their occupation is worthless.[17]

As in England earlier, the antitheatrical movement in France couples the stage itself with a variety of other inadmissible activities. A celebrated tract by the Milanese Cardinal Carlo Borromeo, translated into French in 1662, and often cited by the foes of the theater, heaps much harsh denunciation on the sinfulness of dancing. Borromeo, in his own diocesan orders, commanded priests to preach frequently against dances and balls, but especially to fulminate with all the pious zeal they could muster against plays, "which are the source and the base of nearly all evils and all crimes."[18] Nicole, in a phrase made notorious by the acrimony it stirred up, accused playwrights along with writers of romance of being "public poisoners."[19] And as the Puritans had assailed May games, wassails, bowling, and other diversions, along with vain plays and filthy interludes, so the French moralists denounce gaming,

16. Nicole, *Traité*, p. 53; Conti, *Traité*, p. 30.

17. André Rivet, *Instruction chrestienne touchant les spectacles publics des comoedies et tragoedies* (The Hague, 1639), Sigs. B3–B3ᵛ, B5, C5.

18. Quoted in Conti, *Traité*, pp. 59–60: "Les Comedies, qui sont la source et la base presque de tous les maux, et de tous les crimes."

19. *Les visionnaires*, #1 (Jan. 1666), quoted in Racine, *Oeuvres*, ed. Ad. Regnier, 2d ed. rev. Paul Mesnard, IV (Paris, 1886), 260: "Un faiseur de romans et un poëte de théâtre est un empoisonneur public."

card-playing, and other fashionable amusements of polite society, always reserving the brunt of their condemnation for plays. Senault, outlining the diversions open to a responsible monarch like the young Louis XIV, will allow gaming, hunting, tournaments, and dancing, in limited degrees and under proper conditions. Only "la comédie" receives the full weight of a categorical prohibition.[20] Similarly, for Thiers, in his *Traité des jeux*, and for Frain du Tremblay, in *Conversations sur les jeux*, various accommodations are introduced to soften the ban on dicing and other games, but none to lift the interdiction on theatergoing.[21] Doubtless, for such unbending hostility the stage could thank not only the peculiar intensity of the pleasure it afforded, but even more its social and ontological subversiveness. If gambling aroused the passions and unsettled the reason, at least it offered no glimpses of an alluring world in which so many of the taboos of the real world fell away, in which jealous husbands could be tricked with impunity, misers hoodwinked out of their gold, religious hypocrites unmasked, and in which impious grandees set themselves up against the powers that ruled the universe. It did not threaten to replace the rule of law with that of the senses and the unbridled will of the individual.

Jansenist austerity, which more than matched that of English Puritans, traced its psychic lineage even more directly to St. Augustine. The prevailing gloominess of Nicole's view of life comes out in a passage in which he compares human existence to "a universal sore, or rather a mass of sores, of plague spots, of carbuncles, with which a man's body is entirely covered in a frightful and hideous manner . . . among these sores are some which appear more envenomed and enflamed, others which seem as if deadened and lacking in heat . . . . That is the image of the state in which we are born and of what we are by nature."[22] In such a world, human freedom has little place.

20. Jean François Senault, *Le monarque, ou les devoirs du souverain* (Paris, 1664), pp. 205–208.

21. Jean-Baptiste Thiers, *Traité des jeux et des divertissemens* (Paris, 1686), pp. 255–356 passim; J. Frain, Seigneur du Tremblay, *Conversations morales sur les jeux et les divertissemens* (Paris, 1685), pp. 312–313.

22. *De la connoissance de soi-même*, in *Essais de morale*, III (Paris, 1755), 69–70: "Qu'on s'imagine donc une plaie universelle, ou plûtôt, un amas de plaies, de pestes, de charbons, dont le corps d'un homme soit tout couvert; qu'entre ces plaies, il y en ait qui paroissent plus envenimées et plus en-

Notoriously, and even heretically, the Jansenists denied the freedom of the will. Man could do nothing—could not so much as obey the ten commandments—without an express interposition of grace, and when grace came, its force was irresistible. Jansenism shares the Puritan aversion to pleasure, but rationalizes it more lucidly. Pleasure, says Nicole, makes addicts of us. It softens and enervates, leaving our hearts vulnerable to the whisperings of sin. All gaiety distances us from God, and for anyone to suppose that he is immune to its hurtful effects is prideful and temerarious. To expose oneself wantonly to temptation is to repeat the sin of Eve, who insisted on testing the prohibition instead of obeying it. Goodness, then, consists not (as with Milton) in seeking trial and surmounting it, but in fleeing temptation. Nicole goes so far as to suggest that we make it a rule never to follow any opinion that favors our natural impulses, if it has been condemned by respectable people.[23] For natural impulse, thanks to our fallen state, can be trusted only to mislead. In the theater our pleasure amounts to a secret approbation of vice. We share shamefully in the passions being unfolded before us. Pursuing this venture into audience psychology leads Nicole into one of his infrequent false steps. When we truly detest an action, he suggests, we cannot bear to see it performed, and from this it follows that what we like seeing performed we are effectively approving and endorsing.[24] But this is to make Tertullian's error, to confound a play with the rest of life, and to ride roughshod over Aristotle's more down-to-earth view of what actually happens in the theater, a view confirmed repeatedly by experience. Many painful and upsetting events which we would indeed shudder to witness, or even to hear about, in our daily lives, please us precisely because they are taking place on stage, within a charmed circle that exempts them from the fatal and irreversible consequences of daily life. Moreover, even on the ground of elementary consistency, we can hardly approve of *all* we see on stage, since so much of what we see there is contradictory; our approval would be bound to cancel itself out a dozen times within the course of a single

flammées, d'autres qui semblent comme amorties et sans ardeur. . . . Voilà l'image de l'état où nous sommes nés, et de ce que nous sommes par la nature."

23. *Connoissance de soi-même*, III, 81.
24. *Traité*, p. 51.

evening. From which it would seem to follow that we approve what we wish to approve, or, perhaps more pertinently, what the playwright has with his art contrived that we shall approve.

Bossuet's conception of spectator complicity may be designed to avoid this pitfall. For him the spectator becomes a "secret actor" in the play. He lives out its passions in his inner spirit, and until he does so, the events of the story remain cold and uninteresting to him.[25] We seem to hear in this analysis the words of a man who has had some genuine experience of the theater. We may even be reminded of Augustine's discussion of his own youthful theatergoing in the *Confessions*. But Bossuet is not writing his confessions. He makes no mention of the fact that he had, according to his secretary, been a devotee of the drama in his younger days, or that even as bishop—unlike more scrupulous clerical dignitaries, who wished to avoid giving scandal and setting a bad example to their parishioners—he had frequented court theatricals, including two performances of Racine's *Esther*.[26] The contrast between his own self-indulgence in this regard and the ferocity with which he denounces all playgoing in the *Maximes et réflexions* may leave a disagreeable impression, but it doubtless also reflects the unwelcome reality with which the antitheatrical clergy had perforce at this moment to live: on the one hand, the universal addiction to plays, on the other the fierce traditional enmity of the Gallican church toward the theater. "If these directors of the Christian conscience could tolerate the fact [i.e., of the widespread frequentation of the theater], they could not allow their doctrine on this point to be cast into doubt, or contrary principles to be opposed to their principles, or the grounding in justice of the legitimacy of the most pernicious diversions of the century."[27] They were, in short, fighting a rearguard action without

25. *Maximes et réflexions*, pp. 178–179: "On se voit soi-même dans ceux qui nous paraissent comme transportés par de semblables objets: on devient bientôt un acteur secret dans la tragédie, on y joue sa propre passion; et la fiction au dehors est froide et sans agrément, si elle ne trouve au dedans une vérité qui lui réponde."

26. Urbain and Levesque, eds., *L'église et le théâtre*, pp. 33, 39.

27. Louis Bourquin, "La controverse sur la comédie au XVIIIe siècle et la lettre à d'Alembert sur les spectacles," *Revue d'histoire littéraire de la France* (1919), 43–86, p. 53: "Si ces directeurs de la conscience chrétienne pouvaient tolérer le fait, l'habitude définitivement enracinée, ils ne pouvaient admettre qu'on mit en doute leur doctrine sur ce point, qu'on opposât à

perhaps altogether realizing it. Hence the fury with which Bossuet fell upon the innocuous Father Caffaro toward the century's end, and the sweaty arm-twisting and hammer-locking with which he tried to twist Aquinas' dictum in favor of plays into a condemnation of them.

Even more overtly than in England, French clerical antitheatricalism betrays a misogynist tinge. Playgoing is viewed as a vice to which women are particularly prone because of their emotional natures, and on whom it is particularly damaging, since it fills their heads with romantic notions and unfits them for their duties as wives and mothers. This view, which persists well into the eighteenth and nineteenth centuries, brings into sharp focus the difference between the enemies of the stage on the one hand and the Italian Neoplatonists on the other. For the latter, and quintessentially for Castiglione, women are admired and sought after because of their life-enhancing power. Their presence turns the meanest routine to prettiness and to favor. For the reformers, both English and continental, antitheatricalism joins hands with antifeminism as part of the war against pleasure. In this life-denying syndrome, all worldly delights are suspect, as souring men's palates for the more enduring delights of eternity. It is one consequence moreover of the nature of the stage as they see it that the reformers and their allies refuse to believe in the possibility of its reform. Since it attempts to make us laugh or to arouse our passions, and so in either case to spoil our hopes of salvation, nothing is to be gained from attempts to purify it, which simply disguise the evil, trick it out with a spurious innocence and make it all the more insidious. The more honest it appears, the freer of gross situations and immodest language, the more criminal it must be judged to be.[28] Nothing less than total suppression will do.

---

leurs principes des principes contraires et qu'on fondât en droit la légitimité des pires divertissements du siècle." Bourquin's excellent article is misleadingly titled. It deals almost wholly with the quarrel of 1694 and its immediate aftermath, up to about 1710. Evidently a later installment was planned, but never reached print.

28. Senault, *Le monarque*, p. 206: "Plus elle [la comédie] est charmante, plus elle est dangereuse; Et . . . plus elle semble honneste, plus je la tiens criminelle." The argument actually goes back to Lactantius, *Institutes*, VI, 20: "And the more eloquent they are who have composed the accounts of these disgraceful actions, the more do they persuade by the elegance of their sentiments; and harmonious and polished verses more readily remain fixed

As the foes of the stage argue their case more incisively than their English counterparts, so too do its defenders. In place of the inconsistent Lodge and the bumbling Heywood we find the thoughtful Balzac, the orderly and level-headed Chappuzeau, and the moderate, sensible Caffaro. Balzac confronts the ancient canard that plays are merely deception by admitting it and making it a point of pride. Plays deceive, he observes, the better to instruct. Deception enables them to teach without dogmatizing, to convey valuable lessons while seeming merely to tell stories: "O la bonne trahison que celle-là!"[29] The argument resembles Sidney's in defense of poetry. But Sidney shows a purist's distaste for live theater, a fastidious preference for the printed page, which Balzac does not share. Chappuzeau bases much of his defense on an intimate acquaintance with actual theatrical conditions. To the charge of loose living brought against the actors, he retorts, out of his own experience, that most actors lead lives of churchwardenly respectability, which it would be hard to distinguish from those of other well-regulated bourgeois. And he appends an enlightening description of how they actually conduct their affairs—the administration of their business, the allocation of the proceeds of performances, etc. —so as to create an image of middle-class punctiliousness and sobriety. In answer to those who condemn the wearing of women's clothes by men, on Deuteronomic grounds, he notes that in the plays done in the ecclesiastical colleges it was common for the collegians to dress as women, and thus to defy the prohibition as flagrantly as any actor on the public stage, yet not to be censured or called to account for this infraction. He refrains from adding what other writers imply, that Jesuit hostility to the public theater sprang in part from professional rivalry: the Jesuits wished their own productions to be well attended, and disliked the competition from the regular actors. And in answer to those who tax the theater with disrupting and disordering the lives

in the memory of the hearers" (*Works*, trans. Wm. Fletcher, Ante-Nicene Library, eds. Alex. Roberts and Jas. Donaldson [Edinburgh, 1871], I, 408). See J.-P. Migne, *Patrologia latina*, VI (Paris, 1844), 710: "Et quo magis sunt eloquentes, qui flagitia illa finxerunt, eo magis sententiarum persuadent, et facilius inhaerent audientium memoriae versus numerosi et ornati."

29. Guez de Balzac, "Responce a deux questions, ou du charactere et de l'instruction de la comedie," in *Oeuvres diverses*, ed. augmentée (Paris, 1658), pp. 73–96, p. 94.

of its practitioners, Chappuzeau observes that war does the same, but that the church has never ceased to regard soldiering as an honorable and praiseworthy occupation, if practiced under the right conditions.[30]

Chappuzeau's points are neither definitive nor necessarily irrefutable, but they signally constitute steps in a genuine argument. They do not simply reshuffle the same well-thumbed cards, or offer picturesque anecdotes to counter the anecdotes of the opposition. They raise questions which the antitheatricalists ought to have felt it necessary to reply to, but which in fact they ignored. And in so doing they remind us once more of how deep-seated and deep-rooted the opposing views are, how they spring from the total life-views of their respective proponents, preceding and dictating, rather than following, the use of reasoned argument. Reasoned argument in these cases is not an exploratory instrument like Socratic dialectic, but a weapon, not a means of arriving at the truth so much as a way of jamming hotly held beliefs down an antagonist's throat.

A somewhat livelier response to antitheatrical agitation than that of formal commentary comes occasionally from the dramatists themselves, in plays in which they undertake to explain and exemplify the beneficent power of their medium. Such plays characteristically depict actors going about their work, pausing from time to time to defend it. A clumsy instance would be Gougenot's *Comédie des comédiens* (1633), in which a group of theater amateurs form themselves into an acting company. In the course of rehearsal, a discussion arises concerning actors. A spokesman for the group cites their versatility as a reason for honoring them. Most people, he points out, need only be themselves, whereas actors must be universal spirits, capable of representing a wide variety of human types. To this end they must also be "well informed, bold, cooperative, humble, and well mannered, sober, modest, and above all hard-working" ("docte, hardy, complaisant, humble, & de bonne conversation, sobre, modeste, & sur tout laborieux")[31]—the exact reverse, in short, of the shiftless rascals their detractors take them to be. Toward the end of what becomes a rather tedious prologue, the same speaker launches into a more systematic apology, in which various familiar arguments are reviewed: the antiquity of the stage, the phi-

30. [Samuel Chappuzeau,] *Le théâtre françois* (Paris, 1674), pp. 17–18, 26, 131, 134–135, and passim.
31. Gougenot, *La comédie des comédiens, tragi-comédie* (Paris, 1633).

losophers who have praised it, the princes who have patronized it. Unfortunately, the defense lacks any necessary connection with the rest of the prologue, having very much the air of something forcibly thrust into it, while the prologue as a whole lacks any connection with the play proper, the romance intrigue which is being rehearsed and which is afterward acted out in its entirety. The defense of acting, then, instead of issuing naturally from the action, comes to little more than a laborious digression, awkwardly fitted into a context that has no need of it.[32]

Corneille's *Illusion comique* (1636) does much better. Here the prologue introduces us to a father, Pridamant, consulting a magician, Alcandre, in order to discover the whereabouts of his missing son. The magician uses his wizardry to conjure up a spectacle for the grieving father in which he sees his son first as the servant of a braggart, then as the wooer of a young girl, then as her philandering husband, and finally as a victim of the outraged husband of one of his mistresses. Pridamant, watching intently, genuinely believing his son dead, cries out in dismay at this cruel conclusion, but when Alcandre raises the curtain for the last time, it is to reveal the son, along with the other characters of the story, seated around a table, counting out money and

---

32. A play with the identical title, by Georges de Scudéry (Paris, 1635), attempts even more clumsily to expound the virtues of the theater and defend the good name of its practitioners. Like Gougenot's, Scudéry's play consists of two essentially unrelated parts: the prologue, and a romantic tale enacted by the troupe that has been discussing its own *métier* in the prologue.

Comparable plays may of course be found in the English drama of the period. Apart from earlier instances like Edwardes' *Damon and Pythias* (1565), *The Taming of the Shrew* (1594), and *Every Man Out of His Humor* (1599), each of which implicitly takes up the defense of the theater as a mode of education and ethical instruction, a more explicit genre of apology evolves in the seventeenth century. Massinger in *The Roman Actor* (1626) places a formal plea for the stage in the mouth of the actor Paris, in answer to charges of subversion brought by hostile Senators. In *The Muses' Looking-Glass* (1630), Thomas Randolph brings two Puritan bigots directly into the action. By witnessing a morality-like play of the passions, they are brought to give up their antipathy to the theater and come to acknowledge its corrective power. Richard Brome, finally, in *The Antipodes* (1638), devises an intricate plot to demonstrate the therapeutic virtue of the theater on characters suffering from a variety of delusions and obsessions.

dividing it up among themselves. They are a troupe of comedians who have just finished playing the comedy seen by the father; his son is a member of the troupe. Pridamant, at first, reacts with as much chagrin to find his son an actor as he did when he thought him killed, but a eulogy of the theater from Alcandre makes him change his mind. He ends quite converted, confessing that his son's métier, if anything, surpasses his own.

In several respects the play seems designed as an apology for the theater. Alcandre, the master of illusion, is clearly a theatrical impresario. He shows Pridamant the story of his son's life in a series of theatrical scenes, causing curtains to rise, scenery to appear, and time and space to be abbreviated and manipulated. He even introduces each new scene with the customary *coups de bâton* of the public stage. Moreover the spectacle works powerfully on Pridamant, who enters into it passionately, rejoicing and lamenting with the rise and fall of his son's fortunes. He receives it, that is, as truth. And truth it is, though an illusion, and an at least partly imaginary tale. For even the imaginary tale is really and truly being played by the son, Clindor, and his companions, while the final reality of the last scene shows us the down-to-earth facts behind the tale. Yet at the same time all is illusory, since what Pridamant sees is a series of events that have taken place in the past, or are taking place miles away, in Paris, thanks to the power of Alcandre's magic. That magic, we may note, is benign. It aims at consolation and reassurance. When the session is concluded, Alcandre will not even accept payment from Pridamant, declaring that all he cares about is his guest's peace of mind. And he offers a remarkable explanation for the cheerful spirits of the actors. Not only do they share equally in the day's receipts, so that none has any cause for envy, but as soon as they leave their roles, they leave behind the passions of those roles, the rages and jealousies and frustrations. Alcandre thus defends the theater as a means of psychic purgation for its practitioners. Having spent the afternoon hurling violent tirades at each other in make-believe, they have no further need to do so in reality. Playing has effected a welcome catharsis of their inflamed aggressions and swollen egoisms.

Moreover, as Marc Fumaroli has shown, Clindor's rise from rebellious son to wandering adventurer, in which he takes up the successive trades of secretary, notary, mountebank, huckster, composer, solicitor, etc., to servant of the egregious Matamore, to lover and then husband of Isabelle, can be seen to correspond to a moral ascent, in the course of which he learns to speak a progressively nobler language, to behave with greater and greater fidelity to principle, and most notably to despise death. As he gradually comes to turn his natural metamorphic talents to worthier uses, he arrives at a fully adult and responsible consciousness of himself.[33] The final consolation offered to the skeptical Pridamant is that the theater, once so ill viewed, is now esteemed by all. His son's rise in the theatrical world, in dignity of language and in moral worth, reflects a social rise as well, since the theater is now an affair not merely of idlers in villages but of kings and courts. The theater, Pridamant is at length driven to admit, is not what he thought it was: "J'en ignorais l'éclat, l'utilité, l'appas, / Et la blâmais ainsi, ne la connaissant pas."[34] With this realization, the demonstration is concluded, and audiences both within the play and without—Pridamant and ourselves—have been led to appreciate the stage for the ennobling and emancipating force it is.

Finally, in *Le véritable Saint Genest* (1645), Rotrou shows the theater in the most exalted role of all, as the incubator of miracles. The action concerns the conversion of the actor Genest from a persecutor of Christians to a Christian martyr, brought about while playing the part of an earlier persecutor who had similarly turned martyr. We might see this as one rejoinder to those who alleged that actors became infected with what they imitated. So be it, says Rotrou in effect; let us consider an instance. And he proceeds to chronicle the story of an actor who undergoes a conversion to sanctity while playing the part of a saint, and who then sets the seal on his conversion by embracing in reality the martyrdom he has so often flippantly counterfeited. Genest, the actor, himself recognizes that his frequent enactment of the martyr's role has infused some of the martyr's spirit into him, and that heaven

33. Marc Fumaroli, "Rhétorique et dramaturgie dans *L'illusion comique* de Corneille," *Dix-septième siècle*, Nos. 80–81 (1968): 107–132, pp. 126–128. As its title suggests, this essay views Alcandre as both dramatic impresario and rhetorician, primarily as rhetorician, employing as one traditional device of his art the use of vivid enactment to move and persuade his listener.

34. V.v. in *Théâtre complet*, I, 743: "I didn't realize its brilliance, its utility, its appeal, and so censured it, not knowing what it was."

has capped the process by a direct intervention, "prompting" him to take up the tribulations and the glories of true martyrdom.

> Je sais, pour l'éprouver, que par un long étude
> L'art de nous transformer nous passe en habitude;
> Mais il semble qu'ici des vérités sans fard
> Passent et l'habitude et la force de l'art,
> Et que Christ me propose une gloire éternelle
> Contre qui une défense est vaine et criminelle. . . .
>
> (II.iv.405–410)[35]

The fact that heaven chooses to intervene and bestow grace upon Genest should by no means be taken to mean that his profession as actor is irrelevant. On the contrary, it is clear that he has been singled out for favor precisely *because* he is a brilliant actor, able to translate himself so eloquently into new and unfamiliar roles. The theater has *fitted* him for martyrdom. Earlier, we have heard testimony from Diocletian pointing to a theatrical impact of a different kind. Not only can a powerful performance, he tells us, revive his spirits when he is depressed, but the heroes played by Genest can actually, through Genest, reassume some of the power they wielded when alive. For in the vividness of their theatrical incarnation, they seem to come back to life, "plutôt ressuscités/Qu'imités," and are able to offer fresh guidance to their imperial descendant, helping him win new battles and pass new laws, centuries after their deaths.[36]

35. Jean Rotrou, *Le véritable Saint Genest*, ed. R. W. Ladborough (Cambridge, 1954), p. 15: "I know, from experience, that through much study the art of transforming ourselves becomes habitual; but it seems that here unadorned truths are reaching beyond both habit and the power of art, and that Christ is offering me an eternal glory, against which resistance would be vain and criminal."

36. *L'Illusion comique*, I.v.239–240. Apart from Lope de Vega's earlier play on the Genest legend, *Lo fingido verdadero* (1621), which Rotrou probably knew and utilized, there was also an earlier French treatment of the theme, Desfontaines' *L'illustre comédien, ou le martyre de sainct Genest, tragédie* (Paris, 1645). Here Genest, playing out the story of his *own* early life before the emperor, relates how his father tempted him, and his sister urged him, to become a Christian, and how he resisted their pleas, consenting to be baptized only in order to save his inheritance. But the baptism worked, by miracle, and made him truly a Christian. The outraged Di-

One difference between the English and French antagonists to the stage lies in the greater social sophistication of the latter. The antitheatrical Puritans tend to come from a lower social stratum. They reflect a tradesman's mentality in their concern for the chastity of citizens' wives, the good order of the shopkeepers' apprentices, and the authority of the London magistracy. The Jansenists and their friends, on the other hand, form a clerical intelligentsia that maintains close links with polite society, including in some instances the highest reaches of the aristocracy. Perhaps it is partly on this account that whereas in England the Puritan movement found itself repeatedly thwarted by the court in its efforts to censor or suppress the stage, in France clerical opposition managed to infiltrate the inner sanctum of the court itself, winning first the queen and then at length the king himself to its cause. One is not surprised therefore to find links between Port-Royal itself, the stronghold of Jansenism, and such brilliant worldlings as Pascal and La Rochefoucauld. In the latter's *Maximes* and *Réflexions diverses* we find a complete antitheatrical morality worked out by one who has grasped at first hand the virtually inescapable theatricality of everyday life.

La Rochefoucauld resembles Machiavelli, Gracián, and also Hobbes in the unsparing nature of his insight and the bleak conclusions it leads him to about human behavior, but he differs from them in his refusal to approve the unpleasantly real merely because it is real. Like theirs his vision springs more from observation than from metaphysical the-

---

ocletian, having listened quietly so far, orders the leading lady of the troupe to use her beauty to win Genest back to reason, and paganism. But Genest's sweetheart, another actress in the company, is converted by him to his new faith and resolves to join him in martyrdom. At this point, with the play only half over, the theatrical motif is all but dropped, and after Genest's arrest nothing more is heard of it. By having Genest play out his own *past* conversion, Desfontaines sacrifices what for Rotrou becomes the heart of the matter, a conversion taking place before our eyes as a consequence of the theatrical setting, the transformation, as we watch, of a theatrically assumed identity into a real one.

For an illuminating account of how Rotrou's play works, with its three superimposed levels of theater, Roman empire, and heavenly empire, and the intricate analogies that develop among these realms, see J.-D. Hubert, "Le réel et l'illusoire dans le théatre de Corneille et dans celui de Rotrou," *Revue des sciences humaines*, New Series, no. 91 (1958): 333–350, esp. 338–344.

orizing, but in his case it is also backed by a conservative moralism whose ultimate sanction is, at least by his own claim, religious. What the *Maxims* contain, we learn in the preface to the first edition of 1665, "is nothing other than the summary of a moral doctrine conformable to the views of several Fathers of the Church . . . he who wrote them had good reason to think that he could not go wrong in following such good guides, and that it was permissible for him to speak of man as the Fathers have done."[37] The implicit claim here, that La Rochefoucauld was following his religious authorities, has been disputed on plausible grounds,[38] but one can agree that nothing in his analysis of the human condition contradicts what might have been said about it by Augustine or Jansenius. Indeed, as Paul Bénichou has made clear, La Rochefoucauld's whole enterprise of demystification, his reducing of ethical concepts to their animal basis in passion and egoism, has close links with the psychological and moral pessimism of Port-Royal, which refused to honor such secular ideals as *gloire*, or to allow the least trace of the heroic or divine in fallen human nature.[39] What is conspicuously missing from his account, as critics have always noticed, is any reference to a supernatural realm, any appeal to prayer or grace as a way out of the labyrinth of our own selfishness, or any suggestion of the *necessity* for supernatural intervention, an omission which gradually alerted his Jansenist acquaintances to the essentially secular basis of his vision.[40] But on this point as well La Rochefoucauld took pains to anticipate and mollify his critics. The preface to the second edition of 1666 declares explicitly that "The Author of these Maxims has con-

37. La Rochefoucauld, *Réflexions ou sentences et maximes morales*, ed. Dominique Secretan (Geneva, 1967), p. 2: "Ce qu'elles [les *Maximes*] contiennent n'est autre chose que l'abrégé d'une morale conforme aux pensées de plusieurs Pères de l'Église . . . celui qui les a écrites a eu beaucoup de raison de croire qu'il ne pouvait s'égarer en suivant de si bons guides, et qu'il lui était permis de parler de *l'homme* comme les Pères en ont parlé."
38. As in, e.g., Louis Hippeau, *Essai sur la morale de La Rochefoucauld* (Paris, 1967). Hippeau sets forth an erudite and closely argued case for seeing La Rochefoucauld as an Epicurean, continuing the antistoical Pyrrhonism of the later Montaigne. Enlightening and convincing as it often is, however, Hippeau's study seems to make too little allowance for the kinds of maxim cited below (pp. 214–216), in which virtue is seen as more than simple prudence or the skilful manipulation of unavoidable vices.
39. *Morales du grand siècle* (Paris, 1948), pp. 76–111.
40. On La Rochefoucauld and the Jansenists see Hippeau, pp. 97–119.

sidered men only in the deplorable state of nature corrupted by sin; and ... thus the manner in which he speaks of the infinite number of faults which join together in their apparent virtues does not apply to those whom God preserves by a particular grace."[41]

Considering men, then, "only in the deplorable state of nature corrupted by sin," La Rochefoucauld sees them, like Machiavelli and Hobbes, or the doctors of Port-Royal, as ruled by self-interest, only he translates this into the psychologically subtler concept of self-love.[42] Self-love differs from self-interest in that it can conflict with it; it can blind its possessor to his own truest advantage, and that in the most worldly sense. Like Gracián, to whom he may be indebted for his aphoristic method, La Rochefoucauld sees that men are engaged in games, in performances, in an endless round of deceptions and dissimulations: "On all occasions we assume the look and appearance we want to be known for, so that the world in general is a congregation of masks" (256).[43] Unlike Gracián, however, La Rochefoucauld never views this situation complacently. He never sees these masks as models, nor does he ever recommend using other men's weaknesses against

41. *Réflexions*, p. 4: "Celui qui les a faites [les *Maximes*] n'a considéré les hommes que dans cet état déplorable de la nature corrompue par le péché; et ... ainsi la manière dont il parle de ce nombre infini de défauts qui se rencontrent dans leurs vertus apparentes ne regarde point ceux que Dieu en préserve par une grâce particulière."

42. The chief precedent for this notion seems to have been a popular English tract of the early seventeenth century, *The Mystery of Selfe-Deceiving, or A Discourse and Discovery of the Deceitfulness of Mans Heart*, by Daniel Dyke (1614; rpt. London, 1615), reprinted at least seven times in English and translated into French in midcentury by Vernulius. Like La Rochefoucauld, Dyke tends to see immorality largely in terms of falseness, "of *histrionicall* and *hypocriticall*" pretense (Sig. D2ᵛ). More pertinently, after canvassing some familiar forms of falsity, he comes at length to "the second part of deceitfulnesse, and that farre more deepe and dangerous then the former; namely, that which wee may call *selfe-deceit*, whereby we deceive even *our selves*, sometimes together with, sometimes againe without deceiving others besides" (Sig. D3ᵛ).

43. La Rochefoucauld, *Maxims*, trans. Louis Kronenberger, Modern Library ed. (New York, 1959), p. 81. See *Réflexions*, p. 104: "Dans toutes les professions, chacun affecte une mine et un extérieur, pour paraître ce qu'il veut qu'on le croie: ainsi on peut dire que le monde n'est composé que de mines." Parenthetical numbers in the text will refer to the conventional number of the maxim in question.

them, scoring points off them by outmaneuvering them at their game. He never, that is, translates his chill insights into a program of worldly one-upmanship, an invitation to yield to the whirligig of appearances. Rather than join it, indeed, the wise man abstains from it entirely.

If society is a maze of masks, in which men habitually try to screen themselves from each other, the irony of the situation lies in the high percentage of failures: "However carefully we disguise our passions to look like piety and honor, the mask proves of no avail" (12).[44] Of no avail, that is, except to ourselves. For our power to delude ourselves, while seeking to deceive others, is boundless. "We get so much in the habit of wearing a disguise before others that we finally appear disguised before ourselves" (119).[45] We thus come to form our own best audience, and are most completely taken in by our own act. Our efforts to hoodwink the rest of the world amount to a prolonged essay in self-deception, which succeeds all too well. This is a more radical version of the theatrical theory of personality than any we have so far encountered, since it introduces the element of *inadvertent* theatricality. When Machiavelli promotes deceit as a political weapon, when Castiglione recommends the artful display of the self, they are thinking in terms of conscious purpose. La Rochefoucauld recognizes a deeper layer of unconscious theatricality, which makes life a delusion imposed by the actor on himself, a desperate tactic by which he tries to foist a certain sense of himself onto himself, with whom he is far more likely to succeed than with others who lack his reasons for cooperating, and who are engrossed in similar designs on their own selves. "It is as easy to deceive ourselves without knowing it as it is hard to deceive others without their finding it out" (115).[46] If for no other reason than for its unworkability, then, La Rochefoucauld cannot, like Castiglione, calmly outline a plan for self-ostentation, or, like Gracián, coolly compose prescriptions for cunning in the conduct of affairs.

44. *Maxims*, p. 35; *Réflexions*, p. 11: "Quelque soin que l'on prenne de couvrir ses passions par des apparences de piété et d'honneur, elles paraissent toujours au travers de ces voiles."

45. *Maxims*, p. 55; *Réflexions*, p. 52: "Nous sommes si accoutumés à nous déguiser aux autres, qu'enfin nous nous déguisons à nous-mêmes."

46. *Maxims*, p. 54; *Réflexions*, p. 50: "Il est aussi facile de se tromper soi-même sans s'en apercevoir, qu'il est difficile de tromper les autres sans qu'ils s'en aperçoivent."

There is much to suggest that La Rochefoucauld, despite the acid of his analysis, which regularly decomposes virtues into their constituent vices, has kept faith in virtue as a true possibility for men. Ordinary friendship may be, in his devastating account, "just an arrangement for mutual gain and an exchange of favors . . . a business where self-interest always sets out to obtain something" (83), yet the maxim immediately following hints at a less mercenary bond: "It is more shameful to distrust our friends than to be deceived by them" (84).[47] Here the strongly evaluative word *shameful* (*honteux*) pitches us out of the realm of detached observation into that of moral judgment. It rejects any cynical acquiescence in the way of the world. The innocence of the dove, we are sharply reminded, is to be preferred to the wisdom of the serpent, even if the serpent is engaged in eating the dove. Likewise, "when our hatred is too violent, it puts us beneath those we hate" (Ed. 3, 338).[48] Here "beneath" refers not to any scale of worldly benefits, but to a moral scale. We fall "beneath" the objects of our hatred not in the sense of losing some competitive advantage to them, but in degrading ourselves spiritually. Again, "Our worth wins us the regard of the worthy, our success the regard of the world" (165). "Worth," an ethical quality, earns us the esteem of the few, the moral elect, while "success," a purely external and theatrical quality, compels the attention of the many, who are also the morally coarse, the reprobate. It is typical of the world, moreover, that it "oftener rewards the appearance of merit than merit itself" (166),[49] and the context leaves us in no doubt that we are to value the reality over the illusion. All these precepts have a surprising tinge of unworldliness, emerging as they do from such a congeries of worldly insights. Disillusion with the world never leads to a surrender to the world's values.

The primary virtues, then, most of them, emerge unscathed as valid goals. Though most men may be corrupt, not all are. Though most

47. *Maxims*, p. 48; *Réflexions*, pp. 38–39: "Ce que les hommes ont nommé amitié n'est qu'une société, qu'un ménagement réciproque d'intérêts, et qu'un échange de bons offices; . . . un commerce où l'amour-propre se propose toujours quelque chose à gagner"; "Il est plus honteux de se défier de ses amis que d'en être trompé."

48. *Maxims*, p. 96; *Réflexions*, p. 126: "Lorsque notre haine est trop vive, elle nous met au-dessous de ceux que nous haïssons."

49. *Maxims*, p. 63; *Réflexions*, p. 65: "Le monde récompense plus souvent les apparences du mérite que le mérite même."

men spend their hours grimacing and posturing, not all do. Worthy
alternatives exist; a few, even, adopt them. Though sincerity may be
rare, and often shammed, it is not on that account a mere sentimental
fiction; it does inhabit a few upright souls. "Sincerity comes directly
from the heart. One finds it in very few people; what one usually finds
is but a deft pretense designed to gain the confidence of others" (62).[50]
Honesty likewise exists in both genuine and counterfeit forms: "Men
who but pretend to be honest hide their faults from others and themselves alike; men who are really honest thoroughly recognize their
faults and confess them" (202).[51] As for humility, though it may frequently be "just a feigned submissiveness employed to dominate others
. . . a strategem of pride, which lowers itself that it may raise itself"
(254),[52] it is also, in its authentic manifestations, "the true test of
Christian virtue," without which "we persist in all our faults, concealing them, under a cloak of pride, not only from others but often
from ourselves" (358).[53] True humility helps dispel the mists of self-
deception. It shows us to ourselves as we really are, stripped of the
theatrical tinsel in which our pride arrays us, and true honesty lends
us the courage to show ourselves so to others. And as with sincerity,
honesty, and humility, so with the more comprehensive quality of
"virtue" itself. However rare it may be in uncontaminated form, it is
no mirage. As Jonathan Culler has pointed out, commenting on maxim
200 ("Virtue would not go nearly so far if vanity did not keep her
company"[54]), "The confident use of 'vertu' cannot but suggest that
virtue exists, that it can go certain distances in our relations with others;

50. *Maxims*, p. 44; *Réflexions*, p. 31: "La sincérité est une ouverture de
coeur. On la trouve en fort peu de gens, et celle que l'on voit d'ordinaire
n'est qu'une fine dissimulation, pour attirer la confiance des autres."

51. *Maxims*, p. 70; *Réflexions*, p. 78: "Les faux honnêtes gens sont ceux
qui déguisent leurs défauts aux autres et à eux-memes; les vrais honnêtes
gens sont ceux qui les connaissent parfaitement, et les confessent."

52. *Maxims*, p. 81; *Réflexions*, p. 102: "L'humilité n'est souvent qu'une
feinte soumission, dont on se sert pour soumettre les autres . . . un artifice
de l'orgueil qui s'abaisse pour s'élever."

53. *Maxims*, p. 100; *Réflexions*, p. 129: "L'humilité est la véritable preuve
des vertus chrétiennes: sans elle, nous conservons tous nos défauts, et ils
sont seulement couverts par l'orgueil, qui les cache aux autres, et souvent
à nous-mêmes."

54. *Maxims*, p. 70; *Réflexions*, p. 77: "La vertu n'irait pas si loin si la
vanité ne lui tenait compagnie."

that it can find itself in different sorts of company which may reflect badly on it; but that it is still virtue."[55]

Certain of the maxims set up a standard of naturalness from which disguises and imitations are seen as deviations and distortions. They distinguish between what we are by nature and what we affect to be through mimicry. "We are better off exhibiting ourselves as we are than trying to seem what we are not" (457).[56] "Nothing is so contagious as example, and we never commit good or evil acts without their propagating themselves. We imitate good deeds in an effort to equal them; we imitate bad ones from inherent ill nature, which our sense of honor restrains but which the power of example sets free" (230).[57] Little in such sentiments would need to be amended to make them conform to Plato or be acceptable to the directors of Port-Royal. La Rochefoucauld sees imitation, as they do, as a potent force in human life, dangerous precisely in proportion to our "inherent ill nature." It prompts us to copy the worse rather than the better, and leads to every kind of affectation. The notorious maxim 136—"There are people who would never have fallen in love but for hearing love discussed"[58]— conjures up a whole society of apes and parrots, trying to reproduce not only the outer gestures but the inner experiences they presume others to have had. Maxim 134—"We are never so ridiculous for the qualities we have as for those we pretend to"[59]—might serve as epigraph to the collected comedies of Jonson or Molière. "Imitation," indeed, "is always a mistake: the counterfeit displeases for the same reasons that what proves natural, charms" (618).[60] The best that can be

55. Jonathan Culler, "Paradox and the Language of Morals in La Rochefoucauld," *Modern Language Review* 68 (1973): 28–39, p. 36.

56. *Maxims*, p. 117; *Réflexions*, p. 149: "Nous gagnerions plus de nous laisser voir tels que nous sommes, que d'essayer de paraître ce que nous ne sommes pas."

57. *Maxims*, p. 76; *Réflexions*, p. 89: "Rien n'est si contagieux que l'exemple, et nous ne faisons jamais de grands biens ni de grands maux qui n'en produisent de semblables. Nous imitons les bonnes actions par émulation, et les mauvaises par la malignité de notre nature, que la honte retenait prisonnière, et que l'exemple met en liberté."

58. *Maxims*, p. 57; *Réflexions*, p. 56: "Il y a des gens qui n'auraient jamais été amoureux, s'ils n'avaient jamais entendu parler de l'amour."

59. *Maxims*, p. 57; *Réflexions*, p. 56: "On n'est jamais si ridicule par les qualités que l'on a que par celles que l'on affecte d'avoir."

60. *Maxims*, p. 152; *Réflexions*, p. 193: "L'imitation est toujours mal-

said for it is that artfully employed it may serve to caricature an unworthy individual who deserves to be pilloried: "The only good copies are those that reveal what is silly in the bad originals" (133).[61]

So the drastic reduction of life to its theatrical basis goes hand in hand with a clear conviction that such a life—life as it mostly is lived—is not, on that account, life as it need be, still less as it should be, lived. If the self is to come into its own, the theater must be discarded. And as it is more shameful to mistrust one's friends than to be duped by them, so "The wise man does better by not playing at all than by coming out winner" (549).[62] It is not, finally, dignified or honest to play society's stupid games; the prizes it has to offer are not worth the sacrifice of self-respect they require.

The antitheatricalism of the *Maxims* receives powerful reinforcement in the posthumous *Réflexions diverses*, published in 1731. One passage speaks of the "airs" and "tones" and "manners" native to us, how they show forth unaffected in small children, who charm us with their naturalness, but who then, as the imitative instinct gains sway, begin to ape their elders and lose their integrity. When we copy others, we forsake what is authentic to us and sacrifice our own strong points for alien ones that may not suit us at all.[63] Though La Rochefoucauld disclaims any desire to discourage us from trying to perfect ourselves by following good examples, example itself nevertheless remains under something of a cloud. This comes out in a scathing paragraph in Passage 7:

Whatever difference there may be between good and bad examples, we will find that both have almost exactly the same ill effects. I don't even know if the crimes of Tiberius and Nero don't carry us farther *from* vice than the estimable examples of the greatest men move us *toward* virtue. How many braggarts has Alexander's valor created! How many enterprises against one's native country has Caesar's glory sanctioned? How many ferocious virtues have Rome and Sparta not

---

heureuse, et tout ce qui est contrefait déplaît, avec les mêmes choses qui charment lorsqu'elles sont naturelles."

61. *Maxims*, p. 57; *Réflexions*, p. 56: "Les seules bonnes copies sont celles que nous font voir le ridicule des méchants originaux."

62. *Maxims*, p. 137; *Réflexions*, p. 172: "Le sage trouve mieux son compte à ne point s'engager qu'à vaincre."

63. *Réflexions*, p. 210.

praised! How many importunate philosophers has Diogenes made, Cicero babblers, Pomponius Atticus lazy and indifferent creatures, Marius and Sulla vengeful ones, Lucullus voluptuaries, Alcibiades and Antony debauchees, Cato opinionated bigots! All these great originals have produced an infinite number of bad copies. The virtues are the frontiers of vices: examples are guides which often mislead us, and we are so filled with falsity that we use them no less for departing from the path of virtue than for following it.[64]

The sweeping negativity of this gives the lie to those apologists for the stage, like Nashe, Heywood, and Scudéry, who held that great deeds reenacted theatrically might serve as models for the young, and in so doing it betrays an antimimetic bias perhaps even sterner than Plato's. Plato assumes a fairly straightforward equation between the nature of the thing imitated and the imprint it leaves on the imitator. The imitator will absorb and ultimately embody the qualities he imitates. If he copies violent or irrational men, he will make himself violent and irrational; if he emulates temperance and courage, he will instill temperance and courage in himself. What most of the reformers deplore about the stage is that it affords so few good examples, so many bad ones. It creates a rogues' gallery of dangerous models to tempt the unwary beholder. Even ostensible saints, like Polyeucte, may on inspection turn out to be radically defective, remarkable more for vainglory than for piety. And our sinful nature, as Nicole, Conti, and the

---

64. *Réflexions*, pp. 221–222:

Quelque différence qu'il y ait entre les bons et les mauvais exemples, on trouvera que les uns et les autres ont presque également produit de méchants effets; je ne sais même si les crimes de Tibère et de Néron ne nous éloignent pas plus du vice, que les exemples estimables des plus grands hommes ne nous approchent de la vertu. Combien la valeur d'Alexandre a-t-elle fait de fanfarons! Combien la gloire de César a-t-elle autorisé d'entreprises contre la patrie! Combien Rome et Sparte ont-elles loué de vertus farouches! Combien Diogène a-t-il fait de philosophes importuns, Cicéron de babillards, Pomponius Atticus de gens neutres et paresseux, Marius et Sylla de vindicatifs, Lucullus de voluptueux, Alcibiade et Antoine de débauchés, Caton d'opiniâtres! Tous ces grands originaux ont produit un nombre infini de mauvaises copies. Les vertus sont frontières des vices; les exemples sont des guides qui nous égarent souvent, et nous sommes si remplis de fausseté, que nous ne nous en servons pas moins pour nous éloigner du chemin de la vertu, que pour le suivre.

others stand ready to insist, spurs us to follow the bad examples and neglect the good.

But for La Rochefoucauld, who applies a systematic method of close scrutiny, there are really no good examples. In examples, as in living men, the virtues break down into compounds of vices. Moreover, even when genuine they border on neighboring vices so closely, across such a tenuous boundary, that only the lynx-eyed observer can distinguish them. The result is that most imitation of the good simply caricatures it. The imitator ends by culling the bad and ignoring the genuinely good. The imitative impulse, deformed by self-interest, distorted by self-love, unscrupulous in catering to our weaknesses, will find in the most exemplary of heroes some unsuspected encouragement to vice. Even when we most solemnly intend it for our betterment, it can contribute to our confusion. Since men, then, are incapable of sifting the wheat from the chaff, since our malign souls lead us almost inevitably to *prefer* the chaff, it would be best if we could give up imitating altogether. And this is a conclusion, or an inference, that even Plato would have hesitated to draw, convinced as he was that for all its dangers imitation had a key role to play in the formation of good citizens. La Rochefoucauld's account is probably the most totally unfavorable one can find anywhere, even from among the enemies of the theater. Certainly it is the most urgently articulated, the one that probes most deeply into our foundations as social beings, and finds us unsound.

At the same time, it is the one that paradoxically is the likeliest to command a wide acceptance. For it diagnoses in implicitly antitheatrical terms a social and psychological malady without reference to the theater at all. La Rochefoucauld is not thinking about the stage, but about the stagey quality of life in urban Paris. He is antitheatrical not in objecting to plays or players, but in recoiling from the histrionic falsity—the deceitfulness and covert exhibitionism—of so much ordinary behavior. What appears in other antitheatrical writers, often, as petulance or "stubborn initial prejudice," or as a desperate casting about for reasons to justify an irrational dread, appears in La Rochefoucauld as the recognition of a lasting dilemma, of which the theater cannot in any case be more than a symptom. His own route of escape from the dilemma, moreover, lies not along the path of austere intellection recommended by Plato, or in the contempt of earthly things, but in opposing to the life of social mimicry and self-deception an ideal of self-respect, of freedom from the despotism of custom. One could not, certainly, be a *précieuse ridicule*, a *femme savante*, or a M. Jourdain, and approach the ideal, but on the other hand one would not have to be a Socrates. Unsparing as La Rochefoucauld's exposition may seem, it contains its crumb of comfort, its modest hope of amendment for those who have the energy to apply its lessons. The still bleaker insight that men are almost fatally cursed with mimicry from the cradle awaited the arrival on the scene, a century later, of a more ambivalent moralist, Jean-Jacques Rousseau. La Rochefoucauld we may credit with exposing the ugly underside of everyday mimicry, everyday exhibitionism, and thereby of implying what kind of validity, despite its frequent excesses and crankiness, the antitheatrical prejudice must be allowed to possess.

· VIII ·

Immorality
and Profaneness

ANTITHEATRICAL POLEMICS seem to occur in streaks, or bursts. A single letter or pamphlet, printed at the right moment, will set off a chain reaction, provoking a rebuttal which in turn will provoke a rejoinder, the rejoinder a surrejoinder, until the bookstalls crackle with furious treatises like strings of firecrackers, some of them lit by persons remote from the original issues and only peripherally interested in them. Nicole's reference to playwrights as public poisoners ignited a fiery train of charges and countercharges between the partisans of the stage and the doctors of Port-Royal. Father Caffaro's letter to Boursault, in 1694, affirming the harmlessness of the theater as a recreation for Christians, brought down on his head the terrible thunderbolts of Bossuet, which were followed for more than two decades by angry rumblings from obscurer quarters. Rousseau's letter to d'Alembert, in 1758, protesting the proposal to build a theater in Geneva, lifted the floodgates of an absolute cataract of response, of every conceivable degree of agreement and abhorrence, from the most fervent congratulation to the most maddened repudiation.[1] Jeremy Collier's *Short View of the Immorality and Profaneness of the English Stage* (1698) raised a storm of its own, which raged intermittently for over a generation.[2] Collier

---

1. According to one authority, "The number of pamphlets or articles hurled against his *Lettre à d'Alembert* went beyond four hundred" (Lester G. Crocker, *Jean-Jacques Rousseau*, II [New York, 1973], 18).

2. The bibliography in Sister Rose Anthony, *The Jeremy Collier Stage Controversy 1698–1726* (New York, 1937), pp. 300–307, lists nearly eighty contributions to the controversy during the years 1698–1726.

himself kept it alive by relentlessly answering his critics, first with *A Defence of the Short View* (1699), then with *A Second Defence* (1700), then with *Mr. Collier's Dissuasive from the Playhouse* (1703), and finally with *A Farther Vindication of The Short View* (1708), each time, by renewing the attack, creating new antagonists and mustering fresh advocates.

As a nonjuring parson with Jacobite sympathies, Collier occupied a far different place in the ecclesiastical spectrum from that of his Puritan forebears, and also from that of many of his own followers, a circumstance which doubtless lent weight to his campaign, causing it to seem to be coming from the conservative, royalist wing of the clergy rather than from its antimonarchical lunatic fringe, which had been discredited since the Restoration. Yet his tirades often recall those of the more fanatic Puritans in their humorless grimness and in the bulldog tenacity with which he keeps returning to the attack. The likeness did not go unnoticed. One opponent calls attention to the resemblance between Collier and "his famous Predecessor Mr. *Prynne*, whose Arguments and *way of* Reasoning Mr. *Collier* inherits as well as quarrel, with a double portion of his Spirit."[3] The comparison may be unjust to Collier on the score of "Arguments" and "Reasoning," but with respect to "Spirit" it hits home. Collier has more than his share of Prynne's rage, of Prynne's fierceness and anticontextualism, his imperviousness to rational argument, and his power to sustain the note of high-pitched vituperation over hundreds of pages. Although not himself a dissenter, he had, in the words of one critic, "A Dissenter's puritanical ideas about many things," with the result that he "rekindled puritanic fires slumbering in many a fanatic heart."[4]

At the same time, much has changed in the sixty-five years since *Histriomastix*, and Collier's crusade differs in some signal respects from that of his forerunners. It is more sharply focused on the matter at hand, and less flagrantly anachronistic in its procedures. Collier saves until the end of his book the heaping up of citations from the Fathers, the Councils, the pagan historians, and the decrees of Christian com-

3. [James Drake], *The Antient and Modern Stages Survey'd, or, Mr. Collier's View . . . Set in a True Light*, etc. (London, 1699), p. 247.

4. Alexandre Beljame, *Men of Letters and the English Public in the Eighteenth Century 1660–1744, Dryden, Addison, Pope*, trans. E. O. Lorimer, ed. Bonamy Dobrée (London, 1948), p. 244.

monwealths. Nowhere does he on his own account rake up the charges of idolatry, falsehood, and hypocrisy that had formed the stock in trade of earlier antitheatrical polemicists. Moreover he adopts a relatively mild view of the drama as a social force. Instead of clamoring for its suppression, he advances a distinct, if moralistic, notion of what it should be, a prescription to which he demands that the theater of his day conform. "The business of *Plays*," he declares, at the outset of the *Short View*,

is to recommend Virtue, and discountenance Vice; To shew the Uncertainty of Humane Greatness, the suddain Turns of Fate, and the Unhappy Conclusions of Violence and Injustice: 'Tis to expose the Singularities of Pride and Fancy, to make Folly and Falsehood contemptible, and to bring every Thing that is Ill Under Infamy, and Neglect.[5]

Needless to say, it is the shame of the current stage that it has failed to do these things. Although Collier's critics found this formula harsh and grudging, omitting as it does all reference to pleasure, it sets forth a positive rationale for the stage such as the friends of the stage had themselves often advanced, and does so in no contemptuous or dismissive terms. In due course, moreover, pleasure itself makes an appearance as a legitimate concern. If moral instruction is to be the first and overriding aim even of comedy, "Delight," we are told, may be allowed to be at least a "secondary End." Only it must not be mistaken for the supreme law: "Vice must be under Discipline and Discountenance, and Folly shown with great Caution and Reserve. . . . If there must be Strumpets, let *Bridewell* be the *Scene*. Let them come not to Prate, but to be Punish'd."[6] As the final phrase may suggest, Collier's precepts in practice would no doubt have made the drama hopelessly preacherly. They would have leached out of it the rich coarse strain of realism that made it vivid and lifelike. A recent critic has pointed out that Collier's assumptions about the nature of dramatic action are Platonic: "He simply will not tolerate any realistic imitation of evil in the theater," fearing contagion by example, as Plato feared it, and

5. *A Short View of the Immorality, and Profaneness of the English Stage, together With the Sense of Antiquity upon this Argument* (London, 1698), p. 1.

6. *A Defence of the Short View of the Profaneness and Immorality of the English Stage* (London, 1699), pp. 8–10.

it is precisely on the question of the nature of dramatic representation that he locks horns most strenuously with his opponents the playwrights, who insist on the need for the stage to render life as it is, so that it may accomplish its moral ends, and who invoke Aristotle to testify to the value of arousing the passions.[7] Nevertheless, the worst that can be said of Collier's view at this point is that it is excessively moralistic, and when we recall that he was in this same moment engaged in translating Bossuet's *Maximes et réflexions* into English (1699), with its categorical anathemas against all plays and all playgoing, its theological rejection of all mimesis as evil, we may be tempted to regard Collier's own view as positively benign.

It is only after affirming the educational mission of the stage that Collier moves to consider particular plays, to ask whether they serve or subvert the high cause he has assigned them. He commences with a retrospective glance at earlier times, vigorously exempting both the drama of antiquity, and—more surprisingly—that of Elizabethan and Jacobean England from the blast he is about to discharge against his own contemporaries. His retrospect leads in fact to the unexpected conclusion that it is only "the *Present English Stage*" which is "superlatively Scandalous," its forerunners having been sufficiently chaste and wholesome. The stage, he hence concludes, "stands in need of a great deal of Discipline and Restraint"[8]—but not, it would appear, of suppression.

Collier resembles Prynne in one obvious respect—in the maniacal thoroughness with which he has done his homework. As Prynne had spent a decade mastering the enormous literature of antitheatricalism, along with anything else that might be construed as contributing, however remotely, to the question, so Collier shows himself to be a formidable student of dramatic literature, minutely acquainted with the Greek and Roman classics, in the original languages, as he never lets us forget; conversant with Aristotle, Horace, and Tacitus; with Boileau, Dacier, and Rapin; *au courant* with the critical controversies of his day and eager to add his voice to the views of his own chosen faction. Frequently, and rather disarmingly, he seems to forget his role as antitheatrical polemicist in order to take up the more interesting one as

7. Aubrey Williams, "No Cloistered Virtue: Or, Playwright versus Priest in 1698," *PMLA* 90 (1975): 234–246, p. 235.
8. *A Defence*, p. 26.

dramatic critic, sometimes straying far from the point in order to do so. At one moment he ponders what Aristotle may have meant by the distinction between tragedy and comedy. At another he vindicates the morality of the fables of ancient tragedies, or defends them from the charge of licentiousness through a scrutiny of pertinent passages. He summons Dacier to his aid to help settle the meaning of a disputed passage in Horace. He debates the classification of *Plutus* as "Old" or "New" Comedy. Coming to indict the plays of his own time, he shows the same close knowledge and the same disposition to enter the lists as dramatic critic, condemning *The Relapse*, for instance, as much for violating the unities, for implausibility in character and incident, and for mistaking the proper end of comedy, as for its alleged immorality and profaneness. Nor does he hesitate to take the playwrights harshly to task for their purely stylistic shortcomings, as when he ridicules a speech in Congreve for the excesses of its figurative language: its "Litter of *Epithetes* makes the *Poem* look like a Bitch overstock'd with Puppies, and sucks the Sence almost to skin and Bone."[9] It matters nothing to Collier that such digressions have no bearing on the point at issue and carry him far from his announced purpose, to expose the moral derelictions of the playwrights. As Oldmixon suavely noted, "the Unities may be broken, and the Author never the worse Christian."[10] The most incompetent playwright in London stands as good a chance for salvation as the most accomplished. But Collier is either writing at such fever pitch that he cannot resist the opportunity to score, however irrelevantly, off his opponents, or else he has somehow succeeded in persuading himself that anything he can lay to the poets' charge— faulty dramaturgy, stylistic blundering, etc.—will add to the dreadful ledger he is compiling against their moral turpitude.

No doubt Joseph Wood Krutch is right in suggesting that Collier adopts the critic's guise partly in order to confound his critics,[11] to make his diatribe appear a reasoned contribution to debate rather than simply a din of abuse. This was certainly the opinion of many of Collier's contemporaries, who regarded him as slowly taking off the wraps of his

9. *Short View*, p. 34.

10. [John Oldmixon], *Reflections on the Stage, and Mr. Collyer's Defence of the Short View* (London, 1699), p. 6.

11. *Comedy and Conscience after the Restoration* (1924; rpt. New York, 1961), pp. 108–109, 114, 120.

hostility to reveal it in its full extent only at the end of the book.[12] It is true also that his specific critical comments can be grotesquely inept, with a Tertullianesque literalness that suggests a kind of tone-deafness to all imaginative experience.[13] Yet it is hard not to suspect, from the scores of pages and the quantities of energy lavished on topics like decorum, verisimilitude, and the morality of dramatic fables, that these interest him for their own sake, that he is as powerfully attracted as he is violently repelled by the phenomenon he is investigating. Spingarn long ago pointed out how much Collier owes to Rymer—in style, method, and even content—how he borrows Rymer's method for anatomizing Elizabethan tragedy and uses it to conduct an inquest into Restoration comedy.[14] Rymer too seems flatminded and tone-deaf to us today, impervious to the essential qualities of imaginative writing. Yet no one would think to deny him his own lunatic brand of commitment, and the same allowance ought to be made for Collier. Why, indeed, should he have made himself a disciple of Rymer in the first place unless he was genuinely interested in the issues raised by Rymer? Why should he have so gluttonously wolfed down such indigestible masses of critical commentary unless they satisfied a real hunger? For much of the *Short View*, he writes about the stage less as a hostile outsider bent on wrecking it than as a slightly demented devotee bent on reordering it, sworn to make it over—if necessary by violence—in conformance with some unworkable visionary scheme of his own. How else explain the countless hours he has spent poring over playbooks, tabulating the minutiae of plot and language, or the pedantic absorption with which he plunges into his critical digressions? In this respect he

12. [Elkanah Settle], *A Defence of Dramatick Poetry: Being a Review of Mr. Collier's View*, etc. (London, 1698), p. 1; John Dennis, *The Usefulness of the Stage, to the Happiness of Mankind*, etc. (1698), in Edward Niles Hooker, ed. Dennis, *Critical Works* (Baltimore, 1939), I, 146; Oldmixon, *Reflections on the Stage*, pp. 2–3; and Edward Filmer, *A Defence of Plays: Or, the Stage Vindicated, from Several Passages in Mr. Collier's Short View*, etc. (London, 1707), pp. 5–7, 38, 45, 101, 157, 167.

13. See Beljame, *Men of Letters*, p. 234: "He is completely lacking in artistic feeling. . . . He has no spark of sympathy for dramatic literature of any kind," and Krutch, p. 114: "He shares to the fullest extent the ascetic Christian hatred of all art."

14. J. E. Spingarn, *Critical Essays of the Seventeenth Century* (London, 1907), I, lxxxvi–lxxxvii.

differs strikingly from authors like Rainolds and Prynne, who show neither interest in nor knowledge of the plays they are condemning —who boast, indeed, of their own ignorance. But even if we allow— which seems doubtful—that Collier's indulgence toward certain epochs of theater and his zeal for solving problems of dramatic criticism represent a lapwing effort to distract us from his darker purpose, we are still faced with a changed cultural situation, in which mere protracted frenzy, of the sort typified by *Histriomastix*, is no longer viable. Perhaps we may most plausibly reckon Collier as one of a number of antitheatrical writers who betray in their very rhetoric the fact that the theater exerts a primitive and powerful pull on them, which they must make it part of their program as pamphleteers to deny and to exorcise, being unable to acknowledge it openly.

He differs also from his own more plodding followers. One, the anonymous author of a tract entitled *The Stage Condemn'd*, traces all the evils of the theater to the faults of English education, calling for the removal from the school curriculum of *"Amorous Passages* of *Ovid, Terence, Plautus,"* and others, whom Collier takes pains to exempt from his censure of Congreve, Dryden, and Vanbrugh. *The Stage Condemn'd* in fact examines the supposedly correct uses of the stage allowed by Collier and pronounces them indefensible, since they poach on the preserve of the appointed leaders of the community—the magistrates, the ministers of God, and the holy Scriptures. Collier is found guilty of arrogating to the theater an illegitimate authority, and so of thwarting the right agencies of church and state in their task of moral instruction. *"God,"* the anonymous pamphleteer reminds Collier sharply, *"hath appointed sufficient Means for Recommending Vertue, and Discountenancing Vice* without the STAGE." In accord with the more reactionary temper of his treatise, the author also engages in a furious comparison between "the Church of Christ and the Play-house, which *Tertullian* and others call the Church of the Devil," going on to note, with a characteristic stroke of misogyny, that "In the former Women are by Apostolical Prohibition forbid to speak, and commanded to learn in silence, but in the latter their Discourses, Songs and Parts are the principal Entertainment, which is certainly inconsistent with the Natural Modesty of the Sex," etc.[15] One point of superiority of the church

15. *The Stage Condemn'd* (London, 1698), Sig. A2ᵛ, pp. 1, 45, 158.

over the stage, then, is that with no uncertain emphasis it holds women in their canonically inferior place.

Collier is thus rebuked, if not repudiated outright, by one of his own party, and even allowing for his frequent bungling, it is hard to imagine that he would have introduced critical digressions into his pamphlets as a deliberate red herring, if they could so easily confuse and alienate his own followers. To the very end, in *A Farther Vindication*, he is claiming to defend the Idea of a Theater, and even alleging the existence of an actual theater corresponding to that Idea: "I still affirm . . . that *Plays*, where the Argument and Manner are religious and solemn, are *Acted* in Monasteries in *France*, and in other Countries too."[16] Perhaps Collier had picked up a reference in Bossuet to the theater of the French Jesuits, which formed a spectacular part of the program of religious instruction in their colleges,[17] and perhaps he transformed the colleges into monasteries in order to heighten the effect of holiness and solemnity. In any case, in doing so he was extending aid and comfort to the champions of the stage, and depriving its enemies of one of their sharpest weapons. Perhaps, had he been living in France himself, or in England a generation earlier, he would have been as horrified as the bitterest Dissenter at the blasphemous attempts to import a "religious and solemn" subject matter into the drama. That is, we may well be dealing with yet one more subterfuge of the antitheatrical prejudice, affecting to dislike only a particular kind of play at a particular time, while in truth being deeply hostile to the mimetic principle in any form and at any time. Ostensibly, however, Collier is professing to believe what his Puritan ancestors, and many of his own more zealous supporters, would have died rather than admit—that under certain circumstances and with proper controls, the theater might still hope to become a "religious and solemn" adjunct to the Christian life.

16. *A Farther Vindication of the Short View . . . in which the Objections Of a late Book, Entituled, A Defence of Plays, Are Consider'd* (London, 1708), p. 33.

17. A point on which Dennis seems to be uninstructed. See *The Usefulness of the Stage*, in Hooker, ed. *Critical Works*, I, 185, where he lumps "the Jesuits" with "the Fanaticks" as "inveterate Enemies to Plays." On Jesuit theater see Ernest Boysse, *Le théâtre des jésuites* (Paris, 1880).

His pamphlets unexpectedly reverberate with another, and different, set of echoes, from the Battle of the Ancients and Moderns. Collier goes needlessly far—astonishingly far, for the needs of his thesis—in clearing the ancient playwrights of all imputation of immodesty and profaneness, using them as a stick with which to beat his own contemporaries. As he picks furious quarrel with innocuous passages in Dryden, Congreve, and Vanbrugh, so he as furiously denies the least deviation from propriety in the plays of Aeschylus, Sophocles, and Euripides, and labors to exonerate Terence and Plautus from the objections of earlier commentators. His lopsided treatment of this issue incurs reproof from at least one answerer, James Drake, who in *Antient and Modern Stages Survey'd* remarks how Collier, "to inflame the Reckoning of the Modern Poets . . . enlarges very much upon the great Modesty and Regard which the *Antients* had to Vertue, and *Decorum*, falsly insinuating thereby as great Neglect and Violation of 'em among the *Moderns*." Drake thus ascribes the position to purely polemical motives. Collier "caresses the Antients in pure spight to the Moderns." Drake himself, an impassioned and at times intemperate Modern, credits his own generation with inventing, or at least first systematically practicing, poetic justice, whereby virtue is taught in plays by being seen to be rewarded, and vice discouraged by being seen to be punished. "The *Modern* Stage," for him, is on this account "infinitely preferable to the *Athenians*."[18] Collier, excessive and intemperate on his own side, exaggerates the purity of the old drama as he blackens the drama of his own time, to sharpen the contrast and aggravate the indictment. Yet it is hard to believe, once again, that he would digress so lengthily, harp so remorselessly on critical issues so remote from the purpose, unless in some strange way he genuinely cared about the old plays. He answers Drake on the subject of poetic justice much as French controversialists had done:

A formal Piece of Justice at the end of a Lewd Play, is nothing but a Piece of Grimace, and a Politick Hypocrisy. 'Tis much such a strain of Conduct, as it would be to let a Mad Dog loose among the Crowd, and then knock him on the Head when he has bitten a great part of them.[19]

18. *Antient and Modern Stages Survey'd*, pp. 124, 41, 230.
19. *A Second Defence of the Short View* (London, 1700), p. 84.

The fact that this rebuttal—very likely adapted from Bossuet on the subject of eleventh-hour marriage in comedies—is couched in what Coleridge would term Collier's "Black-guard Slang," or what the authors of the *Peri Bathous* would aptly dub the "Pert Style,"[20] need not blind us to the element of common sense in it. There are plays of the period to which it all too clearly applies.

Collier's master, Rymer, we may recall, viewed all modern tragedy as degenerate, and the tragedies of the ancients as the only suitable models. It is likely that Collier shared this view, and extended it to features of the drama other than tragic form. The fact that the *Short View* appeared just as the quarrel between the Ancients and Moderns was beginning to drift toward specifically literary issues suggests that Collier may have found himself more or less accidentally swept into its orbit. With his nose for controversy—to change the metaphor—he could hardly have failed to pick up the scent, and with his boisterous combativeness he could hardly have refrained from flinging himself, yelping and barking, along the trail with the rest of the pack. Once launched on his antimodern crusade, he must have found it natural and inevitable to compare current plays with the acknowledged classics, and to make of the ancient drama a high-water mark of excellence from which all subsequent drama had receded. For him to have done so, for whatever reason, affords a telling reminder of how times had changed since Prynne's day, of how deeply classical culture had infiltrated the English consciousness. That a hotheaded nonjuring parson, leading an antitheatrical crusade, should measure the theater not against the teachings of Christ or the lessons of the Gospel, but against the theatrical achievements of ancient pagan authors, and even against the very English playwrights who had themselves so often been denounced by their Puritan adversaries as limbs of Satan, constitutes a minirevolution in itself.

Collier innovates in still a further respect, in the microscopic scrutiny he bestows on his play texts. The standard earlier attacks had traded in generalities, denouncing plays *en masse* as obscene and irreverent, ruinous of order, wasteful of time, subversive of salvation, and the like. If a more specific indictment seemed called for, it might take the form

20. George Williamson, *The Senecan Amble: A Study in Prose Form from Bacon to Collier* (Chicago, 1951), pp. 361, 363.

of a horrified catalogue of the subject matter of the dramatic genres. Thus Gosson:

The argument of Tragedies is wrath, crueltie, incest, injurie, murther eyther violent by sworde, or voluntary by poyson.
   The persons, Gods, Goddesses, furies, fiendes, Kinges, Quenes, and mightie men. The ground worke of *Commedies*, is love, cosenedge, flatterie, bawderie, slye conveighance of whoredom. The persons, cookes, queanes, knaves, baudes, parasites, courtezannes, lecherous olde men, amorous yong men.[21]

Gosson, as a lapsed playwright, could hardly have been better placed to divulge the iniquities of particular plays, and yet, in common with the rest of his generation, he never thinks to do so, other than by scornfully summarizing the plot of a single lost morality in order to ridicule it for its silliness. In midcentury France, writers began to allude more pointedly to the actual fare of the playhouses, occasionally conducting brief *examens* of particular plays in order to establish the gulf between the sensuality of the stage and the purity of true Christianity. But it is Collier, following Rymer, who seems to have turned close analysis into a weapon of controversy, combing through the printed playbooks for instances of his various categories of abuse—disrespect of the clergy, profanation of Scripture, smuttiness of language, etc.—and then launching into a scene-by-scene scrutiny of a few plays chosen to exemplify all the vices in combination.

   Collier's chivvying style and his amassing of evidence seem to have had more impact than his relatively restrained theoretical views. *The Defence of Dramatick Poetry* (1698) accuses him of gradually coming out from hiding to reveal himself in his true colors as a root and branch enemy of the stage, his aim being "not *Reformation*, but *Eradication*: For here he throws by the Pruning Hook, and takes up the Axe."[22] Actually, what Collier does at the point in question is simply to assemble, in a lengthy appendix, a series of quotations from the Fathers, the Church Councils, the ancient historians, and the statutes of various governments, to show how past ages have solicited the elimination of

21. *Plays Confuted*, in Arthur F. Kinney, *Markets of Bawdrie: The Dramatic Criticism of Stephen Gosson*, Salzburg Studies in English Literature, no. 4 (Salzburg, 1974), p. 160.
22. *Defence of Dramatick Poetry*, p. 1.

the theater. He himself, with almost ostentatious forbearance, refrains from drawing any such categorical conclusions.

His followers, to be sure, showed no such restraint, and Collier's own growing irritation with the failure of the theater to amend itself according to his instructions must have incensed them further. Far from taking his warnings to heart, he protests, the stage goes on stubbornly repeating the same faults, mulishly refusing to put his wholesome remedies into practice. "We must not forget," he writes in 1703, "the Incorrigibleness of the *Stage* . . . . Their ill Plays have been some of them examin'd, their licentious Extravagance mark'd, and repeated Instances produced upon them. . . . However, all this Conviction and Discouragement wont do. They are Proof against Reason and Punishment, against *Fines* and Arguments, and come over again with their old Smut and Profaneness."[23] Lest any were tempted to forget, there were those who stood ready to remind them—Arthur Bedford, for example, a dissenting parson, whose *Evil and Danger of Stage-Plays* (1706) exposes upward of two thousand abominations raked from plays of the two previous years alone, "to prove the *Stage* to be a *Sink of Sin, a Cage of Uncleanness*, and the Original Cause of all our Profaneness." Bedford takes over Collier's method intact, utilizing it with a truly horrendous grimness and humorlessness, multiplying Collier's categories of offense and citing endless wicked phrases from the plays under scrutiny. He is more indignant even than Collier over the stage's refusal to physic itself. Far from purifying their texts, he complains, the poets have affixed prefaces to them, "in Vindication of *Plays* in General," and "in their *Acts*"—i.e., in the dialogue of their plays—have often inserted "Speeches to this Purpose."[24] Bedford cites with hearty approval a "presentment" addressed to the grand jury of Bristol protesting the erection of a playhouse in that town and demanding the cessation of all theatrical activity, a document one may suspect Bedford himself, a citizen of Bristol, of having authored, since he has discussed it already with detailed knowledge and warm approval in two earlier tracts, the second of which, *A Second Advertisement concerning the Profaneness of the Play-House*, expresses disgust at the fact

23. *Mr. Collier's Dissuasive from the Playhouse; in a Letter to a Person of Quality; Occasion'd by the Late Calamity of the Tempest* (London, 1703), p. 9.
24. *The Evil and Danger of Stage-Plays* (London, 1706), p. 16.

that a previous "advertisement" has been disregarded by the players. With predictable restraint and delicacy, Bedford thereupon concludes that players are *"Persons bold in Sin, and openly addicted to the Service of the Devil."*[25] The Devil indeed plays a more prominent role in Bedford's imagination than in that of any antitheatrical writer since the Restoration. As a hard-shelled fundamentalist, he reverts with a crashing emphasis to the old Puritan charge of idolatry, laying the existence of the theater squarely at the door of heathen gods and wicked spirits. Its sole purpose, he opines, is "to promote *Atheism* in the World," "to undermine *Religion*, and render both the sacred Majesty of *God* and his Judgments contemptible." Plays "shew to the World many dreadful Examples of all Sorts of *Impiety*, and expose *Vice* (as they tell us) not for Reproof, but for Imitation; not to suppress it, but to increase the Fashion."[26]

A dozen years later he is at it again, with perhaps the most Prynnian of all antitheatrical tracts since Prynne:

A Serious Remonstrance in Behalf of the Christian Religion, Against the Horrid Blasphemies and Impieties which are still used in the English Play-Houses, to the great Dishonour of Almighty God, and in Contempt of the Statutes of this Realm. Shewing their plain Tendency to overthrow all Piety, and advance the Interest and Honour of the Devil in the World; from almost Seven Thousand Instances, taken out of the Plays of the present Century, and especially of the five last Years, in defiance of all Methods hitherto used for their Reformation.

The title itself carries us back to a day when a title page could contrive to compress into its restricted compass a whole volume of furious objurgation. And the work bears out its forbidding frontispiece. It consists of an interminable and impenetrable jungle of citations of offensive extracts from plays mostly of the 1690s and 1700s, with a flood of marginal references to the texts quoted, and, by way of preamble or appetizer, a "Catalogue of above Fourteen Hundred Texts of Scripture, which are mentioned in this Treatise, either as ridicul'd and expos'd by the Stage, or as opposite to their present Practices."[27]

A somewhat more analytical polemicist, William Law, sees plays as

25. *A Second Advertisement concerning the Profaneness of the Play-House* (Bristol, 1705), p. 2.
26. *Evil and Danger of Stage-Plays*, pp. 101, 83, 195.
27. (Bath, 1719), pp. v–xx.

radically hostile to religion by their nature, since they utilize "Discourses," which "entertain the Heart, and awaken and employ all our Passions," and so "more fatally undo all that Religion has done, then several other Sins." Where Collier, if only out of tactical cunning, had been willing to distinguish the right use of a thing from its abuse, Law will admit of no such distinction, at least where plays are concerned. "Now it is to be observ'd," he declares, in drawing up his indictment, "that this is not the State of the *Play-House* through any accidental Abuse, as any innocent or good thing may be abused; but that Corruption and Debauchery are the truly natural and genuine Effects of the *Stage-Entertainment*."[28] Unhappily for the validity of his argument, Law proceeds to enliven it with little prose dialogues, in which imaginary personages answer the apologists for the playhouse with sallies against it. Whereupon an anonymous opponent bitingly takes notice that Law's "own Words are his best Condemnation. He exclaims against personating, or drawing Characters, and yet himself draws three Characters under the borrow'd names of *Lovis*, *Trebonia*, and *Jucunda*. This is the very Sin he cries against, yet cannot see the Beam in his own Eye."[29] The answerer is of course perfectly correct. The speeches of the characters in Law's dialogues constitute "discourses" every bit as much as the speeches of characters in plays. Even with the illustrious example of Plato behind him, it is hard to understand how a debater could so recklessly flout his own principles, so unconcernedly resort to mimetic dialogue in the very pamphlet in which he is uttering such vehement invectives against it. Plainly we are faced, as so often, with a prejudice deep enough to blind its exponent to the simplest illogicalities in his own dialectic.

However quaint they may sound today, it can hardly be claimed that Collier, Law, Bedford, and their adherents were merely quixotic. For they seem to have accomplished on a smaller scale what their antitheatrical grandfathers had accomplished so sweepingly in 1642. First

28. *The Absolute Unlawfulness of the Stage-Entertainment Fully Demonstrated* (London, 1726), pp. 5, 15.

29. Mrs. S— O—, *Law Outlaw'd: or, A Short Reply to Mr. Law's Long Declamation against the Stage. Wherein the Wild Rant, Blind Passion, and False Reasoning of that Piping-Hot Pharisee are made apparent to the meanest Capacity*, etc. (London, 1726), pp. 9–10.

they mobilized the free-floating suspicion of the theater always present in the merchant class, putting the theaters on the defensive; then they wiped them out as a significant cultural force. Doubtless they could not have done so without the unexpected aid of the Walpole government, smarting from the satirical gibes of opposition playwrights. Well before the government showed any interest in the matter, however, the copybook morality of the dissenters was already exerting its pressure on the stage, converting libertine comedy into sentimentalism. The clamors of the citizenry against the lewdness of the playhouses must have made it relatively easy for the authorities to step in and pass the terrible Licensing Act of 1737, which killed the free theater and drove its most gifted writer, Fielding, from the stage altogether. Henceforth control over plays was vested in the whim of a Lord Chamberlain, all but the two officially approved patent theaters were closed down, and—in a particularly odious regression—unattached actors once more reverted to their ancient status as rogues and vagabonds.[30] With the debate over the stage thus won in practical terms by the party of the negative, all serious debate came to a standstill.

Students of the antitheatrical movement have often drawn attention to the economic aspect of Puritan hostility, the charge that the theater encourages, or is thought to encourage, idleness, perverting youth from its business of learning a trade, hindering thrift and diligence, and (coincidentally) competing with the pulpit for the leisure of its parishioners, not to mention promoting an unsavory underworld of petty criminals—pimps, prostitutes, pickpockets, and their like—who batten on the presence of pleasure-seeking crowds with money in their purses. Unquestionably this impulse plays its part in the antitheatrical complex, and it is one that has been recognized, not always unsympathetically, by defenders of the stage itself. Dennis, for example, attempting

30. For the impact of the reform movement on the drama, see Krutch, *Comedy and Conscience*, ch. vii, pp. 150–191. For the Licensing Act, see P. J. Crean, "The Stage Licensing Act of 1737," *Modern Philology*, 35 (1938): 239–255; David H. Stevens, "Some Immediate Effects of *The Beggar's Opera*," *The Manly Anniversary Studies in Language and Literature* (Chicago, 1923), pp. 180–189; and Emmett L. Avery, "Proposals for a New London Theatre in 1737," *Notes and Queries* (May 23, 1942): 286–287.

a historical view of his subject, ascribes the measures taken against the Elizabethan theater to precisely such considerations, and approves: "For since the Interest of *England* is supported by Trade, and the chief Trade of *England* is carry'd on by the Citizens of *London*, it was not convenient that the young Citizens should have a Temptation so near them, that might be an Avocation to them from their Affairs"[31]—not, it is to be feared, a very intelligent comment from one setting out to champion the stage against its detractors. One sign of Collier's relative modernity is that he allows this ancient grievance to lapse. He shows no disposition to lament the plight of apprentices caught in the toils of the theatrical siren, and it is one sign of Bedford's regressiveness that he returns so heavily to this well-worn theme: "When *such* [i.e., as apprentices] leave their *Callings* to go to the *Plays*, it is but seldom that the Masters have any Command of those who are under them. . . . By this Means Families are disordered, and forced to keep unseasonable Hours, and therefore they cannot be so early about their lawful Callings."[32]

But Bedford can hardly be said to be alone in his alarm. We find the same chord struck loudly in a tract of Samuel Richardson's, *The Apprentice's Vade Mecum*, one of a number of handbooks that aimed to teach apprentices how to conduct themselves in their master's houses and discharge their duties properly.[33] Richardson expatiates lengthily on the perils of the stage. He stops short of condemning it on principle, advancing indeed what root-and-branch antitheatricalists would have thought an impious thesis: that "under proper Regulations, the Stage may be subservient to excellent Purposes, and be an useful Second to the Pulpit itself," and even confessing that as it is already conducted, with all its faults, it may be "a tolerable Diversion to such as know not how to pass their Time, and who perhaps would spend it much worse, either in Drinking, Gaming, &c. if they did not go to the Play-

31. *Critical Works*, I, 179.

32. *Serious Reflections on the Scandalous Abuse and Effects of the Stage,* etc. (Bristol, 1705), p. 29.

33. For the attribution to Richardson, and an analysis, see Alan D. Mc-Killop, "Samuel Richardson's Advice to an Apprentice," *Journal of English and Germanic Philology* 42 (1943): 40–54. A portion of this article reappears in the introduction to McKillop's edition of the *Vade Mecum* (see note following).

house."[34] The stage, then, cannot be said to be what so many of its ancient foes had declared it to be, the worst of all possible sins, the most unredeemable, the most pleasing to the Devil and hateful to God. But for apprentices it is quite bad enough, bound to conflict with the performance of their duties, and also to instill in them a mockery of the very calling in which most of them are destined to live out their days. Richardson rehearses some of Collier's strictures on the libertine hero of stage comedy, bringing the picture up to date with reference to plays about Jack Sheppard and Jonathan Wild, and instancing Lillo's *George Barnwell* as the sole example of a truly acceptable stage entertainment. He adds his voice to the outcry against the new playhouse in Goodman's Fields, which neighboring merchants had objected to for fear it would lead their households into disorder. This was the same Goodman's Fields Theater, founded in 1729, which was to be instrumental in launching David Garrick on his acting career, and which became the pretext for the imposition of the Licensing Act of 1737, as the result of a scurrilous play offered to the management, though never produced or printed.[35]

Richardson's objections to plays, in any case, concern their unsuitability for young citizens. Plays waste time and money; they tend to be performed during business hours, and so hurt trade; they expose young men to lewd women; and they portray sober men of business as fools and the dupes of the hero, who often specializes in cuckolding citizens. This last objection applies above all to comedies "written in a late licentious Reign, which are reckon'd the best, and are often acted" (p. 11). Clearly, even if libertine comedy was being supplanted by sentimentalism, the Restoration masterpieces still held the stage and still filled the theaters. They have the peculiar disadvantage, from Richardson's point of view, of being "calculated . . . for the Condition of Persons in high Life, and are therefore entirely unsuitable to People of Business and Trade, who . . . are always represented in the meanest and most sordid Lights in which the human Species can possibly ap-

34. *The Apprentice's Vade Mecum* (1734), ed. Alan Dugald McKillop, Augustan Reprint Society, nos. 169–170 (Los Angeles, 1975), pp. 9–10. Page references in the discussion that follows will be to this edition.

35. See Frederick T. Wood, "Goodman's Fields Theatre," *Modern Language Review* 25 (1930): 443–456.

pear." Though the theater may be tolerable "for the Amusement of Persons in upper Life," it must be "of pernicious Consequence when set up in the City, or in those Confines of it, where the People of Industry generally inhabit."

Public taste, clearly, while it disapproved the immorality of libertine drama, also welcomed it. On the one hand it craved revivals of the Restoration classics. On the other it saw them as a threat to its own values. It wished access to the theater, but not to have the theater at its doorstep, where it could become a standing temptation to the young to neglect their work. Despite the increasing influx of the middle class into the theater,[36] Richardson continues to regard it as an aristocratic pastime, in which the children of the citizenry have no place. In some ways the situation resembles that of Elizabethan London: then, while the ministers thundered from the pulpits, the people, unresponsive, betook themselves to their favored amusements. Now it is the compilers of guides to conduct who raise the alarm, while the apprentices stream to such playhouses as are within reach and within their means. Richardson worries that they will learn foppery, of which he gives a vivid sample in the portrait of a young shopkeeper's assistant he has encountered recently, decked out in elaborately modish attire, and he fears that the daughters of honest tradesmen may be taught vanity. The theater, which should be teaching "wholesome Rules" to its auditors with plays like *George Barnwell*, has instead planted among them:

An infamous Troop of wretched Strollers, who by our very Laws are deem'd Vagabonds, and a collected String of abandon'd Harlots . . . impudently propagating, by heighten'd Action and Scenical Example, to an *underbred* and *unwary* Audience, Fornication, Adultery, Rapes and Murders, and at best teaching them to despise the Station of Life, to which, or worse, they are inevitably destin'd; this must surely have fatal Effects on the Morals both of Men and Women so circumstanc'd. (pp. 17–18)

It was "fatal Effects" such as these which respected burgesses like the magistrate Sir John Barnard thought to forestall when he lent his support in 1735 to a bill "for restraining the Number of Houses for playing of Interludes and for the better regulating common Players

36. See Allardyce Nicoll, *Early Eighteenth Century Drama*, 3d ed. (Cambridge, 1952), pp. 412–413.

of Interludes." Sir John reflected the concerns of the merchantry. He "represented the mischief done to the city of London by the playhouses 'in corrupting the Youth, encouraging Vice and Debauchery, and being prejudicial to Trade and Industry.' How much more would these evils be increased if yet another playhouse were built in the very heart of the city."[37]

For Sir John Barnard, as for Richardson, economic, social, and moral considerations interpenetrate. Plays may injure the citizens as a class, but they also upset the moral equilibrium of susceptible young serving-men and apprentices, whose psychic health depends on their performing cheerfully their roles as well-governed members of the business community. If they cause trade to suffer, they also mar the happiness of the individuals misled by them. A more extreme instance of the economic point of view, divorced from any interest in the well-being of playgoers, appears buried among the early eighteenth-century pamphlets in the British Museum, in a remarkable "Letter to the Right Honourable Sir Richard Brocas, Lord Mayor of London, from an unidentified Citizen,"[38] which in the nakedness of its economic concerns might have been cited by Marx as a naive instance of the spirit of early capitalism, written in a day before employers had learned to cloak their predatory intentions under a guise of benevolence—before, indeed, it had even occurred to them that such a disguise might have its uses.

The aim of the letter is to urge Sir Richard to close down the playhouse newly opened in Goodman's Fields, and—to judge from the intensity of the author's disapproval—already doing a thriving trade. The stated grounds of the complaint are baldly and exclusively economic. England's prosperity, it is argued, depends on its manufactures, particularly its exports, and these, in turn, require a reliable supply of labor, which plays are bound to disturb. For in the first place, by painting the matrimonial condition as they do in such *"ridiculous Colours"* and with such "insolent Reflection[s]," plays encourage the male members of the audience "to gratify their Inclinations in a lewd and unlawful Way," and so distract them from their work, as well as hindering their capacity to reproduce their kind. Trade, after all, depends

37. Crean, "The Stage Licensing Act," pp. 241–243.
38. (London, 1730). Page references in the discussion that follows will be to this text.

on "the *Increase* of *useful and laborious Subjects*. . . . It is not . . . enough considered, that every *working Subject* is a real *Advantage* and a real *Treasure* to the Kingdom; and whatever is done to hinder the Increase of these, is a real Detriment to the Publick." It is all very well for fine gentlemen to waste their time and spoil their reproductive powers with profligacy; such fine gentlemen are already useless to the kingdom. Not so the working class: "In all good Policy the labouring, and the trading Part of the People should be engag'd by every possible Inducement, to marry, and educate a Race of healthy and laborious Children. By this Means there will be *more Work* done, as there are *more Hands* to perform it; and consequently the *Manufactures* will be *cheaper*; we shall make *greater Exports*, and gain more at foreign Markets" (pp. 6–10). The labor pool, in short, exists for the convenience of employers, to help lower the cost of exported goods, and enable manufacturers to compete successfully on the international market.

Plays not only interfere with marital function and procreative energy, they tend also to "*destroy all Notions of Religion*, and spread Prophaneness and Infidelity, and a total Disregard for every thing serious or sacred" (p. 11). This too can have grievous consequences for trade. For those who frequent plays will come to disbelieve in the reality of the moral laws, which depend upon a belief in punishment, which in turn depends upon a belief in religion.

Can there be a more strong, compendious, and intelligible Way of influencing the *whole* Behaviour of all Mankind, than by convincing, and inculcating upon them, that if they commit any Act of Villainy; if they cheat, lie, or forswear themselves; if they neglect the proper Duties of their Station; in short, if they are not honest Men, and useful Subjects, they will *suffer* the everlasting Displeasure of an *Almighty and All-knowing God* . . . . (p. 14)

The writer shows no interest in the soul's health of the workers. What matters to him is that they remain "honest Men, and useful Subjects." Religion, for him, is the opiate of the people, and therein lies its value. It maintains law and order among the potentially unruly. It is not its truth that matters, but its utility to the employer class, and did it not exist, it would be necessary to invent it. Plays, therefore, which weaken its grip, must be abolished.

The theater forms an unfit diversion for working people in other ways as well,

Not only as it brings them too much acquainted with that kind of Life, and those Ways of acting, which are above their Sphere, and therefore improper for their Knowledge; not only as it gives them Notions of Greatness and Pleasure, unfit for their Employments and Stations, in the World, or as it may occasion great Injuries to their Health; but also in that it is a Diversion that interferes with their Work, and *breaks* in upon their *Hours of Labour.* (pp. 18–19)

Ignorance, thus opines the worthy Citizen, is better than knowledge. Plays have an unfortunate tendency to acquaint the worker, in his lowly paradise, with lives far different from his own, which constitute a source of temptation and of idle ambition. The Citizen paints an affecting contrast between two kinds of worker, one the *"careful honest Man,"* all industry and sobriety, and the other "your *Mechanick* of *Pleasure,"* who frequents the theater, and, in consequence, works less, or, if given a fixed task, "will slubber it over in a hasty, slight, and careless Manner"; who leaves work early so as to be at the Playhouse, riots it half the night, and then rises distempered the next morning, his body disordered and "his *Mind* fill'd with *Scraps of a Play"* (p. 19).

The theater, however, not only jeopardizes the labor supply of manufacturers, it also threatens nearby merchants, whose clerks and apprentices risk being debauched by its proximity. At this point the Citizen attempts a rough computation of the loss suffered by the country as a consequence of the new playhouse, arriving at a startling estimate of between £200,000 and £300,000 per annum. He worries particularly about the effect on the silk trade, giving rise to the suspicion that he may be himself a prosperous silk merchant, unnerved by having a house of pleasure like the theater operating so close to his own place of business. The perils of foreign competition concern him greatly.

'Tis therefore, in a particular Manner, the *Interest of our Country,* that effectual Care be taken, that those concern'd in the making of *Silks* should be *constant* in their Labour, and do as much Work as can be done; that they should *live as cheap* as conveniently they can; and that their *Expences* be as *small* as possible. But notwithstanding this, shall we carry *Idleness, Debauchery,* and *expensive Diversions* into *that Quarter of the Town* which is concerned in this very Trade! (p. 25)

Marx himself could hardly have stated the case for the employer's attitude toward his workers more plainly. As a final inconvenience, the Citizen mentions the servant problem: "I will only add, that the universal Complaint of the *Badness of Servants,* seems to be in some Measure owing to the Liberty they enjoy at the Play-houses; for I can't help thinking, that if they had not the Privilege of the Footmens Gallery, they would be as little conceited and sober as they are at present" (pp. 27–28). So the defects of domestic service are laid at the door of the playhouse as well. As a stopgap remedy, until it can be closed entirely, the Citizen proposes a stiff tax on all seats. This will discourage impecunious spectators, who will then be unable to afford the price of admission.

Just as, in the earlier Puritan attacks, one often discerns social and economic motives behind the clatter of the rhetoric, so here one sometimes suspects the presence of deeper, more visceral prejudice, of a simple fundamentalism that would break out into biblical quotations if it thought they would help. Nevertheless, the Letter constitutes a remarkable document in the exclusively economic view it takes of the question. It assumes it as axiomatic that workers may be deprived of their pleasures by law, if those pleasures, in the opinion of employers, impair their efficiency as workers. The profit of the employer is unabashedly equated with the welfare of the nation as a whole. Though the workers' welfare is alluded to from time to time, it is instanced only in the way in which the health of farm animals might be mentioned in a treatise on animal husbandry. Like beasts of burden, workers must be kept free of disease, well enough fed to be able to endure toil and to reproduce abundantly, but expected to be "laborious" up to the limit of their strength, and to cost as little as possible to maintain. Stability in their marriages is desirable because it insures a good crop of offspring. Religion helps instill a dread of punishment which will inhibit selfish or subversive thoughts. Nowhere is the faintest concern expressed for their dignity as human beings in their own right, whose minds might make them discontented with their harsh lot, or whose tastes might legitimately conflict, on occasion, with the efficient performance of their jobs.

The theater, on this view, becomes a menace not because it fails to educate, but because it educates too well. It acquaints the worker with a sphere of existence different from his own, with a whole range of attitudes and sentiments other than those he encounters in his daily rounds. And so, as a vitalizing, interest-creating activity, it is "not proper for their Knowledge," because it makes them see the defects of their own lives so much more clearly. Jean Duvignaud's thesis, that the stage provides models, imaginary roles for the spectators to try on in their minds,[39] seems strikingly confirmed by the fears of the Citizen. For what the Citizen really dreads is that the worker, imagining himself leading the life shown on the stage, will learn to think past the confines of his own life, and having first ventured beyond it in imagination, will one day be tempted to abandon it in sober fact.

Adam Smith's *Theory of Moral Sentiments* (1759) provides a strange instance of a theatricalist morality which manages to sound like a product of eighteenth-century benevolism. Or perhaps it is a benevolent morality which adopts the vocabulary of the theater as its basic idiom. In either case it is an anomaly. One ordinarily associates the theatrical perspective with manipulators of illusion like Machiavelli and Castiglione, studying to create spectacular effects for purposes of power or self-realization, or with disillusionists like La Rochefoucauld, seeking to strip the gilding from a society that corrupts our relations with each other and falsifies our relations with ourselves. Smith, who repudiates the "hard" morality of Hobbes and Mandeville—the morality of self-interest—and who insists strongly on the native goodness of his kind, nevertheless contrives to found his own softer theory on a theatrical basis. Instead of promoting egoism or self-interest, his theatricalism manages to reinforce the premises of eighteenth-century optimism. A faint preacherly aroma drifts from the pages of Smith's treatise, possibly as a result of the fact that it originated in a course of lectures written for schoolboys. The tone, indeed, is that of one who while ostensibly investigating the foundations of ethics in a spirit of disinterested inquiry is actually waging an energetic campaign in favor of the received morality of his day, a morality heavily tinged with sentimentalism.

39. *L'acteur, esquisse d'une sociologie du comédien* (Paris, 1965).

Smith sees the moral sentiments, first of all, as responses to the behavior of others. They are essentially reactive. As we observe our fellows in action, their passions communicate themselves to us by a kind of natural instinct or sympathy.[40] Certain kinds of behavior, moreover, tend to induce "admiration and applause" in us—exactly as if we were at a play. We sit entranced as spectators of each others' lives, and nature has so contrived matters that we are perpetually "changing places in fancy" with those we watch, while those we watch change places, in turn, with us.[41] One immediately useful result of this interchange is that we learn to abate the violence of our own passions, for we wish to avoid appearing unseemly in the eyes of our companions.

Now this essentially theatrical construction, which casts us all as viewers and viewed, and puts the condition of spectatordom at the heart of the moral experience, might be interpreted in an ecumenical spirit, so as to minimize national and cultural boundaries, but Smith tends to interpret it parochially. He is aware that moral codes vary greatly from age to age and from nation to nation, and that an extremely relativistic anthropology might be based on them, but he nevertheless chooses to view them, when all is said and done, entirely as an eighteenth-century English or Scottish gentleman of comfortable means would view them, and implicitly to make that view the standard for humanity. He assumes, for instance, that men must curb the vehemence of their passions, that a high degree of self-restraint forms a necessary feature of the moral life, without troubling to inquire whether the higher value placed on self-expression, expansiveness, self-manifestation, and the like in other cultures might not be, from the viewpoint of his own spectator morality, an equally valid ideal. At the same time, his essential indifference to the customs of other cultures does not in itself invalidate his theory of their origins. The same mechanism, operating

40. Smith is here elaborating on Hume's doctrine of sympathy, as set forth in the *Treatise* and the *Enquiry concerning the Principles of Morals*, though dispensing with most of Hume's epistemological preoccupations. See Glenn R. Morrow, "The Significance of the Doctrine of Sympathy in Hume and Adam Smith," *Philosophical Review* 32 (1923): 60–78, esp. 69–70; Luigi Bagolini, *La simpatia nella morale e nel diritto: aspetti del pensiero di Adam Smith* (Bologna, 1952), passim; and A. L. Macfie, *The Individual in Society: Papers on Adam Smith* (London, 1967), pp. 50–51.

41. *The Theory of Moral Sentiments*, new ed. (London, 1853), pp. 20, 4. Page references in the discussion that follows will be to this edition.

in different ages and climates, might produce differing configurations of belief and behavior. What Smith often seems to be doing indeed is preferring one form of theatrical behavior to another. Clamorous grief, for example, he suggests, which "calls upon our compassion with signs and tears, and importunate lamentations," rightly disgusts us, but "we reverence that reserved, that silent and majestic sorrow, which discovers itself only in the swelling of the eyes, in the quivering of the lips and cheeks, and in the distant, but affecting, coldness of the whole behaviour" (p. 27). Might he not here be describing two schools of tragic acting, each with its own way of expressing grief, as well as two modes of sensibility, which we can for convenience call the Mediterranean and the Anglo-Saxon? One favors a reserved and tight-lipped style, which conveys feeling through the tremors that escape from an only partly successful effort at control, while the other gives way unashamedly to passionate outcries and vehement gestures. Whichever we prefer, we are in the theater, transmitting signals from the stage of ourselves, and receiving the signals being transmitted by our watchers. What is odd in Smith's discussion is his unexamined assumption that the Anglo-Saxon style is the right one, that it is natural and proper for "us" to prefer a "silent and majestic sorrow" to the more clamorous sort, when the same question, asked in Southern Italy, might receive the opposite answer, and yet the same mechanism of spectatordom lie at the heart of that also.

Smith often backs up his rules about our "normal" reactions with explicit reference to our experience in the theater, or of reading plays, poems, and histories, of looking at paintings and listening to music. We judge of the actions of our comrades, he tells us, exactly as we judge of "the productions of all the arts which address themselves to the imagination" (p. 30). We apply identical standards. Instead of explaining or justifying our aesthetic responses with reference to our moral sentiments, that is, Smith proceeds in the reverse direction. He elucidates our moral sentiments with reference to our aesthetic responses, and so ends by giving the latter a certain paradoxical primacy, making them fundamental to our entire moral constitution.

It is English as well as Aristotelian of Adam Smith to think of the "propriety" of the passions as lying in the mean between two extremes. Perhaps it is English of him to concern himself with "propriety" at all. It is certainly theatrical, since it has to do with our impact on others.

For those who believe in virtue as an absolute, the extremes hold no danger. One cannot be too holy; one cannot be too honest; one cannot be too engrossed with heavenly things or too disdainful of earthly. One can, however, make oneself ridiculous in the eyes of one's fellow creatures. The very concept of a mean between extremes seems to imply a watcher, assessing the decorum, which is to say the stageworthiness, of our performance. We know from *The Wealth of Nations* that Smith himself strongly favored the theater. He wished to see it liberated from the fanaticism of its adversaries, partly in order to check the exaggerations of fundamentalist morality at large. He counted on "dramatic representations and exhibitions" to dissipate "that melancholy and gloomy humour which is almost always the nurse of popular superstition and enthusiasm."[42] The fundamentalists, the antitheatricalists, he would imply, are insufficiently alive to the foolish figure they cut among their fellow mortals.

It will be noticed that Smith leans toward a somewhat coercive use of the first-person plural pronoun. No doubt most of his propositions would have been unhesitatingly endorsed by the bulk of his original readers. But by repeatedly declaring that "we" react in such and such a fashion, in such and such kinds of circumstance, he tends to prejudge questions, to settle them in advance before they have even been clearly perceived *as* questions. One feels, moreover, that the "we" stands not even so much for the inhabitants of the English-speaking world as for the much narrower élite of classically educated readers with whom Smith makes common cause. It is this audience that is being invoked when he illustrates the desirability of the mean by citing "our" reactions to pain in Greek tragedy (p. 37), or to love in the poems of Cowley and Petrarch (which "we grow weary of"), or in Ovid or Horace (whose gallantry and gaiety are "always agreeable" to "us"), or in Otway and Racine (pp. 40–41). It is this audience that reacts with indignation to the plight of Othello or the inhumanity of Iago (p. 44), this too which enjoys looking at "trophies of the instruments of music or of agriculture, imitated in painting or in stucco" (p. 46), or which reacts as it does to the various passions imitated in musical compositions (p. 49). While claiming to be mapping out a universal grammar, in short, Smith is actually compiling a regional dialect, applicable to only a small

42. *The Wealth of Nations* (Oxford, 1904), II, 435.

portion of a country which itself occupies only a small corner of the linguistic world.

One has the impression, even so, that the dialect has itself been rather carelessly patched together, that its rules lack a basis in systematic observation, being at the same time too subjective and too stereotyped— too much a reflex of Smith's private prejudices, and that those prejudices in turn are too obedient to sentimental clichés. We tend, says Adam Smith, to sympathize with others' joys more readily than with their sorrows, just as we more readily allow ourselves to laugh in company than to weep. We therefore "struggle against that sympathetic sorrow" which the tragic drama seeks to arouse in us (p. 64). The "mob," again, "never bear any envy to their superiors," and hence can enter wholeheartedly into the pleasure of triumphs and entries, while being unable fully to feel the grief of a public execution (p. 65). Now every one of these assertions might be challenged—both the observations themselves and the reasons given to account for them. It would take a quite different order of insight to persuade us so bluntly that we sympathize with others' joys more readily than with their sorrows. We might as bluntly counter with Rousseau's maxim in *Émile*, which declares the exact opposite: that "it is not in the human heart to put itself in the place of people who are happier than we, but only of those who are more to be pitied."[43] But even if we granted Smith's rule rather than Rousseau's, we might still find the reasoning hard to swallow. If it is true that we laugh in company more easily than we weep, is this really because we think our mirth will be more acceptable than our tears? Whatever the correct explanation of laughter may be—whether it comes from a sense of superiority and "sudden glory," or an unexpected revelation of the mechanical possibilities of human behavior, or a discharge of libidinal energy—it ordinarily involves a tinge of self-satisfaction, whereas weeping, which springs from frustration, places us in the humiliating posture of weakness, helplessness, and loss of control. It is hard, indeed, not to suspect that Smith's preference for his own axiom, and the explanation he offers for it, do not so much represent a con-

43. *Émile, ou de l'éducation*, ed. François et Pierre Richard (Paris, 1939), p. 262: "Il n'est pas dans le coeur humain de se mettre à la place des gens qui sont plus heureux que nous, mais seulement de ceux qui sont plus à plaindre."

clusion based on a sifting of the evidence as a wishful improvisation based on certain prior assumptions about our moral instincts.[44]

The difficulty reflects itself in the fact that (as one astute critic has put it) "many of Smith's examples of sympathy . . . assume the context of an eighteenth-century drawing-room or meeting-place, where the sociable nature of the gathering puts a premium on agreeableness and concord."[45] This is certainly the milieu Smith understands best, and it is the one that generates his definition of "the natural and ordinary state of mankind" as that of the man who is "in health, who is out of debt, and has a clear conscience" (pp. 62–63). Even assuming "clear conscience" to be an unambiguous and measurable quantity, can conditions such as these be satisfied by the spectators at an execution, the bulk of whom may be mangy, ragged, and dependent on petty crime for their survival? Smith attributes a state of peaceful well-being to the millions of a race who have probably lived in fear and need throughout most of that race's history. While claiming to speak for humanity at large, he is in fact speaking only for a tiny, privileged minority. As for the mob, far from feeling concern for the condemned man, the mob is more likely to view him with a mixture of triumph and gloating —triumph to the extent that they admire and recognize themselves in him, and welcome him as their champion, gloating to the degree that they reject such an identification, and wish to see him suffer. The mob, moreover, is curious. The mob is bloodthirsty, and welcomes the execution as a diversion, as Roman mobs enjoyed gladiatorial shows. The spectacle of violent death inflicted ritually on a victim designated by law would seem to be one of the oldest sources of gratification known to public man. Whatever the explanation for this unsettling state of affairs, it can hardly support a thesis of universal sympathy. Yet Smith never raises the question as to why, if we cannot enter into another's grief so easily as into his joy, public executions should for so long have been the mass entertainments history shows them to have been. Michel

44. Cf. R. F. Brissenden, "Authority, Guilt, and Anxiety in *The Theory of Moral Sentiments,*" *Texas Studies in Literature and Language* 11 (1969): 945: "Despite his originality, Adam Smith never departed too radically from what the ordinary educated *homme moyen sensuel* of the day wanted to believe about the moral character of himself and his society."

45. T. D. Campbell, *Adam Smith's Science of Morals,* University of Glasgow Social and Economic Studies, no. 21 (London, 1971), p. 123.

Foucault commences his study of prisons with an account of the execution, in 1757—two years before the first edition of the *Theory of Moral Sentiments*—of the regicide Damiens, whose long drawn-out and ingeniously varied tortures testified to the nature of executions in the eighteenth century—carefully ordered ceremonials in which the lesson of royal supremacy was inscribed on the body of the criminal, triumphal reconstitutions of royal sovereignty after the offender's assault on it, a "theater of hell" in which the victim's cries and struggles and blasphemies provided a foretaste of the torments he was destined to suffer in the afterworld. In this theater the public were required not only as spectators—to witness the rite, performed with much military panoply, of power restored—but also as participants, to add their own extemporized revenges to the formalized vengeance of the crown. The contemporary reformers cited by Foucault show themselves keenly aware of the cruel curiosity that drew people to such spectacles, and one chief aim of the penal reforms of the Revolution was to eliminate the theatricality of these occasions, which Smith views with such disconcerting blandness.[46] Smith seems too quick to improvise comfortable maxims about mob response, too ready to attribute goodness of heart to human nature at inappropriate moments, too anxious to avert his gaze from what is ugly and threatening in it—too prone, in short, to sentimentalize, too deficient in a sense of evil. The texture of his analysis lacks the quality of insight we find in moralists like Pascal or La Rochefoucauld, whose axioms carry painful conviction because they spring from both disciplined observation and unsparing introspection. Smith sometimes seems to be reaching out for observations to fit his theory, rather than evolving a theory from scrupulous and dispassionate observation.

Public executions, public humiliations of various kinds provide a major source of evidence about the moral sentiments for Smith, doubtless because of their inherently theatrical character. Much hinges on the claim that "we" identify ourselves with the great, that we incline naturally to "go along with" the passions of the rich and the powerful simply because they *are* rich and powerful (p. 73). If the logic of this seems dubious, it also seems unduly complacent about the hierarchical attitudes it might be subjecting to scrutiny. Unquestionably, many of Smith's pronouncements have a validity for his own time that they

46. Michel Foucault, *Surveiller et punir: naissance de la prison* (Paris, 1975), pp. 9–11, 49–55, 61–64.

would no longer have for ours. Social attitudes do change, and the superstitious reverence accorded a lord in the eighteenth century would doubtless find few echoes in Western society today. Nevertheless one is struck by the uncritical way Smith tends to underwrite an ethic based on clichés. Speaking, for example, of the hero reduced to humiliation, he tells us:

If he should be reduced to beggary and ruin, if he should be exposed to the most dreadful dangers, if he should even be led out to a public execution, and there shed one single tear upon the scaffold, he would disgrace himself for ever in the opinion of all the gallant and generous part of mankind. (p. 68)

But would he, in truth? Would the shedding of a single tear really blot out a lifetime of courage, even in the eyes of those most wedded to the dogma of the stiff upper lip? More important still, should it? Smith, we notice, does not on this occasion pretend to speak for the "mob," but for "all the gallant and generous part of mankind." At this moment he is not so much investigating morality as dictating it, prescribing his comfortable stoic stereotypes and attributing them to the other enlightened souls he claims to speak for, little interested in determining what the generality of men would actually feel under such circumstances.

Again, and still with reference to the victims of public correction,

A brave man is not rendered contemptible by being brought to the scaffold; he is, by being set in the pillory. His behaviour in the one situation may gain him universal esteem and admiration. No behaviour in the other case can render him agreeable. The sympathy of the spectators supports him in the one case . . . . There is no sympathy in the other . . . . Those who pity him, blush and hang down their heads for him. (p. 82)

Now whether this is or is not a correct account of how onlookers can be trusted to react at a beheading or a pillorying, it is quite plainly how Adam Smith *thinks* they react, and, what is more, how he thinks they *ought* to react. But why should the humiliation of standing in the pillory be more "contemptible" than that of being beheaded—or crucified? Should our esteem and our contempt depend so spinelessly on the whims of public officials? Smith seems almost to assume that all punishment is condign, and that it is proper for us to adopt the official view according to which the offender is to be honored or degraded by his penalty. In short, he seems to subscribe without debate, and without awareness, to the very defects of the theatrical, other-directed view we might have wished him to call into question.

His comments on social rank from the viewpoint of the socially well born betray a similar touch of complacency, a similar wish to see the situation as the assiduous frequenter of sentimental plays might see it. The young nobleman, Smith opines, is trained from infancy to live in the public gaze, and, in consequence, "as he is conscious how much he is observed . . . he acts, upon the most indifferent occasions, with that freedom and elevation which the thought of this naturally inspires" (p. 75). Bizarre consequence! Does the awareness of being observed actually inspire "freedom and elevation"? Might it not as easily constrain and inhibit? Who has not, at one moment or another in his life, felt his freedom and self-possession leaking away under the gaze of others? Nor does the young nobleman's case differ essentially from our own. For we all, *ex hypothesi*, live like the young nobleman, surrounded by spectators, by whose reactions we learn to adjust our behavior. Our experience is an attenuated version of his. Smith seems on this point wilfully to ignore the implications of his own theatrical scheme, just as on other occasions he too uncritically endorses them.

Having surveyed the moral sentiments as they concern our assessments of others, Smith goes on to ask how we arrive at judgments about ourselves. How do we regulate our own behavior? He finds that here we operate in the same way, except that instead of being the witness of our neighbor's actions, we turn our glance inward onto ourselves. As we judge our outward appearance with the aid of a looking-glass, which serves as an impartial eye, so when we come to assess our conduct, we examine it "as we imagine any other fair and impartial spectator would examine it" (p. 162). We divide ourselves into two beings, actor and spectator, judged and judging.

But the inner witness to whom we appeal is an *impartial* spectator. Not only do we instinctively crave the approval of our comrades, we also wish to deserve it. We wish their praise to be validated by something more than itself, and for this reason we are forced to become not merely spectators but *disinterested* spectators of our own acts. As so often, the psychological rules adduced in support of this proposition seem rickety: "The most sincere praise can give little pleasure when

it cannot be considered as some sort of proof of praise worthiness";
"Ignorant and groundless praise can give no solid joy"; "A woman
who paints could derive, one should imagine, but little vanity from
the compliments that are paid to her complexion," etc. (pp. 167–168).
Smith, once again, seems to be speaking for that putative "gallant and
generous part of mankind" whose spokesman he has appointed himself. The slackness of "one should imagine," in the case of the woman
who paints, suggests that a stereotype of the vain woman is being
foisted on us in place of actual analysis or observation. For Smith and
his gallant and generous associates it may be true that ignorant and
groundless praise can give no joy, but does this hold for the "mob"?
May there not be those who have never outgrown the childish craving
for praise whether it has been earned or not? Does not the desire for
praiseworthiness in fact form part of a powerful set of learned responses, not necessarily reducible to instinct at all? Who, indeed, can
know at all times whether the praise bestowed on him is well-founded?
Are we not often uncertain about the value of our own deeds until
they are praised or dispraised by others?

Praise, in any case, is the spur. "Nature, when she formed man for
society, endowed him with an original desire to please, and an original
aversion to offend his brethren. She taught him to feel pleasure in their
favourable, and pain in their unfavourable regard" (p. 170). Here we
touch bedrock in the theatrical morality, in the form of an instinctual
need to please, and hence to organize our lives so as to placate others.
But, as Smith's critics have had occasion to notice, such a purely theatrical mechanism at the base of our moral sentiments contains disturbingly relativistic implications, for the structure of spectatordom
and sympathy can in itself afford nothing either to confirm or discon-
firm the rightness of a given course of action, nothing to validate the
moral sentiments of one group against those of another.[47] Smith cannot
leave matters purely to the chance operations of such a principle, since
he himself subscribes so unequivocally to the morality of his own culture, and so plainly rejects that of other cultures or other climes where
they conflict with his. He requires some more trustworthy sanction for
the morality he takes to be true. He wishes, in short, to maintain that
"moral laws, despite the fact that they are inductively derived . . . from
experience, have a special status. They represent the will of the Deity,

47. See Campbell, *Smith's Science of Morals*, pp. 134–135.

and we are therefore obliged to obey them in any case."[48] At least, we are obliged to obey the moral laws as understood in England and Scotland, however we may choose to regard those governing Africa or Asia. To the supposition, then, that nature has endowed us with a desire to please, and an aversion to offend, Smith adds another: nature has endowed man "not only with a desire of being approved of, but with a desire of being what ought to be approved of; or of being what he himself approves of in other men" (p. 170). What *ought* to be approved of? What he himself approves of in other men? These criteria introduce new confusions and complications. For one thing, they seem phrased almost as restatements of one idea, yet clearly they must be distinct. What men approve of in others cannot always be identical with what *ought* to be approved of, since the auxiliary *ought* implies reference to some external measure, some objective and absolute standard, which could not possibly be derived from the hall of mirrors Smith has imagined the moral life to be. Smith is having trouble, it would seem, in maintaining the purely theatrical basis of the moral sentiments. The actor-spectator relation leaves man too much the creature of appearances, as La Rochefoucauld had already made clear. It holds us to no more rigorous standard than the wish to propitiate others. It takes no formal account of traditional moral imperatives, and contains every possibility of flouting these. It is to restore them, then, that Smith smuggles in the *ought* clause. What *ought* to be approved of sneaks in by a back door, having arrived there by way of the whole ethical tradition of Western Europe, and not at all by way of Smith's theatricalist psychology.

Hence the distinction, now drawn sharply, between two types of inner monitor, one the "indulgent and partial spectator," the other the "indifferent and impartial spectator"—or, in the apt terms of a recent commentator, between judgment based on a "*norm* of performance" and one based on an "*ideal* of performance" (emphasis mine).[49] The

---

48. Brissenden, "Authority, Guilt, and Anxiety," p. 954. Despite its eccentric-sounding title, this article contains an illuminating account of Smith's moral theories. On the problem of relativism and subjectivism, see also Macfie, *Individual in Society*, pp. 90–93.

49. J. Ralph Lindgren, *The Social Philosophy of Adam Smith*, International Archives of the History of Ideas, Series Minor, no. 3 (The Hague, 1973), p. 26.

appeal to the latter enables Smith to introduce a semblance of moral rigor into his scheme while at the same time clinging to its theatrical scaffolding. It is only the indifferent or impartial spectator who embodies both the severe conscience inherited from Judaeo-Christian and Graeco-Roman tradition and the watchful observer. This spectator serves as "the man within the breast, the great judge and arbiter of [our] conduct," or, as he is elsewhere termed, "the demigod within the breast." "Like the demigods of the poets," he is partly mortal but partly immortal also (pp. 185, 187). Immortal in that he originates in some autonomous and invisible realm. Mortal in that he sits within us as an incorruptible judge before whom we must plead our cause. It is this demigod, our conscience, to whom we appeal when the sentence of mankind goes against us, or who, conversely, ratifies the sentence in favor of our accusers. And it is this same inner judge who rules the actions of the man of "real constancy and firmness." Such a heroic man lives always in the view of the impartial spectator, whose decrees he not merely respects but fervently adopts for his own, almost becoming himself that spectator (p. 206). He thus is an actor of a special sort. He has trained himself to shape his performance to meet the expectations both of his playhouse audience, in the social world, and of the exacting audience lodged within the playhouse of his mind. If the inner audience serves as the truer guide, however, it nevertheless depends on the other. It exists to review the other's verdicts, and either uphold or overturn them. It decides whether the applause is genuine, or the blame fairly placed, but often in its turn it needs to be "awakened" and "put in mind of [its] duty by the presence of the real [i.e. the outer] spectator" (p. 216).

So the moral life, as Adam Smith reconstructs it, involves a perpetual oscillation of our attention between the real spectators in the world around us and the invisible one installed in the theater of our minds, who sifts and evaluates the evidence brought to it. The upright man is one whose conduct is "principally directed" by the inner spectator. Smith thus fuses outer and inner into a single system. With the theatrical arrangement he gains the advantage of a social standard, which acknowledges that men seek to ingratiate themselves with other men, and perform their parts in the world in the consciousness of being watched. It acknowledges also that a healthy fellow feeling lies at the basis of much of our activity. With the demigod conscience, on the other hand, the presumably well-informed and impartial spectator in the breast, he devises a pseudotheatrical adjunct which in fact derives its ultimate sanction from the absolutes of religion. Despite a certain adroitness in fitting these two essentially incompatible concepts together, they remain rather awkwardly superimposed. Smith manages to escape the relativistic consequences of his theatrical construct only by splicing onto it a quite alien system of values and giving this primacy over it.

From Smith's other-directed morality one may infer that the animus against the theater has begun to diminish. We have travelled far in fact from Collier—from the scourging of an actual stage for its baneful effects on morals, through the ambivalence of a moralist who also wishes to remove hindrances to moneymaking, to the selfish practicality of a Citizen interested *only* in moneymaking, to Smith's view of the moral life as a genteel theater of mutually self-correcting passions. Even in Collier we can sense some softening of the old rigid positions. Collier —not, after all, himself a Puritan—abandons the heavy-handed emphasis on the chain of interlinked abuses that had engrossed his predecessors: not only plays but playbooks and poems, not only acting but face-painting, hair-curling, and "lascivious, effeminate" music. Collier restricts himself almost abstemiously to the stage itself and its putative consequences. In the Citizen, we find the old nexus between antitheatricalism and morality, still evident in Richardson, ruptured. What remains is a cold pragmatism from which all nonmaterial considerations have been banished, and only the immediate goals of the inveterate moneymaker are treated as real or valid. In Adam Smith, finally, we find the theatricality of society, so scathingly anatomized by La Rochefoucauld, turning into something as innocuous as an invalid's pudding, and acquiring, in the process, some of the same faintly nauseous flavor. Smith's reluctance to face the implications of his own theatrical scheme almost ends by provoking an antitheatrical outburst from the reader. His complacency toward it, in any case, we may take as one advance signal of a changing climate, a harbinger of the more devious and complex attitudes destined to emerge in the following century.

· IX ·

The Case of
Jean-Jacques Rousseau

MAN IS BORN GOOD, declares Rousseau at various junctures in his career, and nature has taught him to desire the good; it is society that has corrupted him. Once upon a time—so runs the tale in the improvised anthropology of the *Discourse on the Sciences and the Arts*—mankind was nobler, simpler, more vigorous, more virtuous than it is now; women in particular were more modest and more chaste. Men's dealings with each other were marked by openness. There was no pretense because there was no need to pretend. Then came luxury, and in its wake came vice, injustice, and conspiracy, fomented by the development of the very arts whose products we now admire but which have helped to rot the social fabric. Today no man approaches his neighbor frankly and fearlessly, but there hangs like a pall over all our relations with each other a "uniform and perfidious veil of politeness"[1] behind which we conceal our true feelings—our mistrust, our rancor, our envy. Egypt, Greece, Rome, China, Byzantium—each of the great civilizations of the ancient world succumbed in turn to the debilitating effects of the arts. As men acquired a taste for luxury they ceased to devote themselves to tillage and soldiership, ceased to live simply, hardening their bodies with toil, and learned instead to compete with each other in vain display. They became "artists"—which is to say men whose existence is predicated on the desire to please, and who to be praised by their fellows will sell their talents at any price. Only the

1. "Ce voile uniforme et perfide de politesse" (*Discours sur les sciences et les arts*, in *Oeuvres complètes*, ed. Bernard Gagnebin and Marcel Raymond, III [Paris, 1964], 8).

rare incorruptible outpost, like Sparta, resisted. To its undying credit Sparta chased the arts and the artists, the sciences and the scientists, from its walls, and instead of the pompous marbles and other worthless trophies of degenerate Athens, left nothing to posterity but the memory of its heroic deeds.

With all its schoolboyish exaggerations and sophomoric paradoxes, the *Discourse on the Arts* sounds themes that will reverberate through Rousseau's later writings, notably that of the antagonism between civilization and virtue. The second *Discourse, On the Origins of Inequality among Men*, speculates anew on the transition from primitive "transparency" to civilized "opacity,"[2] tracing it to that imagined moment in prehistory when men, having long lived in isolation from one another, first banded together for mutual aid. At this moment, as the forests turned into agricultural settlements tilled by communal effort, the division of labor came into existence, and with it a hierarchy among men according to their capacities. Wit, strength, talent, good looks, property, all became necessary, first for survival and then for status. Those who lacked them took to counterfeiting them, and the end result was that condition of perfidious and self-serving politeness described in the earlier *Discourse*, in which Seeming parted company forever from Being.

Men's need for each other having led them to pretend, and so commit the first cardinal sin of dissimulation, their itch to excel produced the second great sin, of exhibitionism. It is to the "burning desire to have oneself talked of," the "fury to distinguish oneself," that Rousseau traces most of the failings, as well as the pitifully few benefits, of civilized society. For individual men, the lamentable consequence is that they have lost the knowledge of themselves.

. . . the savage lives only in himself; social man, always outside himself, only knows how to live in the opinion of others; and it is so to speak, entirely from their judgment that he draws the sense of his own existence.[3]

2. I borrow these terms from Jean Starobinski, *Jean-Jacques Rousseau, la transparence et l'obstacle* (Paris, 1957), passim, who, of course, derives them from Rousseau.

3. *Discours sur l'origine, et les fondemens de l'inégalité parmi les hommes*, in *Oeuvres*, III, 189: "C'est à cette ardeur de faire parler de soi, à cette fureur de se distinguer qui nous tient presque toûjours hors de nous mêmes, que

Rousseau thus views exhibitionism as a basic psychological datum. Almost by a law of our beings we consult others, and our perpetual referral of ourselves outward results in a radical falsification of our inner experience, until it is from others that we derive even "the sense of our own existence." On this point Rousseau anticipates the stress placed by psychoanalysis and phenomenology on the degree to which our beings are founded in our interaction with others. But for Rousseau this remains a deformation of civilized life, capable of being corrected. He holds in reserve a possibility his successors would view with skepticism—that by an effort of will, or a social reform, or a reconstructed education, we can tear our gaze away from our fellows, look into our own hearts, and refound our lives on a more autonomous basis. If the savage is capable of living "only in himself," it should not, presumably, be hopeless for civilized man to aspire to do the same.

Meanwhile, if society is cursed at the root by its theatrical origins, if it is itself only a perpetual charade of illusion, created by self-interest and self-love, the theater proper quintessentializes the evil. It takes a man already conditioned to be a hypocrite and an exhibitionist and makes him one by profession. It takes the ceremonial politeness of which social life is composed and makes it a model to be copied instead of a vice to be shunned. It submerges the actor's very identity in the masks he must assume in order to amuse. All the arts, for Rousseau, are tainted with the same infection. "Every artist wishes to be applauded; the praises of his contemporaries are the most precious part of his reward."[4] Art in any form is the one occupation Rousseau will not permit his protégé Émile to adopt. Émile is not to become a lace-maker, a gilder, a lacquerer, a musician, or a maker of books. "I would rather have him a cobbler than a poet; I would rather have him pave highways than make procelain flowers."[5] Stylistic refinement, the lav-

nous devons ce qu'il y a de meilleur et de pire parmi les hommes . . ."; p. 193: "Le Sauvage vit en lui-même; l'homme sociable toûjours hors de lui ne sait vivre que dans l'opinion des autres, et c'est, pour ainsi dire, de leur seul jugement qu'il tire le sentiment de sa propre éxistence."

4. *Oeuvres*, III, 21: "Tout Artiste veut être applaudi. Les éloges de ses contemporains sont la partie la plus précieuse de sa récompense."

5. *Émile, ou de l'éducation*, ed. François and Pierre Richard (Paris, 1939), p. 229: "J'aime mieux qu'il soit cordonnier que poète; j'aime mieux qu'il pave les grands chemins que de faire des fleurs de porcelaine."

ishing of attention on nuance and detail—not only are they useless and effeminizing, they all betray the same sick craving for the approbation of others.

Other playwrights have renounced the stage, have scourged and humbled their muse, have brought it into line with a sterner morality or a more rigorous piety. None has plunged from such extravagant success to such bitter apostasy as Rousseau, who, after the *succès fou* of *Le devin du village* (*The Village Soothsayer*), and his other lively ventures toward a theatrical career, went on to become one of the most dogged enemies the theater has ever had. In the process, his own highly theatrical temperament had clearly to be tamed and mortified by an infusion of antitheatrical moralism. Just as Plato reveals a nocturnal side of himself in the *Symposium* and the *Phaedrus*, an unexpected hankering after frenzy and mysticism, so Rousseau's whole career betrays a taste for the whimsical and the fantastic, a craving for irresponsible metamorphosis, a theatrical penchant for allowing himself to be totally transfixed and transformed by the objects of his imagination. A well-known passage from *Le persifleur* (*The Banterer*) describes his instability in markedly theatrical terms:

Nothing is more dissimilar from myself than I am myself. . . . At times I am a hard and ferocious misanthropist; at other moments, I wax ecstatic amid the charms of society and the delights of love. Now I am austere and devout . . . but I soon become an arrant libertine. . . . In a word, a Proteus, a chameleon, a woman are less changeable creatures than I am.[6]

At moments like this Rousseau comes close to sounding like Montaigne, a writer he often disparaged for his deficient candor. It is as if this protean quality, this wish to transform himself into successively dif-

6. Quoted in Henri Peyre, *Literature and Sincerity* (New Haven, 1963), p. 86. See Rousseau, *Oeuvres*, I, 1108: "Rien n'est si dissemblable à moi que moi-même. . . . Quelquefois je suis un dur et feroce misantrope, en d'autres momens, j'entre en extase au milieu des charmes de la societé et des délices de l'amour. Tantôt je suis austére et dévot . . . mais de deviens bientot un franc libertin. . . . En un mot, un protée, un Caméléon, une femme sont des êtres moins changeans que moi." For comment on this passage, and on the contradictions it points to, see Marcel Raymond, "Deux aspects de la vie intérieure de J.-J. Rousseau (intermittences et permanence du 'moi')," *Annales de la Société Jean-Jacques Rousseau* 29 (1941–42): 6–57, pp. 19–20 et seq.

ferent states of being, represented something at the same time infinitely seductive and terribly threatening, which had to be both appeased and violently denounced—indulged in his own person, violently denounced on behalf of his fellows, especially his fellow townsmen of Geneva. Geneva, which he revisited in imagination oftener than in reality after leaving it at the age of twelve, remained for him throughout his life a symbol of the vanished honesty in the world, a haven of innocence in a vicious society, and threatened with engulfment from that society as Sparta had been threatened by Athens.

The *Letter to d'Alembert Concerning Spectacles* (1758) owes its genesis to a few lines in Volume VIII of the *Encyclopedia*, which had just appeared. There d'Alembert ventures to suggest that Geneva might become an even more admirable center than it already is, might further cultivate the taste and refine the sensibilities of its inhabitants, if it possessed a resident theater. Rousseau, who detected in this proposal the Machiavellian hand of Voltaire, scheming to persuade the Genevan magistracy to allow him to continue his private theatricals unmolested, regarded it as a gauntlet flung down to virtue.[7] Appointing himself the champion at the same time of virtue and of his native city, he met the challenge with a furious counterattack in the form of a *Letter* to the author of the article, from a "citizen of Geneva." The *Letter* addresses itself in fact to two slightly different issues. One is the theoretical question of the theater as such. The other is the more immediate problem of the desirability of establishing one in Geneva. The two questions are not identical, for Rousseau is ready to concede that where manners have already decayed, as in Paris, the theater may actually help arrest the decay. It may help prevent idlers from turning into ruffians, whereas in Geneva, where manners retain their original simplicity, it can only deprave and adulterate.

Like most antitheatrical tracts, the *Letter to d'Alembert* advances few new arguments. Most of its positions had been staked out by Nicole, Conti, Bossuet and others in the previous century, as well as earlier by Plato and the Fathers. What distinguishes Rousseau's treatment is the

7. See *Correspondance générale*, ed. Théophile Dufour, IV (Paris, 1925), 17, 91. Rousseau also believed that d'Alembert's reason for printing the article was to pay court to Voltaire. He renders a scathing judgment on both: "Voilà les auteurs et les Philosophes! Toujours pour motif quelque intérest particulier, et toujours le bien public pour prétexte."

impetuous eloquence of his pleading, and the vigor with which he fashions a secular framework for what had long been primarily a theological argument. The theater is now judged not for its service to God but its utility to men. The quarrel with the theater merges into the larger quarrel with civilization itself for its hurtful effects on morality. Instead of lamenting our exile from Eden, or the fall of our first parents, Rousseau bends his efforts toward forestalling a second fall, that of Geneva, another Eden, demiparadise, worth defending to the death against the attempts of the serpent Voltaire to introduce into it the venom of the outer world.

Much of the central argument of the *Letter* stems directly from Plato, whom Rousseau had been rereading and restudying in preparation for his antitheatrical campaign. An essay entitled *"De l'imitation théâtrale,"* done in conjunction with the *Letter to d'Alembert*, conducts a tendentious inquiry into the nature of mimesis by way of a cento of paraphrases from Plato himself, whose positions are systematically resumed and reaffirmed.[8] Despite its derivative nature, and Rousseau's own indifferent opinion of it when he allowed it into print, this essay nevertheless revives with amazing energy the case against imitation. Though the basic steps in the argument retrace Plato's, the fiery expression is Rousseau's own, and bears witness to the responsive chord struck in him by the antitheatrical theses of the *Republic*. One favorite technique of adaptation is to rework Platonic insights as epigrams. "Imitation," for instance, "is always one degree farther from the truth than it is thought to be."[9] Or, again, "the art of representing things is very different from the art of making them known. The first pleases without instructing; the second instructs without pleasing."[10] Here Rousseau gives an aphoristic twist to Plato's distinction between false knowledge ("representing things") and true ("making them known"), managing to strike a sidelong blow against pleasure in the process. To make known means to disclose the essential nature of things, to see

8. "De l'imitation théatrale, essai tiré des dialogues de Platon," in *Oeuvres*, ed. Petitain and Musset-Pathay, III (Paris, 1846), 183–191.

9. Ibid., p. 184: "L'imitation est toujours d'un degré plus loin de la vérité qu'on ne pense."

10. Ibid., p. 184: "L'art de répresenter les objets est fort différent de celui de les faire connoître. Le premier plaît sans instruire; le second instruit sans plaire."

them as they really are, stripped of the accidents of color, shape, and timbre. Our senses may delude us, but then we have recourse to the arts of measuring and weighing and counting and comparing, to rectify our errors and rescue us from the tyranny of appearance. For Rousseau as for Plato, truth lies not in concrete particulars nor in what possesses the accent and the beat of life, but in the silent, invisible essences that underlie it. And just as Plato's own bent for abstraction seems often to clash with the mimetic world he summons so vividly into being, so Rousseau's commitment to the truths of quantity and measurement seem to clash with the highly particular, intimately personal accounting he makes of his own most fugitive emotions, conferring on them a reality we have no hesitation in conceding.

Following Plato, Rousseau calls the poet's alleged pretensions to knowledge sharply into question. He asks cuttingly, "If someone could have at his choice the portrait of his mistress or the original, which do you think he would choose? If some artist could make equally well the thing imitated or its simulacrum, would he give the preference to the latter, in objects of some worth, and content himself with a painted house when he could make a real one for himself?"[11] Rousseau thus finds damning equivalents of his own for the bed, the horse gear, and the flute which the Platonic artist is alleged, by painting, to be claiming to know something about. And one might be prompted to ask, as one asked of Plato, whether the artist really designs his imitation as a replica of the thing imitated, as a substitute for it. Does a painter paint a house in order to "have" a house? In order to "make" a house? Or in order to have a *painting* of a house. Does not the fact that he will in truth neither have a house nor make one free him from certain practical constraints, enable him to fashion one of a quite different character from that of the actual builder? Might he, again, not wish to "have," in addition to his mistress herself, her portrait? And for quite different reasons? Is there not, indeed, an equivocation on "have" which invalidates the whole argument? A mistress can never be "had" in the same sense as her portrait, except in the proprietary vocabulary

11. Ibid., p. 185: "Si quelqu'un pouvoit avoir à son choix le portrait de sa maîtresse ou l'original, lequel penseriez-vous qu'il choisît? Si quelque artiste pouvoit faire également la chose imitée ou son simulacre, donneroit-il la préférence au dernier, en objets de quelque prix, et se contenteroit-il d'une maison en peinture quand il pourroit s'en faire une en effet?"

of male chauvinism of which Rousseau himself was so dogged an exponent. Is there any but the thinnest and most inconsequential sense, then, in which the painting substitutes for the thing painted?

But Rousseau, like Plato, carries the argument directly into the realm of poetry. "As for the tragic author, if he really knew the things which he claims to paint, if he had the qualities which he describes, if he knew how to do himself everything he made his personages do, would he not himself exercise their talents?"[12] But—once again—what tragic author could ever have wished to "do" the things done by Clytemnestra, Orestes, Medea, Phaedra, Oedipus, or Creon? When did the writing of tragedy ever faintly imply the poet's capacity to *do* the things he depicts? And what would his power to do them in the real world have to do with his ability to represent them in words? What strikes one above all, in Rousseau's paraphrase, is the regressive nature of his imagination on this point, how heavily and literally he returns to Plato's own literalism, to the assumption that the aim of imitation is to turn out duplicates of things, and that this aim betrays an impotence to create the things themselves in the real world.

But Rousseau has fallen under what Karl Popper terms "the spell of Plato,"[13] and in this condition of bewitchment he tries to revive for Geneva the rigorous moral climate of the *Republic* and the *Laws*. Respecting mimesis, his antipathy is even more extreme than Plato's, since for Plato mimesis must of necessity form the basis of education, whereas the whole educational enterprise of *Émile* is an attempt to circumvent it as a formative principle. Nature may have planted the impulse in us —Rousseau will grant as much—but men have so distorted it that they imitate today only in order to ridicule others and degrade themselves, or else to impose on their fellows by fraud. "The basis of imitation among us comes from the desire always to transport ourselves beyond ourselves"[14]—to de-authenticate ourselves, as it were. No good

12. Ibid., p. 185: "Si donc l'auteur tragique savoit réellement les choses qu'il prétend peindre, qu'il eût les qualités qu'il décrit, qu'il sût faire lui-même tout ce qu'il fait faire à ses personnages, n'exerceroit-il pas leurs talens?"

13. K. R. Popper, *The Open Society and Its Enemies*, vol. I, *The Spell of Plato*, 2d ed. (London, 1952).

14. *Émile*, p. 99: "Le fondement de l'imitation parmi nous vient du désir de se transporter toujours hors de soi." There nevertheless does seem to be some exaggeration in Cassirer's statement that "Rousseau categorically de-

can come of it, in Rousseau's bitter view, and *a fortiori*, no good can come of the art that makes of it a mainspring.

Some of the same Platonic themes reappear in altered form in the *Letter to d'Alembert*. In addition, Rousseau transposes into a secular key some of the theses of his ecclesiastical forerunners—the proposition, for example, that the theater is an amusement, and that amusement is essentially harmful, that we should give up the craving for empty pleasures and find our pleasure in the satisfaction of our family duties. Without dwelling on the fact that these precepts come from a man who on his own admission had never willingly missed a performance of Molière,[15] and who had discharged his own family duties by turning over his (approximately) five children one by one to foundling homes, we may observe simply that this is one point, among several, which is not argued but assumed. The theater is categorized as a mere diversion, and all diversion is judged, without debate, as dispensable distraction.

The *Letter* begins, in its substantive part, by affirming that the theater affects us much less than we think. Spectators are interested only in seeing mirrors of themselves on the stage, in seeing their own passions reproduced and flattered. Whatever morality we find in plays we have brought to them ourselves. To the extent that they do affect us, therefore, they affect us for the worse, reinforcing and intensifying our existing weaknesses. Concerning our supposed identification with dramatic

---

nies the educational power of example" (Ernst Cassirer, *The Question of Jean-Jacques Rousseau*, trans. Peter Gay [New York, 1954], p. 124). For while Rousseau does claim that imitative virtues are merely "vertus de singe," and that the only good actions are those performed for their own sake and not because someone else has been seen doing them, still, "at an age when the heart as yet feels nothing, it is necessary to make children imitate those acts to which one would habituate them, while waiting for the time when they can perform them through discernment and the love of good" (*Émile*, p. 98): "Dans un âge où le coeur ne sent rien encore, il faut bien faire imiter aux enfants les actes dont on veut leur donner l'habitude, en attendant qu'ils les puissent faire par discernement et par amour du bien." This innocent-seeming concession is in fact tantamount to a major modification in Rousseau's whole educational program.

15. An anonymous Jesuit writes to Rousseau that "We could, Sir, be much more edified by all the fine things you say against the spectacles, if you did not at the same time tell us that it is in frequenting them that you have learned all those fine things" (*Correspondance générale*, IV, 132).

characters, Rousseau advances an odd notion: the masterpieces of the
past have no hold over us at all, since we have no power to put ourselves in the place of people who don't resemble us: Sophocles' best
plays would fail miserably on the current stage. Rousseau could hardly
have foreseen that time would refute him on this point, that the masterpieces of the past would regain some of their ascendancy over us,
but what really matters is his way of treating "resemblance" as an all-
or-nothing proposition. In Rousseau's scheme, the characters on the
stage either resemble us, or they don't. But this oversimplifies with a
vengeance. Resemblance in the theater, as elsewhere, is a highly elastic
phenomenon, coming in all shapes and sizes, all degrees of intensity,
and having to do not only with historical epochs but with rank, sex,
age, occupation, family circumstances, as well as the hundreds of subtler
categories through which men have been able to perceive a bond with
each other. And in its variableness, just as surely, lies one secret of the
stage, which can coax us into feeling a kinship with creatures who at
first sight may seem to have nothing at all in common with us. With
a scrap of resemblance the playwright can weave a dense tissue of identification, making us enter passionately into the fates of the most remote
and unlikely beings. Rousseau in effect concedes as much when he dis-
putes the playwright's claim to teach virtue. Would not any playgoer,
he demands, hearing of the crimes of Medea or Phaedra, detest them
far more *before* seeing them in action than after? And if so, do not the
plays, far from rendering vice odious, actually reconcile us to it?

Needless to say, the answer to the first of these questions would have
to be yes. A bare recital of the crimes of these characters would, and
indeed should, appall us, just as, thereafter, the witnessing of their
histories enacted on the stage would soften our antipathy and mitigate
our censure. But herein lies one aim of the plays in question, which
are not simply designed to make us declare vice vicious and virtue
virtuous. They reconcile us, as Marmontel nicely puts it, not to the
crime but to the criminal.[16] They make us feel what it might be like
to *be* Medea or Phaedra, and so dissolve some of our moralistic rigidity. The spectator who starts by thinking of Phaedra as a monster

16. Jean François Marmontel, "Apologie du théâtre, ou analyse de la
lettre de Rousseau," in Rousseau, *Oeuvres* (Paris, 1826), II, 269–384, p.
288: "Ce ne sont pas les crimes, ce sont les criminels que l'on déteste moins
à la fin de la pièce."

changes his mind as he comes to apprehend the intensity of her suffering. Rousseau, like other guardians of public virtue, wishes us to apply fixed and unvarying standards. He wishes us to judge the action only in its outward and visible bearings, as a presiding magistrate would judge it, not in its inner human meaning. He wishes us, that is, to *pre*judge it, to endorse with our minds the penalties of the law, against offenders who are to be excluded from human sympathy. But the theatrical process works to complicate our judgments and disarm our vindictiveness. It makes us apprehend these criminals as feeling beings like ourselves, in whom virtue may be as strong or nearly as strong as vice, but for whom circumstances may have been stronger, who have struggled painfully but at length unsuccessfully against their passions. And so, as it makes us less judgmental, it validates its claim to be teaching us something. It educates by widening our imaginative range. The fact that Rousseau wishes to keep our sympathies in a permanently contracted and hardened state means that he thinks of morality as something given, something complete and definitively fixed, rather than as something to be explored and revaluated.

With respect to *Bérénice*, a tragedy without a criminal, Rousseau complains that it makes us relent toward the protagonist. We start by condemning Titus for vacillating between love and duty, and demeaning with "effeminate complaints" the quasi-divine character assigned him in history.[17] We end by concerning ourselves sympathetically with his plight, pitying the passion that at first we rightly judged to be a crime. Once again, in Rousseau's view, our instinctive and natural reaction has been spoiled by our experience of the play. Now it may or may not be true that we start out blaming Titus so severely. But there is no doubt that as the action proceeds we identify more closely with him in his dilemma. And this involvement of ours, which Rousseau rejects, is precisely what the play labors to bring about. We start with a prior judgment, an official view, a formal prejudice inherited from "history." We end with the discovery that our initial reaction *was* a prejudice, that the "divine character" given the emperor may have had other and better reasons for it than the ones ordinarily given, that the

17. *Lettre à M. d'Alembert sur les spectacles*, ed. M. Fuchs (Geneva, 1948), p. 70. The *Letter* has been translated by Allan Bloom under the title of *Politics and the Arts* (Glencoe, Ill., 1960).

nature of his divinity may need to be redefined. Perhaps the claims of empire do not, indeed, outweigh the claims of love, or perhaps, if they do, one is called upon to regret the terrible cost involved, at which the dry facts of history, with their emphasis on the outward event, can barely hint. One of Rousseau's interlocutors, the actor Dancourt, alleges that the only authentic heroism would have been for Titus to prefer the virtuous Bérénice to the splendors of empire, and that his yielding to ambition rather than to "so legitimate a passion" degrades him in our eyes.[18] At very least, we may agree, his choice forms a tragic comment on the constraints of public life and the dehumanizing possibilities that lurk in the concept of *gloire*. But Rousseau wishes to see official morality reinforced, and quarrels with the play for subverting it. One might equally well be tempted to find in this subversion a sign of imaginative freedom and emotional generosity. The play refuses to rubber-stamp the moralistic meanings bequeathed by history; it insists on reassessing the situation afresh, developing its morality as it goes along. To see it, or wish to see it, as a vehicle for maxims about the folly of passion is to wish to reduce it to precisely the copybook truisms it is striving to transcend.

Again, Rousseau manages to wax indignant about the nature of the crimes depicted in ancient plays, professing a positive preference for gladiatorial combats. In the latter, he grants, real blood flowed, but at least one's imagination was not soiled by deeds that make nature tremble. But he himself has told us that we take away from the theater essentially only what we bring to it; the morality lies in ourselves, not in the plays. So too, then, must the immorality. The terrible crimes can hardly soil our imaginations. What might far more plausibly soil them would be the sight of human blood shed for our amusement. Which, we may wonder, would be the likelier to provoke imitation: the imagined crime, however horrendous, from which its victims rise up to have it inflicted on them again the following day, and the day after that, or the actual butchering before our eyes of men who, having

18. L. H. Dancourt, Arlequin de Berlin, *À Mr. J. J. Rousseau, citoyen de Genève* (Amsterdam, 1760), p. 206. It has been doubted whether either this, or another reply purporting to come from "P. A. Laval, *comédien*," were actually written by the actors in question, or indeed by actors at all. See Rousseau, *Lettre*, ed. Fuchs, p. 206.

amused us by dying, are then carted out of the arena to be shoveled into the earth? Sometimes it is the ferocity of Rousseau's own imagination that startles.

His strictures on comedy take us back to the dichotomizing didacticism of the Puritans, for whom vice is something to be denounced in pamphlet and pulpit, not ridiculed in theaters. The good, says Rousseau, do not use ridicule against the wicked; they crush them with contempt. Ridicule is the favored weapon not of virtue but of vice, and nothing diverts less than virtuous indignation. But Rousseau's own psychology has taught us that men are moved by the itch to display themselves, and comic technique, one supposes, might be entitled to avail itself of the fact for purposes of moral instruction. Ridicule, moreover, offers a more telling weapon than anger. It deprives the victim of his dignity, whereas anger magnifies him. If it is true that the wicked use ridicule against "us," perhaps it is because they have discovered how devastating it can be.[19] All the more reason, one might think, to wrest it from their grasp and wield it against them. But Rousseau, on this topic as on so many, thinks in Manichean absolutes. Indignation, his preferred weapon, is by its nature a reaction of outrage, an extreme. It tends to view its enemies as diabolic; it erases them from the book of life and casts them into the burning pit. It takes no account of the fact that vices, like resemblances, come in many shapes and sizes, not all of which require the ultimate penalty. Here ridicule has the edge. Unlike outrage, which admits of no gradations, it can range from the mild to the scathing. It does not imply, and still less does it clamor for, the dismissal of its victims from the human race, but rather, tries to heal them and restore them to the community. And as one aim of tragedy may be to soften our inflexible moral stances, so one aim of comedy may be to mitigate harsh correctives like contempt, to chastise while keeping the objects of chastisement well within the human pale.

Of the bravura discussion of Molière's *Misanthrope* it is perhaps enough to observe, together with Rousseau's other critics,[20] how in-

19. In fact, of course, as one of Rousseau's remonstrants points out, "La raillerie n'est pas l'arme favorite du vice," and "L'emportement est le plus souvent l'arme de l'hypocrisie et du fanatisme" ([Claude Villaret], *Considérations sur l'art du théâtre* [Geneva, 1759], pp. 27–28).

20. E.g., among others, Robert L. Politzer, "Rousseau on the Theatre and the Actors," *Romanic Review* 46 (1955): 250–257, esp. 253, and Ber-

tensely Rousseau identifies himself with Alceste in the play, and how totally this identification rules his analysis. What Rousseau sees is a man of heroic honesty, and virtuous contempt for the world's double dealing, being laughed at and making a fool of himself. He sees also, but at a less conscious level, what George Meredith has described so well: a "melancholy person, the critic of everybody save himself; intensely sensitive to the faults of others, wounded by them; in love with his own indubitable honesty, and with his ideal of the simpler form of life befitting it." He sees, in short, his own mirror image, and that the image has activated some of his deepest fantasies about himself there can be little reason to doubt. The result is that the whole discussion follows the lines of force created by this identity. Alceste, treated as a real type with whom Molière had no business to tamper, is praised for the respects in which he resembles Jean-Jacques—for being, in Meredith's memorable phrase, "a Jean Jacques of the Court"[21]—and Molière is reprimanded for holding him up to ridicule merely to amuse the patrons of comedy.

A more telling complaint concerns the nature of audience involvement. Tragic drama, Rousseau argues, draws tears from us when the equivalents in real life would leave us unmoved. It prompts us to lavish our pity on unrealities, so that we can escape committing ourselves to the relief of the miseries that lie all about us. And in so doing it constitutes a falsification, a perversion of the pity which, as he has elsewhere maintained, forms the basis of moral action.[22] True humanity would require persistence, the painstaking involving of ourselves in others' troubles in a way we are all too willing to be dispensed from. The theater salves our conscience by giving us a form of surrogate

nard Waisbord, "Rousseau et le théâtre," *Europe*, nos. 391–392 (1961): 108–120, pp. 116–117. Waisbord suggests further that Rousseau's theatrical imagination casts Voltaire as Philinte (p. 118).

21. George Meredith, *An Essay on Comedy and the Uses of the Comic Spirit* (London, 1897), p. 44.

22. See *De l'inégalité, Oeuvres*, III, 156: "La pitié est un sentiment naturel, qui modérant dans chaque individu l'activité de l'amour de soi même, concourt à la conservation mutuelle de toute l'espéce. C'est elle, qui nous porte sans réflexion au secours de ceux que nous voyons souffrir: c'est elle qui, dans l'état de Nature, tient lieu de Loix, de moeurs, et de vertu, avec cet avantage que nul n'est tenté de désobéir à sa douce voix," etc. For further comment, see Politzer, "Rousseau on the Theatre," p. 252.

pity, enabling us to substitute easy tears for difficult action. To this charge, which echoes one of Augustine's, there is no ready answer, since even today we know so little about audience psychology. The subject would require an exact and finely tuned sociology of a sort that has never been undertaken. From time to time a lynx-eyed observer, an Augustine or a Rousseau, will introspect his own reactions and try to generalize about the nature of the experience, but when it comes to the crucial matter of how we react in a group, how in mysterious fashion we cease being our individual selves and merge with the others around us, we remain largely ignorant. Nor do we have much evidence as to how the theater affects us once we have left it. We remain ignorant of what the effect is, on our behavior of Tuesday, of having wept in the theater on Monday. It is hard to believe, however, that the piteous aspects of tragedy make us *less* responsive to actual trouble than we would otherwise be. Reports on the effects of television violence seem to suggest that we respond (or nonrespond) in life situations as we have learned to do while watching the tube. If we have been schooled to gaze with unconcern on imaginary violence, we will do the same when confronted with real violence. Our normal channels of sympathy will have atrophied. If, on the contrary, we have learned to shed tears—as audiences of eighteenth-century pathetic drama had certainly learned—then it seems likely that we will respond so in similar situations in the real world—with an increase, rather than a decline, in sympathy. To be sure, there is much in Paul de Man's observation that pity, "the arch passion in Rousseau," is also itself "inherently a fictional process," which "transposes an actual situation into a world of appearance, of drama and literary language: all pity is in essence theatrical."[23] Pity, it would seem, intrinsically involves spectatordom, and passive spectatordom at that. We look upon the vexations of another and identify with him as we would if witnessing his sufferings in the theater. The more helpless we feel to come to his aid, the sharper our pity. The moment we reach out to grapple actively and energetically with his problems, we lose the theatrical distancing, the

23. Paul de Man, *Blindness and Insight: Essays in the Rhetoric of Contemporary Criticism* (New York, 1971), p. 132, elaborating on Jacques Derrida, *De la grammatologie* (Paris, 1967), pp. 247–250, 262, 269–272. See *Of Grammatology*, trans. Gayatri Chakravorti Spivak (Baltimore, 1976), pp. 172–175, 184–185, 189–192.

ingredient of imagination, that pity requires. Pity dissolves into something quite different, a direct confrontation with a real condition. Hypothesis for hypothesis, nevertheless, the one that posits some continuity between our response to the actors and our behavior at other times would seem more plausible than the one that posits a sharp disjunction between them, and Diderot's hope of using the theater to soften our feelings and teach virtue would seem to have a firmer psychological basis than Rousseau's view of it as a school for the hardening of the heart.

On the question of love in plays, and women in the theater, Rousseau's nostalgic primitivism equals in intensity even the antifeminist fervor of his priestly predecessors. In the cobbled up anthropology of the *Discourses*, it is women who have foisted the whole morality of love onto the world, and that morality, in its turn, which has so grossly inflated the importance of women. The code of courtship has for Rousseau little basis in nature. It is a factitious sentiment, born of custom, and fostered by women themselves in order to preserve their illegitimate empire and "render dominant the sex that should obey." From which it follows, logically if ungallantly, in the *Letter*, that women in plays are shown as exercising a wisdom which they do not in truth possess, and wielding an authority they have done nothing to deserve, just as the young are shown, in another condition contrary to fact and repugnant to good order, as outwitting their elders and triumphing over them. Rousseau's disapproval on this score does much to validate Jean Duvignaud's view of the theater as a kind of laboratory of the spirit, in which new social roles are tested.[24] By enabling new versions of humanity to be projected experimentally, plays aid in the process of social evolution. They help stake out the road to the future, and for this reason must appear uniquely dangerous to those bent on preserving or restoring some order—real or imagined—of the past.

Morality, for such backward-looking moralists, consists in a system of fences and No Trespassing signs. For them, the theatrical vision of women as images of authority subverts all order since it violates one of the most sacred of boundaries. It also gives undue prominence to love, which is virtually synonymous with a shameful abandonment to sensual pleasure. Rousseau cites with harsh satisfaction the driving of Manilius from the Roman Senate for having kissed his wife in the

24. *L'acteur, esquisse d'une sociologie du comédien* (Paris, 1965).

presence of his daughter.[25] Even if the embrace in question had been a frankly sexual one, which Rousseau is far from claiming, the Senate would seem to have been guilty of an emotional meanmindedness alongside which Manilius' open and easy affection appears entirely attractive. Needless to say, his expansive behavior corresponds much more closely to the ideal "transparency" of primitive man than to the code-ridden opacity of man in society. It is Manilius and not the Senators who gives evidence of the forthrightness Rousseau professes to admire, and the Senate which is busy forging the chains of a repressive social system. But in the conceptual world of the *Letter to d'Alembert*, "love" tends to reduce itself to a single, unvarying, and for the most part negatively charged concept, a matter of seduction and sensuality: "It seduces," says Rousseau, "or it is not love."[26] Now this motto may apply to these characters who experience love in plays, as it certainly applies to Jean-Jacques himself, with his lifelong fantasy of being swept away by tumultuous and irresistible passion. But does it apply to the *spectators* of plays? Does the playgoer find himself "seduced" by Phaedra's love? By Medea's? Does love in these instances not rather inspire horror and aversion? Does it not, in Rousseau's own favorite comedy, *The Misanthrope*, inspire derision? There can be no fixed formula for it, in life or in letters, except for those who are determined to reduce all of existence to formula.

With respect to the actors, the *Letter* rehearses, with much Jean-Jacquesque embroidery, a number of hoary prejudices. Actors lead disordered lives. The hostility to them, being universal, must be well-founded; it must reflect the inherent baseness of their trade. That trade consists of counterfeiting, obliterating their own identities in order to assume alien ones, turning themselves into ciphers, into nonpersons. That the same charge, as Marmontel, d'Alembert, and Dancourt all subsequently point out,[27] would have to be lodged against poets and playwrights, who must also and perhaps even more radically transform themselves into the persons they would cause to speak on the stage,

25. *Lettre*, p. 69; *Politics and the Arts*, p. 52.
26. *Politics and the Arts*, p. 55; *Lettre*, p. 74: "Il séduit, ou ce n'est pas lui."
27. Marmontel, "Apologie," pp. 377–380; d'Alembert, "Lettre à M. Rousseau, citoyen de Geneve," in Rousseau, *Oeuvres* (1826), II, 217–267, pp. 248–250; Dancourt, *À M. Rousseau*, p. 269.

is not a consideration that recommends itself to Rousseau, even if he had happened to come across it in the epistolary skirmish between Racine and one of the minor spokesmen for Port-Royal. A certain Dubois, defending the Jansenist translation of Terence against Racine's raillery, had distinguished fiercely between a translator and a poet of the theater. The former, he argues, is concerned solely with the rules of grammar; the latter has more dangerous things on his mind.

He feels all the passions he imagines, and even tries to feel them so as the better to imagine them; he grows heated, he is carried away, he plays the flatterer with himself, and waxes so impassioned that he ceases being himself altogether in order to enter into the feelings of the persons he depicts: he is sometimes Turk, sometimes Moor, now man, now woman, and only leaves one passion behind in order to take up another: from love he falls into hate, from anger he passes to revenge, and at all times he wishes to make others feel the same interior stirrings that disturb him; he is angry when he does not succeed in this miserable aim, and grows despondent over the evil he has not done.[28]

However peculiar may be the notion that a translator is interested only in the rules of grammar, and however inept the passage may be for its purpose of exculpating the translator while incriminating the playwright, its kernel of truth can scarcely be disputed, and it applies directly to Rousseau. But for Rousseau to have acknowledged it, or the principle behind it, would have involved not only the incrimination of Jean-Jacques Rousseau, playwright, composer of *Le devin du village* and other theater pieces, but also of Jean-Jacques Rousseau *romancier*, at this very moment deep in the gestation of *La nouvelle Héloise*, a whole enormous novel based on the principle of ventriloquism, in

28. Dubois, "Première réponse," in Racine, *Abrégé de l'histoire de Port-Royal augmentée de deux lettres du même, à l'auteur des hérésies imaginaires, avec les réponses de Mm. Dubois & Barbier d'Aucourt* (Cologne, 1770), p. 38: "Il sent toutes les passions qu'il conçoit, & il s'efforce même de les sentir, afin de les mieux concevoir; il s'échauffe, il s'emporte, il se flatte, il s'offense & se passionne jusqu'à sortir de lui-même pour entrer dans le sentiment des personnes qu'il représente; il est quelquefois Turc, quelquefois Maure, tantôt homme, tantôt femme, & il ne quitte une passion que pour en prendre une autre; de l'amour il tombe dans la haine, de la colere il passe à la vengeance, & toujours il veut faire sentir aux autres les mouvements qu'il souffre lui-même; il est faché quand il ne réussit pas dans ce malheureux dessein, il s'attriste du mal qu'il n'a pas fait."

which the author speaks now through the voice of one character and now another, but never (explicitly) in his own.

Rousseau will grant that the actor's transformations cannot be set down as criminal impostures. The actor does not necessarily deceive maliciously, but his art does consist in knowing *how* to deceive, and though he may practice it innocently enough in the playhouse, how is he to be prevented from turning it to evil on the outside? Having acted the thieving valet on stage, will he not be tempted to pick pockets in the street? Rousseau preserves silence on professions that wield more dangerous powers. He says nothing of kings or magistrates or clerical dignitaries, with their license to kill and crush and excommunicate, or of physicians, with their charter to cut, bleed, and purge. All these hold the power of life and death over their fellows, yet no one thinks to denounce them or pass persecutory laws against them. Only the actors, devoted to pleasing, and unprotected by status, come under the lash. The "guardians" of society may use violence as they please. Its humble entertainers must avoid the slightest suggestion that they have acquired any understanding of those vices on the representing of which their art and survival depends.

And if the actor, instead of playing scamps and rascals, happens to play saints and heroes, what then? Does his familiarity with the gestures of sainthood help him to achieve sanctity offstage, as his supposed intimacy with the techniques of pickpocketing enables him to turn thief outside? Naturally, the question is never raised. Two contradictory assumptions remain simultaneously in force, as they have in antitheatrical literature since the days of Tertullian: first, that when the actor imitates wicked actions he is revealing the truth about himself, or taking lessons in how to do evil, but that when he imitates good actions his imitation is a sham, since he is, after all, acting a lie, pretending to be what he is not. Sir Richard Baker, in 1662, had already remarked on the absurdity of this proposition, to no avail. Antitheatrical writers like Law and Bedford had simply turned a deaf ear. Now another theatrical apologist, the actor Dancourt, again exposes the puerility of the reasoning, and again the enemies of the stage close their eyes and stop up their ears. "Just a moment ago," Dancourt reminds Rousseau, "you reproached the actors for appearing what they are not, and for putting on a character not their own. Now you wish to make the public afraid that they are what they represent."[29] And Dancourt goes on to spell out the requirements of elementary consistency: if the actor's craft has such an impact on his moral self that when he portrays a knave or villain he must actually become that knave or villain, then it follows that he who plays the saint—plays Joad, Polyeucte, or Mardochée—must himself become a saint.

Actors, again, mean luxury, vanity, and display. They intensify the vices to which society is already prone. In the *Année littéraire* for 1759 appears an ironic commentary on Rousseau's treatise in the form of an unsigned letter from a draper, worried lest his own trade place his soul in a danger as great as that of the actor.[30] He too, confesses the draper, lives by catering to the taste for pleasure. He too must pander to his customers' vanity, only (he admits) he lacks the actor's extenuation in that he is in no position to reprove or ridicule the fops and gallants who frequent his shop. If he does not exactly make vice attractive, as the actor does, he does the next worst thing: he supplies all the trappings for it in the luxurious stuffs he vends. Moreover he wrecks many an honest citizen by tempting him into expenditures beyond his means. Even those whom he does not ruin he manages to seduce from the path of good works, for his regular customers must buy new materials for their clothes every season so as not to fall behind the fashion, and this means that they are unable to relieve the poor with alms, as actors regularly do. His shop, furthermore, is a seat of scandal and a court of calumny, like the theater, but, unlike the theater, it is a place where one can defame with impunity. Is not his soul then in greater danger than the actor's?

Without claiming that this *jeu d'esprit* gets far in the way of logical refutation, one may say that it exposes adroitly the prejudicial nature of the attack. Whoever seeks evidence to confirm a prejudice can usually find it. One can, indeed, find reason for anything, as the classical rhet-

29. *À M. Rousseau*, p. 275: "Vous venez de reprocher tout à l'heure aux Comédiens, de paroître ce qu'ils ne sont pas, et de revetir un autre caractere que le leur. Vous voulez ici faire craindre au Public, qu'ils ne soient ce qu'ils représentent."

30. *Année littéraire*, III (8 mai, 1859), 29–36, "Lettre d'un marchand d'étoffes d'or et de soie, à M. Desprez de Boissy," cited and excerpted in M. M. Moffat, *Rousseau et la querelle du théatre au XVIIIe siècle* (Paris, 1930), pp. 136–138.

oricians understood when they composed their eulogies on flies, parasites, and other trivial and contemptible objects, or as Sidney understood when he reminded his readers that "a playing wit can prayse the discretion of an Asse, the comfortablenes of being in debt, and the jolly commoditie of beeing sick of the plague."[31] In the same way, anything can be made the target of execration and obloquy. Rousseau, if not exactly a playing wit, is never at a loss for specious reasons to defend his prejudices. What the self-styled draper reminds us is that the animosity to actors springs less from reasons than from a deep-seated existential aversion, a visceral distrust of those who refuse to submit to the customary restrictions on identity, and whose profession thereby seems to be inviting the rest of the world to do likewise.

Rousseau, we should add, is guilty of perpetuating an old confusion which others in his day were beginning finally to disentangle. Those who addressed themselves to the problem of the actor's psychology in the seventeenth century usually assumed that the actor really felt the emotions he portrayed. To some degree, while he played, he actually became the character he was impersonating. The claim that acting could corrupt him hence acquired a certain plausibility, since with enough repetitions of a role he might be thought in danger of absorbing its qualities permanently into his own nature. Obviously, some such danger was felt by Plato to lurk in all mimetic activity. In the eighteenth century, belief in the actor's identification with his role became a cliché, to be laboriously parroted not only by the enemies of the stage but by its friends and well-wishers and successful practitioners. It led to a kind of Stanislavskian attitude toward the creation of character on stage—to the belief that, as Luigi Riccoboni put it, by speaking the *"Language of the Soul,"* or, in other words, by *"feeling the thing he pronounces,"* an actor could lend such an "Air of *Truth* and *Sincerity"* to his part as would make an irresistible appeal.[32] For Aaron Hill, adapting Sainte-Albine, "The performer, who does not himself feel the several emotions he is to express to the audience, will give but a lifeless and insipid representation of them," from which it follows,

31. *Apology for Poetry*, in *Elizabethan Critical Essays*, ed. G. Gregory Smith (Oxford, 1904), I, 181.

32. Luigi Riccoboni, "Reflections upon Declamation, or, The Art of Speaking in Public," in *An Historical and Critical Account of the Theatres in Europe*, etc. (London, 1741), pp. 1–36, 25–27.

absurdly but pseudologically, that *"No Man who has not naturally an elevated Soul, will ever perform well the Part of a Heroe upon the Stage"*; more absurdly still, that *"Players who are naturally amorous, are the only ones who shou'd perform the Parts of Lovers"*; and that if a tragic actor would:

Strongly impress the illusion of his performance upon us, he must first impress it as strongly upon himself . . . . In order to his utmost success, it is necessary that he imagine himself to be, nay that he for the time really is the person he represents, and that a happy frenzy perswades him that he is himself in his own person betray'd, persecuted, and exposed to all the unmerited injuries, for which we are to pity him.[33]

In Germany, following the same line of reasoning, the director Heinrich Gottfried Koch once "refused to give the role of Phaedra to an actress because he felt that she had not yet experienced true love and would thus be incapable of rendering the part convincingly."[34]

For those holding such views, which we may once again anachronistically term Stanislavskian,[35] the importance of mimicry dwindles, and the old charge against the actor—that he is a hypocrite, merely feigning sentiments he does not feel—becomes increasingly contradictory and pointless. The more level-headed among the antitheatrical controversialists therefore tend to drop this charge. With Cibber, Garrick, and the younger Riccoboni, on the other hand, we find the opposite thesis beginning to take shape: that the actor does *not* in any significant degree take on the identity of the character he is imitating. Garrick himself owed his success to a new acting style, which depended less on sensibility or declamation than on mimicry. Contemporary theater-

33. *The Actor: A Treatise on the Art of Playing* (London, 1750), pp. 16, 96, 115, 106.

34. Theodore Ziolkowski, "Language and Mimetic Action in Lessing's *Miss Sara Sampson*," *Germanic Review* 40 (1965): 261–276, p. 265.

35. Anachronistically, but by no means irrelevantly, since Stanislavsky, it appears, "shared the view of the great German actor Iffland who used to say that if an actor wanted to appear noble on the stage, he had to be noble in his private life too" (David Magarshack, ed. *Stanislavsky on the Art of the Stage* [London, 1950], p. 82), and he seems to have gone into transports of approval when he read Riccoboni's *Réflexions historiques et critiques* for the first time, in 1914—Edwin Duerr, *The Length and Depth of Acting* (New York, 1962), p. 214, quoting David Magarshack, *Stanislavsky, A Life* (New York, 1951), p. 336.

goers marvelled at his power to transform himself into a galaxy of characters, each different from all the others and from his normal self. When he was criticized, it was for being "overactive, overpantomimic, overvisual."[36] For such acting, a surplus of sensibility might well have seemed more of a defect than an asset. François Riccoboni's *Art of the Theater* argues indeed that "sensibility" is incompatible with acting, since acting requires control. If an actor has the misfortune genuinely to feel what he must act, then he is in no condition to command the changes of emotion which succeed each other so rapidly and explosively in plays. If, for example,

In a tender passage, you allow yourself to be carried away with the feeling of your role, your heart will suddenly contract and your voice will choke off almost entirely; if a single tear falls from your eyes, involuntary sobs will encumber your throat; it will become impossible for you to advance a single word without ridiculous hiccups. If you then must pass suddenly to the greatest anger, will that be possible?[37]

On the stage, again, true surprise is out of the question. The actor knows by heart everything that is going to be said to him. Often he arrives on stage for the express purpose of hearing it said. Nevertheless, his face, his voice, his body must still be able to register astonishment vividly enough to be believable to spectators. Rather more adroitly than the luckless Heywood, Riccoboni presses into the argument an incident from antiquity when an actual killing took place during performance. The actor Aesop was once roused to such a pitch of fury in his role as Orestes that he killed a slave who happened to be crossing the stage. But why, asks Riccoboni acutely, did he never kill any of the other actors who played with him? Because the life of a slave counted for nothing, whereas that of a citizen had to be respected, and at the peril of his own life. In other words, the rage was not entirely authentic; it was certainly not all-consuming; it left his judg-

36. Duerr, *Length and Depth of Acting*, pp. 225, 247–248.
37. François Riccoboni, *L'art du théâtre* (Paris, 1750), pp. 37–38: "Si dans un endroit d'attendrissement vous vous laissez emporter au sentiment de votre rôle, votre coeur se trouvera tout-à-coup serré, votre voix s'étouffera presqu'entierement; s'il tombe une seule larme de vos yeux, des sanglots involontaires vous embarrasseront le gosier, il vous sera impossible de proférer un seul mot sans des hocquets ridicules. Si vous devez alors passer subitement à la plus grande colere, cela vous sera-t-il possible?"

ment free enough to distinguish between a safe victim and an impossible one. The strain, then, which an actor feels while playing comes not from experiencing the actual emotion of the part but from the effort required to reproduce the external signs of it. According to this view, it would be consistent, if not necessarily correct, to accuse the actors of being hypocrites and impostors, but not of becoming the monsters and criminals they portray.

Two incompatible accusations, that is, formerly brought more or less indiscriminately against the actors, are now in process of being disengaged, but Rousseau, as we have seen, bent on making his own indictment as sweeping as possible, ignores the developing debate, and instead of helping to sort out the two positions, implicitly muddles them together once more. Nevertheless, the *Letter to d'Alembert*, on the whole, favors the "sensibilist" or "emotionalist" view, sufficiently so that it seems to have provoked a brilliant (though unpublished) riposte from Diderot, in the celebrated *Paradoxe sur le comédien*. Diderot carries Riccoboni's thesis as far as it can go, into a full-scale theory of the actor's phlegmatic calm and coldbloodedness. The great actor, says Diderot, is always self-possessed. In the midst of the most tragical tirades he can count the buttons on his partner's coat; while expressing the most poignant suffering he can take cool note of imperfections in the décor.

... I require in this man [the actor] a cold and tranquil spectator; I demand, therefore, penetration, and no sensibility, the art of imitating everything . . . . Great poets, great actors, and perhaps in general all the great imitators of nature . . . are the least sensitive of beings . . . they are too engaged in observing, in recognizing, and imitating, to be vitally affected within. . . . all his talent [the actor's] consists not in feeling, as you imagine, but in rendering so scrupulously the external signs of feeling, that you are taken in.[38]

38. ". . . il me faut dans cet homme un spectateur froid et tranquille; j'en exige, par conséquent, de la pénétration et nulle sensibilité, l'art de tout imiter . . . Les grands poètes, les grands acteurs, et peut-être en général tous les grands imitateurs de la nature . . . sont les êtres les moins sensibles. . . . Ils sont trop occupés à regarder, à reconnaître et à imiter, pour être vivement affectés au dedans d'eux-mêmes. . . . tout son talent consiste non pas à sentir, comme vous le supposez, mais à rendre si scrupuleusement les signes extérieurs du sentiment, que vous vous y trompiez" (*Oeuvres*, ed. André Billy [Paris, 1951], pp. 1036, 1038–39, 1040).

The great actor, in short, is magnificently, consummately a hypocrite, and to be admired as such. By reviving emphasis on the element of calculation, Diderot also rehabilitates acting as an art and discipline, against the emotionalists with their insistence on self-expression and identity between actor and role.

James Boswell reports a conversation in which the actor Thomas Sheridan espoused the cause of the sensibilists. "An actor," opined Sheridan, "ought to forget himself and the audience entirely, and be quite the real character." Sheridan's interlocutor, one Captain Maud, thought otherwise, "because an actor in that case would not play so well, as he would not be master of himself," a judgment endorsed by Boswell himself.[39] For Doctor Johnson, also, the notion that the actor transforms himself into the personage he plays is a vulgar error. If true, it would be a black mark against actors. "If Garrick really believed himself to be that monster, Richard the Third, he deserved to be hanged every time he performed it"[40]—a characteristic touch of common sense followed by a characteristic stroke of brutality, reminding us of Tertullian's equation of the real crime with the feigned one. Johnson makes the inner persuasion of evil as heinous as the evil itself, though in the first case the murdered dukes and strangled princes rise cheerfully from the stage, to be sacrificed again on the following night. Johnson's notorious scorn for the stage has Platonic overtones. On the tour to the Hebrides, he tells Boswell that "the action of all players in tragedy is bad. It should be a man's study to repress those signs of emotion and passion, as they are called."[41] Acting, then, in accord with sound Platonic doctrine, unleashes those impulses in us that most urgently need to be restrained, and it must, in consequence, be reckoned "bad," morally, and hence aesthetically as well.

Diderot, we may note in passing, is not without a tinge of antitheatrical sentiment of his own. This comes out in his comments on the actors, which can be almost as devastating as Rousseau's. Admiring their art, he nevertheless confesses that he holds them in low esteem

39. *Boswell's London Journal 1762–1763*, ed. Frederick A. Pottle (London, 1950), p. 109.

40. *Boswell's Life of Johnson*, ed. G. B. Hill, rev. L. F. Powell (Oxford, 1934), IV, 244.

41. *Boswell's Journal of a Tour to the Hebrides*, ed. G. B. Hill, rev. L. F. Powell (Oxford, 1950, 1964), p. 38.

as people. Even their greatest practitioners, he declares, are little better than clever puppets; all of them must be admitted to be essentially devoid of character. In Rousseau's eyes, the actor's trade corrupts him, alienating him from his true self. Diderot reverses the order: for him, the actor lacks a self to begin with, and it is because he has no character of his own that he is able to assume so many imaginary ones. In their offstage lives he finds them repellent: "Polite, caustic, and cold; ostentatious, dissipated, wasteful, self-interested . . . isolated, vagabond, at the beck of the great; few morals, no friends, almost none of those sweet and holy ties which bind us to the pains and pleasures of another, who in turn shares our own." Why do they go onto the stage in the first place? "Lack of education, poverty, a libertine spirit. The stage is a resource, never a choice. No-one ever became an actor out of love of virtue, from desire to be useful in the world, or to serve his country and family; or from any of the honorable motives which might lead a right mind, a warm heart, a sensitive soul, to so fine a profession."[42] And Diderot goes on to paint a harsh picture of the indigent rake (or the abandoned courtesan) turning to the stage as a last resort, there heightening the public's scorn for the profession, and, in response to that scorn—however mingled, in some cases, with adulation—sinking deeper than ever into self-hatred, and perpetuating in his own treatment of others the ruinous treatment he has received from the world.

Diderot's antitheatricalism, however, vivid as these extracts may make it seem, remains benign, since it views the low condition of actors as a historical accident, "an unlucky heritage from the old actors." As it springs from no necessity, it is capable of being dispelled by a reform of the stage, by making the drama truly a school of virtue. On this

---

42. *Oeuvres*, p. 1066:

Dans le monde, lorsqu'ils ne sont pas bouffons, je les trouve polis, caustiques et froids, fastueux, dissipés, dissipateurs, intéressés, . . . isolés, vagabonds, à l'ordre des grands; peu de moeurs, point d'amis, presque aucune de ces liaisons saintes et douces qui nous associent aux peines et aux plaisirs d'un autre qui partage les nôtres.

Qu'est-ce qui leur chausse le socque ou le cothurne? Le défaut d'éducation, la misère et le libertinage. Le théâtre est une ressource, jamais un choix. Jamais on ne se fit comédien par goût pour la vertu, par le désir d'être utile dans la société et de servir son pays ou sa famille, par aucun des motifs honnêtes qui pourraient entraîner un esprit droit, un coeur chaud, une âme sensible vers une aussi belle profession.

crucial point Diderot confronts Rousseau in absolute opposition. For Rousseau, the frequenting of the theater can be nothing but an exercise in self-indulgence. The citizen enters the playhouse in order to have his prejudices flattered, his passions aroused, his unworthiest instincts inflamed. For Diderot, he leaves his vices at the door when he goes to his seat. Under the mediation of the stage and his fellow spectators, he becomes a better man, newly susceptible to the impact of improving fictions, ready to respond with indignation to villainies he would be quite capable of committing himself in his daily rounds. What is needed is for playwrights to exploit this favorable psychological situation, to write plays that will speak to the best in the public, and cause it to bring its everyday actions into line with the feelings it can be made to experience in the playhouse. This once effected, the whole nightmarish cycle of degradation and self-loathing and public contempt into which the actor has been locked for centuries will melt away overnight. The actor will take part not as an idle entertainer, amusing society by pandering to its vicious side, but as a citizen making a valued contribution to social order, and his present shortcomings will come to be recognized as no more than a regrettable contingency, a temporary byproduct of his unfortunate past, in no way a brand of Cain setting him eternally apart from his fellows.

As plays mean love, so love means women, and women, in turn, mean actresses, against whose alleged immodesty Rousseau launches one of his most injurious diatribes. Women, he informs us, were meant by nature for modesty and a retired life. When they try to copy men they become odious; they deform themselves and dishonor their sex. When, as in the theater, they display themselves publicly for money, they become little better than prostitutes. Nothing is offered by way of reasoned argument for these and similar scathing assertions. Instead, we are offered a tableau of the happy mother, surrounded by her children, adored by her husband, obeyed and respected by her servants, making her domestic rounds as nature intended—as if this sentimental vignette constituted a crushing and definitive refutation of all known arguments in favor of a wider sphere for feminine activity—this, and a harsh comparison between the submissive, self-effacing wives of antiquity and the strident Amazons of Rousseau's own day, who combine the manners of the gutter with the sexual mores of camp followers.

It is hard to know what to say about this extraordinary outburst, except to notice how deeply it shares the primitivist patriarchal fantasies of *Émile* and the two *Discourses*, and how tightly it links antitheatrical-ism with antifeminism, how in the name of a "natural" morality it makes common cause with the Christian exponents of a divinely or-dained hierarchy between the sexes, and thus issues a challenge to the progressivism of the *Encyclopedia*. With the *Letter* as a whole, indeed, Rousseau breaks with the philosophes, and on no single issue does he oppose them so vehemently as on the question of women. Marmontel, for the Encyclopedists, then d'Alembert, and later Dancourt, all grap-ple more successfully with this problem than with the more familiar one of the morality of plays,[43] perhaps because on this point their thinking is less encumbered by tradition, less ready to bog down in cliché. What they see, the *philosophes*, is that inherited attitudes toward women must be understood as a consequence of the roles women have been required to play in society, and that those roles, having long since become fixed, in their turn perpetuate the inherited attitudes. This insight one might have hoped for from Rousseau himself, who seems almost to stumble onto it in the *Discourse on Inequality*. He is sketching the rise of despotism as one consequence of the establish-ment of inequality, precisely in the context of those differences between men which seem like the work of nature but in fact are the product of custom. Despotism, he says, came about when the rich man:

Conceived the most deeply pondered plot which has ever moved the human mind: to employ in his favor the same forces that were assailing him, to make his adversaries into his defenders, to inspire them with other maxims, and give them other institutions which were as favorable to him as natural right was contrary.[44]

The rich, that is, contrived to make the downtrodden cooperate in their own downtreading; they taught them to internalize their own servitude, to equate it with natural law, and then to consent to see

43. Marmontel, "Apologie," pp. 337–357; d'Alembert, "Lettre," pp. 250–256; Dancourt, *À M. Rousseau*, pp. 161–208.

44. *De l'inégalité, Oeuvres*, III, p. 177: "Conçut enfin le projet le plus réfléchi qui soit jamais entré dans l'esprit humain; ce fut d'employer en sa faveur les forces même de ceux qui l'attaquoient, de faire ses défenseurs de ses adversaires, de leur inspirer d'autres maximes, et de leur donner d'autres institutions qui lui fussent aussi favorables que le Droit naturel étoit con-traire."

it formalized into political institutions. Now exactly the same hypothesis might have been invoked to explain the inequality between the sexes. As the wretched of the earth have been coopted into perpetuating their own wretchedness, so women have been made to believe that nature meant them to obey, to sit by the fire and spin, to dread using their minds or bodies in any vigorous or creative way.

At one point in the *Discourses* the inference seems on the verge of crystallizing. Rousseau is discussing the different roles of the sexes, tracing these to the moment in prehistory when men first gathered together stable communities. Before this, men and women had lived identically. Now they took up differing tasks, the men becoming warriors, farmers, and planners, the women settling into household affairs. Differentiation of function, then, on this account, can hardly be reckoned among the primordial facts. It arises in the course of a social evolution; it owes its existence not to nature but to nurture. But Rousseau, far from drawing the inference, passes it by as if with blinkers on, and we find him, in the *Letter to d'Alembert*, opposing the theater for Geneva because it would bring the sexes too much together. Nature, he informs us, has prescribed for women a "sedentary and homebound life," for man a strenuous and active one.[45] If we wish to follow nature, therefore, we will separate the sexes as much as possible. Otherwise, men will be softened and effeminized by too much frequenting of women, as women rendered immodest by too freely consorting with men. The theater threatens to demolish the No Trespassing signs which Rousseau sees as essential to the preservation of society.

It also, of course, brings the sexes together not only as members of an audience but on the stage, a condition he regards as "scandalous." One of his antagonists inquires, pointedly, where lies the scandal in seeing men and women together? What could more plainly belong to the order of nature? Would it not be more scandalous to imitate the Greeks, and cast men in women's roles?[46] The issue beautifully illustrates the nature of prejudice. For who can doubt that if men actually had played women's parts on the eighteenth-century stage,

45. *Politics and the Arts*, pp. 101–102; *Lettre à d'Alembert*, p. 136: "La Nature, qui impose aux femmes cette vie sédentaire et casaniere, en prescrit aux hommes une toute opposée."
46. [Eugène Eléonore de Béthisy, Marquis de Mézières], *Critique d'un livre contre les spectacles* (Amsterdam, 1760), pp. 46–47.

no one would have been more shocked and horrified than Rousseau? What more heinous nullification of the self, what greater derangement of nature could be imagined, than the parading in public in the garments of the other sex? What practice more calculated to debauch and effeminize? Who can doubt that Rousseau would have resumed all of the most furious reprehensions of the Fathers and the English Puritans on this topic, and added a few picturesque ones of his own? But prejudice operates on the principle of the double bind: it will admit as valid, will proclaim as valid, arguments antithetical to its own arguments, so long as what it argues is allowed to be right.

It is always tempting, in behalf of a deeply rooted prejudice, to invoke the authority of nature. A belief intensely held seems like God-given and self-evident truth to the believer. If Rousseau, wishing to maintain the segregation of the sexes, appeals to nature, so his opponent, wishing to promote their mingling, likewise invokes nature, and, we may think, with greater plausibility. What surprises and discourages, in the *Letter to d'Alembert*, is to find this technique wielded so sophistically by someone of such powerful and probing intellect, who is normally so disinclined to coast in the grooves of received opinion. He tells us, at one point, that "according to the order of nature," resistance in courtship belongs to women; it is men who must play the aggressors. But the pigeons outside his study window, which he cites in illustration, tell a different story.

The white female goes following her beloved step by step and takes flight herself as soon as he turns around. Does he remain inactive? Light pecks with the bill wake him up; if he retires, he is pursued; if he protects himself, a little flight of six steps attracts him again. Nature's innocence arranges the provocations and the feeble resistance with an art which the most skillful coquette could hardly attain.[47]

Of this repellently charming vignette, one may say first that it shows the female to be at least as forward as the male. If one were impartially analyzing patterns of aggression and passivity, one might easily con-

47. *Politics and the Arts*, p. 87; *Lettre à d'Alembert*, pp. 116–117: "La blanche colombe va suivant pas à pas son bien-aimé, et prend chasse elle-même aussi-tôt qu'il se retourne. Reste-t-il dans l'inaction? De légers coups de bec le réveillent; s'il se retire, on le poursuit; s'il se défend, un petit vol de six pas l'attire encore; l'innocence de la Nature ménage les agaceries et la molle résistance, avec un art qu'auroit à peine la plus habile coquete."

clude from the doves' behavior that it was the female's role to pursue, and the male's to resist and delay. It is hard, in fact, to magine Rousseau, with his puritanical views about feminine modesty, actually endorsing behavior of such unabashed flirtatiousness as a model for his own kind. He himself has warned us, in the *Discourse on Inequality*, against drawing inferences about human sexual habits from the study of animals, for "one must start by excluding all those species where Nature has manifestly established in the relative power of the sexes other relations than among us . . . the combats of game cocks form no basis for induction concerning the human species."[48] How, then, does one decide which species can safely be supposed to shed light on human behavior? How does one decide to argue from the observation of pigeons, but not of game cocks? Obviously, only by making prior judgments as to what constitutes natural human behavior. Nature, in short, emits confusing and contradictory signals, which it is left to the interpreter to decode. The reasoning is thus perfectly circular. Rousseau has decided, prior to all experiment, that men are meant to pursue and women to resist. Then he has decided that pigeons can be used to illustrate the thesis among the lower animals. Finally, he has proceeded to describe a scene in which the more plausible conclusion would in fact be the reverse of the one he draws. The appeal to "nature" turns out to be a disguised appeal to his own prejudices, a picking and choosing among the kinds of evidence to be admitted, and a misrepresenting of the evidence actually selected, in order to bend it to his polemical purpose.[49]

Something of the same coerciveness distorts his equation between Geneva and Sparta, which exploits a few tenuous likenesses while ignoring a host of profound differences. His fixation on Sparta had long ago drawn raillery from his friend Bordes, following the publication

48. *De l'inégalité, Oeuvres*, III, p. 159: "Il faut commencer par exclure toutes les espéces où la Nature a manifestement établi dans la puissance relative des Séxes d'autres raports que parmi nous: Ainsi les combats des Cocqs ne forment point une induction pour l'espéce humaine."

49. Lionel Trilling, speaking of the "anti-Parisian and antimodern tendency" of the *Letter to d'Alembert*, and "its resistance to the influence of women," says that "it cannot be called anti-feminine" (*Sincerity and Authenticity* [Cambridge, Mass., 1972], p. 62, n. 1). But I would say it can *only* be called antifeminine.

of the *Discourse on the Sciences and the Arts*. In response to Rousseau's eulogy of Spartan virtue, Bordes had suggested that Spartan valor, poverty, frugality, and patriotism "cease to be virtues when . . . subordinated to the lust for domination," and he had gone on to enumerate bitingly the Spartans' well-known vices, "their tolerance of adultery and sexual inversion; their inhumanity toward their slaves and prisoners of war; their base flattery of the Persian satraps."[50] This time, following the publication of the *Letter*, it is Marmontel who chides him for trying to superimpose upon a peace-loving modern state like Geneva the ethos of an ancient military city.[51] One of his own Genevan compatriots hastens to correct the misapprehension according to which Sparta refused to harbor a theater. Not only did Sparta have its theater, closely resembling the theater of Bacchus in Athens, "it was the finest ornament of that city so renowned for the courage of its inhabitants."[52] In short, the supposed incompatibility of the theater with civic valor lacks all basis. But Sparta casts a hypnotic spell over Rousseau that no amount of sober evidence can undo, and Geneva, similarly, remains in his mind an image swathed in nostalgia and impervious to the claims of reality. He pastoralizes Geneva as he has pastoralized Sparta, projecting onto them both his fantasies of a golden age in which hard work prevailed, luxury was unknown, and men dealt plainly and openly with one another. In Geneva, as in Sparta, the enemy is time. For the ravages of time to be held at bay, all change must be resisted. "The least change in customs," he has avouched much earlier in the preface to *Narcissus*, "even if advantageous in certain respects, always ends as prejudicial to manners. For customs are the morality of the people, and

50. F. C. Green, "Rousseau and the Idea of Progress," The Zaharoff Lecture for 1950 (Oxford, 1950), p. 9.

51. "Apologie," pp. 347–348.

52. *Correspondance générale*, IV, 105: "Non seulement il y avoit un théatre à Sparte, absolument semblable à celui de Bacchus à Athènes, mais il étoit le plus bel ornement de cette ville si célébre par le courage de ses habitans." Rousseau, it should be added, replied humbly and courteously to this reproof, promising to correct the error in a second edition, and requesting the writer's permission to quote him (*Correspondance*, IV, 106). In the event, he left the passage as it was. This may have been an inadvertence, although he made another correction of some importance at about the same point in the text.

as soon as it ceases to honor them, it no longer obeys any rule but its passions or any restraint but its laws."[53] Custom, then, is sacred because it is. In its realm, whatever is, is right, and whatever threatens to alter it poses a deadly threat to the moral health of its votaries. For Rousseau as for Plato, the ideal is one of immobility and stasis; whatever promotes change must be combatted with every available weapon of logic and persuasion.

As severe Sparta stood in austere contrast to decadent Athens, so simple, rough-hewn Geneva silently rebukes corrupt Paris. In one rhapsodic passage Rousseau eulogizes the rustic ways of the old Neuchâtel mountaineers, living out their lives remote from the urban centers, finding their recreation in family activities like woodworking, ironworking, tapestry weaving, sketching, flute playing, and the singing of four-part psalms. Geneva, too, has its "circles," or clubs, which preserve the antique customs. In the circles one can speak out in praise of virtue or of country without being thought a bore. Men and women can go off to their separate recreations, the ones to their outdoor sports, their drinking and gambling and rough talk, the others to their fireside schools of slander and censure, each in their own way marking once more the difference between the sexes imposed by nature. Characteristically, Rousseau all but ignores the actual facts about the circles: they had been found troublesome by the Genevan consistory for promoting "drunkenness, disorderly conduct and neglect of family duties," and were in disfavor with the ruling oligarchy as well, which thought them "centers of subversive discussion and criticism."[54] For

53. Preface to *Narcisse, Oeuvres*, ed. Gagnebin and Raymond, II (1964), 971: "Le moindre changement dans les coutumes, fut-il même avantageux à certains égards, tourne toujours au préjudice des moeurs. Car les coutumes sont la morale du peuple; et dès qu'il cesse de les respecter, il n'a plus de régle que ses passions ni de frein que les loix."

54. Lester G. Crocker, *Jean-Jacques Rousseau*, II, *The Prophetic Voice (1758–1778)* (New York, 1973), p. 11. The eulogy of the circles stirred protest from a number of Rousseau's private correspondents as well. His friend Dr. Tronchin pronounced them "a source of distraction, of loss of time and of dissipation, which exceed the honest bounds of a needed amusement, and distinctly injure home education." With the fathers gone, the children grow up undisciplined, in some cases even delinquent (*Correspondance*, IV, 117–118). Another writer points out that while certain of the circles may be irreproachable, others include people of no principles and no morals, occasioning abuses of order and of morality (IV, 121). Still

Jean-Jacques, nevertheless, they are made to symbolize a vanishing innocence. Allow the theater into such a milieu, he warns, and the idyll will collapse. The "rudely simple" manners of the honest Genevans will quickly succumb to affectation. The thirst for inequality will once more reassert itself. Tragedy will make the citizens yearn vainly for power and grandeur, acquainting them with the duties of kings while teaching them to neglect their own. As for comedy, instead of curing old follies, it will provide instruction in new ones. Plato banished Homer from his Republic; are we to allow Molière in ours? One may note, parenthetically, the habit among antitheatrical writers of referring to Plato's Republic as if it actually existed—as if Plato were recommending the destruction of all copies of Homer and the banishment of the tragedians from his own Athens, instead of from a visionary utopia designed to provide a blueprint and an ideal. Athens, in fact, adds Rousseau in an extraordinary sentence, perished through the fury of the theater; we must prevent the same thing from happening to Geneva.[55]

But, he asks at length, if we may not have theatrical spectacles, must we give up spectacles altogether? By no means. Let us, he urges, expand and enhance those spectacles we already have, our republican fêtes, those outdoor gatherings at which we celebrate our collective well-being. Let us hold athletic contests, gymnastic games, naval tournaments, and chaperoned balls at which the young can dance under the benevolent eyes of their elders—but let not the elders themselves dance, for that, adds Rousseau with a gratuitous touch of prudery,[56] would be to profane their conjugal dignity. Let us award an annual prize to the best-behaved young girl in town. And let us model these pageants on the civic festivals of Lacadaemon, in their simplicity, their freedom from pomp, and their patriotism. So we shall satisfy at once our wish for spectacle and our craving for community.[57] Rousseau offers sim-

---

another regards the circles as politically suspect, especially when composed of young people (IV, 140).

55. *Politics and the Arts*, p. 121; *Lettre à d'Alembert*, p. 163.

56. On which see Mézières, *Critique*, pp. 61–63.

57. Like the praise of the circles, the proposed annual ball arouses resistance, even pique, among Rousseau's Genevan correspondents. One informant declares that balls are already too frequent as it is; multiplying them could only work to the detriment of religion and virtue (*Correspondance*, IV, 186). Another quotes extensively from his sister, a maiden lady living in the country, who reacts with indignation to the proposal. Do not

ilar advice, years later, to the framers of the Polish constitution, when they consult him, in his capacity as sage and political architect, about the structure of their new state. Let all ordinary amusements, he tells them, all gambling, all theater, all comedy, all opera, be abolished, even at court—or rather, especially at court, since it is from the court that the rest of the country will take its bearings. Instead, let there be instituted fêtes and solemnities of a more democratic kind, open-air festivities in which all the people will take part, as they did in classical days.[58]

The key to this newer, and at the same time older, form of spectacle is total participation, the breaking down of the arbitrary barrier between stage and audience. All the actors now become spectators, and all the spectators actors. No one any longer *represents* anyone other than himself. One is reminded of Rousseau's dislike of representation in the political sphere, against which he argues vigorously in *The Social Contract*. "Sovereignty," he says there, "cannot be represented, for the same reason that it cannot be alienated; its essence is the general will, and will cannot be represented."[59] In other words, free men cannot surrender their freedom to agents and deputies. Nor can they do the analogous thing in the theater: they cannot surrender their power to be themselves, and to manifest themselves fully, to surrogate creatures like the actors. In traditional drama, the actor stands for other men—

---

mothers have enough to do already, demands this lady, watching over their daughters, averting the dangers that threaten them, regulating their manners, without having their task doubled by this inventing of new occasions? Will they not have to devote even more time than they do now to adorning their daughters instead of teaching them household duties? Will not the balls produce a disagreeable rivalry between mothers as well as between the daughters? Even now, in winter time in Geneva one hears of little else but dances. Are we not to be allowed to preserve what is left of our natural modesty and simplicity? etc. (IV, 123). In short, many of his correspondents may be said to out-Rousseau Rousseau in their unwillingness to allow change, their eagerness to preserve their own archaic simplicity.

58. "Considerations sur le gouvernement de Pologne," *Oeuvres*, III, 962–963.

59. *The Social Contract*, III, 15, trans. Maurice Cranston (Harmondsworth, 1968), p. 141. *Oeuvres*, III, 429: "La Souveraineté ne peut être réprésentée, par la même raison qu'elle ne peut être aliénée; elle consiste essenciellement dans la volonté générale, et la volonté ne se réprésente point."

either for mankind at large, as in the English morality drama, or mankind reduced to certain moral and social categories—king and commoner, hero and villain, saint and sinner. Even the most intensely individualized stage figure always retains something of this exemplary character. As we watch him we find that we are gazing at ourselves, entering into his actions and his passions as if they were our own. But in the public festivals imagined by Rousseau, no man will represent anyone but himself or be represented by anyone but himself. The spectacle will constitute an expression of the general will, pouring itself out in a communal joy in which all artificial distinctions between persons will disappear.

A close analogue to the patriotic festival projected for Geneva appears in the festival of the wine harvest in Book V of *La nouvelle Héloise*, which Jean Starobinski rightly sees as one of the master keys to the whole work of Rousseau.[60] In this vision, composed at about the same time as the *Letter to d'Alembert*, we find a similar festival, an affair of the open air rather than the indoors, which in its rustic simplicity expressly recalls the golden age. It involves the same improvisatory spirit, the same temporary obliteration of social distinctions, as those who have cooperated in the winemaking enterprise gather together to share the fruits of their toil—those fruits themselves, needless to say, being virtually synonymous with conviviality and the dissolving of the barriers between men. All classes participate, and all ages as well: at a given moment each day the children are brought in to complete the community. Everyone eats the same rough but nourishing peasant soup and drinks the wine that all have labored to produce. Like the proposed Genevan festival, the *vendange* is accompanied by dancing and music, by the raucous sound of rustic instruments and the sweeter one of the harvest-women singing in unison—unison because, for Rousseau as for Plato, simplicity means purity and innocence, whereas the complexity of harmony spells the onset of corruption. If the theater, in Starobinski's terms, is the world of opacity, the *fête* is that of transparency. The true meaning of the occasion lies not in the wine but in the opening of hearts, in the people's freeing themselves from the alienation imposed on them by a falsifying society. The note struck by the writer is rhapsodic:

60. *Jean-Jacques Rousseau*, pp. 116–121, et seq.

One forgets one's century and one's contemporaries; one is transported back to the time of the patriarchs; one longs to lend one's own hand to the work, to share the rustic toil and the happiness that one sees to be linked to it. O time of love and innocence, when women were tender and modest, when men were simple and lived content![61]

All social obstacles and falsities melt away, in short, and all the deformations that the theater not only reflects but aggravates. From the alienating solitude of the darkened auditorium, where our liberty was captured and nullified by the spectacle, we move to the exhilarating, liberating out-of-doors, where the community "expresses itself in the very act of communication, and takes itself for the theme of its exaltation."[62]

Jean Duvignaud has seen in Rousseau's proposal the vision of a new form of theater.[63] The old élitist theater, with its cube set, which gathered its audience into darkened halls to tell them of man's fixed nature and his tragic helplessness to control his destiny, is to be done away with and replaced by a popular theater, which will express man's freedom to remake himself and his world in accord with his desires and needs. Such a theater, of course, is very much what Rousseau's revolutionary disciples labored to bring about more concretely later on, in their festivals of the Supreme Being, the Goddess of Liberty, and the like. But the festivals disintegrated into something as fragmented as the theaters they were meant to replace, with ideological factions representing various shades of revolutionary opinion replacing distinctions between rank as a principle of division and a breeder of discord.[64] Furthermore, they quickly took on allegorical trappings which

61. *Oeuvres* (1964), II, 603–604: "On oublie son siècle et ses contemporains; on se transporte au tems des patriarches; on veut mettre soi-même la main à l'oeuvre, partager les travaux rustiques, et le bonheur qu'on y voit attaché. O tems de l'amour et de l'innocence, où les femmes étoient tendres et modestes, où les hommes étoient simples et vivoient contens!"

62. Starobinski, *Rousseau*, p. 118.

63. *Les ombres collectives: sociologie du théâtre*, 2d ed. (Paris, 1973), pp. 359 ff.

64. Jean Duvignaud, "Idéologie dans la fête, le fête dans l'idéologie," in *Fêtes et civilisations* (Geneva, 1973), pp. 120–143. See also David Loyd Dowd, *Pageant-Master of the Republic: Jacques-Louis David and the French Revolution*, University of Nebraska Studies, New Series, no. 3 (Lincoln, 1948); and Joseph Butwin, "The French Revolution as *Theatrum Mundi*," *University of Washington Research Studies* 43 (1975): 141–152.

linked them to the *ballets de cour* and other older aristocratic divertissements. They strikingly failed, then, to embody the unity and fra-
ternity they were supposed to be celebrating, and they failed equally
to preserve the spontaneous and nonmimetic character crucial to Rousseau's own conception.

In theory, no doubt, such patriotic manifestations as those dreamed
of by Rousseau would have drawn on certain elements of theater: the
community's admiring fascination with its own image, the reinforcing
of common beliefs and shared instincts, the self-rejoicing and self-
renewal implied by the displays of prowess, the voyeuristic pleasure
involved in watching others perform. But such spectacles would also
of necessity have sacrificed much that we may regard as intrinsic to
the theater, and especially the element of fiction and impersonation,
the assumption by the actor of an identity not his own, with all the
possibilities for imaginative exploration this permits. Doubtless the
mimetic instinct is too strong within us to be abolished by a stroke
of the philosopher's pen, or even by parliamentary statute. To banish
it from the theater would in any case be to leave the theater denatured
and devitalized, deprived of one of its life-giving ingredients. The
Rousseauesque fête, indeed, would impoverish even the element of
exhibitionism itself, since the kind of display it proposes is largely
acrobatic and athletic, leaving no room for the expression of the full
personality of the total man, with his inner life, his existential per-
plexities, and his temperamental idiosyncrasies. Doubtless, with stretch-
ing, one can make the theater into an umbrella term covering a multitude of loosely related activities: baseball games, boxing matches,
sailing regattas, square dances, spelling bees, cakebaking contests, and
high masses. But these, in truth, deserve the term largely by courtesy
of analogy. At best they represent a truncated form of theater. They
inhabit the fringes of a concept whose center must permit disguise
and play and fabulation as well as full revelation of human identity.
It must encompass not only the cheerful stare of patriotic well-being,
but the more quizzical gaze of skeptical inquiry; it must be able to
interrogate and unsettle as well as to affirm. To restrict it to simple
affirmation, and to prescribe the mode of that affirmation, as Rousseau
would do, as Plato wished to do when he recommended that the poets
be allowed only to offer hymns to the gods and odes in praise of heroes, is to decorticate it and save the husk instead of the kernel, to

throw away its germinal principle. It is to make it over, after so many centuries, into a communal rite in which neither imagination nor intelligence is allowed a voice.

Rousseau cannot, then, be really said to be offering a program for the reform of the theater, but a prayer for its suppression. The new society is not in fact to be encouraged to evolve its own morality but to revert to an earlier one, to that paradisal time when men were hardy and virtuous, women housebound and obedient, young girls chaste and innocent. In such a reversion, the theater—with all it symbolizes of the hatefulness of society, its hypocrisies, its rancid politeness, its heartless masqueradings—has no place at all.

· X ·

Antitheatrical Prejudice
in the Nineteenth Century

ROUSSEAU'S HARSH ELOQUENCE, reinforcing the civic prejudices of the Genevans, found its mark. So much one may infer immediately from the letters of congratulation that streamed in on him from his fellow townsmen upon the publication of his book.[1] It effectively blocked the creation of a theater in Geneva for another generation, and it helped delay for as long a time the lifting of the official stigma from actors in France. The players of the French national theater, though applauded and acclaimed as never before, continued also to endure a persecution as senseless as that of the *infamia* of the late Roman Empire. Under the laws of the crown, they were forbidden, like the Roman comedians, to leave their profession, and subject to a variety of grotesque indignities from their immediate overseers, the Gentlemen of the King's Chamber, who regulated their lives with capricious despotism, determining when they should play and where and in what, and throwing them into prison, even the most illustrious of them, at the slightest hint of re-calcitrance. At the same time, while chained to their profession by the crown, they were denounced for it by the church, forbidden the sacraments, and stamped with opprobrium at every turn.[2] The result of incessant harassment from the authorities, and the public scorn that mingled with the public adulation, was to make them insolent and overbearing in their turn to those who in some sense depended on them,

1. See Jean-Jacques Rousseau, *Correspondance générale*, ed. Théophile Dufour, IV (Paris, 1925), 103 ff.

2. See Gaston Maugras, *Les comédiens hors la loi*, 2d ed. (Paris, 1887), pp. 215–221 et seq.

notably the dramatic authors, including such devoted champions of their cause as Voltaire.³ When the Revolutionary Assembly finally came to annul the old prohibitions—not without protest from one member who had read the *Letter to d'Alembert* and could report that its writer, a patron saint of the Revolution, regarded actors as inherently vicious⁴ —when it finally admitted actors to citizenship along with the rest of the population, permitting them to be married without having to go through the humiliating farce of renouncing their profession one day and being ordered back into it by the Gentlemen of the Chamber on the next, when the whole savage system of sanctions began to be dismantled, at least on the part of the secular authorities, then actors themselves began quietly to emerge into the light of day as honest creatures like their neighbors, equally undeserving of the wild adulation and the cruel impairments that had been their lot for over half a century.

In England, where no comparable impairments had been inflicted, and the actors had been allowed a tolerable measure of human decency, no such spectacular stroke of rehabilitation was needed. But the fierce Protestantism of the English clergy continued to scorch the theater with its hot breath, and to muster adherents among the pious laity when it could. As Geneva refused to allow a theater in its midst, so the Congress of the United States passed a resolution in 1778 condemning all theatrical representations, along with gambling, horse racing, and cock fighting, as sinful and intolerable; with the result that theatrical activity, for the next decade or two, retreated into the universities, where even so it could fall under the lash of precisians like Timothy Dwight, who warned his students at Yale that to frequent the theater was to lose their souls.⁵

We have glanced at Doctor Johnson's retrograde sentiments already. Further instances of his lifelong dislike for the actors might be cited, but it is hard to escape the suspicion that the dislike stemmed less from principle than from resentment at the failure of his own tragedy on the stage, and envy at the meteoric career of his pupil David Garrick. More typical of midcentury antitheatricalism would be that of John Witherspoon, later Principal of Princeton College, whose *Serious Inquiry into*

3. Ibid., pp. 359–364.
4. Ibid., pp. 418–419.
5. Leónie Villard, *Le théâtre américain* (Paris, 1929), pp. 3, 12, 104.

the Nature and Effects of the Stage energetically resumes all the familiar arguments on the subject and adds a few unfamiliar ones for
good measure. Like his predecessors, Witherspoon assigns the theater
a preeminent place in the history of sins. It outdoes gambling in wickedness, he insists, because it is so much more public, so much more institutionalized. It represents sin codified and reduced to system.[6] To
the suggestion that the stage might be reformed rather than abolished
he replies that there never was a well-regulated stage, since the nature
of the thing did not admit it (p. 6). To the claim that men need amusement he rejoins tartly that "the need of amusement is much less than
people commonly apprehend, and, where it is not necessary, it must be
sinful" (p. 15). We hear in this a familiar ground bass, the fundamentalist antipathy to pleasure. The fact that amusement is amusing suffices
to discredit it. Witherspoon shows no interest in considering what
true need might mean in such a context. How does one determine
what is "necessary" in the matter of recreation? By what criteria?
Using what kind of measurements? And by what rule is that which is
"not necessary" stigmatized as "sinful"?

On one point Witherspoon departs startlingly from standard antitheatrical doctrine. Instead of berating the stage for its lies and its
fictions, he arraigns it on the opposite charge: it is too truthful, and
therefore "an improper method of instruction." Drama, he informs
us, is "a picture of human life, and must represent characters as they
really are. An author for the stage is not permitted to feign, but to paint
'and copy. . . . Now are not the great majority of characters in real
life bad? Must not the greatest part of those represented on the stage
be bad? And therefore, must not the strong impression which they
make upon the spectators be hurtful in the same proportion?" (p. 45).
One rubs one's eyes at this reversal of traditional teaching. "An author
for the stage is not permitted to feign, but to paint and copy"! How
often, and how vainly, had the defenders of plays struggled to make
the same point, only to be told sternly that their plots consisted of nothing but lies and delusions! Suddenly the playwright's strongest defense
is torn from his hands and turned into a weapon of attack. Witherspoon may be remembering Jeremy Collier's anger against the plays

6. John Witherspoon, *A Serious Inquiry into the Nature and Effects of
the Stage: And a Letter Respecting Play Actors* (Glasgow, 1757), p. 21.
Page references in the discussion that follows will be to this volume.

of his day on the score of their implausibility. If so, however, he is forgetting Collier's main point, which is that such implausibility constitutes a *fault* in plays. Witherspoon makes it a fault that they *aim* at a lifelike portrayal, since this means acquainting their audiences too convincingly with the true facts of life. One could hardly find a more signal instance of the protean nature of the antitheatrical prejudice, its indifference to consistency and its power to take on protective coloration from the times. For the playwrights of the eighteenth century, like their forerunners, certainly claimed to be copying nature, but never before had the adversaries of the stage taken the claim so seriously. On the other hand, rarely had the claim been so ill substantiated by those who made it. For the eighteenth-century theater, far from presenting a bleak or hardheaded view of social reality, or a powerful vision of evil, had come to specialize in the presentation of virtuous characters, noble renunciations, improving sentiments, and whatever might make mankind appear naturally benevolent and good. Witherspoon, in short, accepts the formal aims of the practitioners of drama as equivalent to the successful execution of those aims, without concerning himself with the actual practice of the drama at all.

It is strange to find the stage rebuked for its truthfulness; it is stranger still to find history itself dealt with in such terms. History, says Witherspoon, is filled with unedifying events of which men might better have remained in ignorance. "Perhaps . . . it had been better for the world that several ancient facts and characters, which now stand upon record, had been buried in oblivion" (pp. 48–49). Instead of being a guarantee of worth, as in the past, the truth has now become an object of suspicion. Truth is no longer to be prized, no longer to be sought after, either in history or in drama. Instead, it would appear, a program of brainwashing is to be instituted, in which the world is to be described in whatever terms authority chooses to describe it, in order to perpetuate whatever it may choose to construe as a desirable morality.

Nevertheless, given the increasing secularism of the intellectual world, the atmosphere is beginning to change. Adam Smith may adopt the theatrical metaphor as a way of explaining our moral sentiments, and then fall back upon traditional religion as the ultimate sanction, but for Schiller, in the *Letters on the Aesthetic Education of Man*, play constitutes the most characteristic activity of our species, and needs no supernatural validation. "Man only plays when he is in the fullest sense of the word a human being, and *he is only fully a human being when he plays*."[7] It is hard to imagine a more frontal challenge to the whole antitheatrical movement, in which play in all forms has been so systematically downgraded, and even, at moments, proscribed. Bunyan might torment himself for having yielded to a round of cat on the village green, but for Schiller it is precisely the delight in play that distinguishes us from savages. It distinguishes most men also from saints, for it is at both the extremes of exceptional stupidity and exceptional intelligence that men insist on the "real" and refuse to be mollified by the pleasure of appearances. Schiller may be said to portend a whole revolution in favor of pleasure, which makes a similarly conscious and emphatic appearance in England, as Lionel Trilling has demonstrated, with Wordsworth.[8]

At the same time, romanticism, as one of its prime attributes, also fostered a cult of inwardness and privacy which fed the puritanical distrust of qualities like mimicry, ostentation, and spectacle, and was fed by it. The stream of antitheatricalism continues to run strong in both the ecclesiastical establishment in France and the low church sects in England. Even in its old-fashioned form, suspicion of the stage and of actors continues to smoulder, bursting out from time to time into sudden and disconcerting blaze.

One such outburst occurs near the beginning of the nineteenth century in an unlikely place, Jane Austen's novel *Mansfield Park* (1814). Here, it may be recalled, the grown sons and daughters of Sir Thomas Bertram devise, for a pastime, some amateur theatricals during their father's absence on a business trip. They choose a play, distribute roles to themselves and their friends, and rehearse; they build a little stage within the house, cut a curtain, order scenery painted. Unexpectedly, Sir Thomas returns from the Indies, shows his disapproval, and the whole undertaking collapses overnight. The point of the episode lies in the fact that all the right-thinking characters in the story regard the

---

7. "Der Mensch spielt nur, wo er in voller Bedeutung des Worts Mensch ist, und *er ist nur da ganz Mensch, wo er spielt*" (Friedrich Schiller, *On the Aesthetic Education of Man*, ed. Elizabeth M. Wilkinson and L. A. Willoughby [Oxford, 1967], pp. 106–107).

8. Lionel Trilling, "The Fate of Pleasure," in *Beyond Culture: Essays on Literature and Learning* (New York, 1965), pp. 57–87.

project as self-evidently immoral from the outset. This applies to Sir Thomas's younger and more responsible son, Edmund, and above all to his niece, Fanny Price, the heroine. On the other hand, it is the fatuous aristocrat Mr. Yates who proposes the theatricals in the first place, and the idler Henry Crawford who becomes their most enthusiastic promoter, since they represent an "untasted pleasure" in "all the riot of his gratifications."[9] Crawford proves to be the one talented actor of the group, and also, at the climax of the story, the blackguard who runs off in an adulterous elopement with Maria Bertram, after having flirted with her during the rehearsals of the play.

The thing that has puzzled readers of the novel is the intensity of the disapproval visited on the acting scheme, and the shadowiness of the objections against it. From the moment the idea is broached it arouses acute anxiety in Edmund. It makes him "uncomfortable"; he "listens with alarm" as the others discuss it (p. 124), and tries to persuade his older brother to abandon the project. "In a *general* light," he argues,

> private theatricals are open to some objections, but as *we* are circumstanced, I must think it would be highly injudicious . . . . It would show great want of feeling on my father's account, absent as he is, and in some degree of constant danger; and it would be imprudent, I think, with regard to Maria, whose situation is a very delicate one . . . . I am convinced that my father would totally disapprove it. . . . He would never wish his grown up daughters to be acting plays. His sense of decorum is strict. (pp. 125–127)

But this argument, which has been cited as though it were a definitive statement of principle, self-evidently valid and unanswerable,[10] seems in fact a tissue of cobwebs. It makes no attempt to specify the objections to which private theatricals are open "in a *general* light," nor what about them is calculated to give offense to Sir Thomas. Why should this particular amusement show any greater want of feeling toward their father than the riding, shooting, visiting, and other diversions unguiltily pursued at Mansfield Park during his absence? Needless to say, Edmund's prediction proves correct: Sir Thomas does deeply dis-

9. *Mansfield Park*, ed. R. W. Chapman, 3d ed. (Oxford, 1934), p. 123. Page references in the discussion that follows will be to this edition.

10. David Lodge, "A Question of Judgement: The Theatricals at Mansfield Park," *Nineteenth Century Fiction* 17 (1962): 278.

approve, but he is even less able than Edmund to articulate the grounds of his displeasure. We overhear muttered phrases about "unsafe amusements," "noisy pleasures," "glaring impropriety," "wrong measures," "bustle and confusion," "much to offend his ideas of decorum" (pp. 184–190), but these, it will be observed, either refer to the disruption of Sir Thomas' domestic convenience, or else they evade the issue. Why "unsafe"? Why "wrong"? Why "improper"? The appeal in each case can only be to the prior prejudice of the character, and the reader. A heavy censure does in due course fall on the play chosen for performance, Kotzebue's *Lovers' Vows*, as "altered" by Mrs. Inchbald, but the censure occurs belatedly, long after the initial proposal has aroused such passionate protest from Fanny and Edmund.

In short, the theatricals come charged with a mysterious iniquity that challenges explanation. The mystery deepens, as Lionel Trilling observes, "when we know that amateur theatricals were a favorite amusement in Jane Austen's home."[11] It deepens further when we turn to the play that excites so much indignation. Edmund views *Lovers' Vows* with unfeigned horror as "exceedingly unfit for private representation" (p. 140). Fanny, likewise, finds in the situation of one heroine and the language of the other an impropriety that makes her cousins' acquiescence mystifying: "That it could be proposed and accepted in a private Theatre!" (p. 137). When we glance at *Lovers' Vows*, it is we who are mystified. We have been led to expect a gamey morsel of continental libertinism; we find instead as pious a tale of vice repentant and virtue triumphant as ever maiden yawned at, done in the vein of tearful humanitarianism that Diderot had promoted across the channel. Only in the coxcomb Count Cassel, and only for an instant, is the libertine point of view even given a hearing, and then only to be scathingly repudiated. With the doubtful exception of the scene in which Amelia takes the lead in wooing Anhalt (in the demurest tones—Mrs. Inchbald has seen to that), nowhere does it contain anything faintly licentious or *osé*. By turns and in concert the characters avouch sentiments of the most unimpeachable propriety—and act on them. The seduction episode on which the plot is based has occurred twenty years ago; its perpetrator has long since been penitent. Its victim, his cast-off mistress, appears in the opening scene of the play reaping the rewards of sin—sick, ragged, and begging, spurned by a heartless innkeeper, and on bended knee

11. *The Opposing Self* (London, 1955), p. 218.

imploring Providence for the safety of her son and her former lover. The revelation of her identity leads to her lover's final remorse, her own rehabilitation, her son's assumption of his heritage, and the definitive righting of all old wrongs. Only the exacerbated sanctimoniousness and overwrought propriety of the 1800s, or the grim determination to exact retribution at all cost, could have found anything to complain of in the morality of the action. Mrs. Inchbald, in some "remarks" prefaced to one of the later editions, informs us of the "grand moral,"

to set forth the miserable consequences which arise from the neglect, to enforce the watchful care, of illegitimate offspring; and surely, as the pulpit has not had eloquence to eradicate the crime of seduction, the stage may be allowed an humble endeavour to prevent its most fatal effects.

The analogy with the pulpit is well taken, for the play promotes in every line an ethic of irreproachable orthodoxy. But there are, continues Mrs. Inchbald, "some pious declaimers against theatrical exhibitions, so zealous to do good,—they grudge the poor dramatist his share in the virtuous concern."[12] Pious declaimers—or exclaimers—there had indeed been. Some were political reactionaries incensed by the play's supposed portrayal of members of the aristocracy as libertine and the humbler folk as virtuous; others were puritan zealots chronically inflamed against the stage and eager to find excuses for denouncing it.[13] What is disconcerting is to discover Jane Austen in such company. Her own complex moral awareness in most circumstances

12. August Kotzebue, *Lovers' Vows*, trans. [Elizabeth] Inchbald (London, 1808), p. 7.

13. See William Reitzel, "*Mansfield Park* and *Lovers' Vows*," *Review of English Studies* 9 (1933): 451–456. On puritan objections to home theatricals, see Sybil Rosenfield, "Jane Austen and Private Theatricals," *Essays and Studies* (1962), p. 43. For the Evangelical protest against the corrupting influence of German drama, see Hannah More, *Strictures on the Modern System of Female Education* (London, 1799), I, 42–45. In 1800, it may be added, Wordsworth lent his voice to the case against German drama by complaining that the English classics were being "driven into neglect by frantic novels, sickly and stupid German Tragedies, and deluges of idle and extravagant stories in verse" ("Observations prefixed to *Lyrical Ballads*," 2d ed.). But his comment suggests no prejudice against the drama or the stage as such, of the sort so emphatically present in the writings of the Evangelicals.

makes *Lovers' Vows* look like a dance of cardboard cutouts. The idea that anything in Mrs. Inchbald's adaptation of Kotzebue could seriously threaten the virtue of a character in Jane Austen is almost laughable, yet Sir Thomas marches solemnly about Mansfield Park, seizing and burning every copy he can lay hands on, as though a radical purification were required to combat a mortal contagion.

In her introduction to the novel, Queenie Leavis provides a bit of clarifying biographical information. Jane Austen's letters, she points out,

reveal that whereas Jane was hostile to "the Evangelicals" in 1809, by 1814 she has changed and is "by no means convinced that we ought not all to be evangelicals." The change-over to sponsoring a conventional moral outlook must be associated with this change of opinion about Evangelicalism . . . .

Furthermore,

She seems to have felt that hitherto she had set too high a value on liveliness of mind, . . . and had differed from conventional moral theory too confidently. Why otherwise should she endorse Sir Thomas's and Edmund's objection to private theatricals? The Austens and their friends had performed questionably decorous plays in their barn without any ill effect on their conduct.[14]

Why indeed? Mrs. Leavis sees rightly that the antagonism to the theatricals, in the novel, goes with a retreat to a more stringent morality, akin to that of the Evangelicals, whose leading spirit, William Wilberforce, had hotly castigated the theater in his most celebrated tract, *A Practical View of the Prevailing Religious System of Professed Christians . . . Contrasted with Real Christianity*. For Wilberforce the theater is a place haunted by debauchees bent on gratifying their appetites, from which modesty and regularity have retreated, "while riot and lewdness are invited to the spot,"[15] where God's name is profaned, and the only lessons to be learned are those Christians should shun like the pains of hell, to which indeed they will inevitably lead. For the creator of Elizabeth Bennett to have adopted this dour view of a pleasure to

14. *Mansfield Park*, with an introduction by Q. D. Leavis (London, 1957), p. xii.

15. William Wilberforce, *A Practical View of the Prevailing Religious System of Professed Christians, in the Higher and Middle Classes in this Country, contrasted with Real Christianity*, 2d ed. (London, 1797), p. 307.

which she had herself owed so much is a tribute to the stubborn puritanism that seems to lodge in the marrow of even the most independent spirit. As critics have noticed, the character in *Mansfield Park* who most resembles Elizabeth Bennett in her vivacity, freedom from cant, and readiness to challenge received opinion—Mary Crawford—is also one who comes close to being a "bad woman" in the conventional sense, while the role of the heroine is occupied (some might say usurped) by a figure of almost unnatural docility and sluggishness. The antitheatricalism in the story, then, involves not only an espousal of severer moral standards, but an abdication of the freedom the author had implicitly claimed for herself and her heroine in the earlier book.

A more recent critic, A. Walton Litz, has remarked on the suggestive parallel between the situation of Edmund and Mary Crawford in the novel and that of Jane Austen's own brother Henry and her cousin Eliza de Feuillide. Like Edmund, Henry had aspired to the priesthood. Like Mary, the beautiful and flirtatious Eliza had tried to dissuade him from it. Unlike Mary, she succeeded. A later tradition of the Austen family had it that "Eliza's marriage to Henry in 1797 was the outcome of renewed theatrical parties at Steventon"—that Henry, that is, had abandoned his high calling as a result of private theatricals. To these events there had also been, as in *Mansfield Park*, a disapproving witness, a friend of Eliza's named Philadelphia Walters, whose letters contain some of Fanny's distaste for play-acting and some reproach for the "dissipated life" of her friend. "In this exchange," observes Litz, "Phila's moral scruples and spectatorial attitude are strongly suggestive of Fanny Price, and the arguments against amateur theatricals are those of *Mansfield Park*."[16] Uncomfortable personal memories, then, contributed to Jane Austen's defection from the theater. But defection, and even apostasy, it must be reckoned. The former believer is not merely giving up her childhood diversions in the barn, she is disavowing them, burning them in effigy, setting them down as forbidden games. And while memories of Henry, Eliza, and Philadelphia Walters may well have helped stiffen her in her more straitlaced attitude, they could hardly have done more than reinforce a process already under way. For why should Jane have blamed her brother's abandonment of his priestly vocation on the theatricals? Why should she have reacted

16. A. Walton Litz, *Jane Austen: A Study of her Artistic Development* (New York, 1965), pp. 120, 118–119.

so primly, so many years after the fact, against an imaginative pleasure that had taught her so much? The real springs of disapproval must lie deeper, and even in fictional form, it would seem the author can hardly tap them or articulate them. To convince us, and perhaps herself, of the sinfulness of the case, she heaps up the specific indictments of time, place, and manner, of noise and bustle and frivolity, the damage done to Sir Thomas' billiard room, and the supposed indelicacy of the play itself in encouraging indiscreet familiarity between the sexes. All the trivial incidental annoyances are invoked in turn and massed together, to substantiate after the fact the immediate instinctive revulsion felt by Fanny and Edmund and Sir Thomas.

Lionel Trilling rightly concludes that "What is decisive is a traditional, almost primitive, feeling about dramatic impersonation." Perhaps he is slightly less right when he defines the feeling, platonically, as "the fear that the impersonation of a bad or inferior character will have a harmful effect upon the impersonator, that, indeed, the impersonation of any other self will diminish the integrity of the real self."[17] The point at Mansfield Park is not so much that Henry or Maria Crawford will mar their integrity by taking roles in the play as that their flair for impersonation already signifies the erosion or even the absence of such integrity. They are, as Leo Bersani has wittily termed them, "ontological floaters." Only because they already suffer from a "disintegrated" personality in the first place do they throw themselves with such furious gusto into the theatricals. "Their liveliness is the style of beings without definition, actively ready to jump from one entertaining performance to the next."[18] To return to Trilling, "The real reason," he continues,

for not giving the play . . . is that Sir Thomas would not permit it were he at home. . . . And Sir Thomas, when he returns before his expected time, confirms their consciousness of sin. It is he who identifies the objection to the theatricals as being specifically that of impersonation. His own self is an integer and he instinctively resists the diversification of the self that is implied by the assumption of roles. It is he, in his entire identification with his status and tradition, who makes of Mansfield Park the citadel it is—it exists to front life and to repel life's mutabilities. (pp. 224–225)

17. *The Opposing Self*, p. 218.
18. *A Future for Astyanax* (Boston, 1976), p. 76.

It is not clear what Trilling means by saying that Sir Thomas "identifies the objection to the theatricals as being specifically that of impersonation." For Sir Thomas does nothing of the sort. His frown of inquiry quells the whole enterprise in an instant, but he never divulges the reasons for his annoyance, and all we are properly entitled to conclude on our own is that the theatricals interfere with his privacy. Hostility to impersonation, however, assuredly hangs in the air. It could hardly be more convincingly expressed than by the fact that the trifler and future profligate, Henry Crawford, is made the one confident impersonator of the group, secure in his ability to transform himself into whatever is required by his part.

"I really believe," said he, "I could be fool enough at this moment to undertake any character that ever was written, from Shylock or Richard III down to the singing hero of a farce in his scarlet coat and cocked hat. I feel as if I could be any thing or every thing, as if I could rant and storm, or sigh, or cut capers in any tragedy or comedy in the English language." (p. 123)

Fanny herself, later, must admit the justice of this boast. To her surprise she finds that Crawford's readings teach her for the first time some of the pleasure to be had from a play. But his talent is portentous of ill. For it is precisely his ready command of these other, imaginary selves that reflects Crawford's lack of a firm self of his own, and as a result his disastrous lack of fixed moral standards, long before these manifest themselves to the world at large in his elopement with Maria. Maria herself is comparably malleable and indeterminate. In the improvised theatricals she plays her part "well—too well," thus early betraying the instability that will bring about her ruin, accepting too casually a role incompatible with the one she has chosen for herself as wife to Mr. Rushworth. The power to act a part, then, becomes, as Litz observes, "a touchstone to insincerity, so that Fanny's early, horrified protest, 'No, indeed, I cannot act,' finally becomes a moral accolade." As in the case of Cordelia, the inability to feign becomes an emblem of rectitude. The road that leads from the play-acting at Mansfield Park to the adultery in town, then, far from being mysterious or circuitous, could hardly, in the author's eyes, be more unmistakable or direct. And what is true of the theater seems true of the imagination in general. Previously thought of by Jane Austen as "a possible source of enlightenment and love," it now appears "bound . . . to the service of hypocrisy,"[19] a serpent introduced into the paradisal world of Mansfield Park.

Metamorphic talent such as Crawford's had long been a staple of the gifted criminal in literature. It belongs to such rascals as Richard III in the sixteenth century, Jonson's Volpone in the seventeenth, and Fielding's Jonathan Wild in the eighteenth. In the nineteenth it lodges to an almost dazzling degree in the antiheroine of *Vanity Fair*. Becky, child of a Bohemian artist and a French "opera-girl," is conceived throughout as an actress, and especially as a virtuoso in mimicry. As a child, she deludes the sanctimonious Miss Pinkerton with her capacity to "perform the part of the *ingénue*," proceeding thereafter to amuse her father and his friends with unkind impersonations of her benefactress. Upon the death of her father and her definitive removal to Miss Pinkerton's, she pursues her bent for acting. "She had not been much of a dissembler, until now her loneliness taught her to feign,"[20] and the remainder of her remarkable career is predicated on her prowess as a mimic. In the scenes of sisterly tenderness with Amelia, "one person was in earnest and the other a perfect performer" (p. 66). As Queen's Crawley, for the entertainment of the rich Miss Crawley, she caricatures Sir Huddlestone's wheeze, Sir Giles Wapshot's "particularly noisy manner of imbibing his soup," and Lady Wapshot's tic-like wink of the left eye. "As for the Misses Wapshots' toilettes and Lady Fuddleston's famous yellow hat, Miss Sharp tore them to tatters, to the infinite amusement of her audience" (p. 104). Later she finds matter for ridicule in Miss Crawley's companion, Miss Briggs, whom she imitates impudently to her face, and when installed, after marriage, in her own house in Mayfair, she regales her visitors with burlesques of Lady Southdown prescribing undrinkable potions:

She put on a night-cap and gown. She preached a great sermon in the true serious manner: she lectured on the virtue of the medicine which she pretended to administer, with a gravity of imitation so perfect, that you would have thought it was the Countess's own Roman nose

19. *Jane Austen*, pp. 126, 128.

20. *Vanity Fair, A Novel Without a Hero*, ed. Geoffrey and Kathleen Tillotson (London, 1963), p. 22. Page references in the discussion that follows will be to this edition.

through which she snuffled. "Give us Lady Southdown and the black dose," was a constant cry amongst the folks in Becky's little drawing room in May Fair. (p. 406)

Becky's impersonation, we may note, includes a few key props, the "night-cap and gown," to make the illusion more vivid. The climax of her career, therefore, we are not surprised to discover, comes in an evening of private theatricals, the charades at Gaunt House. Becky acts Clytemnestra on this occasion so brilliantly, and with such "ghastly truth," that the spectators are stricken into silence, after which, in a swift metamorphosis, she reemerges "in powder and patches, the most *ravissante* little Marquise in the world" (p. 497). Lord Steyne, her rich admirer, overcome with wonder at the whole performance, tosses flowers to her, which, "with the air of a consummate comedian," she presses passionately to her heart (p. 498).

Becky remains the performer even with her nearest and nominal dearest, ostentatiously fondling in public the son she ignores in private. When the moment comes to recount for Amelia's benefit her separation from the child, a fresh performance takes place, a pathetic one this time, forcing Amelia to retire "altogether behind her pocket-handkerchief, so that the consummate little tragedian must have been charmed to see the effect which her performance produced on her audience" (pp. 638–639).

Play-acting, in short, carries strong negative implications in *Vanity Fair*. Central in Becky's case, they are underlined by being extended to the coarse and caddish George Osborne. After the disastrous evening with the rum punch at Vauxhall, George and Dobbin visit Joseph Sedley in his rooms, still suffering horribly from a hangover, where the "ruthless young fellow [George], seizing hold of Dobbin's hand, acted over the scene, to the horror of the original performer, and in spite of Dobbin's good-natured entreaties to him to have mercy" (p. 62). On another occasion, George dispatches his new bride home alone to her mother's house, ostensibly for reasons of business, but actually in order to continue his convivial drinking. As Dobbin finally returns to his own quarters after the merrymaking, George,

when he had taken wine enough . . . went off to half-price at the play, to see Mr. Kean perform in Shylock. Captain Osborne was a great

lover of the drama, and had himself performed high-comedy characters with great distinction in several garrison theatrical entertainments. (p. 249)

Their flair for acting creates a bond between George and Becky, making the flirtation at Brussels seem like the natural outcome of a temperamental affinity.

With Dobbin, the case is reversed. As he tries to dissuade George
from mocking Jos, as he remains uninterested in going to the theater
to see Kean, so also, at the opera, he manages to express himself forcibly
on the subject of Becky. Becky, during the interval, spends her time
posturing for the benefit of General Tufto in the box opposite.

She bustled, she chattered, she turned and twisted, and smiled upon
one, and smirked on another . . . . And when the time for the ballet
came (in which there was no dancer that went through her grimaces
or performed her comedy of action better), she skipped back to her own
box, leaning on Captain Dobbin's arm . . . . "What a humbug that
woman is!" honest old Dobbin mumbled to George . . . . "She writhes
and twists about like a snake." (p. 273)

Like the aboriginal snake, Becky can writhe and twist expertly enough
to deceive most people, even such beady-eyed men of the world as Lord
Steyne, who confesses himself half admiring, half aghast, when he discovers the full extent of her duplicity. "Honest old Dobbin," by contrast, whose simple uprightness rejects all pretense, sees through her at
once, creating an antagonism that persists undiminished on both sides
throughout the story. The natural alliance between Becky and George,
on the one hand, and the instinctive antipathy between Becky and
Dobbin, on the other, confirm our impression that play-acting, in this
world, is as clear a sign of moral dereliction as it is in *Mansfield Park*.
If anything, it is more unappetizing, since it suggests not so much an
amorphous and too malleable personality as a hard and ruthless one.
Becky is not simply pleasure-loving and self-indulgent, like Henry
Crawford, but cold and scheming. She combines Crawford's metamorphic talents with a calculating deceptiveness, a systematic con-
cealment of her true intentions. And yet, as most readers of the novel
have long since agreed, Thackeray implicitly pays his heroine the tribute due her energy, resourcefulness, and verve. It is she who gives the

novel its edge and its vitality. Alongside her, most of the other characters, and perhaps especially the sentimental Amelia, seem limp and vapid. Like Lord Steyne, we remain half aghast, half admiring at her audacity. If Thackeray is the puppet master of the show, Becky is the puppet master's puppet mistress, for whom others serve mainly as under-puppets, to be hauled from the box and manipulated, not only for her advantage, but also for our own ambivalent amusement.

Nothing in *Vanity Fair* suggests that Thackeray himself thought ill of the theater, or disapproved of its practitioners. When the coxcomb Sir Pitt Crawley, prudishly offended by the charades, "reprobate[s] in strong terms the habit of play-acting and fancy-dressing, as highly unbecoming a British female," and takes his brother Rawdon "severely to task for appearing himself, and allowing his wife to join in such improper exhibitions" (pp. 508–509), we understand, as we have already understood, that Sir Pitt is as egregiously an ass as Becky is consummately a knave. Nor do we need to draw invidious conclusions from Arthur Pendennis' infatuation with the good-natured but vacuous Miss Costigan, "the Fotheringay," in *Pendennis*, who not only had never heard of Kotzebue (in whose play she was then acting), but "had never heard of Farquhar, or Congreve, or any dramatist in whose plays she had not a part"—of whom, further, it was a wonder how she could be so stupid and act so well, yet who could judge so excellently of a pudding, or a piece of needlework, or anything pertaining to her domestic affairs.[21] From his letters we know that Thackeray himself frequented the theater assiduously, and felt deprived without it.[22] What the portrait of Becky implies is neither enmity to the theater as an art form, nor hostility to actors as a profession, but rather an unmasking state of mind, which aims to expose the hypocrisies of the social scene, those against which Becky is reacting, those to which she devotes herself in order to master a hypocritical world. Like La Rochefoucauld, Thackeray sees life as a game of masks and disguises, in which the successful gamesters are those skilled in feignings and concealments, and in which his own role as moralist is to lift the curtain and make his creatures reveal themselves for what they are.

21. *The History of Pendennis* (London, 1849–50), I, 2, 52, 58, 111.
22. See Gordon Ray, ed. *The Letters and Private Papers of William Makepeace Thackeray* (Cambridge, Mass., 1945–46), I, 154, 160; II, 44; III, 460–461; and passim.

PROTHÉE ET ARISTÉE.

Prothée étoit Fils de l'Océan et de Téthys, né à Pallène en Macédoine. Neptune pour le récompenser du soin qu'il prenoit de ses Veaux
Marins qu'il menoit paître sous les eaux, lui donna le don de connoître le passé, le présent et l'avenir. Ceux qui le consultoit ne devoit pont
espérer d'en tirer de réponse sans l'avoir lié et serré avec violence. Alors il prenoit toutes sortes de formes, se changeant en Lion, en Tigre, en
Feu, en Eau &c. mais plus il prenoit de figures différentes, plus il falloit le serrer. On voit ici Aristée Fils d'Appollon et de Cyrène occupé à
consulter de cette manière. Ce jeune homme avoit beaucoup aimé Euridyce, qui fuyant ses poursuites le jour de ses noces avec Orphée, fu-
piquée d'un serpent et mourut sur le champ. Les Nymphes touchées de ce malheur, tuèrent toutes les mouches d'Aristée. Sa Mère lui con-
seilla d'aller trouver Prothée, et celui-ci, après avoir été surpris, lui dit qu'il falloit appaiser les mânes d'Euridice, en faisant un sacrifice de 4. Génisses et de 4 Taureaux, des entrailles desquels il sortit des Essains d'Abeilles   Voy. Georg. 4.   27

1. Abraham van Diepenbeeck, the binding
of Proteus by Aristaeus, who is consulting him
about the future. Emblem based on Virgil, *Georgics* 4.
From Michel de Marolles, *Le tableau du
temple des muses* (1655; re-edition, 1768), Plate 27.
Reproduced by courtesy of the Warburg Institute.

Proteus Oceani & Tethyos filius.

Audiit ambiguis Aegyptus Protea Verbis
Narrantem summi mystica sensa Jovis.

2. Theodore de Bry, the Egyptian Proteus.
From Jean Jacques Boissard, *De divinatione*
(Oppenheim, n.d.), p. 148. Reproduced by
courtesy of the Warburg Institute.

HISTRIO-MASTIX.

THE

PLAYERS SCOVRGE,

OR,

ACTORS TRAGÆDIE,

Divided into Two Parts.

Wherein it is largely evidenced, by divers *Arguments*, by the concurring Authorities and Reſolutions of *ſundry texts of Scripture*; of the *whole Primitive Church*, both under the *Law and Goſpell*; of 55 *Synodes and Councels*; of 71 *Fathers and Chriſtian Writers*, before the yeare of our Lord 120c; of above 150 *foraigne and domeſtique Proteſtant and Popiſh Authors*, ſince; of 40 *Heathen Philoſophers, Hiſtorians, Poets*; of many *Heathen*, many *Chriſtian Nations, Republiques, Emperors, Princes, Magiſtrates*; of ſundry *Apoſtolicall, Canonicall, Imperiall Conſtitutions*; and of our owne *Engliſh Statutes, Magiſtrates, Univerſities, Writers, Preachers.*

That popular *Stage-playes* (the *very Pompes of the Divell* which we renounce in *Baptiſme*, if we beleeve the Fathers) *are ſinfull, heatheniſh, lewde, ungodly Spectacles, and moſt pernicious Corruptions; condemned in all ages, as intolerable Miſchiefes to Churches, to Republickes, to the manners, mindes, and ſoules of men. And that the* Profeſſion of *Play-poets*, of *Stage players*; together with the penning, acting, and frequenting of *Stage-playes*, are unlawfull, infamous and misbeſeeming Chriſtians. All pretences to the contrary are here likewiſe fully anſwered; and the unlawfulnes of acting or beholding Academicall Enterludes, briefly diſcuſſed; beſides ſundry other particulars concerning Dancing, Dicing, Health-drinking, &c. of which the Table will informe you.

By WILLIAM PRYNNE, *an Utter-Barreſter of* Lincolnes Inne.

Cyprian. De Spectaculis lib p.244.
Fugienda ſunt iſta Chriſtianis fidelibus, ut tcm ſrequentes dixim.us, tam vana, tam pernicioſa, tam ſacrilega Spectacula: qua, etſi non haberent crimen,habent in ſe et maximam et parum congruentè fidelibus vanitatẽ.
Lactantius de Verò Cultu c.p. 20.
Vitanda ergo Spectacula omnia, non ſolum ne quid vitiorum pectoribus inſideat, &c. ſed ne cuius nos voluptatis conſuetudo delineat, atque à Deo et à bonis operibus avertat.
Chryſoſt. Hom. 38.in Matth.Tom.2. Col.299 B & Hom. 8 De Pœnitentia, Tom.5. Col.750.
Immo vero, his Theatralibus ludis everſis, non leges, ſed iniquitatem extercis, oc omnem civitatis peſtem extinguetia: Etenim Theatrum, communis luxuria officina, publicum incontinentia gymnaſium, cathedra peſtilentia; poſſ.c. uus locus; plurimarumque morborum plena Babylonica fornax, &c.
Auguſtinus De Civit. Dei, l.4 c.1.
Si tantummodo boni et honeſti homines in civitate eſſent, nec in rebus humanis Ludi ſcenici e ſſe debuiſſent.

LONDON,
Printed by *E.A.* and *W.I.* for *Michael Sparke*, and are to be ſold at the Blue Bible, in Greene Arbour, in little Old Bayly, 1633.

3. Title page of William Prynne,
Histriomastix (1633).
Reproduced
by courtesy of the Bancroft Library,
University of California, Berkeley.

LA SVPPLICA
DISCORSO FAMIGLIARE
DI Nicolò Barbieri detto
BELTRAME
diretta à quelli che scriuêdo
ò parlando trattano de Comici
trascurando i meriti dellè
azzioni uirtuosè.

Lettura per que galanthuomini
che non sono in tutto critici,
ne affatto balordi

IN VENEZIA
Con licenza dè Superiori
e Priuilegio

PER MARCO GINAMMI

L ANNO MDCXXXIV

4. Title page of Nicolò Barbieri,
La supplica (1634). Reproduced by
permission of the British Library.

On whether fide foe're I am,
I, ftill, appeare to bee the fame.

5.   Emblem of the cube.
From George Wither, *A Collection
of Emblems, Ancient and Modern*
(1634), Sig. 2H2ᵛ. Reproduced
by permission of the British Library.

6. First in a series of three etchings by Giuseppe Maria Mitelli, c. 1680, likening human life to the theater in its most negative aspects of impermanence, illusion, and futility, with men cast as stock figures from the *commedia dell'arte*. (See detail in Plate 8.)

7. The third and last in the series, showing the *zanni* tearing off his mask and leaping into the grave. Both etchings reproduced by courtesy of the Keeper of Prints and Drawings, the British Museum.

MONDO
È Proteo 'l mondo, e con sue forme infide
Le sperate delude, e le sue frodi,
Vlisse non conobbe, Argo non uide.

Gioseffo Maria Mitelli inuentore, g f.   TEMPO

La vita è una comedia, il mondo è scena;
Il Tempo è 'l maestro Atropo hà 'l fin de l'opra,
chi ben recita hà onor, chi male hà pena.

8.   Detail of Plate 6 showing paraphernalia
of the arts of the theater—music, painting,
poetry, literature, and costume—arts which
in their turn symbolize the worthlessness
of earthly life.

A more ambiguous and puzzling case than that of Becky Sharp would be the disturbing, elusive, slightly sinister figure of Melville's Confidence Man, trying, through a dizzying series of mutations, to induce his fellow travelers to give or lend him their trust. Like his predecessors, the Confidence Man owes much of his success to the credulity or rascality of his victims, many of whom deserve to be cozened, or who need to be taught the flabbiness of their own skepticism. He differs from the others in the startling range and thoroughness of his transformations. Can he, indeed, be only a single character, a quick-change artist endowed with extraordinary powers of metamorphosis? Or does his bewildering variety of guises point to a supernatural, perhaps a subterrestrial, origin, which releases him from the ordinary confines of personality?

Both the Confidence Man, in certain of his masquerades, and his fellow voyagers, in some aspects, tend to see the world as a stage and its inhabitants as players. The jeering wooden-legged skeptic of the opening scenes carries disbelief so far as to suggest that the Negro cripple Black Guinea is actually a white man in disguise. More startling still, he refuses to think of such a humbug as in any way remarkable, given the fact that all men are actors. "How?" demands the solemn solicitor of funds for the Seminole Widow and Orphan Asylum, the momentary incarnation of the Confidence Man, "Does all the world act? Am *I*, for instance, an actor? Is my reverend friend here, too [alluding to the young Episcopalian minister nearby], a performer?" "Yes," retorts the skeptic. "Don't you both perform acts? To do, is to act; so all doers are actors."[23] Such a point of view, reminiscent of the tautologies of the first grave-digger in *Hamlet,* disposes radically of the whole concept of simple sincerity, since it ascribes a taint of the theatrical to all action. Nor does the skeptic make difficulties about imagining motives other than mercenary ones for Guinea's alleged disguise. There are other reasons, he points out, for "pains and hazard, deception and deviltry, in this world. How much money did the devil make by gulling Eve?" (p. 50). The question is an unsettling one, even if we question the skeptic's right to pose it, since it was he who earlier had suggested "financial purposes" for Guinea's disguise (p. 15); his

23. *The Confidence Man: His Masquerade,* facs. ed. John Seelye (San Francisco, 1968), p. 49. Page references in the discussion that follows will be to this edition.

present proposal seems rather like a spiteful afterthought. In any case, if all doers are actors, then all men are engaged in deceiving. Some, however, deceive more deliberately, more programmatically, and more hurtfully than others.

The skeptic himself, like the Confidence Man, appears in numerous guises. One is that of a misanthropic bachelor who, conversing with the amiable cosmopolitan, insultingly likens his interlocutor to "Signor Marzetti in the African pantomime," except that Marzetti had the honesty to wear a tail, and was no hypocrite (pp. 205–206). The cosmopolitan, in rejoinder, vigorously approves the principle of playing a part in life:

Trust me, one had better mix in, and do like others. Sad business, this holding out against having a good time. Life is a pic-nic *en costume*; one must play a part, assume a character, stand ready in a sensible way to play the fool. To come in plain clothes, with a long face, as a wise-acre, only makes one a discomfort to himself, and a blot upon the scene. (p. 208)

The sentiments are ingratiating, and plausible, except that they come from the Confidence Man in his most extravagant incarnation, who proceeds to gull as many of the other passengers as he can, and who ends by quenching the light with which the simple old man of the last scene cons his Bible, so that ship and passengers are left in total darkness. Neither the wooden-legged skeptic, "a limping, gimlet-eyed, sour-faced person" (p. 15), nor the morose cripple Thomas Fry, nor most of the other doubting Thomases of the tale, are presented as attractive figures. Most of them, despite an initial resistance, succumb at length to the blandishments of the Confidence Man. Many are would-be confidence men in their own right. Thomas Fry, the embittered paralytic, in order to coax out a compassionate shilling, tells a different hard-luck story to each listener, on the theory that the true one would never be believed. The businessman Charlie Noble slyly attempts to hoodwink the cosmopolitan as the latter is placidly expatiating on the virtues of confidence. So much merely underscores the harsh assertion of the first skeptic: all men act, all have a spice of the confidence man in their natures. The protagonist's own transformations, his varieties of syrupy cant and pious insinuation, merely illustrate the proposition that with some men, their penchant for deceit is not accidental but a trade.

It is worth recalling that on at least two other occasions Melville uses the theatrical situation as a metaphor for evil. The action of *Benito Cereno*, written just prior to *The Confidence Man*, consists of an elaborate charade in which, for the benefit of the gullible Captain Delano, the other characters perform parts that essentially reverse their true ones, the captive commander of the Spanish vessel rather badly misplaying his assigned role as master of his own ship, and the true master, the rebel slave Babo, brilliantly acting the part of the obsequious valet. Whatever else may be concealed in this sinister parable, the masquerading of Babo and Don Benito illustrates the ease with which evil can pose as its opposite, affixing the humblest demeanor while perpetrating the most ferocious cruelties, and the ineptitude with which even imperfect good is condemned to play a feigned part. The most innocent of the three principals, Captain Delano, would be incapable of playing any part at all, and has difficulty penetrating the deceptions of others. Again, in Melville's last story, *Billy Budd*, the innocence of the hero is declared by his perfect transparency, his total inability to counterfeit, while his deadly antagonist Claggart possesses precisely that faculty in diabolical measure, as the imagery of the serpent in the garden serves to underscore.

At the same time, Melville, as creator, must own himself beholden to the same talent, because it is that which enables him to speak through so many personages, to shift both scene and character so multifariously. Addressing us directly as readers, he assures us that he belongs not with those who wish fiction to be a mere dull copy of a dull reality, but with those:

Who sit down to a work of amusement tolerantly as they sit at a play, and with much the same expectations and feelings. They look that fancy shall evoke scenes different from those of the same old crowd round the customhouse counter, and same old dishes on the boarding-house table, with characters unlike those of the same old acquaintances they meet in the same old way every day in the same old street. And as, in real life, the proprieties will not allow people to act out themselves with that unreserve permitted to the stage; so, in books of fiction, they look not only for more entertainment, but, at bottom, even for

313

more reality, than real life itself can show. . . . In this way of thinking, the people in a fiction, like the people in a play, must dress as nobody exactly dresses, talk as nobody exactly talks, act as nobody exactly acts. (pp. 285–286)

"In real life, the proprieties will not allow people to act out themselves with that unreserve permitted to the stage." Life, then, inhibits; the stage exhibits. The stage strips off the layer of diffidence beneath which men cloak their true selves; it completes gestures that normally remain arrested. In so doing it actualizes life's potential, revealing a truer reality than the one we daily witness. What is morally reprehensible in the Confidence Man, then, his mastery of change, his whirligig of shapes, and his flamboyance, becomes an aesthetic virtue for his creator, who is thereby empowered to confer a bolder energy on his tale. Even Jane Austen might have admitted, had she wished, that the skill she reprehended in Henry Crawford was one which she, as a novelist, could hardly do without.

A further masquerade, one of the Confidence Man's most bravura performances—to carry the tale briefly forward into our own century —confronts us in Thomas Mann's unfinished comic novel, *The Confessions of Felix Krull*. Here, in an imagined retrospect from his own pen, we have the apologia of the metamorphic artist, proudly chronicling the growth of his own talent. Krull practices his self-mutations with a disdain for bourgeois scruple that he also extends to bourgeois notions of property. He will no more rest content with the insignificant identity society has fobbed off on him than with the paltry income he can acquire by socially approved means. When young, the rapturously received performances of the music-hall comedian Müller-Rosé teach him of the human craving to be deceived, and of the existence of talents like Müller-Rosé's to cater to the craving. The crowds desire to feel the vicarious joy of life that Müller-Rosé sheds on them; Müller-Rosé needs to be adored by the crowds he pleasures. In the mutuality of the need lies the secret whereby this miserable mountebank—who offstage proves ugly, pustular, and bad-tempered—nightly transfigures himself into an adorable luminous butterfly. Krull regards his own exploits as similar feats of self-creation. When, by a brilliant performance as an invalid, he hoodwinks the family doctor into prescribing absences from school, when he dupes a panel of army medics into diagnosing him as epileptic, and so barring him from military service, he feels the unspeakable satisfaction of having "improved upon nature, realized a dream."[24] In both cases he has made his body the servant of his will, and his will the servant of his imagination. During his term of service as waiter at the Hotel St. James et d'Albany in Paris, he leads a double life, thanks to an irregularly acquired bank account, appearing on his days off elegantly dressed in fashionable places, a mysterious man of distinction. Much of the charm of this split existence lies in the ambiguity as to which of his selves is real, and which the artifact. "I masqueraded in both capacities," he tells us, "and the undisguised reality behind the two appearances, the real I, could not be identified because it actually did not exist."[25] Perhaps we should conclude from Felix's case that all our identities reflect the same indeterminacy, as we learned from Melville's skeptic that all doers are actors. But Felix himself would discourage the inference. He would class himself with the circus clowns, as a unique being whom only sentimentalists would try to reduce to the level of ordinary, humdrum humanity. All artists, in Felix's view, are marked men, fixated imperiously on their own needs. In his own case, the need is to remake himself: "It was the change and renewal of my worn-out self, the fact that I had been able to put off the old Adam and slip on a new, that gave me such a sense of fulfilment and happiness."[26] "Put off the old Adam"! Felix's phrase gives a wry, subversive twist to the old Protestant doctrine that a man must be reborn in order to be saved. For what Felix aims at is no final state of innocence, purity, or beatitude, but simply the ecstasy of change for its own sake. The very condition of mutability that the putting off of the old Adam was designed to arrest, by translating the changed crea-

24. *Confessions of Felix Krull, Confidence Man*, trans. Denver Lindley, Penguin Books (London, 1958), p. 34; *Bekenntnisse des Hochstaplers Felix Krull* (Frankfurt, 1954), p. 48: "Ich hatte die Natur verbessert, einen Traum verwirklicht."

25. *Confessions*, p. 205; *Bekenntnisse*, p. 266: "Verkleidet also war ich in jedem Fall, und die unmaskierte Wirklichkeit zwischen den beiden Erscheinungsformen, das Ich-selber-Sein, war night bestimmbar, weil tatsächlich nicht vorhanden."

26. *Confessions*, p. 231; *Bekenntnisse*, p. 298: "Die Veränderung und Erneuerung meines abgetragenen Ich überhaupt, dass ich den alten Adam hatte auszuziehen und in einen anderen hatte schlüpfen können, dies eigentlich war es, was mich erfüllte und beglückte."

ture into a new country of the spirit, becomes itself the goal of the rebirth. Instead of removing himself from the river of flux, in order to walk on the sands of eternity, Felix plunges back into it over and over again.

Certainly when he declines the invitation of the rich Lord Strathbogie to return to Scotland with him and become his heir, he does so precisely in order not to surrender the power he has won over himself. Lord Strathbogie promises instant, effortless translation to a sphere of luxury and status, with the prospect of still greater grandeur for the future. But the temptation weighs as nothing against the threat to Felix's creative freedom. "A confident instinct within me," he tells us, "rebelled against a form of reality that was simply handed to me and was in addition sloppy—rebelled in favour of free play and dreams, self-created and self-sufficient, dependent, that is, only on imagination."[27] Felix, in brief, is an artist, an artist of the self, committed to ceaseless experiment with his own identity. It costs him little to reject the ducal splendors offered by Lord Strathbogie in order to pursue his destiny, to await new occasions to mint new selves and melt them down again as whim and circumstance permit.

Critics have seen in Felix a version of Hermes, the alchemist, the light-fingered rascal, the mercurial creator, whose mutations enact the novel's theme—"life is a continual process of transformations in which all living things must joyfully participate."[28]—and certainly it would be hard to find a more total antithesis to the spirit of Mansfield Park, where integrity of the person is so stubbornly cultivated. For Mann's hero, the worst torment he could be condemned to would be that of having to remain forever the same man, his limits marked out for him by some force beyond himself. And the greatest joy he can experience is the dissolution of the self; the process of self-change becomes the very goal of existence. Somewhere between Felix's game of perpetual self-transcendence and the unbudging rectitude of Fanny Price

27. *Confessions*, p. 197; *Bekenntnisse*, p. 256: "Ein Instinkt, seiner selbst sehr sicher, Partei nahm in mir gegen eine mir präsentierte und obendrein schlackenhafte Wirklichkeit—zugunsten des freien Traumes und Spieles, selbstgeschaffen und von eigenen Gnaden, will sagen: von Gnaden der Phantasie."

28. Frank J. Kearful, "The Role of Hermes in the *Confessions of Felix Krull*," *Modern Fiction Studies* 17 (1971): 92. For the detailed parallels see pp. 91–108 passim.

moves the equivocal figure of Melville's Confidence Man, reminding us simultaneously of the insidious theatricality of life and of the exhilarating theatricality of art.

Through all such instances runs the recognition that the actor, or impostor, practices a perilous art, and tempts other men to do the same. The age-old dread of mutability, the longing for a state of perfection akin to the immobility of God, the enmity of Christianity to what it regards as sacrilege against the creation persist, though with diminishing intensity, in the nineteenth century, at both ends of the ecclesiastical spectrum. At one end we have a continuing clatter of protest kept up by the low church sects, in the form of fiery pamphlets with titles like *The Church and the Stage*, or *Christians and the Theatre*. These rehearse, with varying degrees of adroitness, the well-worn theses inherited from Plato and Augustine and the Puritans, and they show a continuing incapacity for historical thinking, for reexamining the question in the light of the contemporary scene. Edmund Gosse, attempting to fathom the peculiar rigidity of his mother's moral temper, finds it in her unbudging attitude toward the Scriptures.

. . . she had formed a definite conception of the absolute, unmodified and historical veracity, in its direct and obvious sense, of every statement contained within the covers of the Bible. For her . . . nothing was symbolic, nothing allegorical or allusive in any part of Scripture, except what was, in so many words, proffered as a parable or a picture. Pushing this to its extreme limit, and allowing nothing for the changes of scene or time or race, my parents read injunctions to the Corinthian converts without any suspicion that what was apposite in dealing with half-breed Achaian colonists of the first century might not exactly apply to respectable English men and women of the nineteenth. . . . Both my parents, I think, were devoid of sympathetic imagination.[29]

"Devoid of sympathetic imagination": very much the state of mind, reaching at least as far back as Tertullian, which has characteristically underlain the more abusive varieties of antitheatricalism. A minor consequence of this heritage for Gosse was that when he came to read Shakespeare, the plays never seemed to him to be "bound by the exigencies of a stage or played by actors. The images they raised in my

29. Edmund Gosse, *Father and Son: A Study of Two Temperaments* (1907; rept. Penguin Books, London, 1949), pp. 57–58.

mind were of real people moving in the open air" (p. 217). Here the legacy of Puritan literalism combines with romantic incomprehension of the stage to dissolve the theatrical core of Shakespearean drama, turning it into a series of adventures staged in the theater of the mind, without reference to its being acted in public by live players. Something of the sort, we may add, had already become one standard response to Shakespeare's uncomfortable theatricalism. It had left its mark on the stage itself in the form of a passion for archaeologically correct reconstructions of costume and scenery, as though the purpose of staging a play was to build a museum on stage, to give audiences lessons in period dress and the architecture of past epochs.

Very few writers of intellectual consequence subscribed to the more clamorous antitheatricalism of the fundamentalists. One who did was Charles Kingsley, whose essay, "Plays and Puritans," undertakes to rehabilitate not only the lives and main doctrines of the old Puritans, but their specific odium of the stage. Looking back on the repertory of the Jacobean playing companies, Kingsley finds himself in total agreement with their Puritan enemies: "We should not allow these plays to be acted in our own day, because we know that they would produce their effects." They would, that is, presumably, prompt viewers to wish to imitate the horrors contained in them. "We should call him a madman who allowed his daughters or his servants to see such representations. Why, in all fairness, were the Puritans wrong in condemning that which we now have absolutely forbidden?" It is not entirely clear for whom Kingsley is speaking here, or who has absolutely forbidden what. What is clear is that because Kingsley himself would favor such prohibitions, the Puritans were right in vociferating as they did against all plays, in all theaters, at all times. The claim of the old dramatists to be "holding a mirror up to vice" [sic] is derided by Kingsley as pious cant. "If the poets had really intended to show vice its own deformity, they would have represented it . . . as punished, and not as triumphant. It is ridiculous to talk of moral purpose in works in which there is no moral justice."[30] The "deformity" of vice, then, can only be recognized in the theater if it is plainly labelled and properly punished. Kingsley subscribes without reserve to the neoclassic,

30. Charles Kingsley, *Plays and Puritans, and Other Historical Essays* (London, 1873), pp. 25–27. Page references in the discussion that follows will be to this volume.

or pseudo-classic dogma, according to which the moral purpose of a play is to be measured by the strictness with which the poet assigns rewards and penalties. The Jacobean playwrights are chastised for not making their plays into parsonical exercises in retribution, and the playwrights of Kingsley's own day applauded for their more wholesome and salubrious doctrine. What I think one must infer from this prescription, as perhaps also from Jeremy Collier's, is that an extreme moralism tends by its nature to verge on root-and-branch hostility, since its primary purpose usually proves to be the ruthless elimination of whatever does not conform to its canons. Whoever wishes to set bounds so closely, to legislate so tightly what the plot of a play should do or not do, and to rule out of court whatever does not conform to its exact specifications, must be reckoned an essential enemy to the whole enterprise, which can only grow in freedom.

It is hardly a surprise, under the circumstances, to find Kingsley announcing, with evident complacency, that "the temper of the British nation toward 'Art,' is simply that of the old Puritans, softened, no doubt, and widened; but only enough to permit Art, not to encourage it" (p. 5). The satisfaction with which Kingsley puts "Art" in its proper place may remind us that animosity to the stage often constitutes only the most obvious symptom of an antagonism toward all art. The theater being the most volatile of the arts, the most telling in its impact, the most provocative of mass emotion, as well as the most productive of visible disorder in the lives of its practitioners, who must move in a perpetual glare of artificial light and public curiosity, it tends to provoke the sternest dismissals from those whose true suspicion is of the unfettered imagination in any form. Those who have most darkly mistrusted the theater—Plato, the Puritans, the Jansenists, Rousseau—have tended to see in it a paradigm case for what is baleful in all the arts. Kingsley, giving the old demonology a peculiarly John Bullish twist, aligns himself happily with those descendants of the "old Puritans" who will magnanimously "permit," though never foolishly "encourage," "Art." If anything, he would harden the temper and narrow the bounds once more. He shares the scandal of Elizabethan Puritans for whom playwrights were wantonly defiling the minds of their audiences by transmitting the latest immoralities from Italy, and he subscribes also to the Puritan view that it was sinful for boys to play feminine parts. "One would fancy that the practice was forbidden by Moses' law, not arbitrarily, but because it was a bad practice, which did harm, as every antiquarian knows that it did." One antiquarian who knew no such thing was John Selden, who, being consulted on the matter by Ben Jonson, had cleared up the meaning of the Deuteronomic prohibition, as applying to the ceremonial not the moral law, more than two centuries earlier. But for Kingsley, as for Gosse's parents, what was forbidden to the ancient Israelites under special ritual conditions must also be forbidden seventeenth-century Englishmen under all conditions, "allowing nothing for the changes of time or scene or race." The Puritans, therefore, were "perfectly right. . . . to make a boy a stage-player was pretty certainly to send him to the Devil." Not a claim, perhaps, that would have survived an unbiased acquaintance with Nathan Field's *Remonstrance*, which, coming from the most renowned boy actor of his day, shows more charity and generosity of spirit than any of the un-Christian vituperations of the sermoneers with whom Kingsley does not hesitate to make common cause. Doubtless, as with the Puritans themselves, Kingsley's abhorrence rests partly on a Platonic fear of the power of impersonation: "Would any father allow his own children to personate, even in private, the basest of mankind?"

The conclusion, in any event, ringingly reaffirms the old Puritan anathemas, and pays tribute to their most agitated exponent: "Honour to old Prynne . . . for his passionate and eloquent appeals to the humanity and Christianity of England."[31] When one recalls the eye-bulging fanaticism stamped on every one of the thousand-odd pages of *Histriomastix*, one finds it hard to believe that this abusive lunatic is the same "old Prynne" whom Kingsley is saluting for his humanity and Christianity.

At the other end of the ecclesiastical spectrum, joining hands in mutual abhorrence with those whom in so many other respects they themselves abhorred, we find the solemn warning of Cardinal Manning that acting involves "the prostitution of a body purified by baptism,"[32] or the entry in Abbé Migne's 1847 *Encyclopédie théologique*, explaining

31. Ibid., pp. 35–37.
32. Gordon Craig, *On the Art of the Theatre* (1911; 5th impression, New York, 1957), p. 81, n. 1.

and defending the sanctions against actors still practiced in the French church:

The excommunication pronounced against comedians, actors, actresses tragic or comic, is of the greatest and most respectable antiquity. . . . it forms part of the general discipline of the French Church. . . . This Church allows them neither the sacraments nor burial; it refuses them its suffrages and its prayers, not only as infamous persons and public sinners, but as excommunicated persons. . . . One must deal with the comedians as with public sinners, remove them from participation with holy things while they belong to the theater, admit them when they leave it.[33]

From which one can only conclude that so far as the conservative wing of the Gallican church was concerned, the French Revolution might as well never have happened. We have also the more strident denunciations of Léon Bloy in his novel *Le désespéré*. Bloy's protagonist and mouthpiece, Caïn Marchenoir, is given to furious diatribes against the press, the priesthood, and the Jews. At a banquet in his honor, Marchenoir stoically endures the flutings and flutterings of the venal literati assembled to meet him, but when, after the reading aloud of his article, the host, his editor, compliments him on its tragic power and ventures to suggest that he has a métier for the stage, Marchenoir's eyes blacken with fury. Ragingly he explains,

I regard the state of an actor as the shame of shames. . . . The vocation of the theater is, in my eyes, the basest misery of this abject world, and passive sodomy is, I believe, slightly less infamous. The male whore, even when venal, is obliged to confine his debauchery to cohabitation with a single other person, and can still—in the midst of his frightful

33. Quoted in Maugras, *Les comédiens hors la loi*, pp. 476–477:

L'excommunication prononcée contre les comédiens, acteurs, actrices tragiques ou comiques, est de la plus grande et de la plus respectable antiquité. . . . Elle fait partie de la discipline générale de l'Église de France. . . . Cette Église ne leur accorde ni les sacrements, ni la sépulture; elle leur refuse ses suffrages et ses prières, non seulement comme à des infâmes et des pécheurs publics, mais comme à des excommuniés. . . . On doit en agir avec les comédiens comme avec les pécheurs publics, les éloigner de la participation des choses saintes pendant qu'ils sont sur le théâtre, les y admettre dès qu'ils le quittent.

ignominy—preserve a certain freedom of choice. The actor abandons himself, without choice, to the multitude, and his industry is not less ignoble because it is his *body* which serves as instrument of the pleasure given by his art.[34]

Marchenoir goes on to denounce the recent lifting of the legal and ecclesiastical stigmas on actors, the restoration to them of their rights as citizens and Christians. There is no excuse for receiving with honor and festooning with decorations "abominable hams whom respectable people of an earlier day would have refused to allow to sleep in the stable, for fear that they might infect the horses with the glanders of their profession."[35] After administering a further tongue-lashing to his auditors, Marchenoir storms out, his bile as thick and bitter as ever, and his prejudices not only unaltered but unchallenged. In view of the violence with which Bloy hurls himself on all the objects of his disapproval, one ought not perhaps to place too solemn an interpretation on his invectives against the actors. Still, it is characteristic of such attacks that they belong to a pattern of attack. It would be anomalous to find such a furious repudiation of one form of social behavior coupled with permissiveness toward the rest. Cardinal Manning, a dogged foe of the stage throughout his life, was also a fierce teetotaler, "a Puritan under the purple," in the words of his biographer, who took the pledge publicly, and led the battle for temperance with intemperate fanaticism.[36] Kingsley's unbridled attacks on Newman have made his name almost a byword for injurious bigotry. The denunciatory fervor of the French writer and the moral fundamentalism of the Englishmen

34. *Le désespéré* (Paris, 1887), pp. 474–475:

Je regarde l'état de comédien comme la honte des hontes. . . . La vocation du théâtre est, à mes yeux, la plus basse des misères de ce monde abject et la sodomie passive est, je crois, un peu moins infâme. Le bardache, même vénal, est, du moins, forcé de restreindre, chaque fois, son stupre, à la cohabitation d'un seul et peut garder encore,— au fond de son ignominie effroyable,—la liberté d'un certain choix. Le comédien s'abandonne, sans choix, à la multitude, et son industrie n'est pas moins ignoble, puisque c'est son *corps* qui est l'instrument du plaisir donné par son art.

35. Ibid., pp. 475–476: "D'abominables cabots, que les bonnes gens d'autrefois auraient refusé de faire coucher à l'écurie, par crainte qu'ils ne communiquassent aux chevaux la morve de leur profession."

36. Sidney Dark, *Manning* (London, 1936), pp. 72–74.

belong to the same psychological category, that of the zealous corrector of sin in others, and this probably forms a closer bond between them than any doctrinal agreements. Doctrine plays a lesser part, though not a negligible one: all subscribe to the dogma that the human self must be, in Trilling's term, an "integer," which nature forbids us to alter or diversify. When we alter or diversify for pleasure, when the body is made the instrument of that pleasure, when the pleasure is available to anyone who can pay for it, as with the actor, the activity turns into a form of metaphysical prostitution for which no loathing can be too strong and no repudiation too absolute.

An analogous streak of rigidity helps explain the measures contemplated by Auguste Comte for his projected positivist utopia. Utopian writers in general tend to be uneasy with the theater. They see it as a concession to our weakness, a symptom of our irrationality, a kind of placebo of the spirit with which the good society will be able to dispense. In their zeal to promote freedom among the people, they start by restricting them in their pleasures. Comte, himself an assiduous frequenter of the theater, with a box at the Opéra and one at the Comédie Française, an acquaintance among theater people, and an enviable collection of playbooks, nevertheless does not hesitate to ban the theater from his ideal state. The theater being, in his theory, merely a surrogate religion, it follows that, when traditional worship is abolished and the religion of humanity instituted in its place, the spiritual needs of the people will be fully met. The theater will wither away, or, if it will not, it will have to be eliminated. Those who care about drama as literature will seek it in the printed texts, undistracted by the trumpery of the playhouse:

It is for Positivism finally to suppress the theatre, as an institution at once irrational and immoral; and it will do so by reorganising the common education, and by founding, by Sociolatry, a system of festivals calculated to bring unprofitable satisfactions into contempt. Since reading has become so general that all can enjoy by themselves the master works of dramatic literature, the protection given to theatrical representations is solely an encouragement to mediocrity, and the factitious support in no way conceals the fact of their instinctive abandonment.[37]

37. *System of Positive Polity*, trans. J. H. Bridges, et al. (London, 1875–77), IV, 384; *Système de politique positive* (Paris, 1830–42), IV, 441–442,

Comte thus sees the theater as an instance of what, borrowing a term from T. E. Hulme, we may call "spilt religion," something to be replaced by a rational apparatus of public worship. He also sees it as a deteriorated, demotic form of drama: performance amounts to little more than an alluring method of conserving the heritage of dramatic poetry, which rectified spirits will prefer to savor in pure form, on the printed page. As a votary of reason, Comte will do away with the irrationality of the stage; as a reader, he will dispense with the foolish bedizenment of scenery and costume. As the arbiter of his own utopia, he will of course make the decision for others. Conceptual links between Comte and the Puritans may be slight, but the psychological affinity, as between Bloy and Manning, is close. Comte's scheme in general, observes John Stuart Mill,

Makes the same ethical mistake as the theory of Calvinism, that every act in life should be done for the glory of God, and that whatever is not a duty is a sin. . . . Like the extreme Calvinists, [Comte] requires that all believers shall be saints, and damns them (after his own fashion) if they are not.[38]

Whatever the mechanism behind it, Comte's line of reasoning drives a wedge between the drama and the theater, extending a sheltering wing over the one while grimly barring the other. And this attempt to separate out and exclude the element of live theater from the drama represents a recurrent illusion of the antitheatrical prejudice in all ages. Faced with the well-known fact that Gregory of Naziansen had composed a play about Christ, and that John Buchanan had written one on Saint John the Baptist, Gosson, in *Plays Confuted*, had had recourse to the distinction between plays for acting and plays for reading, approving the latter on the precedent of Moses and David, who "sett downe good matter in numbers, that the sweetenesse of the one might

---

quoted in Henri Gouhier, *L'essence du théâtre*, nouvelle ed. (Paris, 1968), p. 99: "Le positivisme doit irrévocablement éteindre l'institution du théâtre, autant irrationnelle qu'immorale, en réorganisant l'éducation universelle, et fondant, par la sociolâtrie, un système de fêtes propres à faire dédaigner de vaines satisfactions. Depuis que la lecture est assez répandue pour qu'on puisse partout goûter isolément les chefs-d'oeuvre dramatiques, la protection accordée aux jeux scéniques ne profite qu'aux médiocrités, et ce secours factice n'empêche pas d'apprécier la désuétude spontanée."

38. *Auguste Comte and Positivism* (London, 1865), pp. 142, 145.

cause the other to continue, and to bee the deeper imprinted in the mindes of men." The authority of Moses and David, together with the scarcely less august precedent of Plato and Cicero, who wrote "in numbers with interloquutions dialoguewise," enabled Gosson to conclude that "whatsoever such Playes as conteine good matter . . . may be read with profite, but cannot be playd, without a manifest breach of Gods commaundement."[39] It is the playing, then, the physical presence of live actors performing the scene before one's eyes, that constitutes the danger. Plays, when sufficiently edifying, are acceptable if they are not played. Similarly, the author of *The Stage Condemn'd*, a disciple of Jeremy Collier, declares it to be "very well known" that in antiquity, plays were "repeated for the Instruction of the Audience, but not acted with profane and villanous Gestures to corrupt the Morals of the Spectators . . . it being accounted a disgrace for the Authors to have them acted in Stage-Plays."[40] It hardly matters where this writer derives his strange notions concerning ancient dramatic performance —perhaps from the confused mediaeval tradition about recitations of Terence[41]—but it is clear that to separate script from performance in this manner provides a way of salvaging a venerated text while at the same time keeping up the hue and cry against live theater. An English contemporary of Comte's, in *A Rational Inquiry concerning the Operation of the Stage on the Morals of Society*, makes it clear that in his mind too the danger lies in performance, in the seductive and compelling vividness of what is presented to the eye and ear. There is, with respect to their relative degrees of impact, "a material difference between a play perused in the closet, and seen as performed."[42]

Renaissance writers of neo-Senecan tragedy, composing their plays to be "perused in the closet," or recited at private gatherings by coteries of initiates, had nursed a similar illusion. Presumably they hoped to exploit what was valuable in dramatic form without having to concede anything to the vulgarity of the playhouse. But the lifelessness of most

39. Stephen Gosson, *Plays Confuted in Five Actions* (1582) in Arthur F. Kinney, *Markets of Bawdrie: The Dramatic Criticism of Stephen Gosson*, Salzburg Studies in English Literature, no. 4 (Salzburg, 1974), pp. 177–178.
40. *The Stage Condemn'd* (London, 1698), p. 193.
41. See E. K. Chambers, *The Mediaeval Stage* (Oxford, 1903), II, 208.
42. David M'Nicoll, *A Rational Inquiry concerning the Operations of the Stage on the Morals of Society* (Newcastle-upon-Tyne, 1823), p. 12.

of their products tended to prove, on the contrary, a close connection between playhouse vices and dramatic virtues. By renouncing the former they usually ended by sacrificing the latter as well.

The process reaches epidemic proportions in the nineteenth century, partly as a result of a natural antipathy between romanticism and the theater. Romanticism, like Puritanism, leans toward inwardness, solitude, and spontaneity. It shares with Puritanism a belief in an absolute sincerity which speaks directly from the soul, a pure expressiveness that knows nothing of the presence of others. It takes as its models the guileless folk of the earth, who "know not seems": the peasant, the savage, the idiot, the child—those in whom the histrionic impulse remains undeveloped. To be sure, as Irving Babbitt has devastatingly shown, romantic expressiveness can be very impure; it can produce the posturings of a Chateaubriand, a Heine, or a Byron.[43] Here the craving to demonstrate individuality leads to a histrionic turning outward: the unique spirit collects spectators, wraps itself in picturesque costumes, executes magniloquent gestures. More characteristically, however, the romantic artist retreats within himself, or into solitary nature, shunning self-presentation. For John Stuart Mill, the peculiarity of the poet lies in his "utter unconsciousness of a listener." Poetry is "feeling confessing itself to itself, in moments of solitude." Confessing itself to itself—that is to say, self-engrossed, self-encapsulated, solipsistic. Mill distinguishes between public speech or eloquence, addressed to the world, and true speech or poetry, addressed only to the speaker's self: "Eloquence is *heard*, poetry is *over*heard. . . . Poetry . . . is the natural fruit of solitude and meditation; eloquence, of intercourse with the world."[44] Instead of a sage, the poet becomes a dreamer; instead of the theatrical setting of the marketplace, where the presence of others falsifies feeling, we have the uninhabited wilds, where only the clouds and trees can listen. True communion occurs with nature, or with others in imagination, as when a solitary reaper is heard across the fields singing in an unknown tongue. Here the communion is validated by the fact that the listener does not comprehend the language, and that it is not addressed to him—or to anyone—in the first place.

Mill's distinction between poetry and eloquence, of course, neither

43. *Rousseau and Romanticism* (New York, 1919), pp. 56 ff.
44. *Essays on Literature and Society*, ed. J. P. Schneewind (New York, 1965), pp. 109–110.

begins nor ends with Mill, but forms a cardinal tenet of romanticism. Blair admires Ossian because his poetry "deserves to be styled, *The poetry of the heart*. It is . . . a heart that is full, and pours itself forth. Ossian did not write, like modern poets, to please readers and critics. He sung from the love of poetry and song." Johann Georg Sulzer, ruminating specifically on poetry and eloquence, tells us that only eloquence "constantly has the listener, upon whom it wants to produce an effect, before its eyes," whereas the "poet" is one who "can not resist the violent desire to utter his feelings; he is transported. . . . He speaks, even if no one listens to him, because his feelings do not let him be silent." And Carlyle, similarly, declares of Burns that "He speaks forth what is in him, not from any outward call of vanity or interest, but because his heart is too full to be silent."[45] For a modern echo of the same distinction we may cite Pablo Casals, in conversations published in 1956. Speaking of J. S. Bach, Casals tells his interlocutor approvingly that "the theatre never tempted him. There was no room for concessions to showmanship in any of his works. . . . In the science of obtaining effects Handel was a great master . . . . Bach never thought of an effect: his music came out of the most intimate part of his mind and never aimed at anything but the purest."[46] What Casals is saying, in effect, is that Bach's music is a form of prayer, of introspection. Any consciousness of listeners introduces an impurity into it, cheapening the musical thought. Handel's mastery of "effects" places him in the inferior category of the eloquent, those seeking to address themselves to the public. Bach's music would be a species of self-communing, like a lyric poem, which we as it were accidentally overhear, whereas Handel's was frankly designed to be listened to and feasted on. Bach opens a window onto his soul; Handel mounts a platform and transfixes us with grandiose gestures.

What applies to the poet applies as well to the characters of fiction. Among romantic writers, Auden has pointed out, "there is . . . an agreement that the hero should be solitary, or if he does enter into relations with others, the relations should be very temporary."[47] Ro-

45. Cited in M. H. Abrams, *The Mirror and the Lamp* (Oxford, 1953), pp. 83, 89, 72.

46. J. Ma. Corredor, *Conversations with Casals* (New York, 1956), pp. 111, 116.

47. W. H. Auden, *The Enchafèd Flood* (New York, 1950), p. 108.

mantic narrative tends to involve confrontation with the sea, the mountains, the forests, or wild creatures, more than with other men. In Babbitt's formula, "there is . . . no object in the romantic universe—only subject" (*Rousseau and Romanticism*, p. 225). But drama, as traditionally defined and practiced, had always placed *action* at its center —men making moral decisions about their relations with other men, finding themselves precisely caught in the tension *between* their private and subjective selves and their roles as members of society.

M. H. Abrams has charted the displacement, in romantic critical theory, of tragedy from its traditional preeminence among the genres, and its replacement by lyric poetry.[48] The process involves a turning away from the theater. Lyric poetry strives toward the condition of the cry, the upwelling of the impassioned soul, accidentally preserved, as it were, in the recording medium of language. Tragedy falls from its high estate because it concerns men in their outward dealings with one another, and also because it requires physical means for its realization—a stage, scenery, costumes, and players.

It follows that though tragedy continues to elicit a formal respect, if only because of the rising tide of bardolatry, it also becomes increasingly a nontheatrical genre. The process touches Shakespeare himself in Lamb's essay "On the Tragedies of Shakespeare, Considered with Reference to their Fitness for Stage Representation." Lamb's notorious negative conclusion—that Shakespeare is *not* fit for the stage —springs from the conflict between his veneration for Shakespeare and his impatience with what he saw of the plays when acted. His impatience we may in turn set down partly to the unsatisfactory stage conditions of his day, which offered bleak prospects for intelligent revival of the classics, and this despite the presence of powerful actors like Kemble, Kean, and Mrs. Siddons. As an intellectual force the stage in England had been declining for a century; except for Coleridge, no writer of the first rank had written for it for decades. An institution that existed to mount lachrymose comedies like *Lovers' Vows* and sentimental tragedies like *The Iron Chest*, together with farces, pantomimes, and comic operas, whose very texts of Shakespeare were still tainted with the inauthenticity inherited from the Restoration, and which moreover was beginning to develop a fixation on scenic archae-

48. *The Mirror and the Lamp*, pp. 84–88, 145–146, and passim.

ology,[49] was unlikely to be able to do even fractional justice to the Shakespeare Lamb had learned to revere while poring over the plays in his library. Lamb's disgust with what he terms the "hateful incredible,"[50] the gross tricks whereby the stage sought to impose its childish illusions on the spectators, may be construed partly as the justified dismay of a man of sense confronting a deal of incompetent nonsense. If the actress playing Imogen really did, while nominally addressing Posthumus, aim crudely beyond him at the audience, she was violating a convenant of her art that Stanislavsky, at the century's end, would have to bend all his energy toward renewing, and Lamb was being made the victim of a kind of surplus exhibitionism that must assuredly have spoiled the effect.

But his objections strike deeper. Where Shakespeare is concerned, Lamb recoils from the very essence of theater, from its necessity to externalize, in which he finds intolerable coarseness. Plays themselves may be miracles of delicacy; character may disclose itself in language of haunting subtlety and reticence. The theater takes all this and renders it with harsh lights, violent gestures, and braying voices. "The things aimed at in theatrical representation," says Lamb, "are to arrest the spectator's eye upon the form and the gesture, and so to gain a more favourable hearing to what is spoken: it is not what the character is, but how he looks; not what he says, but how he speaks it" (p. 186). Even if, as in the case of Hamlet's soliloquies, the very meaning of a scene lies in its inwardness, the theater necessarily fixes our gaze on surfaces. How can the anguish of Hamlet be conveyed by a hired player gesticulating and mouthing before hundreds of people? How can the intimacies between lovers or the tenderness of husbands and wives be other than deformed and travestied when bawled out to row upon row of gaping groundlings? "The practice of stage representation," protests Lamb, "reduces everything to a controversy of elocution" (p.

49. See, for example, the stage history of *Macbeth*, as summarized by C. B. Young in J. Dover Wilson, ed. *Macbeth*, New Shakespeare (1947; rev. Cambridge, 1960), pp. lxix–lxxxii; and Dennis Bartholomeusz, *Macbeth and the Players* (Cambridge, 1969), pp. 98–180 passim.

50. *Essays of Elia*, ed. Robert Lynd and William Macdonald (New York, 1929), II, 195. Page references in the discussion that follows will be to this edition.

184). Even if we doubt the ultimate conclusion, we can hardly dispute the validity of the observation on which it is based. The stage does magnify, coarsen, and distort. Acting does crush some of the delicacy out of poetic language, but—and one would not suspect this from Lamb's discussion—it is also capable of introducing unsuspected riches of its own.

If Lamb, however, takes offence at the impostures of the theater, at the puerility of its scenic devices and the exhibitionism of its actors, at all that spoils the illusion, he nevertheless registers dismay when the illusion succeeds. Far from welcoming the reality created by the physical presence of live actors, he finds it threatening and oppressive. The vividness of mimetic representation becomes an assault on the viewer's peace of spirit, robbing him of the pleasure, so readily experienced in solitude, of savoring the poetry in his mind. If the play is *Macbeth*, and the player is Kemble, the intensity of the dagger scene can arouse acute distress:

... when we no longer read it in a book, when we have given up that vantage-ground of abstraction which reading possesses over seeing, and come to see a man in his bodily shape before our eyes actually preparing to commit a murder, if the acting be true and impressive, as I have witnessed it in Mr. K.'s performance of that part, the painful anxiety about the act . . . the too close pressing semblance of reality, give a pain and an uneasiness which totally destroy all the delight which the words in the book convey . . . . (pp. 191–192)

As if anxiety, pain, and uneasiness were not precisely the feelings Shakespeare wished to arouse in his audience! As if Macbeth's soul-searchings had nothing to do with his outer life, with the world of action and of other people—nothing to do with crime, blood, and terror! Similarly on *Othello*: here Lamb retreats into a benighted racism at the spectacle of the black man (or feigned black man) wooing the heroine.

I appeal to every one that has seen Othello played, whether he did not . . . sink Othello's mind in his colour; whether he did not find something extremely revolting in the courtship and wedded caresses of Othello and Desdemona; and whether the actual sight of the thing did not overweigh all that beautiful compromise which we make in reading. (p. 193)

Precisely the state of mind Iago labors to bring about in Brabantio in the opening scene! The very thing that gives and is meant to give the play its jolting impact, the physical proximity of the actors, black and white, together on stage, unnerves Lamb and makes him long for the quiet of his fireside, where all that is unpleasant and unsettling may be blotted out. It is odd indeed to find a professed admirer of the drama reacting so squeamishly to the emotional arousal that is one prime goal of histrionic art. But for Lamb, deeply sunk in his attachment to the printed page, the theater is blasted if it falls short of the illusion it aims at, and blasted if it achieves it.

An astute commentator has attempted to exculpate Lamb, along with Coleridge and Hazlitt, from the charge of being "closet critics," on the ground that they always measure the actual performance against an imagined ideal, and that "judged by this standard, *all* actual performances . . . are bound to fail in some respect." In their case, therefore, "the usual distinction between closet criticism and theatrical criticism must be set aside. The ostensible anti-theatrical bias . . . grows out of an assumption that these writers share about the nature of the drama itself and the qualities it manifests to an intelligent and sympathetic observer."[51] But the conviction that "*all* actual performances . . . are bound to fail in some respects" is one with which very few devotees of the theater would quarrel. If, however, it leads to the conclusion that actual performances had better not be attended, or (worse) attempted, at all, or that they remain somehow intrinsically inferior to the invisible, inaudible performances played within the theater of the mind, then it must be accounted an unmistakable symptom of antitheatrical bias. For only the physical stage, whatever its shortcomings, can be the true site of performance. The theater of the mind is no substitute. What Lamb and his colleagues, with their keen eye for the defects of particular productions and individual players, signally fail to convey is a sense of the *indispensability* of performance, the fact that the script *must* be incarnated by live actors, or it remains forever impalpable and wraithlike, subject to every misunderstanding and distortion of which readers are capable. No musician, however persuaded of the inability of human pianists to do justice to Beethoven's last sonatas, would ever choose to content himself with simply reading the

51. Joseph W. Donohue, Jr., *Dramatic Character in the English Romantic Age* (Princeton, 1970), p. 285.

score, or could ever be imagined as saying, "We do not like to hear our master's sonatas played, and least of all Opus 106." Yet, given the fact that Beethoven was deaf and isolated when he wrote them, locked up in anguish in a private world of his own, such an attitude would make better sense than Lamb's toward the plays of Shakespeare, designed not only for *the* theater, but for a specific theater, of which Shakespeare himself was an honored member and active participant.

Characteristically, the writers of the romantic generation hold themselves aloof from the theater even when they wish to practice the art of tragedy. Wordsworth composed *The Borderers*, he tells us, "without any view to its exhibition upon the stage." When, as it chanced, the script was submitted to Covent Garden, the poet "entirely concurred" with the manager who "*judiciously*" refused it as "not calculated for the Stage."[52] In Byron's case, after exposure to the sordid side of the workaday theater in his capacity as member of the managing committee for Drury Lane, and after a stinging rebuff from Edmund Kean, whom he had admired to the edge of idolatry, he ended with a furious dislike for the whole operation. Rather than renounce dramatic form in his writing, however, he recast his material so as to frustrate in advance any attempt to bring it onto the boards. He writes in 1817, with reference to his dramatic poem *Manfred*, that though he has no high opinion of it, he has "at least rendered it *quite impossible* for the stage, for which my intercourse with Drury Lane has given me the greatest contempt." "The thing," he pursues,

could never be attempted or thought of for the stage . . . I composed it actually with a *horror* of the stage, and with a view to render the thought of it impracticable, knowing the zeal of my friends that I should try that for which I have an invincible repugnance, viz. a representation.

As to the correct designation of the work, he adds, "You may call it 'a Poem,' for it is no Drama, and I do not choose to have it called by so d——d a name,—'a Poem in dialogue,' or—Pantomime, if you will; anything but a green-room synonyme. . . ."[53] There is perversity in an

52. *Poetical Works*, ed. E. de Selincourt (Oxford, 1940), I, 342–343.
53. *Poems and Plays*, ed. W. P. Trent, Everyman ed. (London, 1910), 11, 263–264.

author's first choosing play form, and then consciously emasculating it of its play element. But there is greater perversity in what followed, for beginning with *Marino Faliero* in 1821, Byron wrote a series of more straightforward tragedies, relatively conventional in structure, with clear opportunities for stage spectacle and physical action, which he then struggled to keep from the hands of producers, the voices of actors, and the gaze of the public.[54] *Marino Faliero*, when it appeared in print, came accompanied with a sharp repudiation of any interest in the theater, or any desire on Byron's part to see it acted:

I have had no view to the stage . . . . I cannot conceive any man of irritable feeling putting himself at the mercies of an audience. The sneering reader, and the loud critic, and the tart review, are scattered and distant calamities; but the trampling of an intelligent or of an ignorant audience on a production which, be it good or bad, has been a mental labour to the writer, is a palpable and immediate grievance, heightened by a man's doubt of their competency to judge, and his certainty of his own imprudence in electing them his judges. Were I capable of writing a play which could be deemed stage-worthy, success would give me no pleasure, and failure great pain.[55]

With due regard for the independence and energy of these sentiments, and for the specific disillusion with the theater that they reflect, they suggest that their author does not think of the theater as an artistic medium in its own right, with its own laws of expression. John Marston, reluctantly allowing *The Malcontent* to be printed so as to forestall a piracy, lamented that a play, "invented merely to be spoken,"

54. See David V. Erdman, "Byron's Stage Fright: The History of his Ambition and Fear of Writing for the Stage," *English Literary History* 6 (1939): 219–243, for the well-argued proposition that Byron's hostility to the theater masked an intense desire to succeed as a playwright, coupled with an equally intense fear of failure. Peter J. Manning, "Edmund Kean and Byron's Plays," *Keats-Shelley Journal* 21–22 (1972–73): 188–206, elaborates, with special reference to Byron's strong identification with Kean, the effect of Kean's acting style on his own playmaking, and the disenchantment suffered as the result of an affront from Kean, supinely concurred in by the Drury Lane management.

55. *Works*, ed. Ernest Hartley Coleridge, rev. ed. (London, 1901), IV, 337. See also the Preface to *Werner* in *Works*, V, 338, n. 1.

should be "enforcively published to be read."[56] Byron, by contrast, denies that his plays were ever "invented to be spoken" at all, and goes to law to prevent their being pirated—in the playhouse. Production, in his eyes, not only trivializes plays and introduces irrelevancies, it desecrates; it defiles the artistic integrity of the original script.

In part, no doubt, the divorce between serious writers and the stage may be ascribed to the unfavorable conditions prevailing in the popular theater—the growing size of playhouses, the increasing demand for spectacular scenic effects, the all but total indifference on the part of audiences to exploration of moral questions. Any self-respecting artist who tried to conform to the requirements of the theatergoing public would probably have had to sell his artistic soul in the process. But it lies also in part in the prevailingly untheatrical, excessively inward conception of drama itself on the part of the poets. Moody Prior has remarked how ineptly most nineteenth-century playwrights handle the soliloquy. Instead of being, as it had been for the Elizabethans, a device for uncovering hidden motives, for connecting the inner will with the outer deed, the soliloquy now becomes simply "a signal for the expatiation of the sensibilities."[57] By contrast, one virtue of *The Cenci*, and one explanation of its superior survival power, lies in the fact that Shelley desired it to be performed, and wrote it for a specific actress whose art he admired, consciously avoiding "the introduction of what is commonly called mere poetry."[58] "Mere poetry," for most other poetic dramatists, constituted the chief reason for writing. They wrote as "custodians of a noble art, or as reformers," in open contempt for the stage of their day.[59]

A vein of antitheatrical tragedy is thus initiated, which persists throughout the nineteenth and into the twentieth century. A commentator in 1887 describes the following odd state of affairs:

Shakespeare's plays are so much more frequently read in private than seen on the stage, that it is almost forgotten that they were ever intended to be acted and hence a tendency has arisen to regard the drama, from

56. "To the Reader," *The Malcontent*, ed. George K. Hunter, Revels ed. (London, 1975), p. 5.

57. *The Language of Tragedy*, 1947 (Bloomington, 1966), p. 218.

58. *Complete Poetical Works*, ed. Thomas Hutchinson and Benjamin P. Kurtz (New York, 1933), p. 277.

59. Prior, *The Language of Tragedy*, p. 220.

a purely literary point of view, as a distinct form of literary art, independent of the concrete associations of stage and actors once germane to it. Thus Taylor calls Philip van Artevelde a 'library' play . . . .[60]

This somewhat complacent acknowledgement of the unconcern of dramatic authors toward the stage echoes Sir Henry Taylor's own remarks in the preface to *Philip van Artevelde*: "As this work, consisting of two Plays and an Interlude, is equal in length to about six such plays as are adapted to representation, it is almost unnecessary to say that it was not intended for the stage. It is properly an Historical Romance, cast in a dramatic and rhythmical form."[61] Unfortunately for such writers as Taylor, the indifference to the stage that led them to project their works as "historical romances" also encouraged a prolixity that leached out of the plays whatever vitality they might otherwise have possessed as literature. *Philip van Artevelde* is deader than Queen Anne, and so are the interminable dramatic *oeuvres* of Taylor's much more talented younger admirer, Algernon Swinburne. Taylor wrote Swinburne a eulogistic letter on the latter's *Mary Stuart*, which Swinburne cherished as coming from "the one English poet living for whose opinion as an authority on poetic drama I care a cracked farthing."[62]

But the conjunction is ominous. Although, like Taylor, Swinburne disliked the theater—partly because of his deafness[63]—throughout his career he championed the neglected Elizabethan dramatists, collecting their plays, furthering fresh scholarly editions of their works, writing critical studies of them, and entering into passionate correspondence about them with fellow admirers. He also wrote five volumes of bookish imitations, in the course of which he worked out a neo-Elizabethan poetic idiom of his own, of considerable expressive power. Yet he cares nothing for the Elizabethans' concreteness, for their feeling for phys-

60. J. B. Bilderbeck, *Sir Henry Taylor and his Drama of Philip van Artevelde* (Madras, 1887), p. 14.

61. *Philip van Artevelde; A Dramatic Romance*, 3d ed. (London, 1844), p. ix. In 1849 Taylor also wrote two plays by which he hoped "to revive the Elizabethan comedy of romance" (*Autobiography 1800–1875* [London, 1885], II, 39).

62. Edmund Gosse, *The Life of Algernon Charles Swinburne* (London, 1917), p. 257.

63. See Cecil Y. Lang, ed. *The Swinburne Letters* (New Haven, 1959–62), I, xxxi; VI, 59.

ical gesture and carnal presence. His own most ambitious drama, *Bothwell*, he alludes to most often as a "poem" or a "work" or an "epic," almost never as a play. His career as dramatist, then, resembles Taylor's: play after endless play on historical themes, none meant to be acted—only one, by a fluke, brought to the stage in his lifetime—and nearly all, in their self-indulgent prolixity, as unreadable as they are unactable.

Swinburne's biographer, Edmund Gosse, writing eight years after Swinburne's death, confesses that "readers are now almost as impatient of unactable 'poetic' drama as playgoers are." In Swinburne's youth, says Gosse, "the question had hardly begun to be asked in England whether theatrical literature not intended for the theatre had any right to exist."[64] If not in England, however, it had certainly been raised by Wagner in Germany. Wagner, musing on the art-work of the future, had turned a withering gaze on the whole phenomenon of closet drama. Thanks to Goethe, who had attempted to revive poetic drama by an effort of the will, a whole generation of insignificant closet playwrights had spurned the stage in order to court the favors of art critics and solitary readers.

> Where Goethe shipwrecked, it could but become "good tone" to look upon oneself as shipwrecked in advance: the poets still wrote plays, but not for the unpolished stage; simply for their cream-laid paper. Only the second- or third-rate poetasters, who here and there adapted their conceits to local exigence, still busied their brains with the players; but not the eminent poet, who wrote "out of his own head" .... Thus happened the unheard-of: *Dramas written for dumb reading*!
>
> Did Shakespeare, in his stress for unadulterated Life, take shelter in the uncouth scaffold of his People's-stage: so did the egoistic resignation of the modern dramatist content itself with the bookseller's counter ....

Closet drama, then, in Wagner's devastating account, comes down to a refusal to bow to the realities of theaters and actors, in the name of a freedom which is self-pampering and illusory. Even the decadent virtuosity of French and Italian opera represents a healthier form of "the bent to artistic exhibition, than where the 'abstract' poet would fain usurp this bent for his own self-glorification." The only road to redemption, insists Wagner, lies through submission to the brute facts

64. Gosse, *Swinburne*, pp. 216–217.

of stage performance, "for only that which wills to *live*, must hearken to necessity,—but that which wills to do much *more* than live, namely to lead a *dead* existence, can make of itself what it pleases."[65] The fate of most of the closet drama of the nineteenth and twentieth centuries testifies to the prophetic accuracy of this analysis.

In France, we encounter a more bizarre situation: not antitheatrical drama, but antitheatrical theater, with, as its prime exponent, the high priest of symbolism and Wagnerian disciple, Mallarmé. Mallarmé's relations with the theater form a study in self-contradiction and a lesson in the unattainable, a quixotic attempt on the part of the antitheatrical principle to capture the theater. There is something absurd and heroic in the spectacle of the master of silence, inwardness, and immobility trying to impose these qualities onto the bustling world of the public stage, trying to force the theater, against its grain, to give up action, narrative, and physicality. All that remain of Mallarmé's cherished the-

65. "The Art-Work of the Future," in *Prose Works*, trans. William Ashton Ellis (London, 1892–98), I, 143, 146. See *Das Kunstwerk der Zukunft* (Leipzig, 1850), pp. 119–120:

Wo ein *Göthe* gescheitert war, musste es guter Ton werden, von vorne herein sich als gescheitert anzusehen: die Dichter dichteten noch Schauspiele, aber nicht für die ungehobelte Bühne, sondern für das glatte Papier. Nur was so in zweiter oder dritter Qualität noch hier oder da, der Lokalität angemessen, herumdichtete, gab sich mit den Schauspielern ab; nicht aber der vornehme sich selbst dichtende Dichter, der von allen Lebensfarben nur noch die abstrakte preussische Landesfarbe, Schwarz auf Weiss, anständig fand. So erschien denn das Unerhörte: *für die stumme Lectüre geschriebene Dramen!*

Behalf sich Shakespeare in Drange nach unmittelbarem Leben mit dem rohen Gerüste seiner Volksbühne, so genügte der egoistischen Resignation des modernen Dramatikers die Buchhändlertafel, auf der er sich lebendig todt zum Markte auslegte. Ibid., pp. 124–125: Nichts desto weniger ist dennoch da, woselbst nur diese *Virtuosität des Darstellers* für das Publikum den Begriff der Schauspielkunst ausmacht, wie in den meisten französischen Theatern und selbst in der Opernwelt Italiens, eine natürlichere Aeusserung des künstlerischen Darstellungstriebes vorhanden, als dort, wo der abstrakte Dichter dieses Triebes zu seiner Selbstverherrlichung sich bemächtigen will. . . . nur was *leben* will, hat der Nothwendigkeit zu gehorchen,—was aber viel *mehr* als leben, nämlich *todt* sein will, das kann mit sich machen, was es Lust hat.

atrical projects are a sheaf of notes and jottings and a few fragments of superby immobile, elliptical poetry. By the time he reaches the planning of his most ambitious play, *Igitur*, the presence of an actual theater has retreated like a mirage. The action has become something designed for the theater of the mind rather than the boards of the physical stage.[66] But failure did not deter Mallarmé from continuing to pursue his uncompromising dream. In some conversations with George Moore, he outlined a dramatic project similar to that for *Igitur*. One night, says Moore,

I ventured to ask him what new work he was producing.
"A drama," he replied with visible pride. That evening our talk was of the theatre and he reproached Victor Hugo for wishing to revive Shakespearean drama in Alexandrine verse.
"Then, your play is not at all like 'Hernani'?"
"Not at all," he replied with the howl of a dog whose tail has been stepped on.
"In how many acts is your play, Master?" "Three." "How many characters?"
"Two; myself and the wind."

It would be hard to imagine a more radical contradiction in terms than a "play" with only two characters, "myself and the wind." As for the action, the fable, it was to have been along these lines:

"A Young man, the last of his race, is dreaming in his ruined castle. Dreams, dreams . . . he dreams of battles, duels, adventures in distant forests . . . . of Life itself . . . . his life . . . he makes plan after plan and prays his ancestors to direct his course. But always it is the wind in the old tower which answers, which tries to answer, for it is a tribute to the genius of the French language that the wind in an old tower always desires to whisper the word ou . . . i (oui, yes)." And the dreamer listens . . . without ever being sure if it is "yes" that the wind wishes to say.

The untheatrical nature of the conception hardly needs underlining. Dreams, memories, reveries, on the part of the young man in his *tour abolie*; and, for answer, the fragmentary mutterings of the wind, which may or may not be the "oui" that the dreamer thinks he hears. It

66. Haskell M. Block, *Mallarmé and the Symbolist Drama* (Detroit, 1963), p. 38 and passim.

stretches one's imagination to the breaking point to think how such a play might be staged, yet Mallarmé, according to Moore, wished it to be produced and acted:

When I would ask him where he wished to give it, in what theatre, he would always speak of travelling in a caravan, and of himself playing the role of his hero in all the fairs of France. He would grow enthusiastic over the idea that the poet should be his own mountebank.[67]

A critic has suggested that Mallarmé was teasing his visitor, who was too dense to get the joke,[68] and Moore's notorious unreliability might prompt us to view the whole anecdote with skepticism. But assuming Moore has reported it accurately, would he have missed the point night after night, in what was evidently a continuing discussion? Does the proposal, moreover, as Moore transmits it, differ so greatly from Mallarmé's own plan for a "great work" of theater in which he himself, as unique recitant, would perform before a select audience of only eight people?[69] In both cases, it is more likely, Mallarmé was indulging in fantasies of the kind of purified theater he would like to have been able to summon into existence, but which he increasingly understood to be incommensurate with the practical possibilities.

Equally bizarre is the case of a more authentic man of the theater, Maeterlinck—authentic in that he wrote plays to be acted by professional actors, in professional theaters—in whom we find not Mallarmé's slightly febrile enthusiasm but rather a strange, regressive distaste for his own chosen medium. Visiting London with the Théâtre de l'Oeuvre in 1895, he told *The Daily Chronicle* that "with the greatest admiration for the talents of my interpreters, I cannot say that any theatrical representation, whether of my own plays or of others, gives me real pleasure. . . . I think that almost all plays that are not mere stage-carpentry can be better appreciated in reading than on the stage." To the *Sketch* he confided further, "I myself take little or no interest in the practical side of dramatic life. I always enjoy reading a play far more than I do seeing it acted, for on the stage the delicate symbolic essence of what

67. Allen Carric, "Mallarmé and the New Drama," *The Mask* 2 (1909–10): 172. All ellipses indicated here originate in the text cited. They are not, of course, ellipses at all but typographical renderings of hesitation and dreaminess.
68. Block, *Mallarmé*, p. 46.
69. Ibid., p. 78.

every thoughtful writer wishes to convey cannot but escape." The sentiments vividly recall those of Lamb on Shakespeare, with the astonishing difference that this time it is the playwright who is speaking, and on the occasion of a public performance of his most celebrated play, *Pelléas et Mélisande*, for the production of which he had come to London himself to serve as consultant. It is true that Maeterlinck aimed, and more programmatically as his career advanced, at "a drama of silence and gesture rather than one of violence and action,"[70] and that in his hands symbolism meant the creation of a mood, a fragile, tenuous poetic atmosphere, which he found difficult to achieve in the physical theater. Nevertheless, it remains odd that a playwright who harbored such views should have concerned himself with production at all. Why should he not, like Byron, have applied himself to the composition of plays meant only for reading, and even perhaps tried to balk production, so as to protect his plays from the deformations attendant *on* production? Perhaps because in spite of his doubts, he nevertheless dreamed of creating, in the theater, the effects of charged silence and muted intensity to which his plays so palpably lend themselves. Perhaps he was ready to risk a measure of theatrical coarsening in order to arrive at a greater degree of theatrical delicacy. Whatever the explanation, what seems crystal clear is that at least in his professed doctrine this epigone of the Wagnerian movement has utterly renounced Wagner's own cardinal conviction that the life of the theater lies in the theater, and not on the printed page.

The persistence of "closet" drama, the continuing alienation of poets from the stage, reflects a persisting antitheatricalism on the part of writers, no doubt, but also the quandary of the theater as an artistic medium. Victor Hugo, in 1827, writes *Cromwell* in the immense, unwieldy, unplayable state in which we have it because of his despair over the stage of his day, and his resolve to remain aloof from it until it could raise itself out of the swamp of its own corruption and triviality. As the nineteenth century wears on, the theater comes under increasingly vitriolic attack from men of the theater themselves. Probably no more scathing diatribe against actors has ever been written than Octave Mirbeau's notorious *feuilleton* of October 26, 1882, in *Le Figaro*, which

70. Quoted in John Stokes, *Resistible Theatres* (London, 1972), pp. 171–173.

nearly led to duels with the outraged *sociétaires* of the Comédie Française, as well as with Mirbeau's own editor, who meanly backed down
on the support he owed his maverick writer. According to Mirbeau, the
player lives wrapped in an unreality that drains all truth from his life.
His joys, his sufferings, even his death, are cheapened and dishonored
by the falsity to which his profession commits him.

In a later, suaver excursion on the same subject, Mirbeau recounts
an imaginary interview with the retired matinée idol Frédéric Febvre.
After telling the young reporter of his conviction that he need only
bide his time in order to be named emperor by acclamation, Febvre
confesses gloomily that he has fallen victim to a strange visitation.
Everything in his life—all tangible and visible phenomena, his books,
his furniture, his newly purchased clock, the sky itself—has turned
into stage décor. "I live in a horrible nightmare," he laments. At this
moment a servant appears to set lunch before Febvre, but the roast
chicken that steams and sputters savorously as it is being carried in
turns into a papier-maché prop as soon as Febvre tries to cut it, and
the knife itself, with which he tries to cut it, scratches spiritlessly against
it, a stick of painted cardboard. Febvre's own explanation for this disquieting phenomenon is that the souls of his admirers are flocking
around him, imploring him to return to the stage, in which his departure has left such a void. And he assures his visitor that he has every
intention of yielding, of playing his greatest triumphs over again in
all the capitals of Europe, if only this persecution of love will cease.
Meanwhile—in despair, the wretched actor drops a tear, but the tear,
instead of drying up or wetting his cheek, condenses into a solid little
ball which drops to the floor with a sharp click. At length Febvre disappears, "behind an illusionistic door-curtain," and the visitor listens
for some time to the tears that rattle onto the floor like dried peas in the
adjoining room.[71] The whole anecdote is a fierce parable of the actor's
existence, seen as so radically false that it lends him a negative Midas
touch. Everything he approaches derealizes itself into stage trumpery,
into canvas, tinsel, and paste. At the same time—and here Mirbeau
delivers the *coup de grâce*—the actor himself, sunk in the boundless
egoism of his kind, can see in it all nothing but one more sign of the
adulation of his public.

Another *feuilleton* describes an interview with another sacred mon-

71. Octave Mirbeau, *Gens de théâtre* (Paris, 1924), pp. 110–117.

ster, Constant Coquelin. Coquelin, "our great national ham," is discovered by the reporter at home, surrounded by 2,809 painted portraits of himself and 3,046 sculptured busts, multiplied to infinity by mirrors that reflect them in every direction. The reporter learns that each provincial museum in France, as well as every major gallery abroad, has its own collection of such effigies, a gift from Coquelin himself. The collection at hand is destined for the Louvre, and Coquelin hopes that after his death the government will see fit to institute a cult to him—in fact to the trinity composed of himself, his brother, and his son. While a secretary performs cosmetic ministrations on his feet, Coquelin confides that in his opinion the French press has at last redeemed itself from triviality, by the energy with which it is addressing itself to the question, "Should Coquelin act in Germany or should he not?" Since Coquelin incarnates France and France symbolizes Coquelin, the question has universal resonance.[72]

Mirbeau's satiric ferocity may be understood partly as the resentment of a skilled playwright against the cabals tyrannizing over the theatrical life of the country. Against his biting accounts of the actors of the national theater, and his relentless mockery of the most established dramatic critic of the day, Francisque Sarcey, we need to place his impassioned tribute to Sarah Bernhardt, his eulogy of playwrights like Henri Becque, and his warm appreciation of the art of the theater when its exacting standards are met. His quarrel with the theater is in part at least a lover's quarrel; the actors are arraigned for betraying a sacred trust. But their betrayal has brought the theater to the point where nothing can save it short of total revolution. Similar sentiments are beginning to be voiced elsewhere; they grow stronger as the century wanes. The most sacred of all the sacred monsters, Eleanora Duse, revolted by the falseness of the theatrical milieu, longs for a cleansing holocaust that will enable the true votaries to build a new temple:

To save the theatre the theatre must be destroyed: the actors and actresses must all die of the plague. . . . They poison the air, they make art impossible.[73]

And to this voice from the altar we may add that of Bernard Shaw from the aisles:

72. Ibid., pp. 118–124.
73. Gordon Craig, *On the Art of the Theatre* (1911, 1957), p. 79.

The curse of our stage at present is the shameless prostitution of the art of acting into the art of pleasing. The actor wants "sympathy": the actress wants affection. They make the theatre a place where the public comes to look at its pets and distribute lumps of sugar to them.[74]

Through all the protests runs a single thread: revulsion from the actors. The antitheatrical prejudice battens on the stubborn centrality of the theater's human raw material, the fact that the stage must work not mainly with wood or paint or marble, or even words, but with treacherous, imperfect men. Artists dream of creating something permanent, fixed, and exempt from the ravages of time, well-wrought urns and mosaic saints. Inert matter they can force to do their bidding; they can impose their shaping wills on it, stamp it with their signatures. But how subdue human beings in the same way, who have wills of their own? How control a medium recalcitrant not with the brute heaviness of inanimate matter but with the wild rebelliousness of flesh and blood? Alice's croquet game with hedgehogs and flamingoes seems pedestrian and mechanical by comparison. Disgust with the actors leads some of the more radical innovators to dream of doing away with them entirely. Gordon Craig longs for a race of supermarionettes who will do the actor's work without any of the sickening egoism that the actor himself pours into it.[75] For Anatole France, it is pointedly not the bad actors, but the good ones, who spoil plays: their egregious individuality spills over and drowns everything. He too yearns for the impersonality of the marionettes.[76] And Joseph Conrad, in a letter, confesses that though he greatly desires to write a play, he:

Can't conceive how a sane man can sit down deliberately to write [one] and not go mad before he has done. The actors appear to me like a lot of *wrong-headed* lunatics pretending to be sane. . . . To look at them breeds in my melancholy soul thoughts of murder and suicide,—such is my anger and my loathing of their transparent pretences. . . . But I

74. *Our Theatres in the Nineties* (London, 1948), II, 283.

75. *On the Art of the Theatre*, pp. 54–94.

76. "The Marionettes of M. Signoret," *Mask* 5 (1912): 99–102. Earlier, France had endorsed Lamb's view that Shakespeare is unsuited to theatrical representation, believing that "the greatest dramatic compositions are addressed to the inner theatre of the mind, wherein their symbolic value is not destroyed by the accidents of physical performance" (Block, *Mallarmé*, p. 110).

love a marionette-show. Marionettes are beautiful,— . . . I love the marionettes that are without life, that come so near to being immortal![77]

Just so! The marionettes are beautiful because without life, without the soiling passions and ugly malice of real people. They hold out the hope that the theater will be able to free itself once and for all of its humiliating dependence on live players, and take its place alongside the other arts, where the artist's will is law. Partly, no doubt, the vogue for marionettes and masks at the turn of the century reflects an attempt to retheatricalize the theater, to rescue it from a paralyzing realism. But it also constitutes an effort to *de*theatricalize it, to divest it of the kind of theatricality implied in the eternal posturing and grimacing of the actors. As reforming poets set out with the weapons of anti-poetry to destroy the merely "poetical," so the reformers of the theater approach with their own wrecking implements, their hatred for what Gordon Craig termed the "monster called The Theatrical,"[78] eager to smash it so that the theater can settle down once more to the pursuit of its true artistic mission.

Craig and his associates, then, wish to reform the theater by rebaptizing it in a truer theatricalism, dispensing both with the outworn artifices of the nineteenth-century stage and with the offensive histrionicism of the actors. The other great theatrical reformer of the day, Stanislavsky, wishes to detheatricalize the theater entirely, by reimmersing it in a truer, more authentic naturalness. The Stanislavskian actor undergoes an arduous discipline to learn how *not* to mimic, *not* to exhibit himself, *not* to allow the spectators to control his performance. Instead, he is to copy the romantic poet. He is to look into the deep well of his own consciousness. Rather than fashion a stage personality

77. G. Jean-Aubry, *Joseph Conrad, Life and Letters* (London, 1927), I, 213. Not surprisingly, Conrad did ultimately try his hand at playwriting, despite his suspicions of the actors. In 1905, his one-act play *One Day More* was performed by an amateur drama society, and earned a *succès d'estime*; G. B. Shaw, who attended, was "ecstatic and enthusiastic." In 1919, spurred by a successful stage adaptation of *Victory* (prepared by someone else), Conrad turned *The Secret Agent* into a full-length play, and dramatized one of his stories as a play in two acts, *Laughing Ann*. See Gérard Jean-Aubry, *The Sea Dreamer*, trans. Helen Sebba (New York, 1957), pp. 248, 277.

78. Shaw, *On the Art of the Theatre* (1911, 1957), p. 183.

as one would construct a mask, he is to urge it into being as one would preside over the birth of a natural creature. *"Our type of creativeness is the conception and birth of a new being—the person in the part. It is a natural act similar to the birth of a human being."*[79] Once this act has taken place, the actor will have succeeded in infusing his own natural person into the playwright's imagined one, effecting a kind of vital juncture between them. But he still will be obliged to exert the most rigorous restraint so as not to be tempted by the presence of an audience to slide back into mimicry or exhibitionism.

For Strindberg also, the art of acting is emphatically *not* the art of pretense, since low comedians can often dissimulate brilliantly through mask and costume, and it is *not* imitation, since poor actors are often superb mimics, but something "honest, true, and natural."[80] When we look at what was said about Eleanora Duse by her contemporaries, we see that Mill's distinction between poetry and eloquence now extends to the art of the stage itself. For the greatness of Duse, according to Bernard Shaw, Arthur Symons, and others, is her supreme naturalness. She is, or seems, wholly without artifice. She does not *pretend* to play such and such a part; she simply inhabits that part, lives the life of the character, thinks the very thoughts of that character, for the duration of her performance. She has made herself great as an actress "through being the antithesis of the actress . . . . She loves art so devotedly that she hates the mockery of her own art." "When she is on the stage she does not appeal to us with the conscious rhetoric of the actress; she lets us overlook her, with an unconsciousness which study has formed into a second nature." Just as the lyric poet eschews eloquence and allows us to "overhear" his reveries, so Duse shuns all "conscious rhetoric," permitting us simply to "overlook" her. And in this respect her art has launched a revolution. Previously, acting has always meant "an art wholly rhetoric, that is to say, wholly external." It is the "dramatised oratory" of Sir Henry Irving that has always been understood as acting. With Duse's advent, "rhetoric disappeared," to be replaced by an art "wholly subtle, almost spiritual, a suggestion, an evasion, a secrecy." Symons, it is clear, is seeking a formula analogous to Mill's to suggest

79. Constantin Stanislavski, *An Actor Prepares*, trans. Elizabeth Reynolds Hapgood (London, [1937]), p. 294.
80. August Strindberg, *Open Letters to the Intimate Theater*, trans. Walter Johnson (Seattle, n.d.), p. 21.

that Duse, when she acts, unlocks a secret chamber of her being, like the lyric poet, allowing its fugitive and impalpable emanations to drift outward toward the public. Duse, quite plainly, is an antitheatrical actress, an anti-actress, who plays "with hardly a suggestion of the stage, except the natural woman's intermittent loathing for it." And one result of her wholly triumphant, wholly natural presence is that all other acting now shows itself for the "mechanical, forced, and unnatural" thing it is.[81]

Her naturalness shows itself most clearly of all when she is compared to her celebrated rival Sarah Bernhardt. Bernhardt represents the older kind of rhetorical acting at its transcendant best. Next to Duse, she seems the epitome of artifice. Her acting is "a perfect mechanism." She comes on stage "like a miraculous painted idol,"[82] never for a moment failing to mark the gulf between nature and art. "The fact is," says Symons, "that we do not sufficiently realise the difference between what is dramatic and what is merely theatrical,"[83] but Duse and Bernhardt exist to symbolize the difference for us. Bernhardt, whose acting is always "artificial," stands as the supreme exemplar of the "merely theatrical," but Duse teaches us what is truly "dramatic."[84] "Dramatic,"

81. Arthur Symons, *Eleonora Duse* (London, 1926), pp. 1, 6, 7, 9.
82. *Plays, Acting, and Music: A Book of Theory* (London, 1909), pp. 18–20.
83. Ibid., p. 170.
84. See also Shaw's comparison between Bernhardt and Duse in the role of Sudermann's Magda, *Our Theatres in the Nineties*, I, 148–154. Bernhardt's, says Shaw, is a doll-like beauty, "entirely inhuman and incredible," the result of cosmetic wizardry (p. 149). Duse's lines and wrinkles "are the credentials of her humanity; and she knows better than to obliterate that significant handwriting beneath a layer of peachbloom from the chemist's" (p. 150). Yet paradoxically, "in the art of being beautiful, Madame Bernhardt is a child beside her," and her acting acquires its "indescribable distinction" from the fact that "every stroke of it is a distinctively human idea" (p. 151). It is because of Duse's tremendous moral range that her compass "so immeasurably dwarfs the poor little octave and a half on which Sarah Bernhardt plays such pretty canzonets and stirring marches" (p. 152). Shaw has in effect transposed Mill's terms "poetry" and "eloquence," and the nineteenth-century opposition between "nature" and "theater" into his own preferred terms "human" and "inhuman," but the intent is very much the same: to distinguish between an art (in this case acting) that seems simply to grow out of nature and one which frankly utilizes every device to make itself stunning and spectacular.

here, means approximately what Mill means by "poetic"—natural, human, powerfully expressive of inner feeling. And "merely theatrical" means something much less, means "eloquent," means consciously and artfully turned toward an adoring public. Duse, in her naturalness, her poetry, her dramatic power, is unique. And if one can draw any moral from the testimonials to her greatness, it is that such genuine and deeply felt antitheatricalism in the theater is rarer than the phoenix. Yet impossible as her achievement must be acknowledged to be, and bizarrely self-contradictory as some of Stanislavsky's antitheatrical prescriptions for his actors must sound, both possess the utmost authority, since they reckon with the fullest complexity of the art to which they have devoted their lives. Both not only acknowledge but exemplify the antitheatrical prejudice. Both recognize in the circumstances of the theater something inherently corrupting, which threatens to defeat the whole enterprise, and which must be energetically combatted and neutralized before it can begin to be turned into an asset.

One might draw the same moral from the career of another theatrical genius of the epoch, Giuseppe Verdi, whose relation to his art, whose whole character indeed, embodied the same paradox as Duse's. "Great grief," he wrote to a friend in 1897, after the death of his wife, his lifelong companion, "Great grief does not demand great expression; it asks for silence, isolation, I would even say the torture of reflection. Words dull, enervate, and destroy feeling. There is something superficial (*poco sentito*) about all exteriorization . . . a profanation." This from the absolute master, the undisputed wizard, of the expression of passion in all its most blazing and volcanic forms, whose entire artistic existence has been dedicated to the incarnating—the exteriorizing —of feeling. "With an unsurpassed instinct for the theater," remarks Verdi's biographer, "he hated everything the theater stood for, just as he despised the race of singers while rating the human voice as the most potent means of musical expression." Verdi's whole career, indeed, as we apprehend it through his letters, consisted of an endless struggle *against* the theater, and in his struggle against it lay his triumph over it. The "compelling sincerity" rightly regarded as the cardinal feature of his art is "perhaps more, not less, indispensable for a writer for the artificial medium of the theater than any other."[85] The theater,

85. Francis Toye, *Giuseppe Verdi: His Life and Works* (1931; rpt. New York, 1972), pp. 192, 413.

that is, lays exceptionally powerful and insidious snares for its votaries; it constantly threatens to sap their authenticity, and its inescapable artificiality must be combatted with all the naturalness at the artist's command. Only the strong can bend it to their will, instead of being cheapened or debilitated by it.

If men are to realize their full potential, then, even within the theater, they must first face up to the demon of theatricality in themselves and find ways of exorcising it. The theater, no doubt, is always in crisis, begotten by despair upon impossibility. Nevertheless, it seems during the nineteenth century to have been undergoing a crisis that made it ugly even to its friends. The old stigma on the actors having been removed, in law and to some extent in custom, an older stigma reappeared: original sin. The actors turned tyrannous; they sat cross-legged at the entrance to theaters, barring the way against art and intelligence. Clement Scott the critic told an interviewer,

that he was the worse for his thirty-seven years of playgoing . . . that the theatrical profession "induces the vain and egotistical that is in all of us to a degree that would be scarcely credited by the outsider,"[86]

and that those who condemned the theater, on whatever religious or philosophic grounds, were right. Shaw himself, with characteristic iconoclasm and penetration, endorses the judgment in its main points. The very nature of the theater, one would conclude, brings out the worst in its votaries, and turns its aesthetic triumphs into human defeats, or at least into human disabilities. It does so by licensing, and hence nurturing, our penchant for self-display. It cannot be said that Craig or Stanislavsky, Duse, Verdi, or Shaw himself fear the mimetic side of theater. What they shrink from is the uncontrollable egoism it unleashes in actors, the self-regarding mania it induces in those whose lot it is to parade, night after night, before crowds of clamorous admirers. Kean, puffed up with his own renown, and contemptuous of poets, dealt out a mean rebuke to Byron who had in all admiration proposed that they collaborate in a tribute to Sheridan. Playwrights in every age including our own have turned away, nauseated, from the insatiable narcissism of the actors to whom they have confided their texts. It is not the gift of mimicry as such, nor the lively metamorphic imagination, that disturbs them—which they must indeed share—but

86. *Our Theatres in the Nineties*, III, 274.

the addiction to the limelight, the quenchless exhibitionism without which, however stunning his powers of mimicry, the actor would only be half himself.

From our present point of vantage in time, nineteenth-century attacks on the theater frequently have the air of a psychomachia: the artistic conscience, struggling against the grossness of the physical stage, striving to free itself from the despotism of the actors, resembles the spirit warring against the flesh, the soul wrestling with the body, or the virtues launching their assault on the vices. But the persistence of the struggle seems to suggest that it is more than a temporary skirmish: it reflects an abiding tension in our natures as social beings. On the one hand we wish to license the fullest mimetic exploration of our own condition—for self-understanding, delight, and self-mastery. But to do so through the medium of other human beings like ourselves means licensing the liberation of much that we wish ultimately to control. We foment our very vices and weaknesses, lend them shape and amplitude, in order to confront and, it is hoped, master them. So long as this situation prevails, so long as actors rather than marionettes occupy the central place in theatrical experience, so long also as in life "all doers are actors," so long will the ethical ambiguities of the situation be likely to trouble us. So long as we seek to render the quality of our existence in voice, gesture, and color, the simple integrity to which we all at heart aspire will continue to haunt us. To this integrity the antitheatrical prejudice will continue to pay its wry tribute, preserving our awareness of the corruption we risk in the very act of attempting to express and subdue it.

· XI ·

Crosscurrents
and Countercurrents

ANTITHEATRICAL PREJUDICE, however, is far from having the last word in the nineteenth century. As the century advances we begin to encounter not only a tolerance for the theater, and an enthusiasm for the theater, but a cult of the theater—if not for the theater as an institution, at least for theatricality as a mode of existence. Baudelaire's artistic credo, set forth in *The Painter of Modern Life* (1862), expounds a kind of Platonism in reverse: Platonic theses are embraced and elaborated in a wholly anti-Platonic spirit. "A man's idea of what is beautiful imprints itself upon all his attire and bearing," proclaims Baudelaire. "A man ends by resembling what he would like to be."[1] Propositions such as these, varying the Platonic axiom that the soul sets its seal on the shape of the body, extend it so as to include not only the body itself, the soul's vesture, but "attire," the vesture of the body, and not only attire, but all that accompanies it—jewelry, perfume, and make-up. Where Plato would have been horrified by the attempt to promote mere dress to the level of a significant reality, Baudelaire lavishes on it the most protracted and loving attention. As the body to the soul, so the clothes to the body. Clothes alone express, in visible and enticing form, the inner being that otherwise remains veiled. Fashion itself, in con-

1. *The Painter of Modern Life*, trans. Norman Cameron, in Charles Baudelaire, *The Essence of Laughter and Other Essays, Journals, and Letters*, ed. Peter Quennell (New York, 1956), p. 21. See *Le peintre de la vie moderne*, in *Oeuvres*, ed. Thierry Maulnier (Paris, 1948), III, 214–215: "L'idée que l'homme se fait du beau s'imprime dans tout son ajustement .... L'homme finit par ressembler à ce qu'il voudrait être."

350

sequence, the changing styles of dress from generation to generation, becomes a source of value, and fashion drawings, at one further remove from the soul to which they ultimately refer, acquire preciousness in their own right. Apart from their intrinsic grace and attractiveness, they contain indispensable archaeological data, which enable us to reconstruct the life styles of previous epochs. What has value for Plato is what endures, what resists change. For Baudelaire, what has value is what most changes, what is evanescent, whatever drifts, shifts, passes, and disappears. Beauty, to be sure, is a duality. It contains at its heart an element that is "invariable" and "eternal." But this is "exceedingly difficult to assess," and can only be made known to us through the mediation of the other element, the temporary, transitory one, without which the first remains "indigestible and beyond our powers of appreciation."[2] Beauty cannot be addressed directly to the spiritual part of us, nor can artists concern themselves solely with the impalpable and the inaccessible. Nor does Baudelaire envisage any system of transcendence by which we may rise from earthly beauty to heavenly, from the visible to the invisible, or the transient to the eternal, as with the Neoplatonists. He rests, and is happy to rest, in the visible, the transient, and the earthly.

For Plato and the traditional moralists, the world was a prison house in which the sick soul languished while awaiting its release into eternity. To be *worldly* was a term of bitter reproach for those who allowed themselves to be seduced by ephemera. But for Baudelaire it is the glory of Constantin Guys, the "painter of modern life," that he lives with unaffected delight in the realm of change and illusion, of color and glitter and movement. He is praised precisely for being "a man of the world," for joying in the endless cascade of appearances that constitutes the life of the senses. And not only a man of the world, but—in the unflagging intensity of his responses—a perpetual child as well. He is the "child-man" for whom the world is a glittering toyshop, for whom "no aspect of life has become stalely familiar," the "perfect spectator" who loves to wander incognito, like a prince in disguise, revelling in the

2. *The Painter*, p. 22; *Le peintre*, p. 216: "Le beau est fait d'un élément éternel, invariable, dont la quantité est excessivement difficile à déterminer, et d'un élément relatif, circonstanciel. . . . Sans ce second élément, . . . le premier élément serait indigestible, inappréciable, non adapté et non approprié à la nature humaine."

carnival of existence. His quest is to go "wherever light shines, poetry thunders, life teems, music throbs; wherever any human passion can 'pose' for his inspection,"[3] impatient to transcribe it into the leaves of his notebook.

He can be termed, therefore, the painter of "modernity," for what he pursues is precisely the "ephemeral, fugitive, contingent" element in art, by which alone the eternal element can be unlocked. It is his task to wrest the mysterious poetry of creation from the flux of life. Guys possesses special gifts as a war artist. He specializes in scenes of battle, soldiers, and the pomps and ceremonies of the military life. He "excels at painting the pageantry of officialdom . . . with all the ardor of a man in love with space, with perspective, with light that comes in floods or sharp bursts, attaching itself in drops or sparkles to the severe uniforms and gowns of a court."[4] For us, no doubt, children of a greyer and more cynical era, the pageantry of officialdom can hardly be separated from the vain and tendentious rhetoric that often accompanies it. We can hardly forget that that pageantry is often in itself a vain and tendentious rhetoric, designed to persuade by pomp, to compel by dazzling, and that the oaf or bully can glitter as well as the hero: on parade they may be all but indistinguishable. Even a lukewarm moralist might hesitate to discount the possibility of some kind of inner spiritual reality beneath the shining surfaces. But Baudelaire's gaze is purely theatrical, purely fastened on surfaces. It contents itself with the shimmer of phenomena, taking it as complete and satisfying in itself, remaining casual to the point of indifference about possible discrepancies between outer and inner reality.

Inner reality does, nevertheless, make an occasional hesitant entry. Military men, suggests Baudelaire, are addicted to their own appearance, and governments love to deck their troops in splendid, eye-catching

3. *The Painter*, pp. 28, 31; *Le peintre*, p. 225: "Prenez-le . . . pour un homme-enfant . . . pour lequel aucun aspect de la vie n'est *émoussé*"; p. 229: "M. G . . . restera le dernier partout où peut resplendir la lumière, retentir la poésie, fourmiller la vie, vibrer la musique; partout où une passion peut *poser* pour son oeil."

4. *The Painter*, pp. 32, 42; *Le peintre*, p. 246: "M. G . . . excelle à peindre le faste des scènes officielles, les pompes et les solemnités nationales, . . . avec toute l'ardeur d'un homme épris de l'espace, de perspective, de lumière faisant nappe ou explosion, et s'accrochant en gouttes ou en étincelles aux asperités des uniformes et des toilettes de cour."

costumes. As each profession derives its outward beauty from some moral quality peculiar to it, the soldier's springs from a martial imperturbability, a mixture of calm and boldness, "from the need to be prepared to die at any moment." What one misses from this account of the basis of soldierly beauty is some acknowledgment of its exclusively external character, of the fact that the martial serenity may itself be only a pose, the bravado feigned, the readiness to die a sham, and the entire effect the product of a bovine sensibility. One also detects a pronounced strain of snobbery. Baudelaire is thinking exclusively of the officer class, and of the higher officers at that, of the privileged upper stratum of the soldiery, with the money, and the leisure, and the freedom, to bedizen itself and dazzle the populace. He is thinking of a level on which the swaggering grace he admires has already become a mark of caste, and he explicitly exempts from his concern those more menial trades "in which monotonous and violent labor deforms the muscles and stamps the face with the mark of servitude."[5]

Akin to the soldier, with his elegance and his aplomb, is a closely related species, the dandy. The celebrated digression on the dandy praises him for his concern for appearances, his "serious devotion to the frivolous." It also leaves Constantin Guys himself somewhat to one side. For the dandy's creed involves not only the desire to cause astonishment in others, but the resolve not to betray, preferably not to feel, astonishment. *Nil admirari* is the dandy's watchword. *His* characteristic beauty arises from his glacial impassivity, "his unshakeable resolve not to feel any emotion."[6] As Baudelaire expounds it, dandyism embodies a sociological protest, a last heroic flare-up, on the part of a self-appointed élite, against the levelling, brutalizing encroachments of democracy. Traditional aristocracy having collapsed following the Revolution, the dandy would forge a new one based on personal distinction. Instead of striving to please his prince or a noble patron, however, he aims to startle the bourgeois, but by similar means: by a cult of the self expressed in an endless preoccupation with his own

5. *The Painter*, p. 45; *Le peintre*, p. 250: "Une beauté qui dérive de la nécessité d'être prêt à mourir à chaque minute"; "on trouvera naturel que je néglige les professions où un exercise exclusif et violent déforme les muscles et marque le visage de servitude."

6. *The Painter*, pp. 48, 50; *Le peintre*, p. 255: "Cette gravité dans le frivole"; p. 257: "L'inébranlable résolution de ne pas être ému."

elegance. We might be reminded of Castiglione, whose courtier is similarly devoted to the formation of a brilliant self, similarly driven by the need to arrest the gaze and compel the admiration of his beholders. Like the courtier, the dandy is an essentially theatrical construct, created for the values of parade, about whose inner life we possess only fragmentary hints. He aspires to indifference, it would appear, not so much for its own sake as because it enables him to satisfy two contradictory conditions simultaneously: it imposes a patrician distance between himself and the crowd, while at the same time riveting their attention onto his own ornamental person. It provokes their admiration while declaring his independence of them, his awareness of belonging to a class which they cannot aspire to approach. As for Guys, he eludes the category of dandy because he is ruled by an opposite impulse, by an inexhaustible passion for seeing and experiencing, an unfeigned delight in the state of spectatordom.

As with military men, as with dandies, so with women: appearances are all, and surfaces alone possess a reality that deserves veneration. Not only does Baudelaire exalt "woman" as divinity, idol, and enchantress, he refuses to distinguish between her and her clothes. Who indeed, he demands, would dare to do so, since all that adorns her and illuminates her beauty belongs as indissolubly to her as her own flesh? Here the misogyny of traditional moralists is set smartly on its head. In this scenario women are still seductresses, temptresses, lascivious daughters of Eve. They dwell still in an intoxicating aura of cosmetics, jewels, perfume, and diaphanous garments. Now, however, this witchery acquires all the most perversely positive connotations. It is not only clothes that are to be accorded the same dignity and reverence as the body, but anything whatever that helps enhance the body's allure.

Baudelaire's eulogy of cosmetics starts from a philosophical view that the severest antitheatrical moralists would have endorsed, and which stems, as critics have noted, from his own upbringing in traditional religion. Nature, in his account, teaches us only to satisfy our animal needs. If it can be said to have moral consequences, those consequences are negative. It drives us to rival our neighbors, to covet and confiscate their goods, to torture, kill, and even eat them. The moment we move from the realm of natural necessity to that of luxury or pleasure, we find that nature counsels crime. It is philosophy, argues Baudelaire, and religion, that teach us to cherish the sick and the poor;

nature advises us to knock them on the head, rather as Edmund's nature, in *King Lear*, directs the young animal to throw its parent out of the nest when it becomes strong enough to do so. But in *Lear* another kind of nature teaches other laws, of love and solidarity and selflessness. Baudelaire admits of one nature only, which can be only cruel and amoral; virtue springs only from conscious human design. Now whether this view is right or wrong—and it leaves conspicuously out of account all reference to pity, thought by eighteenth-century philosophers to provide a natural basis for morality—it does accord with traditional Christian teaching. In the world of Augustinian Christianity, unaccommodated man is vicious. Left to himself he remains perverse, requiring the interposition of an unearned grace to redeem him from his native foulness. The world is also the place whose prince is the Evil One. The theater, then, which deals with fallen man, and makes his fallen condition attractive and amusing, becomes an epitome of all that is evil. For Rousseau, nature is innocent, and man is good; it is society that has misshaped us. But the theater remains evil none the less, because it focuses and heightens the evil of society, as in a burning glass. For Baudelaire, by contrast, society and its theatrical manifestations represent a praiseworthy effort on the part of men to fashion something beautiful and excellent from their coarse and ugly selves.

If nature is evil, then the artifices which embellish it help mitigate the evil. Fashion itself becomes "a symptom of that attachment to the ideal which is superimposed in the human brain upon all the coarse, terrestrial and foul accumulations of natural life; it should be regarded as a sublime deformity of nature, or rather as a continual and ever-renewed attempt to reform nature." So art competes with nature. In defiance of conservative moralists, for whom cosmetics represent a lewd interference with the creator's handiwork, a blasphemous assault on our divinely ordained identities, for Baudelaire they represent a means of self-perfection. Women are "performing a sort of duty, in studying to appear magical and supernatural."[7] Baudelaire does not hesitate to

7. *The Painter*, p. 53; *Le peintre*, pp. 262–263: "La mode doit donc être considérée comme un symptôme du goût de l'idéal surnageant dans le cerveau humain au-dessus de tout ce que la vie naturelle y accumule de grossier, de terrestre et d'immonde, comme une déformation sublime de la nature, ou plutôt comme un essai permanent et successif de la réformation de la nature. . . . La femme est bien dans son droit, et même elle ac-

comment approvingly on specific cosmetic practices, such as the use of rice powder to mask blemishes; this undoes the flaws that nature has "outrageously sown" on the skin, substituting an "abstract unity" of texture and color. It makes the human creature into something nearer a statue, something superior and divine. On the other hand he disapproves of the attempt to disguise the signs of age. These should not try to hide themselves, but rather flaunt themselves, "if not with ostentation then at least with a sort of frankness."[8] The whole passage reads like a high-spirited challenge to old-fashioned anathemas against face-painting, an iconoclastic attempt to confer value not only on the disgraced body, on the treatment of it as a work of art, but on the most flagrant artificialities that adorn it, and on a basis that the ancient anathematizers could only have endorsed, that of the radical imperfection of nature.

Half a century later, a much less alienated, less rebellious soul than Baudelaire could enthusiastically endorse the same principle. Max Beerbohm, speculating on the persistent prejudice against cosmetics, ascribes it to the "tristful confusion man has made of soul and surface." Man has come "to think of surface even as the reverse of soul," instead of as a welcome and delightful elaboration of it. Beerbohm audaciously likens the cult of the dressing table itself to the "tangled accrescency" of pleasures and feelings by which man, in a sophisticated era, achieves "that refinement which is his highest excellence." By thus making themselves partly independent of nature, men come nearer to God, in a way of which Pico della Mirandola could not possibly have approved. One specifically theatrical conclusion to which Beerbohm's musings lead is that in the theater, masks are preferable to facial expressions. Instead of transmitting the soul, they create it, and very much to our advantage. Since expression itself so often betrays us, the "safest way . . . is

---

complit une espèce de devoir en s'appliquant à paraître magique et surnaturelle."

8. *The Painter*, pp. 54–55; *Le peintre*, p. 264: "Qui ne voit que l'usage de la poudre de riz . . . a pour but et pour résultat de faire disparaître du teint toutes les taches que la nature y a outrageusement semées, et de créer une unité abstraite dans le grain et la couleur de la peau"; p. 265: "Le maquillage n'a pas à se cacher, à éviter de se laisser deviner; il peut, au contraire, s'étaler, sinon avec affectation, au moins avec une espèce de candeur."

to create, by brush and pigments, artificial expression for every face."[9]

Guys is right, in any event, to devote his pencil to the recreation of feminine beauty in all forms—to sketch courtesans, swathed in evil, and actresses, living in their element of poetry, spirituality, and exhibitionism. He is right to enhance with all the potency of his brush the same women who had drawn the sharpest objurgations of the Fathers, the Puritans, the Jansenists, and the canon law.

In his essay on Baudelaire, Jean-Paul Sartre has suggested that Baudelaire lived his life haunted by the unreachable and unrealizable, that it was his mission—his "project"—to live on the plane of the unsatisfied, and that much of the peculiar poignancy of his poems stems from their evocations of impermanence. Along with the flickering gleams and vanishing glints that arrest him in Guys's drawings, Baudelaire is captivated by odors, which, as the most volatile and insubstantial of all sensory excitants, almost by their nature defy full realization, remaining always teasingly beyond the threshold of full apprehension, incapable of being arrested or transfixed.[10] A similar tantalizing impermanence marks the moods inspired by drugs. The blessing conferred by hashish, in Baudelaire's account, lies in the gorgeous visions it induces, the parades of phantasms filled with brilliant shapes and colors, as transitory as they are irresistible. Colors assume a preternatural intensity, paintings take on "a terrifying life," grammar turns into "a sorceror's conjuration," and "music . . . recites to you the poem of your life."[11] For an instant, all desire seems totally transformed into reality, and in this state of entranced euphoria, man arrives at the ultimate fulfillment: he feels himself to be God. But then the vision fades and vanishes. Like De Quincey's opium dreams, Baudelaire's narcotic reveries recall the great masques and triumphs of the Renaissance, splendid almost beyond description, whole universes of festive spectacle, but as perishable as shadows in their splendor, and precious exactly in proportion to their perishability.

9. *A Defence of Cosmetics* (1896; rpt. New York, 1922), pp. 5–6, 22.

10. Sartre, *Baudelaire*, trans. Martin Turnell (New York, 1950), pp. 96, 174–178.

11. *The Poem of Hashish*, trans. Norman Cameron, in Quennell, ed. *The Essence of Laughter*, pp. 94–95; *Les paradis artificiels*, in *Oeuvres*, II, 97–99: "Les peintures . . . revêtiront une vie effrayante"; "la grammaire . . . devient quelque chose comme une sorcellerie évocatoire . . . . La musique . . . vous raconte le poëme de votre vie."

When it comes to the nature of the poet, Baudelaire's mimetic conception strongly recalls the celebrated letter of Keats which traces the poetical character to the poet's ability to become all things.

As to the poetical Character itself . . . it is not itself—it has no self—it is every thing and nothing—It has no character—it enjoys light and shade; it lives in gusto, be it foul or fair, high or low, rich or poor, mean or elevated—It has as much delight in conceiving an Iago as an Imogen. What shocks the virtuous philosop[h]er, delights the camelion Poet. . . . A Poet is the most unpoetical of anything in existence; because he has no Identity—he is continually in for—and filling some other Body—the Sun, the Moon, the Sea and Men and Women who are creatures of impulse and are poetical and have about them an unchangeable attribute—the poet has none; no identity . . . .[12]

"What shocks the virtuous philosopher, delights the camelion Poet"— this might serve as epigraph to the history of the antitheatrical prejudice, a chronicle of virtuous if not self-righteous philosophers, who have reproached poets with being chameleons, and actors of being chameleons to the edge of damnation. For Keats, the ductility that the moralists reprehended becomes the prime fact in the creative sensibility. The power to lose oneself imaginatively in evil becomes as needful as the capacity to identify with the good; otherwise the poet forfeits his status as creator. Baudelaire, captivated by change, flux, and metamorphosis, strikes a similar note in a comparable context.

The poet enjoys the incomparable privilege of being, at will, both himself and other people. Like a wandering soul seeking a body, he can enter, whenever he wishes, into anyone's personality. . . . He takes as his own all the professions, rejoicings and miseries that circumstance brings before him.

Even more unmistakably than in Keats's letter, the metamorphoses of the poet here resemble those of the actor. His cardinal talent is his power to shed his own identity and adopt alien ones, like garments. The sentence that follows, with its hint of erotic abandon, carries us into an even more ambiguous, quasi-demonic realm, akin to that inhabited by Guys in the moments of his passionate absorption in the courtesans and their ambience of evil:

12. *Letters*, ed. Hyder Edward Rollins (Cambridge, Mass., 1958), I, 386–387.

What men call love is a very small, restricted and weak thing compared with this ineffable orgy, this holy prostitution of a soul that gives itself utterly, with all its poetry and charity, to the unexpectedly emergent, to the passing unknown.[13]

Baudelaire officiates over an anti-Platonic cult of surfaces, a sacralizing of all that is transitory in a deliquescent world. Oscar Wilde carries the process to its preposterous conclusion, this time with open reference to Plato. More programmatically than Keats or Baudelaire he rejects the concept of sincerity. "Is insincerity such a terrible thing?" he inquires, in *The Picture of Dorian Gray*. "I think not. It is merely a method by which we can multiply our personalities."[14] The cultivation of the self, then, instead of being the pursuit of integrity and constancy, becomes a cultivation of the selves, in the plural, the deliberate abandonment of fixity as a goal in favor of the pleasure of merely circulating through an endless succession of alternate identities. "The Decay of Lying" (c. 1886)—the very title of which cocks an impudent snook at received canons of morality—sets forth the perverse thesis that truth, so venerated throughout the ages, is only a nuisance and a burden, an offense against what is free and beautiful, while lying deserves to be the aim of all who aspire to vitality or expressiveness. Plato is maliciously invoked in support of the proposition that "Lying and poetry are arts—arts . . . not unconnected with each other," and then promptly turned on his head in the sequel—"and they require the most careful study, the most disinterested devotion."[15] Wilde sets about methodically to up-end all accepted polarities. "The only real people are the

13. "Crowds," from *Short Poems in Prose*, trans. Norman Cameron, in Quennell, ed. *The Essence of Laughter*, pp. 139–140. See "Les foules," *Petits poèmes en prose*, in *Oeuvres*, III, 33–34: "Le poëte jouit de cet incomparable privilège, qu'il peut à sa guise être lui-même et autrui. Comme ces âmes errantes qui cherchent un corps, il entre, quand il veut, dans le personnage de chacun. . . . Il adopte comme siennes toutes les professions, toutes les joies et toutes les misères que la circonstance lui présente.

Ce que les hommes nomment amour est bien petit, bien restreint et bien faible, comparé à cette ineffable orgie, à cette sainte prostitution de l'âme qui se donne toute entière, poésie et charité, à l'imprévu qui se montre, à l'inconnu qui passe."

14. *The Picture of Dorian Gray*, 1890 (Paris, 1905), p. 208.

15. *Intentions* (New York, 1888), p. 7. Page references in the discussion that follows will be to this edition.

people who never existed, and if a novelist is base enough to go to life for his personages he should at least pretend that they are creations, and not boast of them as copies" (p. 12). With this, the ontological rug is pulled out from under our feet, the accepted order of being is sharply inverted, and that which is fabricated by man, whether in verse or in more tangible materials, is accorded the primacy over what exists in nature. Nature's creations now constitute only degraded copies of human artifacts, and for an artist to try to utilize this degraded world in his art becomes the deepest possible betrayal. For art originates in itself and has reference only to itself. "She is not to be judged by any external standard of resemblance. . . . Hers are the 'forms more real than living man,' and hers the great archetypes of which things that have existence are but unfinished copies" (p. 29).

Life, then, can be no more than rough material, the stuff from which Art is fashioned. Instead of Art holding the mirror up to nature, as Shakespeare made Hamlet say (in order to make his madness plain to the dullest observer, Wilde slyly opines), "Life holds the mirror up to Art." Either it "reproduces some strange type imagined by painter or sculptor, or realizes in fact what has been dreamed in fiction" (p. 38). The great world around us itself may be said to be our own creation. "Things are because we see them, and what we see, and how we see it, depend on the Arts that have influenced us." If the first half of this assertion sounds like an extreme version of the romantic theory of the creative imagination, the second half gives it a distinctively Wildean twist: not only do we beget what we behold in nature, we do so in the image of those works of art we have seen before. "One does not see anything until one sees its beauty. Then, and then only, does it come into existence" (p. 39). The brown London fog did not exist until painters discovered it, nor did the quivering white sunlight of France. Human life, even more obviously, apes Art with all possible diligence, even on the level of the "silly boys who, after reading the adventures of Jack Sheppard or Dick Turpin, pillage the stalls of unfortunate apple-women, break into sweet-shops at night, and alarm old gentlemen who are returning home from the city by leaping out on them in suburban lanes, with black masks and unloaded revolvers" (p. 32). With Plato, then, Wilde believes in the power of mimetic art to foster further mimicry in its turn. Knowingly or not, the young blackguard models himself on Dick Turpin or Jack Sheppard, but for Wilde this does not merely mean that art has modified him: it has virtually created him, or recreated him, in its image. The only valid form of creation is that whereby Art engenders likenesses of itself in Nature. "Literature always anticipates Life. It does not copy it, but moulds it to its purpose" (p. 33). In the domains both of human action, then, and of external nature, art, far from occupying an inferior post in the ladder of being, remote from the archetypes, stands at the very top, has in fact forged those archetypes, and given shape to the natural world, which can only clumsily caricature it, much as in Plato the work of art can only ineptly travesty the archetypes themselves.

By logical extension, lying becomes not merely an art and a craft, but the organizing principle of reality, the foundation of all humanity and all civilization. By lying, however, Wilde takes pains to make it clear he does not mean some of the activities that sometimes pass for lying, such as the mean falsehoods of politicians, who merely "misrepresent," and do not scruple to buttress their untruths with argument and proof; or the sophistries of lawyers, unashamed to amass facts and cite precedents in their cases; or the fabrications of newspapers, increasingly (and odiously) given to reliability in their stories; nor, certainly, does he mean lying for the sake of the improvement of the young, the advantages of which "are so admirably set forth in the early books of Plato's *Republic* that it is unnecessary to dwell upon them" (p. 50). (Wilde here wickedly uses the same injurious term that Plato had cast at the poets' fables to describe the brainwashing recommended by Plato himself for the education of the guardians.) No, the form of lying in question is the sole one that is beyond reproach, because it is totally disinterested—lying for its own sake, or Lying in Art, precisely the kind that Plato found so deeply objectionable. What society needs is to return to "its lost leader, the cultured and fascinating liar" (p. 26)—such as Herodotus, "who, in spite of the shallow and ungenerous attempts of modern sciolists to verify his history, may justly be called the 'Father of Lies'" (p. 24). To say this is to say more than that poets are the unacknowledged legislators of the world, or that beauty springs from the attempt to correct the imperfections of nature. It is to claim that the poet's special status rests on his express rejection of the realm of fact, his scorn for the veracity that has become a ruling passion among the moderns. Wilde offers an ingenious explanation for the materialism and philistinism of America: they are "entirely due to that country having adopted for its national hero a man who, according to his own confession, was incapable of telling a lie" (p. 25).

There seems little need to dwell at length upon the cardinal role of the theater in Wilde's whole approach to existence. "One sees," says Arthur Symons,

that to him everything was drama, all the rest of the world and himself as well; himself indeed always at once the protagonist and the lonely king watching the play in the theatre emptied for his pleasure. . . . one can understand that to him sin was a crisis in a play, and punishment another crisis, and that he was thinking all the time of the fifth act and the bow at the fall of the curtain. For he was to be the writer of the play as well as the actor and the spectator. "I treated art," he says, "as the supreme reality, and life as a mere mode of fiction." A mode of drama, he should have said.[16]

Pursuing the course charted by Keats and Baudelaire and Wilde, we discover, in recent generations, an ever more explicit respect for artifice and impersonation, for the joys and indeed the necessity of self-invention. Santayana, in a brilliant series of essays on masks, makes theatricality into one pole of existence, with substance as the other. Substance, which is fluid, amorphous, and indeterminate, lacks coherence and meaning until it manifests itself in the illusions and illuminations of the world. The world, whatever it may ultimately be, is proximately at least a stage, a theatrical show from which it would be folly to turn aside, and bad philosophy as well. The deepest truth of things undoubtedly remains invisible. It is right for us to value it and wish to fathom it, for it must correspond in some way to the deepest part of our own selves, but at the same time "the roots of things are properly and decently hidden under ground, and it is as childish to be always pulling them up, to make sure that they exist, as it is to deny their existence."[17] It is the itch to be always pulling them up that Santayana ascribes to the "iconoclasts," the implicit adversaries of his argument. What the iconoclasts cannot understand, or will not acknowledge, is that the very words in which they set forth their beliefs comprise a set of metaphors, just as do the visual designs of the painters and sculptors whom they would denounce. Religion, like the arts,

16. *A Study of Oscar Wilde* (London, 1930), pp. 84–85.
17. George Santayana, *Soliloquies in England and Later Soliloquies* (London, 1922), p. 128.

deals in figuration, except that the figures—words—have rooted themselves so deeply into our lives that we think of them as "natural," setting them in opposition to the "artificial" figuration of the painters and sculptors, when in truth they stand on the same footing, as schemes for structuring experience. One reason why philosophers dislike each other's systems so heartily, and theologians detest each other's theologies, is that they will not recognize the arbitrary, playful, artful character of *all* systems.

The wise balance here struck between the claims of the visible and the invisible, between crystallized form and inchoate substance, recurs repeatedly in the essays. In "Solitude and Society" Santayana sees another set of opposites as both mutually antagonistic and mutually self-engendering, each forever collapsing into the other. The saint craves solitude, but he immediately peoples it with his own thoughts, like Richard II in prison, in order to create an ideal society, because natural society has proved corrupt. But even as all of us depend on society, and wish to make it ideal, so we long equally for the isolated comfort of our own warm moist cell, unaccountable to anything but itself, living out unmolested its self-absorbed and self-sufficient existence. Santayana sees the two terms as engaged in a perpetual choreography of thesis, antithesis, and synthesis. Similarly with his other dichotomies. In "Masks" we start with the childish love of masquing, the liberating delight it brings, "the pleasing excitement of revising our so accidental birth-certificate and of changing places in spirit with some other changeling." But swiftly comes the counterturn, the reversal. The game tires. The mask refuses to stay in place. The part no longer seems to suit. Playing turns out to involve irksome commitments and persistences of its own. "Now you begin to think your speeches ridiculous and your costume unbecoming. You must pull off the mask to see clearly and to breathe freely." Once the mask has been cast aside, "what a relief to fling away your wig and your false beard, and relapse into your honest self!" (p. 130). "Your honest self!" There is an "honest self" after all, under the sportive grimace, and substance takes its revenge by showing the mask to be no less constricting and falsifying than the "honest" self it wished to escape. If all the world were playing holidays, to sport would be as tedious as to work!

"The Tragic Mask" advances a slightly different, though related proposition: our personalities are not given, we must create them for ourselves. It is as inevitable for us to assume roles, or wear masks, as for molluscs to grow shells, and proper also for us to adorn and inscribe them with emblems of what we are underneath. Substance pure and simple is too unfixed to represent us in our unique separateness. The mask permits us to compose ourselves. Through it we project our ideals, our serious and exalted purposes. Beneath it we can hide "all the inequalities of our mood and conduct, and this without hypocrisy, since our deliberate character is more truly ourself than is the flux of our involuntary dreams" (p. 133). These last merely connect us uninterestingly with others of our species, and with animals too, whereas our "deliberate character," what we have chosen and willed ourselves to be, alone can express us truly. Wilde had made the same point, that beneath our disguises "we are all of us made out of the same stuff,"[18] so that what confers individuality are such accidentals as the cut of a man's cloak or the color of his waistcoat. In the same way, for Santayana "the primary impulses of nature . . . are monotonous," and a man who wishes to be no more than "unaffectedly himself" risks ending up "uncommonly like other people" (p. 136). What counts, then, what distinguishes us, is the artfulness with which we can construct our mask.

The comic mask, not surprisingly, activates our less solemn selves. It provides an expressive outlet for our tendency to see things in caricature, and for all the random impulses in us, of "brute habit and blind play," which clamor for expression. Objections to the comic mask, Santayana points out,

to the irresponsible, complete, extreme expression of each moment—cut at the roots of all expression. Pursue this path, and at once you do away with gesture: we must not point, we must not pout, we must not cry, we must not laugh aloud; we must not only avoid attracting attention, but our attention must not be obviously attracted; it is silly to gaze, says the nursery-governess, and rude to stare. Presently words, too, will be reduced to a telegraphic code. A man in his own country will talk like the laconic tourist abroad; his whole vocabulary will be Où? Combien? All right! Dear me! (pp. 137–138)

This sly reductio ad absurdum knocks the props out from under postromantic objections to ostentation and spectatordom. If expressive-

18. *Intentions*, p. 13.

ness is valuable, argues Santayana, with a trace of defiant sophistry, then the more the better. The man who realizes himself will be the man who can theatricalize himself. And his licensing of his own expressive potentialities will free him to take up a healthy role as spectator when it is others who happen to occupy the center of the stage. A moment later the hidden antagonist, the hater of life, comes into view again. Of the enemies of comedy Santayana observes that irony overtakes them. They become hypocrites; their reserve freezes into a pose; their mincing speech turns to cant. Moreover they misrepresent their own authorities, for the Decalogue, whatever "Biblereading Anglo-Saxondom" may think, does not forbid the art of innocent make-believe as embodied in comic masks. "To embroider upon experience is not to bear false witness against one's neighbour, but to bear true witness to oneself" (p. 138). Once again we detect, if not an echo, at least a strikingly suggestive resemblance to Wilde's paean to lying, except that Santayana's "embroidery," unlike Wilde's "lying," carries no implication of deliberate sabotage or impish subversion.

The sequence of essays climaxes in "Carnival," in which existence is perceived somewhat as it is for Constantin Guys, as an endless revelry, an inexhaustible spectacle. It has in fact no specific character in itself, but represents an opportunity which may be turned either to good or evil. If we take the longest view of things, then life must inevitably appear tragic, for like all of existence it must some day be no more. But on a shorter and saner view, it appears a vivid comedy of random haps and mishaps, incongruities, expedients, and merry solutions, which the full-blooded soul partakes of in lusty appreciation. Behind the welter of phenomena that compose existence may lurk Platonic essences, but existence differs from these precisely in being "a conjunction of things mutually irrelevant," a congeries of contingencies and absurdities. What philosophers however have always done is to "deny that any of those things exist which we find existing," because they see that they are unintelligible and have no reason for existing, and "their moral and religious prejudices do not allow them to say that to be irrational and unintelligible is the character proper to existence" (pp. 142–143). Philosophers, that is, have dealt with the unintelligibility of existence by declaring it to be an illusion, and locating reality in some invisible beyond. Camus, later, will make the same complaint even about the existential philosophers. Having concluded,

365

on the basis of observation, that existence is absurd—that man is doomed to struggle fruitlessly to understand a universe that refuses to be understood—these philosophers end by taking the leap across the gulf, into faith. They embrace irrationality as an ideal, they abandon the here and now for a chimerical absolute, whereas the truer way, the way of "absurd man," would be to remain in permanent perplexity and make what one can of life as it offers itself.

Camus, moreover, takes the step which neither Keats nor Baudelaire nor Santayana had taken: he makes the polymorphism of the actor a pattern for humanity. *The Myth of Sisyphus* designates the actor as a hero of the absurd. All men, in Camus' bleak exposition, are doomed to live in the shadow of death, in essential ignorance of life, powerless to make anything intelligible of the fact of their being thrown into an alien, uncomprehending universe. This terrible fate confers a certain freedom on them, however, if they accept it unflinchingly and live out its implications in full lucidity. One implication is that a man is responsible for what he makes of himself, and this also means that he "defines himself by his make-believe as well as by his sincere impulses,"[19] so that what he wishes to be or plays at being becomes, in effect, what he is. Another implication is that belief in the absurd amounts to "substituting the quantity of experiences for the quality. . . . What counts is not the best living but the most living."[20] Perhaps this is tantamount to saying that quality has now been redefined *as* quantity. That life which contains the most of life becomes the life to be admired and emulated. Don Juan leads such a life. He does not so much "possess" women as he "exhausts" them. With his innumerable seductions he packs a dozen lifetimes into one. And such a man is the actor. By his constant changing of roles he builds into his métier the universal condition; he immerses himself in the fleeting, and passes through a hundred lives while the ordinary man toils to complete a single one. Like Keats's or Baudelaire's poet he practices the art of Proteus. "Entering into all these lives," says Camus, "experi-

19. Albert Camus, *The Myth of Sisyphus and Other Essays*, trans. Justin O'Brien, Vintage Books (New York, 1955), p. 9; *Le mythe de Sisyphe*, 1942 (Paris, 1961), p. 25: "Un homme se définit aussi bien par ses comédies que par ses élans sincères."

20. *Myth of Sisyphus*, p. 45; *Le mythe de Sisyphe*, p. 84: "La croyance à l'absurde revient à remplacer la qualité des expériences par la quantité . . . . Ce qui compte n'est pas de vivre le mieux mais de vivre le plus."

encing them in their diversity, amounts to acting them out."[21] The actor thus becomes the traveller in time, the haunted voyager among souls. Like the traveller, he "drains something and is constantly on the move."[22] The more deeply he enters his roles, and the more intensely he can realize them while they last, the more fully he may be said to be enacting the common lot and raising it to heroic proportions. His art, moreover, encourages him to play his roles to the hilt. The feelings that the rest of us express only hesitantly and imperfectly, the gestures we curb, the words we choke back or the sentiments we muffle—the actor takes all these and triumphantly realizes them. What ordinary people merely sketch out, the actor executes with all his training, all his resources of voice and technique, all the extravagant and full-bodied poetry conferred on him by the playwright.

Camus, then, consciously overturns the older attitudes. For Renaissance Neoplatonists like Pico, even the most audacious self-creator was confined by a tradition that lodged human felicity in the attempt to resemble the angels and to disown one's likeness to the brutes. "Whatever seeds each man cultivates will grow to maturity and bear in him their own fruit. If they be vegetative, he will be like a plant. If sensitive, he will become brutish. If rational, he will grow into a heavenly being. If intellectual, he will be an angel and the son of God. And if, happy in the lot of no created thing, he withdraws into the center of his own unity, his spirit, made one with God, in the solitary darkness of God, who is set above all things, shall surpass them all."[23] For a believing Christian, the choice of the earthly self constituted a rehearsal for eternity, the claiming of as high a place as possible on the ladder

21. *Myth of Sisyphus*, p. 57; *Le mythe de Sisyphe*, p. 196: "Pénétrer dans toutes ces vies, les éprouver dans leur diversité, c'est proprement les jouer."

22. *Myth of Sisyphus*, p. 59; *Le mythe de Sisyphe*, p. 108: "Il épuise quelque chose et parcourt sans arrêt."

23. Elizabeth Livermore Forbes, trans., in *The Renaissance Philosophy of Man*, ed. Ernst Cassirer, Paul Oskar Kristeller, and John Herman Randall, Jr. (Chicago, 1956), p. 225; Eugenio Garin, ed., *De hominis dignitate, Heptaplus, De ente et uno* (Florence, 1942), p. 106: ". . . quae quisque excoluerit illa adolescent, et fructus suos ferent in illo. Si vegetalia, planta fiet. Si sensualia, obrutescet. Si rationalia, caeleste evadet animal. Si intellectualia, angelus erit et Dei filius, et si nulla creaturarum sorte contentus in unitatis centrum suae se receperit, unus cum Deo spiritus factus, in solitaria Patris caligine qui est super omnia constitutus omnibus antestabit."

of being. But for Camus there is no eternity. Men fulfill themselves in the present alone, through their self-assumed roles, and the concept of self-elevation, of climbing the rungs of a cosmic chain, has lost all meaning. One is whatever one elects to be, and the man whose livelihood consists of a perpetual series of becomings touches the heroic through the very number of his self-transformations. Instead of a hypocrite, seeking to dissemble his true nature, or a fickle chameleon, vainly striving to mimic its surroundings, instead of a social outcast and an ontological nullity, the actor becomes a larger-than-life symbol of what life is all about: the bringing to birth, enactment, and ready relinquishing of a role that has no other justification than the energy and *élan* with which it is played.

By the same token the theater, instead of being an illusion, a lie, a meaningless parade of appearances, becomes a quintessential symbol of existence. Camus is eloquent on the historical antagonism between the church and the actor, which he views as inevitable.

How could the Church have failed to condemn . . . the actor? She repudiated in that art the heretical multiplication of souls, the emotional debauch, the scandalous presumption of a mind that objects to living but one life and hurls itself into all forms of excess. She proscribed in them that preference for the present and that triumph of Proteus which are the negation of everything she teaches. Eternity is not a game. A mind foolish enough to prefer a comedy to eternity has lost its salvation.[24]

The point is apt, as are the terms in which it is phrased. Still, if in the past the foes of the stage seem often to have been blinded by bias, goaded by obscure ontological promptings to reject the whole theatrical enterprise uncomprehendingly and unreservedly, in Camus' panegyric we seem to encounter the opposite extreme, a schoolboyish infatuation with greasepaint raised to the dignity of a philosophical

24. *Myth of Sisyphus*, p. 61; *Le mythe de Sisyphe*, p. 112: "Comment l'Église n'eût-elle pas condamné dans l'acteur pareil exercice? Elle répudiait dans cet art la multiplication hérétique des âmes, la débauche d'émotions, la prétention scandaleuse d'un esprit qui se refuse à ne vivre qu'un destin et se précipite dans toutes les intempérances. Elle proscrivait en eux ce goût du présent et ce triomphe de Protée qui sont la négation de tout ce qu'elle enseigne. L'éternité n'est pas un jeu. Un esprit assez insensé pour lui préférer une comédie a perdu son salut."

principle. Not only does Camus find no place for the persistent residual antitheatricalism in all of us, he also fails to make sufficient allowance for the purely parabolic, purely emblematic nature of his own absurdist heroes. For the testimony of men of the theater themselves points to conclusions almost the reverse of his—that the actor's existence, in harsh fact, may be predicated not on a heroic confrontation *with* reality or an exhilarating immersion *in* it, but on a neurotic flight *from* it, on a desperate search for an identity felt to be incomplete, or insecure, or lacking altogether. Camus ignores, similarly, the pathology of Don Juan, whose thousand and three conquests in Spain alone are most convincingly understood not as satisfaction joyously repeated but as satisfaction perpetually eluded and vainly sought. He ignores, too, the compulsive and driven quality that seems to mark so many specimens of his third kind of hero, the adventurer—T. E. Lawrence, for example. In short, his images of absurd man leave the familiar conditions of life too far behind, leave us no wiser than we were before when it comes to plotting our own destinies. Camus also fails to pursue other problems raised by his schema. What, for example, about Bluebeard? Does he, or any other serial murderer, qualify for the ranks of absurd man? If what counts is not the best living but the most living, who has a better claim? He too lives out his chosen destiny to the full, exhausts something and moves on. He too slakes his thirst at the same well over and over, uninterested in extracting meanings or imposing cadences on his experience. One could even improvise the sophistries Camus might use to justify his exploits: "He knows that there is no eternity and that his victims will shortly be as dead from other causes as he can cause them to be right now." "He releases them from the burden of the absurdity with which he himself has chosen to live," etc. Camus, one suspects, has not truly faced up to the moral questions raised by his doctrine, and one consequence is that his exalted view of the actor is difficult to take as anything but a high-spirited metaphor.

The growing commitment to the theatrical that we find in Baudelaire, Wilde, and Santayana, and some of the equivocal morality with which it is associated, may be traced in more direct form in the defenses of the theater conducted in a number of novels and stories of the nineteenth century. Unlike Thackeray, Dickens would not have portrayed evil as theatricality, or made mimicry a synonym for hy-

pocrisy. Thackeray appreciated the theater as a discriminating spectator; Dickens brought to it a devouring passion. His own extraordinary
histrionic gifts made it into the chief medium through which, apart
from his fiction, he could best express himself, and once the writing
of fiction had become his trade, the exercise of his theatrical talent became a necessary form of psychotherapy to which he turned when he
wished to exorcise depression. "Whenever he felt in need of distraction, whenever he was restless, bored, or unhappy, he broke out in a
violent bout of theatricals," with the result that alongside his career
as novelist he pursued "what amounted to a brilliant second career as
an amateur actor and producer,"[25] utilizing his inexhaustible energy
and his prodigious mimetic powers to organize benefit performances
for needy theater folk, revivals of old plays and productions of new
ones, in which he served as manager, director, coach, and actor all at
once. On one occasion he played the lead in his friend Wilkie Collins'
melodrama *The Frozen Deep* with such hair-raising intensity that
the audience was terrified; on another he took no fewer than six different parts in the same evening, aided by rapid changes of costume
and make-up.

Throughout his life, moreover, Dickens in his own person espoused
the cause of actors, whom he saw as victims of prejudice, bound to a
harsh profession to begin with, and then reviled for it by the legions
of the respectable. If the actor's nature, he remarks,

like the dyer's hand, becomes subdued to what he works in, the actor
can hardly be blamed for it. He grinds hard at his vocation, is often
steeped in direful poverty, and lives, at the best, in a little world of
mockeries. It is bad enough to give away a great estate six nights a-week,
and want a shilling; to preside at imaginary banquets, hungry for a
mutton chop; to smack the lips over a tankard of toast and water, and
declaim about the mellow produce of the sunny vineyard on the banks
of the Rhine; to be a rattling young lover, with the measles at home;
and to paint sorrow over, with burnt cork and rouge; without being
called upon to despise his vocation too.[26]

25. Edgar and Eleanor Johnson, eds. *The Dickens Theatrical Reader*
(London, 1964), p. 13.
26. "The Amusements of the People," from *Household Words* (Mar.
30, 1850), in *The Dickens Theatrical Reader*, p. 239.

One would look far for a more understanding account of the unreality of the actor's life which provokes such scathing dismissals from Rousseau and Mirbeau, and even from such friends of the stage as Diderot. Dickens, with far more direct experience of the stage than most of its detractors, defiantly champions both actors and theaters against the assaults of Evangelical zealots and their associates. If Bible-thumping preachers denounce the theater as a place of idleness, Dickens retorts by applauding the actors as pillars of the community, who respond to one of its deepest and most blameless needs. "It is probable," he declares, "that nothing will root out from among the common people an innate love they have for dramatic entertainment in some form or other." But even were such a rooting out possible, society could only be the loser by it. For men, says Dickens, can be trusted only when their sympathies are alive, and sympathy requires an active imagination, which "no amount of steam-engines will satisfy." These considerations apply with especial force to the members of the working class, who cannot read, or who, if they could, would be unable to afford the price of a book or find a quiet corner in which to read it. For them, plays form an indispensable source of imaginative nourishment. The pleasures of the theater being "at once the most obvious, the least troublesome, and the most real, of all escapes out of the literal world" (pp. 237–238), the literal world is greatly beholden to it. Instead of persecuting the stage, society should cherish it for the sake of its own stability and survival. Dickens shows small patience with attacks on the idleness of the workers. "We consider the hours of idleness passed by this class of society as so much gain to society at large; and we do not join in a whimsical sort of lamentation that is generally made over them, when they are found to be unoccupied" (p. 240).

It is clear that the mode of attack to which Dickens is replying has altered since the day when the Mayor of London could be asked to close down a playhouse because it threatened to turn factory workers into philandering drones. The attack has evolved its subtleties and subterfuges, its pretense of solicitude for the soul's health of those laborers whose laboriousness it wishes to safeguard, as also its high-minded concern for the welfare of the social organism. An anonymous Layman writes in 1819 that the morality of the lower classes must be protected against the ill effects of the theater for the good of all:

Whatever may be the effects of frequenting theatrical exhibitions to the higher orders of society, to the lower, they must be, and are, almost inevitably ruinous. . . . On the lower classes, the higher are built. . . . If you sap or corrupt the foundation, the superstructure must be endangered. Of the lower classes, is the foundation of society formed. Here then, in the theatre, is engendered the dry-rot, which, penetrating to the heart of the English oak, . . . destroys its very nature, and renders it not only useless, but highly insecure and dangerous.[27]

Dickens remains not only impervious to such pleadings but roused to indignation by them. "We do not join in a whimsical sort of lamentation" is as much as to say, we reject the crocodile tears that are shed over the idleness of the workers out of the fear that if they enjoy a few hours of leisure the more they will profit their employers a few pennies the less; we reject the implication that every moment of their pleasure is a moment snatched from their toil, to the detriment of the whole industrial enterprise. The only concession Dickens will make to those who croak "corruption" and agitate for the shutting down of the theaters is to urge that theatrical amusements be made as wholesome as possible, with "a good, plain, healthy purpose" to them.[28]

Apart from the deep imprint which his early years as a playgoer left on the plots of his novels, Dickens' lifelong passion for the stage comes out, in his fiction, in his indulgent portraits of theater folk and their milieu. Without at all glamorizing them, he makes them embody qualities of freedom and imagination that contrast sharply with the stuffiness and drabness of society at large. Sleary's Horse-Riding Circus, in *Hard Times*, almost takes on the qualities of a magic country into which the beleaguered denizens of the land of Gradgrind can escape, from the tyranny of fact to the freedom of fantasy, from the prosy, literal world in which a horse is nothing but a "Quadruped. Graminivorous, Forty Teeth," etc., to a dreamland in which a horse may sprout wings ("The Pegasus Arms") or wear magnificent caparisons and be ridden by ladies swathed in pink gauze, or in which the stolid language of things and facts is replaced by such surrealistic jargons as that of E. W. B. Childers. Everything about Sleary's Circus stamps it as a haven of vitality, including Mr. Sleary himself, with his

27. [Anon.,] A Layman, *"Facts, but not Comments;" being Strictures on the Stage: in a Letter to Robert Mansel, Esq.,* &c. (Sheffield, 1819), p. 19.
28. *The Dickens Theatrical Reader* (April 30, 1850), p. 247.

asthmatic gasping and wheezing, his loose rolling eye, his brandy tippling, and his irrepressible energy and good will. In the final moments, it is this domain of fantasy that rescues the sordid world of fact from its own implacable rules: Mr. Sleary hides the fugitive Tom from the law, disguising him as a black servant in a pantomime of Jack the Giant Killer, and then, when Tom has been discovered in that guise, and is about to be led off and locked up, contrives his definitive escape with the aid of a trained horse, a trained dog, and a trained pony. Even on the level of practical action, then, the circus world triumphs over its repellent rival, and redeems it from its own philistinism.

Earlier, in *Nicholas Nickleby*, the contrast is in some respects still sharper between the Crummles troupe of travelling actors and its surroundings. After Nicholas' sojourn in Yorkshire with the ferocious Squeers clan, after his brushes with his villainous uncle, his encounter with the dishonest M. P. Gregsbury, who wishes to hire a flunky at starvation wages to ghost-write his parliamentary speeches, after Miss Knags and her persecution of Kate Nickleby, the troupe of Vincent Crummles seems like the salt of the earth. They are in truth a raffish lot, much given to strutting and posturing, absurdly puffed up with their merit as artists, and no more immune than respectable, God-fearing folk to petty spites and jealousies. Yet they are also diamonds in the rough, essentially decent, kindly souls who take care of each other and live as a genuine community. They show Nicholas the first spontaneous kindness he has ever received from strangers, even going so far as to admit into their calling the half-witted Smikes, once Nicholas has coached him in his part. Despite their numerous follies, and the insubstantiality of much of their experience, they project a positive image of humanity, quite different from that presented by the rapacious creatures Nicholas has met up with earlier, or from that embodied in such selfish drones as the Wititterlys or Sir Mulberry Hawk and his toadies.

Their theatrical world, indeed, suggests a harmless and nonthreatening counterpart to the vicious world from which Nicholas has escaped. It serves as a "comic and Arcadian" interlude among his adventures,[29] in which the problems and challenges of life can be posed playfully, and be playfully confronted. It is from this point of view

29. Joseph Mazo Butwin, "The Actor as Artist in English Fiction" (Ph. D. diss., Harvard University, 1971), p. 52.

that we can understand Nicholas' otherwise implausible success on the stage. For nothing in Nicholas' behavior has given us any reason to believe that he will pass muster, let alone excel, behind the footlights. Apart from having enough presence of mind to hold his tongue under trying conditions, he has been more remarkable for his forthrightness than for his capacity to conceal or counterfeit his feelings. It is only by an effort that he manages to restrain his indignation at Dotheboys Hall or when goaded by his malevolent uncle. Unlike Becky Sharp, he shows no childish bent for mimicry or caricature. As G. K. Chesterton puts it, "Nicholas Nickleby is a proper, formal and ceremonial hero. He has no psychology; he has not even any particular character; but he is deliberately made a hero—young, poor, brave, unimpeachable and ultimately triumphant."[30] This is all well said, and one result of Nicholas' purely formal and ceremonial character is that we really do not believe it when Mr. Crummles tells him, "There's genteel comedy in your walk and manner, juvenile tragedy in your eye, and touch-and-go farce in your laugh,"[31] or when shortly afterward he hands Nicholas the part of Romeo to learn, along with that of Rover, and Cassio, and Jeremy Diddler, with the bland assurance, "You can easily knock them off" (p. 298). Even allowing for Mr. Crummles's exaggerations, we are likely to find this confidence startling. But Dickens regards both his hero and his theater folk as humanly alike in their essential decency; both embody the goodness of the species in an engagingly unsanctimonious form, and he wishes to forge an alliance between them. He does so by arbitrarily allocating a generous measure of histrionic ability to Nicholas, so that during the company's season at Portsmouth he becomes a starring actor in the troupe, impersonating "a vast variety of characters with undiminished success" (p. 374). But as one cannot find substantial reasons in Nicholas' character for this turn of events, so one does not find, either, that his sojourn with the actors alters him in any conspicuous degree. It provides a moment of diversion and recreation from the grimmer challenges he must finally cope with, and it enables him quietly to establish himself as a valued member of a working community. He learns something, we presume,

30. Introduction to *The Life and Adventures of Nicholas Nickleby*, Everyman ed. (London, 1907), p. ix.

31. *The Life and Adventures of Nicholas Nickleby*, with intr. by Dame Sybil Thorndike (Oxford, 1950), p. 283.

about the nature of life in such a quasi-picaresque, somewhat disorganized milieu; he learns, by observation, something about mimicry, exhibitionism, theatrical artifice, and theatrical illusion. But he leaves them, when he does, the same goodhearted, right-minded, rather colorless young man he has been all along, enriched now with an acquaintance among the curious subculture of "artists."[32]

Considering the skeptical treatment of mimetic activity in *The Confidence Man*—not to mention the terrifying performance of "Babo" in

32. For reasons this discussion will have made clear, I find myself skeptical of the thesis of J. Hillis Miller, *Charles Dickens: The World of His Novels* (Cambridge, Mass., 1958), pp. 89–90, and of Bernard Bergonzi, "Nicholas Nickleby," in John Gross and Gabriel Pearson, eds. *Dickens and the Twentieth Century* (London, 1962), pp. 68–71, that theatricality supplies a major structural motif for the novel as a whole. According to Miller (p. 89), Crummles and his troupe "have no solid existence in themselves. Even when they are off the stage, their every gesture and phrase is a theatrical pose. They live lives which are sheer surface, sheer cliché, the perpetual substitution of one assumed role for another. . . . We come to recognize that the other characters in the novel have the same kind of existence, make the same theatrical gestures and speeches, and that the central action . . . is the elaborate performance of a cheap melodrama." The first part of this statement seems to gloss over the genuine differences between the actors and the others. The communal solidarity and familiar closeness that animate them, despite the rivalries and jealousies, have all too little counterpart in the world at large, apart from Nicholas' own immediate family and (much later) the oppressively benevolent Cheeryble brothers. As for the assertion about the central action, whatever its truth, would it not apply to any of Dickens' novels? What is more melodramatic than the plot of *Great Expectations*? Yet we do not conclude on that account that melodrama is itself being weighed in the balance and found wanting. Nor should we so conclude, I suspect, in the case of *Nickleby*, so that Miller's summary proposition, that "The scenes of the provincial theatre thus act as a parody of the main plot, and of the life of the characters in the main story," seems to me doubtful, as does the kindred assertion of Bernard Bergonzi (p. 73) to the effect that "the theatricality of *Nickleby* is a substitute for actual social relationships." Again, to the extent that this is true, it does not seem to distinguish *Nickleby* from most other Dickens novels. Much more to the point, it seems, to me, would be Butwin's comment that "The theatrical setting releases Dickens from the narrow limitation of the melodramatic morality. . . . By continually reminding his audience that these are only actors, he is free to do with them what he pleases" ("The Artist as Actor," p. 59).

Benito Cereno—an earlier story of Melville's entitled "The Two Temples" (written by 1854 but not published until the present century) offers a surprisingly affirmative view of the theater itself. The narrator ventures, one Sunday morning, into a large and handsome church in a fashionable quarter of New York, hoping to join the worshippers. Not being a member of the congregation, he is refused entrance, and must sneak up into the tower to observe the proceedings by stealth. From aloft he gazes down upon what has all the earmarks of "some sly enchanter's show."[33] The white-robed priest reminds him of Talma; having intoned the hymn, he vanishes through a side door, only to reappear shortly, 'his white apparel wholly changed for black" (p. 154), in what is doubtless a suitable counterpart to his spiritual condition. The entire service is described in the terms of a theatrical performance, of exits and entrances and changes of costume, until, when it is over, the speaker unluckily finds himself locked in the belfry. Discovered at length by the beadle, he is turned rudely over to the police, haled before a court of justice, and there reprimanded and fined for illegal entry and disturbance of the peace.

Some time later he finds himself in London, penniless and famished. A kind stranger gives him a ticket to the top gallery of a theater in which Macready is playing as Cardinal Richelieu. Before the curtain rises, a ragged boy selling penny ale, seeing him to be a stranger and in need of refreshment, provides him with a charitable cup to warm himself. Macready himself, known to be "an amiable gentleman, combining the finest qualities of social and Christian respectability, with the highest excellence in his particular profession," recalls irresistibly, when he appears in his cardinal's costume, the stately priest of the New York church. When he speaks, "Hark! The same measured, courtly, noble tone. See! the same imposing attitude." When he disappears, through a side door, he returns, like the priest, "somewhat changed in his habiliments." As the curtain falls, a thunderous roar of approval bursts from the crowd, "deafeningly; unmistakably sincere. Right from the undoubted heart" (pp. 164–165). In church, the priest's final benediction had been followed by a hushed silence, "as if the congregation were one of buried, not of living men" (p. 154), so that his memory, which retains so many vivid visual similarities, provides "no duplicate" for the joyful responsory din of this occasion. "In earnestness of re-

33. *Complete Stories*, ed. Jay Leyda (London, 1951), p. 153.

sponse, this second temple stands unmatched. And hath mere mimicry done this? What is it then to act a part?" With this question beating in his mind, the narrator goes home to a sleepless night, during which he ponders the difference between the two temples, and "how that, a stranger in a strange land, I found sterling charity in the one; and at home, in my own land, was thrust out from the other" (p. 165). The point of the story, then, lies in how closely the church and the theater resemble each other in externals—the solemn music, the high gallery reached by a low door (the needle's eye), the throngs below, the priest with his solemn mien and changes of garment—but how profoundly they differ in spirit, the theater being a true church in which the acting is heartfelt and the responses genuine, the church being a mere theater in which nothing is sanctified but externals, the make-believe cardinal of the stage presiding over a more truly Christian assembly than the ordained priest officiating at the altar.[34] "Mere mimicry" in both cases, but addressing itself in one case, in church, only to the senses, only to the sensual man, and in the other case, the theater, addressing itself to the heart, with the votaries of pleasure more humane and charitable by any reckoning than the congregation assembled for its pompous Sunday morning worship. Doubtless a further irony lurks in the fact that the cardinal of the second temple, the Machiavellian Richelieu, notorious for his guile, is being portrayed by an actor who in Christian decency and simplicity far exceeds him. What the audience applauds, of course, is not Richelieu's craftiness at all but Macready's expert re-enactment of it. And unlike the congregation of the first temple, which believes, or pretends to believe, in the piety of its priest, the theater audience is not deceived by the spectacle offered to it, which does not pretend to be other than a spectacle.[35]

34. Cf., half a century later, the comparable opinion of Bernard Shaw: "Unfortunately this Christian Church, founded gaily with a pun, has been so largely corrupted by rank Satanism that it has become the Church where you must not laugh; and so it is giving way to that older and greater Church to which I belong: the Church where the oftener you laugh the better, because by laughter only can you destroy evil without malice, and affirm good fellowship without mawkishness" (*Our Theatres in the Nineties* [London, 1948], I, vi).

35. Behind both temples, however, it has recently been argued, we find only "the ambiguous, illusive, stage-like nature of the world, which hides its secrets well from the prying human actors" (Frederick Asals, "Satire

and Skepticism in *The Two Temples,*" *Books at Brown* 24 [1971]: 7–18, p. 16). Asals perceives several layers of moral, ecclesiastical, and philosophical meaning in the tale: a calculated contrast, first of all, between the Hebrew temple, the sanctified architectural structure, with its implications of Pharisaism, and the Christian temple of the spirit, and, consequently, between the Old Testament rule of Law and the New Testament rule of Charity. He finds, in addition, a progress in the roles assumed by the narrator, from committed Christian to alienated Ishmaelite to gratified humanist, and finally, beyond all these contrasts, an epistemological mystery, since in neither temple is it clear "who is running the show and what is the meaning of the plot." "Emotionally and psychologically, the second temple is more 'real' than the first; metaphysically, both are houses of illusion which reveal nothing of the nature of reality" (p. 16). This all seems to me wisely spoken. I would stress only that for mundane "emotional and psychological" purposes, the theater is given an unequivocal edge over the church, which is allowed little dignity or reality of any kind.

A more strenuous, and somewhat less persuasive essay, which nevertheless contains much valuable material, is that of Beryl Rowland, "Melville Answers the Theologians: The Ladder of Charity in 'The Two Temples,' " *Mosaic* 7 (1971): 1–13. Rowland too sees the tale as a gloss on the Pauline concept of charity, but also as a specific attack on the creeds of some of Melville's contemporaries, notably Pusey and Emerson. She reminds us aptly that it is dedicated to Sheridan Knowles, the actor, who had acquired a certain celebrity from his pamphlets against popery and Puseyism. Knowles specialized in accusing the papists of being theatrical. Their church " 'deluded [its] flock by theatrical practises.' Its rituals were 'a plausible dumb show,' " its mass little better than a "cunningly spun out melodrama"; its priests "grave enacters of an elaborate alluring pantomime . . . palming off fiction for truth and absurdity for consistency" (p. 5). And as Knowles charged the church with being illicitly theatrical, so he defended the theater as a valid form of representation, akin to that found in the Gospels. Presumably he would have endorsed the main features of Melville's contrasting temples. Whether he would also have approved the "perversely sympathetic" account of the unruly working-class audience, whose habit of revelling in the theaters past Saturday midnight had led to attempts to ban performances that infringed on the Sabbath, is viewed as doubtful by Rowland, but here we enter the realm of supposition and conjecture. We do so even more with the claim that Melville is castigating Emerson's Unitarianism in the tale, and most of all with the harsh view of the narrator, who is perceived as "presumptuous," "full of hate," gazing down "with envy, injured pride, and fear" on the first congregation, and able to muster only "a kind of jaunty self-pity" with the second (pp. 9, 12). When we reach this point, we find the critic beginning to rewrite the story in order to make it fit her thesis.

Melville's little parable, setting up as it does a paradoxical crisscross between church and stage, recalls not only the time-tarnished Protestant view of popery as theatricality, but also a newer and more surprising likeness between Evangelical Protestantism itself and the theater. Mrs. Frances Trollope, visiting Cincinnati in 1828, was startled to find that although respectable ladies of puritanical scruple avoided playgoing, they flocked to church in their most pretentious finery in order to enjoy the equivalent of a theatrical performance, the sermon, which was likely to consist of a piece of virtuoso acting on the part of the preacher. The aim of the preacher was to make his parishioners' flesh creep, and he accomplished this with a wide repertory of histrionic effects: shrillness, hysteria, sweating, and foaming at the mouth. "The acting was excellent," reports Mrs. Trollope drily of one such performance, adding it as her own opinion that "the coarsest comedy ever written would be a less detestable exhibition for the eyes of youth and innocence than such a scene."[36] The pulpit, plainly, has here absorbed some of the sensationalism of the stage. The public craving for mimetic entertainment, unable to satisfy itself with the theater in the ordinary sense, has led to an unhealthy spillover of theatricality into the inappropriate context of a religious service. "So, if you do not have a theater, or if you have one but do not or cannot make use of it, you run the risk that your church will become the theater."[37]

Similar in purport is the complaint of the actor Robert Mansel, earlier in the century, who defended his scenical brethren from the intolerance of the Methodist pulpit. The Methodists, still after more than two centuries relentlessly campaigning against the stage, are accused in their turn of borrowing effects from the tiring-house, and scoring points in the pulpit with devices learned from the players. Their motives for attacking the actors, suggests Mansel, spring from "a sort of jealousy," "a dread of rivalry." The preachers, too, "study stage effect, and are very attentive to costume. We confess," says Mansel, "that . . . they

36. *Domestic Manners of the Americans*, quoted in Philip W. Edwards, "The Devil's Chapel and the Function of Comedy," *Berkshire Review* 5, 2 (Winter, 1969): 23–32, pp. 23–24. This excellent article proposes an analogy between the Litany of the Anglican Church, with its formal "deprecations" and "supplications," and the staging of satiric and festive comedy, each being seen as a public ceremony designed to ward off malice and insure a bountiful future.

37. Ibid., p. 24.

keep up to the character they have assumed better than we do." That is, they are better actors than the actors. The preacher arrays himself for his role in "a suit of black, or sombre colour—polished boots, without tops—hair smoothly combed," assuming "a gravity of deportment." Once costumed, he is "conducted to his theatre," where he receives "the sighing approbation, and groaning acquiescence of all his auditors. . . . He performs his limited engagement, and then," in the manner of an itinerant entertainer, "proceeds to the next place appointed by his managers."[38] So much for the being whom Mansel terms the "equestrian saint in one theatre"—the admired and successful performer considered to be beyond reproach because of his clerical cloth. His counterpart, "the pedestrian sinner," also, like the saint, "experiences A Call, mistaking intoxication for inspiration—and enthusiasm for vigour and capacity," but once enrolled in the ranks of the Roscii, he finds the board of plenty whisked away and replaced by the platter of indigence. "*He* finds no suppliant host to greet his efforts with welcome and approbation! *He* finds no chearful fire side—no gentle courtesies. . . . He finds himself an isolated being in the midst of bustle . . . . Banished from all respectable society," until, in despair, he meekly "submits to the opprobrious name of Player, with every disgraceful epithet which illiberality and ignorance can bestow" (pp. 164–166).

Mansel's accent falls on the bitterness of the actor who sees his talent meagerly rewarded and his profession despised, while his rival, the preacher, living in the odor of sanctity, wins the adulation of his public by exercising the very talents he castigates the actor for possessing. Melville goes a step farther. He not merely convicts the church of the heartless theatricality commonly imputed to the stage. He finds in the theater the very human concern and benevolence traditionally accounted the special province of the church. In part his comment is a social and Dickensian one: the church belongs to the cosseted few, whose ease has insulated them from their poorer brethren and chilled their fellow feeling, while the theater, frequented by the simple and the humble, has become a natural haven for the charity once thought to find its proper home in churches.

Doubtless one ought not to generalize the tale too sweepingly, not

38. Robert Mansel, *A Short Struggle for Stage or No Stage; Originating in a Sermon, Preached by the Reverend Thomas Best* (Sheffield, 1818), pp. 158–163.

take it too flatly as a defense of the theater, even if it embodies a clear attack on churches. In Henry James, however, we find a defense not only of theater, but of theatricality and all it implies, the more telling in that it comes from a fastidious artist whose own temperament contains so much that is untheatrical. That James should have accepted, and for a time even welcomed, the vulgarity inseparable from the theater, speaks eloquently for his understanding of it, and for the intensity of his own hopes to conquer it. "An acted play," he ventures in his scenic commentary, "is a novel intensified; it realizes what the novel suggests, and, by paying a liberal tribute to the senses, anticipates your possible complaint that your entertainment is of the meagre sort styled 'intellectual.'"[39] That an acted play is a "novel intensified" is a half-truth at best. Perhaps the misapprehension it implies helps explain why James failed in his efforts to write a good play. But that a play must pay "a liberal tribute to the senses" is of course profoundly true, and accounts in part for the relentless antagonism historically shown toward plays by those to whom the life of the senses remains suspect. James recognizes that the theater is compounded of coarse ingredients. He knows that it can be no fine-spun enterprise, no gossamer tissue of impalpable subtleties, and that it must be able to attract those of blunt sensibility as well as the refined. "It may be," he goes so far as to speculate at one moment, putting the drama and the novel again into the same category, "that the drama and other works of art are best appreciated by people who are not 'nice'; it may be that a lively interest in such matters tends to undermine niceness; it may be that, as the world grows nicer, various forms of art will grow feebler."[40]

Here James is improbably allying himself with those who are not "nice," who enjoy plays and "other works of art" in all their garishness and crudity. And he seems to consolidate the alliance in one representative short story and one massive novel. The story, "The Real Thing," tells of a painter's search for models to help him illustrate a novel about high society. A down-at-heels major and his wife, named Monarch, present themselves at his studio as ideal for his purpose: they themselves, in their better days, have moved in high society. Even now, they remain the perfect gentleman and lady. Their dress, though worn, is

39. *The Scenic Art, Notes on Acting and the Drama: 1872–1901*, ed. Allen Wade (New Brunswick, 1948), p. 3.
40. Ibid., p. 102.

fashionably correct; their talk is of horses, railway schedules, and weekends in country houses. They are, in short, "the real thing." The painter hires them with obscure misgivings, touched by their plight but mistrustful of their amateur status as sitters, and confessing to "an innate preference for the represented subject over the real one," since the real one seems so often to lack representation. "I liked things that appeared; then one was sure. Whether they *were* or not was a subordinate and almost always profitless question."[41] Like Constantin Guys, James's artist prefers the accidental to the essential, the latter being unknowable except as it makes itself felt in the former. For his purposes his usual model, the nondescript Miss Churm, possesses the happy knack of being able to transform herself at will into whatever role he chooses to place her. Her "real" self matters not at all. It would be only an encumbrance.

I scarcely ever saw her come in without thinking afresh how odd it was that, being so little in herself, she should yet be so much in others. She was a meagre little Miss Churm, but was such an ample heroine of romance. She was only a freckled cockney, but she could represent everything, from a fine lady to a shepherdess; she had the faculty, as she might have had a fine voice or long hair. (p. 239)

Mrs. Monarch, by dispiriting contrast, "had no variety of expression —she herself had no sense of variety. . . . She was the real thing, but always the same thing." Reality, in her case, a fixed and settled quantity, proves a handicap rather than an asset.

After I had drawn Mrs Monarch a dozen times I perceived more clearly than before that the value of such a model as Miss Churm resided precisely in the fact that she had no positive stamp, combined of course with the other fact that what she did have was a curious and inexplicable talent for imitation. (pp. 244-245)

"No positive stamp"—precisely the reproach that generations of antitheatrical writers had levelled against actors, or others histrionically endowed. Miss Churm's indeterminacy, as against the high distinctness of the Monarchs, is linked to her power to inhabit so many alternate selves so easily, and affords the key to her success as a model.

41. Leon Edel, ed. *The Complete Tales of Henry James*, VIII (Philadelphia, 1963), 237.

The crisis comes when the Monarchs are supplanted not only by Miss Churm but by an indigent Italian named Oronte. "He was sallow but fair, and when I put him into some old clothes of my own he looked like an Englishman. He was as good as Miss Churm who could look, when requested, like an Italian" (p. 249). Both of them, needless to say, despite their humble station, can capture the moods and gestures of high society more vividly, from the artist's point of view, than the former inhabitants of that society themselves. Their undefined suggestiveness enables him first to imagine and then to create, for himself, the artistically real thing. The inevitable upshot is that the inadaptable, pathetic Monarchs must be cashiered, sinking first to the humiliating position of domestic helpers, then vanishing altogether in their misery. One moral to be drawn from their fate is that not only are they too rigid and unbending to make satisfactory artist's models, despite their authentic gentility; they are too inflexible even to cope with the altered requirements of their own circumstances. They can never be anything other than the stiff, cast-iron lady and gentleman they have always been, and their inability to adapt themselves to the artist's needs reflects a failure of human resilience, an incapacity to change even enough to ensure their own survival. Significantly, when they first appear at the studio they have already been unsuccessful in a number of other attempts to find work, and when, in the course of their sittings for him, the painter tries to help them to further employment, introducing them to other artists, nothing comes of it. They fail to "take," for reasons the narrator can appreciate. By contrast, the "meagre" Miss Churm and the "sallow" Oronte come mysteriously charged with the life force, endowed with a saving spirit of play which enables them to undergo limitless transformations. Oronte, indeed, appears on the scene through a happy faculty of intuiting his way through circumstances. "He had had no other introduction to me than a guess, from the shape of my high north window, seen outside, that my place was a studio, and that as a studio it would contain an artist. He had wandered to England in search of fortune, like other itinerants, and had embarked, with a partner and a small green handcart, on the sale of penny ices. The ices had melted away and the partner had dissolved in their train" (pp. 248–249). Oronte thus has a smack of the picaresque about him, a generous measure of the ready plasticity that the Monarchs so woefully lack, and James seems to be making of his talent, as of Miss Churm's, not a practical asset only but a point of moral superiority.[42]

More ambitious and probing is James's "theater" novel, *The Tragic Muse* (1890), which explicitly debates the status of the theater as an art and as a way of life. One way of looking at the story is to see it as a study of the tenacity of the antitheatrical prejudice in the person of the amiable young diplomat Peter Sherringham. Sherringham, for the greater part of the story, dotes fiercely on the theater. The theater bewitches him; it lures him into loitering in Paris while his career idles, first so that he can hover close to the Comédie Française, later so that he can take the heroine, Miriam Rooth, under his protection, lend her his money, his moral support, and his entrée into the theatrical world, to help her become what in time she does become, a great actress. But when it comes at last to the logical, inevitable consequence of marrying her, he recoils. He does fall in love with her, does greatly desire to marry her, but only on his own terms, on the impossible condition that she renounce the stage. For he can't, as he says on two widely separated occasions, conceive of having an actress for a wife. He wishes to further his own career with the aid of a brilliant and accomplished partner, for whom he promises to do more than has ever been done for a woman. His commitment to his own calling, however, has always been tepid compared to Miriam's. He has dallied in Paris, haunting the *coulisses* of the Comédie Française long past the time when a more active ambition would have sought advancement elsewhere, preferring to remain in the theatrical capital as a subordinate rather than go to

42. As a subtle and elusive writer, James has often been the victim of commentators who will take nothing at face value, who insist on discovering ironies behind every bush and tree. David Toor, in "Narrative Irony in Henry James' 'The Real Thing,'" *The University Review* 34 (Dec., 1967): 95–99, sees the teller of the tale as an instance of the "unreliable narrator" —a shallow, callous, mercenary creature, who enjoys the discomfiture of the Monarchs and tries to blame them for his own shortcomings as a painter. Nothing in the story seems to me to support such a reading. That the artist is the central figure has been better argued by Earle Labor, in "James's 'The Real Thing': Three Levels of Meaning," *College English* 23 (1962): 376–378. Labor points out, correctly, that the narrator changes in the course of the story, learning compassion for the Monarchs, whom at first he tends to view with detached amusement, so that ultimately he is able to see the setback to his own artistic projects as recompensed by this increase in human understanding.

Honduras as a principal. Yet it is he, with his relatively perfunctory interest in his own work, who asks her to give up hers, to sacrifice the destiny to which she is burningly devoted, though he himself has nurtured that devotion. When the moment comes for him to follow through on the premises of his own acts, he reverts to a benighted male chauvinism and a reflexive English philistinism, implicitly claiming the right to abort Miriam's career so as to make her into an ornament of his. As James puts it, many years later, in his preface,

Sherringham's whole profession has been that he rejoices in her as she is, and that the theatre, the organised theatre, will be . . . irresistible; and it is the promptness with which he sheds his pretended faith as soon as it feels in the air the breath of reality, as soon as it asks of him a proof or a sacrifice, it is this that excites her doubtless sufficiently arrogant scorn. Where is the virtue of his high interest if it has verily never *been* an interest to speak of and if all it has suddenly to suggest is that, in face of a serious call, it shall be unblushingly relinquished? If he and she together, and her great field and future, and the whole cause they had armed and declared for, have not been serious things they have been base make-believes and trivialities—which is what in fact the homage of society to art always turns out so soon as art presumes not to be vulgar and futile.[43]

James thus links the fate of the theater firmly with that of all the arts, makes the theater into a paradigmatic case *for* the arts, and sees society's downgrading of it as a symptom of its hostility to art in any form that presumes to be serious. Miriam herself, in this climactic scene, points out to Sherringham how essential the theater is to his feeling for her—that what enthralls and magnetizes him is the histrionic self she projects, the self mobilized in the service of the histrionic art. What we see, in addition, is that Miriam, who enters the story obtuse and hoydenish, animated chiefly by drive and a kind of coarse energy, has become, under Sherringham's tutelage and that of her coach Madame Carré, not only a great actress but a great person. She has acquired moral insight, moral intelligence, even grandeur. The discipline of the theater, to which she has submitted with fanatical patience, has refined her, bringing her to full cultivation. It has served her as a school of sensibility, of taste and discrimination, of a multitude of qualities that James always respects in his characters and expects us

43. *The Tragic Muse*, 1908 (New York, 1936), pp. xix–xx.

to respect. Not only Miriam's destiny, but her very identity, all that she has become by the time she triumphs as Juliet, is inextricable from her life as an actress, and it is a painful sign of denseness in Sherringham that he fails to understand this, or a mark of shallowness that, understanding it, he fails to be able to act on it.

Sherringham forms a sharp contrast, in this regard, with his cousin Nick Dormer, who possesses a genuine bent for public life, but comes to acknowledge in himself an even profounder and more abiding need to paint, and who makes, in consequence, a renunciation far more difficult than anything asked of Peter. He sacrifices his fiancée, with whom he is deeply in love, sacrifices her great wealth and splendid political connections, sacrifices the huge settlement being readied for him by his rich patron Mr. Carteret, and sacrifices also, in a different but even more painful sense, his mother, who is utterly bewildered by what she regards as a mortal betrayal and a calculated attempt to destroy the family. The contrast is glaring between Nick, who gives up every shred of worldly advantage and social prestige in order to be able to paint, and Sherringham, who finds his commitment to the theater, intense as it has seemed to him and to us to be at times, too frail to withstand the weight of ancestral taboos, the canons of social correctness he has absorbed in his English upbringing, canons according to which all *filles de théâtre* and the whole theatrical milieu must ultimately be judged as unacceptable. James has endowed him, early on, with some of his own most distinctive sentiments—a preference for "representation, the representation of life," over "the real thing," and an exalted vision of the future of the theater as an art form. He endows him at the same time with a deeply rooted distaste for the intemperances and irregularities of the theatrical life, and a concurrence, therefore, at last, in the stigma attached to the theater by people who, like Nick's mother and fiancée, actively "hate art," or can tolerate it only so long as it confines itself to trifling. When the two impulses collide under the pressure of a practical dilemma, it is the Parisian hobby, the belief in the theater, that crumbles, and the ingrained prejudice, the English aversion to frivolity, that wins out.

James heightens the contrast between his two ambivalent protagonists by recording the stinging impact of Nick's renunciation on Peter. "He felt as if he had heard the sudden blare of a trumpet, and he felt at the same time as if he had received a sudden slap in the face." Peter feels, that is, both challenged and shamed, called forth to battle and at the same time rebuked for his slackness. He feels humbled "at having placed himself so unromantically on his guard, rapidly saying to himself that if Nick could afford to allow so much for 'art' he might surely exhibit some of the same confidence."[44] In the event, of course, that confidence fails him, his adventurousness deserts him, and it is Miriam who must point out to him, like an echo of his own conscience, how heroic his cousin appears in the difficult, lonely course he has chosen: "Oh, it's refreshing to see a man burn his ships in a cause that appeals to him, give up something for it and break with hideous timidities and snobberies! It's the most beautiful sight in the world" (p. 552). But by this time Peter is too deeply enmeshed in his own hideous timidities and snobberies. The only effect of Miriam's invocation of the high "cause," added to Nick's example and the unexpected eloquence of Nick's sister Biddy, is to drive him desperately and definitively into the camp of the philistines: "Art be damned: what commission, after all, had he ever given it to better him or to bother him?" (p. 555)—a terrible betrayal, we can only feel, of the values and ideals he has at an earlier stage so highmindedly professed to believe in.

As for Miriam, one early mark of her distinction of character is the clear-sighted view she takes of herself and her chosen profession. She recognizes that it makes her, as Sherringham puts it, "strange." "Doesn't one have to be," she tells him, "to want to go and exhibit one's self to a loathesome crowd, on a platform, with trumpets and a big drum, for money—to parade one's body and one's soul?" (p. 130). No foe of the stage could have put the case more trenchantly. Miriam understands, and understanding, manages to transcend, the vileness, the "strangeness" of being gaped at by crowds for money. James stands ready, moreover, to subscribe to the familiar antitheatrical view that the actor has no true self of his own, but is forever playing a part, whether off stage or on. Even before Miriam's talent becomes evident, Sherringham perceives a form-creating or "plastic" quality in her that fits her for her vocation (p. 105). He sees more clearly, later, that she has, as he tells her, "no nature of [her] own," that she is "always playing something; there are no intervals" (p. 167). And he tells himself that:

44. *The Tragic Muse*, 1890 (London, 1948), p. 272. Citations will be to this edition.

A woman whose only being was to "make believe," . . . and whose identity resided in the continuity of her personations, so that she had no moral privacy . . . but lived in a high wind of exhibition, of figuration—such a woman was a kind of monster, in whom of necessity there would be nothing to like, because there would be nothing to take hold of. (p. 150)

Behind the phrase "a kind of monster" no doubt lurks the French notion of the actor as a *monstre sacré*, to whom all "strange" things are permitted because of the strangeness of his calling. With majestic sympathy, James refuses to see in the absence of a fixed identity any moral defect. On the contrary, Miriam's kaleidoscopic quality, maintained partly for us by our being excluded from her consciousness, so that we see only her external self, her endless protean manifestations, this kaleidoscopic quality comes at length to affect Sherringham "not as a series of masks, but as a response to perceived differences, an intensity of sensibility, or still more as something cleverly constructive, like the shifting of the scene in a play or a room with many windows" (p. 447). Her infinite variety, then, far from implying shallowness or a trivial scattering of energy, suggests instead intensity and concentration, a heightened responsiveness to those she is with, and also (as another passage makes plain) a power to live to the fullest in the present moment, with a minimum of reference to either past or future—a quality we have seen to be characteristic of Falstaff.

Even on the narrow grounds of social correctness, James is ready, in the person of Madame Carré, to do battle with the philistines. Responding to the anxious respectability of Mrs. Rooth, who is worried about the people her daughter will have to meet and the places she will have to go to, the old actress admonishes her that "to be too respectable to go where things are done best is, in my opinion, to be very vicious indeed; and to do them badly in order to preserve your virtue is to fall into a grossness more shocking than any other" (p. 100)—that discipline, technique, and excellence, in short, are morally positive qualities, that aesthetic judgment implies an ethical one as well.

Most of the familiar antitheatrical positions are thus rehearsed, sifted, and weighed in the course of the story, usually in the end being somehow mysteriously assimilated and purified, converted from minuses into pluses. And in this prolonged focus on the antitheatrical motif, James goes far beyond his "source" story, Mrs. Humphrey Ward's

Miss Bretherton (1884). *Miss Bretherton* chronicles the slow awakening to artistic consciousness of a young American actress. To the extent that antitheatrical attitudes enter the story, they do so in the person of the heroine herself. Isabel Bretherton desires a great career on the stages of Europe. At the same time, as a consequence of her Scotch Presbyterian upbringing, she loftily despises the theatrical culture of France, of which she knows nothing. To the world's admiration of the great Desforêts she counterpoises her own ignorant bias:

... not that I don't believe she's a great actress; but I can't separate her acting from what she is herself. It is women like that who bring discredit on the whole profession . . . who make people think that no good woman can be an actress. . . . there is not one of you [i.e., men] who would let your wife or your sister shake hands with her, and yet how you rave about her . . . as if there were nothing in the world but genius—and French genius!

Where Miriam is bent on becoming a great artist, and is ready to seek out the most exacting teachers and submit to months of harrowing toil to arrive at that goal, Miss Bretherton aspires to little more than to captivate her audiences—an aspiration all too easily satisfied—and to turn acting into a calling suitable for respectable women. It is only under the sympathetic tutelage of her admirer Kendal that she begins to perceive that "it is the actress's business to *act*, and that if she does that well, whatever may be her personal shortcomings, her generation has cause to be grateful to her."[45] And it is only the tactful refusal of a serious playwright to invite her to star in his new play that brings home to her how far short she falls, in the judgment of those who have come to matter to her, of possessing the needful equipment. She springs from a half-barbarous society that sees in actors little more than personal magnetism, and lacks all sense of the theater as an institution with a history, a tradition, and a discipline of its own. Her progress in the story is to become aware of this, and to place herself at length under the sponsorship of those who can teach her what to read and how to read, how to recite, how to exercise intelligence and exert control in the management of her stage self.

What is said against the stage, in *Miss Bretherton*, therefore, comes

45. Amelia (Mrs. Humphrey) Ward, *Miss Bretherton* (London, 1884), pp. 89–90, 91.

from the uninstructed Miss Bretherton herself, in her moments of benightedness, and not at all from such deep vessels of antitheatrical snobbery as Nick Dormer's mother, his fiancée Julia, his friend Gabriel Nash, or his cousin Peter Sherringham, all of whom, in their various ways, profoundly distrust the theater, and make their distrust intensely felt at the pressure points of the story. James gives us both the attitude toward theater exemplified in France, where it ranks as a splendid department of national culture, with a rich and ordered life of its own, and the casual, belittling English view of it as a demeaning activity best left to people whom one would not admit into one's drawing room. No one can doubt that James himself is vividly aware of the vulgarities of the theater. He reverts to them too often and with too much evident conviction.[46] At the same time, he is eager to charge them with positive meanings, and with a kind of conspicuous gallantry to leap to the defense of actors, to make excuses for whatever shortcomings they may be thought to possess as a class. This comes out most explicitly in the preface:

The trade of the stage-player, and above all of the actress, must have so many detestable sides for the person exercising it that we scarce imagine a full surrender to it without a full surrender, not less, to every immediate compensation, to every freedom and the largest ease within reach.[47]

That is, the harshness of the actor's lot licenses him in whatever self-indulgences he may choose to yield to. It is as handsome, even as chivalrous a tribute as Dickens' insistence on the actor's economic and social tribulations, and it acquires a special poignancy from the fact that it was written so long after the first publication of the novel, which is to say after James's own crushing defeat as a writer for the stage. Instead of rancorously turning against the muse he had wooed in vain, or developing a fixation on its seamy side, James continues to hold it as uncompromisingly in reverence as ever, as an ideal worth spending one's life in the service of.[48]

46. On this point see Butwin, "The Actor as Artist," pp. 148–153.
47. *The Tragic Muse* (1908), p. xxi.
48. *The Tragic Muse* has had rather a bad press in James criticism, beginning with Edmund Wilson and continuing with Oscar Cargill, F. W. Dupee, and others. By far the most intelligent reading I have encountered, and one very much to the point of the present discussion, is that of Dorothea

A more ambivalent story, George Moore's *A Mummer's Wife* (1885), explores the impact of a troupe of visiting actors on the life of a provincial draper's wife, the collision between her inherited puritanism and the bohemian mores of the travelling artists. Kate, attempting to cross over from one world into the other, finds that she cannot completely make the transition. The world of antitheatrical puritanism, which she thinks she has left behind forever, returns to wreak a terrible revenge in the form of guilt feelings that pursue and at length destroy her.

She starts as the hardworking wife of an asthmatic invalid, whose asthma seems to symbolize everything constricting and oppressive about the moral climate of the town in which they live. She tends her husband, minds the shop, and keeps to the tight routine of business and domestic affairs imposed by her code and their economic needs. Her mother-in-law, a spokesman for the values of the provincial community, has

---

Krook, *The Ordeal of Consciousness in Henry James* (Cambridge, 1962), pp. 62–105. A recent attempt to defend the novel against its detractors, from the structural point of view, "*The Tragic Muse*: Henry James's Loosest, Baggiest Novel?" by Robert Falk, in R. B. Browne and Donald Pizer, eds. *Themes and Directions in American Literature* (Lafayette, Ind., 1969), pp. 148–162, discusses the constructive difficulties intelligently, but tries to solve them by imposing a rather too rigid schematism on a novel which is already schematic enough in its own right.

On the other hand, an otherwise illuminating account of the imagery in the novel, "The Theme of Freedom in James' *The Tragic Muse*," by Daniel J. Schneider, *Connecticut Review* 8, 2 (1974): 5–15, seems to me to be vitiated by a marked *parti pris* concerning the characters, above all concerning Nick Dormer. Nick is described as "hopelessly torn between the political life and the artistic life," whereas in fact he gives up his political career gladly, and without regrets, and as "tainted by compromise," because it looks in the end as though his fiancée may return to him, on his own terms. Schneider's insistence on reading the action, through the imagery, as an indictment of art and politics for their coerciveness, selfishness, lust for power, dehumanizing properties, preoccupation with Vain Appearance, etc., seems to assign an arbitrary set of negative valences to a configuration from which one can draw quite different inferences.

An extremely rewarding account of the book, in its relation to the theater conditions and theater debates of the late nineteenth century, is that of D. J. Gordon and John Stokes, "The Reference of *The Tragic Muse*," in John Goode, ed. *The Air of Reality: New Essays on Henry James* (London, 1972), pp. 81–167.

small love for theater people. Mrs. Ede "could rate play-actors for a good half-hour without feeling the time passing." When the travelling opera comes to town, she warns Kate against letting out rooms to the actors, even though the extra money would be greatly welcome. "Don't you know, dear, that actors have always a lot of women after them, and I for one am not going to attend on wenches like them. If I had my way I'd whip such people until I slashed all the wickedness out of them."[49] Mrs. Ede thus echoes an earlier, more virulent prejudice, which passed laws condemning actors as vagrants, and closed the theaters when those in authority found them inconvenient and could overrule public demand.

Kate herself is not altogether free from prejudice. She worries about the fact that her assistant chatters about theaters and actors, fears that the girl is "losing her character," and wonders whether "to have her coming about the house would give it a bad name" (pp. 41–42). On the other hand, Kate's inner life does contain "one bit of colour" to offset its prevailing greyness. She is "dreamy, not to say imaginative" (p. 44)—having been addicted, as a child, to tales of goblins and fairies, and later, as a young girl, to stories of knights and princesses. Now, as an adult, she reads sentimental novels about the loves of doctors and nurses. Predictably, then, the presence of the theater in town, and of its manager, Mr. Lennox, in her house, touches a spring that unlocks a long-closed chamber of her being.

Mr. Lennox, to her mystified amazement, is fanciful. She cannot understand how he thinks of the things he says, as when he likens the pottery ovens to boys in a Christmas pantomime and wonders if they might not be included in the next show. He is gallant, flirting recklessly with her when opportunity presents itself, interspersing kisses with scraps of half-remembered dialogue from romantic parts he has once played in. He is also an accomplished liar, able to improvise freely in order to extricate himself and Kate from an awkward situation. He is, as Kate finally concludes, "coarse and largely sensual," yet at the same time kind and protective. "The very intonation of his voice was comforting. He was, in a word, human, and this attracted all that was human in her" (p. 92).

Kate's ignorance of the ways of the theater is at first comically complete. She cannot understand why her sweetheart should deliberately

49. George Moore, *A Mummer's Wife* (1885; rpt. London, 1918), p. 16.

play clownish parts in which he looks foolish, wearing unbecoming clothes and allowing himself to be beaten.

... when she saw her hero fall down in the middle of the stage and heard everybody laugh at him, she felt both ashamed and insulted. The romantic character of her mind asserted itself, and, against her will, forced her to admire the purple-cloaked Marquis. (pp. 196–197)

She assumes, that is, that because Dick Lennox has become "her hero," he should play the hero's part on the stage, that the purpose of his playing is somehow to exhibit himself to her in heroic guise, and that for him to be laughed at represents a humiliation for them both. She has as yet, in short, an extremely undeveloped sense of what impersonation in the theater is all about.

But such innocence is quickly and painlessly dispelled. Much more momentous is the series of moral crises she faces after her elopement. At the railway station in Preston, where Dick tricks the restaurant into serving them breakfast free of charge, Kate suddenly enters a new and terrifying realm. Her old life had coupled a narrow existence to a peaceful conscience. The new life is to reverse the formula, to bring her a freer, less constrained existence but along with it an anguished conscience.

... though love had compensated her for virtue, nothing could make amends to her for her loss of honesty. She could break a moral law with less suffering than might be expected from her bringing up, but the sentiment the most characteristic . . . of the middle classes is a respect for the property of others; and she had eaten of stolen bread. Oppressed and sickened by this idea, she shrank back in her corner, and filled with a sordid loathing of herself, she moved instinctively away from Dick. (p. 210)

Kate finds, in short—and we as readers find with her, if we believe that Moore is writing about a social reality—that from the point of view of bourgeois morality the prejudice against actors is not entirely unfounded. The decent and likable Dick Lennox has an imperfect sense of *meum* and *tuum*; the troupe as a whole lives much in the free and easy manner imputed to them by their more straitlaced fellow citizens. Sexual liaisons spring up casually among them, and as casually wither away; seriousness is reserved for the getting of their living. Even Sundays they spend "playing 'nap,' smoking cigarettes, and talking of

393

wigs, make-ups, choruses, and such-like." Aside from the hard work they must put in to make their opera go, they lead as aimless and indolent an existence as the most pinch-nosed Mrs. Ede could imagine.

Kate becomes, in consequence, a battleground of conflicting impulses. On the one hand, she gives up many of her old scruples, learning to enjoy experiences she had long thought of as sinful.

... once the ice of habit was broken, she ... began to abandon herself thoroughly to the pleasures of these rich warm breakfasts, and to look forward to the idle hours of digestion which followed, and the happy dreams that could then be indulged in. (p. 212)

On the other hand, she reverts repeatedly in memory to the narrow, secure, conscientious life she has left behind. Moments of crisis tend to provoke accesses of nostalgia and upwellings of regressive day-dreaming.

For the twentieth time since she had donned them the robes of the Bohemian fell from her, and she became again in instincts and tastes a middle-class woman longing for a home, a fixed and tangible fireside where she might sit in the evening by her husband's side, mending his shirts, after the work of the day. (p. 314)

For a time, bohemianism triumphs. As the vicissitudes of the company begin to multiply, for a time so often solved almost magically in un-foreseen ways, Kate ends by becoming convinced "that there was no knot that chance, luck, or fate would not untie" (p. 333)—that con-trary to all the teachings of her bourgeois upbringing, hard work, thrift, and careful planning are pointless and futile. But the triumph of bo-hemianism over her will, the paralysis of her capacity to act, can do nothing to arrest—can in fact only accelerate—the remorseless hound-ing of her by inner anxiety and guilt. As the company's fortunes crum-ble, Kate's spirit crumbles with them, leaving her at length a confirmed and hopeless alcoholic, a dead weight for herself, her husband, and all who face the impossible task of trying to save her from destruction.

What is remarkable, and admirable, about the story is the balance Moore succeeds in maintaining between the two ways of life, and the degree of imaginative sympathy he manages to extend to both. Kate's original existence is depicted in all its constraint and narrowness, yet with a sure feeling for its moral substantiality, its sustaining security. The life of the travelling opera, likewise, is depicted in its inviting freedom, its capacity to kindle the imagination and please the senses, yet with an equally sure feeling for its shallowness, its equivocal morality, its failure to provide adequate spiritual sustenance. And the simultaneous pulls and repulsions of both poles are beautifully embodied in the plight of Kate, who can respond to the values of both, but whose hold on herself is too weak to enable her to make a decisive choice. In one world, she yearns for the glamor and adventurousness of the other; in the second, she longs for the stability and security of the first. If the tale points a moral, it is perhaps that the taboos imposed by her childhood environment, and so deeply rooted in her personality, are too strong to be surmounted, except by a much more decisive nature than hers, or else by some exceptionally lucky combination of circumstances such as she is never destined to encounter.[50]

Some years later Moore turned in a more devastating report, in his essay "Mummer-Worship." The burden of this text is a scathing account of the morality of actors and the low state of the profession. Acting, declares Moore at the outset, is an intrinsically second-rate, parasitic occupation, since it consists in parrotting dialogue from a story invented by someone else. Actors in consequence are vain, self-willed creatures, impatient of social restraint and interested only in indulging their appetites. Suddenly, however, they have developed a raging thirst for status, as fierce as their need for applause. Once upon a time they were bohemians, who took to the stage partly in revolt against respectability. "Then a great and drastic change came; the mummer grew ashamed of his hose and longed for a silk hat, a villa, and above all a visit from the parson."[51] As actors now wish to be pillars of the community, so actresses now wish to be vestals. For its part the public, incapable of discriminating good acting from bad, applauds its favorites not for what they do but for what they are. And Moore proceeds to a withering survey of the low state of a craft

50. It will be plain from this discussion that I do not subscribe to John Stokes's view of *A Mummer's Wife* as "a satirical attack on the acting profession" (*Resistible Theatres* [London, 1972], p. 126), any more than to the common view of it as a pedestrian and derivative exercise in Zolaism, for which see, e.g., Milton Chaikin, "George Moore's Early Fiction," in Graham Owens, ed. *George Moore's Mind and Art* (Edinburgh, 1968), pp. 29–31.

51. *Impressions and Opinions* (London, 1891), p. 154.

which every ignorant amateur thinks himself entitled to practice, for "ability is required to compose even a bad opera, a bad epic, a bad picture—but any one can play Juliet or Hamlet badly" (p. 171). Not only ability, but solitude and concentration, which "young people of today" abhor. So the theater is crowded with young men and women of small talent who shrink from hard work, with the result that many who might have led satisfying if unglamorous middle-class lives succumb to the glitter of the stage and end up as pathetic castaways, as so many Kate Lennoxes. "The stage was once a profession for the restless, the frankly vicious—for those who sought any escape from the platitude of their personality; the stage is now a means of enabling the refuse of society to idly satisfy the flesh, and air much miserable vanity" (pp. 176–177).

Whatever may be the validity of this view, in so far as its basic thesis is concerned—that the stage has always attracted the restless, the vain, and the self-indulgent—the cold, censorious tone rings disagreeably compared to the words of James and Dickens on the same subject. Like Dickens and James, Moore was a habitué of theaters, and had tried, without success, to write for the commercial stage. One may reasonably suspect an element of personal pique in the intensity of his dislike for the actors. Beyond that, one senses also the lingering antitheatrical conviction, still widespread among men of letters, that where drama is concerned the "real" play lodges not in performance but in the text, that what the actors do is distort and deform that text to suit their own vanity, so that the accolades showered on them—like Sir Henry Irving's knighthood—come not from their service to their art but from their crass exploitation of it.[52] Whatever the reason, Moore is incapable at this moment (as in *The Confessions of a Young Man* shortly after) of maintaining the more generous appreciation that kept *A Mummer's Wife* in balance. Dickens and James, while not blinking the shortcomings of the theatrical milieu, see them as a response, in large part, to the harsh conditions of the actor's life, its combination of clocklike regularity with spasmodic irregularity, and to the contempt of an ignorant public. Moore, who managed in *A Mummer's Wife* to enter

52. Stokes, *Resistible Theatres*, p. 128. For an enlightening review of Moore's various theatrical activities, as journalist, critic, playwright, and entrepreneur, see Stokes, pp. 120–148 passim.

into that precarious condition with such sympathy, now gives evidence of a streak of prejudice as coarse as that of a provincial housewife.

An even more sympathetic, but also more enigmatic, account of the impact of travelling actors on a small-town English girl than that in Moore's novel appears a generation later with D. H. Lawrence's *The Lost Girl* (1920). Like Kate Ede, Alvina Houghton becomes a mummer's wife following the visit to her town of a troupe of strolling entertainers. As a daughter of the local theater owner, she has the occasion to encounter a succession of actors, or, as they prefer to call themselves, "artistes." Even if they are "very much of a type," these artistes, and even if that type itself is "a little frowsty, a little flea-bitten," as well as "indifferent to ordinary morality," with "a certain fund of callous philosophy," it is also bracingly different from anything Alvina has known in her Midland town, "where everything was priced and ticketed. These people [the actors] were nomads. They didn't care a straw who you were or who you weren't. They had a most irritable professional vanity, and that was all. . . . They weren't very squeamish." Their immorality, so far as Alvina can make out, consists largely of a familiar manner, a mild impudence in the relations between the sexes, and a tendency to drink too much. They are even slightly pitiable. "Most of them had a streak of imagination," and "an abstracted manner; in ordinary life, they seemed left aside, somehow. Odd, extraneous creatures, often a little depressed, feeling life slip away from them." Lawrence is of course describing a generation later than that of Dick Lennox, at a time when provincial theater was being killed by the rise of the movies—hence the nostalgic note in "left aside" and "extraneous"—but the cardinal traits seem not to have changed much: the oddness and eccentricity, the aimless frivolity, the "streak of imagination." Lawrence is markedly less judgmental than Moore, however. He refrains from implicating his actors in anything like the shabby confidence trick played by Dick Lennox at the railway restaurant. There is no moral squalor about the troupe to which Alvina attaches herself as there is about Dick. Yet the theater proves nearly as destructive for Alvina as for Kate.

Alvina, having grown up herself a misfit, is attracted to the actors' oddity. She welcomes the chance to become acquainted with people who live with a casualness and relaxed freedom she has never seen among her townsfolk. "She liked being *declassée*. She liked feeling an outsider. At last she seemed to stand on her own ground."[53] Starting from a position more marginal than Kate's, Alvina finds the very "extraneousness" of the actors a source of strength, and utilizes it almost consciously as a mechanism of escape from her straitlaced milieu. Liberation, however, ends in extrusion. Increasingly unable to endure the proprieties of English bourgeois life, and rendered apathetic by the prospect of marriage to a stiff English doctor, she marries instead the vagabond actor Cicio, whom she then must follow (when he ceases to be an actor) back to his lonely Calabrian village, to the discomforts of a harsh climate and the rigors of a poverty-stricken, peasantlike existence, as well as to the humiliation of being a woman in a far more fiercely male-dominated society than the one she has left. The theater has helped focus Alvina's discontent with her native place, has enabled her to detach herself from it, but has given her no positive role, no secure new identity of her own. It has plunged her into a radically alien element in which she must reconstruct herself from scratch—without, in the end, even the comfort of her husband, who as the story closes is marching off to join the Italian army, with little chance of returning. Alvina is "lost," now, because, separated from her home, her childhood, and all that has shaped her, she can no longer expect ever to find herself.

Lawrence offers, in the course of *The Lost Girl*, some acute incidental speculations as to why the theater is losing out to the movies as the favored recreation of the people. Mr. May the theatrical impresario wonders gloomily why people run to the films when they can still see live actors, "artistes," who are so endlessly fascinating and who in fact excite them more than any film. Alvina opines—for Lawrence we suspect—that however intense their excitement, people don't really wish to be excited that way. They resent having to envy the human actors, with their acrobatic and balletic and histrionic skills. They resent having to respond to them as personalities different from themselves. The figures on the screen, by contrast, remain unthreatening. As pictures, explains Alvina, they

have no feelings apart from their own feelings . . . the feelings of the people who watch them. Pictures don't have any life except in the

53. *The Lost Girl* (London, 1955), pp. 122–123.

people who watch them. And that's why they like them. Because they make them feel that they are everything .... they take it all to themselves—and there isn't anything except themselves. ... they can spread themselves over a film, and they *can't* over a living performer. They're up against the performer himself. And they hate it. (p. 120)

In short, the very element of confrontation between performer and spectator that creates excitement in the theater, the human fire that attracts Alvina to the actors, disturbs her townspeople, who prefer not to be hotly scorched. It requires the onlooker to take account of another human being, distinct from himself, with a prickly otherness that can never be entirely soothing, as the image on the screen can be soothing, over whose unresisting flicker the watcher may pour without hindrance whatever he will of his own feelings.

Perhaps we may also detect in Alvina's analysis a partial counterpart to the animus against actors expressed by playwrights like Mirbeau and Shaw, and directors like Craig. To Mirbeau, Shaw, and Craig, actors grow irksome, even abhorrent, because they cannot or will not curb their egoism in favor of the characters they are supposed to be impersonating. Instead of shaping themselves to their roles, they wantonly seize the roles as pretexts for exhibiting themselves. If Alvina is right, audiences sense this underlying self-assertion on the part of the players, and though exhilarated by it, find it alarming. They prefer the shadow-play of the screen, from which live human presence has been deleted, so that what remains is only a ghostly simulacrum of reality, a dance of wraiths, onto which they can project what reality they will, and onto whom they can father such feelings as will soothe and comfort them.

· XII ·

The Nietzschean Apostasy

THE CASE OF GEORGE MOORE, capable in one moment of a warm imaginative kinship with the actors, and in the next of a cold and contemptuous withdrawal from them, may serve to remind us of the instability of even the protheatrical bias, its frequently conflicted and unresolved nature. Almost inevitably, it seems to contain the seeds of its own opposite. Aside from those renegade playwrights, like Plato, Gosson, and Rousseau, who abandon the theater only to denounce it, aside from those who renounce the stage in the throes of a religious conversion, like Calderón, Racine, and Jean-Baptiste Gresset, we also find renegade patrons like the Prince de Conti: having energetically furthered Molière's career at one time, he went on to become one of the most resolute and eloquent antitheatricalists of his generation. More strikingly and disturbingly we see the same ambivalence on a mass scale, in the theatergoing public of the late Roman Empire or of eighteenth-century France, which mingles hysterical adulation of the actors with cruel legal proscription. Attitudes toward the stage, quite plainly, come fraught with passion and charged with contradiction. Keats, who urged a state of metamorphic versatility for poets, also found actors to be "a set of barren asses."[1] For an eccentric, and in many ways unique instance of late nineteenth-century antitheatricalism we may consider the case of Friedrich Nietzsche, in whom we find yet one more variation on the theme of fervent espousal followed by apostasy.

We start with the Nietzsche of *The Birth of Tragedy from the Spirit of Music*, in Thomas Mann's words "the most complete and irredeemable aesthete known to the history of the human mind,"[2] for

1. *Letters*, ed. Hyder Edward Rollins (Cambridge, Mass., 1958), II, 149.
2. Thomas Mann, "Nietzsche's Philosophy in the Light of Recent His-

whom tragedy is the ultimate art, and music a direct emanation from
the deepest reality of the universe, who justifies existence itself as an
aesthetic phenomenon, a perpetual entertainment devised for himself
by the Author and Spectator of all being. We ourselves, in this view,
are merely aesthetic projections of this Being, and derive such dignity
as we possess from our own status as art works. An individual human
creature becomes an artist himself to the degree that he partakes of
the aesthetic spirit, and his vocation will announce itself to him in essentially theatrical terms:

At bottom, the aesthetic phenomenon is simple: let anyone have the
ability to behold continually a vivid play and to live constantly surrounded by hosts of spirits, and he will be a poet; let anyone feel the
urge to transform himself and to speak out of other bodies and souls,
and he will be a dramatist.

The drama that results—the tragic drama that emerges in ancient
Greece, expressive of the anguish of the human Many striving to become One again under conditions of Dionysiac ecstasy—constitutes for
Nietzsche the supreme human experience. It has the power to transmit
itself to all:

The Dionysian excitement is capable of communicating this artistic
gift to a multitude, so they can see themselves surrounded by such a
host of spirits while knowing themselves to be essentially one with
them.[3]

tory," in *Last Essays*, trans. R. and C. Winston and T. and J. Stern (New
York, 1959), p. 32.

3. Walter Kaufmann, trans. *The Birth of Tragedy and The Case of
Wagner*, Vintage Books (New York, 1967), p. 64; Nietzsche, *Werke*, ed.
Giorgio Colli and Mazzino Montinari, III.i (Berlin, 1972), 56–57: "Im
Grunde ist das aesthetische Phänomen einfach; man habe nur Fähigkeit,
fortwährend ein lebendiges Spiel zu sehen und immerfort von Geister-
schaaren umringt zu leben, so ist man Dichter; man fühle nur den Trieb,
sich selbst zu verwandeln und aus anderen Leibern und Seelen heraus-
zureden, so ist man Dramatiker.

Die dionysische Erregung ist im Stande, einer ganzen Masse diese
künstlerische Begabung mitzutheilen, sich von einer solchen Geisterschaar
umringt zu sehen, mit der sie sich innerlich eins weiss."

The tragic genius thus restores humanity to its primal unity with itself and the rest of creation.

But—and at once we begin to glimpse Nietzsche's more evolved attitude—the history of the tragic drama is in fact a degeneration. Decline sets in with Sophocles, who dislodges the chorus from its central position and begins to introduce psychological portraiture, moving away from Dionysian ecstasy toward Apollonian objectivity. Euripides, advancing under the standard of Socrates, the destructive critical intelligence, launches a ruinous assault on myth, reducing it to pettiness and triviality. Instead of gods, demigods, and heroes, Euripides brings mediocrity onto the stage in the person of the common man, the ordinary spectator, until nothing remains of the Dionysian spirit. Music, once a direct embodiment of "will," a pure secretion of Being, dwindles to a wretched copy of phenomena, a cheap imitation of *things*.

Even at this moment Nietzsche's theatricalism may be seen to have a strong antimimetic tinge. It strives to obliterate the distance between player and role, actor and spectator, instinct and consciousness. Since the world is unknowable to man, since the laws of time, space, and causality are only devices by which appearance is delusively raised to the status of reality, that art alone is great which can ignore space, time, and causality, so restoring our original oneness with elemental existence. That art, on the other hand, which brings appearances into focus, which takes space, time, and causality as true categories, and seeks to imitate and duplicate them, is an art of lies, carrying us away from all that is profound and invigorating.

The dry rot that sets in with Euripidean drama reaches epidemic proportions in modern opera. Opera, for Nietzsche, is an essentially Socratic art, which is to say an art from which the irrational has been wilfully excluded, and in which nonartistic, nonmusical considerations have come to tyrannize over music itself. Florentine declamation aims to make the text heard and understood. This immediately misplaces the emphasis, and singers put the finishing touches to the perversion by themselves treating words as primary, "intensifying the pathetic expression . . . by means of this half-song,"[4] so that music becomes a lackey to meaning. Recitative alternating with aria forms such an unnatural convention that its origins must be assumed to lie "outside all

4. *Birth of Tragedy and Case of Wagner*, p. 114; *Werke*, III.i, 117: "Dass er den pathetischen Wortausdruck in diesem Halbgesange verschärft."

artistic instincts" entirely.[5] Pastoral opera, the characteristic Florentine form, instead of expressing the grief proper to tragedy, conveys only "the comfortable delight in an idyllic reality";[6] a shallow Socratic optimism replaces the deep but exultant pessimism of authentic art. And as one consequence of this vacuous optimism, opera seeks busily to copy the external world, pressing into its service the low mechanical skills of the stage designer and the machinist. It becomes the creature, finally, not of the artist at all but of the theorist and the critic.

In opera, then, music abandons its dignity as "Dionysian mirror of the world"[7] and ignobly places itself in thrall to imitation, reflecting only the trivial stream of phenomena. If music in its right role is "the true idea of the cosmos," drama can be "but a reflection of that idea." Nevertheless, out of the rebirth of German philosophy with Kant and Schopenhauer, and out of the achievements of Wagnerian music drama, a rebirth is on the way. For the philosophers have taught us once more what the Greeks knew all the time, that we apprehend the world only through a veil, darkly, through our limited powers of perception. And Wagner, in *Tristan*, like Aeschylus and the pre-Aeschylean tragic dramatists, has begun to pierce through the veil, reinstating the unconscious and irrational in their old primacy, and so at last dispelling the glib optimism of the long Socratic interregnum. The odious "critic" of the era of opera, who wielded despotic powers over a debilitated genre, has once again been replaced by the "aesthetic spectator," true descendant of his ancestor who sat on the hillside at Athens or at Delphi.

It is clear, from so much, that although Nietzsche's vision is aesthetic, it is also antimimetic. Nietzsche turns sharply away from whatever attempts to imitate the outer world, from whatever adopts our blinkered categories of space, time, and causation. The more imitative music or drama becomes, the more intensely Nietzsche dislikes it. When the composer, or the dramatic poet, instead of secreting his poetry like a vital fluid, attempts to copy the natural world, when he aims at psy-

5. *Birth of Tragedy and Case of Wagner*, p. 115; *Werke*, III.i, 117: "Ausserhalb aller künstlerischen Instincte."

6. *Birth of Tragedy and Case of Wagner*, p. 118; *Werke*, III.i, 121: "Die bequeme Lust an einer idyllischen Wirklichkeit."

7. *Birth of Tragedy and Case of Wagner*, p. 119; *Werke*, III.i, 122: "Dionysischer Weltspiegel."

chological realism, when he seeks narrative or conceptual clarity, he is betraying the essence of his art. The essence of his art lies precisely, one might say, in the fact that it is an essence, an emanation of being, which takes no account of accidents or particularities. True tragedy, in fact, is to be found only in early Greek culture, where it has not really yet become fully theatrical. The chorus suffers, but does not act. The actor, the spectator, can scarcely be said yet to exist. The various elements of the theatrical situation have hardly begun to disengage themselves, to acquire separate and distinct identities, and, to the extent that they have, the current of the tragic occasion serves to sweep them back into an undifferentiated unity. The principle of individuation is dissolved in an action that has the character of a rite rather than a mimetic event. The key to the situation is Dionysian "presentation" rather than Apollonian "representation," "participation" rather than spectatorly "contemplation."[8] The moment the element of illusionism and portraiture begins to crystallize, the moment tragedy begins to consist of an action *shown* to onlookers—the moment, in short, when it begins to resemble what for more than two millennia in Western European history has passed for theater—Nietzsche's approval begins to cool. It freezes entirely when he encounters a writer like Euripides, a master showman, skilled in the creation of spectacular effects.

We start, then, in the Nietzsche of 1873, with life conceived as an aesthetic phenomenon and the early Greek drama as a triumphal moment in the history of the human race. Wagner's *Tristan*, we are assured, heralds a revival of that moment, when two millennia of falsehood will be swept aside, and music will resume its ancient dominion, breaking down the dikes between man and man, to use Yeats's striking phrase. We end, in 1888 and 1889, with *The Case of Wagner* and *Nietzsche contra Wagner*, in which Nietzsche explains and defends his apostasy against his one-time hero, upbraiding him with the injurious names of mime, histrio, and stage player. That these are meant

8. For a systematic and intelligent unravelling of the meanings of Dionysus, Apollo, and Socrates in Nietzsche's views on the theater, see Bernard Lambert, "Les grandes théories: Nietzsche et le théâtre," *Littérature* 9 (1973): 3–30. This valuable article is the only item I have discovered in the commentary on Nietzsche that addresses itself to the concerns of the present chapter.

as opprobrious is beyond question: "The musician now becomes an actor, his art develops more and more as a talent to *lie*."[9] With this astonishing statement Nietzsche stretches out a hand to the puritanical Plato of the *Republic*, whose own métier as tragic poet had been blighted, in Nietzsche's view, by the corrosive rationalism of Socrates. It is not so much art as such that is being impugned, in this passage, as the way it has been degraded into mimicry. Wagner is rebuked for abandoning musical style in order to devise something purely instrumental, a "theatrical rhetoric, a means of expression, of underscoring gestures, of suggestion, of the psychologically picturesque,"[10]—in short, for following in the footsteps of Euripides and the inventors of the *stile rappresentativo*. Like theirs, his approach to dramatic action is that of the impresario. He never starts with music itself, with Dionysian spirit seeking Apollonian form. Instead, he starts with story, with a sensational situation or a gripping incident, for which music becomes accompaniment, rhetorical buttressing. In true drama, music occupies the secret center of all. Wagner debases it into a mere accessory.

Wagner, thus, is fixated on effect. Far from being a musician, he is "a first-rate actor . . . an incomparable *histrio*, the greatest mime, the most amazing genius of the theater ever among Germans, our *scenic artist par excellence*,"[11] who became a musician only as it were incidentally, and secondarily, in order to be able to heighten his theatrical effects. For drama, declares Nietzsche, "requires *rigorous* logic; but what did Wagner ever care about logic?"[12] He was not even enough of a psychologist for drama, and the very word, *drama*, when it appears in his writings, is a misnomer. The discussion seems strange. Nietzsche

9. *Birth of Tragedy and Case of Wagner*, p. 169; *Der Fall Wagner*, in *Werke*, VI.iii (1969), 20: "Der Musiker wird jetzt zum Schauspieler, seine Kunst entwickelt sich immer mehr als ein Talent zu *lügen*."

10. *Birth of Tragedy and Case of Wagner*, pp. 172–173; *Werke*, VI.iii, 24: "Eine Theater-Rhetorik, ein Mittel des Ausdrucks, der Gebärden-Verstärkung, der Suggestion, des Psychologisch-Pittoresken."

11. *Birth of Tragedy and Case of Wagner*, p. 172; *Werke*, VI.iii, 23–24: "Ein ganz grosser Schauspieler . . . ein unvergleichlicher Histrio, der grösste Mime, das erstaunlichste Theater-Genie, das die Deutschen gehabt haben, unser *Sceniker* par excellence."

12. *Birth of Tragedy and Case of Wagner*, p. 175; *Werke*, VI.iii, 27: "Das Drama verlangt die *harte* Logik: aber was lag Wagnern überhaupt an der Logik!"

seems to be distinguishing between theater and drama in the latter's favor, and he seems to be defining it as a product of plot, incident, and character ruled by logic and psychological consistency. But, we may ask in our turn: what did *Nietzsche* ever care about plot, incident, or psychological consistency? He had exalted Greek drama for the opposite qualities, for being *ir*rational, "full of causes apparently without effects, and effects apparently without causes; the whole, moreover, so motley and manifold that it could not but be repugnant to a sober mind, and a dangerous tinder for sensitive and susceptible souls."[13] The whole purpose of the evil Euripidean revolution, according to the earlier Nietzsche, was to dethrone the murky, ecstatic pre-Socratic tragedy and replace it with something obedient to the laws of ordered thought. Now those maligned laws seem to be taking their revenge. They seem to have acquired a modest virtue: at least they are preferable to Wagnerian trickery.

Wagner, furthermore, stands for everything cheap and specious in musical declamation, for "oratory" rather than true utterance. As Mill found "eloquence" inferior to poetry, and saw in Rubens an example of rhetoric despotizing over vital expression, so Nietzsche sees a precursor of Wagner in another baroque artist, Bernini, who "ruined" sculpture with his flamboyant histrionic gestures. Wagner, in fact, is a seducer on a grand scale. One detects a faint theological aroma in the charge, a whiff of brimstone. Wagner is Lucifer, lighting souls the way to hell—even if that hell occupies a purely secular site. Nietzsche climaxes his tirade with the threefold plea: *"That the theater should not lord it over the arts. That the actor should not seduce those who are authentic. That music should not become an art of lying."*[14] The theater, then, quite as traditional antitheatricalists had always claimed, is a place of danger, where damned souls, in the shape of actors, lurk

13. *Birth of Tragedy and Case of Wagner*, p. 89; *Werke*, III.i, 88: "Etwas recht Unvernünftiges, mit Ursachen, die ohne Wirkungen, und mit Wirkungen, die ohne Ursachen zu sein schienen, dazu das Ganze so bunt und mannichfaltig, dass es einer besonnenen Gemüthsart widerstreben müsse, für reizbare und empfindliche Seelen aber ein gefährlicher Zunder sei."

14. *Birth of Tragedy and Case of Wagner*, p. 180; *Werke*, VI.iii, 33: "*Dass das Theater nicht Herr über die Künste wird. Dass der Schauspieler nicht zum Verführer der Echten wird. Dass die Musik nicht zu einer Kunst zu lügen wird.*"

to seduce others, trying to make them actors in their turn and so rob them of their authenticity.

It is also a place ruled by the herd, the mob, the mass. Nietzsche bitterly disapproves of Wagner's powers as a hypnotist. In *The Birth of Tragedy*, we recall, genius manifested itself precisely in its transfusing energy, its power to weld the scattered Many back into the primordial One. One might, in consequence, expect a favorable, even an admiring view of Wagner's hold over his listeners. But Wagner's sway over audiences has now become something malign, because it really means *their* sway over *him*. "Wherever the decision comes to rest with the masses, authenticity becomes superfluous, disadvantageous, a liability."[15] Instead of leading, the pseudo-artist, like Wagner, slavishly follows. Instead of constituting himself true prophet and seer, he lets his audience call the tune. He dances to their pipe. Furthermore, adherence to Wagner—Wagner*ism*—produces arrogance among the ignorant, and contempt for all discipline. It leads, finally, to the most abysmal condition of all,

theatrocracy—the nonsense of a faith in the *precedence* of the theater, in the right of the theater to *lord it* over the arts, over art. . . .

But one should tell the Wagnerians a hundred times to their faces *what* the theater is: always only *beneath* art, always only something secondary, something made cruder, something twisted tendentiously, mendaciously, for the sake of the masses. . . . The theater is a form of demolatry in matters of taste; the theater is a revolt of the masses, a plebiscite *against* good taste.[16]

---

15. *Birth of Tragedy and Case of Wagner*, p. 179; *Werke*, VI.iii, 31: "Überall, wo den Massen die Entscheidung in die Hände fällt, die Echtheit überflüssig, nachtheilig, zurücksetzend wird."

16. *Birth of Tragedy and Case of Wagner*, pp. 182–183; *Werke*, VI.iii, 36: "*Theatrokratie*—den Aberwitz eines Glaubens an den *Vorrang* des Theaters, an ein Recht auf *Herrschaft* des Theaters über die Künste, über die Kunst . . . Aber man soll es den Wagnerianern hundert Mal in's Gesicht sagen, *was* das Theater ist: immer nur ein *Unterhalb* der Kunst, immer nur etwas Zweites, etwas Vergröbertes, etwas für die Massen Zurechtgebogenes, Zurechtgelogenes! . . . Das Theater ist eine Form der Demolatrie in Sachen des Geschmacks, das Theater ist ein Massen-Aufstand, ein Plebiscit *gegen* den guten Geschmack."

Theatrocracy! Plato's very word, used in Book III of the *Laws* (701a), to designate the mania of a citizenry intoxicated with complex and varied kinds of music, licentious in its tastes, complacent in its lawlessness, and as a result losing respect for its rulers, breaking away from the control of father, mother, elders, and ultimately the law itself, in a universal anarchy similar to that foretold by the Ulysses of *Troilus and Cressida*. Like the writers of closet drama whom Wagner had pilloried in *The Art Work of the Future*, Nietzsche distinguishes sharply between art and theater, construing the latter as a cheapened, demotic substitute for the former, in which truth is abandoned, taste degraded, and the herd instinct triumphant. The elitism implicit in this view had been smoldering for years in Nietzsche's writings, and had already burst into full blaze in *The Gay Science*, in a passage to be reprinted in *Nietzsche contra Wagner*.

What is the theater to me? What, the convulsions of [Wagner's] "moral" ecstasies which give the people—and who is not "people"?—satisfaction? What, the whole gesture hocus-pocus of the actor? It is plain that I am essentially anti-theatrical: confronted with the theater, this mass art par excellence, I feel that profound scorn at the bottom of my soul which every artist today feels. *Success* in the theater—with that one drops in my respect forever; *failure*—I prick up my ears and begin to respect.

But Wagner was . . . essentially . . . a man of the theater and an actor, the most enthusiastic mimomaniac, perhaps, who ever existed, *even as a musician*.[17]

"I am essentially anti-theatrical"! This from the writer who in *The Birth of Tragedy* imagined the demiurge looking on with delight as

17. Walter Kaufmann, ed. *The Portable Nietzsche* (New York, 1954), pp. 664–665; *Werke*, VI.iii, 417: "Was geht *mich* das Theater an? Was die Krämpfe seiner 'sittlichen' Ekstasen, an denen das Volk—und wer ist nicht 'Volk'!—seine Genugthuung hat! Was der ganze Gebärden-Hokuspokus des Schauspielers!—Man sieht, ich bin wesentlich antitheatralisch geartet, ich habe gegen das Theater, diese *Massen-Kunst* par excellence, den tiefen Hohn auf dem Grunde meiner Seele, den jeder Artist heute hat. *Erfolg* auf dem Theater—damit sinkt man in meiner Achtung bis auf Nimmer-wieder-sehn; *Misserfolg*—da spitze ich die Ohren und fange an zu achten. . . . Aber Wagner war . . . wesentlich noch Theatermensch und Schauspieler, der begeisterste Mimomane, den es vielleicht gegeben hat, *auch noch als Musiker* . . . ."

his creatures played before him, and thought of lesser creature-creators as imbued with the same instinct. What is Greek drama, as Nietzsche once imagined it, if not an art of the masses? The writer who once exulted at the thought of the populace transported by Dionysian frenzy now vituperates that same populace for the transports it experiences in the modern theater. Or perhaps the populace is no longer the same? The moment for the theater in the history of a people, Nietzsche elsewhere suggests, comes when its imagination has begun to shrivel, when instead of fully living its myths it is content to see them represented scenically.[18] In this perspective even the high noon of Greek tragedy appears vestigial and debilitated, the shrunken version of an earlier, more authentically heroic age. In this perspective even Aeschylus appears as the first of the decadents, and Euripides as the end-product of a long decline. In short, the only masses acceptable to Nietzsche would appear to be those shrouded in the mists of prehistory, about whom nothing definite can really be said, and the only admissible art of the masses would be that which has not survived in any historical record.

In any case, his attitude toward the audiences of his own day is more Augustinian than "Nietzschean." With Augustine, Nietzsche now differentiates between man as an individual and man in the mass. "In the theater," he tells the "upright Wagnerian,"

one is honest only in the mass; as an individual one lies, one lies to oneself. One leaves oneself at home when one goes to the theater, one renounces the right to one's own tongue and choice, to one's taste, even to one's courage . . . . No one brings along the finest senses of his art to the theater . . . . There one is common people, audience, herd, female, pharisee, voting cattle, democrat, neighbor, fellow man; there even the most personal conscience is vanquished by the leveling magic of the great number; there stupidity has the effect of lasciviousness and contagion; the neighbor reigns, one becomes a mere neighbor.[19]

18. *The Dawn of Day*, Section 265, trans. J. M. Kennedy, in *Complete Works*, ed. Oscar Levy, IX (London, 1911), 249.

19. Walter Kaufmann, trans., *The Gay Science*, Section 368, Vintage Books (New York, 1974), pp. 325–326; *Die fröhliche Wissenschaft*, in *Werke*, V.ii (1973), 300: "Im Theater ist man nur als Masse ehrlich; als Einzelner lügt man, belügt man sich. Man lässt sich selbst zu Hause, wenn man in's Theater geht, man verzichtet auf das Recht der eignen Zunge und Wahl, auf seinen Geschmack, selbst auf seine Tapferkeit . . . . In das Theater

The theater, that is, not only confronts us with actors, human beings who have lost their identities in their roles, it erases *our* identities as well. It obliterates all distinctions; it merges us into an undifferentiated bulk; it makes us purely "relational," existing only as adjuncts to the others around us. By a kind of sinister contagion we become "mere neighbors" having left our true selves at home. Again one is struck by the strangeness of this account coming from Nietzsche. Is he not here describing, in fearful and invidious terms, something like the loss of separate identity he once thought of as a terrible joy, a legitimate goal and the supreme achievement of ancient tragedy? Then, the principle of individuation was an obstacle to the surge of the Dionysian spirit, something to be triumphantly annulled as that spirit overflowed. Now, it becomes something to be anxiously and jealously guarded, against the forces threatening to break it down.

A passage in *The Gay Science* in which Wagner makes no appearance expounds an antitheatricalism remarkably similar, in some respects, to Plato's. Nietzsche is musing on the fact that what has always provided most men with their sense of role has been their calling, the means by which they make their living. For centuries men have tended to confound their very essence with roles which for the most part were imposed on them rather than chosen by them. Their very characters have issued from those roles, yet they have persisted in thinking of themselves as obscurely destined to play them, not acknowledging the element of accident and caprice and self-will involved. In certain ages, however, the process has been reversed, and notably in really democratic ages,

where people give up this faith, and a certain cocky faith and opposite point of view advance more and more into the foreground—the Athenian faith . . . the faith of the Americans today . . . . The individual becomes convinced that he can do just about everything and *can manage almost any role*, and everybody experiments with himself, improvises,

---

bringt Niemand die feinsten Sinne seiner Kunst mit . . . da ist man Volk, Publikum, Heerde, Weib, Pharisäer, Stimmvieh, Demokrat, Nächster, Mitmensch, da unterliegt noch das persönlichste Gewissen dem nivellirenden Zauber der 'grössten Zahl,' da wirkt die Dummheit als Lüsternheit und Contagion, da regiert der 'Nachbar,' da *wird* man Nachbar."

makes new experiments, enjoys his experiments; and all nature ceases and becomes art.

After accepting this *role faith* . . . the Greeks . . . went step for step through a rather odd metamorphosis . . . . *They really became actors.* As such they enchanted and overcame all the world . . . .[20]

Whereupon Nietzsche records his gloomy conviction that the modern world is travelling the same road. Men are again becoming conscious of the fact that they play roles. They are beginning to learn that they can control those roles to some extent, and the result is that like the Greeks they are becoming actors. A new society is in process of formation, in which "the 'actors,' *all* kinds of actors, become the real masters."[21] This means that an older, more valuable human species is being discredited and discarded: the great "architects" of humanity, the creative spirits capable of fashioning a new society. For as an architect needs stones, so the social visionary needs a human component that corresponds to stone—something durable, hard, sharply defined. How can one embark on long-range planning when the very raw materials needed for building have lost the qualities that make them usable?

For what is dying out is the fundamental faith that would enable us to calculate, to promise, to anticipate the future in plans of such scope, and to sacrifice the future to them—namely, the faith that man has value and meaning only insofar as he is *a stone in a great edifice*; and to that end he must be *solid* first of all, a "stone"—and above all not an actor! . . . What will not be built any more henceforth, and *cannot* be

20. *The Gay Science*, Section 356, pp. 302–303; *Werke*, V.ii, 277–278: "Wo man diesen Glauben mehr und mehr verlernt und ein gewisser kecker Glaube und Gesichtspunkt des Gegentheils in den Vordergrund tritt, jener Athener-Glaube . . . jener Amerikaner-Glaube von heute, . . . wo der Einzelne überzeugt ist, ungefähr Alles zu können, ungefähr *jeder Rolle gewachsen* zu sein, wo Jeder mit sich versucht, improvisirt, neu versucht, mit Lust versucht, wo alle Natur aufhört und Kunst wird. . . . Die Griechen, erst in diesen *Rollen-Glauben* . . . eingetreten, machten . . . Schritt für Schritt eine wunderliche . . . Verwandlung durch: *sie wurden wirklich Schauspieler*; als solche bezauberten sie, überwanden sie alle Welt . . . ."

21. *The Gay Science*, Section 356, p. 303; *Werke*, V.ii, 278: Die 'Schauspieler,' *alle* Arten Schauspieler, die eigentlich Herren sind."

built any more, is—a society in the old sense of that word; to build that, everything is lacking, above all the material. *All of us are no longer material for a society* . . . .[22]

Men, in short, have turned into hedgehogs and flamingos, who refuse to keep their shapes, and with whom an orderly pattern of action, played by accepted rules, is no longer possible. They have turned into stage players, who cannot be trusted to stick to their assigned roles because they no longer believe that those roles have been conferred on them by anyone but themselves. They are becoming a race of Felix Krulls, each one restlessly tinkering with his identity, so that there is no longer the stable human unit, with solid contours, needed for social architecture.

Not the least offenders in this drift toward polytropism are the artists. In one remarkable passage Nietzsche considers the scholars of the world, how deformed and crippled they are with the lifelong effort to master their respective disciplines, how grotesque, even, and yet, at the same time, how admirable in their fierce drive for mastery, how infinitely preferable to their opposites, the dexterous, "polydexterous" men of letters, who *are* nothing, but spend their lives "representing" everything, "playing" and "substituting" for the true experts. The scholars represent nothing but themselves. Their sole aim is to learn. They revere competence, and bear an "uncompromising opposition to everything that is semblance, half-genuine, dressed up, virtuosolike, demagogical, or histrionic in *litteris et artibus*."[23] Their physical and mental deformities look heroic when compared to the slippery evasiveness of the men of letters.

22. *The Gay Science*, pp. 303–304; *Werke*, V.ii, 278–279: "Es stirbt eben jener Grundglaube aus, auf welchen hin Einer dergestalt rechnen, versprechen, die Zukunft im Plane vorwegnehmen, seinem Plane zum Opfer bringen kann, dass nämlich der Mensch nur insofern Werth hat, Sinn hat, als er ein *Stein in einem grossen Baue* ist: wozu er zuallererst *fest* sein muss, 'Stein' sein muss. . . . Vor Allem nicht—Schauspieler! . . . was von nun an nicht mehr gebaut wird, nicht mehr gebaut werden *kann*, das ist—eine Gesellschaft im alten Verstande des Wortes; um diesen Bau zu bauen, fehlt Alles, voran das Material. *Wir Alle sind kein Material mehr für eine Gesellschaft.*"

23. *The Gay Science*, Section 366, p. 323; *Werke*, V.ii, 297: "Mit rücksichtslosester Ablehnung alles Scheinbaren, Halbächten, Aufgeputzten, Virtuosenhaften, Demagogischen, Schauspielerischen in litteris et artibus."

We are back, startlingly, in the world of the *Republic*. As the Platonic utopia depended on the lifelong adherence of each man to one sole calling, with the result that mimesis, inviting men to forsake their roles, became a threat, to be narrowly watched and closely regulated, so, for Nietzsche, the good society also requires permanency of its members, a permanency being undermined by men's discovery that they are no longer at the mercy of rank, hereditary status, or unfathomable destiny, but can constitute and reconstitute themselves as they please. The menace of the actor, for Nietzsche as for Plato, lies in the unwholesome example he sets for others, his refusal to confine himself to a single fixed role, so that the projecting of a coherent social order becomes impossible.

Very much like Plato, Nietzsche at this moment in his career assimilates the concept "artist" to that of "actor," making of the artist one who trades in illusion.

Falseness with a good conscience; the delight in simulation exploding as a power that pushes aside one's so-called "character," flooding it and at times extinguishing it; the inner craving for a role and mask, for *appearance*; an excess of the capacity for all kinds of adaptations that can no longer be satisfied in the service of the most immediate and narrowest utility—all of this is perhaps not *only* peculiar to the actor?[24]

It thrives, "all of this," in certain areas of society—in the lower classes, in people who have lived lives of absolute dependence, under changing constraints, "who had to cut their coat according to the cloth, always adapting themselves again to new circumstances, who always had to change their mien and posture, until they learned gradually to turn their coat with *every* wind and thus virtually to *become* a coat."[25] The

24. *The Gay Science*, Section 361, p. 316; *Werke*, V.ii, 290: "Die Falschheit mit gutem Gewissen; die Lust an der Verstellung als Macht herausbrechend, den sogenannten 'Charakter' bei Seite schiebend, überfluthend, mitunter auslöschend; das innere Verlangen in eine Rolle und Maske, in einen *Schein* hinein; ein Ueberschuss von Anpassungs-Fähigkeiten aller Art, welche sich nicht mehr im Dienste des nächsten engsten Nutzens zu befriedigen wissen: Alles das ist vielleicht nicht *nur* der Schauspieler an sich?"

25. *The Gay Science*, p. 316; *Werke*, V.ii, 290: "Welche sich geschmeidig nach ihrer Decke zu strecken, auf neue Umstände immer neu einzurichten, immer wieder anders zu geben und zu stellen hatten, befähigt allmählich,

consequence was that they became masters of an eternal game of hide and seek, "which in the case of animals is called mimicry." The mimetic instinct in them at last became "domineering, unreasonable, and intractable,"[26] turning them into a crew of actors, artists, buffoons, pantaloons, Merry Andrews, and Jack Puddings. The same instinct can of course develop in the upper classes, especially among diplomats, obliged by their work to take on a kind of protective coloration from their environment. It thrives among the Jews also, because of their long history of adaptation, and among women, who are often obliged to be adaptable to the point where they must put on roles even when they take off their clothes.

Elsewhere Nietzsche makes it clear that for the individual of his day, the time for theater is the time of childhood. As one becomes a man, one must put away childish things and learn to see with the "third eye," the inner vision that views the world as a stage, but has no need of literal costumes, paint, or scenery.[27] The actor, in another aphorism, "is nothing but an ideal ape—so much of an ape is he, indeed, that he is not capable of believing in the 'essence' or in the 'essential': everything becomes for him merely performance, intonation, attitude, stage, scenery, and public."[28] With these sentiments, which have so much to do with the tawdry late nineteenth-century stage, and so little with, e.g. the tragic actors of antiquity, Nietzsche simply echoes the centuries-old suspicion of the falsity of all players, and their incapacity to live in the world of the real.

Nietzsche himself explains his disaffection from Wagner—and Schopenhauer—partly as the result of a belated understanding of romanticism. Originally—i.e., in *The Birth of Tragedy*—he had thought of Wagner's music and Schopenhauer's pessimism as stemming from "the

---

den Mantel nach *jedem* Winde zu hängen und dadurch fast zum Mantel werdend."

26. *The Gay Science*, p. 316; *Werke*, V.ii, 290: "Das man bei Thieren mimicry nennt . . . herrisch, unvernünftig, unbändig."

27. *The Dawn of Day*, Section 509; *Works*, IX, 353.

28. *Dawn of Day*, Section 324; *Works*, IX, 275; *Morgenröthe*, in *Werke*, V.i (1971), 233: "Der Schauspieler eben ein idealer Affe ist und so sehr Affe, dass er an das 'Wesen' und das 'Wesentliche' gar nicht zu glauben vermag: Alles wird ihm Spiel, Ton, Gebärde, Bühne, Coulisse und Publicum."

over-fullness of life," which produced a need for Dionysian art and tragic insight. Later he came to recognize that they stemmed instead from *romanticism,* from "the *impoverishment of life,"* with its consequent search for rest, calm, and redemption.[29] In Dionysian art it is *superabundance* that becomes creative; in romantic pessimism it is merely *hunger.* So the break with Wagner, the rejection of Schopenhauer, are explained in purely philosophical terms.

No doubt there is a measure of truth in the explanation. No doubt, also, Nietzsche's disgust with Wagner for having espoused, in *Parsifal,* a regressive Christianity in which he could not possibly have believed, was perfectly genuine. No doubt too the spectacle of *Gesamtkunstwerk,* at Bayreuth, proving to be not the rebirth of tragedy out of the spirit of music but only a colossal piece of public relations showmanship, attended with all of the most repellent trappings of popular opera, truly nauseated him. Moreover, in place of one rejected masterpiece—*Tristan* —now viewed as the embodiment of everything to be loathed in art— Nietzsche now polemically installed as counterideal the hardly less sensational and theatrical *Carmen,* confiding privately in a letter that he was doing so only to provide an "ironical antithesis" to Wagner.[30] In letters to his musician friend Peter Gast, furthermore, he continues to display the liveliest interest in opera even of the most demotic kind— Offenbach, Halévy, etc.—right down to the final days of his sanity.

We must reckon, also with the *fluctuating* nature of Nietzsche's pronouncements, the notorious contradictions that fill his pages. Gilles Deleuze has observed that Nietzsche's empiricism is a *jouissance,* which stands in opposition to the *work* of dialectic. "Nietzsche's 'yes' challenges the 'no' of dialectic; joy, *jouissance,* challenges dialectic labor; lightness, dance, dialectic heaviness; splendid irresponsibility dialectic responsibility."[31] As the terms imply, contradiction may be expected to be built into the very structure of Nietzsche's thinking. The axioms

29. *The Gay Science,* Section 370, p. 328; *Werke,* V.ii, 302: *"Ueberfülle des Lebens . . . Verarmung des Lebens."*

30. See Mann, "Nietzsche's Philosophy," p. 33.

31. Gilles Deleuze, *Nietzsche et la philosophie,* Bibliothèque de la philosophie contemporaine (Paris, 1962), p. 10: "Que la dialectique soit un travail et l'empirisme une jouissance, c'est les caractériser suffisamment. . . . Le 'oui' de Nietzsche s'oppose au 'non' dialectique; la joie, la jouissance, au travail dialectique; la légèreté, la danse, à la pesanteur dialectique; la belle irresponsabilité, aux responsabilités dialectiques."

unfold in a dance of strophe and antistrophe, turn and counterturn, positive and negative, under no constraint to march in a single rigorous line to a preordained destination. Karl Jaspers has amassed an imposing catalogue of conflicting statements in Nietzsche about Christianity, the church, the priests, the Bible, the Jesuits, and everything which it is common to suppose he rejected definitively and without appeal.[32] We should not perhaps be surprised if we found comparable oscillations and equivocations in his ruminations on the theater. And in fact, in Section 77 of *The Gay Science*, we find that after first praising Italian opera and other popular arts for their healthy vulgarity, their frank delight in masks, especially as against the offensive squeamishness of German art, he goes on to express gratitude more generally toward the artists of the theater for having "given men eyes and ears to see and hear with some pleasure what each man *is* himself, experiences himself, desires himself," and for teaching us "to esteem the hero that is concealed in everyday characters, . . . the art of viewing ourselves as heroes—from a distance and . . . simplified and transfigured"[33]—observations that would do credit to the most passionate believers in the theater as an intellectual force. Nevertheless, a moment later (Section 86) he is turning away in disgust from the music and art "that tries to intoxicate the audience and to force it to the height of a moment of strong and elevated feelings." For his own part he feels in no need of such artificial stimulants: "Whoever finds enough tragedy and comedy in himself, probably does best when he stays away from the theater," since theater and music, when all is said and done, are merely "the hashish-smoking and betel-chewing of the European!"[34]

32. Karl Jaspers, *Nietzsche and Christianity*, trans. E. B. Ashton (n.p., 1961), pp. 2–5.

33. *The Gay Science*, Section 78, pp. 132–133; *Werke*, V.ii, 109–110: "Erst die Künstler, und namentlich die des Theaters, haben den Menschen Augen und Ohren eingesetzt, um Das mit einigem Vergnügen zu hören und zu sehen, was Jeder selber ist, selber erlebt, selber will; erst sie haben uns die Schätzung des Helden, der in jedem von allen diesen Alltagsmenschen verborgen ist, und die Kunst gelehrt, wie man sich selber als Held, aus der Ferne und gleichsam vereinfacht und verklärt ansehen könne."

34. *The Gay Science*, Section 86, pp. 141–142; *Werke*, V.ii, 119–120: "Alle jene . . . welche ihre Zuhörer berauschen und zu einem Augenblicke starken und hohen Gefühls *emportrieben* möchte . . . . Wer an sich der Tragödie und Komödie genug hat, bleibt wohl am Liebsten fern vom

Like religion, then, the theater represents for Nietzsche an opiate of the masses, and his appreciative understanding of it regularly dissolves into fury at its character as a herd activity, of which such strong and lonely souls as himself have no need. For such souls, the world itself presents a sufficient spectacle, a world moreover which by their contemplation they have helped create. As for the Attic theater, so lovingly and nostalgically evoked in *The Birth of Tragedy*, that remains a moment of unrecoverable splendor. What has succeeded it in subsequent ages of history, including Nietzsche's own age, is a debased form, valuable no doubt for *l'homme moyen sensuel*, but too offensively rank with the smell of the community to have anything essential to say to the man of the future.

Theater. . . . Und Theater und Musik das Haschisch-Rauchen und Betel-Kauen der Europäer!"

· XIII ·

Yvor Winters and
the Antimimetic Bias

A SIMPLER and less conflicted rejection than Nietzsche's of all that the theater stands for, including the mimetic principle itself, may be found in the work of a recent American critic, Yvor Winters, perhaps partly in response to the disintegration of personality that forms so marked a feature of twentieth-century culture. Amid the commentary that has already accumulated on Winters' criticism, little mention has been made of his deep-seated prejudice against the drama. That his attitude involves prejudice is not difficult, I believe, to show, but if it were merely prejudice it would hardly be worth extended discussion. What lends it interest is first of all the fact that Winters, characteristically, was not content to leave it a simple matter of taste or a personal idiosyncrasy, but elaborated it strenuously into an article of dogma, and made it an integral part of his whole critical system. As with his other heterodox theses, he did not hesitate to push this one to its most bizarre extremes, so that what may have started as a temperamental quirk grows into the most sweeping attack on the mimetic principle since Plato, an attack perhaps more sweeping than Plato's since it admits of no contradiction or qualification, and since it is never couched, as it is in Plato, in the quasi-mimetic form of dialogue, which leaves a certain amount of breathing space for dissent and irony, but advances like a military campaign, flanked and buttressed with all that the author can muster of argument and counterargument. Rather like Renaissance antitheatricalists—the Puritans, the Jansenists, the clerical reactionaries—but with far more intellectual power than most of them, Winters promotes a constrictingly narrow view of life, and a view of literature that rules out most of the richness of life, with the certainty of one who feels in secure possession of the truth. A critic who could lay the blame for Hart Crane's suicide on the theories of Emerson and the permissiveness of Walt Whitman would hardly have hesitated to trace the ills of modern man to the increasing theatrical fixation of our epoch.[1]

Winters may be thought to have been preceded, or accompanied, in his coldness toward the theater by an English critic whose name is often linked with his, F. R. Leavis. In Leavis' case, however, one must speak of implicit rather than overt antitheatricality. Instead of attacking the stage, or theorizing about its shortcomings, Leavis simply ignores it— rather pointedly, as it would seem, where we might most expect him to address himself to it, in discussions of plays. His interest in plays, indeed, begins and ends with Shakespeare, perhaps sufficient indication in itself of a lack of sympathy with the dramatic medium. When he analyzes Shakespeare, he attends to matters such as imagery, symbolism, the rhythm of the verse, and "the bearing of all these on the way we are to take character, action and plot." Leavis plumes himself, along with his generation, on having "left Bradley fairly behind"—on having cast overboard the old-fashioned portrait-gallery approach to Shakespeare, and replaced it with a study of poetic texture. "We know,"

1. One or two disclaimers may here be in order. A shrewd critic has observed that "Winters' critical limitations are at their most marked when he is writing of drama" (Andor Gomme, *Attitudes to Criticism* [Carbondale, Ill., 1966], p. 82), so that to isolate his views on the drama is inevitably to see him at his weakest, and to neglect most of what is really valuable in his writing. It is also to focus on a relatively small portion of it. Still, Winters' objections to mimesis are basic, and form a keystone of his critical system, with the result that their defects imperil the stability of the whole structure. The present essay will also ignore the chronology of Winters' writings. His early books, as his readers already know, set forth their theses in relatively measured, judicious terms, while the later ones are disfigured by a growing harshness and crankiness. But the later books simply bring into high relief what was already there. Even the earliest pieces, recently published as *Uncollected Essays and Reviews*, ed. Francis Murphy (Chicago, 1973), show all the basic critical positions already staked out. See, for example, the "Statement of Purpose" from the first issue of *Gyroscope* (1929), pp. 216–217. What happened as time passed was that Winters came to insist on certain features of his system—the antimimetic strain among others—with a more and more querulous emphasis. Little distortion is risked, then, by treating his theories as a single unbroken totality from the start.

he writes, "that poetic drama is something more than drama in verse, and that consideration of the drama cannot be separated from consideration of the poetry." We also know, however, and Leavis rather too unconcernedly forgets, that poetic drama is something more than dramatic poetry, and cannot be separated from consideration of stagecraft. Leavis is Bradleyan himself in his disregard for the theater. He has no more than Bradley to say about the fact that plays, even Shakespeare's, are meant to be performed by live actors. The organization of a play, he notifies us, is "a matter of a strict and delicate subservience to a commanding significance, which penetrates the whole, informing and ordering everything—imagery, rhythm, symbolism, character, episode, plot—from a deep centre."[2] By omitting the stage from his list of crucial elements, Leavis effectively consigns it to marginality, and turns a play into a nontheatrical reading experience, into closet drama. He is less excusable than Bradley in this, in that he belongs to a generation tutored by Harley Granville-Barker in the indispensability of performance for a just appreciation of Shakespeare. A personal antipathy, here, would seem to be inducing a critical myopia. Leavis shares with Winters a certain strenuous, embattled, defensive moralism, a solemn view of literature from which playfulness and frivolity and high spirits have been rather severely excluded.

But it is Winters with whom we are now concerned. Winters' main critical position has been summarized many times, by himself and by others, but it may be useful to rehearse those points that bear on the issue at hand. Winters holds that "poetry," i.e., literature, is "a definable method of understanding human experience and judging it,"[3] or, to put it another way, that its primary function is evaluation. Criticism, in turn, is an evaluation of that evaluation. In both imaginative literature and critical discourse the factor of judgment must predominate, and judgment means rationality. Winters espouses, as is well known, a strongly rationalist view of literature. He specifies a logical structure, or at least a paraphrasable content, as the essential basis for a good poem. The poem must also contain emotion, but not for its

2. "The Criticism of Shakespeare's Late Plays, A Caveat," *The Common Pursuit* (London, 1952), pp. 173–181, p. 174.

3. *The Function of Criticism* (Denver, 1957), p. 16. This title will be abbreviated hereafter as FC.

own sake. Emotion enters as an accompaniment, a validation in the realm of feeling of what reason and judgment are proffering in their own domain. The primary or denotative aspect of words leads to the paraphrasable content; the secondary or connotative aspect produces the overtones that lend richness and power. In a good poem, moreover, the emotion aroused by the connotative side of language has a special propriety; it is the emotion that "ought" to be aroused by the logical configuration; it is adequately "motivated" by the rational substructure.

This, I trust, is not a prejudicial account. The spurious neatness and coerciveness of it have often been remarked by commentators, and at least one acute critic has pronounced it, on close scrutiny, logically indefensible.[4] But the main trouble with it lies in the inflexibility of its application. Winters' schemes, whether logical or not, are marked by a forbidding scholastic rigidity. They depend on hard and fast categories and absolute alternatives. For purposes of casual talk we continue to rely on rough and ready distinctions such as that between "reason" and "emotion," or between "denotation" and "connotation." But for Winters these constitute substantial entities; they are invested with the attributes of being, and assigned strict territories from which they may not stray. When they then go on to become key terms in a critical system, falsification becomes inevitable, of poetry and indeed of life. For the terms in question are more than unbending, they are outworn and discredited. No reputable theorist of personality today could manage with such blunt instruments as the dichotomy of "reason" and "emotion." They belong to an obsolete faculty psychology that entered the museum decades ago, along with chloroform, pneumothorax, and Dakin's solution. For a critic claiming to speak authoritatively on the moral life to use them seriously, for him to speak, as Winters does, of the "rational soul" and the "sensible soul," is virtually to foreclose from the outset on any credible account of behavior, and hence of poetry that aims to evaluate behavior. Similarly, no self-respecting student of language could get far on the tight antithesis between *denotation* and *connotation*. These rubrics ignore too much of how language works. Too much of how literature works is certain, in consequence, to escape. Winters' conceptual vocabulary, like some

4. John Holloway, "The Critical Theory of Yvor Winters," *Critical Quarterly* 7 (1965): 54–68.

of his tastes, is *reactionary* (a term he has proudly claimed), or (another preferred term) *counter-romantic*. One might also call it counter-insurgent.

The work of literature, in any event, is for Winters a statement about a human experience and a rational judgment on it, together with the emotional effect proper to the judgment. The more vigorously a given work promotes this end, the better it must be judged to be. In an essay entitled "Problems for the Modern Critic of Literature," first published in 1956, Winters undertakes to consider how well the various literary genres fulfill this aim. Marching through the genres like a general reviewing troops, he registers his displeasure with most of them, and with the mimetic component as it enters into any of them. He reserves his severest disapproval for the drama, and bestows his unqualified praise only on the expository short poem. The short poem, in Winters' view, is the supreme genre, the one best equipped to do what literature ought to do. The drama, on the other hand, is an intrinsically second-rate form, incapable of mustering the full intellectual resources of its practitioners. Inferior also, in varying degree, are the other genres that utilize mimesis in part: the novel, the dramatic monologue, etc.

A certain number of practical absurdities would seem to follow from this, and one need not dwell on them. One consequence is that Paul Valéry becomes a greater writer than Shakespeare (to say nothing of Homer or Sophocles), since "Ébauche d'un serpent" is "the greatest poem which I have ever read, regardless of kind" (FC 74), whereas *Macbeth*, the masterpiece among Shakespeare's tragedies, is badly flawed by defects inherent in its medium. Winters does not in so many words prefer Valéry to Shakespeare, but it is hardly likely that he would have flinched from doing so, not having hesitated to confer "immortality" on Adelaide Crapsey or to have declared the action and details of the Homeric poems "simply incapable of resulting in a great work" (FC 42).

But it is the theoretical issues which are of interest. In his tour of the genres, on which we should like to accompany him part way, Winters does not reach the drama immediately, but he begins nearly at once to challenge the virtues of the mimetic principle. One objection raised against it is that it cripples the exercise of "evaluation" on the part of both poet and critic. This we infer from the discussion of R. S. Crane's comments on Gray's *Elegy*. Crane asks us, says Winters, to regard the *Elegy* as "an imitative lyric of moral choice rather than of action or of mood, representing a situation in which a virtuous, sensitive, and ambitious young man of undistinguished birth confronts the possibility of his death," and so on. Yet if I understand this account of the poem, we would have in Crane's terms a kind of dramatic monologue appropriate to the speaker and his peculiar combination of talent, education, defects, and the like; and we would know what kind of young man he was solely from the poem; and the poem would therefore be inescapably a perfect achievement, and criticism would be forestalled at the outset. (FC 21)

But the conclusion here does not seem to follow from the premise. The fact that we would know what kind of person the young man was solely from the poem does not at all mean that the poem is placed beyond criticism. We could not, certainly, measure the young man's portrait against a historical original, or a composite historical type, but there would be nothing to prevent us from assessing its consistency and vividness, its subtlety, its clarity of articulation, the scope and significance of the human issues raised by it, and much else. Exact correspondence with some presumptive historical model, indeed, is one of the last things we would normally look for. Winters' objections, if valid, would have to apply to all dramatic monologues and all plays, apart from those based on history, for the same thing would need to be said of all of them: no external criteria could be invoked by which to verify them. On the other hand, his dictum would seem to enforce an impossible historical literalism on such works as do attempt historical portraiture.

Speaking of Crane's criticism as a whole, Winters points out that it betrays "an unexamined preference for the mimetic principle" (FC 24). No doubt the charge is just, and could be brought against many of us; it is a virtue in Winters to have brought the principle so fiercely under the microscope. But he does not stop to ask why Crane, and hundreds of thousands of readers and critics along with Crane, should be guilty of such a preference. What is there in mimetic activity that so insidiously seduces us? Is it merely that—as Plato thought—it appeals to our passionate selves, which we love to indulge? Is it no more than a wish to abandon ourselves to our most disreputable desires? According to Aristotle, the instinct of imitation is implanted in us from childhood; it forms one chief difference between ourselves and the lower animals. Men learn through imitation, says Aristotle, and learning is pleasurable, with the result that the pleasure taken in the imitation even of things in themselves ugly or repellent can be intense. Winters has nothing to say of this, nor of any implications that might be drawn from it. Perhaps mimesis satisfies us because it extends our experience, amplifies and enriches it, giving us, in effect, two lives for one. Perhaps it momentarily frees us from the cage of our own egos or our own limited circumstances, enabling us to become in imagination the others we could never be in actuality. Especially in the drama, one may suspect, mimesis provides a direct entry into a surrogate existence, a short circuit between the current of our own life and that of another, from which we find our own being recharged. One of the moldiest clichés about reading depends on this fact: "I didn't read that book, I lived it." The trite phrase expresses the rapt engrossment with which we enter a life other than our own in all its absorbing particularity, adopting momentarily its consciousness, but without having to pay its penalties in actual illness, suffering, or death. We return to ourselves thereafter with expressive capacities renewed and sympathies dilated.

Winters has nothing to say of any such possibilities because he has from the outset declared the evaluation of experience, rather than experience itself, to be the valuable thing, the moral judgment rendered on life rather than the living or the reliving of it. As Denis Donoghue has recently phrased it, "Winters had very little feeling for an experience until it was finished and there was nothing left of it but its meaning. He judged a story primarily by its moral. In a hurry to reach conclusions, he was irritated by the detail of processes and transitions, he was concerned with the gist of things rather than the things themselves."[5] Mimetic art concerning itself as it does so intimately with "processes and transitions," so sparing as it often is about "conclusions," it must necessarily remain, for Winters, a radically unsatisfactory enterprise.

Winters is stern on the subject of catharsis. Responding to Crane's claim that imitation "affords us a particular pleasure through awakening and allaying our emotions," he rejoins that "if we were to tell him that we prefer to keep our emotions allayed from the beginning, there

5. Review of *Uncollected Essays and Reviews*, *The Times Literary Supplement*, no. 3,782 (Aug. 30, 1974), p. 918.

is nothing . . . in [Crane's] system, which would provide him with the materials of an answer" (FC 20). Winters does not in so many words declare that he would prefer to keep his own emotions allayed, but he implies as much, and the implication seems confirmed at other places in his writing where he views emotion as a menacing force, straining to burst the dam, and having to be held in check by reason. "The basis of Evil is in emotion," he announces bluntly in the early "Notes on Contemporary Criticism," "Good rests in the power of rational selection in action, as a preliminary to which the emotion in any situation must be as far as possible eliminated, and, in so far as it cannot be eliminated, understood."[6] The consequences for literature are obvious. "All feeling," he tells us in a later essay, "is a way of disintegration," and "poetic form is by definition a means to arrest the disintegration and order the feeling."[7] The proposition that all feeling is necessarily "a way of disintegration," and that the basis of Evil lies in emotion, is one that might have surprised a good many traditional moralists, but it suggests how threatening Winters finds feeling to be. For him it is something to be curbed, not indulged, and literature would do better to order it than arouse it.[8] In these conditions, one of the prime attributes of mimetic art—its power to summon up strong feeling, to create a powerful emotional identification between the stage figure or the represented character and the viewer—turns inevitably, for Winters, as for Plato, the Puritans, the Jansenists, and antitheatricalists of all ages, into a vice.

Uninterested as he is in experiencing other lives, Winters is also uninterested in—is confessedly bored by—the particularity of life, which mimetic art tends to offer in abundance. He is concerned, he tells us, not with details but with the conclusions that may be drawn from them—not with experience, again, but with the evaluation of experience. Evaluation, for Winters, means abstraction, and his fondness for abstraction is notable; he envisages a world of absolutes toward which,

6. *Uncollected Essays*, p. 221.

7. *In Defence of Reason* (New York, 1947), p. 16. This title will be abbreviated henceforth as DR.

8. See Delmore Schwartz, "Primitivism and Decadence," *Southern Review* 3 (1938): 604: "[Winters'] own beliefs . . . so far as they are available, seem to relate mainly to a conception of nature as full of sensuous temptation, which must be resisted."

in our grovelling particularity, we haltingly move. Though he has emphatically denied being a Platonist,[9] one can understand why critics have sometimes mistaken him for one. Mere phenomena hold little interest for him; what counts are the permanent truths which can be perceived beyond them. What attracts Winters is not becoming, but being, not the uncompleted or the inconclusive, which he tends to think of as illusory, but that which is fully formed, fixed, and final. Mimetic art, dealing as it inevitably does with process, tending as it does to resist finalities and certainties, does not simply move him to indifference; it provokes active antipathy.

Touching on prose fiction, Winters chides the practitioners of the technique of interior monologue for wishing to reproduce "the processes by which [they believe] that people really think." The kind of association and sensory perception utilized by these writers "is only one kind of thought, and it is thought at the most elementary level. There are other ways of thinking. . . . But many of our novelists have decided that the thought of the conscious author is somehow unworthy of the serious author, and should be eliminated," to be replaced by the "fragmentary and unguided thought" of presumably uninteresting characters engaged in trivial activities. Winters himself opts for "the complete thought of the great mind" (FC 37–38). But would the complete thought of the great mind not be more appropriately sought in works of systematic philosophy? Should not one who truly wished wayward particularity, flukishness, and triviality expunged from literature turn to Feuerbach rather than George Eliot, to Locke rather than Sterne, to St. Thomas rather than Dante? Winters' inference that the use of the interior monologue signifies a repudiation of conscious thought seems a wilful refusal to understand. Of course "other ways of thinking" exist; they have been exploited for centuries by traditional techniques. What the writers in question are attempting is nothing less than a revaluation of the nature of consciousness.[10] They would sound its depths, unfold its plighted cunning, trace its links with the unconscious. Winters very rarely alludes to Freud (except, for example, to belittle the "Freudian mysticism" of the surrealists

9. "The Critical Method of T. Weiss," *Quarterly Review of Literature* 2 (1945): 136.

10. See Delmore Schwartz, "A Literary Provincial," *Partisan Review* 12 (1945): 140.

[DR 56]), but virtually all he says of the workings of the mind stamps him as a dogged enemy of psychoanalysis and a grim upholder of psychological law and order, with rationality as a police force and the irrational as a mob of troublesome dissenters, and no inkling of the possibility that the two realms intersect too densely to be separated at all in any final accounting. The danger, it would appear, in the interior monologue, for Winters, is that it leads toward a view of human nature to which he is programmatically opposed in advance. The kind of insight implicit in the Joycean stream of consciousness is something he will not allow to operate on him, and which, for its apparent formlessness, he sees as a threat of chaos. The fact that Joyce and writers like him are investigating that realm of experience which we share "with sea-anemones, cabbages, and onions" (DR 56)—to the extent that this picturesquely stated proposition is true—means simply that they are asserting and exploring the nature of our kinship with these lower realms, and the inescapable ways they impinge on our higher faculties. The impact may be unwelcome, but it is a datum that even a rigorous moralist might do well to reckon with.

Coming to drama, Winters starts, predictably but unpromisingly, by classifying it as "primarily a form of literature," for the following reason: "We reach the action by way of the speech, for even if we see the play performed before having read it, it has still been necessary for the performers to read it and thus understand it before performing, and it is the speech which gives meaning to the action when we see it performed" (FC 51). Undeniably, an actor must first read and, with luck, understand a script before acting in it. This fact confers on the written text a certain pragmatic priority: first words, then action. But the pragmatic priority in no sense constitutes a logical priority, nor does the written word enjoy any transcendent rights conferred by God over all other elements of performance. Considering the ritual origins of the drama, considering the role of dance, music, costume, light, and architecture, it is simply parochial to assume that because plays have been transmitted mainly through printed texts, they are therefore primarily a form of literature, and that the text enjoys some mystical primacy in the theatrical enterprise. The most one can say is that at certain epochs, when language held a central place in culture, the written word acquired a temporary working ascendancy in the theater also. It acquired it a few centuries back in western Europe, and now seems to be on the point of losing it again; increasingly, playwrights today seem to feel themselves to be working in a nonverbal medium.[11] Winters' definition arrogates an unwarranted sovereignty to language in the drama, and denies the independence of the theater as an art form in its own right, with its own canons of realization. The drama for him, indeed, is not simply "primarily" a form of literature. It is exclusively such, and as such he will criticize it, with no interest in its other potentialities. His infrequent references to the theater are always hostile. He regards actors as debasers of poetry and as boring people; he has "never witnessed a performance of Shakespeare without more of pain than of profit or of pleasure." "I think," he admits,

the world would be well enough off without actors: they appear to be capable of any of three feats—of making the grossly vulgar appear acceptably mediocre; of making the acceptably mediocre appear what it is; and of making the distinguished appear acceptably mediocre. In any event, they cannot read poetry, for they try to make it appear to be something else. . . . (FC 84–85)

All of us, no doubt, have groaned through inexpert readings of Shakespearean verse. All of us have misspent hours listening to the players wrench accents, flatten vowels, and coarsen poetic texture in order to make it "acceptably mediocre." It may be even that dramatic verse, uttered aloud on the stage, must be intrinsically less complex and subtle than the same verse studied in silence by the lone reader, since the actor, choosing among various ways to speak a given passage, must adopt some and reject others; the actualizing of certain possibilities necessarily eliminates certain others. By his facial expressions and bodily gestures he may make still further exclusions. But at the same time he will be lending warmth, color, shape, and concreteness to his chosen version, releasing its kinetic power, making it part of an active pattern of theatrical movement. The presumptive losses need to be measured against the potential gains, but this Winters never thinks of doing. Nor will he concern himself with any phase of the actor's art other than the recitation of the text. Alluding to Charles Churchill's

11. By now, of course, the divorce between text and performance has reached a point where "the act of reading is, to an unprecedented degree, discredited as a substitute for (or even a complement to) the theatrical experience" (Leo Bersani, *A Future for Astyanax* [Boston, 1976], p. 275).

satiric poem *The Rosciad*, which ridicules some of the actors of Churchill's day, Winters opines that "the poem is tedious. The poem satirizes people whom we have forgotten and who were unimportant at the time. In fact, actors are always unimportant and their qualities are unimportant, and it seems foolish to devote so much attention to them."[12] So much for the profession of Shakespeare, Ben Jonson, and Molière. "Their qualities are unimportant": Nothing the actors do while on stage has beauty, power, or significance. Their only conceivable contribution can be the voicing of a dramatic text, and that they can be counted on to do badly.

We confront at the start, then, a radically antihistrionic sensibility, for whom there is no excitement, but only irritation, in the fact of live players incarnating dramatic characters. But even with respect to a purely literary drama, Winters holds the mimetic ingredient in disrepute, and extends his approval only grudgingly to particular plays in despite of their unfortunate genre. The section in which he elaborates most fully his objections to dramatic form deals with one tragedy, *Macbeth*, and one comedy, *Volpone*, both chosen as exceptional specimens of their kind, but shown to suffer from defects inherent in that kind. A play, like a poem, for Winters, must provide evaluation, not merely experience. Action must be accompanied by judgment; what makes *Macbeth* great is that it presents not simply the imitation of an action, but a moral judgment on the action, a "rational grasp of the theme." The judgment comes about in several ways, one of which is "explicitly in the form of the action: that is, Macbeth is destroyed as a result of his sins" (FC 51). We may note in passing the homiletic bluntness of this, the evident satisfaction with which Winters extracts a hard moral from the play, turning it into an object lesson against crime, as well as, of course, the fact that *Macbeth* is virtually unique among Shakespeare's mature plays in the degree to which it can be construed as homiletic. The two other main methods of rendering judgment are through the comments of the other characters on Macbeth, and through Macbeth's comments on himself; but these methods, Winters tells us, are seriously compromised and their efficacy impaired by the use of the mimetic principle. For a dramatist, in Winters' view, has saddled himself with an impossible task.

12. *Forms of Discovery* (n.p., 1967), p. 127. This title will be abbreviated hereafter as FD.

Let us suppose that the dramatist is imitating the speech of a character of moderate intelligence in a situation of which the character does not in any serious sense understand the meaning. This presents an almost insoluble problem. If a poet is endeavoring to communicate his own best understanding of a human situation, that is one thing. If he is endeavoring to communicate approximately a plausible misunderstanding of a situation on the part of an imaginary character much less intelligent than himself, that is quite another. He can only guess at the correct measure of stupidity which may be proper to such a character in a given situation . . . and whether he is successful or not, he will still be writing poetry which as poetry will be of an inferior kind. Exactly what is the target? It seems to me that the whole business must in the nature of the case be a rough approximation—and rough approximations are unfortunate affairs in the fine arts. (FC 52–53)

The aim of poetry, that is, is to achieve the finest moral judgments of which the poet is capable, but the nature of the dramatic medium forces him to do so through the agency of characters less insightful than himself. In order to portray the mind of a fool, a bully, a toady, or a mediocrity, he must cramp himself into the diminished frame of such a character, and this is not only undesirable, since it requires him to suppress a portion of his own intelligence, it is also impossible, since it requires him to guess at the right degree of stupidity, criminality, or foolishness appropriate to the character.

Before rejecting this proposition out of hand, we should acknowledge its meed of truth. Experience supports Winters in at least one respect: we tend to respond most strongly to those characters in whom we feel the playwright has put most of himself, characters of exceptional moral or intellectual stature, such as Falstaff or Hamlet. We find a special exhilaration in participating in their multiplicity, freedom, and wit, and we can hardly restrain the conviction that they provide a vehicle for some of the playwright's own thoughts. When we hear Hamlet tell Polonius, "Use every man after his desert, and who should scape whipping? Use them after your own honour and dignity. The less they deserve, the more merit is in your bounty," we suspect we hear not only Hamlet speaking, but Shakespeare. And the same would be true, in varying degree, of Dante's Virgil, or Molière's Alceste.

But character, only one way in which the playwright organizes his material, is for Winters the sole way. He pays lipservice to plot; setting, atmosphere, rhythm, stage spectacle he passes over in silence. And character itself he treats entirely from the standpoint of the individual speech, which he approaches as a separate poem, and measures by the canons previously laid down for all poems. He makes perfunctory reference, from time to time, to the fact that dramatic characters are creatures in transit—acting, suffering, evolving—but without in the slightest relenting his criteria on that account. A speech delivered at the beginning of a play is judged in the same terms as one spoken toward the end. And as for the fact that characters speak not only at different moments in the action but in differing circumstances, now alone, now with friends, now among enemies, now harboring one purpose and now another—none of these or any of the countless other ways in which dramatic context leaves its imprint on a given speech are accorded the dignity of mention. Each speech is judged wholly in itself. It is as though one were to judge a building only by the workmanship of individual stones, and call only those stones "good architecture" which were attractive as separate objects. As though a thousand beautifully sculptured stones might not on occasion produce an awkward and ugly building, or an equal number of rough-hewn stones a graceful and beautiful one. It is not that local texture, the craftsmanship of the individual stone, can be disregarded, but that to gaze on it so myopically is to lose sight of why it is there in the first place, and so in a real sense to fail to see it. To approach drama exclusively from the point of view of the texture of single speeches, and to judge that texture exclusively by nondramatic criteria, is to guarantee the rejection of the mimetic method in advance by imposing on it standards alien to it.

Winters begs a serious question, moreover, in his phrase "understand the meaning." What does it mean to understand the meaning of a situation? For Winters it means to be able to formulate a rational, paraphrasable attitude toward it, to be able to articulate a judgment on it. But there might be more intuitive forms of understanding, less translatable into declarative statement, which—on occasion—might be arguably as valuable as or more valuable than the more formal rational sort. It is a suggestive fact that Winters refrains, for the most part, from referring in print to *King Lear*, as though something about that play offended him, but he hesitated to say so. One wonders whether he was not displeased by its too favorable account of madness and its unflattering view of reason, whether he did not recoil from the spectacle of the mad Lear and the distracted Fool and the antic Edgar in possession of more true wisdom than the "lucid" Goneril, Regan, and Cornwall. For if Winters mistrusts feeling, as "a way of disintegration," madness disturbs him profoundly. He sees it as an unmitigated evil, unyieldingly arrayed against its mighty opposite, sanity, the two bolted together in an eternal antithesis like that between "reason" and "emotion" or "denotation" and "connotation." The idea that reason and unreason interpenetrate, that they are socially and historically conditioned, that madness is a social judgment, so that what is mad for one epoch may be sane for another, and what is good sense in one society may be wild lunacy in another—that, in short, there is no absolute and unalterable gulf fixed by God or Nature between them—all this seems beyond his reckoning. For Winters, the "insane" may sometimes "perceive and feel with great intensity, but [their] feelings and perceptions are so improperly motivated that they are classed as illusions." Along with the feeble-minded, they belong to the category of "obviously unfulfilled human nature" (DR 370). To "understand the meaning" of a situation, then, for Winters, is to understand it in ways predefined by him, with no allowance for the possibility that the madman, so designated, might, in certain respects and according to the case, "understand" better than the sane man.

A poet imitating the thought processes of a character of smaller intelligence than his own will inevitably, concludes Winters, even if he succeeds, "be writing poetry which as poetry will be of an inferior kind." Shakespeare, accordingly, in Macbeth's dagger soliloquy, "cannot employ the best poetry of which he is capable, for such poetry would be out of character." "The situation," says Winters of the troubled protagonist, "calls for powerful statement; but the statement must be made by an imperfect intelligence" (FC 53). If we rewrote this so as to make it read, "The situation calls for powerful realization, such as requires an exceptional sensibility," we would have a fairer account of the case, and of what Shakespeare provides. For Macbeth is certainly superior as a sensibility, in the energy and activity of his imaginative life, and the swiftness with which his feelings take shape and struggle with each other. Winters' views on character would seem to require that a hero be of an intellectual stature comparable to that of his creator. The capacity to feel on an unusual scale, to learn pity, to change with suffering, to embark on untried areas of experience—all the traits that Shakespeare characteristically signals to us as marks of heroism—do not appear on Winters' docket at all. Shakespeare tends to teach us precisely that heroism does not lodge in "rational apprehension," but in qualities of feeling, so that a Lear, an Othello, may be heroic despite a clouded intelligence, while a Richard of Gloucester, an Iago, an Edmund, may be vicious despite exceptional mental alertness. Needless to say, it is no romantic sentimentalism on Shakespeare's part to draw this inference, but a deeply pondered view of the nature of the moral life, closely related to some of the most familiar tenets of traditional ethics.

But further problems remain. "The poet," says Winters, "can only guess at the correct measure of stupidity which may be proper to such a character in a given situation," and therefore "the whole business must in the nature of the case be a rough approximation." True enough, in all likelihood, but the consequences reach farther than Winters contemplates. If the playwright's attempt to inhabit a lesser mind is doomed to failure or imperfection because it commits him to "rough approximations," so equally must be the attempt to render *any* mind other than his own, including one of comparable intellectual dimensions. Here too he will have to improvise; here too he will have to conjecture what it might be like to have sprung from different parents, into a different milieu, to have had different experiences as child and man, and now to hold different views and feel different emotions. In each case the challenge is the same: the poet must perform an imaginative leap into the skin of another creature, divesting himself momentarily of his own habitual thoughts and feelings. His task is to devise new human forms, and render them plausible by the imaginative energy he can infuse into them. Any mimetic poem, whether designed for the stage or not, must be so written. Winters has high praise for some of Edwin Arlington Robinson's dramatic monologues, such as "Rembrandt to Rembrandt." Here the painter, grown old, is imagined as gazing into a mirror (or into an earlier self-portrait), musing despondently on his past career and present isolation. Rembrandt is represented, certainly, as intelligent, but he is also represented *as Rembrandt*, as another soul with his own history, to enter which, to create which, requires an imaginative assault analogous to that required to invade the spirit of a dwarf, a cripple, a murderer, or a child.

Do we not, indeed, encounter a version of this rough approximation even in nonmimetic poems about the lives of other people, as in several of the Robinson lyrics most warmly endorsed by Winters? In "Eros Turannos," for instance, or in "Veteran Sirens," or in "The Poor Relation," we have feelings *imputed to* the characters, and an evaluation imposed from without onto their alleged inner experience. "Eros Turannos," Winters tells us, is "a universal tragedy in a Maine setting. In the first three stanzas there is an exact definition of the personal motives of the actors and an implication of the social motives; in the fourth stanza the tragic outcome; and in the last two stanzas the generalized commentary."[13] But can the "motives," whether "personal" or "social," assigned to the actors be any less a matter of guesswork than if the poet were to make the actors talk and gesticulate on their own? Does the imputation of feelings from without not very much reduce the density and specificity of the portraits, so that the "generalized commentary" emerges from a relatively meager context? Are we not ourselves forced simply to take the writer's word for the validity of the presumed motives?

In the case of "The Poor Relation," Robinson attributes a fairly detailed sequence of feelings to the title character: fears, doubts, childish hurts and bewilderments, dependency coupled with a reluctance to be patronized by her comfortably off kinfolk, and a keen sense of the shallowness of their pity. All is sharply observed, and, as Winters requires, evaluated. One drawback, however, of the poem is precisely that it apprehends its subject so exclusively from the outside. It could be taxed with some of the condescension it ascribes to the visiting relations, with some of their sentimentalism and defective identification. For it conceives of the poor relation largely as a victim, as an object of pathos, whereas a mimetic representation, by reconstructing her feelings from within, might discover truly fresh possibilities and lead to a less stereotyped portrayal. The mere effort to recreate the experience at its source might disclose a domain of consciousness barred to an outsider, and such an attempt might have a chance to alter our awareness fundamentally, to shift our angle of vision. Plainly, if the mimetic method involves its penalties, the nonmimetic method incurs other, perhaps more grievous, ones of its own.

The character of Rembrandt, in the poem, it might be claimed,

13. *Edwin Arlington Robinson* (Norfolk, Conn., 1946), p. 32.

actually stands for Robinson. In Rembrandt, Robinson examined the plight of the alienated artist, which he felt as his own. Winters also informs us that in Valéry's "Ébauche d'un serpent," the mind of the serpent is Valéry's mind, and his metaphysics are Valéry's metaphysics (FC 66). Granted this close identity between author and character, one is prompted to ask: If the mimetic principle is such an albatross, why should the poet hang it around his neck in the first place? Why, to ruminate on his own problems as isolated artist, should Robinson saddle himself with Saskia and Titus and the Burghers of Amsterdam? Why should Valéry portray himself as a viper coiled in a tree, with a triangular emerald head, a forked tongue, and deadly venom, a hatred for the sun and the human race, a memory of the beauty of the newly created Eve, and all the rest? Surely "the greatest poem that [Winters] has ever read, regardless of kind," does not adopt all this mimetic apparatus as mere décor? And why, moreover, *"Ébauche d'un serpent,"* with its deliberate suggestion of the tentative and fragmentary? Valéry, at least, believes he is gaining something by the method, and part of what he gains is spelled out by Winters himself in his brilliant pages on the poem—the use of intense physical details which "live in the texture" of the rest "with a kind of electrical energy" (FC 70). In addition, Valéry gains a useful distancing, a displacement of some of his own meditations onto an imagined other, who can be endowed with traits that will keep the meditation ordered and focussed. By making the speaker a serpent, Valéry sharply restricts the range of possibilities, and circumscribes the area for meditation. He rules out scores of irrelevancies that might otherwise clamor for entrance. The narrative context delimits the situation further, and supplies motives for the meditation. Perhaps also, in creating this second voice Valéry permits himself to pursue certain speculations farther than he would care to in his own name. But in doing all this, he has invented a new character, who is neither Paul Valéry nor a simple dummy, but an independent construct, whose very opinions must be looked at as something other than the private views of their writer. Before Winters can convince us that the mimetic principle is a hindrance, or a danger, he must explain why it occurs so prominently in so many of his own favorite poems—why, indeed, he uses it himself, in dramatic monologues like "Socrates," "John Sutter," or "Sir Gawaine and the Green Knight," or in lyrics such as "To be Sung by a Small Boy Who Herds Goats."

There is an element of retributive irony in Winters' ambivalence toward the dramatic monologue, which clearly fascinates as much as it repels him. For the monologue, one of the chief legacies of Romanticism, is by its nature a mimetic form. Virtually in its essence it requires the writer to project himself into an alien consciousness, to give facts "from within," to derive meaning "from the poetic material itself rather than from an external standard of judgment," so that he is enabled not only to "dramatize a position the possibilities of which he may want to explore," but also to "dramatize an emotional apprehension in advance of or in conflict with his intellectual convictions." The lyrical element in the form, moreover, characteristically forbids us to judge the speaker or to "find in his utterance the counterpart to everything we understand about him."[14] There is always, then, in the case of the dramatic monologue, a discrepancy between what our judgment might conclude from a situation as perceived from the outside and what our more intimate knowledge, resulting from the lyrical immediacy with which the speaker is presented, leads us to feel. This discrepancy, exploited by all the best writers of the form, is plainly inherent in it—otherwise the adoption of the alien persona would make no sense—yet at the same time it is clearly what makes the form abhorrent to Winters.

Continuing to confine ourselves, however, to Winters' own terms, we may ask whether even in the case of his own favored model for prose writing, the historical narrative, the same conditions of rough approximation, guesswork, and imaginative projection that obtain in the dramatic monologue do not also prevail here. "The historian such as Gibbon or Macaulay," Winters speculates, "examines his material to the best of his ability, and on the basis of that examination forms a fairly definite idea of the characters and actions involved. In this stage of his work, he is comparable to the novelist who has long meditated his characters and outlined his plot. The final literary form of the history represents an evaluation, a moral judgment, of the material which he has held in his mind" (DR 415). But must not the historian, scanning his sources, coming to know his characters however intimately, resort to the same guesses demanded of the dramatist? Can Macaulay's portrait of the Duke of Monmouth, or of the Earl of Argyle, or of James II,

14. Robert Langbaum, *The Poetry of Experience: The Dramatic Monologue in Modern Literary Tradition* (London, 1957), pp. 78–79, 104, 201, and passim.

be more "exact" than Shakespeare's of Macbeth (who is also, of course, an historical character)? Apart from fidelity to the documents—and one is surprised to find Winters so positivistically wedded to such particularities—against what do we measure such portraits, if not against the same canons of vividness and consistency, lifelikeness and human substance that we apply to the drama? The fact that the characters are not allowed to speak for themselves can do nothing to enhance the accuracy of the portraits. It can only mean that the historian has transfixed them with his all-judging eye and undertaken to speak for them. The evaluative conclusion, to which Winters attaches such weight, can have no validity other than what is lent it by the energy of the portraits themselves.

But even when attempting to speak directly in his own person, the poet is still committed to approximations. Let us suppose he wishes to recreate, poetically, some fragment of his own experience in which conscious deliberation played little part—a dream, a childhood memory, a moment of passion. Will the recreation be much less approximate than the creation from nothing of the imagined experience of someone else? He must in this case repossess what he has never quite fully possessed in the first place, capture it and drag it into words, with as much as possible of its remembered quality. In both cases an act of imaginative appropriation is involved, and the degree of definiteness possible under the circumstances seems about the same. But let us suppose even that he is writing about his present self—his alert, reflective, adult self, in which conscious deliberation enters strongly. Does he not have quirks and moods and temperamental vicissitudes, which elude the grasp, and require similar strategies of approximation to fix in words? Winters himself regards language as essentially conceptual. If he is right, the translation of our perceptual existence into verbal discourse must always involve tactics of accommodation.

Winters would doubtless deny that poetry ought to concern itself with quirks and moods, except perhaps to disapprove them. He censures Laforgue for his use of the double mood, and quotes approvingly an acquaintance who said that Laforgue reminded her of someone who spoke rudely and then apologized, whereas he ought to have made the necessary subtractions beforehand. "The whole issue," according to Winters, "comes down to the question of how carefully one is willing to scrutinize his feelings and correct them" (DR 72). "Scrutinize his feelings and correct them": this would prove a useful rule of thumb in many life situations. To blurt out whatever crosses our minds in whatever company is neither civil nor decent. But one cardinal advantage of poetry is that it permits the acting out of fantasies of rudeness that would be intolerable in real situations, permits them to be dramatized and explored, understood and in this very process evaluated. If poets traditionally deliver a golden world instead of nature's brazen one, on occasion they also do the reverse. To imply that a poet should regularly and on principle edit his feelings before writing (or during writing), that he should somehow repress or dismiss them from his consciousness—this is to place an intolerable censorship on the expressive function of literature.

But Winters disapproves of the expressive side of literature, of its power to simulate lived life. Poets praised by others for their conversational naturalness of style, like Donne and Frost, are castigated by Winters for the same talent. Poetry, he would make clear, "is not conversation, and I see no reason why poetry should be called upon to imitate conversation. Conversation is the most careless and formless of human utterance; it is spontaneous and unrevised, and its vocabulary is commonly limited. Poetry is the most difficult form of human utterance; we revise poems carefully in order to make them more perfect" (FC 160). Winters neglects here a well-enough-known fact: some poets revise precisely in order to catch the accent of the speaking voice more closely, and they regard *this* as a way of perfecting. Winters himself sometimes objects to inversions and archaisms and other departures from idiomatic speech, so that it is evident he expects a poem to conform, in some measure at least, to the norms of conversation. His championship of the "plain style" in English poetry would seem to involve the assumption that poetic language should not vary too widely from spoken language; his rejection of the "ornamental" style would seem to show a disapproval for the promiscuous way in which that style violates the patterns of ordinary speech. To the praise bestowed on Donne, however, for the colloquial vividness of his openings, Winters can only retort, "I am not interested in the petulant conversation of Donne or of any other man, and I see no reason why Donne should have to inflict his on me in order to prove his sincerity" (FD 76). The divergence, here, from the experience of most readers is immense. For most readers the sense of human presence produced by the illusion of spontaneous speech seems self-evidently valuable, a guarantee that the poet is engaged with realities. For Winters it lacks all virtue, either in itself or as an adjunct to the function of judgment: it is merely slovenly or petulant or boring. "The abuse of the effect of dramatic speech," he writes elsewhere, "is one of the commonest defects of recent poetry: it is very easy, apparently, to write in meters which simulate the looseness of conversation in the belief that they simulate the effect of dramatic speech" (DR 549). The implication seems inescapable that the effect of the living voice is more than a matter of unconcern to Winters; it is an affront. One need not wonder at his antipathy toward the actors, for nothing they could do to a play could interest him. Neither the warmth of the voice, nor the expressiveness of the face, nor the eloquence of the limbs, nor any of the means by which actors make expressive instruments of themselves, could exert any hold on him. The only feature apprehensible is the verse, and that only in the degree to which it has been denatured of its kinship to living language.

We may suppose, finally, that the poet does wish to communicate his own "complete thought," from the most thinking level of himself. Here too he will face pitfalls. From Montaigne onward our most prized writers have taught us how frail and unstable our reason is. We are not, today, the beings we were yesterday; we are undulating and diverse; our very powers of ratiocination hinge on trifles beyond our control. Except on the level of mathematical symbolism or formal philosophizing, from which concreteness and particularity have been systematically strained out, we must, when we write, take up the burden of what is fleeting and impalpable in ourselves, and this will entail accommodations and approximations before it can be rendered in language.

Winters approves guardedly of forms like the novel and poetic drama when he can assure himself that their mimetic component is mimimal, or strictly controlled by the watchdog of reason. In fiction he favors the device of the omniscient narrator, freely commenting on the story; otherwise the reader must depend on what the characters themselves say and do, as in the novels of Joyce or James, or as in the drama. For drama, Winters prefers the sort of closet play produced by writers like

439

Robert Bridges.[15] The remoteness of Bridges' plays from the stage greatly enhances their acceptability to Winters, since it ensures that they will not be contaminated by passion. "They are not independent works; they are not dramatic in form; they could not be staged," he states reassuringly. Bridges' own essay on Shakespeare[16] reveals him as a fastidious distaster of the popular element in Shakespearean drama, which he takes to be a capitulation to a brutal public. The jokes and obscenities, the exhibitions of cruelty, the casual poetic justice, the coarse manners and inconsistent motivation—all of these gross faults, as he considers them, he blames on an audience which has extorted them from the playwright, and reproaches the playwright for yielding to their blackmail. To Shakespeare's unhampered choice he assigns only those portions of the plays of which he himself thoroughly approves. Bridges' own plays, not surprisingly, combine a certain fineness of texture with a feeble emotional temperature. One would hardly recognize, in the well-bred personages of his tragedies about Nero, the horrendous creatures who stalk the pages of Tacitus and Suetonius, but for Winters, their tepid emotionality is a virtue. "The style becomes unfortunately excited on a few occasions," he confesses, "but only on a few" (FD 204).

The analysis of the dagger speech in *Macbeth* is intended to illustrate the drawbacks of the mimetic method by showing that at this juncture in his career, Macbeth's understanding of his situation is imperfect, and Shakespeare therefore cannot write his best poetry. We must, as we proceed, remind ourselves that Winters will be judging each detail of the speech entirely on its own merits. He does not, like most critics, distinguish "idea" from "execution" or "execution" from "structure" merely as a critical convenience, and, as it were, apologetically. He does so in sober meanings, never hesitating to damn or praise an individual passage without reference to anything beyond itself. He commences his discussion, oddly, by praising the first seven lines:

> Is this a dagger which I see before me,
> The handle toward my hand? Come, let me clutch thee.

15. See *Uncollected Essays*, p. 148, where he declares it to be "beyond all question that Bridges' two plays on *Nero* are the greatest tragedy since *The Cenci* and . . . quite possibly superior to any English tragedy outside of Shakespeare."

16. Robert Bridges, *The Influence of the Audience* (New York, 1926).

> I have thee not, and yet I see thee still.
> Art thou not, fatal vision, sensible
> To feeling as to sight? Or art thou but
> A dagger of the mind, a false creation
> Proceeding from the heat oppressed brain?

These, Winters informs us, "are fine lines, plain in style, and definitive of [Macbeth's] perplexity." One is prompted to inquire at once whether anything said against the rest of the speech can outweigh this initial concession. If the mimetic method is capable of a success here, why should subsequent lapses be blamed on the method rather than on faults of execution? "But these lines," Winters pursues,

are somewhat quiet and speculative, and Macbeth is on the brink of murder. The subsequent lines about the dagger add little to what has been said . . . but they come closer to "imitating" the distraught state of mind and they give the actor an opportunity to "ham" it. The imitation resides partly in the redundancy, partly in the broken rhythm, partly in the violent detail at the end, the gouts of blood. Now these lines may transform the passage into a plausible imitation . . . of a second-rate intelligence in a distraught condition, or it is possible that they fail to do this—I confess that I am unable to say. But they are not very good poetry. (FC 53-54)

The lines in question are these:

> I see thee yet, in form as palpable
> As this which now I draw.
> Thou marshall'st me the way that I was going;
> And such an instrument I was to use.—
> Mine eyes are made the fools o' th' other senses,
> Or else worth all the rest: I see thee still;
> And on thy blade, and dudgeon, gouts of blood,
> Which was not so before.[17]

Now it seems to me certain that if the first seven lines of the speech can be described as "somewhat quiet and speculative," so can these. Alternatively, either passage might be described as tense and "distraught." An actor could probably read them convincingly either way.

17. Kenneth Muir, ed. *Macbeth*, New Arden Shakespeare, rev. ed. (London, 1955), II.i.40-47.

The notion that there is some emphatic and unarguable shift in tone from the first passage to the second seems an invention of the critic. Second, if, as between the first seven lines and those that follow, one group more than the other invites the actor to "ham" it, it is the first group. The line "Come, let me clutch thee" requires Macbeth to grasp convulsively at empty air, whereas the only physical movement dictated by the second passage is the drawing of the dagger, and this, an accustomed gesture with a familiar solid object, is likely to be more composed and unexcited than the other. Nor is any sort of rhetorical hamming more in order for the second passage than for the first. As for "broken rhythm," it is difficult to know what Winters means by this: except for the single elision ("o' th' other") and the extra light syllable at the end of two of the lines, the passage is composed of perfectly regular iambics. There are no displaced accents, no bunched or crowded stresses, no heavy or irregularly positioned cesuras—nothing to interfere with the steady iambic beat. Finally, to have nothing to say of the gouts of blood but that they are a "violent detail" is to be anticontextual with a vengeance. Of course they are a violent detail, as *Macbeth* is a violent play and a play about violence. Moreover they form one link in a chain of "blood" images that criticism of recent decades has shown to be central to the language and stagecraft of the play. They link back to the bleeding sergeant of the first scene and forward to the blood on Lady Macbeth's hands in the sleepwalking scene, and to much else. They show the blood that Macbeth has not yet shed beginning to possess his imagination in terrifying form; they contain prophetic warning as well as psychological validity. And they mark a distinct stage in the progress of his derangement, since they appear in the course of the soliloquy itself. They show the process of hallucination and disintegration taking place before our eyes. In the face of such plain facts, one can only conclude that Winters' comment represents prejudice elaborately masquerading as analysis. What is extraordinary is how complacently Winters caters to his prejudice, how unconcernedly he pushes his distorted account of the speech onto the reader. Most extraordinary of all is that such coercive and inaccurate criticism could have proceeded from a critic who spent a lifetime insisting on the intimate connections between prosody and morality, who preached, even if he did not always successfully practice, the most scrupulous attention to the particulars of versification, and taught his readers to do the same.

Similar repressive critical tactics might be illustrated from the discussion of the rest of Macbeth's speech, but perhaps the point has been sufficiently made. Proceeding to the observations on Racine, we find that Winters views the tragedies as "elaborate and precise mechanisms for exhibiting action which rises at certain moments to great poetry; but there is a great deal of mechanism in proportion to the great poetry" (FC 56). Here we have a striking instance of the divorcing of speech from context, the uncoupling of the tirades from the narrative, which is then abandoned in orbit. Winters thinks of the plot rather as an assembly line, designed to turn out a certain amount of a specified product—great poetry—and then censured for not filling its quota. Perhaps if one were to adopt a less mechanical view, seeing it (in a romantic trope that Winters would doubtless abhor) more as a live organism, one might find it beautiful in itself, and not accuse the root or the stem of failing to be a blossom. One curious upshot of Winters' insistence on line-by-line evaluation is that in practice he comes to sound like Edgar Allan Poe, a writer he detested. Like Poe, who disbelieved in the possibility of a long poem, Winters requires every instant of every poem to be a high spot, and every poem to consist, as nearly as possible, of an unbroken succession of great lines. Is there not, in this fixation on the individual moment, something faintly hedonistic? Is this not the hedonism of the plain style?

In comedy, according to Winters, some of the flaws inherent in poetic drama show up more clearly. He turns therefore to *Volpone*. After describing very well the peculiar intensity of the opening lines, he observes:

But Volpone is trivial in spite of his intensity. He represents a limited and contemptible passion. Hence, in the opening speech and in others, Jonson is bringing his brilliant poetic talent to bear upon a subject of minimal importance. Jonson, of course, knew this: this is a comedy, and comedy is a minor form; furthermore, not only did Jonson know this, but his whole intention in the play is to demonstrate this, to convince us of this for our own improvement. But the fact remains that in spite of brilliant writing we have an extended elaboration of trivial material, and eventually it becomes tedious. Jonson, like Shakespeare, is handicapped by the mimetic principle: Dryden was able to depict Shadwell in Dryden's language and to relate him directly to Dryden's principles; Jonson was forced to depict Volpone in Volpone's language and with relation to Volpone's principles. Jonson did a remarkably brilliant piece of work, if one considers the limitations of his medium, but Dryden did a better . . . . (FC 57)

Here we have a good instance of Winters' preference for what can be squarely and unambiguously stated. He is right to think of drama as basically an inexplicit medium. Once character has been set against character, and allowed the freedom of its author's mind to pursue its own destiny, the sum total must end perforce as something relatively unstable, even when individual speeches are highly explicit, as in Shaw. Even a seeming raisonneur or authorial spokesman must take his place at length as one more element in a larger design; his authoritativeness can never be more than conditional, and is forever qualified by the rest of the design.

The charge of triviality seems peculiar, though characteristic. It leaves out of account our sense that Volpone's intensity in itself raises him above triviality, and it reflects Winters' belief that there are inherently trivial subjects which ought not to be imitated at all. Winters' view of imitation in fact reverses Aristotle's: instead of seeing it as part of an educative process, he sees it, Platonically, as a yielding to, and hence an invitation to chaos. Nowhere in his account of the moral life is there room for the idea of play, or play-acting, for childish fantasy or indulged illusion—as if even the most severely sane and rational of individuals could subsist wholly on a diet of sanity and rationality, with never a moment's return to the waters of flux and indeterminacy. Freud pointed out long ago in *Beyond the Pleasure Principle* that fantasied reenactment of the past might constitute an effort on the part of the injured mind to regain control of its own history, and Fenichel suggested later[18] that performance of the sort familiar in stage-acting and mimetic play had as one of its meanings the building of beachheads into the future. By experimenting with the imaginary, we learn to master the real; we discover, in fantasy, how to make the right moves in actuality. We learn to *utilize* our trivial or negative impulses. But Winters sees all

18. Otto Fenichel, "On Acting," *Psychoanalytic Quarterly* 15 (1946): 144–160.

enactment as luring us toward disaster, dangerous in the degree to which it kindles live feeling. His preferred role for literature is that of the schoolmaster dispensing precepts, from which ambiguities and dissonances have been filtered out, and all traces of the problematic and the tentative leached away.

One might suggest, further, that to see Volpone as representing only "a limited and contemptible passion" is itself prejudiced and limiting, very much at odds with what recent criticism has seen—that this character is governed by an *un*limited and far from contemptible passion for self-transformation.[19] Even if one assented to the proposition that Volpone was trivial because bent on acquiring gold, it still remains doubtful whether a play whose characters obey trivial impulses must itself be trivial. Is it trivial of moralists to denounce *cupiditas* as the *radix malorum*? Is *Plutus* trivial? Is *The Pardoner's Tale* trivial? Trivial men have worshipped money since the world began, but the fact (alas!) is not trivial. But of course Mosca and Volpone are far more than simple schemers for coin. Jonson makes them burningly, flagrantly alive, so that they arouse subversive feelings in us—the craving for power, for intrigue and wit and voluptuousness, for imaginative variety and sensual indulgence. He makes us guilty of their fantasies and their triumphs, corrupting us partly through the power of the poetry Winters signalizes, so that when at the end they are sentenced and judged, we find ourselves sentenced along with them, accomplices and secret sharers rather than simple spectators. How could any of this begin to come about if Jonson had simply written a didactic poem in Winters' preferred genre of the expository short lyric? The drama has a power to enlist our complicity in a way that an expository lyric can never have. The inherent openness of play form, along with its inherent reticence, makes for an exceptionally dynamic set of possibilities. It seems worth remembering that on any roster of the representatives of the great cultures of our own tradition, the names of one or more dramatists will usually figure.

Yet for Winters, literature improves as it moves further from mimesis. Volpone is a great comic creation, no doubt, but hampered by being presented mimetically, whereas (to complete the quotation interrupted above):

19. See, e.g., Thomas M. Greene, "Ben Jonson and the Centered Self," *Studies in English Literature, 1500–1900* 10 (1970): 337–343.

It would not be hard to devise a very good argument to the effect that Dryden's Shadwell, as we get him in *MacFlecknoe* and in the portrait of Og in the second part of *Absalom and Achitophel*, is the greatest comic figure in our literature. (FC 57)

One wishes that Winters had taken a moment to complete this easy assignment. For one's first reaction must be that Shadwell, in the poems named, is hardly a character at all. Or if he is, it is only in the Theophrastian sense in which the figures in Earle or Overbury are characters—thumbnail sketches wherein a few salient traits are stroked in, and a quick verdict delivered. Winters apparently assumes that summary judgment is more demanding and difficult than imaginative penetration, but the reverse seems more likely. To describe a character bitingly from the outside, to impute a foolish appearance and some eccentricities of behavior to him, and then to proceed to withering judgment—nothing, morally speaking, could be easier. But to conceive of a strange creature like Volpone, to breathe the breath of life into him, to make him vivid and believable to us even for an instant, is to open a window in our sensibilities, to make us feel, momentarily, what it might be like to inhabit a different form of life, as well as to intimate the degrees of cousinship which already, all unsuspecting, we share with him. We can see ourselves in Volpone, for dramatic form forces us in some sense to become him as we watch, but we can never see ourselves in Dryden's Shadwell, at whom we laugh as from an Olympian height, scornfully aware that the midwife has cursed him from the cradle with the fatal gift of dullness.

One puzzling element in the picture is Winters' fixation on character. A judicious critic has noticed that "Winters is always hampered in his (rather rare) discussion of drama by taking the mimetic principle very solemnly indeed, and by talking always in terms of 'character.'"[20] We may understand this fixation better, perhaps, if we notice what another critic has observed about the dramatic medium, that it "lacks . . . that incessant *voice* which, in poetry, prose fiction and the essay, never stops implying the presence of a stable and structured self as the center to which the world always returns and from which it receives its own reassuringly stable designs."[21] Drama, that is, cuts us

20. Gomme, *Attitudes to Criticism*, p. 164, n. 57.
21. Bersani, *A Future for Astyanax*, p. 258.

off from direct access to the poet's self, which is a source of coherence, and replaces it with the competing selves of the various characters, who in their turn become the closest thing to the poet, the more so the more we can believe they embody his own views and feelings. As the only available substitutes for the direct authorial presence, they afford at least a partial reassurance. Hence the taking solemnly of the mimetic principle, and the talking always in terms of character. When characters fail to speak for their authors, when they begin to speak only for themselves, or for some subterranean layer of their author's consciousness, they become rebellious, even dangerous. At this point Winters begins to think of them as real people who have somehow broken loose, and can no longer be taken simply as fictions, as projections of their authors' minds. He prefers characters like Dryden's Shadwell because they are tame, unthreatening, closely bitted and curbed by their creators, and not in danger of bolting, like Macbeth or Volpone. When an author allows a character to speak for himself, when he refrains from crowding in at his elbow and interpolating his own opinions, he encourages an independence that threatens to subvert his own designs; one might say that he licenses a fuller participation of his own unconscious. Winters' disturbance at the fact of such participation, at the capacity of characters to embody impulses not necessarily intended by their authors, would seem to constitute an unwilling tribute to the drama's power, and an expression of deep uneasiness toward it.

The link is close between Winters' prejudice against drama and his distrust of what he has memorably christened "the fallacy of imitative form," that is, "the procedure by which a poet surrenders the form of his statement to the formlessness of his subject-matter" (FC 54). According to this view, any attempt to render disordered experience mimetically involves a capitulation to disorder; a poem trying to mimic the shapes of feeling and thought in any but their most highly rational form will inevitably suffer from the fragmentary, elusive, inchoate nature of those thoughts and feelings. In the drama, where the mimetic principle prevails, the process is doubly pernicious, since there is no formal control over it. Not only will a speech reproducing Macbeth's confusions share in those confusions, there is no authorized witness who can call this fact to our notice. We confront the creatures of the author's imagination directly, and it is the directness that Winters seems to find intolerable. He does not take very seriously the role of convention as a mediating force, though criticism has customarily recognized that any structured form imposes controls over its material in the very fact of its structure. Winters looks only at local texture, at what is going on in the individual line, or speech, and so fails to see larger patterns operating—the shape of the narrative, the order of events, the arrangements of tone and mood and image and gesture, the whole continuum which produces an evaluation too dense to be summed up in sententious formulae like "Macbeth is destroyed as a result of his sins." At the same time, rather like the naive playgoer, Winters seems to respond strongly to the concrete immediate presence of the characters, and to find it alarming.

It may be suggested, finally, that Winters' ideal of the plain style, especially in sixteenth-century poetry, steers a narrow middle course between two forms of theatricality, both felt as threatening: the mimetic style of passion, on the one hand, and the no less theatrical style variously referred to as "courtly, ornate, aureate, sugared, or Petrarchan" (FD 8) on the other. The ornate style tends to be ceremonial; its practitioners are often engaged in performing certain rhetorical rituals, and the effects of splendor they aim at resemble some of the spectacular effects of the Elizabethan public stage. We have then both an existential kind of theatricality, which imitates men in crisis, and a more ceremonial and pageantlike kind, which subsumes them into a cosmic order. In the one case life seems throbbingly close and immediate, and form seems ready to disintegrate into formlessness; in the other life seems hieratically solemn, and form a too elaborately preestablished harmony. The one kind might be thought of as akin to the psychodramas of Protestantism, the other to the rites of traditional religion, and Winters seems equally repelled by both. One is too naked, too intimately responsive to instinct and feeling, the other too gorgeous and sensuous and carnal. Winters prefers to move in an area abstracted from carnality, from the pleasures it can afford and the fears it can engender. What is exceptional in him, and indeed unique, is the energy with which he turned his repugnances into a critical dogma, refusing to countenance either form of theatricality, and seeking to forge a literary tradition in which the theatrical element would play the smallest possible part. The success of his curious enterprise may be gauged partly by the number of superb poems he plucked from oblivion, of a kind that more theatrically given readers had ignored or dismissed. Its failure must be reckoned partly by the number of unworthy poems he tried to promote to greatness for the same reason, and by his inability ever to work out a satisfactory rationale for the antipathy toward all forms of mimesis that seems increasingly to have ruled him, blocking his access to an essential aspect of our nature, our culture, and our literature.

· XIV ·

The Theater against Itself; Jews, Actors, and the Survivors of Hiroshima

IF WINTERS may be said to have reared a last futile bastion against the theater, as symbolized in protean man, protean man has gradually been battering down the walls of the theater from within. The theater has certainly never lacked a streak of antitheatricalism of its own. Perhaps a vigorous dose of it forms an essential ingredient in its vitality. When the theater grows self-satisfied, when it ceases to question itself, when it believes too uncritically in its own pomps, it begins to suffer from a kind of fatty degeneration. Craig's "monster of the theatrical" broods heavily over it then, while intelligence, wit, and insight flee the stifling air. Most of the pioneers of the modern drama, who brought the theater out of its long winter of Victorian discontent, were actively engaged in combatting this decaying theatricality, and one preferred method was to build into their very plays a critique of the theater, redeeming their better characters from it as they wished to redeem society at large.

Ibsen fashions heroes out of those who, like Brand, can commit themselves unreservedly, even fanatically, to their life enterprises, heedless of how these may appear to others, or who like Peer Gynt can experiment playfully with various roles, trying them on like so many hats, falling prisoner to none. We might designate Brand as the antitheatrical hero, and Peer as the theatrical hero, in the Ibsen canon. In Ibsen's social plays the heroines are those who reject the mold in which society casts them—Nora Helmer, Mrs. Alving, Ellida—while the failures tend spinelessly to recite parts they have accepted without protest from the world—Torvald Helmer, Pastor Manders, Hjalmar Ekdal, Jörgen Tesman—or else they are posturing dissenters who make of their quarrel with society an occasion for histrionic display—Gregers Werle, Eilert Lövborg. The weak characters define themselves in accord with clichés inherited from popular drama. To set them before the footlights as Ibsen does is to expose the hollowness of their theatrical self-images. To confront them with the more energetic characters is to reveal them as creatures of paint and cardboard, reacting with a Bergsonian automatism to the crises that confront them—incapable, indeed, of recognizing them as crises. Freedom consists in the struggle to fashion one's self anew, in defiance of social expectation, as Mrs. Alving struggles, however belatedly and timidly, to shake off the conception of herself she has had foisted on her by her elders and has hitherto tried to live by. Bondage consists in slavish fidelity to one's prescribed role, as with Pastor Manders, or in the cultivation of a self-image wholly at odds with observable reality, as with Hjalmar Ekdal. The theater thus serves implicitly as a standard of narrowness and artificiality, and the rejection of it as a sign of inner substance and power. The search for authenticity involves a denial of theater, because the theater itself is a denial of reality.

With Shaw, whose proudly affixed puritanism extends to a mistrust of all art, the antitheatrical motif moves into sharper focus. Declaring war on the theater in the preface to *Mrs. Warren's Profession*, he readies himself to fight it "not with pamphlets and sermons and treatises, but with plays." Along with his Puritan ancestors Shaw believes in the power of the stage to stir men's souls and alter their lives. He is therefore determined to wrest it from the hands of those who have abused it. It has fostered a false and unnatural view of the world, prompting men to behave falsely and unnaturally themselves. Ibsen himself has offended in this respect. Even he has spuriously "theatricalized" his characters, making Hedda Gabler, for example, kill herself when in real life she would have lived on. The remedy is not to suppress the theater but for men of good will to seize it and make it serve morality and truth. All art, in Shaw's view, should be used so, but the theater, because of its exceptional potency, constitutes a uniquely powerful pedagogical instrument, an ideal agent of moral reform. "By exhibiting examples of personal conduct made intelligible and moving to crowds of unobservant unreflecting people to whom real life means nothing,"[1] it can work a revolution in consciousness. For the generality of the populace, then, "real life means nothing." Most people are already debauched by their frequentation of the theater, or by absorbing at second hand the kind of lesson promoted in the theater. Since they derive their sense of reality, and their standards of conduct, from what they are shown in plays, plays must show them something better. Shaw determines to use plays, therefore—not at all, of course, to the exclusion of pamphlets, sermons, and treatises, but in addition to them—to inculcate the antitheatrical spirit in his audiences, to replace the unreal and unworkable examples that have oppressed the public for so long with models of independence and sound judgment. Shavian iconoclasm boils down to a cool rejection, on the part of the clear-eyed characters, of the various codes—heroic, romantic, respectable, or puritanical—by which their fellows live, or affect to live, a persistent testing of those codes by the canons of common sense, and the exposure of them as gaseous folly. Hence the deflation of such stage stereotypes as the overbearing vice magnate Sir George Crofts, in *Mrs. Warren's Profession*, or the stilted picture-book soldier Sergius of *Arms and the Man*, his worshipful fiancée Raina, and her romance-bedazzled mother, or the wealthy society matron Lady Britomart in *Major Barbara*. To fight the theater with plays is to hold such figures up to scorn, to make audiences recognize their own follies in them. It is to ridicule the fustian conventions, derived mainly from cheap melodrama, by which most men live. As with Ben Jonson, for whom he should have had more sympathy, Shaw's assault on the theater involves an attack on stage claptrap and a return to the honest realities of life as lived outside the theater.

Chekhov, too, specializes in characters made to look foolish because they cannot control their penchant for preening. Sometimes his dramatis personae almost compose themselves into a rogues' gallery of poseurs. The Arkadinas, the Trigorins, the Vanyas, the Kuligins, the Vershinins, the Gaevs, the Trofimovs—all, in their various ways, given to strutting and posturing, all eager to don stilts or climb soapboxes —stand in dire need of an antitheatrical purgative. Chekhov's compassion for them comes mixed with a certain distaste. They strike us, these characters, as unattractively narcissistic, in contrast to such

1. *Plays Unpleasant* (1898, rpt. London, 1934), p. 151; *Preface to Three Plays by Brieux* (New York, 1910), p. 7.

forthright figures as Sonya, in *Uncle Vanya,* or the old family retain-
ers, nurses, and butlers, who command our respect because they never
put on airs, never show any wish to attract attention or collect onlookers, and go about their business without exaggeration or extravagancies of manner.

With Pirandello commences a more disintegrating movement, a
challenge to the theater as an expressive medium, a rebuke to its age-
old claim to be able to instruct us about our true natures. Pirandello
attempts to demonstrate, in a hundred ingenious theatrical ways, that
human character lacks anything approaching the consistency, the co-
herency, and the knowability it has always been assumed to possess.
He sees it as a mirage with which we have deluded ourselves, a shadowy, impalpable essence, forever in flux, forever fleeing our grasp. It is
only the characters of fiction, in fact, those imprisoned in the pages of
books or strutting on stages, who truly exhibit the fixity and intelligi-
bility we would like to attribute to ourselves. It is they who display the
changelessness that for Plato formed the touchstone of reality, and we,
the persons of flesh and blood, who are the proteans, the chameleons,
the delusory phantoms, utterly unable to compete in reality with our
own appointed surrogates. Those surrogates, at our bidding, have in
fact told lies about us. In trying to represent us, they have misrepresented us.

The doctrine meets us in play after play, often through an ironic
transposition between stage and life. The distraught family of *Six
Characters in Search of an Author* possesses a distinctness, a substantiality, which the "real" actors who surround them utterly lack. By virtue of their fictive origin, and the burning imagination of their creator,
they are bound to repeat their terrible history over and over, with no
hope of ever advancing beyond it, and in their obsessive replaying of
that history they acquire a hallucinatory intensity that makes the nondescript actors who try to reproduce them seem like the pallidest of
ghosts. At the same time, they too, the six characters, are trapped in
unknowability. They cannot agree on the simplest facts about their own
collective existence. Each remains caught in a web of self-justifications
that none of the others will accept for a moment. Similarly, the haunted
Ponzas of *It Is So* acquire a tragic pathos from their attempts to protect
their anguished concern for each other from the prying eyes of the town
busybodies, yet that concern prompts them, or seems to prompt them to

proclaim totally different and incompatible versions of their mutual experience. Over the literal facts falls a veil which we can never hope to penetrate. As for the characters of *Each in His Own Way*, they prove unable to sustain the least confidence in their own self-images. With each fresh impulse of skepticism or credence from the outside, they revise their judgments about their own motives, their own desires, their own deepest drives, responding with a chameleonlike rapidity to the suggestions of the others around them.

Pirandello, to be sure, is by no means applauding or promoting the breakdown of the personality. He is simply registering it, recording it, seeing it as a fatal irony of our lives that we can never begin to fathom, still less truly to possess, our own inmost selves. In each case, by stressing the superior reality of the illusion to the merely illusory reality of the real, Pirandello reverses a basic premise of classical drama, the claim of the theater to be an image of truth in which we can see our own lives mirrored. In Pirandellian theater, *life* becomes the watery, inconstant, flickering reflection of what the *theater* vainly tries to persuade us to see as final and unchanging, and the enactment of the thesis involves a persistent challenge to the received tenets of traditional theater. In the very process, however, of subverting the customary claim, Pirandello paradoxically reasserts it. For he shows us what our lives are like by showing that they bear little resemblance to the lessons we thought we had learned about them from the theater of the older kind.

Much more aggressive tactics—shock tactics indeed—are espoused by Antonin Artaud, whose title for the second of his theatrical ventures, the Theater of Cruelty, tells us much about his approach to theatrical experience. Following the symbolist, expressionist, and surrealist theaters, with their masks, marionettes, and fantastic decor, their varied techniques of dislocation and dehumanization, Artaud strives to turn his actors too into puppets or mechanical dolls by giving them deliberately unnatural gestures. The Balinese dancers, in whom he found his theatrical ideal embodied, did not actually wear masks, but they used their faces in a peculiarly masklike way, rolling their eyes, pouting their lips, and contorting their facial muscles so as to depersonalize their faces. Similarly, they used their limbs not to simulate real gestures but in a vocabulary of ritual motion that "excluded all idea of pretence, or cheap imitations of reality." Instead of external events they portrayed inner states, "ossified and transformed into gestures—diagrams." The whole purport of their art was magical, symbolical, "absolute." When it came to the designing of a physical theater, Artaud planned to abolish the duality of stage and auditorium and replace them with a single continuous site, without boundary or partition. The spectator, a detached observer no longer, would be engulfed by the spectacle, bombarded by colors, lights, and sounds. About him would swirl huge masks, giant mannekins, hieroglyphics, objects "of strange proportions," and creatures "in ritual costumes."[2] All this so as to subvert his judgment and unseat his normal sense of himself, send seismic shock waves coursing through him, to teach him his helplessness in the face of the powers that rule human life. Though Artaud's doctrine of helplessness stands at the opposite pole from the message of freedom which Rousseau wished to promote through his civic festivals—though indeed it recalls the antique doctrine of fate which Rousseau regarded as one of the most odious features of classical drama, and made him long to abolish it— nevertheless Artaud shares with Rousseau, as also with the backward-looking Nietzsche of *The Birth of Tragedy*, a vision of theater as a mass event in which impersonation disappears, fiction vanishes, and the spectator loses himself amid the swarm of sensory excitants that assail him. With the actor discarded as a representative of humanity, or swallowed up in his distorting masks and exaggerating costumes, with the division annulled between stage and spectator, theater becomes a participatory rite meant to arouse and overwhelm the spectator with intense states of consciousness. Whether in joy or in panic, he is made to merge directly with his fellows, to *sub*merge his consciousness in theirs, to experience reality unmediated, instead of seeing it transferred or delegated to others.

Brecht, once more concerned with humdrum external reality, with the social, the economic, and objective, reconstitutes it by restoring the mimetic component to its central place. Instead of a dream kingdom or a nightmare world, with its elements deliberately pushed out of place, Brecht seeks to confront us with a simulacrum of our waking experience. At the same time, in order to balk our craving to enter too deeply into the lives of his characters, in order precisely to prevent us from losing ourselves as we watch, he sets out to undermine the illusion he is creating. Through devices of distancing like sudden songs and jingles,

2. *The Theatre and Its Double*, trans. Mary Caroline Richards (New York, 1958), pp. 96, 53.

the use of narrators or placards or didactic captions flashed on screens, of masks and other extravagancies of costume, of top-lighting that floods every nook and cranny of the stage and forbids all mystery, he calls our attention to the element of artifice in his fables. We are gazing not at a slice of life but at an artfully composed fiction, designed to teach us certain momentous truths about our lives and to challenge us to change them. Brecht would foster judgment rather than self-abandon or emotional participation in his audiences, and to this end he interrupts the current of sympathy whenever it threatens to flow too strongly between stage and onlookers. In spite of which, as playgoers have learned by now, the most powerful and affecting moments in Brechtian drama continue to be those in which the illusion commands, in which—doubtless contrary to Brecht's formal intentions—we drop our judicial impartiality and become impassioned partisans—when Mother Courage stoically refuses to admit kinship with the son whose body lies before her on the stage, when the dumb Kattrin madly bangs her drum on the rooftop to arouse the villagers, when Shen-Te, the good person of Setzuan, allows herself to be victimized by her airman lover, or, in more comic vein, when the peasant Azdak, pressed into service as a judge, doles out justice with an unpredictable mixture of rascality and horse sense. In such moments, it hardly matters that we know we are being told a story. Our sympathy jumps the gap, as it does in such comparable moments as the recognition scenes in *Pericles* or *The Winter's Tale*. It brushes aside the conventions meant to hold us at arm's length, reaching out toward the suffering creatures on the stage quite as if no mechanism of alienation had thrust itself between them and us at all.

In *The Resistible Rise of Arturo Ui*, the theater implies degeneracy. The horrible protagonist learns to grimace and gesticulate before the crowds he would sway by taking lessons from an old ham actor, and striking attitudes before a mirror. Earlier, his courtship of Dollfoot's widow over the body of her husband, murdered by his thugs, alludes pointedly to the similar scene in *Richard III*, in which Richard woos the Lady Anne over the hearse carrying the corpse of her father-in-law, whom he, Richard, has likewise killed. As though to suggest, in both cases, how imitative evil is, how empty of resource, how helpless to proceed except by pillaging stale tricks from a tired art. At the same time, just as the mechanisms of alienation fail to prevent our identifying with characters like Kattrin, or the beleaguered Grusha, so the self-transforming powers of Shen-Te, or Azdak's slipping in and out of his allotted roles, or the survival techniques that carry the good soldier Schweik safely if ignominiously through the Second World War, all betray an ambivalent admiration of the protean instinct which to some degree undoes the official antitheatricalism Brecht would have us espouse.

Brecht and Pirandello both work with one vital element of traditional theater, a strong narrative framework. The characters of their plays may harbor opacities and secrecies, but they also have histories, which they struggle to tell us. Pirandello's characters are locked in an endless repetition-compulsion. They revert over and over, in speech, in imagination, to the traumatic events of their past. We find them entangled in family quarrels, social commitments, subject to bureaucratic harassments and geographical displacements. Brecht's characters, even more unmistakably, live in the workaday world. They possess skills, trades, idiosyncrasies, class allegiances, "philosophies of life." With Beckett, a new radicalism operates: the tissue of plausible event is stripped away; character is scraped down to the bone of consciousness, cut off from past and future, home and family, education and occupation, and all the other reassurances of quotidian life. What remains is simply the universe in its brute incomprehensibility, its stubborn refusal to speak to man, the desolation produced in us by our futile efforts to interrogate it, and the struggle to survive even when all familiar guideposts have been swept away. Little enough, no doubt, yet sufficient, as was discovered at a famous performance of *Waiting for Godot* in San Quentin prison in 1957.[3] The audience of convicts instantly grasped its kinship with the two tramps going through their time-killing rituals, and after a short time the rest of the world grasped it as well. However little we may learn of the daily circumstances of the two, however fragmented, elliptical, and nonconsequential their speech, however arbitrary and baffling the comings and goings of their peculiar visitors, we recognize in the clownish routines by which they get from one moment to the next a symbol of our own predicament. The expectations of the theater audience, waiting for the play to begin, are subtly transferred to Didi and Gogo, waiting for their own more cosmic play to take a decisive turn.

3. Martin Esslin, *The Theatre of the Absurd* (New York, 1961), pp. xv–xvii.

In Beckett's later plays, the scraping away process continues remorselessly, attacking the characters in their vitals, leaving them not only without memory, or with only the merest shred of memory, but—according to the case—without locomotion, without speech, or even without visibility. They come imprisoned in urns or ashcans or pyramids of earth, reduced to trunkless heads or legless torsos, or else deprived of language so that they can only gesticulate frantically in pantomime, or reduced to a single disembodied mouth hysterically jabbering away in shrill monologue, or—extremest of all—reduced to total absence except for two faint cries and an intake of breath heard on a bare stage with nothing on it but a pile of rubbish. It is hard to imagine a theater more negative, more calculatedly eviscerated of everything the world has always thought of as theater. It is hard to imagine human substance coming so close to absolute nullity and yet retaining, in some weird and stunted fashion, a meaningful semblance of humanity.

In all these cases the playwright assaults the theater, undermines it with high explosives, in order to delve to the bedrock of consciousness. He wishes to blast the theater loose from its specious theatricality, from its complacent reliance on mimicry, from its slavish clinging to spectacle, and its facile trust in the rational, the social, and the objective. But in so doing he topples one by one the stones that held the edifice together. With personality challenged as a value and even as a reality, with impersonation less and less honored as an art, the actor undergoes a transformation into a ritual vessel, an impersonal symbol of existence, a depersonalized building-block with which the architect of the theater tinkers his constructions together. Antitheatricalism links itself with antihumanism, as it does when with Artaud it aims to offend rather than please. Robert Brustein's comment on Jerzy Grotowski, that he "operates on the anti-pleasure principle,"[4] would apply to much recent theater, which views the ancient wish to please as a discredited symptom of bourgeois prejudice and capitalist exploitation, which it is necessary to resist. Antitheatrical also, along with Rousseau's projected civic festivals, Nietzsche's vision of Dionysian intoxications in ancient Greece, and Artaud's wish to create epidemics of the plague within the walls of his theater, would be the repeated attempts of recent theater to wring "audience participation" from playgoers, whether by hector-

4. Quoted in John Simon, *Singularities* (New York, 1975), p. 154.

ing or cajolery.[5] The most striking stage experiments of recent decades —the Living Theater, the Open Theater, the self-crucifixions of Grotowski's "holy actors," the extravaganzas of Robert Wilson—for their part reject narrative, continuity of person, and sometimes formulable meaning of any kind. In one case, the Open Theater's production *Mutations*, the actors are reduced to collections of tics, jerks, and animal noises. Strange whines and wheezes and guttural grunts issue from them as though to realize every conceivable possibility of the human vocal apparatus—except that of normal speech. Speech, along with text, has been discarded, not merely as inessential, but as a tyrannous system of prefabricated meanings that must be overthrown if new meanings are ever to be found. The theater seems to be committing itself to a science-fiction-like attempt to reinvent the human, as if we were all suddenly to wake on a new planet, and had to recommence the history of the race anew, with no reference to the past other than that of repudiation.[6]

One explicit and devastating gesture of sabotage occurs in the plays of Peter Handke, whose work (much influenced by Brecht) we may take as paradigmatic of the effort to dismantle the theater within the theater that has been going on since Pirandello. *Offending the Audience*, one of his early *Sprechstücke*, or speak-pieces—"speak-ins," as the translator calls them—confronts us with four actors, unnamed, wearing whatever they happen to be wearing, addressing us from an empty stage, in turn, according to no fixed rule. What they tell us, not once but many times in the course of the hour or so they spend with us, is that they have not come to present a play. They are not here to tell a story, to enact events, or to create a picture, not even a verbal picture. Nor are they about to engage in anything resembling impersonation.

5. On audience participation in contemporary theater see Helene Keyssar, "I Love You. Who Are You? The Strategy of Drama in Recognition Scenes," *PMLA* 92 (1977): 297–306, who analyzes acutely (pp. 297–298, 301–303) some of the problems created by the demand that a spectator confront an actor (a "character"?) and "reveal" himself.

6. For a more sympathetic view of the phenomenon of the "deconstructed self" see Leo Bersani, *A Future for Astyanax* (Boston, 1976), p. 258—"In art, the theater is a privileged arena for testing the viability of a fragmented and collectivized self. It can enact modes of escape from the ideology of a full and fully structured human character"—and passim.

459

They will play no roles, not even the roles of themselves. Their assignment is merely to recite some words written for them by the author. The stage on which they stand is neither more nor less than what it appears to be, an unadorned platform. It contains neither entrances nor exits, nor are we being asked to imagine doors or windows (as in, for example, Thornton Wilder's *Our Town*). No other space is signified by the stage. It is simply a part of the building, lit just as the rest of the building is lit. Time is not, here, being represented either, any more than space or events. There is no imaginary time, no difference between time as lived by the audience and as experienced by the actors. It is possible indeed for the actors to claim that they are observing the classical unities, because of their refusal to split the theater into two halves. By speaking directly to the audience, without interruptions, intervals, pauses, or significant silences, they maintain a perfect unity of action. Of place as well, since "there are no two places here. Here is only one place": a single unbroken spatial continuum links actors and spectators. And of time for the same reason: there is no dividing of the occasion into two separate time schemes, one real and one make believe. "Only one time exists here."[7]

Nor, furthermore, do the stage figures wish to *express* anything, to arouse feelings in the audience, to involve them emotionally in grief or laughter. They are theatrical, the actors, "because [they] are speaking in a theater"[8]—i.e., in a building called a theater—and for no other reason. They will offer us no visual effects, no appeals to the senses or to the imagination. Nor will anything that happens on stage *signify* anything, as is usual in plays, where nonsense itself must mean something, and even "conspicuous meaninglessness" is designed to convey a meaning—where the action, whatever it may be, always points to some ulterior reality (p. 24). Here, neither reality nor any part of it is

7. Peter Handke, *Kaspar and Other Plays*, trans. Michael Roloff (New York, 1969), p. 20; see *Prosa Gedichte Theaterstücke Hörspiel Aufsätze* (Frankfurt, 1969), pp. 197–198: "Es gibt hier nicht zwei Orte. Hier gibt es nur einen Ort. . . . Hier gibt es nur *eine* Zeit." On the self-evident anti-Aristotelianism of this, which links Handke directly with Brecht, see Johannes Vanderath, "Peter Handkes *Publikumsbeschimpfung*; Ende des Aristotelischen Theaters?" *German Quarterly* 43 (1970): 317–326.

8. *Kaspar*, p. 20; *Prosa*, etc., p. 197: "Wir sind theatralisch, weil wir in einem Theater sprechen."

being played. *Nothing* is being played. Reality simply *is*. Appearance, on this occasion, is nothing but appearance.

Unlike the actors and the stage, however, the audience does represent something. All its members have made certain preparations to attend the performance; they have made their way to the theater at the same time, have sat down in seats disposed according to a certain plan, and in so doing have created an order, a community distinct from that of all the other people in the world who have not come to the theater this night. By virtue of their dress, the position of their bodies, the direction of their glances, the community expectations they bring with them, the spectators form "a theater society." They form a pattern. In fact, they are "putting on a masquerade so as to partake of a masquerade."[9] With this suggestion Handke begins slyly to transfer the theatricality of the moment from the stage to the audience. To the extent that theatrical values are anywhere in evidence on this strange occasion, they lodge not in the actors but in us. It is the audience which becomes the "topic," which provides the "initial impulse" and the "words," which undergoes changes of consciousness, becoming newly aware of itself as a result of being addressed by the actors, and which ends up as a complete cast of theatrical characters, as the "playmakers and the counterplotters . . . the youthful comedians . . . the youthful lovers . . . the ingénues . . . the sentimentalists . . . the stars . . . the heroes and the villains of the piece."[10]

Handke succeeds in maintaining this negation of all illusion, all story, and all impersonation, by the rigorous use of a single simple device: the actors speak only to the audience, never to each other. They gaze out over the audience, but never at each other. No interplay of any kind takes place among them, except for the reciting of their lines in orderly sequence, though the specific order in which they speak is of no interest and no importance. The only interaction, if it may be

9. *Kaspar*, p. 17; *Prosa*, p. 194: "Sie betreiben einen Mummenschanz, um einem Mummenschanz beizuwohnen."

10. *Kaspar*, p. 21; *Prosa*, p. 199: "Sie sind das Thema. . . . Sie sind das auslösende Moment. . . . Sie sind die Spielmacher und die Gegenspieler. Sie sind die jugendlichen Komiker, Sie sind die jugendlichen Liebhaber . . . die Naiven . . . die Sentimentalen . . . die Salondamen . . . die Bösewichte und Helden dieses Stücks."

called such, occurs between actors and audience, reaching a bizarre climax in the "offending" speeches. The audience is reviled with the kind of epithets it might itself use—including terms used by the Nazis to savage their opponents, and terms used by the Left to abuse the political Right, terms taken from sickness and death, from tales and stories, terms of deference, terms from Scripture[11]—all in order to create an "acoustic pattern" (*Klangbild*) which will narrow the gap between actors and onlookers, but not create (or imply) any kind of fictive situation. What the audience is chiefly berated *for*, however, in the increasingly violent outpouring of invective that ends the piece, is precisely for being theatrical, for being skilled impersonators, for being brilliant Stanislavskian inhabiters of their parts. "Your parts were well rounded," we are told. "Your scenes were unforgettable. You did not play, you *were* the part. . . . You lived your roles."[12] We recognize in this language the worn currency of journalistic play-reviewing and social chatter about the theater, which praises actors for *being* rather than merely acting their parts. In the present case, of course, by a witty stroke, the audience in the most literal sense *is* its part and does live its role. For its role, here and now, is simply to be an audience. "You were thoroughbred actors. . . . You were true to life. You were realistic. You put everything under your spell"[13]—another stream of cliché plaudits maliciously apt for the present occasion, in which the bourgeois decorousness of the audience, its paltry "reality," its own taste for realism, its malign hold over the stage, are brought to the verge of the opprobrious. Opprobrium breaks out shortly in earnest: "Your playing was of exquisite nobility. . . . You showed us brand-new vistas. . . . You outdid yourselves. . . . You were born actors. Play-acting was in your blood, you butchers, you buggers, you bullshitters, you bullies, you rabbits, you fuck-offs, you farts."[14] Here the stream of obscene

11. Vanderath, "Handkes *Publikumbeschimpfung*," p. 323.

12. *Kaspar*, p. 29; *Prosa*, p. 208: "Ihr habt eure Figuren plastisch gemacht. Ihr habt unvergessliche Szenen geliefert. Ihr habt die Figuren nicht gespielt, ihr seid sie *gewesen*. . . . Ihr habt eure Rolle *gelebt*."

13. *Kaspar*, p. 30; *Prosa*, p. 208: "Ihr wart Vollblutschauspieler. . . . Ihr wart lebensecht. Ihr wart wirklichkeitsnah. Ihr zoget alles in euren Bann."

14. *Kaspar*, pp. 30–31; *Prosa*, p. 209: "Euer Spiel war von seltenem Adel. . . . Ihr habt uns ganz neue Perspektiven gezeigt. . . . Ihr seid über euch hinausgewachsen. . . . Ihr wart die geborenen Schauspieler. Euch streckte die Freude am Spielen im Blut, ihr Schlächter, ihr Tollhäusler, ihr

taunts leads off with the most vicious insult of all: "You were born actors. Play-acting was in your blood"; more and more the name-calling expresses an antitheatrical loathing for the phoniness of the theater. "You had perfect breath-control. . . . You are accomplished actors. . . . You wax figures. You impersonators. You bad-hats. You troupers. You tear-jerkers. You potboilers. You foul mouths. You sell-outs. You dead-beats. You phonies. You milestones in the history of the theater."[15] So the audience is first harshly praised, then savagely castigated for its theatricality, for its falling into all the stock-company stereotypes of sentimentality, melodrama, and cheap exhibitionism. The actors, having washed their hands, so to speak, of the stigma of theatricality, have now succeeded in transferring it to us. It is we, at last, who are the play, the illusion, the story, the conspicuous meaninglessness masquerading as a meaning, and it is the empty stage and the nondescript, expressionless figures standing on it, reciting their nonrepresentational words to no one in particular, who thus constitute the naked reality.

It is hard to imagine a more radical reversal of the normal order, or a more far-reaching application of the Pirandellian premise that reality, as customarily construed, is more theatrical than the stage. It is hard to think of a more sweeping refusal to admit into the theater any of the things that for centuries have been assumed to be integral to it. We have come to watch a play, only to be told that there is no play, or rather, that we are the play, that it is we who are being watched, we who "represent" something other than what we appear, we who are insincere, inauthentic, and theatrical in the worst senses. By the calculated rejection of every one of the conventions whereby the theater has traditionally played reality, we are placed in the disgraceful position of playing it ourselves, and of showing ourselves to be little better than cheap hams, escapees from a Grade B movie, mouthing and grimacing our tawdry parts.

Mitläufer, ihr ewig Gestrigen, ihr Herdentiere, ihr Laffen, ihr Miststücke, ihr Volksfremden, ihr Gesinnungslumpen."

15. *Kaspar*, pp. 31–32; *Prosa*, pp. 209–210: "Ihr habt eine gute Atemtechnik bewiesen . . . . Ihr seid profilierte Darsteller . . . . Ihr Kabinettstücke. Ihr Charakterdarsteller. Ihr Menschendarsteller. Ihr Welttheatraliker. Ihr Stillen im Land. Ihr Gottespülcher. Ihr Ewigkeitsfans. Ihr Gottesleugner. Ihr Volksausgaben. Ihr Abziehbilder. Ihr Meilensteine in der Geschichte des Theaters. Ihr schleichende Pest."

When we reach this point, we may feel that the antitheatrical prejudice, which has so often attacked the theater from within in order to revive it, has here infiltrated its very beating heart and all but killed it, that the rage for authenticity on which the prejudice in its more enlightened version is founded has all but annihilated its object, to the point where if, in future, the theater is to exist at all, it must either return in shame to its bad old ways, imitating, impersonating, storytelling, dealing in illusions and pretenses, or else painfully and grimly carve out for itself some form of antitheatrical self-transcendence in the deepest cavern of its own being.

Probably it would be a mistake to see Handke as too apocalyptic a portent. The theater has always possessed its own saving salt of antitheatricalism. Furthermore, what appears at first as antitheatrical may reveal itself later as simply an impulse of renovation, a breaking of the windows to let in fresh air. By tilting against what they see as the falsely theatrical, theatrical creators attempt to topple it in order to make room for the truly theatrical. They burn down the ornate, overloaded theater of the past in the hope that a purified theater will rise from its ashes. At present, after the disturbances of the nonsense theaters, the Dada theater, the expressionist, surrealist, and absurdist theaters, after the deconstructive fantasies of Chaikin and Wilson, and the disruptive maneuvers of fringe and underground groups, the dominant sources of theatrical energy seem still to be the familiar, traditional ones: representation of the observed and the actual, intelligible configurations of character, narrative coherence, meaningful patterns of action. Men seem hardly likely, after so many centuries, to give up their addiction to storytelling, their love of gorgeous spectacle, sumptuous rhetoric, and all the vulgar panoply that has provoked so much disapproval in so many impassioned purists.

The workings of what we may term hard-line, fundamentalist antitheatricalism may perhaps be further clarified by comparing it with old-style antisemitism. The historical connection between them, indeed, goes back to a day when Jews and actors were lumped together as undesirable members of society, like prostitutes. Visions of the ideal republic consistently excluded them both from participation. "I have always regarded as most pernicious in republics those two sorts of men, the Jews and the charlatans," writes the doctor Scipione Mercurio in the late sixteenth century. "The former because although our slaves they enrich themselves with the blood of the poor," and the latter because, with their japing and joking "they deprive stupid people of their money, earned with so much toil, which ought to have supported the needy family."[16] Both Jews and itinerant entertainers, in this view, are predators. The wandering Jew joins with the vagabond mountebank to exploit the poor, and move on. When, on occasion, actors are defended, it is likely to be because, like Jews and prostitutes, they constitute a lesser evil in the absence of which a worser might prevail. A plentiful supply of prostitutes helps deter sensual males from molesting respectable women; the presence of the Jews reduces the temptation for Christians to engage in usury. Just so, the arrival of the actors helps dissuade simple folk from following even more vicious pastimes than the one the players offer. All three groups are seen as essentially alien to the good society, outsiders who by definition have no positive role to play and no proper contribution to make, who can at best be grimly tolerated. Beltrame, defending his fellow players, struggles to differentiate them from those groups to which odium rightly belongs, the Jews and the courtesans. The Jews are tolerated, he suggests, not really because they practice a usury which Christians might otherwise be tempted to embark on, but because in their own persistent infidelity they bear witness to Christian faith, as they await their own conversion. Actors, by contrast, true sons of the church already, stand in no need of such insulting, humiliating tolerance.

At the time of the Revolution, again, in France, when the National Assembly came to address itself to the cause of certain persecuted minorities, it debated the Jewish question and the case of the actors at the same time.[17] We have noted the virulence with which the hero of Bloy's novel *Le désespéré* vituperates both the Jews and the actors, seeing them as equally poisonous to all good people and all social order.[18]

16. Nicolò Barbieri, *La supplica: discorso famigliare a quelli che trattano de' comici*, ed. Ferdinando Taviani, Archivio del teatro italiano, no. 3 (Milan, 1971), p. lxxiv.

17. See Gaston Maugras, *Les comédiens hors la loi*, 2d ed. (Paris, 1887), pp. 413–414.

18. We have given above (pp. 321–322) a sample of Bloy's vein of invective against the actors. Here is a sample of his vein against the Jews: "Ce Monsieur Nathan était une petite putridité judaïque, comme on en verra, paraît-il, jusqu'à l'abrogation de notre planète. Le Moyen Age, au moins,

We have noted, furthermore, in one major novel, *The Tragic Muse*, the fact that the central figure, the title personage, is also Jewish, as is (earlier) the demonic Vashti in Charlotte Brontë's *Villette*, whose acting is at once "a marvellous sight: a mighty revelation," and "a spectacle low, horrible, immoral."[19] Most elaborate of all are the connections worked out between acting and Jewishness in George Eliot's *Daniel Deronda*, where Jews, along with artists—and especially actors—are seen as archetypal outsiders, whose wanderings in the diaspora have conferred on them a special aptitude for the arts, a special affinity for the burden of otherness true artists must always carry.[20] If prejudice

---

avait le bon sens de les cantonner dans les chenils réservés et de leur imposer une défroque spéciale qui permît à chacun de les éviter. Quand on avait absolument affaire à ses puants, on s'en cachaît, comme d'une infamie, et on se purifiait ensuite comme on pouvait. La honte et le péril de leur contact était l'antidote chrétien de leur pestilence, puisque Dieu tenait à la perpétuité d'une telle vermine" (*Le désespéré* [Paris, 1887], p. 266: "This Mr. Nathan was a little Judaic putridity, such as will be seen, no doubt, until the abrogation of our planet. The Middle Ages, at least, had the good sense to quarter them in kennels set aside for the purpose and to impose a special garment on them which enabled others to avoid them. When one absolutely had business to transact with these stinking creatures, one covered oneself up from them as from something vile, and afterward one purified oneself as best one could. The shame and the danger of contact with them was the Christian antidote to the plague they carried, since God insisted on the perpetuation of such a vermin").

The unwary reader should not be deceived by the title of Bloy's tract, *Le salut par les juifs* (1892; rpt. Paris, 1947), into thinking that Bloy ever retracted these sentiments. On the contrary, the tract in question restates them with the most unbridled violence, declaring on page after page their author's physical revulsion from the Jews, for their ugliness, their raggedness, their stink, their whine, their avarice, their hatred of God, etc. Salvation depends on them in the sense that Christ can never descend from his cross until they are ready to receive him. On the other hand, they will never receive him until he does descend (p. 60). The world remains thus locked in an intolerable dilemma, of the Jews' making. They alone have the power to relieve their victim of his burden and so bring peace to the world. It was for this mission that God chose them and still preserves them in all their odiousness, etc.

19. (London, 1949), p. 292 (ch. xxiii).

20. See the excellent (if unorthodox) discussion of this aspect of the novel in Joseph Mazo Butwin, "The Actor as Artist in English Fiction" (Ph.D. diss. Harvard University, 1971), pp. 89–114.

as well as admiration seems to bracket the two categories together, it is because they are felt to go together naturally, the alleged cosmopolitanism, ready adaptability, and linguistic virtuosity of the Jews being felt to have a natural kinship with the mimetic talents of the actors, resulting in such exemplary careers as those of Rachel or Bernhardt. Nietzsche, indeed, in his meditation "on the problem of the actor," expressly likens the actor's malleability to that of the Jews, which makes of the latter "a world-historical arrangement for the production of actors, a veritable breeding ground for actors." Should we not ask, demands Nietzsche, "What good actor today is *not*—a Jew? The Jew as a born 'man of letters,' as the true master of the European press, also exercises his power by virtue of his histrionic gifts; for the man of letters is essentially an actor: He plays the 'expert,' the 'specialist.'"[21]

Borrowing from Jean-Paul Sartre's portrait of the antisemite, we find that many of its features also fit the antitheatricalist.[22] A certain mechanism of paranoia, a certain style of fanaticism, seem common to them

21. Walter Kaufmann, trans., *The Gay Science*, Section 361, Vintage Books (New York, 1974), pp. 316–317; *Die fröhliche Wissenschaft*, in *Werke*, V.ii (1973), 291: "Was aber die *Juden* betrifft, jenes Volk der Anpassungskunst par excellence, so möchte man in ihnen, diesem Gedankengange nach, von vornherein gleichsam eine welthistorische Veranstaltung zur Züchtung von Schauspielern sehn, eine eigentliche Schauspieler-Brutstätte; und in der That ist die Frage reichlich an der Zeit: welcher gute Schauspieler ist heute *nicht*—Jude? Auch der Jude als geborener Litterat, als der thatsächliche Beherrscher der europäischer Presse übt diese seine Macht auf Grund seiner schauspielerischen Fähigkeit aus: denn der Litterat ist wesentlich Schauspieler,—er spielt nämlich den 'Sachkundigen,' den 'Fachmann.'"

22. I am well aware of the shortcomings in Sartre's exposition. They have been brilliantly analyzed by Harold Rosenberg, in "Sartre's Jewish Morality Play," *Discovering the Present* (Chicago, 1973), pp. 270–287, which exposes the inadequacy, not to say the prejudiciality, of Sartre's portrait of the Jews themselves. Readers of the newspapers will recall as well such egregious pronouncements as Sartre's defense of Soviet antisemitism, when he explained that all Jews are automatically entitled to Israeli citizenship, and therefore have a dual loyalty and a place to go if they leave Russia, whereas the ordinary downtrodden Russian non-Jew . . . . But neither Sartre's distortions about Jewishness nor his predictable effort to make common cause with Communism on whatever terms can invalidate his portrait of the antisemite, which remains a searching and powerful account of the workings of the fanatic mind.

both, however divergent their specific aims and purposes. In both cases prejudice takes the form not of a mere opinion but of a passion; while indefatigably seeking to fortify itself with argument and observation, it invariably reverts in the end to a stubborn bedrock of irrationality. In each case the "reasons" advanced for the prejudice serve as pretexts with which the reasoner masks a basic choice of himself. That choice is the decision to live on the plane of the irrational, to embrace prejudice as burning faith. And the faith in question is founded on hatred, immune to logic and experience alike, gaining its strength precisely from its being a visceral self-choice rather than a reasoned position. If, for one society, the Jews are seen as international bankers, for another they are petty shopkeepers mulcting the poor, or cosmopolitan dilettantes with no allegiance to their fatherland, or disaffected intellectuals plotting revolution. If for one society the theater is a house of lies, trading in fraud and falsehood, for another it is a house of blasphemy, insulting holy truth by "playing" it, and for still another a house of immorality, encouraging its audiences in unthinkable fantasies that they would dismiss or disavow in their daily lives. There is no inconsistency to which the standardbearers of prejudice will not resort in order to disguise passion as sober judgment, nor any logical rebuttal of their inconsistencies that will abate the intensity of their passion.

Like the antisemite, again, the antitheatricalist sees the object of his hate as totally evil. The world is explained for both, along Manichean lines, as a battle between good and evil, between which there is no conceivable reconciliation: "One of them must triumph and the other be annihilated." Both think in terms of cataclysms and apocalypses. What they see is "not a conflict of interests but the damage which an evil power causes society. Therefore Good consists above all in the destruction of Evil. . . . The conflict is raised to a religious plane, and the end of the combat can be nothing other than a holy destruction."[23] As Sartre goes on to point out, one advantage of this scheme is that it

23. *Anti-Semite and Jew*, trans. George J. Becker (New York, 1960), pp. 41, 43; *Réflexions sur la question juive* (Paris, 1946), p. 51: "Entre ces deux principes aucun ménagement n'est concevable: il faut que l'un d'eux triomphe et que l'autre soit anéanti"; pp. 53–54: "Il n'est pas question d'un conflit d'intérêts, mais des dommages qu'une puissance mauvaise cause à la société. Dès lors, le Bien consiste avant tout à détruire le Mal. . . . Ainsi la lutte est menée sur le plan religieux et la fin du combat ne peut être qu'une destruction sacrée."

servations rather than the more clinical accounts of patients studied for their evident abnormality—Lifton cautions us against regarding such cases as pathological. On the contrary, in his view they form a natural response to the conditions of our time, to the breakdown in longstanding patterns of culture, to the "flooding of imagery" produced by the mass media, and above all to the menace of nuclear war, with its dissolving of the boundaries of destruction and its consequent threats to the self and the traditional symbolism of the self (pp. 43–44). Yet it is hard for anyone nurtured on that symbolism not to find cases such as that of the young Japanese disturbing, even frightening, in the challenge they seem to pose to our whole sense of reality, based as that is so squarely on our sense of the continuity of our tastes, habits, sentiments, predilections, ethical and social and political commitments.

Lifton cites also the case of an American patient, a gifted young teacher, whose life seemed to him to consist of the wearing of a number of masks which he could put on and take off, and who was uncertain which, if any, was the authentic one, or whether indeed it was necessary for any of them to *be* authentic. The patient in question expressly likened himself to an actor, who "performs with a certain kind of polymorphous versatility" but who cannot distinguish his real self from the fictional selves he projects. "Which is the real person, so far as the actor is concerned? Is he more real when performing on the stage, or when he is at home? I tend to think that for people who have these many, many masks, there is no home. Is it a futile gesture for the actor to try to find his real face?" (p. 45). "There is no home." We seem to encounter here an extreme and desolating instance of the protean man so admired by Pico della Mirandola, and to see how, having abandoned any sense of a certain self, and no longer believing himself part of a beneficent supernatural order, man has shredded himself into an endless series of temporary selves, none of which seems to afford a basis from which a secure sense of the world can be launched. Of man in this state Lifton observes that what has disappeared is

the classic superego, the internalization of clearly defined criteria of right and wrong, transmitted within a particular culture by parents to their children. Freud's original description of the superego, . . . referred to stable moral and psychological structures much more characteristic of traditional cultures than of our own. Indeed, Protean man requires freedom from precisely that kind of superego—he requires a symbolic form of fatherlessness—in order to carry out his explorations. (p. 48)

The loosening of old sanctions, then, has deprived the individual of his anchorage, set him adrift in a sea of identity. Lifton's discussion makes it clear that the "experimental" side of acting, which a classical Freudian like Otto Fenichel could see as a means of mastering experience by playing it,[26] has turned—under irresistible pressure—into a dizzying and dangerous game of self-abandon, which repudiates not only roles approved by tradition, but any fixed or settled role whatever. Lifton notes how the vocabulary of action has been transformed so that experience is now seen in drily theatrical terms "as a 'bit,' 'bag,' 'caper,' 'game' (or 'con game'), 'scene,' 'show,' 'scenario,' or . . . 'put-on'; and one seeks to 'make the scene' (or 'make it'), 'beat the system' or 'pull it off'—or else one 'cools it' ('plays it cool') or 'cops out' " (p. 56). No doubt this vocabulary, compounded from countercultural cant, underworld slang, and the picturesque speech of dispossessed minorities, has already receded into the middle distance, and will shortly disappear altogether. Nevertheless it suggests the intrusion into our language of a newly approving view of acting and spectatordom. If we compare the favorable connotations (for their users) of these terms, the recommendation they imply of controlling experience by keeping it at a distance and toying with it, with the more traditional expressions cited earlier (pp. 1, 155–156), with their deep suspiciousness of anything theatrical, we can begin to measure the extent to which long-held attitudes are in process of dissolving, just as the personalities or characters to which we have so long clung seem also on the verge of deliquescing. Not only nuclear warfare, but all the conditions of modern life have helped accelerate the decomposition of the personality. Psychiatry itself now rarely treats such cases of hysteria as formed the original basis of Freud's practice—the striking distortions of or aberrations from a well-defined self—but rather, vague character disorders the very terms of which are hard to grasp. If, thanks partly to Freud, we have gained an unprecedented freedom of self-creation, an undreamed of power to make and remake ourselves at will, like Proteus or the chameleon or the actor, we have also sacrificed in the process, as Plato, Rousseau, and Nietzsche

26. Otto Fenichel, "On Acting," *Psychoanalytic Quarterly* 15 (1946): 144–160, esp. 151.

all prophesied and lamented, a certain clarity of outline, an integrity of self to which our thoughts and acts could have unambiguous reference. We have given up rectitude for plenitude, and our deeply lodged antitheatricalism is rising up to reproach us for it.

What Lifton observed in young Orientals of the post-Hiroshima generation has increasingly become a feature of the American scene as well. John Lahr, speaking of the "holy" theater of Jerzy Grotowski, with its aim of training the body to a point where it can virtually call into being a new soul, relates this to a cult for transcendence among the young.

What you feel in our culture when you walk down a street is the longing of people to get out of their skins. . . . [Grotowski's] style of continuous change, transformation, and excess mirrors the psychological style of the contemporary youth scene . . . . Rather than commit themselves to one personality, the youth in America take on many different personalities. If you walk around any American city you will see young people dressed up as Indians, Cowboys and gypsies. The name of the game is change.[27]

One consequence of the new situation, as Lifton sees it, is a reaction, a compensatory countersyndrome that takes the form of a retreat into narrowness and fundamentalism—a syndrome that may remind us of Riesman's "inner-directed" man, except that it no longer springs from the shared values of a society, but from nostalgic protest, from the attempt to resynthesize something felt to be coming apart. Some such "reactive or compensatory" mechanism may well have been at work among English Puritans of the sixteenth century, or among the Jansenists and other clerical reactionaries of seventeenth-century France and Spain. Faced with the crumbling of centuries-old structures of identity, with what we might term "identity dispersal," with challenges like that of Pico's self-creating man or Castiglione's self-fashioning courtier, they resort to a narrow specialization in their view of human personality, jamming their fingers in the holes of the dike in a despairing effort to stop the leaks. They gaze at the theater of their time, and it wears the face of Lifton's protean man—mocking, defiant, fascinated with false values and with change for its own sake, addicted to a reckless transformationism that threatens to dissolve all boundaries of identity

27. Quoted in Peter Ansorge, *Disrupting the Spectacle: Five Years of Experimental and Fringe Theatre in Britain* (London, 1975), pp. 29–30.

altogether. Puritan imagery of rebirth may have stressed the cataclysmic effects of a religious conversion on the personality, but that rebirth and that conversion were something that could happen only once in a lifetime, in response to a call sent out by God. If they changed the identity of the individual, it was only by conferring on him a deeper and truer identity, for which he had been destined from all time.[28] For the Proteans of today, by contrast, change becomes a "game" played for its own sake, or as a way of papering over an inner emptiness. In Lifton's young Orientals, as in Lahr's young Indians, cowboys, and gypsies, restlessly tinkering with an identity in which they do not really believe, life begins to approach the condition aspired to by Felix Krull, of never-ending metamorphosis, except that whereas in Felix the metamorphoses satisfy a profound urge for self-mastery, in the gamesters of Lahr and Lifton they seem to signify a compulsive retreat from self-definition of any kind.

A similar pathology is espied, in less flamboyant guises, and in more somber spirit, by Leslie H. Farber. Farber views certain states of distress, notably jealousy, as modes of "promiscuity," by which he means a ceaseless impersonation of the self in which the individual flirts desperately with the world at large, all the while cynically disbelieving in any reality behind his own impersonations. In a number of related psychic ailments—lying, hysteria, despair—he detects a comparable telltale taint of theatricality, a widening gap between the private and public selves wherein the latter is driven increasingly into histrionic exaggeration in order to sustain itself against a conviction of inner worthlessness. Farber belongs among several recent witnesses who have expressed renewed respect for what, borrowing a term from Erik Erikson, we may call "ego integrity"[29]—the willingness to accept ourselves and what we have made of our lives, the sense that we are, in Trilling's phrase once more, though this time with no pejorative overtones, "integers," whose wholeness can be as threatened by theatricality as was that of Fanny Price and her friends at Mansfield Park.

Himself a psychoanalyst, Farber finds even psychoanalysis discon-

28. See Winthrop D. Jordan, "Adulthood in America," *American Civilization: New Perspectives, Daedalus* 105, no. 4 (Fall 1976): 2.

29. *Childhood and Society*, 2d ed. (New York, 1963), pp. 26–29; *Identity, Youth and Crisis* (New York, 1968), p. 139; *Young Man Luther* (New York, 1959), p. 254.

certingly prone to theatricalism. In its quest for traumatic episodes and emotional upheavals, on which aesthetically satisfying interpretations can be reared, it risks losing sight of its primary goal, the truth. Truth does not necessarily take spectacular form. It does not always announce itself in lightning flashes and thunderbolts, and the insistence on revelation tends to discredit the more modest insights that come inch by inch, without dramatic emphasis or intellectual glamor, without triumphal music of any sort. The appetite for revelation must be said to be—surprisingly, perhaps—coarsening, since it prefers the show to the substance, and not only coarsening, but addicting, since it leads to a craving for the spectacular, and spoils the taste for simple truthtelling.[30] The theatrical, then, as it invades our daily lives, as it insinuates itself into our relations with our friends, our wives, our children, our patients, becomes a substitution of what is arresting and exciting for what is true. It hinders the quest for mental health as surely as it hampered the search for the true and the good in Plato's Republic. And with this unexpected relegation of it to the realm of error, we come round to our starting point in Plato, for whom all mimesis was the mistress of delusion, and theatrical mimesis the most disturbing and undermining of all.

The battle of the theater, in its more superficial sense, has been won long ago. Actors now win knighthoods in England, inhabit the seats of government in America, and are revered as sages in France. But the antitheatrical prejudice, tenacious, elusive and protean in its own right, and springing, as it seems, from the deepest core of our being, seems to have taken refuge in the theater itself, as well as in certain outposts of psychoanalysis and certain philosophies of existence. The public may have lost much of its old suspiciousness of the theater. The theater remains suspicious of itself, and so, on similar grounds, do the philosophers. For Jean-Paul Sartre, as for Rousseau, human consciousness arises in a theatrical context. We come into the world encircled by watchful eyes, to whose expressions we quickly learn to adjust our own. Our efforts at self-definition consist of our attempts to cope with this amphitheater of gazes—to accept it, without evasion, as constitutive of us in the first place, but then to refuse to bow to its despotic edicts. We are thrust out as it were onto a strange stage, forced to improvise

30. *Lying, Despair, Jealousy, Envy, Sex, Suicide, Drugs, and the Good Life* (New York, 1976), pp. 53, 86, 89–96, 186–202, 210–220.

our identities as we go along. The props are ready and the rest of the cast is mustered—we can do nothing about that—but the script we must provide for ourselves. In these circumstances, we have two possible courses. We may fulfill ourselves either authentically or inauthentically; we may opt (in the sociologist's jargon) for "role-making" or "role-taking." To behave inauthentically is to settle for a hand-me-down part, one fashioned for us by others, which we ape by performing "gestures," rituals designed to make us feel at ease in our borrowed costumes. To behave authentically is to perform "acts," to invent ourselves from nothing, neither shamed nor frozen into ineffectuality by the sea of faces that surrounds us. In this view, the intrinsic theatricality of our being leaves room for heroic possibilities. A man who can compose his character without being intimidated by the onlookers or the others in the cast, but also without pretending to ignore them, has accepted the hazard of being human, and asserted his humanity to the utmost. We may recognize in him a counterpart of Stanislavsky's matured actor. But the situation contains tragic potentialities as well, since it leads most men to maim themselves, to disavow what is most truly their own in order to avoid unfavorable notice by others.

Is it possible, also, that the theater, where we become voyeurs, owes some of its hold over us to the fact of our having ourselves been at the center of the stage as we entered the world? Freud's "wolf man," we recall, had a recurrent childhood dream of being stared at, silently and intently, by a tree full of wolves. Freud read this as the transposed version of a primal scene. The little boy, reliving the scene in his fantasy, converted the experience of watching into that of being watched. Does the theater derive some of its hypnotic power from a reverse transposition? Does the greediness of our gaze point to a buried memory of the earlier thirst to be gazed *at*, and our satisfaction when that thirst was slaked? Is our desire to sit as beholders merely the other side of the coin of our wish to be beheld, our unacknowledged exhibitionism? If so, perhaps the antitheatrical prejudice reflects a form of self-disgust brought on by our conflicted longing to occupy the center of the stage once more.

By any reckoning, the theatrical analogy would seem an inescapable figure for our relations with the rest of the world. Human existence can hardly avoid resembling in basic ways the experience of actors in the theater, and human consciousness can hardly escape the tinge of bad faith this introduces into our actions, the incitement it gives us to wish to be admired, stared at, made much of, attended to. By living in the theater, as they do, by giving themselves over to mimicry and exhibitionism, men jeopardize the most precious part of their humanness, the right exercise of which would be a relentless campaign to rid themselves of the element of falsity in which they move. If the day ever dawned when men became truly able to live "in themselves," like Rousseau's imagined savages, if the dangers of theatricality ever ceased to threaten us in our daily lives, then perhaps our special need for the theater as an art form might also vanish: it would no longer confront us with an account of our own truth struggling against our own falsity. But since, if the lessons of philosophy are to be believed, that hour can never strike, we may expect that the theater will continue to exert its spell, and that that spell will continue to be felt, at least in part, as baneful. The antitheatrical prejudice, a consequence of the ambiguous facts of our own condition, will continue to confer on the stage, and on theatricality in everyday life, the faint but unmistakable savor of forbidden fruit.

Index

Abrams, M. H., 328

Academic stage, 90–91

Accetto, Torquato, 182–183

Acting, as term of disapproval, 1, 155–157; and prostitution, 2, 42–43, 193–194; truth of, 55–58; as hypocrisy, 91–92, 125, 196–197, 258, 277, 279–280; in Shakespearean characters, 127–131, 186–188; of priests, 161–165, 376–378; psychology of, 195–197, 207, 276–282; therapeutic value of, 206n, 207–208, 370; rival styles of, 277–280; as prostitution, 320, 321–322, 323; naturalism in, 344–348; of Methodist preachers, 379–380; in contemporary language, 472; as self expression, *see* Feelings; Masks; as imitation, impersonation, mimicry, *see each of these terms. See also* Play-acting; Play/playing; Reality; Truth

Actors: legal sanctions against, 39–40, 50, 122, 192–193, 235, 237, 295–296, 321; status in Rome of, 39–42, 43, 63; as hirelings, 40–41, 185; Church fathers on, 44–47, 49, 50; Augustine on, 55–56, 58–59, 63; as liars, 67; defenses of theater by, 81, 122–124, 267, 274–275; early apologists for, 117–121, 124–126, 204, 205–209; offstage lives of, 122, 194–195, 204, 235, 281, 295–296, 370–371, 393–394; psychology of, 195, 196, 207, 276–282; Rousseau on, 272–279, 295; Diderot on, 279–282; in nineteenth century, 296–297, 343–344, 395–396; French church on, 320–323; Mirbeau on, 340–342; egoism of, 341–342, 343, 348–349; Camus on, 366–367; absence of fixed identity of, 366–369, 388; as fictional characters, 369–399; Dickens in defense of, 370–375; Methodist preachers as, 379–380; H. James in defense of, 384–388, 390; in films, 398–399; Nietzsche on, 413–414; Winters on, 454–455; changing nature of in contemporary theater, 458–463; as outsiders, 466–467; as affecting listeners, onlookers, *see* Audiences; Spectatorship; as Proteans, *see* Chameleon; Change; Proteus; as identified with own roles, *see* Feelings; Imitation; Reality. *See also* Garrick, David; Kean, Edmund; Roscius

Actresses, 2, 88, 91, 282–286, 384–389, 466. *See also* Bernhardt; Duse; Women

Aeschylus, 229, 403, 409

Aestheticism: in politics, 14–15; in

479